THE UNITED STATES POLITICAL SPECTRUM

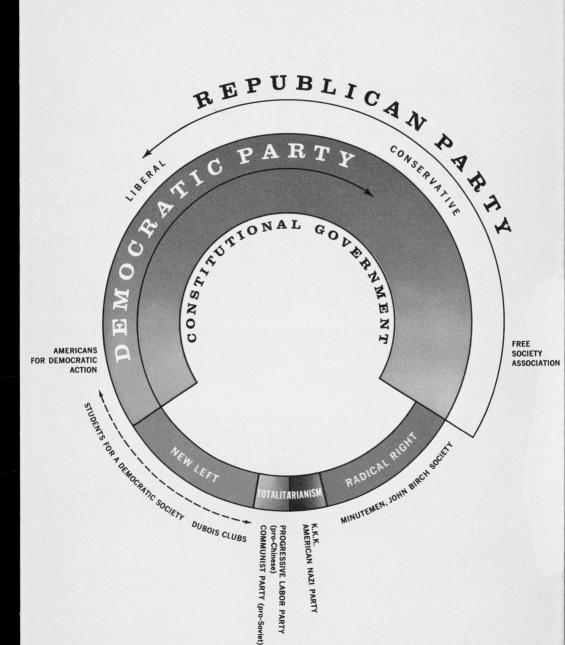

AMERICAN DEMOCRACY

WILLIAM EBENSTEIN

C. HERMAN PRITCHETT

HENRY A. TURNER

DEAN MANN

UNIVERSITY OF CALIFORNIA, SANTA BARBARA

AMERICAN DEMOCRACY

IN WORLD PERSPECTIVE

HARPER & ROW, PUBLISHERS

NEW YORK · EVANSTON · LONDON

AMERICAN DEMOCRACY
IN WORLD PERSPECTIVE

CONTENTS

PART III THE POLITICS OF AMERICAN DEMOCRACY

PREFACE

THIS BOOK APPEARS at a time when American democracy is undergoing vast changes in its domestic ideas, policies, and institutions as well as in its relations with the rest of the world. Not since the 1930s has there been such turmoil and violence in the world. Authoritarian and totalitarian states threaten the very survival of democracy, and within the democratic nations themselves the idea of freedom has been attacked by apathy, doubt, and outright hostility on the extreme Right and Left.

Yet, whereas a generation ago many believed that the United States could stand aside in the worldwide struggle, and that powerful democratic nations like Britain and France could save freedom against its assailants, it has been clear since the 1950s that the United States is now its last—and often first—line of defense. As democracy fares in the United States, so will it, in the long run, fare throughout the world. If American ideas and institutions show vitality and the capacity to innovate, free societies everywhere will gain in strength. By contrast, should the United States fail to meet this awesome responsibility, the worldwide effects of such failure would be quickly felt.

For this reason, we have felt that the study of American government and politics, particularly for the beginning student, must be preceded by a thorough examination of what democracy is all about. The traditional cursory introductory remarks on the subject may have been sufficient when democracy was—correctly or mistakenly—taken for granted. We have long passed that stage. The entire first part of this book, "Perspectives of

Democracy," therefore undertakes to analyze democracy in greater depth. The discussion of democracy as a system of values seeks to show what its operational ideas and ideals are, that is, the ideas that have inspired democracy without ever being fully achieved. The knowledge of these basic democratic values should enable the student to appraise on the one hand what democracy could potentially be like, and to measure, at the same time, the shortcomings and failures of a democratic system as it works in practice.

In addition, we have sought to present the psychological and economic underpinnings of democracy. Like every social system, democracy is linked to recognizable psychological patterns of feeling and behavior, since the irreducible—and probably decisive—ultimate unit of every social system is the individual. However, the individual lives in, and through, groups. In looking at the social forces conditioning the democratic experience, we have primarily stressed the economic environment. In the first place, political systems are more congenial to some economic ideas and practices than to others. Then, the links between politics and economics are particularly important in an age in which, as Alexis de Tocqueville foresaw over a century ago, the economic issue has come to the forefront of democratic politics. Finally, the first part of this book confronts democracy with the challenges of authoritarianism and totalitarianism. No understanding of democracy—American or any other—can be gained without the realization that authoritarianism and totalitarianism are not brief and temporary deviations from the democratic norm but permanent forces that we shall have to reckon with for a long time to come.

Because the world is of concern to the United States, and the United States is a source of immense influence and leadership for other nations, we have tried to go beyond the systematic comparative analysis in the first section and make appropriate comparisons of American ideas and practices with those of leading democratic and nondemocratic systems, throughout the book. There is no area of the American political experience which cannot be illuminated by drawing on similar, or contrasting, experiences of other nations. The traditional method of comparing American government and politics today solely with their historical antecedents is no longer sufficient. While we have sought to provide the essential historical background where it is indispensable to the understanding of contemporary trends, we feel that the beginning student gains even more by looking at the American political experience and performance in world perspective.

In trying to present a fair and balanced picture of American democracy, we have not sought to avoid controversial issues. The United States owes its existence to controversy and conflict, and throughout its history, as today, there has never been a dearth of highly controversial public questions. In addition, we have often tried to pinpoint major issues that are likely to arise in the future in various areas of public policy. If we have not hesitated to express our own views in many places, we have done so, not in order to lay down final certainties, but in order to stimulate thought and discussion.

Although much mutual consultation has gone into the preparation of the book, specific responsibilities of authorship were divided as follows: Chapters 1–4 and 21–24 were written by William Ebenstein, Chapters 5–11 by C. Herman Pritchett, Chapters 12–15 and 18–19 by Henry A. Turner, and Chapters 16–17 and 20 by Dean Mann. We deeply regret that one of our original collaborators, Edgar Lane, died in the very early stages of planning this book. We not only lost a highly esteemed friend and colleague who was deeply committed to what we were trying to accomplish, but American political science, too, lost prematurely a brilliant teacher and researcher at the threshold of a most promising career.

W. E.

C. H. P.

H. A. T.

D. M.

PART I ❧ PERSPECTIVES OF
DEMOCRACY

CHAPTER 1

DEMOCRACY AS A SYSTEM OF VALUES

❧ THE MEANING OF DEMOCRACY

The meaning of democracy was defined by Abraham Lincoln as "government of the people, by the people, for the people." The heart of democracy is the fact that people govern themselves ("Government *of* the people" or "government *by* the people"). Whether self-government always turns out right, whether it is, in practice, always in the best interest of the people ("government *for* the people") is important, but not decisive. This is perhaps the reason why Lincoln put government "*for* the people" at the end of his statement.

In a democracy, there is the hope that self-government will also lead to *good* government because people will generally not act against their own interest; yet if a choice between self-government and good government has to be made by a democrat, he clearly prefers imperfect self-government to a more perfect government imposed from above or from the outside.

We see in the underdeveloped countries of Asia and Africa today that the inhabitants, often illiterate and without much political experience, prefer self-government to government by foreign rulers, although the latter may be more efficient and provide more economic benefits. When Belgium gave independence to the Congo in 1960, chaos and internal strife immediately replaced the orderly life built up by Belgians over many years.

3

Yet the 20 million Congolese preferred their own government—inefficient, corrupt, and ruthless as it might be—to the orderly and smoothly functioning government of the Belgian administration.

The Communist concept of democracy aims at neither government *of* the people nor at government *by* the people, but at government *in the interests of* the people. In the case of Germany, for example, Communist Russia looks upon West Germany as not having any democracy because the capitalistic system of private property operates there. From the Communist viewpoint, West Germany could be a democracy only if her Communist element—about 2 percent of the population—could take over the government and abolish the capitalistic system. The fact that the remaining 98 percent of West Germany is opposed to communism means little to the Moscow version of democracy because the Communists believe that only they know what is in the interest of the people. Even if the capitalist system is upheld by the people in free elections, the Communists still insist that democratic capitalism is a dictatorship because capitalism, they believe, is by definition a dictatorship. The fact that the people living under the system of democratic capitalism want it, proves to Communists only that the majority does not always know what is best for it.

By contrast, Russia considers East Germany as a democracy because productive property is owned and operated by the state. The people of East Germany overwhelmingly reject the Communist tyranny imposed on them, and the Communist government can maintain itself only by secret police methods and "correctional" labor camps. Yet this is of no importance to the Communist version of democracy. The important thing about democracy (in the Communist view) is, not what people want, but what they *should* want. If what they should want can be imposed on them only by force, then freedom means force in the double talk of Communist political language. Or, as defenders of Communist terror have often put it: "You cannot make an omelette without breaking eggs."

Ironically, therefore, the Communist police state in East Germany that can exist only by dint of Russian bayonets, officially calls itself "German Democratic Republic." Similarly, when Russia's Red Army imposed communism on several Eastern European states after World War II, Communist semantics immediately found the appropriate name for them: "People's Democracies."

❧ BASIC PRINCIPLES OF DEMOCRACY

Science and Human Relations

By using reason and experience, man has scored impressive advances in the mastery of nature (such as in physics, chemistry, or biology). Democrats believe that reason and experience can also be fruitfully used in the under-standing and harmonious adjustment of human relations. This belief in reason and experience is considered by many the most important aspect of a free society—and perhaps the most difficult to live up to.

In contrast, dogmatists (such as Communists or Fascists) reject this belief in reason and experience: They are sure they *know* what the truth is, and therefore shut their minds to arguments of reason or to practical lessons of experience.

For Communists, the concept of *class* is the answer to man's ills, whereas for Fascists, *race* and *nation* are the unfailing keys to truth.

Since the political dogmatist knows with absolute certainty, he need inquire no further, and whoever questions him on the basis of contrary evidence supplied by either reason or experience is treated as an enemy. Disdain for reason and experience is thus psychologically reflected in fanaticism; it brooks no compromise, and its political rule of action with respect to opponents is not "live and let live," but "live and liquidate."

By contrast, the democratic way of life is based on the idea that truth (with a small *t*) is tentative, changing, and subject to constant checking and verification. The history of both physical science and social science is full of truths that eventually turned out to be wholly or partly untrue; the rational empiricist—the person who trusts in reason and experience—refuses, therefore, to believe that mankind has ever arrived at the end of its quest for truth and knowledge.

No one can be a scientific investigator without a healthy dose of *profound doubt* or *skepticism*, taking nothing for granted, challenging accepted truths and beliefs, and stopping nowhere in his quest for more knowledge. In the first phase of the development of modern science, the physical sciences were hamstrung by religious fanatics who fought, by force, the onward march of scientific discovery. Later, after the physical sciences became free from any control by church or state, the major obstacles to free inquiry have been raised against the scientific investigation of *social* life by powerful vested economic and political interests. Yet in the areas of both economics and government, the social scientist has only one responsibility: to find the truth.

Similarly, democracy implies the recognition of skepticism as a vital element and attitude in the lives of free men. Whereas totalitarians claim to be in possession of ultimate and changeless truth, the democrat is skeptical of such claims. The free way of life runs parallel here with the Judaeo-Christian religious tradition, which urges man to approach human problems in a *spirit of humility* because no man possesses perfect truth or acts in accordance with perfect justice.

The skepticism of the democrat (so akin to that of the scientist) is based not only on philosophical grounds, but also on the common-sense observation that man is too often inclined to pronounce his interests and passions as universal truths. Because the liberal democrat can have no absolute certainty about his views, he is willing to concede that his opponent may be partly right—and it is out of this realization that the free interplay of rivaling political parties becomes possible.

The issue of skepticism in science and democracy is closely related to that of how to treat opponents. Scientific opinions cannot be accepted as correct on the basis of authority, but must be verified by accurate methods of observation. The scientist is at all times aware of the incompleteness of his data; he therefore feels no animosity against the person who disagrees with him, but at best hopes that the factual evidence will ultimately prove him right. Because he knows that he may be wrong, the scientist does not look upon a fellow scientist who disagrees with him as an enemy or a traitor, a moral delinquent to be silenced or liquidated, but as a colleague and an honorable opponent who is to be respected.

Above all, the scientist is aware of the primary importance of *proper standards of procedure* in scientific investigation: science is doomed if government by law (in this case, verifiable methods of research and experimentation) is replaced by government by men who claim scientific truth on the basis of their personal authority.

A case in point is the Russian biologist Trofim Lysenko, who announced in 1948 an incontrovertible truth: that, contrary to all hitherto available evidence, acquired characteristics can be transmitted by heredity. Because this new "discovery" seemed even to many Communist geneticists rather unsound and unproved, Lysenko, who was unable to present procedures of testing his new truth, buttressed his position at the end of his address by proudly proclaiming that the Central Committee of the Communist party had examined his report "and approved it." Lysenko lost his power and influence only after the Communist leadership, under Brezhnev and Kosygin, stopped supporting him.

The democratic process in politics shares with the scientific process in the laboratory the emphasis on procedure; both prescribe *how* truth is to be ascertained, not *what* specific truth is going to be discovered. The scientist in his laboratory and the democrat in politics both know how they will travel, but they never know in advance exactly where they will ultimately arrive. Thus the Constitution of the United States does not state dogmatically what actions of government are good or bad; instead, it determines what methods are to be used in making, executing, and interpreting the laws. Just as the scientist is eager to discover all evidence on a problem under investigation, the democratic procedure requires that *all* opinions be heard before a policy is adopted.

The English Parliament started out as a High Court, and to this day the

House of Lords has remained the supreme court of Great Britain. As a direct result of British parliamentary procedure, all democracies follow the judicial method of gathering and weighing all available facts and opinions before the legislative decision is rendered.

The process of legislation in Congress would be a simple matter if it were no more than a series of announcements of truth by the majority party. In fact, winning a majority of seats in the House or Senate is only a beginning; what the majority party would like to consider as truth must be subjected to constant checks and criticisms by those, in and out of Congress, who disagree. Authority in democratic politics, as in science, must ultimately rest on persuasion, not on force.

By contrast, authority in totalitarian societies rests on force, and this pattern is easily transmitted from governmental practices to natural science. For example, the German Nazis believed that only "German mathematics" or "German physics" was true, and therefore Einstein's work in physics, the most original since Newton, was rejected as untrue, solely because Einstein was a Jew. Later, the Communists, too, attacked Einstein's theories as "bourgeois" and therefore untrue. The Nazis had no use for Freud's medical theories of psychoanalysis because their author was a Jew; to the Communists, Freud was a lackey of Wall Street because his theories (by stressing the individual nature of the human predicament) were in conflict with the Marxist-Leninist dogma that all of man's ills are the outcome of capitalist exploitation.

It can thus be seen that science and democracy have, both in spirit and procedure, a great deal in common. Above all, there is the principle of *publicity*: secrecy is the death of science as well as of the democratic process. By contrast, government by secrecy is one of the essential principles of totalitarianism.

After fifty years of Communist government and administration in the Soviet Union, the outside world still knows very little about the inner workings of the Soviet system in the field of government, particularly at the top. As far as the Communist party of the Soviet Union is concerned, we know next to nothing about what goes on in the presidium, the top group of the real party leaders. When Khrushchev was ousted in 1964, no one in Russia or outside had any idea that such a momentous development was in the making, or what were the causes behind it.

An important source of information about any country is statistics. In addition to hundreds of specialized statistical materials, the federal government publishes annually the *Statistical Abstract of the United States*, a volume of about 1,000 pages. It contains all important statistical information about the United States—good, bad, and indifferent to the "image" of the country. By contrast, no regular annual statistical collection of Soviet

3/13/57

"Well, we certainly botched this job. What'll we stamp it—'Secret' or 'Top Secret'? From Herblock's *Special for Today* (Simon & Schuster, 1958).

statistics was published at all between 1936 and 1955. Since 1956, the Soviet government has published such statistical volumes—but with a totalitarian slant. First, some of the most important social and economic information is never published: the distribution of the national income, personal consumption, the number of unemployed, and similar data that might appear damaging to the Soviet image. A second feature is the volume and date of such information. When things look good, the Soviet statistical yearbook provides relatively more information (the volume for 1961, for example, had 400 pages), and the information is quickly released. When things look less good, the statistical volume becomes extremely slim (the volume for 1964, for example, had only 160 pages), and the information is released with some delay.

Even a fundamental question such as What is the rate of growth of the Soviet economy? cannot be answered clearly on the basis of available Soviet figures. Economists in the United States and other free nations have written lengthy analyses of this question, so vital to the free world. Such analyses are, in the last resort, combinations of detective sleuthing and guesswork because the Soviet Union has never been willing to publish some of the most elementary economic data, which alone can answer such questions satisfactorily.

Red China has gone even further in its statistical bamboo curtain. In 1966, official figures of Red China's population were 700 million—75 million less than informed estimates of foreign scholars. In agriculture, Red China for nearly a decade published no figures on crop yields and food production after the fiasco of the "Great Leap Forward" in the late 1950s.

The second principal element that links science with democracy is the universalistic principle of *equality of opportunity*. In science, there can be no American versus Japanese physics, nor Communist versus capitalist biology—the only issue in all cases is whether physical or biological principles can be proved by experience. Similarly, the ethics of democracy demands that every person have a chance to make his contribution in life, and that no one be barred because he belongs to a particular social, economic, religious, ethnic, or racial group.

In the long run, therefore, democracy cannot tolerate differentials of advantage that are not demonstrably based on differences of capacity and service. It is no accident that modern science found its strongest early support in seventeenth-century England and in eighteenth-century France, the two major nations in which free thought and government first developed in Europe.

1/17/64
"Psst! Want to see some hot statistics?" From *Straight Herblock*
(Simon & Schuster, 1964).

Compromise Through Free Discussion and Consent

Compromise through free discussion and consent is the method by which a democratic society tries to settle conflicting interests and ideas. Because no one can claim a monopoly in truth, the best possible resolution of arguments and conflicts can be attained by gathering all available facts and by encouraging the expression of the widest variety of ideas.

Experience shows that of two conflicting interests or viewpoints, one is rarely completely right and the other completely wrong. Only men who assume that they are angels—unsullied by pride, greed, and passion—hold their opponents to be devils, in whom there is nothing good or hopeful. In the light of religious belief (which holds all men to be sinners) and of ordinary common sense (which quickly suspects self-righteousness) the human race is made up of individuals who are neither angels nor devils, but who fall somewhere in between these two extremes.

Social life would be a perennial paradise if right were always clearly opposed by wrong, and if the only two colors in human actions were black and white. This view of the world is, in fact, held by children, in whose fantasy the world is inhabited by the "good guys" and the "bad guys." This childish oversimplification forms the background for the totalitarian oversimplification that a Communist (or Fascist) is always right and a non-Communist (or non-Fascist) is always wrong. Compromise is obviously impossible for those who see the world exclusively through lenses that permit them to see only two colors—black and white.

The democrat realizes that there are more than two sides (one good, one bad) to every question, and he tries to explore all possible approaches to an issue. He is aware of the imperfection of all humans, their thoughts and actions, and this understanding includes the painful admission that one's own aims and acts may also be imperfect. This insight makes possible the humility and skepticism without which compromise is impossible.

Whereas the totalitarian classifies all those who disagree with him as *enemies* to be liquidated, the democrat thinks of the other side as *opponents,* who must not only be tolerated in a free society, but whose existence and vigor must be encouraged if a society is to remain free. Opponents of the existing government in totalitarian countries are imprisoned or shot; in a democratic nation such as Britain, the opposition in Parliament is officially styled "Her Majesty's Loyal Opposition," and its Leader receives a special salary to help him carry on his opposition activities in the most effective fashion.

There is another difference here, also, which is important: The totalitarian mind regards the opponents of the government as enemies of the state because of the identification of the government with state and society; by contrast, the democratic view is that an opponent of the government is just as loyal to the state as is the government, and that loyalty to a free society demands opposition because, by definition, no one party can ever be completely right.

Because totalitarian regimes must persist in the unrealistic fiction that they are 100 percent right, they invariably proclaim that all their people are behind them, and election results (at least as proclaimed by totalitarian dictatorships) usually show that 99.6 percent or 99.9 percent of the people have voted in favor of the dictatorship.

Elections in free nations with a two-party system show that the average is roughly 52 percent for the victorious party against 48 percent of the losing party. This has been the average in presidential elections in the United States in the last hundred years; a margin of 60 percent against 40 percent is considered a landslide and most unusual. These close election results in free nations prove that neither party is as right as it would like to think it is, nor as wrong as the opposing party would like to make it out to be.

The vote-splitter in a free society typifies the person who reflects the unwillingness to support any one political party at all times. In a totalitarian state, there can be no vote-splitters by definition—only enthusiastic followers who cheer, or unredeemable enemies whose place is in prison or on the gallows. In a free society, the vote-splitter assumes that neither party is always right nor always wrong; like the man from Missouri, he wants to be shown before he makes up his mind.

In 1952 the Republican party, for example, selected General Eisenhower over Senator Taft as its presidential candidate because it hoped (rightly) that the General would have a stronger appeal to the vote-splitter, the independent voter, and even to Democrats, than the Senator, whose main strength lay with the Republicans who were already convinced.

In 1956, President Eisenhower was re-elected with an exceptionally strong popular majority; yet the Democrats managed to retain the control of both houses of Congress, which showed that many voters did a good deal of thinking before casting their ballots. Millions of voters felt that neither party had a monopoly of wisdom and right, and therefore decided that a Republican should be the Chief Executive, but that the Democrats should be in control of the Congress.

In the elections of 1960, Kennedy did less well than Democratic candidates in congressional elections. In 1964, President Johnson ran ahead of his party in congressional races. This showed again in both cases, that many voters exercised independent judgment in casting their ballots.

Equality in a Free Society

The democratic philosophy does not deny that there are empirical differences between human beings—in size, appearance, intellectual ability, genetic endowment, and character. Yet in spite of such specific differences, the democratic philosophy demands that all human beings should be treated as equals, for they all share the common quality of being members of the human race, which is more universal than any specific difference. Moreover, although no perfectly convincing case for basic human equality has perhaps ever been made, the case for human inequality has been found even less convincing.

Democratic equality means, not the duty to be like everybody else, but the right to be different. At the time of the Declaration of Independence, human beings could be bought and sold like cattle because their color was different from the "right" color; others could not hold public office because their faith differed from the "right" faith (Jews in Protestant and Catholic countries, Catholics in Protestant states, and Protestants in Catholic states); the poor were treated as inferiors, because they were different, in material wealth, manners, and education, from those who were the right people who dominated society; finally, there was the penalty of difference of sex: women were denied equality of status in law and everyday life.

The democratic ideal—not always practiced—is that all these differences are less important than the right of every human being to life, liberty, and the pursuit of happiness. In this fundamental point, all human beings are equal, according to the democratic concept. However, democracy does not promise happiness to the individual, but the right to pursue happiness according to his own lights.

Liberal thinkers and governments had stressed the right to life, liberty, and property before 1776. But the Declaration of Independence, by including the "pursuit of happiness" as a basic human right, was a breakthrough in the development of the democratic concept of equality. For the first time in history, a nation committed itself to the revolutionary proposition that happiness is not the prerogative of only the well-born and well-to-do, but the right of all people.

Totalitarian doctrine makes to its followers the unrealistic promise that happiness can be obtained without personal effort, that a man is entitled to happiness solely (as in the case of Nazi doctrine) because he is the blonde, Nordic type of German, or because (as in the Communist doctrine) he is a loyal proletarian. Promising its subjects such unearned happiness because of a superior inherent quality of race or class, totalitarianism is driven to treat the rest of mankind unequally and unfairly: racialists therefore discriminate against those who are of the "wrong" race, while Communists

have no use for persons of the wrong social background. Despite their
professed belief in equality, Communists invariably end up by acting on
the principle that some are more equal than others.

However, equality does not mean, as Plato charged in the *Republic*,
"dispensing a kind of equality to equals and unequals alike." The contrary
is true, of the ideal democracy at least. The democratic approach is
precisely based on the assumption that there are differences of talent and
ability: all that the democratic doctrine asks is that those who are superior
to others by virtue of character or intellect be given the fullest opportunity
to develop their unequal gifts without artificial obstacles based on racial,
religious, or social discrimination. To deprive such superior (and therefore
unequal) individuals of their chance is, in the democratic theory, not only
morally wrong but also socially wasteful, because it deprives society as a
whole of the potential contribution of such outstanding persons.

For every Ralph Bunche there may be dozens or hundreds of potential
Ralph Bunches among American Negroes. But he had the good fortune of
getting the educational and professional opportunities that enabled a poor,
orphaned Negro boy to get a college education, work for the Department
of State, the United Nations, and finally be honored by the Nobel Peace
Prize as one of the great diplomats and peacemakers of our time.

Because democracy believes in the dignity and uniqueness of each and
every person, its concept of equality does not aim at leveling mankind, but
at allowing each person to develop his personality to the fullest possible
extent consistent with the right of others to do the same. The more
democracy lives up to this ideal, the more it recognizes the reality of
inequality among men.

What democracy opposes is that such inequality be based, not on
demonstrable superiority of character, intellect, or leadership, but on
irrational criteria of birth, status, or violence. To the extent that genuine
superiority is suppressed by custom, fraud, or force, artificial superiority
takes its place. It is the totalitarian society, and not the democratic society,
which seeks to bring about equal uniformity by leveling the whole citizenry
to the condition of serfdom, dominated by a small group of self-appointed
leaders.

Although the totalitarians feel scorn and contempt for democracies
because the latter allegedly neglect the whole problem of leadership,
history does not bear out that that scorn is justified. In World War I, the
Kaiser, Hindenburg, and Ludendorff were by no means superior to Lloyd
George, Clemenceau, Marshal Foch, or Woodrow Wilson. In World War
II, Hitler, Mussolini and Tojo made a poor showing as compared with
leaders like Winston Churchill, Franklin D. Roosevelt, and General de
Gaulle. As to Stalin's quality of leadership in World War II, his pact with
Hitler in 1939 enabled Nazi Germany to conquer the Continent in less

than a year, and then to turn to the invasion of Russia in 1941. Before the Soviet Union could effectively resist, the Germans had occupied Soviet territory four times as large as France. Hitler had said in *Mein Kampf* that Germany must learn from its past mistakes, and never start a two-front war again. Stalin gave Hitler what he wanted in 1939.

Democracy need not pay for its belief in the inherent equality of all men by mediocrity at the top. On the contrary, the democratic belief in equality of opportunity is the best method yet devised in history to get the best type of leaders in peace and war. In the economic sphere, the free market produces more and better goods than the coercive, totalitarian economy. Similarly, in the political arena, the free market of opportunity produces more and better leaders than the coercive, totalitarian polity.

Ends and Means

In the democratic concept, ends, or goals, cannot be sharply separated from means because they constantly influence one another. Experience has shown that the more certain one feels about his ends, the less likely one is to use restraint in the choice of means.

Moreover, it is not always easy to distinguish means from ends, because a means is often also an end, looked at from a different angle. Thus work is for some an end in itself; for others it is but a means to an end—making money, for example. Yet, making money again may be only a means—the end being the support of one's family in comfort; this, again may be only a means to a higher end, such as the realization of deeply felt love.

The fact of war is a constant reminder of how easily means and ends can be confused, and how means have a dynamic and profound effect on ends. At the outset, warring nations generally start with a definite set of objectives, considering war merely as a means to bring about those ends. Yet once war has started, the original ends are often forgotten with amazing haste, and the reality of war begins to permeate every fiber of national thinking, acting, and planning. As the war continues, nations gradually develop objectives that have little to do with the original aims; the new aims largely receive their character from the conduct of the war itself.

Russia entered World War II with the aim of defeating the danger of German imperialism on her western borders; yet by the time the war was over, the Russian goal, as shaped by successful warfare, was broadened to include the subjugation of all of Eastern Europe under her domination and the spreading of Communist regimes throughout Asia and other parts of the globe.

The democratic nations, too, committed acts in World Wars I and II that were out of harmony with their normal objectives, and that could only be explained—as in the case of the wholesale evacuation of tens of thousands of Americans of Japanese descent from the West Coast and their internment in the interior of the country—by fears and hatreds created (or fanned) by the fact of war.

The central position of means in free societies is well entrenched in their living experience. *Magna Carta, habeas corpus,* and *trial by jury,* to mention but a few roots of liberty in the English-speaking world, are originally all procedural devices, or means, and the history of liberty may aptly be described as the history of procedure, of legal techniques. In the United States, the constitutional concept of "due process" has played an enormous role in protecting the citizen's liberty against the government. As the phrase itself suggests, the protection afforded the citizen by due process relates primarily to the means and procedures employed by the government.

The citizen of the totalitarian state lives in a world of constant anxiety and insecurity because he knows there is no due process to protect him against the arbitrariness of the government; he may be sentenced to jail, or even put to death, by administrative agents (such as the police) without any trial whatsoever, or if he gets the benefit of a trial, his sentence may be based on extorted confession following brainwashing, or on false witnesses forced by the state to give false testimony. In his anti-Stalin speech of February 25, 1956, Khrushchev admitted that thousands of persons were executed under Stalin as spies and saboteurs. In most cases, the victims confessed their guilt despite their innocence. How were their confessions obtained? asked Khrushchev, and he answered: "Confessions of guilt of many arrested and charged with enemy activity were gained with the help of cruel and inhuman tortures."

In representative assemblies, too, it is not the legislative *product* that distinguishes a democratic body from a totalitarian one, but the differences of *procedure*. In the one case, procedure aims at the fullest and fairest guarantee of the minority to be heard; in the other, procedure aims at silencing minorities, so that debate is finally replaced by organized cheering for the leader.

Belief in the Dignity of Man

The concept of the dignity and worth of the individual fundamentally distinguishes democracy from communism or fascism. In fascism, the emphasis is on the large group—the nation, the state, or the empire. In communism, the emphasis is again on a large group—the social class. Both totalitarian systems are less concerned with what an individual person *does* than with the larger group he *belongs* to. Both communism and fascism punish and destroy without even the pretext of personal guilt: Fascists discriminate against individuals, and even kill them, solely on the ground that they belong to a different nationality or race, whereas Communists consider "bourgeois" (or middle-class) background sufficient reason for hostile treatment.

By contrast, in the democratic doctrine, no human being is guilty because fate has placed him by birth in one social, national, religious, or racial group, rather than in another. An individual can be held responsible only for wrongs committed by him, and not for belonging to the "wrong" social or racial group. Democratic thought follows here the Judaeo-Christian heritage, according to which every person has the road of salvation open to him if he chooses to take it. He can redeem himself from wrongdoing through good actions; but there is no way of changing the color of his skin or the "bourgeois" background of his parents. There is no "fatal" guilt or crime in this tradition, only personal guilt or crime. Modern totalitarianism rejects this view and goes back to the ancient outlook of paganism, according to which some were born to rule, and others (the natural slaves) to be ruled.

The differences between the democratic and the totalitarian viewpoints with regard to the issue of individual versus fatal or inborn guilt can be illustrated by the differing approaches to the treatment of war criminals after World War II. The United States maintained that individual guilt had to be proved in each case, and that it was not sufficient to have been a member of certain political or military organizations under the Nazi regime. The Soviets were less concerned with individual guilt: imprisonment (and worse) was meted out to all those who belonged to "reactionary" social classes, such as big landowners or industrialists, or to "Fascist" political organizations, a concept flexibly interpreted to include anti-Communists ranging from the Socialists on the Left to the conservatives, nationalists, and Nazis on the Right.

In democratic thought, no social or political institution exists for its own sake. Its sole purpose is to help the individual fulfill himself. The American tradition in this matter is clear. The Declaration of Independence states that the purpose of government is to safeguard inalienable human rights, such as life, liberty, and the pursuit of happiness, and that "whenever any form of government becomes destructive of these ends, it is the right of the people to alter or to abolish it, and to institute new government, laying its foundations on such principles, and organizing its powers in such form as to them shall seem most likely to effect their safety and happiness."

The Principle of Voluntarism: Democracy as a Gamble

Every social system, every method of operating a society in a particular way, prescribes how people are to act. But prescription alone is not enough.

If laws, commands, norms are too far removed from the actual behavior of the people, society breaks asunder. In addition to setting up rules of how people *should* act, every social system makes some assumption as to how they will *in fact* behave. This is the great gamble of every social system, its hope and expectation that a sufficient number of people will act in such a way as to keep the system going. For example, if in a hereditary monarchy the subjects begin to feel and act as if the monarch were just an ordinary mortal, the "emperor's clothes" (as in Hans Andersen's famous story) may fall off quickly, and the gamble of the system collapses, although under existing law the game should go on forever.

The number one bet of democracy is that people will do voluntarily what they would otherwise have to be forced to do. In every group or institution or society, rules of behavior must be established: Some have to lead and others have to follow, money has to be raised, and provisions must be made to defend the existence of the group against internal delinquency and outside aggression. The great gamble of democracy is that people will be ready to take on these responsibilities—some pleasant, others boring, still others dangerous—for reasons of self-respect and intelligence. He who respects himself will prefer to do a necessary job by himself, although it could be done more easily under someone else's direction or compulsion. Second, he who is intelligent enough to understand that some jobs must be done, will more cheerfully tackle them than will the less intelligent person, who persists in wishful hopes that if he keeps on shirking his responsibili-

From *Sick, Sick, Sick,* by Jules Feiffer. Copyright 1956, 1957, 1958 McGraw-Hill Book Company. Used by permission.

ties, the necessary job will somehow go away. In the end, of course, he will have to do what must be done, but he will perform under the dictation of someone else who has fewer illusions.

The principle of *voluntary action* is therefore the very foundation of a democratic society. Democracy can best be practiced in small, voluntary associations. Such associations first evolved in seventeenth-century England for religious purposes, and this tradition in the English-speaking world has resulted in innumerable religious sects that are small and voluntary. Later, the idea of voluntary association was applied to politics, and the state (like the church) came to be looked upon as a voluntary association, endowed with no more authority than the individuals composing it were willing to concede to it.

Within the state, political parties (not mentioned in the Constitution of the United States) express the voluntary principle in a free society. In the field of economic activity, labor unions and employers' associations reflect it, and in education, privately supported schools testify to its enduring strength. In charity, local community chests, the churches, and national organizations, such as the Red Cross, cooperate with government programs designed to relieve distress, want, and loneliness.

Government of Laws, Not Men

The concept of *government of laws, not men* draws on three sources of our Western heritage.

First, there is the source of classical antiquity, as reflected in Aristotle, Cicero, and the Stoics. Aristotle (in the *Politics*) defines the *law* as "reason unaffected by desire," and he adds that "he who bids the law rule may be deemed to bid God and Reason alone rule, but he who bids man rule adds an element of the beast; for desire is a wild beast, and passion perverts the minds of rulers, even when they are the best of men." The rule of law has the advantages of impartiality and calculability, whereas the rule of men is guided by passion, whimsicality, and arbitrariness. Cicero's concept of the state as a "community of law" strongly appealed to the Founding Fathers, to whom the Constitution as the highest symbol of the law seemed the only enduring means of uniting people from different countries into one nation.

The second source of the concept of the rule of law is the Judaeo-Christian religious belief that the law of God is superior to that of man, and that man owes his first loyalty to God, and not to the state.

The third source of the rule of law springs from the federal view of state and society in modern democracy. Society is viewed as the sum total of various voluntary groups, and the state, too, is regarded as an essentially voluntary association, since its authority derives, as in all voluntary associations, from its members, the citizens. If authority is thus conceived, a higher law must define the relations of individual private associations to each other and to the largest association, the state.

In the democratic concept, at least as developed in the United States, this higher law takes precedence over the law made by the state ("positive law"). Basic human rights are not considered a gift of government that it can withdraw at its discretion, but are rooted in higher law that government must respect. Our courts have held that officials in all three branches of government are bound by basic principles of reason and civilized conduct. The strength of the concept of higher law in the United States as compared with other democracies is striking. The American Revolution itself was justified by its leaders through an appeal to a law that was higher than the positive law of imperial Britain. The concept of the higher law is thus closely linked with American freedom from its very birth.

Finally, the concept of the *rule of law* means something different in a totalitarian system as compared with a democratic system. In a free society, the citizen—under the rule of law—may do anything not specifically forbidden by law, and he may not be punished for any act that is not specifically punishable at the time of committing the act. In a totalitarian society, the subject may do only what the state specifically allows him, or wants him, to do. Moreover, he may be punished for acts for which there is no specific penalty, but which the state considers punishable on such vague general grounds as "interest of the state" or "interest of the workers and toilers."

Similarly, the rule of law means something different in democracy and totalitarianism as applied to public officials. In a free society, a public official may do only what the law specifically authorizes or obliges him to do. By contrast, the government official in the totalitarian state may do anything that is not specifically forbidden—either by law or by his administrative superiors. In the free society, the bias is in favor of the citizen against the government. In the totalitarian society, the bias is invariably in favor of the government against the citizen.

In a totalitarian state, officials frequently invoke "state necessity" as a justification for acts that are not permitted by the law. This leaves state officials a wide margin of arbitrariness and discretion because they themselves decide whether "state necessity" exists in a given situation. By contrast, the rule of law does not permit the excuse of "state necessity" for illegal actions of government officials. This principle was established in England in *Entick* v. *Carrington* (1765), in the following words: "With respect to the plea of State necessity, or a distinction that has been aimed at between State offenses and others, the common law does not understand that kind of reasoning, nor do our books take notice of any such distinction."

⚜ DEMOCRATIC GOVERNMENT AND DEMOCRATIC SOCIETY

Democracy Is More Than a Form of Government

One of the weaknesses of modern Western thought is its frequent identification of democracy with democratic government: freedom of thought and speech, freedom of assembly and association, and freedom of the press. This approach is narrow because it equates the part with the whole.

Political democracy is a part (and a very significant one) of democracy, but not all of it. Democracy as a way of life is more than politics and government. A society is not democratic because it has political democracy, but it has political democracy because it is democratic.

Democracy as a way of life must stand the test of scrutiny in such areas as the relations of capital and labor, economic opportunity, racial equality, education, family relations, church organizations, and the position of women—to mention but a few. The perfectly democratic society would be one in which all these forms of human relations are wholly shaped by the democratic principles of self-government based on equality and consent. Such a perfect democracy never has existed, and probably never will exist, as long as human beings are fallible—afflicted with the undemocratic impulses of aggressiveness, greed, and domination.

Why the Political Aspect of Democracy Has Top Priority

Of all the elements of the democratic way of life, the political is probably the most important. The essence of political democracy lies in its emphasis on *how* human beings treat one another, *how* decisions are made, in other words, on *means* and *procedure*, on the rules of the game.

The difference between civilized law and barbarous law is not only that the sentences of the latter are generally stiffer than those of the former but also that civilized law observes predetermined procedures based on fairness and equity; barbarous law knows of no such procedures.

Science begins when the man of magic and wizardry, operating behind the veil of mystery and secrecy, is replaced by the empirical student of nature, whose scientific findings cannot claim serious credibility, much less truth, unless supported by an explanation of the procedures through which the findings were reached.

This sense of procedure, of observing the rules of the game, is not natural to man; children find it hard to obey such rules; hence, one of the purposes of exposing children to organized sports and games under adult umpires is to instill in them a sense of fairness and sportsmanship.

It is therefore no accident that the concept of "due process" is the foundation of constitutional government in the United States. In fact, it can be argued that it is much more than a legal principle: *Democracy as a whole is an enlarged version or paraphrase of due process.*

The essence of political due process in government lies in the fact that all sides to a dispute are given a fair hearing. This principle applies to the two houses of Congress; there it is taken for granted that more than one viewpoint be heard. In modern legislative practice, the Congress will never legislate on labor, agriculture, or in any other area, without giving representatives of the affected interest groups a fair chance to present their point of view before the appropriate congressional committees.

To the unsophisticated mind it may perhaps seem that political democracy is not as important as social and economic democracy because the latter deals with practical aspects of social life (such as wealth and poverty), whereas the former is concerned "only" with the rules of the game. Yet the rules of a game, precisely because they deal with no one aspect of social life in particular, potentially deal with all.

It is not the task of political democracy to prescribe the exact amount of wages to be paid to workers; but by insisting that democratic procedures be observed in dealings between management and labor, such procedures—as in the case of collective bargaining—have a bearing on the question of wages. Political democracy as such has no specific program for education; but if the proper procedures are observed in hiring teachers, in protecting their freedom to teach, in encouraging students to engage in self-government in school activities, then the content of education will thereby be profoundly affected.

Experience supports this line of reasoning. It shows that political democracy, if practiced over any length of time, leads to the extension of the democratic principle to social, economic, educational, racial, religious, and international problems. So far, there is less evidence the other way around. For example, full religious toleration in eighteenth-century Prussia did not lead to political democracy. But political democracy in Britain and the United States in the nineteenth century led to religious freedom and equality.

The case of the Soviet Union is another illustration. When the Communist regime was set up in 1917, Lenin and his followers believed that social and economic democracy had priority, and would inevitably and automatically lead to political democracy. Yet as time went on, events developed otherwise. Instead of social and economic democracy leading to political democracy, the regime of political totalitarianism gradually corroded social and economic egalitarianism. From the early 1930s on, economic inequality became the official policy of the Soviet rulers, the socialist ideal of equality being dismissed as a "petty-bourgeois prejudice."

The contrast with the Western democracies is striking. It could be argued in the nineteenth century that Britain and the United States were "only" political democracies. The discrepancies between the wealthy few and the many poor were staggering. Free labor unions were discouraged and often suppressed by force; higher education was generally limited to persons of means; and there was virtually no governmental protection against the hazards of sickness, unemployment, and old age. Yet the slowly working force of political democracy gradually spread into all other areas of social life—and the masses of the people in the United States and Great Britain today enjoy standards of living, education, security, and leisure undreamed of a century ago.

All this does not mean that political democracy automatically guarantees everything for everybody, through a kind of slot machine operation: put the coin of political democracy in at the top, pull the lever, and the good life comes out of the machine. All that political democracy can do is to provide the challenge and opportunity to make human existence better and happier, by using, on all fronts, more fairness, decency, respect, consent, and liberty. Whether such opportunities are used depends on the intelligence and integrity of the people.

The main difference between political democracy and the other aspects of social life is simply this: With political democracy, the further expansion of democracy into the social, economic, and cultural aspects of society is at least *possible*; without political democracy, the pull in the long run is for less democracy for society as a whole. In fighting for political democracy, people fight for the *chance* to build a better life; where political democracy is absent, the chance itself is lacking.

❦ THE CORE OF FREE GOVERNMENT

Liberty: What It Is and How It Can Be Measured

Political liberty is the first characteristic of political democracy. There are two concepts of freedom: the *positive concept* and the *negative concept*. In the older Greek meaning, freedom was essentially a *positive* concept. It meant the right (and duty) to participate in the making of political decisions, above all the right to vote, to hold public office, to associate with others of like political views, and to criticize the government of the day.

This positive concept of freedom is based on the realization that freedom, if practiced without restraints, would quickly lead to anarchy, the law of the jungle, and to the triumph of the strong over the weak. *Ubi societas, ibi ius:* where there is society, there is law, as the Romans in their practical wisdom so well understood. There can be no civilized and just society without law and order.

The positive concept of freedom admits that there must be compulsion if freedom is to have practical meaning. However, what it demands is that, if there must be law and order, they be *self-imposed.* Government based on consent of the governed is therefore an expression of freedom.

The second meaning of freedom is much more recent: the *negative* concept of absence of constraint. Whereas the positive aspect of freedom expresses the freedom to do something, the negative aspect connotes the freedom from having to do something. This negative meaning of freedom is only about 400 years old; the movement of liberty from the sixteenth century on has been directed against irresponsible authority in religion, government, and economics. This approach to liberty reflects the individualism that found its first modern expression in the Renaissance and Reformation.

Because this negative concept of freedom has been so predominant in the last three or four centuries, it is often forgotten that negation alone can create nothing, and that it must be supplemented by the older Greek positive view of freedom. Above all, the principal shortcoming of the negative view of freedom is the failure to realize that freedom implies obligations as well as privileges, duties as well as rights.

Can political liberty be measured? The crude classification of political systems into democracies and dictatorships is valid in a general way, but provides no accurate standards of measurement for appraising differences of political liberty between specific democracies on the one hand and between specific dictatorships on the other. Moreover, not every political system neatly fits the classification of being democratic or dictatorial. We therefore need a more accurate standard of measurement.

That standard, put briefly, can best be expressed in this way: Political liberty is directly proportionate to the degree of unorthodoxy that is permitted. Obviously, no one was hindered in Nazi Germany from praising nazism as the greatest idea in German history. In Russia today, there is complete freedom of speech for anyone who eulogizes communism. In Red China, there is complete freedom to laud Mao as the most enlightened and most democratic statesman in Chinese history.

"The way I see it, what this college needs is diversity." © 1965 by The New York Times Company. Reprinted by permission.

The same principle also applies, on a smaller scale, to democracies. In a Welsh mining area, sympathies for the British Labour Party do not necessarily testify to geat civic courage. In Vermont, it does not take much civil liberty to be a Republican, nor, in Mississippi, to be a Democrat. In some sections of New York City, the liberal philosophy may be the orthodox thing, whereas in other sections of the same city, the conservative viewpoint prevails.

It can thus be seen that political liberty begins at the point where unorthodox opinions and practices are accepted without legal, social, or economic penalties. Using this yardstick of the margin of tolerated unorthodoxy for a quick survey of the dictatorships, we find the least margin of unorthodoxy in Red China today, in Nazi Germany under Hitler, and in the Soviet Union under Stalin, a somewhat wider margin in the Soviet Union under Khrushchev and his successors, a much wider margin in Fascist Italy (1922–1945) or in Communist Yugoslavia since 1948, and in Poland since the triumph of "national communism" in 1956, and the relatively largest margin of unorthodoxy in the present Spanish, Portuguese, and (traditional) Latin American dictatorships.

Similarly, measuring liberty in democracies with the yardstick of accepted unorthodoxy, we find Britain, Scandinavia, Holland, Australia, and New Zealand probably at the top of the list. However, these positions are not permanent. For example, the United States has been under pressure of conformist tendencies since the end of World War II, such pressures culminating in the years 1950–1954 under the leadership of the late Senator McCarthy. After his censure by the United States Senate in December, 1954, and his death shortly thereafter, there has been a steady movement back to the more traditional American attitude of not obstructing the expression of unorthodox views.

The weakening of liberty in periods of hot and cold war shows that liberty flourishes best in an atmosphere of security, both political and social. Citizens of free societies willingly accept curtailments of liberty in time of war in the national interest; such curtailment, however, must be necessary to win the war, and not to cover up official incompetence and failure. The American Congress and the British Parliament functioned in World Wars I and II with their usual vigor, and differences of opinion were freely expressed in the press, but the gravity of the situation imposed some voluntary self-restraints.

Nor can liberty flourish at its best in times of social and economic crisis. Where the spirit of liberty is strongly ingrained in the body politic, as in the English-speaking world, in Holland, in Switzerland, and in Scandinavia, the impact of social and economic difficulties, as during the Great Depression of 1929–1933, need not be fatal; the peoples of truly free societies showed a remarkable resistance to Fascist and Communist appeals even at the depth of economic depression. Where the roots of liberty are weak and of recent origin, as in Germany, Japan, and Russia, the totalitarian movements of communism and fascism had much more success. However, while social and economic security are important for the maintenance of liberty, other factors are even more important. Liberty is not a luxury of wealthy nations, as is evidenced by the fact that both wealthy and poor nations have succumbed to the appeals of totalitarianism.

The spiritual nature of liberty can best be seen in the fact that its modern origins are primarily *religious*. Long before the English people, for example, gained political liberty, they had achieved the liberty to worship God freely, and to govern their churches without interference from the outside. Although the Puritan Revolution in the 1640s had political and economic aspects, its religious sources and aims were the primary ones. The principle of congregationalism in religion meant that authority lay in the group as a whole, and not in a privileged hierarchy or elite, and that the individual had the right to follow his conscience in his religious beliefs. This *religious congregationalism* of the Puritans and other nonconformists was later applied to politics with results that had tremendous impact. It led to the doctrine that political authority rested with the *people*, who were the true *sovereign*, and that the government was no more than the agent of the community ministering to its communal needs, as its servant and not as its master.

The freedom of conscience in religion as transplanted to politics inevitably led to the concept of basic civil rights as incorporated in the English Bill of Rights (1689) and in the First Ten Amendments to the Constitution of the United States (1791), particularly the First Amendment, which guarantees the freedoms of religion (listed first), speech, press, assembly, and petition.

If citizens of free societies at times underestimate religious liberty as the root of all other liberties, totalitarian states never make that mistake. Both Nazi Germany and Communist Russia clearly understood from their beginning that religious liberty was the first, and most implacable, enemy of human oppression. Yet neither fascism nor communism has been able to eradicate religion.

The refusal of the democratic, liberal state to interfere in religious matters is not based on indifference. On the contrary, precisely because it holds religion in such high esteem, the free society is unwilling to favor one religious viewpoint over another. By granting tax-exemption to religious schools (as to other private schools), the government of free societies indirectly subsidizes them. In some liberal societies, as in Holland and England, the state even directly pays, wholly or partly, for the maintenance of private schools—mostly religious—on the theory that the parents have the right to decide the type of education their children are to receive, because the educational philosophies of public schools may not be valid for all people at all times. For reasons of history and tradition, government in the United States does not go that far in its support of religious schools, but the pressure to go further than has been the customary practice is steadily mounting.

Common Agreement on Fundamentals

The possibility and right to disagree are the very lifeblood of a free society. Yet disagreement alone is something negative and sterile unless there is first the "agreement to disagree."

The most important agreement, going beyond the most solemn constitutional document, is the shared desire to remain faithful to the democratic process. Although there is no written constitution in Great Britain, there are few, if any, nations in which dissenters and nonconformists are as fully protected by law and public opinion as in Britain.

On the other hand, written constitutions do not necessarily safeguard democracy. Fascism came to power in Italy, Germany, Japan, and Argentina in spite of lofty constitutional charters. Communism was established in Czechoslovakia in 1948 in spite of a written constitution dedicated to democratic ideals. The main lesson of history is that the vitality of a democracy is never greater than the capacity of the people to defend it.

If common agreement on fundamentals cannot be attained, tension builds up that may erupt in civil war. In 1860, the disagreement over slavery finally led to civil war in the United States. In 1936, a host of basic issues—the relation of church and state, the question of democracy versus authoritarian government, the issue of tradition versus modernity—led to a cruel civil war in Spain that lasted for three years. In 1965, revolution and civil war occurred in Indonesia over the issue of communism, resulting in Communist defeat.

The great political problem of modern France is not so much the multiparty system as the lack of agreement on the kind of government that is to prevail. Some French parties (such as the Communists and extreme rightists) want dictatorship; others want the traditional parliamentary supremacy over a weak executive; and the Gaullists believe in strong presidential leadership over an impotent legislature.

Much of French public debating and arguing is not over this or that specific political issue, but over the type of government that is best suited for France. After World War II, the Fourth Republic was installed, but it lasted only until 1958, when it was replaced by the Fifth Republic. Many observers—in France as well as abroad—see in the Fifth Republic a temporary expression of the unique figure of General de Gaulle rather than a new and lasting agreement on common political fundamentals in France. After de Gaulle is gone, it is quite possible that new dissensions over fundamentals will produce, in fact if not in name, a new, Sixth, Republic.

By contrast, divisions of political opinion in the United States or Britain are over specific economic or political issues, but not over the form of government itself. No healthy democracy will, of course, ever attain the ideal of 100 percent agreement on fundamentals, and it would perhaps be undesirable were such a condition to prevail. But in a healthy democracy, those who reject democracy itself are usually small in number and enjoy very little social prestige. In a healthy democracy, Fascist or Communist foes of democracy are generally considered the "lunatic fringe" of political life. But when such a fringe begins to reflect 20 or 30 percent of the population, as in contemporary France or Italy, a mild case of political neurosis may eventually turn into a more serious case of political psychosis.

⚘ THE SETTING OF AMERICAN DEMOCRACY

The English Background

The majority of Americans today are descended from non-British stock. This, in part, gives the American civilization that has developed, a distinctive character of its own. Charles Ives in music, William Faulkner in literature, David Sarnoff in industry—all are uniquely American, different from any eminent European counterparts, and characteristic products of the American environment. Yet one area in which the English heritage is still dominant in America and likely to remain so is law and government. The English settlers who came here in the seventeenth and eighteenth centuries brought with them a few fundamental ideas and customs that have withstood the test of time. During the seventeenth century the English people settled—first in the Puritan Revolution of the 1640s and then in the Glorious Revolution of 1688—the question of who was to be boss: King or Parliament. The parliamentarians won. This did not indicate the complete triumph of democracy as yet, because the right to vote was limited to property holders. It did, however, establish the principle of *representative government:* the idea that political authority rests with a freely elected parliament, and not with a king who rules by divine grace. The question of who precisely has the right to vote is much less important than the more basic question of whether government must reflect the wishes of voters or may act independently of them. The bias for representative government was thus as firmly planted on American soil as were the English language, the common law, and the King James version of the Bible.

The Influence of Religious Nonconformity

The religious views of the early English and Scottish settlers were no less important than their political convictions. The victory of Protestantism in England under Henry VIII was at first no triumph of liberty over authority, for it merely replaced the authoritarian Church of Rome with the authoritarian Church of England. In Germany itself, Lutheranism became an ally of authoritarian monarchy. The decisive political impact of Protestantism in England—totally lacking in German Protestantism—was the rise of nonconformist Protestant groups, led by the Puritans. The nonconformists carried Protestantism to its logical conclusions, being opposed to hierarchy in any church, whether Protestant or Catholic. The issue was important enough to cause the only major civil war in English history, that war being decisively won by the Puritans under Cromwell.

The British emigrants to North America in the early colonial days were generally nonconformist rather than Church of England; some of the more affluent nonconformists came over for religious reasons, but most came for economic reasons. The latter, too, were generally nonconformist, since the Church of England had its main support—then as now—in the more established and well-off social groups. Edmund Burke summarized this aspect of the American background in a few striking phrases in his speech in the House of Commons, March 22, 1775, on "Conciliation with the American Colonies": "All Protestantism, even the most cold and passive, is a sort of dissent. But the religion most prevalent in our Northern colonies is a refinement on the principle of resistance: it is the dissidence of dissent, and the Protestantism of the Protestant religion."

While Burke applied his characterization of Americans as "dissenters from dissent" to religion, the radical religious principles of nonconformity were soon to be applied to American government—much faster than in England itself. First, the religious principle that authority resides in the congregation of believers could easily be transferred to government, where it appears as the principle of popular sovereignty—the concept that all political authority resides in "we the people." In this view, democracy is political congregationalism. Second, the nonconformist principle of individual conscience as the ultimate judge of religious faith could easily be transformed into the political principle that the state has no right to dictate or control any personal political or economic views—and much less, moral or religious views. Third, the Puritan bias in favor of society against the state was later carried over into political attitudes. For the Puritan, society meant the numerous *voluntary* associations, whereas government represented the concept of authority and compulsion. According to this view, the role of government is subsidiary and should come into effect only when the free processes of nongovernmental social efforts fail. The government is viewed, not as a moral guide and teacher, but as an *administrative instrument*, always serving society and the individual. Next, the nonconformist emphasis on the small group (the English-speaking countries to this day have thousands of small religious groups and sects) sharpened the awareness that, in government, too, the vitality of democracy is best nurtured in small groups, preferably face-to-face, rather than in the vast anonymity of large national governments. Finally, the nonconformist emphasis on the diversity of social groups implies that behind the law of each group there is a higher law that applies to all. Translated from religion into politics, this principle led to the concept—stronger in the United States than in any other country—that above the law of the land there is the higher law of God and reason which no Congress or President can violate.

The Social Background of Early Immigrants

The social background of the early English and Scottish settlers also had a lasting effect on American society and government. The political revolutions in seventeenth-century England were a reflection of the newly rising middle class of merchants, artisans, and independent farmers. The main impulse for settling North America came from these middle-class groups—

or at least from those who were almost middle class. The wealthy merchant or farmer had no reason to migrate, aristocrats encouraged emigration for patriotic and financial reasons—so long as others migrated—and the lowest on the social scale were often too apathetic and unambitious to uproot themselves and leave their pals, pubs, and parishes. Lower middle-class people of adventurous bent—those who were neither so successful that they did not want to leave nor so down-and-out that they no longer had the spark of rebellion and adventure—provided the mass of English immigrants in the seventeenth and early eighteenth centuries. In addition, there was the small minority of those who were driven by the religious desire for building here the new Jerusalem. Until very recently, these two early groups contributed two of the main streaks of the American character: the drive and restless energy of the economic pioneer and the moral and religious idealism that centered in New England until the end of the nineteenth century.

From its beginning, American society was thus largely middle class, and has remained so to this day. This has happened wherever the English have settled: there is no aristocratic class, since aristocrats rarely emigrate, and there is no proletarian working class in the European sense, because the "frontier," that is, the abundance of economic opportunity—first of land and later of jobs—provided a maximum of social mobility and advancement such as the world had never known before.

In England, the middle classes won their battles, but they have retained the restraining influence of a precapitalist aristocracy and a postindustrial working class. In the American settlements, the ideas, outlook, and style of life of the middle classes have had no such restraining influence, whether it be in government, morals, or social prestige. In Europe, the successful businessman tries to imitate the old-line aristocrat, just as the worker seeks to live like a bourgeois. In American society, the middle class has never known such competition: the scion of an old or wealthy family often behaves as if he were "just one of the boys," and the worker does not need to imitate the bourgeois, because he is a bourgeois, and often earns more.

The social development of America was thus not like that of England, but rather followed its own lines. When Alexis de Tocqueville visited the United States in 1831, nothing attracted him more forcibly, he later wrote in his *Democracy in America*, than the "general equality of conditions." A democratic society—morally and economically—thus existed in America before it became a political democracy: this is perhaps the main reason for its continued success and political good luck. By contrast, many other countries have first ·adopted political democracy in order to create a democratic society of equality, a much more wearisome and complicated process.

The Impact of Mobility on American Attitudes

Another factor in the early English settlements is often overlooked. Even when most newcomers to America were from England, they did not simply transplant their way of thinking and acting. In his hometown, the Englishman was bound by specific local customs, restrictions, and prejudices. Coming to America, he was thrown together with Englishmen from all over the British Isles, in itself a new experience in an age of sparse communications. Studies of contemporary America show that the West has the highest degree of tolerance of nonconformists—largely due to the fact that so many of its inhabitants (the majority in fact) have come there from all over America. The Iowan or Oklahoman who migrates to California or Oregon discovers that Americans from other regions live and think differently than he does, and this experience makes him generally more open minded and experimental. In relation to England, seventeenth-century America was one large California: the minute the Englishman touched American soil, he could start out all over again, no one bothered about his background and family, and every man was judged on his own merit, not by what his great-great-grandfather had accomplished. Something very similar had occurred in ancient Greece: the great liberal movements in thought and philosophy in the sixth and fifth centuries B.C. first occurred in the Greek colonies in the Aegean, settled by Greeks from all over Greece, and from there permeated the Greek mainland itself. The escape from tribal and parochial narrowness is the first condition of liberality of mind.

From the nineteenth century on, as immigrants came here from all over the world, this element of openness and willingness to experiment with new ideas greatly increased in the United States. For a long time, being American meant not so much something fixed and molded by history, as in the case of older nations, but *not* being French, German, or British any longer. In foreign policy, for example, the isolationist attitudes of the nineteenth and twentieth centuries (at least until World War II) expressed more the rejection of Europe than the embracing of a positive, and specifically American, foreign policy. As immigration became a mere trickle since the 1920s, the traditional American hospitality to new and unorthodox ideas was increasingly replaced by an adherence, on the part of some at least, to rigid dogmas and articles of faith of "Americanism."

Democracy: Compatible with Many Specific
Political and Economic Institutions

Because democracy is a very broad term, it is compatible with many specific political and economic institutions. Although the founders of our

Republic thought that monarchy and democracy were incompatible, we have learned in the meantime that some of the finest democracies in the world—such as Great Britain, Holland, Sweden, Denmark, Norway, Australia, New Zealand, and Canada—have developed under the monarchical form of government. Logically, republicanism may seem more consistent with democracy than with monarchy, yet logic does not always win over experience.

As to the issue of federalism versus unitary government, the American preference is in favor of federalism, as practiced also in democracies such as Australia, Canada, and Switzerland. Yet unitary types of government such as Britain, Holland, France, and the Scandinavian states, to mention but a few, are perfectly consistent with the highest degree of democratic self-government. On the other hand, the Soviet Union has a federal government, on paper at least; yet this federalism does not affect the totalitarian rule from the center.

Checks and balances—another favorite device of the American type of democracy—are not a necessary part of a democratic system. To illustrate: In the British political system the House of Commons has almost complete control over the machinery of government, not sharing it to any substantial degree with the judiciary or the House of Lords. The august position of the judiciary in the American system, which Americans cherish and look upon as the last bulwark of liberty, is not known to that extent in any other democracy in the world. It is difficult for Americans to visualize a government based on the rule of law without the interpretation through a Supreme Court, yet other democratic nations have developed the rule of law through different means and customs.

As to the two-party system, the American preference for it is shared by other democracies like Britain, yet the majority of truly functioning democracies in the world—including Switzerland, Holland, Sweden, Canada, Belgium, Israel, and many others—have more than two major parties. The fact that in France the multiparty system has seemed to stifle the operation of democracy has led many persons to assume erroneously that the two-party system is the only possible approach to political democracy.

As to economic institutions, democracy is not tied to any particular types. Among the great democracies in the world, American democracy is most strongly attached to private enterprise or capitalism, albeit diluted by a considerable amount of government regulation and the welfare state. This relatively strong attachment to capitalism is also shared by some other democratic nations—such as Switzerland, Belgium, and Canada. By contrast, strong democracies such as Britain, Norway, Sweden, Denmark, Australia, and New Zealand have been governed by Socialist parties during many of the last thirty years. Although their economic systems cannot be described as full-fledged socialism, they are relatively more Socialist and more welfare-state minded than the United States.

In the world today, there is no democracy that practices pure capitalism, nor any that practices pure socialism. All existing democracies are a mixture of economic principles and practices; some are relatively more attached to free enterprise, whereas others rely relatively more on government responsibility and regulation in the economic field.

Wealth is not a necessary condition or guarantee of democracy. In Latin America, for example, relatively poor countries like Chile, Costa Rica, and Mexico have made great strides toward genuine democracy, whereas the wealthiest Latin American nation, Argentina, has long been plagued by military dictators. The latest was General Perón, whose dictatorship lasted for over a decade, until he was finally overthrown in 1955. In 1966, constitutional government in Argentina was again overthrown by the military. In Europe, the two nations to fall most heavily into the grip of totalitarianism were rich Germany in 1933 and poor Russia in 1917: the high living standards of Germany did not prevent her from developing Hitlerism, and Russian poverty was not necessarily the main cause of Communist totalitarianism.

If some democratic nations, such as Norway or Switzerland, seem relatively well off, it is because cause and effect are frequently confused. In terms of natural wealth, both Switzerland and Norway are extremely poor; the stability and freedom of their democratic institutions over a long period of time have enabled these two nations, however, to slowly build up healthy and strong economies providing high living standards for their people.

In Asia, too, there has been no direct and necessary correlation between wealth and democracy. Before World War II, totalitarianism in Asia was strongest in Japan, then by far the most advanced industrial nation on the Asian continent. After World War II, Asian totalitarianism is most forcefully represented by Red China, one of the poorest nations in Asia. Today, democracy in Asia is hopefully developing in India and the Philippines—two poor nations, but nations dedicated to constitutional government.

CHAPTER 2

DEMOCRACY, AUTHORITARIANISM, TOTALITARIANISM

❦ THE MEANING OF TOTALITARIANISM

The word "totalitarianism" comes from the Latin word *totus*, meaning "all" or "whole." It was first used in the early 1920s, and—like democracy —it is more than a form of government, for it encompasses all aspects of society. Like democracy, totalitarianism is not everywhere the same, but differs from country to country. Yet, despite individual variations, totalitarianism as a way of life and a form of government has a common core: *it recognizes no limits with respect to either goals or means*. The fundamental purpose of totalitarianism is total control of man by the state.

The Goals of Totalitarianism

First, as to goals: Totalitarianism wants all of man, and there is no human activity—political, economic, social, religious, cultural, or educational— that is exempt from government control and domination. The totalitarian way therefore recognizes no *inalienable rights* of the individual. Whatever leeway, or elbowroom, the individual possesses in the totalitarian state, it is his not as a matter of right, but because it suits the state—for its own purposes—to make such arrangements. Liberty and property may be taken away from the individual whenever it suits the state to do so, and even his life may be snuffed out without due process.

34

Similarly, in the totalitarian state nothing is *sacred*. It rejects the Judaeo-Christian concept that man is made in the image of God, and considers man as no more than a tool to be used (or done away with) as seems most useful for the purposes of the state. Religion—to the extent that it is permitted—is but another instrument of state policy.

Finally, totalitarianism completely rejects the sphere of privacy in which the individual may find shelter and comfort. Even the most intimate human relations—friendship, love, family—are not permitted to stand in the way of the all-powerful steamroller, the state. Children are encouraged to denounce parents and teachers, and friends are expected to betray past confidences to the police.

The Means of Totalitarianism

As to means, totalitarianism recognizes no limits to what it is prepared to use: propaganda, imprisonment, terror, slave labor, brainwashing, murder, and even the destruction of entire nations (genocide).

In spirit and intent, modern totalitarianism is akin to many tyrannies of other ages. What is new about twentieth-century totalitarianism is its marriage with technology. Never before in history have antidemocratic rulers had at their disposal such effective means of controlling their subjects and of destroying the populations of other states.

The Importance of Totalitarianism in the Contemporary World

The study of totalitarianism is as imperative today as ever. The emergence of the total state in Russia and Italy during the 1920s was not seen by most people to have any general consequences or implications. As an aberrant and probably transitory political development, it was explained in the West in terms of purely native factors such as Russia's backwardness and semi-Asiatic character. Similarly, poverty and illiteracy and the "theatrical temperament" of Italians were held responsible for the advent of fascism in Italy. Even when nazism came to power in 1933 and caused the threat of totalitarianism to be taken seriously in the West, it was still frequently regarded as a development rooted in the peculiar features of German history and culture. These features included the fact that the Germans had been Christianized later than the rest of Western and Central Europe, that Prussian militarism was a uniquely German phenomenon, and that the modern German economy has never been based on truly private enterprise but on government initiative. It was also widely expected that either its form of "state socialism" would eventually prove to be unworkable, as would the economic collectivism of Russia, or else that Hitler, like

Mussolini, would in the end bring his nation back into the tradition of European conservatism.

The experience of fascism can now be viewed in retrospect with a fuller understanding, and the growth and expansion of communism on a world-wide scale also enables it to be analyzed in a broader historical perspective than was possible twenty or thirty years ago. One conclusion has become certain: in dealing with totalitarianism we confront a general phenomenon of our age, not a peculiar deviation of this or that nation. A billion people, or about one third of the human race, now live under totalitarian communism. If the unlikely had occurred and the Fascist Axis had won World War II, there is a good chance that virtually the whole civilized world might have fallen under the sway of the totalitarian mentality. The main lesson of the political history of the last fifty years is precisely the opposite of what used to be believed about communism and fascism. The experience of these two forms of totalitarianism has revealed aspects and dimensions of human behavior that are more universal than national in character, or it has sharpened our awareness of them.

The mass murders in Nazi concentration camps and gas chambers, the horrors in Soviet and Chinese slave labor camps are important not only because they open up new channels of understanding the Germans, Russians, and Chinese, but also because they reveal that every people is potentially capable of acting in this fashion. Just as every individual lives physically "on borrowed time," constantly confronted with the possibility of death, so does he exist as a moral being "on borrowed time," constantly confronted with the possibility of falling into the abyss of moral nihilism.

Whatever physiological or psychological malformation may occur in one individual human being, may potentially occur in any other. The same truth applies to whole nations: the lesson of the Nazi gas chambers and the Soviet slave labor camps is not how far Germans or Russians could fall, but how far human beings—*all of us*—can fall if critical rationalism, traditional ethics, religious values, or constitutional government has been sufficiently weakened or destroyed.

❧ TOTALITARIAN IDEOLOGY

Despite some minor outward differences, all totalitarian systems show much the same pattern in their political ideologies and practices. Both Fascist and Communist regimes have an officially prescribed ideology, or systems of beliefs and values that must be accepted by every citizen. The principal characteristics of totalitarian ideology are as follows: (1) It embraces all phases of human thought, feeling, and action; (2) it allows no rival set of beliefs or values; (3) it oversimplifies human problems and their solution by reducing them to accord with a single, monolithic principle—that of "race" in the case of nazism and "class" in the case of communism; (4) it is fanatical, demanding complete adherence to its tenets without qualifications and reservations, and justifying use of any means to make it prevail.

In particular, totalitarian ideology goes well beyond politics and economics and seeks to achieve an authority over all of man's life and thought. Thus the doctrine of Marxism-Leninism, as put forth by the current "party line," extends into all areas of human activity and understanding. The dedicated Communist finds a prescription for the "correct" attitude toward painting, poetry, music, architecture, family life, religion, biology, psychology, and so forth. For example, abstract painting and modern architecture are considered "incorrect" in the Soviet ideology. Both are symptoms of "decadent capitalism."

If Marx, Engels, or Lenin did not themselves discuss abstract art or other such aspects of modern life, Communist leaders decree what the "party line" is on these subjects—that is, what Marx and Lenin would have said about them. In all these official decrees, there will be some reference to the "economic interpretation of history," the concept that economic forces are the foundation of everything else. This concept is the basis of Communist ideology.

Similarly, nazism in Germany had an all-embracing ideology based on the concept of *race*. According to this theory, for example, Einstein's scientific concepts had to be wrong because Einstein was a Jew. Just as Marx and Lenin saw world history as the struggle between economic classes, the Nazis viewed world history as the eternal conflict between "superior" and "inferior" races.

Totalitarian ideology, whether Communist or Fascist, has no respect for the mystery of human existence, and therefore no respect for man himself or his countless possibilities. In achieving a monopoly over all aspects of man's life, totalitarianism must of necessity ignore the complexity of human thought and action. Otherwise, it would have to admit to areas of life it could not control.

The One-Party System

The monopolistic ideology of totalitarianism is fully reflected in its political practice. The totalitarian state, Communist or Fascist, permits only *one party*. Actually, it should not even be called a political party, because the very reason for the existence of political parties is to give political representation to different groups of citizens. The monopolistic totalitarian state cannot admit the existence of any group but one—the one in control of the government. An attempt to establish another party is a serious crime, often punished as treason. Thus the totalitarian political party is not an organization of private citizens seeking to have its candidates elected to political office, as in a democracy. It is, in effect, an agency of the government, no more independent than the army or the police.

The main purpose of this kind of "political party" is to provide means of control between the bureaucratic machinery of the state and the mass of subjects who do not themselves take an active part in the government.

The Use of Propaganda

One of the chief instruments of the one-party system is *propaganda*. Whether the Soviet citizen opens a newspaper, listens to the radio, or watches television, he sees and hears only what the Communist party wants him to hear. No foreign newspapers are available except official Communist papers, provided they are friendly to the Soviet Union. Since the Soviet rift with Red China, Chinese Communist publications are more easily obtainable in the United States than in the Soviet Union. Even those foreign papers that are friendly toward communism are not allowed if they are published privately. They must be officially published by a foreign Communist party or government.

The Use of Force

To the extent that propaganda fails to do the job, naked *force* takes over. Nazi Germany's concentration and extermination camps and the Soviet Union's and Red China's slave labor camps (officially called "correctional labor camps") testify to the use of such force. Here torture, beatings, starvation, and disease have, until recently, been the rule. These camps are used not only for punishing political opponents, but as an instrument of control. They are kept before the people as an example of what happens to those who are disapproved of by the government. Where "more direct" means of control are thought necessary, the totalitarian state does not hesitate to use them. Political murder is not an invention of modern totalitarianism, but recorded history knows of no other instance in which mass murder was practiced on a scale even approaching that of Nazi Germany or Communist Russia. Whereas previous types of oppressive government killed individuals, modern totalitarianism has not hesitated to destroy entire nationalities, either by murder or forced dispersal. This crime is now called genocide.

Totalitarian Concept of the Dictator-Leader

The concept of the *dictator-leader* is basic to the totalitarian state. In the case of fascism, it is a point of doctrine. This is understandable, because Fascist ideology in Italy and Germany was decisively molded by the leaders themselves, Mussolini and Hitler. Mussolini's official title was "Il Duce" and Hitler's, "Der Führer"—the Italian and German equivalents of "The Leader." In Fascist doctrine, the leader is regarded as representing in his own person the will and destiny of the nation. Therefore, the nation owes him unquestioned obedience.

Communist doctrine, as set down by Marx, minimizes the role of the leader. Marx's emphasis was on impersonal economic forces, groups, and classes—rather than on outstanding individuals. But on this point, Communist doctrine was fundamentally modified by Lenin with his concept of the "professional revolutionary." According to Lenin, the liberation of the proletariat from the yoke of capitalism would not be accomplished, as Marx had thought, by the spontaneous action of organized workers, but by the planned activity of a select group of leaders—the "professional revolutionaries."

⚜ THE TWO MAIN TYPES OF TOTALITARIANISM

The two main types of twentieth-century totalitarianism are communism and fascism.

The Communist Type of Totalitarianism

In the middle-nineteenth century, communism (derived from the Latin word *communis*, "common") meant the ownership of all productive property by the whole community. Numerous small groups, directed by no central authority, advocated various Communist schemes, and it was not always clear whether public ownership of all property was to be accomplished by force or persuasion, and whether public property should be owned and managed by the national government, local authorities, cooperatives, or the workers themselves.

Since the establishment of Soviet power, communism has been a revolutionary movement that seeks to overthrow existing political and economic systems by subversion or force, and to establish the dictatorship of the Communist party in every country. Whereas a century ago the small Communist groups in different countries were independent of outside authority, today most Communist parties throughout the world are under the influence of either Moscow or, to a lesser extent, Peking.

The Fascist Type of Totalitarianism

The second variety of twentieth-century totalitarianism is fascism. The term derives from the Italian *fascio*, meaning "group," or "movement." The Fascist party was founded by Benito Mussolini in 1919, partly as a reaction to communism, and yet the Fascists showed themselves fast learners and imitators of Communist techniques. Realizing that he could not get into power by constitutional means, Mussolini and his Fascist followers seized power by force in their "march on Rome" in 1922. According to Fascist doctrine, people are too ignorant and emotionally unstable to rule themselves; they must be ruled by a select group of leaders, an elite, superior in moral and mental ability to the mass of the people. In the Fascist doctrine it was not clear who was to decide who was superior to whom in specific cases, but in practice the Fascists had the guns to impose themselves upon the Italian nation. All other political parties but the Fascists were suppressed, and criticism of the government was declared a crime to be punished by imprisonment and even death. Likewise, all free labor unions and business associations were suppressed, and the state undertook to regulate all phases of the economy.

The example of Italian fascism found its imitators and admirers in some other countries, particularly in Germany and Japan. The Nazi party (Nazi is the abbreviation of the German word for *national*[1]) founded by Adolf Hitler in 1919 was a vastly exaggerated version of Italian fascism. Rapidly growing into the largest party in German history, it came into power in 1933. In its domestic policy, it immediately began to persecute many persons for religious or political reasons. In its foreign policy, nazism fanatically believed in the superiority of the Germans over the rest of the world; the aim of Nazi foreign policy was to establish Germany as ruler of the world, leaving a few bits of loot to its Fascist allies, Japan and Italy.

Although the Fascist governments of Germany, Japan, and Italy were vanquished in 1945, their strength during the preceding decades demonstrated that democratic nations must always be sensitive to the danger of Fascist groups at home and abroad. Like communism today, fascism in the 1930s and 1940s was an international movement seeking everywhere to destroy constitutional government by force. In the Western Hemisphere, a Fascist-type dictatorship in Argentina under Juan Perón lasted from 1943 to 1955, when it was overthrown by military leaders opposed to arbitrary dictatorship.

[1] The full party name was National Socialist German Workers' Party.

Fascism and Communism in the United States

In the United States, fascism never made much headway in the 1930s and 1940s. Yet the United States has not completely escaped the influence of either totalitarian fascism or communism. In the 1930s, numerous pro-Nazi organizations—mostly dependent on Germany money and political guidance—sprang up. Some, like the German-American Bund, were led by German-Americans, and others, like the Silver Shirts or the Christian Fronters, by native American Fascists. More important than the openly admitted American Fascists in the 1930s were the sympathizers and fellow travelers of fascism, who admired Hitler's efficiency and his ability "to get things done." Finally, there was a group of loyal Americans who did not like fascism as an ideology, but felt, particularly after the fall of France in 1940, that fascism was "the wave of the future" (this was the title of a famous book by Anne Morrow Lindbergh in 1940), with which the democracies had to live and to which they would have to accommodate themselves.

Similarly, totalitarian communism in the United States has never had an impressively large membership (its peak of about 100,000 was reached in the 1930s, to drop to about 10,000 in the 1960s). Yet, in addition to this relatively small number of Communist activists and militants, there were others who accepted some basic Marxist criticisms of capitalist democracy. Particularly in the 1930s, some Americans saw in communism a possible answer to the world's major ills—economic depression at home and aggressive, imperialistic fascism abroad. After World War II, and especially after the Korean war (1950–1953) and the Hungarian Revolution in 1956, many American sympathizers with communism changed their minds. Just as fascism in the United States was an internal problem primarily as long as some respectable elements in society served as a protective cushion for the self-confessed Fascists, so communism is much less of an internal issue now since the number of American sympathizers with communism has dwindled.

❦ TOTALITARIANISM AND DEMOCRACY

There is a new element in twentieth-century totalitarianism that distinguishes it from earlier forms: some political experience and participation of the masses. It is only since the eighteenth century that the masses of the people have become in many countries an important, or even decisive, factor in the political process. Where there has been no democratic or popular political experience at all, undemocratic government will usually assume the form of traditional authoritarianism or personal despotism based on a loyal army and police. Where there has been some experience— but not enough—in popular participation in politics, totalitarianism finds its most fertile soil.

Totalitarianism borrows from the preceding democratic experience some of the symbols, techniques, and institutions of democratic government and politics. In the language of totalitarianism—both Fascist and Communist—words like "freedom," "true democracy," "rights of workers," "the people's will" and similar expressions and symbols of democratic politics abound. Similarly, totalitarian states call their monopolistic political organizations "parties"—a self-contradiction, because one party, being only part of the body politic, assumes the existence of other parties. Finally, the totalitarian systems of both fascism and communism use all means of political propaganda, first developed by democratic political movements: newspapers, leaflets, mass processions, demonstrations, and all the other techniques of mobilizing the political participation of the people.

The predemocratic authoritarian ruler wanted to rule independently of the consent of the people, and was not even interested in allowing the people to express their consent in any organized fashion, for that might give the people the idea that they possessed a political will of their own. In the postdemocratic phase of totalitarianism, the people are allowed (and encouraged) to express their consent, but consent only. Although there is expression of political will in the totalitarian state, its rulers see to it that only the affirmative expressions of loyalty are heard. By using the democratic techniques of propaganda and mass demonstrations, the totalitarian rulers try to create the fiction that behind these traditionally democratic techniques there is also the substance of democracy.

Freedom of speech implies *freedom of silence*—and this, too, is denied in totalitarian regimes. Totalitarians—whether Fascists or Communists— well understand that silence is not just absence of speech, and that it can often be the most effective form of communication. In a totalitarian regime, a person who wishes to get ahead or often just stay alive must therefore (occasionally at least) praise government leaders and policies in order not to arouse the suspicion that his silence means criticism and hostility.

☙ TOTALITARIANISM AND AUTHORITARIANISM

In popular parlance, the term *totalitarianism* has for a long time been used interchangeably with *authoritarianism*, because both systems are antidemocratic. Yet both differ significantly with respect to goals and means, and these differences are often more important than the similarities between totalitarianism and authoritarianism.

The Meaning of Authoritarianism

As a general term, authoritarianism can be applied to all areas of human relations and institutions, such as the family, education, religion, economics, or politics. Whenever we say that one of these is authoritarian or is run in an authoritarian manner, we mean that the principle of authority prevails over individual freedom and consent. When the term authoritarianism is applied broadly to a system of government and a way of life, it can be contrasted with totalitarianism on the one hand and democracy on the other.

In the division of social and political systems into three main categories —democracy, authoritarianism, and totalitarianism—the degree of individual freedom and the quantity and quality of social control of individual behavior are the key variables. Although this analytical classification is useful as a rough guide, it should again be borne in mind that, in practice, some democratic societies and governments are more democratic than others; the same is true of authoritarian and totalitarian systems. Moreover, no society is static, and there are constant changes in its relation to the dominant system which prevails in it. Thus the Soviet Union is still totalitarian, yet few would deny that it is less totalitarian now than it was under Stalin. Similarly, few would deny that Great Britain is more democratic today than it was one hundred years ago. Or again, Nicaragua today still represents an authoritarian system, but it is much milder than that of the late dictator General Somoza. (See Figure 2-1.)

Although it has been the most neglected form of government as an object of serious study, authoritarianism is undoubtedly the most prevalent of all governments throughout history—including our present age. In antiquity, neither the totalitarian extremism of Sparta nor the unique democracy of Athens was typical either in Greece or elsewhere. The typical form of government was authoritarian. Even in the modern age both democratic and totalitarian governments remain in the minority.

The main reason for the neglect paid to authoritarianism in our own century is probably that the major powers—the United States, Great Britain, Red China, the Soviet Union—happen to be democratic or totalitarian, thus dramatizing the issue of democracy versus totalitarianism as the central political issue of the century. But this should not obscure the fact that the vast majority of nations today—as in the past—are governed by authoritarian systems.

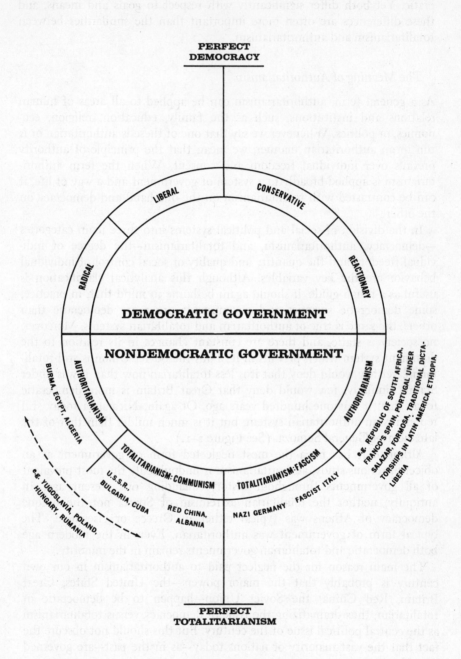

FIGURE 2–1. The World Political Spectrum.

This fact can be quickly grasped by looking at the many underdeveloped nations that have attained independence since the end of World War II. With a few notable exceptions—India, Israel, the Philippines—the pattern is the same everywhere. On receiving independence, the new nation operates for a brief time under a democratic constitution bequeathed to it by its former European master—Britain, France, or Belgium. After a few years, there is a "return to nature" from this state of artificial democracy, and authoritarian government takes over.

The Prevalence of Authoritarianism in History

The reason for the predominance of authoritarianism throughout history is probably psychological. Democracy gives men the maximum of freedom, but in return demands a high degree of responsibility that too few are capable of accepting. Totalitarianism is the opposite extreme. While it relieves men of the burden of responsibility, it grants too little freedom and self-expression to the individual. Authoritarianism denies its subjects the freedom and responsibility of political choice and action, while still leaving them some degree of freedom and self-expression in nonpolitical matters. The only political freedom in some authoritarian states is what is sometimes called the "freedom of the coffee-house." A person may express himself quite freely at his table while conversing with his friends, but he does not have the liberty to stand up and address a group without permission of the police.

In comparison with the all-encompassing control and unrestrained ruthlessness of totalitarianism, life under an authoritarian government may appear relatively tolerable. In comparison with free democratic government, authoritarian government is harsh and oppressive. The fact that authoritarianism has been so prevalent in human history should make one doubly realize that democracy is not something which just happens, a system that naturally grows and develops without much effort and dedication. Far from being natural in this sense, democracy is a bold venture of the human race into a new world of freedom.

The danger of the persistent attraction of authoritarianism has been well understood by the great pioneers of liberty. Because that attraction often takes place on an unconscious level, it has to be resisted by constant and deliberate effort. The founders of the American system of government were apparently aware of this potential pull, because they sought to provide the Constitution with numerous hedges, checks, and balances which would make the subversion of constitutional government in the direction of authoritarian attitudes and institutions impossible or, at least, highly difficult. The separation of powers, the Bill of Rights, and the difficult process of amending the Constitution are but a few examples.

Differences Between Authoritarianism and Totalitarianism

Both with respect to goals and means, authoritarianism sharply differs from totalitarianism. *Authoritarian government* seeks primarily to *control* men's *political activities*, in contrast to the *totalitarian* regime that seeks to dominate *all aspects* of life, *nonpolitical* as well as *political*. In the authoritarian system, the average citizen is left relatively free in his religious, family, and business activities, provided he does not interfere in politics. Thus authoritarianism leaves the citizen a relatively wide sphere of private life, in which he can still retain some of his dignity and self-respect.

This analysis is more applicable to older, established authoritarian states (such as Spain under Franco or Portugal under Salazar) than to some of the newly emerging underdeveloped nations. In Burma and Egypt, for example, authoritarian methods are being carried over from political to economic affairs, thereby moving in the direction of totalitarianism. However, as long as such states do not dominate other primary social institutions (such as the family, religion, and education), they are more properly to be classified as authoritarian than as totalitarian. This example illustrates again that basic categories like authoritarianism and totalitarianism are not absolute but relative, and that there are borderline cases in which one system approaches another.

The difference between authoritarianism and totalitarianism exists also with respect to means. Whereas totalitarianism recognizes no limits to the means employed in pursuit of national policy, and does not shrink from systematic mass murder, authoritarianism does not go to the extreme of moral nihilism. The typical penalty in totalitarian regimes for political opponents has been death or slave labor, whereas the authoritarian regime generally confines itself to the less drastic, although severe, penalty of imprisonment or exile.

Moreover, although the penalties in an authoritarian system may be severe, there is at least some measure of due process in meting out such penalties. The citizen knows where he stands, and if he takes risks, he knows the exact consequences in advance. By contrast, the drastic penalties and persecution in the totalitarian state are often not meted out by judicial procedure, but by a secret police or other administrative agencies that are exempt from any due process.

Finally, there is this fundamental difference between authoritarianism and totalitarianism. Under the former system of government, the citizen is expected to obey without question the political and legal orders of the ruler or rulers: to abstain from oppositional political activities, to pay taxes without representation in a legislative body, to render military service when required to do so, to read only approved books and newspapers, or to travel abroad only with the permission of the authorities. Unpleasant and even oppressive as such authoritarian government may be, the citizen is only expected to comply with the laws and regulations, regardless of what his innermost thoughts may be.

Shakespeare perfectly expressed the essence of the authoritarian ruler when he has King Henry V say : "Every subject's duty is the king's; but every subject's soul is his own" (Henry V). By contrast, the totalitarian ruler is not satisfied with the subject's fulfilling his duties: he wants all of the subject, body and soul, and above all his soul. The authoritarian ruler is not especially disturbed if his subjects are not completely in agreement with his policies as long as they outwardly obey. But they do not have to declare publicly that they love the rod that castigates them. This degradation is added in the totalitarian system: the subject is not only oppressed, but is forced to say publicly that he loves his oppressors.

Totalitarian regimes have periodically staged public trials in which the guilty, before being shot, have to admit their alleged crimes, repent, and then proclaim their undying loyalty to their executioners. The most notorious application of this method was in the Soviet purge trials of the mid-1930s. After the Chinese Communists seized control, there were public trials before tens of thousands of spectators in which former landlords and others suspected of anti-Communist feelings were publicly tried in sport arenas, forced to recant, and then executed on the spot. After Castro came to power in Cuba at the end of 1958, he also held public trials with ensuing executions, a combination of a circus show with real executions thrown in as the top attraction. The Nazis, too, staged public trials and executions—the main purpose being to degrade the victim in his own eyes and in the eyes of his fellow men, rather than merely to kill him.

Totalitarian Nihilism

In line with this argument, it becomes apparent that concentration camps, slave labor camps, and mass murder are more than incidental phenomena in totalitarian systems. They are of the very essence of totalitarianism: for it is in the concentration camps and slave labor camps, where man is completely annihilated as a moral being, and where he is reduced to a mere number, tattooed on his body. The concentration and slave labor camps were not primarily designed to punish ordinary or political criminals: the Nazis filled the concentration camps and gas chambers with victims, such as Jews, who were not even accused of having done anything wrong. Similarly, Stalin filled his slave labor camps with millions of persons who were not guilty of anything specific and who were punished, not for *having done* something wrong but for *being* in the wrong social category (kulaks, sons of former bourgeois elements). The fact that in both Nazi concentration camps and Soviet slave labor camps the vast majority were technically and legally innocent of any wrongdoing was not an incidental by-product of totalitarianism, but of its very essence.

If totalitarian rulers were merely intent on killing certain individuals or groups, such killing could be efficiently accomplished without prolonged suffering and degradation. But in the scheme of the totalitarian mind, degradation was not an incidental by-product of murder; murder was the incidental by-product of the systematic process of degradation.

The following story told by a Negro worker for the SNCC (Student Nonviolent Coordinating Committee) of how he was treated in a Columbus, Mississippi, jail shows that the totalitarian impulse to degrade is not a specialty of any one particular country:

> *At the bottom (of a winding staircase) were two highway patrolmen. One of them pointed to the door, and I walked outside. They stood me against the wall. "You a nigger or a nigra?" one asked. "A Negro," I said. The other hit me across the mouth. Then he asked, "You a nigger or a nigra?" "A Negro," I said again. The first punched me hard on the ear, and I fell down. They took me by the shirt and the arm, and they pulled me up. I could feel two teeth were loose. The first patrolman asked me again, "You a nigger or a nigra?" I looked at their faces, and I knew what they wanted to do to me. "A nigger," I said. Then they smiled, because it was what they wanted to hear.*[2]

❧ TOTALITARIANISM AND ECONOMIC DEVELOPMENT

Recent historical experience has generally shown that communism has seized and held power in poor and economically underdeveloped countries (Russia in Europe, China in Asia), whereas fascism has found its greatest strength in industrially advanced nations (Germany in Europe, Japan in Asia). This generalization does not imply that all underdeveloped countries must go Communist or all developed nations must go Fascist, but merely suggests that, if a poor nation succumbs to totalitarianism *from within*, there is a strong likelihood that it will be of the Communist variety, whereas a wealthy nation is likely to succumb to the Fascist variety. Whether a particular nation, rich or poor, goes totalitarian depends on many other factors besides its level of economic development.

[2] *Look,* September 8, 1964.

Fascism and Economic Development

Italy, the smallest of the former great powers in Europe and the economically least advanced, also developed the mildest form of totalitarian fascism of the Axis. Of course, the relative economic backwardness of Italy compared to either Germany or Japan may not have been the major reason for the mildness of Italian fascism, but it was one of the factors that cannot be neglected in a comparative study of fascism. The development in Italy itself bears out this line of reasoning: fascism in Italy arose in 1919 in Milan, the center of Italian industry.

When totalitarianism invaded the Western Hemisphere, it took the form of fascism in Argentina, the richest Latin American nation. By contrast, communism established its first American beachhead in Guatemala, though it was quickly overthrown by armed rebellion in 1954. In 1959, the victory of Fidel Castro in Cuba inaugurated the first full-fledged experiment in communism in the Western Hemisphere. Both Guatemala and Cuba are among the industrially backward nations of the Americas, and even the proximity of the United States did not prevent the spread of communism in both nations.

The connection between fascism and modern industrial society is very deep. Every industrial society inevitably produces social and economic conflicts. Such conflicts can be dealt with politically either by peaceful conciliation or by forcible repression. The liberal society recognizes that varied and opposing economic interests are bound to collide, and seeks to reconcile such conflicts through bargaining and negotiation. The totalitarian Fascist state denies, as a matter of principle, that there are divergent and conflicting social interests, for there is only one legitimate interest—that of the state. If, in practice, the Fascist state admits the existence of varied interests in the framework of the "monolithic" totalitarian unity, it represses them by force.

Communism and Economic Development

The connection between communism and modern industry is different. Communism is the totalitarian way of industrializing a backward society, whereas fascism is the totalitarian way of resolving social conflicts within an industrially advanced society.

Marx held the view, disproved by history, that communism would first develop within the most advanced industrial societies (such as Germany, Britain, and the United States), and that the triumph of communism would be due to the failure of advanced industrial societies to resolve the problems of social justice and economic progress within the framework of a capitalist economy. Marx has been disproved by events. Wherever advanced industrial societies have resorted to violent solutions in solving major economic and social problems, such methods have taken on the form, not of communism, as Marx thought, but of fascism—a solution that Marx did not even remotely consider as a possibility.

It was Lenin, and not Marx, who correctly foresaw that communism could most successfully develop in the economically backward areas. His own success in Russia confirmed his view, and he forged the strategy of Communist expansion throughout the world on his—rather than Marx's—approach. Particularly in the years since the end of World War II, Soviet propaganda has appealed to the underdeveloped countries on the basis of the key theme: "Under communism, Russia has become the second largest industrial power in the world. Follow our example, and you, too, will be strong and respected."

Experience has shown that a completely backward country that is so poor and illiterate that it is not even "underdeveloped," provides a poor soil for Communist infiltration and growth. In the present-day world, states like Ethiopia, Yemen, and Nepal would probably fall into this category. The reason why such extremely backward societies are not ripe for Communist infiltration is that they do not possess as yet three elements of social ferment that provide the backbone of Communist movements in underdeveloped countries: a frustrated intelligentsia, an urban industrial working class (small as it may numerically be), and a peasantry that has become sufficiently awakened to demand land distribution and a voice in politics. Only after a developing society has undergone the first phase of modernization and industrialization is it ripe for Communist penetration. This was true of Russia, and has been true ever since in other countries. Of course, if a nation can pass through the first phase of industrialization without totalitarian regimes, the chance of such a regime coming into power becomes progressively more remote.

In giving economic aid to extremely underdeveloped nations, the United States takes the calculated risk that the first phase of industrialization promoted by such aid may produce the ferment and upheavals on which revolutionary communism feeds. Yet on the other hand, without such economic development there can, in the long run, be no prospect of economic stability or constitutional government.

Economic underdevelopment is a relative concept, under which various stages of development (or lack thereof) may be subsumed. From the viewpoint of effective Communist infiltration, a society provides the most suitable opportunities if it is neither so backward that there is no nucleus of an urban working class or of an aroused peasantry nor so advanced that it is ceasing to be underdeveloped (Mexico today, for example). Yet even where communism has found the relatively most favorable conditions of internal growth, there is not a single instance in which communism has come to power other than by force—either by internal civil war and revolution (Russia, Yugoslavia, China, Cuba), or by external force (Soviet imposition of Communist regimes in Eastern Europe and North Korea after World War II and the occupation of Tibet by Red China in 1950).

This line of analysis enables one to make tentative forecasts for the future. In countries where democracy is not firmly established by long tradition—such as Japan and India—the possibility of their turning to totalitarianism must always be kept in mind, should things go badly. In that case, it is more likely that an underdeveloped country such as India would turn to the Communist version of totalitarianism, whereas an economically advanced nation such as Japan is more likely to adopt some form of Fascist totalitarianism. Where democracy is firmly established—in countries such as the United States, Britain, or France—any form of totalitarianism is highly unlikely to develop as a result of internal events. Yet should someday the unlikely become real, it is more probable that such economically advanced nations will turn to some type of Fascist totalitarianism rather than to communism. In economically advanced nations, communism can be imposed only by military force, as happened in East Germany in 1945, or by the threat of military occupation, as happened in Czechoslovakia in 1948.

✹ THE APPEALS OF TOTALITARIANISM: FASCISM

Despite the crucial role of the leader in both fascism and communism, totalitarianism is not the product of a leader, but of more complex social forces that, in their turn, enable a Hitler, a Mussolini, or a Stalin to rise to the top and exercise undisputed authority. If we are able to identify the social forces that provide the background for the rise of totalitarianism—Fascist or Communist—we may be in a better position to know ahead of time where trouble is brewing, and what remedies might be employed to prevent it.

Let us first look at fascism. Wherever fascism rose to power in the past, its appeals were relatively most effective in the case of two groups: a small group of industrialists and a much larger group of lower-middle-class people.

Fascism's Appeal to Industrialists

The industrialists who supported and financed Fascist movements were mainly attracted by the Fascist promise to destroy free labor unions.

Ideologically, industrialists are not, as a group, any more vulnerable to Fascist slogans and appeals than are other groups. Where democracy is firmly entrenched in the minds and traditions of a nation, industrialists are just as dedicated to democratic principles as are other people. But where democracy is accepted only by the few rather than by the many (as was the case, after World War I, in Germany, Italy, and Japan), a few wealthy industrialists can greatly contribute to its destruction by supplying Fascist parties with large sums of money.

Fascism's Appeal to the Lower Middle Class

The second social group which has in the past shown itself vulnerable to Fascist appeals is the lower middle class. Economic considerations have been less important here than the anxiety over status. Salaried persons—the numerically strongest group in the lower middle class—have often found themselves, politically and psychologically, in a "no-man's land." Above all, many lower-middle-class people are at a loss as to the powerful or dominant group with which they should identify. From a purely economic viewpoint, salaried persons might find it advantageous to identify with organized labor, but in their intense consciousness of status they generally refuse to do so because joining labor unions means "descending" into the lower world of the working class. From the viewpoint of status, aspirations, and general outlook, salaried and other lower-middle-class persons would like to identify with the solid and prosperous middle and upper classes, but the stark facts of economic reality show that the gap cannot be easily bridged. As a result, salaried persons often develop fears and jealousies in their attitudes toward big business. In many countries, Fascist appeals have effectively capitalized on such fears and jealousies of the lower middle classes. On the one hand, Fascist propaganda attacked the "bossism" and "internationalism" of Big Labor, and on the other, it attacked the "rapaciousness" and "monstrous growth" of Big Business as exemplified particularly by chain stores and big banks. The simultaneous attack of Fascist propaganda against Big Business and Big Labor, against capitalism and socialism, may be logically inconsistent, but such logical confusion merely reinforced the psychological anxiety and confusion of many people in the lower middle classes.

In the United States and Britain, Fascist movements have never been of major political importance. Yet whatever small Fascist groups have sprung up from time to time in both countries, they have more effectively appealed to lower-middle-class people than to the upper and the working classes. The same applies to the Radical Right in the United States. Politically less extremist but numerically much larger than outright Fascist groups, the Radical Right has also concentrated on exploiting status insecurity and political uncertainty among lower-middle-class people.

Fascism's Appeal to Urban Workers

As to the appeal of fascism to urban workers, it was relatively weak, particularly among organized workers, because the crushing of free labor unions was, in many countries, one of the professed aims of fascism. Yet in some cases, fascism did receive strong support from urban workers and some union leaders. The best-known case is that of Argentina. After the ouster of dictator Perón in 1955, it was widely believed that his appeal to Argentine urban workers was but temporary, a product of skillful propaganda and various forms of economic bribes. Moreover, Perón was revealed to have been utterly corrupt, and to have encouraged corruption and personal enrichment of his friends and relatives. Yet the restored democracy under President Frondizi did not enjoy the confidence of the workers, and in the elections of March, 1962, the Peronist Labor party emerged as the strongest party, obtaining one third of the popular vote. In Germany, too, the Nazi party found considerable tolerance and even loyalty among workers. This appeal of fascism to workers—to some workers at least—is based on the fact that Fascist regimes frequently give to the workers more social security than they had before. Some workers, at least, are willing to accept the political authoritarianism of fascism as long as they receive material benefits in exchange. Although American workers have generally rejected fascism as an organized movement, they have often practiced—in the North as well as in the South—racial discrimination, particularly in some highly skilled (and highly paid) occupations like the building trades. The Civil Rights Act of 1964 specifically forbids racial discrimination in labor unions.

Role of the Military in Fascist Movements

Because Fascist movements generally aim at imperialist expansion, the role of the military—both before and after Fascist seizure of power—is necessarily of great importance. In democratic nations, where the principle of civilian supremacy of the military is generally accepted, the military are forbidden to meddle in politics of any kind, Fascist or non-Fascist. Also, as we saw earlier in the case of industrialists, the professional military in a strongly democratic society are in no way different from other social groups with regard to their loyalty and attachment to democratic principles.

But where democracy appeals only to a minority of the population, where society is deeply divided over fundamental political and economic issues, or where a strong Communist movement seeks to foster revolution, significant elements of the military may either openly support Fascist parties or at least display benevolent neutrality toward them. Of the two top military leaders of Germany in World War I, Marshal von Hindenburg was at least benevolently neutral toward the Nazis, and General von Ludendorff sided with the Nazis from the very beginning. In Italy, some leading military figures sympathized with fascism, and a few openly supported it before Mussolini came to power. In Japan, the military class enthusiastically supported the drift toward the Fascist police state in the early 1930s, mainly because they felt that under a Fascist government they could achieve their objective of Asian domination. In Argentina, also, constitutional government was overthrown in 1943 by a group of younger officers under the leadership of Colonel Juan Perón. During the following twelve years Argentina was ruled by Perón's own type of fascism (*peronismo*), a mixture of Italian Fascist methods and intense Argentine nationalism.

Although military elements have often helped Fascist movements to get into power, they have on numerous occasions ousted such regimes. In Argentina itself, Perón was overthrown by the military in 1955, but in 1966 a right-wing group of military leaders seized power, thus ending the experiment in constitutional government that followed Perón. In several other Latin American countries too the military have on several occasions, since the end of World War II, overthrown despotic regimes (Venezuela, Nicaragua), although in a few instances (as in the Dominican Republic) the military have ousted both tyrants and constitutionally elected presidents. The military have also been instrumental in overthrowing dictatorships that flirted with communism, as happened in Indonesia in 1965 and in Ghana in 1966.

In all extreme dictatorships, the army generally remains one of the few institutions that are respected by the people, because the excesses of political repression are committed by the political leaders and the secret police, whereas the regular army is considered one of the few islands left in which the rule of law, or at least a semblance of law and order, prevails. For this reason, dictatorships (both Communist and Fascist) have periodically purged the armed forces of potentially "disloyal" elements. However, such purges are not always successful, and merely increase the feeling of hostility among the military, which may finally explode in attempts to overthrow the dictatorship by armed force.

Fascism's Appeal to the Unemployed

The impact of economic depression as a contributing factor to the rise of fascism is often misunderstood. According to Marxist theory, fascism is basically "advanced capitalism in decay." As a general proposition, this theory is not valid. Economic crises in advanced industrial societies produce varying political consequences. In societies with firmly established democratic traditions, economic depressions often speed up the existing democratic trends, as happened in the 1930s in Scandinavia, the United States, Australia, New Zealand, Uruguay, and other nations. By contrast, where the dominant national tradition is undemocratic or authoritarian, economic crises accelerate and exaggerate such trends, as happened in the 1930s in Germany and Japan. In such societies, economic crises weaken the already weak faith in the democratic process, and fascism—with its promises of economic prosperity and imperialist expansion—is the potential gainer.

The worst feature of unemployment is political rather than economic. An advanced industrial economy can well afford to provide the unemployed with a tolerable level of living and thus eliminate substantial economic suffering. But the psychological and political impact of unemployment on the individual—the feeling of being useless and unwanted—is more serious, for it strikes at the very roots of his self-respect. Fascist movements exploit this spiritual vacuum by assuring the unemployed that they are members of a superior nation or race destined to build a great empire, and that such membership is more important than temporary economic discomfort caused by "impotent democracy." Fascist movements also seek to recruit, in their drive for power, members of their private armies among the unemployed. By putting an unemployed person into a uniform, by having him constantly participate in meetings, marches, and demonstrations, Fascist parties seek to make him feel that he is an activist and one of the saviors of the nation rather than an obscure and useless jobless individual.

Effectiveness of Fascism's Appeal

We thus see that fascism, in its ability to appeal to different social groups, is a more complex phenomenon than is suggested by the Marxist interpretation, according to which fascism is simply the last stage of "capitalism in decay." The effectiveness of fascism's appeal varies from group to group and from country to country. Of the major Fascist regimes, Italian fascism had the relatively weakest mass appeal both before and after seizing power; in Japan, fascism had much broader appeal, particularly in its promise to establish Japan as the leading world power; in Germany, nazism had the widest popular appeal as compared with any other Fascist regime. Starting out in 1919, the Nazi party became the largest political movement in all German history, deeply penetrating all social classes and groups, from royal families down to the lowliest of the lowly. In the last free elections in 1932 and 1933, the Nazi party received nearly half of the total vote, supplemented by other parties that were Nazi in all but name.

The experience of fascism thus belied one of the formerly unchallenged assumptions of conventional democratic wisdom: that no people would ever freely vote for an antidemocratic movement. To a varying degree, Fascist parties were able to attract substantial segments of the people in countries with weak democratic traditions, just as Communist parties after World War II have been able to gain from 25 to 35 percent of the votes in countries such as Italy, Czechoslovakia (before the Communist revolution in 1948), and France. The failure to understand the potential appeal of totalitarian fascism or communism leads not only to incorrect analysis but also to bad policy. Thus, in World War II, many thought at the beginning of the conflict that the German people would rise against the Nazi regime as soon as they had weapons in their hands. This hope proved delusory from the beginning to the end of the war. More recently, the invasion of Cuba by anti-Castro elements in 1961 was predicated, partly at least, on the expectation that the Castro regime had no popular support at all, and that it would collapse at the first sign of an anti-Castro attack supported by the United States. This hope also proved deceptive.

⚐ THE APPEALS OF TOTALITARIANISM: COMMUNISM

The analysis of the significant sources of appeal that favor the growth of communism within a nation is primarily relevant to those countries in which communism has triumphed from within, such as Russia or China. Although in every single case of internal Communist victory, civil war or revolution has been the means by which victory was achieved, such Communist seizure of power even by force is more possible or feasible in some countries than in others. The presence of some typical background factors in the rise of communism does not mean that communism in a particular country is bound to win, but it does serve as a danger signal, indicating that "it can happen here."

Absence of a Competent Governing Class

The first background factor in an underdeveloped country that opens the door to Communist influence is a governing class that possesses neither technical competence nor moral integrity. In the very nature of things, underdeveloped countries depend on a small governing class to a much higher extent than do advanced nations because the mass of the population is neither by education nor economic standards in a position to take an active part in shaping public policy or administering the government. Most people in underdeveloped countries are not too unhappy to be ruled by a small governing class, provided it possesses a sense of public responsibility and is technically competent to carry out the tasks of government. However, when the governing class is incompetent, immoral, corrupt, and concerned with its own privileges more than with the public good, it loses the moral authority, without which there can be no stable government in the long run.

The Russian aristocracy before the rise of communism was probably the worst in Europe. If the Prussian aristocracy was arrogant and caste-conscious, it at least commanded a great deal of respect for its high sense of integrity and its unflinching dedication to public service. By contrast, the Russian aristocracy had neither the ability nor the desire to serve the public interest, and was mostly eager to extract from its privileged position the maximum of pleasure. The contempt which the Russian governing class felt, and publicly displayed, toward the people was reciprocated by the people with increasing hatred. Nor was the Russian governing class intelligent enough to understand that reforms granted in time would make revolution less of a certainty.

In tsarist Russia it would have been inconceivable for wealthy men to give away much of their fortunes to philanthropic foundations—there were, in other words, no Russian Carnegies, Rosenwalds, or Fords. And the Russian counterparts of the Kennedys or Rockefellers preferred to spend their energies on the French Riviera in pursuit of pleasure rather than in government offices and in the thick of election campaigns.

Absence of Constitutional Government

Closely related to the absence of a qualified governing class in tsarist Russia was the absence of a tradition of resolving social conflict through constitutional government. As a result, relations between different social groups were tense, sullen, and hostile. The Marxian theory of class conflict was more in accord with social reality in Russia than in Western Europe, and its promise of a "classless" society strongly appealed to reformers as the cure-all for Russia's social ills. Small as the revolutionary movement was in Russia as early as the 1870s and 1880s, it was then already the most radical in Europe. Russian was the first language into which *Das Kapital* was translated from the original German. It was ironical that Marx, who personally felt contempt for the backward Slavs, should have found his most devoted disciples in Russia rather than in Western Europe.

This absence of constitutional government for the adjustment of social conflicts also characterized pre-Communist China, Yugoslavia, and Cuba. Wherever and whenever free labor unions and democratic Socialist parties are harassed or not tolerated in underdeveloped countries, revolutionary communism gradually appears to be the only alternative to the status quo.

As to the level of economic and educational development, tsarist Russia provided the typically pre-Communist background. In nineteenth-century Europe, Russia was the most backward country. There were only the few well-to-do and educated and the many poor and illiterate, with virtually *no middle class* in-between. Even though industry began to develop toward the end of the nineteenth century, no strong middle class emerged in Russia. Because industry came late to Russia, it skipped the stage of the small workshop or small factory and developed large enterprises from the outset. This was in contrast to Northwestern Europe and the United States, where industrial development was pioneered and carried on over a century through many small enterprises. Here, the small businessman became the main element of the middle class, and, in fact, the dominant element of society as a whole. From a political and social viewpoint, late industrialization in Russia had the exactly opposite effect that it produced in the countries of early industrialization: in Russia, industrialization maintained old social tensions between the rich and poor and created new tensions. By contrast, in the Western countries of early industrialization, the new middle class became the basis of social and political stability, mitigating (and often eliminating) traditional sources of social conflict within the preindustrial economic order.

Late industrialization also had another effect, which is characteristic of all underdeveloped countries embarking on a program of rapid economic progress. Whereas, in the countries of classical capitalism (Northwest Europe and North America), industrialization was planned by no central authority but was the product of individual entrepreneurs seeking profit, industrialization in tsarist Russia was the result of government initiative seeking to enhance the power of the state. Although private property in the means of production was not affected, industrialization under government direction failed to produce a self-reliant middle class, independent of the state. Instead, late industrialization in Russia produced a new *urban working class*, concentrated in a few big cities, such as Moscow and St. Petersburg. This new working class lived in misery, had little political protection, and had little hope of improving its lot by constitutional action. What is more, the concentration of workers in a few places made it easier for Communist propagandists to awaken in these workers a sense of class solidarity. In his *History of the Russian Revolution*, Leon Trotsky points out that Russian industry before 1917, although in absolute volume much smaller than that of Western European countries, was proportionately more heavily concentrated in large enterprises than that of any other nation.

Appeal to the Peasants

Another key factor in the social background of communism is the problem of the peasant. In all underdeveloped countries the mass of the people live on the land—frequently not owned by them but by absentee landowners. For long, Lenin was not too interested in the Russian peasant because Marx—expecting Communist revolutions in the industrially advanced nations—had also paid little attention to the peasantry. But in the spring and summer of 1917, when Communist propaganda was freely allowed in Russia, Lenin emphasized land reform as one of the main aims of communism. The Russian peasant who sympathized with communism did so, not after a careful reading of Marx's and Lenin's writings, but rather because the Communists promised land distribution and immediate relief from the grinding poverty in which the peasants lived. In fact, the majority of the Russian peasants sympathized, not with the Communists, but with the Social Revolutionaries, a democratic Socialist reform party. However, Lenin's slogan of "land to the peasants" appealed to many peasants as an eminently sound proposal, communism or no communism. The Bolshevik leaders, from Lenin downward, made this promise in complete cynicism, for they knew that individual land ownership is incompatible with the long-term objectives of communism. Yet, as on so many other occasions, Lenin acted solely on the basis of practical politics, and he understood that if the peasants yearned for land, the politically smart move was to promise them the land.

In the case of China, the Communists under Mao's leadership leaned on the peasantry more than on the small urban working class for support. Mao persistently cultivated the image of the Chinese Communists as nothing more than a party of "agrarian reform" and thus quite different from the Russian Communist party. This pose was so successful that even foreign observers, including some American experts and policy-makers, were taken in by it.

Exploitation of International Conflict

In all three cases in which Communists fought a successful civil war under the openly proclaimed banner of communism (Russia, Yugoslavia, China), international conflict was an important background factor. From the moment Russia became involved in World War I, Lenin perceptively realized that the Russian government's defeat might provide him with the golden opportunity of conquering power. The Russian state revealed in time of war its inherent weaknesses—lack of leadership, administrative inefficiency, economic backwardness—even more than it had done in time of peace. As the war went badly for Russia, Lenin exhorted the soldiers to quit fighting and go home. As he put it, "the defeat of Tsarist Russia would be the least evil" from the viewpoint of the Russian worker and peasant. This Leninist doctrine of "revolutionary defeatism" was later also applied by Mao in China and by Tito in Yugoslavia.

Exploitation of Nationalism and Racialism

Finally, there is the factor of nationalism and racialism in the social background of communism. In all underdeveloped countries, the Communists exploit a general and widespread desire to turn a backward state and society into a modern one. In the newly independent nations of Asia and Africa, as in the older underdeveloped nations of Latin America, this desire is closely linked with nationalism and—in the case of non-white peoples— with racialism. The peoples of the underdeveloped world want economic progress and political strength in the shortest possible time. But what they want even more is to be recognized by everybody as full members of the human race, erasing the last traces of backwardness or inferiority. As many underdeveloped nations are non-white and were formerly ruled by white European powers, nationalism in the underdeveloped countries easily merges with a strong feeling of racialism. In judging the non-Communist and the Communist nations, the underdeveloped nations take into consideration not only which side supplies more money and technicians, but also which side believes in, and practices, more racial equality.

In theory, communism claims to be above nations and races, and to be international in outlook. Yet in practice, nationalist and racialist propaganda has been an important force in the appeal of communism in underdeveloped countries. Communists have supported nationalist movements in Asia and Africa because they look upon them as expedient means for the spread of communism. More recently, Red China has used race and color as propaganda weapons against both non-Communist states and against the Soviet Union itself. Because traditions of free government are often weak or absent in backward nations, the Communist doctrine of change by violence and terror does not produce the same reaction of shock and opposition that it meets in politically more mature nations.

Moreover, as people in the underdeveloped countries become increasingly proud of their nations' independence and growing importance in world affairs, the temptation to sacrifice other ideals—political equality, constitutional government, the rule of law—to the ideal of national power and glory becomes very strong. Communism exploits these nationalistic feelings by promising that it alone can rapidly create the industrial power and social discipline necessary to gain international respect and recognition.

✺ THE PROSPECTS OF TOTALITARIANISM

Where totalitarianism lies deeply embedded in the national traditions of a people, progress is always difficult. What is required is no less than a radical change of those fundamental forces, ideas, and values in the life of the nation going back to a more or less remote past. This process is slow and painful at best, and there is always the danger of relapsing into the old habits and customs. Yet nations with deeply ingrained patterns of totalitarian behavior, such as Germany and Japan, have shown since the end of World War II that they can abandon their old ways and try out free institutions. The movement away from totalitarianism toward a more liberal concept in countries like Germany and Japan will be the more rapid, the more closely they can be associated with the older liberal societies throughout the world.

In both Germany and Japan, defeat in World War II brought about the destruction of their totalitarian systems and gave both countries the opportunity—and the incentive—to develop gradually liberal and democratic institutions. Yet Communist totalitarianism, too, has undergone considerable changes in recent years. Since Stalin's death in 1953, there has been a marked movement away from rigid totalitarianism toward a milder and more flexible regime both in the Soviet Union and the East European Communist states. The growth of Soviet military, scientific, and economic power has resulted in a heightened sense of self-confidence in these Communist states which, in the eyes of the Communist leadership, makes pressure and constraint of the extreme totalitarian kind less necessary. Also, the rising economic output of goods and services has stimulated the appetite of the masses for a better life, both in terms of material goods and legal security. Finally, it could also be argued that severe totalitarian terror and insecurity, if borne for too long a time, finally becomes well-nigh too heavy a burden.

Just as the totalitarian impulse is not a prerogative of this or that nation but a potential line of development in any nation, the impulse toward freedom and spontaneity, too, is inherent in all human beings. From the viewpoint of an old, established liberal democracy the changeover from harsh Stalinism to the milder totalitarian variety of Khrushchev and his successors may not seem too significant; from the viewpoint of the people living under such a system, such a difference is immensely important. The next stage of this process of "liberalization" may be some form of authoritarianism, as it perhaps has already established itself in Poland and Yugoslavia. Should Red China and her followers some day develop along similar lines of relative liberalization, such changes would not only affect the daily lives of hundreds of millions of people under Chinese control, but would also strengthen the hope for peace and the survival of mankind.

CHAPTER 3

DEMOCRACY: ITS PSYCHOLOGICAL FOUNDATIONS

✳ THE DEMOCRATIC PERSONALITY

Democracy: Not Natural, But a Product of Civilization

Because Americans take democracy for granted, they are inclined to assume that it is the natural way of living, and that nondemocratic ways are the exception. The reverse is the truth.

Man has known democracy for short periods only: in fifth-century Athens, particularly in the age of Pericles, there was a short experience and appreciation of democracy—a unique and isolated incident in ancient history in a small area, no larger than an average county in the United States. During the last three hundred years, there has been a renewed effort to bring democracy to life, and although the effort has not been without its successes, it should be remembered that even today democracy as a way of life exists only in a relatively small portion of the globe.

Whether viewed in time or space, therefore, democracy can hardly be called "natural." This "unnatural" character of democracy is no different from all other creations of civilization: what is civilization but an attempt to lead man away from his natural impulses and inclinations and toward man-made ideals? Reason, equality, liberty, and justice are all inventions of civilization, in opposition to the perfectly natural laws of the jungle—violence and domination by force.

Viewed in this larger context, democracy is more than a set of specific mechanical contrivances, pieces of political machinery; it is, rather, part of the larger impulse and effort of civilization, designed to tame human relations by substituting consent for force, justice for exploitation, equality for domination, freedom for repression, and reason for passion. The more closely a political system approaches these ideals, the more it becomes part of something larger—a liberal civilization.

Emotional and Intellectual Maturity

The emotionally and intellectually mature person is the key to democracy as a way of life—and not constitutions, voting systems, and other devices of this sort, important as they may be. The behavior of the child—before it is tamed and civilized by education and training—is perfectly natural. Similarly, the behavior of the authoritarian (or authority-minded) person is completely natural unless it is changed in a more libertarian, democratic direction of independence. All that is spontaneous in the development of the child into the adult is biological and physiological; social and cultural aspects of this development have to be learned—and very often learned the hard way.

The authoritarian personality is the grownup who still craves the dependence and security of childhood. By contrast, the democratic personality is eager to mold his own destiny. The mature adult does not desire security provided at the price of subservience to outside authority. His inner security allows him to dispense with outside authority to the extent that it is socially possible. Like nations, individuals arrive at their "declarations of independence" at different stages of development. Some individuals assert their independence at an early stage, others at a late stage, and others—never.

The ideally mature individual is not the "organization man" who sees in the "team" the last source of spiritual fulfillment, always ready to adapt to his environment, to "integrate" with his group, to "go along" with others under all circumstances, to be a "regular fellow" without any independent or unconventional thought of his own, to "fit in," even if that can be accomplished only through a mental straitjacket, and, finally, to "be liked" solely for the sake of being liked.

No person can claim to be truly mature unless he realizes that human existence has an element of loneliness and uncertainty, which no fitting-in, no loyal teamwork will wholly do away with. To face courageously this

"Welcome to the team." Porges; in *Saturday Review*, 1966.

loneliness and uncertainty, rather than run away from it by looking for the comfort and shelter of the group or the leader—this is the hallmark of the mature person, without whom there can be no democratic society.

The totalitarian society seeks to destroy whatever individuality exists in man by transforming him into an insignificant atom of the mass. Totalitarianism is therefore hostile to the voluntary group or association made up of individuals pursuing their own private and personal goals. It reduces man to a member of one vast whole—the Nordic master race in nazism, the glorious proletariat in communism. Whereas liberal civilization seeks progress through diverse individuals, totalitarianism seeks to accomplish its ends through the conformist mass. The political uniform is the symbol of totalitarian politics, whereas the democratic society allows (and encourages) the individual to choose his own garb, political and otherwise.

The Ability to Face Reality

Children, adults who have never grown up, neurotics, and psychopaths have one important trait in common: they follow what psychologists have called the "pleasure-principle." Under that principle, a person behaves in accordance with immediate impulsive wishes and desires—not weighing one against another, not reflecting on them critically, but trying to realize each wish as soon as it is born. This pursuit of immediate and temporary pleasure and impulse is accompanied by the avoidance of whatever might cause frustration, pain, or denial. Such behavior is, above all, characterized by the failure to discriminate between conflicting desires on a reasonable or long-term basis; wishful thinking often takes the place of what is reasonably possible or desirable.

By contrast, the mentally healthy and mature person follows the "reality-principle." Under it, a person does not blindly and instantaneously do what his sudden impulse tells him to do, but he considers his desires and needs in a more organized, rational manner by examining their long-range importance. As a result, he will often be willing to undergo present privation or renunciation to achieve some future greater good. The reality-principle implies not only an emotional maturity that enables one to see oneself and one's desires in a cold and detached manner, but also an intellectual maturity that enables one to appraise one's wishes and actions in terms of their probable consequences to oneself and to others.

Generally speaking, what is often called the "easy way out," or the "soft solution," represents the wishful, immature way of solving problems. On second thought, therefore, the mature person shies away from such solutions, and is willing to accept the "hard solution" because he realizes that reality cannot be cheated.

Many persons find it easier to consume (the "soft solution" of what to do with one's money) than to save (the "hard solution"), because it takes a conscious effort of character and intellect to prefer the future larger good to the present smaller one. Voters often prefer to spend on "butter" than on guns, because the butter can be consumed right away, whereas the benefits of guns may only be seen at a much later date. In all such cases, the easy way out is the pleasanter solution, and demagogues will always make their appeal on that basis.

By contrast, statesmen must have the courage to tell the truth, even if the people will be pained by it. As an illustration, the democracies were virtually without armaments when World War II broke out in 1939 because the people had refused to hear the truth as presented to them in Britain by Winston Churchill and in the United States by Franklin D. Roosevelt. The failure of facing reality in the 1930s led to the early disasters of the democratic nations in World War II, which might easily have proved fatal.

The true interests of the individual, as of the nation, are best served by the careful weighing of conflicting wishes and needs in terms of their long-term importance, as well as by the realization that no individual or state can get all it wants, that failure and frustration are an inevitable part of life.

The totalitarian personality is unwilling to accept these limitations of the reality-principle. Far from being "realists," as they often claim to be, totalitarians are addicted to desires which, in the long run, cannot be realized—the final cause of defeat of totalitarian states in the past. At home, the totalitarian state promises everything to everybody, as soon as one big phantasy is realized—liquidating all capitalists, as in the Communist state, or killing all Jews in gas chambers, as in Nazi Germany.

Externally, too, the aims of totalitarianism are unlimited: nazism aimed at world domination by a thousand-year German empire—yet after twelve years the attempt failed. Communism, too, aims at world domination; this unrealistic aim may well be the major cause of its eventual undoing.

All cooperative action involves some renunciation and self-denial; a living democracy, therefore, trains its citizens daily to accept the facts of life as they are, rather than as they ought to be. Knowing that he is neither all-knowing nor all-powerful, the mature democratic person realizes that human existence can never be transformed into a paradise by any "gimmick," and that no totalitarian dictator is godlike enough to fulfill all wishes.

The authoritarian personality remains in the childish hopefulness that somehow the "Leader" will fulfill all his phantasies and wishes, and he is therefore willing to hand himself over, body and soul, to such a dictator. As a result, when the dictator fails, the citizen of the totalitarian system demands death for his leader who has failed him.

The democratic citizen feels less ire toward his political leaders who have failed him because he realizes they are no gods, and are just as subject to failure as he himself is. Blind admiration in success and ruthless hatred in failure characterize the attitude of the authoritarian personality toward his leader, whereas the democrat is more critical of his political leaders in periods of national success and feels less hatred toward them in periods of national failure.

The Right to Make Mistakes

Above all, the mature democratic person realizes that there can be no freedom of choice without making mistakes. Whenever a person is free to act, this means that he can choose between several possible courses of action. By the law of averages, some choices are bound to be erroneous. To eradicate mistakes 100 percent is therefore tantamount to eradicating freedom. This logic is carried through in undemocratic systems, in which the individual is prevented from choosing his own course of action, so that his behavior is always "correct" from the official viewpoint. Democracy is thus inseparable from the inevitability—nay, the right—of erring, of making mistakes. Just as in the progress of science "creative errors" have often stimulated new investigations in a fruitful manner, individual or collective mistakes are often the occasion for more intensive analysis and ultimately for more intelligent action.

Many religions wisely prefer the repentant sinner to the just man who has never been tempted. Implied in this preference is the realization that morality begins with choice, and that acting sinfully is not fatal, provided the sinner can eventually rise above his error and see the good. The untempted just man may, or may not, give in to temptation when it comes along. The repentant sinner will resist sin like a rock.

In the opening of the Bible, God does not remove the apple tree from the Garden of Eden—thus making it impossible for Adam to sin. Instead, he leaves the apple tree, and it is up to Adam to make his choice. Another figure in the Old Testament, Job, would be quite out of place in a totalitarian system. In the tradition of Christianity, Mary Magdalen has a special place in the affection of Jesus, and later St. Augustine (fifth century) tells in his own *Confessions* how sinful his life had been until he saw the light. The "fall of man" in the Judaeo-Christian tradition is a symbol of wisdom: No man can be without sin, and all that man can do is

"They say he has no weakness." Copr. © 1932, 1960 James Thurber. From
The Seal in the Bedroom, published by Harper & Row.

to strive for truth and justice—knowing all the time that he will never fully attain them.

By contrast, the authoritarian personality feels that there are some exceptional supermen who never err, and he therefore puts unlimited trust in them and surrenders to them complete power. Thus, during the Fascist regime in Italy (1922–1943), every schoolroom and public office in Italy was adorned with a picture of Mussolini under which there was one brief line: *"Mussolini ha sempre ragione"* ("Mussolini is always right"). During his lifetime, Stalin, too, was always right.

Attitudes Toward Leader and Group

The authoritarian personality views the leader of his group, party, class, or nation with deep feelings of respect and deference—the emotions he first felt as a child toward his father. The father figure becomes for such a person the unconscious ideal throughout his life, and the allegiance to the father ideal may later be transferred to a political chief ("father of the country") or to abstract ideals, such as empire, class, or revolution. At the same time, such an authoritarian person feels hostility toward the children, that is the people, who seek to overthrow the father—the political ruler.

Yet allegiance to, and identification with, the father is not the only tie between son and father. There is also a basic hostility toward the father, which exists side by side with that of devotion. The common bond of antagonism against the powerful father creates a mutual chain of loyalty among brothers (and sisters), and such loyalty can be transferred to larger groups, and, finally, to the people as a whole. The democratic personality puts his faith more in the group than in the leader, as is clearly expressed in the ideals of the French Revolution: "Liberty, Equality, Fraternity."

These democratic ideals stand midway between authoritarianism and anarchy. On the one hand, these ideals express hostility against any superior authority; on the other, they reflect the need for organized society—but a society which is based on equality and fraternity, not on "paternalism," benevolent as it may be. It is for this reason that the democrat in his individual as well as in governmental affairs, prefers bad self-government to good government imposed from above. Even in a time of crisis, the democrat does not cry for the strong man who will magically remove what causes pain and trouble.

In a group of equals the individual can more easily maintain his individuality than as the subordinate of a leader. The attachment of the democratic person to the group rather than to the leader explains why democracies are often suspicious of great leaders. The Athenian democracy resented in Socrates above all that he was so obviously superior to his contemporaries. He was condemned to death for teaching "un-Athenian" moral and religious precepts, yet his real crime was his greatness. In American history, Abraham Lincoln was besmirched and vituperated by many during his lifetime, although such hatred was justified on political grounds.

Winston Churchill was out of office before World War II because he was too big for his contemporaries. Clemenceau, the greatest French political figure in the first third of this century, was thrust into retirement after World War I because he clearly towered above the other leaders. Throughout the Third and Fourth Republics (from 1871 to 1958) the French consistently elected mediocrities to the presidency, because they see in every real leader a potential "man on horseback." De Gaulle may well prove the exception to the rule rather than the start of a new tradition.

Many Americans opposed Franklin D. Roosevelt not only on partisan political grounds, but also because they resented his great leadership, because he was not enough Main Street. His successor, Harry S. Truman, aroused—particularly at first—much less hostility among his political opponents, possibly because he was a typical small-town American from Independence, Missouri. Much of Eisenhower's immense popular appeal probably was due, among other reasons, to the fact that he appeared as if he had just stepped off a Kansas farm.

All these instances show that the healthy fear and suspicion of leaders or would-be leaders in a democracy can go too far. The difference between democracy and totalitarianism is not that the former can get along without leaders and the latter cannot, but that each system has different methods of selecting leadership and that in each a distinct type of man gets to the top. The great paradox of democratic politics is that the more a nation rejects its predemocratic past (as in France), the less it provides a favorable environment for the growth of strong leadership. By contrast, where predemocratic habits and institutions have not been totally rejected (as in Britain or Sweden), a democratic society seems more receptive to the need for effective leadership. Overreacting to the "cult of the leader" in both fascism and communism, democratic societies in recent decades have often gone to the other extreme of minimizing the importance of leadership.

The Role of the Family

The growth of the democratic personality is crucially influenced by the family. Sigmund Freud's emphasis on the importance of the first five years in a person's life has more than medical and psychiatric implications: it is essentially the application of the historical method to the individual.

In studying collective groups, states and nations, we realize that no group ever starts out from scratch, that we have to go back to its infancy and youth if we are to understand its character of today. Similarly, the individual never starts out from scratch. The roots of his character lie in his past, particularly in his very early years of life.

In his early relations with his parents and brothers and sisters, the child is gradually "socialized"—that is, he finds out that there are other people in this world besides himself, that the world does not revolve around him exclusively, that he must respect to some extent the wishes and feelings of others, and that there are social rules that must be observed. The child also quickly learns various forms of authority and permissiveness, depending on whether he deals with his father, mother, brother, or sister. However, the parents, too, are not completely free agents in dealing with their child.

From the viewpoint of society, the family is its most important agent: through the family, society passes on the prevailing ideals, values, and customs to the new member of society. This method is both economical and effective: no paid employee would be willing to do the 24-hour-a-day job of rearing a child as cheaply as parents do—without vacations, payment for overtime, or collective bargaining by parents' unions. The impact of the family is greatest in the early years of one's life, when there is little competitive influence. Later, there are new sources of influence, such as the street or playground, the school and church, the government, newspapers and books, and all the other stimuli of an expanding world in the life of a growing child.

From the political point of view, the family is of immense interest because the family is also, among other things, a pattern of authority. Unlimited love and permissiveness would turn a child into a tyrant rather than into a St. Francis of Assisi—even if parents were capable of such an attitude. Since a family consists of several members, unlimited liberty for one would inevitably create tyranny over the others. Therefore, some ways have to be found to regulate the relations between the different members of the family.

In some societies, parents possess absolute power over their children; the father, in particular, acts like an absolute monarch, and his word is law. In other societies, democratic family relations give the child the first, and unforgettable, experience of democracy.

Whereas Germany and Japan, for example, traditionally illustrate the predominance of the father in the family (the German *fatherland* is the equivalent for the English *mother-country*), the American family has been likened to a small parliament in which every member takes part in the making of family decisions. American children do not expect to be constantly ordered around, and as they grow up, they expect to decide by themselves how to earn a living, where to reside, and whom they will marry. Parents may try to help and persuade, but generally they cannot dictate. Many students of the American family feel that its exceptionally unauthoritarian structure is possibly the most important single social factor underlying American democracy.

These early influences are the decisive ones, and cannot be as easily changed as later ones. The adult can learn new languages, can adapt himself to new customs, new countries, and can even adopt new ideals and values on a conscious level of action and emotion. But what he cannot change so easily are the emotional attitudes and responses that are deeply embedded in his personality: whether he will be optimistic or pessimistic, cooperative or aggressive, forthright or submissive, generous or stingy, outgoing or withdrawing, tolerant or intolerant, self-confident or suspicious.

The American child does not first learn his attachment to democracy when Lincoln's Gettysburg Address is read to him. It is, instead, the other way around: he appreciates the profound personal meaning of that message because he has lived in a democracy—that of the family and immediate neighborhood—before he ever set foot in his school. The Gettysburg Address spells out for him in clear and poetical language what he has unconsciously learned all along, and serves to reinforce his democratic ideals. But that seed could not grow so well in a less fertile soil.

The Position of Women

Closely related to the issue of the family is that of the position of women in society. In authoritarian societies, the role of the women is best summarized in the traditional German phrase: *Kinder, Küche, Kirche* ("children, kitchen, church"). The Fascist movements in Italy and Germany were frankly antifeminist, extolling the "manly" virtues of force and violence and denigrating the female "defects" of gentleness and kindliness.

Totalitarian communism pays lip service to the ideal of equality for women; in practice, this equality means, for instance, that much of the heavy, unskilled labor in the Soviet Union, from ditchdigging to farmwork, is done by women. Moreover, women are given the opportunity to work for a very practical reason: the wages of the husband and father are kept so low that the wife, too, must work in order to afford the bare necessities of life. When it comes to privileged careers in the Soviet Union, women are generally conspicuous by their absence: the special prep schools and academies that train the Soviet rulers of tomorrow, are for boys only, particularly because many of them also provide a heavy program of military training. From its inception, the top-group in the Communist party, the leaders who really run the Soviet Union, has consistently been made up of men only, while women are used for propagandistic reasons in party and state positions of less importance.

So far, even democracies have promised women more equality than they have actually realized. Although legal barriers are gone, social prejudice is still strong. In politics, there are a little more than a dozen women in Congress, but no woman has ever been a candidate of a major party for the Presidency or Vice-Presidency. President Franklin D. Roosevelt was the first to appoint a woman to a Cabinet post (Miss Frances Perkins as head of the Department of Labor), and President Eisenhower also appointed a woman (Mrs. Oveta Culp Hobby) to head the newly created Department of Health, Education and Welfare. Yet the time is still far off when a woman will be appointed to assume Cabinet responsibility for such "old-line" departments as the Treasury, the Department of State, or one of the Defense Department. Although white women comprise a much larger group in the United States than Negroes, outnumbering them 4 to 1, it will be interesting to see whether a white woman or a male Negro will first be appointed Secretary of State or be elected President or Vice-President.

In higher education, also, there is a sharp distinction between what are considered "soft" fields, in which the feminine touch is appropriate (such as home economics, social work, literature, foreign languages) and "hard" fields (such as the physical sciences, engineering, law, political science, economics), which are generally reserved for men. In the field of medicine, women have gained an entering wedge in pediatrics and gynecology, but have been less successful in making their impact in other areas of medicine, whether in practice or teaching.

In private business, executive positions are generally held to be an exclusive domain of men, and in lower positions women have had to overcome the serious handicap of unequal pay for equal work. In 1964, federal legislation finally established equal pay for equal work.

How the School Can Prepare for Democracy

Next to the home, the school is most influential in shaping a child's attitudes. In the United States, the school has been even more important than in older nations. During the periods of mass immigration, the school was the key institution teaching English to children of non-English-speaking backgrounds and inculcating in children and adults the basic principles of "Americanism." This role of the schools in molding civic attitudes may perhaps explain why American schools are, to this day, more easily drawn into political controversy than is the case in most other democracies.

Recently, a group of leading German educators toured the United States, and then reported its impressions to a group of American teachers.

One German said that his outstanding impression in his visits to American schools was an incident that he would never forget as long as he lived: while attending a classroom, he noticed that a pencil had dropped from a child's desk to the floor. The teacher did not say anything, but simply picked the pencil up and put it back on the desk while listening to another pupil who was reciting. The German educator said that such an incident would be unthinkable in his country, because the teacher would feel that her dignity would suffer if she did such a menial chore for the pupil. The German added that this little incident gave him more insight into American democracy in the school than all the literature about American education he had read before visiting the United States.

In totalitarian societies, the teacher possesses no freedom of thought or speech, and he must teach the children whatever is the official doctrine of the ruling party. The main purpose of such education is unquestioning obedience rather than creative discovery and intellectual exploration.

In a free society, the main function of the teacher is to help the child develop his own personality, because democracy encourages variety rather than uniformity. Whereas in one sense all human beings share much in common, in another, each person is unique, and the aim of a liberal education is to foster, not stifle, individuality.

There can be no progress unless individuals have enough elbowroom to step out of the crowd and do things in a new, untried way. Human beings cannot, as the totalitarians assume, be molded into one shape; this process not only causes pain and frustration that make men uncooperative and sullen, but also obstructs progress, because progress means doing something new and experimental.

All the ideas and material appurtenances of our civilization started out in the mind of a single unorthodox individual, then appealed to a thinking minority, until they were finally accepted by the majority. The truth of yesterday is the truism of today and the commonplace of tomorrow. This is why the ideal democratic teacher will not tell the pupil what to think, but will help him to learn how to think. This permissive attitude of the democratic school is based on the assumption, never fully realized, that people will generally choose the right way if given the proper help and understanding guidance.

The democratic character of the school is also influenced by the relation of teacher and parent, and that of teacher and school board. Parent-teacher associations are another device to run education on a cooperative and harmonious basis. Moreover, teachers have the privilege to join their union (although only a small minority has made use of that privilege in the United States) to defend and improve their professional and economic standards.

Students, also, are encouraged in democratic nations to form organizations of self-government, and thus learn its practices and problems long before they are old enough to participate in local and national politics. In many colleges, for example, students themselves formulate and enforce rules of student behavior. Generally, such self-imposed and self-enforced discipline is found to be more effective than discipline under the control of the school authorities. However, the main value in such self-government lies in the fact that it provides the living experience of democracy rather than indoctrination and exhortation.

American democratic doctrine and custom proudly point to the fact that education is not run by the national government (as in France, for example), but by local school boards that are generally directly elected by the people. In theory, this should ensure a democratically oriented educational system of high quality. In practice, local control—particularly in poor, backward communities—has often meant poorly equipped schools, underpaid teachers, and subservience to powerful economic or political elements. Even if Washington could provide uniformly higher standards of education throughout the nation by direct federal control and operation of schools, the American preference is still for local control. Here we have a practical illustration of the collision between good government and self-government in which, as is so often true in established democracies, the desire for self-government prevails.

Another important element in the educational system of a free society is the private school. In totalitarian societies, the state generally forbids private schools, because education is considered part of the political system which government alone should control. In democracies, educational innovations have often been tested first in private schools before being accepted in public schools. By granting tax-exemption to private schools, the government of free societies indirectly subsidizes them, but it does so because it feels that the encouragement of educational variety is well worth the financial cost. The Elementary and Secondary Education Act of 1965 goes even further. Large federal funds now also benefit children in private elementary and secondary schools.

The Capacity to Cooperate

One of the main purposes of education in a free society is to broaden the horizon of the growing citizen by exposing him to contacts with members of divergent social, religious, racial, and regional groups. Because democracy seeks to solve differences by bringing them out into the open rather than by repressing them, it cannot function unless people learn to accept, appreciate, and work with, the widest variety of persons.

The extent of a person's maturity, of his practice of democracy in his daily life, is largely determined by his range of affection. The child first fixes his attention and affection on himself. Gradually his range of interest and affection broadens as he develops intimate relations with his family, friends, and neighbors. His emotional growth is reflected in his capacity to get to know and befriend persons of the most varied types and backgrounds.

This democratic ideal was aptly summarized by Pericles when he described the citizens of Athens as "open and friendly." This free-and-easy attitude toward everybody has always been a virtue held in high esteem in the United States, and was early noticed by foreign observers, such as Tocqueville and others. By contrast, one of the first effects of totalitarianism is to spread an atmosphere of fear and suspicion among the citizenry. The range of free-and-easy relations constantly shrinks, until one can relax only in one's immediate family or among friends one has known for a lifetime.

Rigid limitation of affection for one's own group (the "in-group") generally conceals an ever deeper hostility for other groups (the "out-group"), such as other parties, classes, or races. Psychologically, it is very difficult to limit hatred to particular groups only. Hitler started out with hatred and hostility toward non-Germans, who were to be subdued by the German master race; he ended up profoundly hating the German people themselves, and was eager to see every German die and every German home destroyed as punishment for their weakness and betrayal of his aims.

In communism, too, the initial theoretical love of the proletariat eventually gave way to contempt and hostility. Thus Lenin pointed out in his pamphlet *What Is to Be Done?* (1902) that the proletariat could not be expected to understand the laws of historical development; he put his hopes in an elite, small groups of professional revolutionaries who would have the intellectual grasp of social developments, and who would be the real leaders of proletarian movements. Even after Communist regimes were set up, the Communist rulers always looked upon the Communist parties as small minorities of the proletariat, or "vanguards of the proletariat," in Communist language.

Since totalitarianism feeds on hatred, it must ceaselessly invent new internal and external enemies if the people at home are to be kept securely in line. This hatred usually starts out with one well-defined enemy, but then it constantly adds to the list. In the case of communism, for example, there was originally nothing but theoretical love for everybody except for "the capitalists." Millions of Russian peasants lost their lives in the early 1930s; they were hardly capitalists in the Marxist sense—just peasants who resisted enslavement by the state. Yet by declaring them as obstinate "enemies of the working-class" the Soviet rulers condemned several millions of peasants to exile and death.

After the last vestiges of capitalism were eliminated in Russia, hatred did not stop. It increasingly spilled over the borders of Russia, and the aim became the destruction of the enemies of communism throughout the whole world. In practice, this means Communist world domination. In recent years, when this militancy has shown signs of declining in Russia, Red China has repeated the pattern of universal hostility—even against its former Soviet ally.

The democratic personality takes a different intellectual and emotional approach to the world. Intellectually, the democratic person understands that no group and no individual—not even he himself—can be perfect. This insight prepares him emotionally to accept others who differ with him in religion or politics, or whose skin or place of birth is different from his own.

❧ FREE COMMUNICATION
AND SOCIAL STABILITY

Frustration and Aggression

Social psychologists have long held that aggression—manifold as its causes are—is closely linked to frustration. Politically, therefore, the more an individual feels he can maintain his integrity against outside dictation, the less likely is he to experience frustration, and the less likely is he to react to such frustration through immediate or delayed acts of aggression.

The democratic society seeks to lessen frustration by attacking its causes and by providing socially useful outlets for aggressive and competitive impulses. William James, the American thinker (1842–1910), brilliantly expressed this problem by stating that if civilization is to survive, we must discover the "moral equivalent of war." He wisely realized that man's aggressive impulses cannot be abolished; rather, what is needed is to provide useful outlets for such impulses, such as fighting the enemies of disease, want, and hunger, or trying to conquer the riddles of nature.

The whole field of education, if based on equal opportunity, provides another outlet for peaceful competition. Competition for scholarships and other academic awards is not only socially just, but is also a safety valve against potential malcontents and revolutionaries. The knowledge that the academic career was closed to them for political reasons was perhaps an important factor in driving Marx and Lenin into revolutionary movements.

Equality of opportunity applies, however, to all fields of endeavor, not only education—although education is perhaps the most important key to individual and social advance. Thus it may be argued that the competitive aspects of the capitalist system cause tensions, ulcers, and premature deaths of some executives. Yet this negative effect may be less serious than the comparative positive gain: the fact that such competitive, aggressive tendencies are directed toward relatively harmless economic activities rather than toward more dangerous political ones. The aggressive and power-hungry type of man who, in a liberal society, lords it over a big bank account is socially preferable to the domineering man who, in a totalitarian state, finds outlets for his aggressive impulses in torturing political prisoners or working slave laborers to death.

In politics, too, the free society provides outlets for competition and aggression that are preferable to the outlets in totalitarian systems. In a free society, political competition often goes beyond the bounds of reasonableness, moderation, and even decency, but such political strife still compares favorably with the methods officially used in totalitarian states: brainwashing, torture, imprisonment, and murder for political reasons. The totalitarian society is unable to provide peaceful outlets for political conflict, and the whole political atmosphere is suffused with fear, suspicion, and terror.

The political technique of self-government is thus not only a response to man's moral urge, but it also satisfies—relatively harmlessly—profound psychological needs on the part of the rulers and the ruled. This technique is also used, in democracies, outside the sphere of government. Collective bargaining between labor and management, for example, does not, in itself, transform feelings of hostility into love. But there is a big difference between allowing such hostilities to be worked out in violent clashes between strikers and the National Guard (as happened only too often before the National Labor Relations Act was passed in 1935) and resolving such conflicts across the bargaining table.

Freedom of Expression as a Safety Valve

The most important safety valve for ineradicable aggressive impulses is free speech and criticism. Freedom of expression fulfills a person's intellectual need to make his opinion known to his fellow men, to have his mind appreciated by others, and to count as a thinker. But man also has the emotional need of getting off his chest all kinds of feelings that lie behind his ideas. This emotional need is satisfied by the mere expression of his ideas—even if nothing much happens as a result.

As long as communication between people flows freely, conciliation is always possible. When people stop talking to each other because they are not allowed to do so for political reasons or because they hate each

"Let's argue—pick a subject." Herbert Goldberg; in *Saturday Review*, 1965.

other too much, then human relations face disaster. This is true as much in a personal relationship such as marriage as in a collective process like politics.

The peasant woman who complained to her neighbor that her husband no longer loved her because he had not beaten her for three months acutely sensed a psychological truth. Silence and indifference are danger signals of accumulating hostility that might end in a fatal blowup, whereas an occasional expression of hostility clears the air and does not affect the basic affection among people.

In democratic government, politicians frequently "knock off" their opponents in a fiery speech, but this act of verbal violence is socially less dangerous than finishing an opponent by the gun or the hangman's noose. Freedom of expression in democratic societies does not remove hostility and resentment, but it allows them to be expressed in small doses, thus contributing to the mental hygiene of the individual and to the social peace of the whole community. True democracy is not afraid of a healthy amount of protest and rebellion, but positively encourages it, because a little individual rebellion expressed today is better than a big mass rebellion tomorrow.

Loss of the ability to communicate can have profoundly disturbing effects on both individual and society. So far we do not know enough about the cure of emotional disturbances through psychiatric help. Yet the different methods of psychiatric therapy have one trait in common: to encourage the patient to talk—thereby partly getting rid of his troubles by expressing them.

A whole society that has lost the ability to communicate cannot go to a psychiatrist for help; social mechanisms must be set up to provide channels of communication that had not existed before.

Maximum communication in a free society implies that there be *no taboo issues*, that is, a set of final truths that must not be questioned. Communism has the taboo of Marxism-Leninism, a set of final social, economic, and political truths that must be accepted—or else. In addition, there are the more passing taboo subjects as defined by the top party leaders.

By contrast, if democracy is true to its principles, it recognizes no taboo issues, not even the validity of democracy itself. In practice, democracies at times violate their own principles, and put restrictions—in fact, if not in law—on the untrammeled discussion and challenge of some political, economic, or moral principles which are accepted by most members of the community to be so true as to be "beyond discussion."

The individual, too, may have taboo issues that he is unable or unwilling to approach and examine in a rational and detached manner. The person with perfect emotional health would have no such taboo issues at all. But no individual is so perfectly mature and rational, just as no society can fully live up to its democratic ideal of taking no truth for granted.

Experience has taught us two lessons about the function of the taboo in the life of the individual as of the group. First, the flight into the security of the taboo is more likely to occur—for an individual as for a group— under conditions of crisis and fear than in normal conditions. Totalitarian regimes need an atmosphere of permanent crisis for their very existence; they claim to be menaced by internal and external enemies who seek their destruction, and they thus justify the continuous need for a highly repressive government. The second lesson of experience is that the security provided by the taboo is only temporary. Postponing the rational attack on real-life problems merely makes their later—and inevitable—confrontation and solution more difficult and painful. This lesson is often learned belatedly in democracies too. The failure of the United States for nearly two centuries to deal rationally and effectively with the problem of racial equality finally led to mass violence in the 1960s.

On the surface, totalitarian societies seem orderly, happy, and united, for no public expression of dissent or discontent is permitted. However, totalitarian systems can only outlaw the expression of such "wrong" feelings, but not the feelings themselves. When totalitarianism loses its grip over the population, the pent-up frustrations may erupt into a volcano of violence and destruction. When Mussolini lost his war, he was killed by a group of anti-Fascists in April 1945, and his dead body was hung, head down, on a lamppost in Milan—the city in which fascism was born in 1919.

The unreality of the outward happiness and unity in totalitarian states is evidenced by their periodic purges. In the 1930s, Stalin staged the Big Purge (roughly from 1934 to 1938), in which most of the Old Bolshevik leaders, the high military, not to speak of millions of subordinate party officials and plain rank and file, perished. In December, 1953, Lavrenti Beria, one of the three top rulers of the Soviet Union, was executed for a long list of alleged crimes, including the charge that he had been working for British and American intelligence all along. True or untrue, the charge was interesting in itself, since Beria had been in command of all police and intelligence organizations.

In Nazi Germany, too, the head of the nation's security system was finally executed as a traitor and spy. Admiral Wilhelm Canaris served as chief of the *Abwehr*, the German military intelligence service, from 1935 until 1944. After the anti-Hitler plot of July 20, 1944, Canaris was arrested, and finally executed in the spring of 1945. Whereas we have no evidence whether Beria, the executed chief of Soviet intelligence, was guilty or not, there is ample evidence that Canaris was involved in the plot to assassinate Hitler in 1944. Moreover, both British and German studies of Canaris have made a strong case for the almost unbelievable probability that Canaris actually worked for the British while serving as the chief of German intelligence![1]

The apparent unanimity of totalitarian states in peacetime is followed by treason in time of war: Hitler was the object of assassination attempts by high-ranking officers on several occasions, and he saw treason everywhere, until, following his attempted assassination on July 20, 1944, he decided to execute hundreds of high officers. Because political change cannot be openly and peacefully advocated in a totalitarian state, those who want such change badly enough must resort to violence and betrayal, the only means left open when the safety valve of free criticism is lacking.

Is Freedom Less Efficient Than Coercion?

Even those who grant that the democratic personality has its appealing traits of openness and friendliness frequently ask this question, Is freedom less efficient than coercion? During the existence of fascism in Italy and Germany, many persons in other countries (who had no sympathy for fascism from an ethical viewpoint) argued that under Mussolini the trains

[1] See Ivan Colvin, *Chief of Intelligence* (London: Gollancz, 1951); K. H. Abshagen, *Canaris* (London: Hutchinson, 1956).

ran on time, and that Hitler had abolished unemployment. These unwitting apologists of fascism were apparently unaware that the Swiss, for example, had managed to run trains on time without the price of political assassination, and that many nations had been able to cope with the problem of unemployment without setting up Nazi-like concentration camps and gas chambers.

Yet after World War II, when the war efforts of both Italy and Germany were examined in terms of efficiency, Italian fascism revealed itself to be just about the most inept and inefficient system of government and administration the Italians had ever suffered from; as to Germany, it was found that her mobilization of manpower, womanpower, and resources was less efficient than that of Britain, for example. This came as somewhat of a surprise, for it had been assumed that totalitarianism could do almost anything because no political resistance was allowed.

Apart from the sullenness and hatred that totalitarianism is bound to produce in a minority of the population (and this minority grows rapidly if the chance of victory fades), there is the effect of passing the buck: the fear of making decisions because the wrong decision may mean death rather than mere loss of promotion. Although there was plenty of administrative confusion in London and Washington during World War II, it was nothing compared to the chaos in Rome and Berlin.

Moreover, there is a *law of diminishing return of totalitarian control:* precisely because it tries to control all citizens in every thought and action, it is bound to fail in the control of essentials. To illustrate: During World War II, a number of British officers successfully escaped from prisoner of war camps in Germany, and then traveled with forged documents throughout the length and breadth of Germany; some even managed to reach England via Sweden or Spain. Wartime travel in Germany required often as many as a dozen documents issued by various authorities. Yet this multiple control made forgery easier rather than harder; there were so many documents that were issued that even security officers could not easily spot forgeries.

In Great Britain, on the other hand, a person had to show only one document—his identity card issued by the National Register. Every official was well familiar with all the fine points of that document, and forgeries could be much more readily discovered.

One escaping British officer, Oliver Philpot, relates that the *verboten* sign was all over the German landscape, but its very frequency invited German civilians not to pay much attention to it. On reaching the naval port of Danzig, for example, Philpot was able to see its secret submarine installations in great detail just by following the German civilian crowd on a sightseeing trip, and he felt amazed by it all, for he felt that a civilian in Portsmouth on a similar mission would run the risk of being shot.[2]

The successful use of forged documents by Philpot (he reached a Swedish ship within 36 hours after his escape from camp) was by no means an isolated incident. After World War II, the British Air Ministry asked Aidan Crawley, himself an escapee, to write a summary history of all escapee activities in German prisoner of war camps for the use of the Royal Air Force. The result was one of the most exciting books about World War II.[3] Based on all the information available to the British Government, Crawley (after World War II a Member of Parliament and Under Secretary of State for Air) concludes that "not even trained members of the Gestapo (German Secret Police) could recognize all passes at sight, and any authoritatively worded pass, well laid out and carrying the necessary police and departmental stamps, was almost certain to survive examination."[4] As a result, forging documents was one of the major enterprises in British prisoner of war camps in Germany. In fact, the vast variety of German stamps, passes, and documents even encouraged the forgery departments to invent new ones so as to make ordinary letters, such as from business firms, appear more official: "It was found that the Germans were impressed by these."[5]

However, excessive administrative control and red tape was not the only cause of totalitarian inefficiency. Political disloyalty was another. Disloyalty of high army officers on a large scale occurred in World War II only in totalitarian Germany and Russia. In Germany, there was first the case of Field Marshal von Paulus. Captured at the Battle of Stalingrad in early 1943, von Paulus organized an anti-Nazi movement among German prisoners of war in Russia, broadcast to Germany appeals to surrender, and helped the Russian war effort in every way he could.

On the Russian side of the war, the most famous case was that of General Andrei Vlasov. Captured by the Germans at the end of 1941 in the defense of Moscow, Vlasov quickly proceeded to organize a Russian Army of Liberation, and begged Hitler to allow him and his army to participate in the war against Soviet Russia. Because he considered Russians *Untermenschen* (subhumans), Hitler was unwilling to grant this request when it might have changed the fortunes of war. Only later, when the war was lost for Germany, Hitler allowed the use of captured Soviet troops, but by then it was too late. According to careful estimates, close to

[2] Oliver Philpot, *Stolen Journey* (London: Hodder & Stoughton, 1950).
[3] Aidan Crawley, *Escape from Germany: A History of R.A.F. Escapes During the War* (London: Collins, 1956).
[4] Aidan Crawley, *ibid.*, p. 76.
[5] *Ibid.*, p. 78.

one million ex-Soviet citizens served with the German armed forces toward the end of the war.[6] Even large numbers of captured Soviet officers joined the Germans against their own country, including 10 out of 50 captured Soviet generals. By contrast, the Germans were unable to interest American, British, or other allied prisoners in the idea of fighting against their own country, and even the French collaborators under Marshal Pétain never dared to declare war on Britain and the United States.

The contrast between totalitarianism and a wartime democracy such as Britain is impressive. As was pointed out above, a person in Britain had to show only one pass—the identity card issued by the National Register. German prisoners of war in Britain who tried to escape were inevitably asked one simple question: "May I see your identity card?" On this simple query escape attempts invariably failed. Despite the absence of totalitarian control in wartime Britain, only a few Germans tried to escape, and those who tried never succeeded. Politically, all parties in wartime Britain were united in the aim of winning the war, and there were no disloyal British who actively aided would-be German escapees, or British officers who would organize an army against their own country.

The Feeling of Being Wanted

In Britain and the United States, controlled educational experiments with children and organizational experiments with adults have shown that performance and productivity can be improved by the greater use of group decisions than was true in the past. In industry, some companies also use other devices—company publications, suggestion boxes, social get-togethers, dances, ownership of company stock, and other material benefits—to make their employees feel that they are members of a community, in which everybody has a personal stake. In some cases, these devices are little more than gimmicks, but in other instances the participation by the group is genuine, and from it important lessons about the relation of democratic group consultation to efficiency have been learned.

Within free societies, prison labor is notoriously the least efficient type of labor; comparing different types of societies, we find that the American worker produces about three times as much as the Soviet worker, while the contrast between production of the American farmer and that of the collectivized Soviet peasant is even greater. When the Soviet government abandoned Stalin's slave labor camps in the 1950s, although still running "correctional labor camps" on a smaller scale, it was motivated by two lines of reasoning. First, there was the realization that Stalin's terror had

[6] George Fischer, *Opposition to Stalin* (Cambridge, Mass.: Harvard University Press, 1952), p. 45.

gone too far from the political viewpoint. Second, there was the fact that, economically, a modern industrial society could not afford the waste of valuable manpower that was rotting to death by the millions in the slave labor camps.

In education, schools and colleges in democratic societies are gradually trying to abandon, or at least to supplement, lectures as the sole teaching method by stressing discussion more strongly as a teaching—and learning— device. In discussion, the teacher no longer does all, or most, of the talking, but sees to it that the exchange of ideas is carried on in an orderly fashion. The students are encouraged to speak their minds freely, and whatever conclusions emerge are the result of their own thinking. The authoritative pronouncement of Truth by a superior to subordinates is replaced by dialogue among equals, the students themselves.

The feeling of being wanted is one of the most powerful sources of inner security, of creative action, and of loyalty to others. It is the greatest source of personal happiness and national strength. He who is treated with trust will act trustworthily, whereas he who is treated as an irresponsible child will act like one. Americans like to think that they "cannot be pushed around." Once things are explained to them, they are capable of any and all sacrifice.

At the end of his essay *On Liberty* (1859) John Stuart Mill says that "the worth of a state, in the long run, is the worth of the individuals composing it," and that "a state which dwarfs its men, in order that they may be more docile instruments in its hands even for beneficial purposes— will find that with small men no great thing can really be accomplished."

Although there is no conclusive proof in this matter, there is reason to believe that, in the long run, a free society is more efficient than an authoritarian or a totalitarian society. Yet we do not value freedom mostly because it is more efficient. Even if it were less efficient, we should still prefer to live under freedom than under tyranny. Freedom needs no further justification: it is an end—for many the highest end—in itself. By contrast, tyranny must always be justified, even by the tyrants themselves, on the ground that it is more efficient or that it will lead to military triumphs.

The supreme task of wise statesmanship in a free society is to prevent situations from arising in which the choice between freedom and efficiency has to be made. The two are perfectly compatible and—in the judgment of many—naturally complement each other.

CHAPTER 4

THE ECONOMIC
ENVIRONMENT
OF DEMOCRACY

❧ DEMOCRACY AND ECONOMIC DEVELOPMENT

In what is perhaps still the greatest study of the United States, *Democracy in America* (1835–1840), Alexis de Tocqueville was one of the first to perceive the intimate relationship between democracy and industrial capitalism. Tocqueville felt that the United States—then a basically agrarian economy—would rapidly develop into a dynamic industrial economy because it operated within a democratic political system recognizing the following basic values:

First, democracy recognizes the "pursuit of happiness" for every human being. This means that democracy is this-worldly rather than other-worldly—a general metaphysical attitude which, economically, stimulates demand. Second, the tendency toward social equality inherent in every democracy favors economic growth, for most persons feel that they are entitled to the good things in life, provided they are willing and able to make the necessary efforts to obtain them. Third, a democracy based on the rule of law provides its members with a sense of security and calculability for the future. In every economic system only consumption is oriented toward the present, whereas the decisive economic activities—private or public—are necessarily oriented toward the future, whether it be in economic planning, saving, investing, or producing. Finally, democracy is not only a system of ideas and values but also a system of utilizing human energy. Where democracy has worked, it has released tremendous energies that only lay dormant in the predemocratic society. It is therefore not surprising that where democracy has flourished, it has generally been accompanied by rapid economic growth. This can most clearly be seen in those societies that are not endowed with abundant natural resources—such as Switzerland and Norway—and that have developed high living standards for their people under the protective shelter of strong social, economic, and political institutions based on freedom and the rule of law. Political democracy provides a favorable framework for economic growth, but does not guarantee it. Other factors, such as the excessive growth of population in India, may inhibit economic growth despite political democracy. Also, attitudes toward work, religious convictions, and ethical commitments may play a role, regardless of the existing political system.

Whereas one frequently hears the statement that democracy is the product of wealth, or "a luxury of the rich," the relationship should more accurately be put in the reverse order—that is, that economic growth and expansion flourish best in a free society. After World War II, Germany and Japan have been two outstanding illustrations. Their economic growth since about 1950 has by far exceeded their economic achievements in their previous history, be it in their semiauthoritarian period of the late nineteenth and early twentieth centuries or during their period of complete totalitarianism in the 1930s. For the first time in modern German and Japanese history, democracy promises to become a living reality. It is perhaps no coincidence that the economy of both nations now flourishes more and grows faster than ever before in their history. Much has been heard of the "economic miracle" of Germany and Japan in recent years. Their "political miracle" of taking democracy seriously is just as important and possibly one of the deeper causes of their economic performance.

In Latin America, too, one of its major nations—Mexico—has shown a surprisingly high rate of economic growth and industrial expansion since the end of World War II. Here again, it is perhaps no pure coincidence that this impressive economic growth has taken place during the very same period when Mexico has moved steadily in the direction of more mature and stable democratic politics and government.

✳ LINKS BETWEEN ECONOMIC AND POLITICAL FREEDOM

In the past, economic and political freedom have generally developed side by side. This does not necessarily prove that one type of freedom—say, the economic—produced another, the political or social. The reverse, too, cannot be affirmed: that political freedom made the rise of a free market economy possible. Instead of trying to determine whether, in the past, economic freedom led to political freedom or vice versa, it is sufficient to note that both developed side by side.

The relation between economic and political freedom is not that one causes the other, but that both are the reflection of jointly shared deeper attitudes and values. In the past, we have never seen the development of a free-market economy without a parallel movement toward political democracy. Whether we shall see in the future one without the other, such as a predominantly collectivized economy within the framework of a political democracy, no one can predict with absolute certainty. So far, it has not happened, and even Socialists, as we shall soon see in greater detail, are in the process of giving up the faith that there can be a fully nationalized economy plus political democracy.

The Individualistic Component

What are some of the common elements that underlie both economic freedom—that is, a capitalist economy—and political freedom—that is, democratic self-government? First, there is the element of rationalist individualism. The individualistic component underlying both capitalism and democracy means above all that the average man in such a society believes he knows best what is good for him. Negatively this means that the individual refuses to be pushed around by his political or economic betters, superiors, or rulers. The ordinary reasonable and sane individual in a capitalist democracy knows that he will never become President of the United States, but he wants to be sure he can turn the President out of office. As Aristotle put it, the guest should be the judge of the meal, and not the cook. Similarly, the average car owner knows he could not step into the place of the men who run General Motors or Ford. But as a customer, he wants to be able to express his negative opinion by buying one year one company's car, and another year some other company's. When the negative votes—in this case, the failure to buy cars—become habitual, a company may go out of business of making cars, as happened to the Studebaker Corporation, which stopped producing cars in the United States in 1963. Yet even big companies must finally bow to the individual preferences of the customers. When the Big Three (General Motors, Ford, Chrysler) failed to produce the small or compact car that the American public wanted in the late 1950s, the car buyers turned to imported cars and then to a smaller American company, American Motors.

From a practical viewpoint, therefore, the freedom of the individual in a capitalist democracy is more important—in both the economic and politi-

cal realms—in what he refuses to do rather than in what he can do. Thus
to most people freedom of the press means in practice, not the use of the
theoretical right to start a new daily in New York or Los Angeles with an
initial investment of $5 million or $10 million, but the freedom to read one
paper rather than another. If enough people stop reading a paper, it
eventually goes out of business. Freedom of association means for most
people, not the practical use of the right to start a new political party, but
the choice between joining existing parties and voting for them—or
forgetting about parties altogether. The same applies to the economic field.
Freedom of trade means for most people, not the right to open a new
department store next to Macy's and Gimbels' in order to compete with
both, but the right to buy in either or neither of the two.

Dispersal of Power

The links between economic and political freedom can also be seen in the
common concept of *dispersal of power*. Neither capitalism nor democracy—even in their most optimistic moods—have ever held the view that
power among men can be eliminated. What capitalism and democracy
have tried to do is to curb and disperse power as much as is practically
possible. In government, this dispersal of power is effected through federalism, checks and balances between the different branches of public authority, separation of state and church, two-party or multiparty systems, the
encouragement of private education as a counterweight to public education—to mention but a few methods long established in the American
tradition. In the economy, this dispersal of power is effected through
ownership of property among many individuals, competition between firms
in the same industry or between entire industries, rivalry between labor
and management, and the absence of a centrally owned and planned
economy.

There is still another link between economic and political freedom. The
fact that government and economic life are not merged, as is the case in a
fully collectivized (Socialist or Communist) economy, makes escape from
one realm into the other much easier. In a government-run economy, a
person who fails in the management of a small haberdashery store would
be through, both politically and economically, because his failure in a
government activity (a government-owned store) would bar him from a
further career of any importance in government, and his failure as a *store*
manager would disqualify him from heavy economic responsibilities. In a
free-market economy, the converse is true. When Harry S. Truman, in his
early manhood, failed in his haberdashery business, he could turn to
politics, where he had more talent, and eventually became President.

Conversely, a person in a capitalist democracy can fail in politics, and then turn to a lucrative and distinguished economic career. This again would be impossible or extremely difficult in a government-run economy.

✻ ECONOMIC INEQUALITY AND POLITICAL UNORTHODOXY

The inequality of property in a capitalist economy has often been an indispensable condition for the propagation of new unorthodox ideas. It is true that the large majority of the economically powerful look askance at new unorthodox or radical opinions. Yet the history of many "little reviews," ultraliberal journals, and radical organizations in both Britain and the United States shows that there is always a minority of the wealthy and influential who are willing to support financially new and unorthodox views in politics, the arts, and education. In a fully collectivized economy, even within a democratic framework of government, it might be more awkward and more difficult for the government to support radical and "subversive" ideas with public funds. Even assuming that relatively affluent individuals existed in a collectivized economy, such individuals would in the nature of things be high government officials, and they would be the last to back ideas and movements directed against the "establishment."

The Fabians in England did so much for the cause of British socialism because they realized that Socialist propaganda addressed to the workers was not enough, and that a major task was to win over a minority at least of the socially influential elements in British society. The same Fabians did not fully see that, under conditions of full-fledged democratic socialism, a new group of procapitalist "Fabians" would find it difficult, if not impossible, to win over members of the Socialist governing class to the cause of capitalism.

Finally, in a capitalist democracy, earning a livelihood is not dependent on political conformity. In the middle 1950s, when a number of individuals lost their government positions in the era of McCarthyism, they could always make a living either in private employment or in independent small business or farming. Many of these persons held political and economic views that were not in sympathy with the principles of a capitalist market economy. Yet when the government, justly or unjustly, deprived them of their livelihood, they discovered that unfavorable political publicity and even disrepute can be submerged in the anonymity of the free market. The free market (at least to the extent that it is free) judges a person only by his productivity and efficiency, regardless of his social and political views, his religion, or his ethnic background. John F. Kennedy's Catholicism was an open issue in the presidential election of 1960, yet his father's Catholicism was never an issue in building up a fortune of hundreds of millions of dollars.

⚜ SECURITY VERSUS RISK-TAKING IN ECONOMICS AND POLITICS

Though most people in a capitalist democracy realize they will never become President of the United States or president of a big corporation, the salient feature in such a system, as contrasted with a closed economic and political system, is that some do make it. In 1964, of 1,000 top American executives only 11 percent (as compared with 46 percent in 1900) came from a wealthy background; 66 percent (in 1900, 42 percent) were of middle-class origins; and 23 percent (in 1900, 12 percent) came from a poor background. Although it is easier for a Roosevelt or Kennedy to become President than for a man born into a family of modest means, we have had many Presidents who came up the hard way: Lincoln—and in more recent times, Truman, Eisenhower, and Johnson.

The Economic Aspect of Risk-Taking

Both capitalism and political democracy thus try to combine two contradictory impulses: the quest for security and the drive for venturing and gambling. The free market is not only—as it is supposed to be in theory—a place where equal meets equal, and where everybody strikes a good bargain, but it is also, in practice, "a financial slaughterhouse, where the strong chop up the weak."[1] The phrase "playing the market" is well known in the United States, where many consider investing hard-earned money in corporate shares a gamble, almost as uncertain in its outcome as playing the horses. Although there is an exaggeration in the phrase, it nevertheless expresses a sound instinct, that engaging in free enterprise is always something of a gamble. The high annual mortality rate of newly started enterprises is a telling testimony—and to many, an effective warning—that venturing into the open fields of free enterprise is dangerous.

True enough, a person who in 1914 had bought 100 shares of International Business Machines for $2,750 would have found in 1964 that his investment (including dividends and other benefits) had risen to about $9,000,000, or nearly a 3,500 times increase in 50 years. A person who had

[1] David T. Bazelon, The Paper Economy (New York: Random House, 1963), p. 52.

TABLE 4–1. *Cost of Investment in 100 Shares of Large Corporations (in 1919) and Value (in 1964)*

	For Each 100 Shares in 1919	
	Cost Then	Value Now
American Beet Sugar	$ 7,113	$ 8,975
American Linseed	5,013	51,300
Amer Tel & Tel	10,000	43,875
Anaconda	6,025	4,713
Baldwin Locomotive	7,513	520
California Packing	5,038	68,503
Corn Products	5,025	203,918
Distillers Securities	5,513	Worthless
Midvale Steel	4,350	19,238
Pan Am Petrol	7,250	16,384
Pierce Oil	1,850	Worthless
United Fruit	16,100	33,469
US Steel	9,313	46,935

SOURCE: *Investor's Reader*, February 5, 1964.

bought 100 shares of General Motors in 1908 would also have increased his investment about 3,000 times by 1964. More recently, we have seen relatively small businesses spring forth rapidly into giants like Xerox, Texas Instruments, and Litton Industries. But for every successful gamble of this sort there are innumerable other gambles in the free enterprise system that have ended less successfully, badly, or even catastrophically. Table 4–1 shows what an investment in 100 shares of large corporations in 1919 cost then and what they were worth in 1964.

Where two investments in 1919 later became completely worthless, others went down in value, others increased, and one star performer in this representative list multiplied its value 40 times in 45 years. Where there is high risk, there is high reward, and this the capitalist system does with its unequal distribution of incomes through incentives for unequal jobs and risks. But the majority of the people are satisfied with relatively mild incentives and more security, buttressed by the comforting knowledge that the opportunity for venture is always there, in case they are ever seized by the spirit of venture. Most Americans enjoy the feeling that the West is wide open for newcomers, but only a small minority in each generation has had the desire or pluck to pull up its roots and move westward. What the West is geographically for the United States, the venture-incentive is economically for the capitalist system.

The Political Aspect of Risk-Taking

In democratic politics, too, there is ample room for both the sedate and the venturesome. The former can confine their political activities, if they so wish, to voting or to political discussions with their friends. But then there are those who are willing to stake their leisure time, hard-earned money, and reputations on running for public office. If the free market of capitalism is for many a "financial slaughterhouse," in which their dreams of making millions come to a quick and disheartening end, the free market of democratic politics is also a "political slaughterhouse," in which in the very nature of things somebody must lose if someone else wins.

❧ QUANTIFIABLE UNITS IN ECONOMICS AND POLITICS

Because both capitalism and democracy stress rational methods of calculation and measurement, a *quantifiable unit* had to be invented in both cases to measure success or failure.

Quantifiable Unit in Economics: Money

In economics, the quantifiable unit is *money*. Although money existed before capitalism, it never played the important role it has acquired under capitalism. Whereas before the advent of capitalism the question, "What is John Smith worth?" might have alluded to his chances of getting into heaven, under capitalism this question refers to his "net assets" in monetary terms. This "cash-nexus" of capitalist civilization has its drawbacks, and it has been under constant attack by those who strive for higher standards of measurement.

If power based on money is not appealing, power based on armed force and the political police is even less appealing. Yet, in a capitalist civilization no one is forced to bow before the omnipresent ruler and quantifier of money. There is the freedom to choose a profession, such as the ministry or teaching or public service, in all of which making money is a means to a higher ideal of service. In fact, capitalist democracies even allow anyone to lead the life of a bum—shirking work, responsibilities, and the need to earn money. Both nazism and communism put bums and hoboes into concentration camps, slave labor camps, or "correctional labor camps," as they are now called in the Soviet Union.

Drawing by O'Brian; © 1966 The New Yorker Magazine, Inc.

Quantifiable Unit in Politics: The Vote

The rational quantifier in democratic politics is the *vote*. Again, the vote as an instrument of deciding political issues or competition between rival political leaders has been ridiculed by its enemies as too mechanical and inimical to true greatness because the vote of a genius counts as much in a democracy as the vote of a merely average person. Democratic theory does not deny that some men are greater than others. But it insists that great men should be able to *convince* the lesser breed of their greatness, and not force such recognition on them. Moreover, democratic theory has been unable to find a rational method by which the experiences of great men and those of ordinary persons can be accurately weighed on some scale and compared.

This difficulty is compounded by the fact that it is not always clear and certain who the great are, for they often seem very small to some of their fellow men. Thus the final justification of the democratic one man, one vote idea—and this is the heart of democratic government—lies, not in the ability of democratic theory to prove that this is the absolutely best way, but in the inability of any other method to prove that some individuals have grasped ultimate truth—be it the concept of race (fascism) or class (communism)—and are therefore entitled to rule regardless of what the majority thinks or feels. Under this "mechanical" quantification of politics in a democracy, the majority will undoubtedly often be wrong—but hardly more often so than minority government that rejects the democratic method of counting heads. Finally, the virtue of the vote-unit—as in the case of money—lies in its simplicity. When the votes are counted, it is all over. When a dispute over the correct interpretation of Marx or Lenin is temporarily settled in an inner clique of self-appointed rulers, all is not over. The hangman's noose or exile to Siberia may be the final method of settling the issue.

❧ CALCULABILITY AND THE RULE OF LAW IN ECONOMICS AND POLITICS

Calculability in Economics

Closely connected with the element of rationalism in both capitalism and democracy is that of *calculability*. The very term "capitalism" points to the future, for capital is being accumulated in the present solely for the purpose of providing goods and services in the future. The key institution of capitalism—property—also points to the future. Property is not, as is so often assumed, a thing (such as a piece of furniture or a home), but a legally enforceable *claim*, measurable in monetary terms. Such a claim may refer to a physical thing, or it may refer to nonphysical objects, such as an invention, a literary or musical composition, goodwill, or an insurance benefit. When a person says, "Such and such is my property," what he is really saying is that he is reasonably certain that courts will prevent others, in the future, from interfering with his claim in a particular object that can be expressed in money.

The content of property claims may vary widely: the owner of a few corporate shares is essentially only the passive recipient of a quarterly dividend; a public utility is more restricted in its rate policies than a manufacturer of candy is in his pricing policies; and the owner of a book may do with it as he pleases. But in all cases the owner—once the scope of his property rights is established—wants to be sure that his expectations will be protected by the law and by the government behind the law.

Two illustrations may demonstrate the extent to which calculability of the future plays a dominant role in capitalist economics. Let us first look at the price of corporate shares. Generally, there is an average "price-earnings ratio" for leading stocks—that is, the price of a share is a given multiple of a year's earning. Assuming the price-earnings ratio to be 20 : 1, this would mean that if a company earns $5 per annum (per share), the price of the share would be $100. Yet the average ratio is only an average; some shares sell below the average and some well above it. Chrysler Corporation or U.S. Steel may sell for 10 to 15 times their annual earnings, because the potential investor is uncertain about the future of these companies; by contrast, companies like Polaroid, Xerox, and International Business Machines may sell for 40 to 100 times their annual earnings because investors seem to see an exceptionally bright future for growth companies of this type. Of course, performance in the past is only one element for evaluating what a company is likely to do in the future. But the past is dead, and this one element can never be decisive. The principal question in appraising a capitalist enterprise from the investor's viewpoint is, "What is this company likely to earn this year, next year, and the year after that?" and not, "What did the company earn ten years ago or five years ago or last year?"

The second illustration of the importance of calculability in capitalist economics is foreign investment. Direct American private investments abroad were over $50 billion in 1966; of this vast sum, about one third was in Canada, and over one quarter in Western Europe—the two wealthiest areas in the world next to the United States. In Latin America, the bulk of American investments was in the Venezuelan oil industry and in various enterprises in Mexico, Brazil, and Argentina—and only paltry amounts in the poorer countries. American investments in the most underdeveloped countries in Asia, Africa, and Latin America are relatively small, although those areas need American capital the most.

What is the logic behind this pattern of American foreign investment—this preference for the relatively low return in advanced countries to the potentially much higher return in poorer countries? The answer lies in the element of calculability. The American investor prefers a reasonably certain, though lower, return in the future to a potentially much higher return in countries with unstable political conditions. In Canada, the American investor feels almost as safe as in his own country, and the same applies to Britain and Western Europe.

This attitude is also true of investors of other nations. In the nineteenth century, Britain concentrated its investments in its own dependent territories and in independent countries like the United States and Argentina, in whose future political stability Britain had confidence. In the years 1900–1914, Britain annually invested about 7 percent of its national income in underdeveloped countries, mostly in its own dependencies. Since

1945, as the former colonies became independent, British investors have invested only a fraction of 1 percent of the national income in the former colonies, and have preferred to invest their capital in Western Europe, Canada, the United States, and other advanced countries. One of the fundamental problems of the underdeveloped countries lies in the fact that, as they have gained political independence, they have not always given sufficient proof of stability and security to attract foreign investors.

Calculability in Politics: The Rule of Law

The concept of calculability in democratic politics is most clearly embodied in the theory and practice of the rule of law. The great virtue of the rule of law is not only that all persons are equally treated by the law according to general rules, but that the citizen knows in advance what legal consequences his actions will produce. To many persons, uncertainty about the future is even worse than the certainty of a relatively harsh legal rule. Although the rule of law is not identical with democracy, it is a step in that direction.

Authoritarian states, too, may have the operation of the rule of law, provided there are clear and general legal rules, and judges can interpret them without political pressure. Yet, in the very nature of things the rule of law in an authoritarian state differs from the democratic rule of law: for in the authoritarian state only the judge and administrative agents need to feel bound by general rules of law. When it comes to the making of the general law itself, the authoritarian ruler is bound by no constitutional or parliamentary limits. By contrast, in a democracy the citizen may not know what the content of future laws is going to be, but he knows that Congress or Parliament will have to observe certain procedures in order to make new laws. The observance of such restrictions is in itself a guarantee against arbitrary legislation. Under the rule of law in a democracy, the citizen may not know what the legislature is going to do in this or that area that concerns him, but he has a good idea of what the legislature is *not* going to do in the future, if past constitutional procedures of lawmaking are continued.

℅ TENSIONS BETWEEN CAPITALISM AND DEMOCRACY

The internal tensions of capitalist democracy can be viewed from two angles: first, those tensions that capitalism and democracy have developed as a result of specific historical circumstances, and, second, the tensions that derive from inherent differences between capitalism and democracy.

Tensions Created by Bigness in the Economy

Looking at the first kind of tensions in capitalist democracy, we find that most of them are due to the success of capitalism and democracy rather than to their failures. For example, the successful business enterprise gets bigger and bigger as time goes on, until it finally becomes one of the few dominant companies in its field (oligopoly) or dominates an entire line of business or industry (monopoly). In this development, one of the main elements (and virtues) of capitalism—vigorous competition—may easily get lost. This concentration of economic power and influence in social and political life then becomes the basis for the demand that such economic concentration be remedied by government intervention. In democratic government, also, the persistent success of an outstanding political personality, group, or party leads to concentration of power or to semiperpetual one-party government, followed by inevitable protests and demands for radical changes.

Next, both big capitalist business and big democratic government seem to produce inevitably the phenomena of bureaucracy and routine. Both capitalism and democracy originally started out with the individual seeking his independence from collective entities, such as the state, church, or nobility. The very success of capitalism and democracy has produced large economic and political organizations, in which conformity has replaced daring, and in which the individual has become a set of digits, whether as a user of the telephone or as a claimant of social security. In the classical phase of capitalism (from the middle of the eighteenth to the end of the nineteenth century), the key figure of capitalism was the adventurous and innovating entrepreneur, whether his innovation consisted in the discovery of new mechanical processes, new methods of production and organization, or the discovery of new markets or sources of supply.

In more recent times, even innovation has become part of an organized routine: technical and scientific research is carried on routinely in special research laboratories, and the researcher or inventor is not a capitalist entrepreneur but a salaried scientist with a fixed salary and pension rights who knows what he is looking for and how to find it. The fact that the bulk of scientific research in many capitalist democracies (in the United States more than in any other country) is financed by governmental resources accentuates this change in the nature of capitalism. As to the discovery of new markets, the merchant-conqueror has often been replaced by professional market research firms that sell market information to anyone who is willing to pay for it.

Tensions Created by Bigness in Government

In democratic government, too, the growth of bureaucracy has been the result, not so much of a conspiracy of power-hungry bureaucrats or of a general breakdown of democracy, but of the success of the democratic system of government. The more people in a democracy require or expect of their government, the more such activities or services lead to new bureaus, new agencies, new organizations, new bureaucracy. Democratic government starts out by being responsible, that is, it can act only in accord with the wishes of the majority. But gradually this political *responsibility* evolves into social and economic *responsiveness*—that is, the people discover that through the vote they can get the state to do many things which cannot, or at least not easily, be done by themselves. In democratic government, as Alexis de Tocqueville saw over a century ago in his *Democracy in America*, the people think that whatever power they bestow on the government, "they bestow upon themselves."

Another manifestation of the corrosion of individuality in the advanced stages of both capitalism and democracy is the development of the *group* as the decisive force in economic and political activity. In the classical stage of capitalism, the individual farmer, artisan, worker, or merchant was the key figure in the economic process. Today, a labor union may bargain for workers in an entire industry, and in most states unions can deny employment to an individual worker who refuses to become a member. The farmer no longer is an independent self-determining entrepreneur, but depends on his organized farm blocs in and out of Congress and state legislatures. The individual businessman has given place, in terms of effective action, to the individual big corporation or to organizations such as the United States Chamber of Commerce or the National Association of Manufacturers. In addition, there are the numerous more specialized economic interest groups, representing particular branches of labor, management, and the independent professions.

In democratic government, too, the individual has been largely replaced by the group. The authors of the Constitution not only did not mention political parties, but looked upon them with great suspicion as a massive force that might dissolve the unity of the state into factions and dissolve the individual in the process. In Britain, also, modern mass parties are only about one hundred years old, and—as in the United States—parties developed as democracy became more pervasive and more successful. In the economy, advanced capitalist societies have tried to stem the tide of big economic power by positive aid given to small business and by negative prohibition of monopolistic trends through antitrust legislation. Similarly, in democratic government, the open primary and other devices have sought to reaffirm the weight of the individual citizen against the monopolistic power of political bosses making vital political decisions behind the back of the public.

Finally, the change of the original capitalist democracy from a predominantly agrarian and small-business society into a highly urbanized industrial society with a corporate style of economic organization has had profound effects on both the economic and political character of the advanced capitalist democracy. First, the nature of property and the emotions and attitudes it engenders have changed profoundly. The property of the middle class in the eighteenth and nineteenth centuries was (1) tangible, and (2) the foundation of the entire social and economic life of the owner. The farmer owned his land, the artisan owned his shop and tools, and the owner of the small factory owned the building and machinery. This type of ownership provided the owner with a feeling of independence and self-reliance, economically as well as politically.

The new middle class of the twentieth century is largely the result of the corporate economy. The main type of property is no longer tangible but intangible, and generally consists of corporate stock and "liquid assets," such as U.S. savings bonds and savings accounts in banks or savings and loan associations. Around the turn of this century, liquid property was about 15 to 20 percent of gross national wealth; now it is well over one half. What is politically, socially, and economically even more important is that the tangible property of the old middle class, although much less in absolute size than today, was "creative property," in the sense that it was the sole source of making a living, and thus defined the whole way of life of a family. By contrast, the stocks and bonds and savings of today's new middle class are an "asset," passive property that merely gives the owner the expectation of dividends or interest, but does not color the family's day-to-day life. The main economic asset of today's corporate middle class is not the property it owns, tangible or intangible, but its position in the hierarchy of corporate employment. Although much wealthier and enjoying a much higher living standard than the old middle class, today's middle class is nevertheless economically dependent, whereas the old middle class was economically independent.

In the eighteenth and nineteenth centuries the economic independence of the property-owning middle class was strongly reflected in its political independence and activism. By contrast, the new middle class of corporate employment tends to be much more nonpolitical. The top corporate executives set an example of not getting "involved" in party politics for fear of losing customers or offending stockholders or government officials with

"Jim and I just don't know who to vote for. Our television has been broken for weeks." Drawing by B. Wiseman; Copr. © 1956 The New Yorker Magazine, Inc.

whom they must deal. The example set by the top executives inevitably colors the behavior of lesser ranks, and staying out of politics becomes second nature. Thus the new middle class, to the extent that it is in the large corporate sector of the economy, becomes a class of "political consumers," generally meeting its voting responsibilities but otherwise watching politics as reported in the newspapers and on television rather than participating as "political producers" in government. This is a far cry from the old middle class of the eighteenth and nineteenth centuries, which was the principal "political producer" in the United States.

Tensions Created by Inherent Differences Between Capitalism and Democracy

In addition to the tensions so far discussed that affect both capitalism and democracy as a result of specific social trends in modern industrial society, there are some tensions caused by inherent differences between capitalism and democracy as such.

First, capitalism puts its stress on performance, on what a person *does*. By contrast, in the democratic view, the fact that man is a human being already gives him certain rights and claims. From a strictly capitalist viewpoint (and also in Communist practice), the man who is incompetent, lazy, or shiftless does not deserve any help from those who work and save. From the democratic viewpoint, the man who is totally ignorant and prejudiced politically still has the right to vote and may even run for public office. Economically, democracy is willing to help the incompetent, lazy, or shiftless person because he is a human being and possibly has a family that depends on him.

Second, capitalism by its very nature emphasizes *private* goals and satisfactions; by contrast, democracy as a way of organizing the body politic focuses more on *public* goals and needs. In recent years, the opinion has frequently been voiced in the United States as in other democracies that the private sector of society has attained considerable affluence, whereas the public sector (schools, hospitals, urban renewal, public transportation) has suffered for the lack of proper attention and support. Whatever the merits of this controversy, it highlights a tension between capitalism and democracy which is not peculiar to this or that country, but grows out of a basic tension between capitalism and democracy.

Third, and lastly, capitalism, in facing the ever-present dilemma of freedom and equality, favors individual freedom at the expense of equality, whereas democracy—both in theory and practice—favors equality relatively more than freedom. Tocqueville saw this clearly in his *Democracy in America*; he noticed two contradictory trends in the United States: the increasing tendency toward equality and the rise of a new "aristocracy of manufacturers." In fact, Tocqueville even saw that the very drive for equality in a democracy creates the mass market, which is the foundation of large private fortunes: "In proportion as the mass of the nation turns to democracy, that particular class which is engaged in manufactures becomes more aristocratic." Whereas in predemocratic, precapitalist societies inequality prevents equality from coming into being, in capitalist democracy inequality evolves out of the spreading equality of opportunity. The inequality in capitalist democracy is the result of the freedom to pursue equal opportunities, rather than of privileges of birth or of legal status.

☙ SOCIALISM: PROTEST AGAINST INEQUALITY, NOT POVERTY

Like capitalism, socialism was intimately related to equality and democracy from its very beginnings. In the early phase of its rise to influence and power, the capitalist middle class had consistently attacked the principle of inequality as expressed in the predominance of the aristocracy. Similarly, the main protest of the working class, after capitalism was firmly entrenched, was against inequality, and not against poverty. After all, at the time when socialism first developed in early nineteenth-century Britain, it was economically the most advanced nation in the world, and British workers enjoyed a level of living that was—by the standards of the time—relatively high.

The social inequality in older European societies goes back to the medieval pattern of feudalism, with its sharp division of society into landlords and landless serfs, with an independent small class of city-dwellers in-between. Although capitalism mitigated some of the traditional differences of class and caste in older societies, it created new social distinctions between the class of capital-owning employers and the class of property-less wage earners. In fighting for the ideal of equality, Socialist workers thus did not invent a new ideal in opposition to the older ideals of the middle class, but merely sought to apply the ideal of equality to the new circumstances of a capitalist economy. This may perhaps help to explain why—in all countries—so much of the Socialist leadership has come from the better educated and morally more sensitive elements of the middle classes. From Robert Owen to Hugh Gaitskell, many of the British Socialist leaders have come from successful middle-class and professional families, and the same was true of India, for example, where Nehru and his closest collaborators came from nonworking-class families. In the United States, too, social reform (although rejecting the label of "socialism") has attracted nonworking-class leadership and in some cases members of leading families like Theodore Roosevelt, Franklin D. Roosevelt, Averell Harriman, and John F. Kennedy.

⚜ SOCIALISM, COMMUNISM, AND DEMOCRACY

The most important difference between socialism and communism is that the former is democratic and the latter totalitarian. When we look at the history of socialism, it can be quickly seen that successful Socialist movements have grown only in nations with strong democratic traditions.

Socialist Attitude Toward Democracy

In Europe, the strongest Socialist movements are therefore in Great Britain, Scandinavia, Holland, Belgium, and Switzerland. In Asia, India and Israel—its two foremost democratic nations—are the strongholds of socialism. In the Pacific, Australia and New Zealand repeat the British experience of powerful Socialist parties. In Latin America, Uruguay and Chile have the longest experience in democratic government, and both nations have had important Socialist movements. In Africa, where there has been little democracy, there has also been little democratic socialism.

Where democracy itself is still an issue, socialism has always fought an uphill struggle. Germany and France provide two illustrations. In the Second Reich (1870–1918), authoritarianism was the order of the day, first under Bismarck and then under the Kaiser. In the 1870s, the Socialists were outlawed as "enemies of the Reich," and many leaders had to flee abroad to escape prison. In the Weimar Republic (1919–1933), the Socialists saw constitutional government menaced by the Nazis on the Right and the Communists on the Left. The main political issue was not this or that social reform within the framework of a democratic government, but the existence of democracy itself.

In France after World War II, constitutional government was also threatened by extremists of the Right and Left. In 1958, the Socialists favored a new political regime with strong executive powers for President de Gaulle in preference to civil war and possible victory by authoritarian militarists. In every crisis of France since 1945, the French Socialists have placed devotion to republican institutions above party interest. But the price for this patriotic attitude was a heavy decline of socialism in favor of the Communist party, which has had a clear field in exploiting social and economic issues.

Socialist parties have shown their respect for democracy and civil liberty not only when in opposition but also when in office. Whatever charges have been made against Socialist governments in Britain, Sweden, Denmark, Norway, Belgium, Australia, and New Zealand, the charge of disrespect of civil liberty has not been made by their opponents. In fact, those who speak of democratic socialism as "creeping communism" would find it difficult to reconcile this nomenclature with the fact that the countries with the strongest Socialist movements are the very ones that practice civil liberty more effectively than do most other democracies.

Yet it should not be overlooked that the Socialist respect for civil liberty in these countries is at least equally matched by the opponents of socialism. If the propertied classes in these nations had shown less respect for constitutional government, the growth of socialism might have been seriously hampered. The anti-Socialist groups in these nations valued their faith in democracy more highly than their pocketbooks, and were willing to pay higher taxes for programs they considered undesirable as well as costly. As was pointed out in the preceding chapters, there is always an element of gamble in the democratic process. Each side assumes that the other will behave decently and not abuse its power. In mature democratic nations with influential Socialist parties, the Socialists have gambled on the expectation that the propertied groups would not destroy constitutional government to save their financial interests (as happened in Germany before 1933, for example). Conversely, the propertied classes gambled on the expectation that Socialist parties would not abuse their political power when in office, but would proceed moderately and pragmatically.

Fundamental Differences Between Socialism and Communism

As mentioned above, the most important difference between socialism and communism is that the former is democratic and the latter totalitarian.

Another major difference concerns the means each favors for bringing about social and economic change. Whereas Socialists seek to bring about such change piecemeal by constitutional means, Communists put the entire economy under state ownership and control by one violent change. No Socialist party has ever run on the election slogan, "Vote for us, and we will give you socialism." At each election, a Socialist party singles out specific issues which are likely to have the largest voter appeal. By contrast, Communists do not wish to change this or that element of the existing social and economic order, but the entire order itself.

Communists are not worried how the majority of the people, or even the majority of the workers, feel about total change, because from the Communist viewpoint the Communist party represents—to use a Rousseauistic concept—the "general will" of the people, by comparison with which the empirical "will of all" is less important. From the Communist viewpoint, it is necessary to impose on the people policies they would choose if they knew what is in their best interest, but which, in their "blindness" and "narrowmindedness," they reject. Under democratic socialism, the leaders can only do what their followers, or the majority of voters, want them to do. Under communism, the people must do what their leaders tell them to do. From the Communist viewpoint, there is only one political reality— class; from the socialist viewpoint, the decisive political reality is *the voter* —whatever class he belongs to. Socialists know that they depend on some, or many, voters who are not workers, since large numbers of workers vote for non-Socialist or anti-Socialist parties.

Because of these fundamental differences between socialism and communism, experience has shown that, where socialism is strong, communism is weak, and vice versa. In Europe, Britain and the Scandinavian countries clearly show the weakness of communism in the face of strong Socialist parties. By contrast, the weakness of socialism in France and Italy is reflected in the strength of communism in both countries.

Finally, the unbridgeable chasm between Socialist and Communist parties can also be seen in the all-important area of foreign policy. No Communist government or party has ever sided with the United States, and no Socialist government or party has ever lined up with the Soviet Union or Red China in aiding Communist imperialism. The most important alliance of free nations ever forged in peacetime—the North Atlantic Treaty Organization—was set up in 1949 under the leadership of the United States and Great Britain, then governed by the Labour party. Similarly, the Socialists in Holland, West Germany, Norway, and other NATO members have steadfastly adhered to NATO.

In June, 1962, the Socialist International met in Oslo. Speaking for 41 parties with 11 million members and 70 million voters throughout the world, the Socialist International stated that the "East-West rivalry has largely been imposed upon an unwilling world by the Communist leaders." A general characterization of Communist policies reads as follows: "Although the Communist countries use the strongest anti-colonial language, they have enslaved scores of millions of people. Misusing the word Socialism, their one-party dictatorships represent in fact tyranny, denying those freedoms of speech, religion, criticism, voluntary organization and contacts with the outside world which are the essence of a democratic society."[1]

✹ CHANGING VIEWS OF SOCIALISTS
TOWARD PUBLIC OWNERSHIP

Public Ownership and a Fully Planned Economy

The growing reliance of Socialist thought and policy on the free market rather than on rigid planning is important because it is one of the factors that have contributed to the decline of the Socialist aim and doctrine of public ownership of productive property. Particularly during the economic depression in the 1930s, Socialists believed that only a fully planned economy could function properly, and that full-fledged planning required public ownership. After World War II, the generally expected postwar depression failed to materialize, and, instead, most capitalist countries experienced a period of unprecedented economic prosperity.

Moreover, the practical experience of planning showed that planning and public ownership were not as closely and inevitably linked as had previously been assumed. Fascism demonstrated that planning by forcible direction could be carried out without public ownership, and the experience of planning by peaceful persuasion and inducement both internally (France, India, Italy, Mexico) and externally (as in the Common Market,

[1] *The World Today: The Socialist Perspective* (London: Socialist International, 1962), pp. 10–11.

the European Free Trade Association) showed that successful planning did not require public ownership, or only partial public ownership in a few selected sectors of the economy.

Public Ownership and Equality

Similarly, the Socialist belief in public ownership as a prerequisite for social equality has been greatly weakened by two lines of development. As the living standards of the masses of workers have risen in many countries—developed and developing—in the last twenty years, the interest in equality has declined. The difference between those who have and those who have more is psychologically less inciting than the difference between not having and having. To illustrate: the difference between a family that has one bathroom and one that has none is greater than the difference between the family that has three bathrooms and one that has only one bathroom. The second line of development that has impressed Socialists with respect to the relation of public ownership and equality is well expressed by a leading British Socialist economist and member of the Wilson Cabinet, C. A. R. Crosland. He writes that "private ownership is compatible with a high degree of equality, while state ownership, as the Russian experience has demonstrated, may be used to support a high degree of inequality."[2]

Public Ownership and Relations Between Labor and Management

Another traditional reason for public ownership—better relations between labor and management—has also lost much of its erstwhile appeal to Socialist parties. The worker in capitalist democracies is no longer the "exploited, impotent wage slave." Organized labor has gradually redressed the balance in his favor. In the United States, for example, labor unions have not lost a single major battle in basic industries such as coal, steel, or automobiles for many years. The absence of a Socialist labor party—as in the United States—may be an advantage rather than a disadvantage, because unions are then not bound to a political party, particularly when that party is in power. Also, the experience of nationalized industries and services in various countries has shown that the relations between labor and management have not significantly changed under public ownership. Socialists themselves admit this, but have so far failed to find a satisfactory answer. Workers still think in terms of "We" and "They," and management—generally the very same persons who ran the enterprises before nationalization—still try to follow what they consider sound policies of running a business, regardless of who the owner is.

[2] *The Future of Socialism* (London: Cape, 1956), p. 89.

In the 1930s, American economists led by A. A. Berle discovered that the real power in the modern corporation lay with the managers rather than with the owners, the stockholders. Socialists have more lately discovered that this phenomenon may also apply to public ownership. As a result, we get this startling admission from a top leader of the British Labour party: "Industrial power in every large, developed economy now rests with a managerial class which is responsible to no one. The form of ownership is irrelevant. State control over nationalized industries is as difficult as share-holder control over private firms."[3]

Public Ownership as a Basic Socialist Concept

Finally—and most important from a practical political viewpoint—public ownership as an overall Socialist concept has faded away because the overwhelming majority of the voters are opposed to it on any large scale.

In Britain, for example, public opinion polls have repeatedly shown that about two thirds of the voters are opposed to further nationalization. Even among Labour party voters the opponents of nationalization outnumber those who favor it. In the victorious general elections of 1964 and 1966, the Labour party changed the traditional emphasis on public ownership and more equality to the newer concept of accelerated economic growth through intensified efforts in research, scientific development, and education. By shifting its historic emphasis on equal distribution of the national product to the urgent demand for increasing the size of the national product, many Socialist parties have come closer to the non-Socialist point of view that the size of the cake is more important than the method of its distribution, and that a relatively unequal cutting up of a large cake is likely to give larger slices to the masses of the people than fairly shared slices of a small cake. In other words, the problem of increased economic output is beginning to concern Socialist parties more than the traditional concern with distribution of wealth.

New Trends in Socialist Views of Public Ownership

Official Socialist party programs have not in all countries reflected as yet the recent changes of public opinion on the issue of public ownership, but the practical policies and policy statements have done so. In some cases, the newer thinking has already been incorporated into basic party programs. Thus, in the "Basic Program" of the Social Democratic Party of the (West) German Federal Republic of 1959, we read that the fundamental

[3] Denis Healey, *The New Leader*, August 17, 1957.

values of socialism are freedom, justice, and solidarity—no mention of public ownership. The three roots of socialism are listed as Christian ethic, humanism, and classical philosophy—again no mention of public ownership. In the more specific discussion of ownership of property and its relation to power, we read that "economic power, rather than ownership, is the central problem today." In line with this new philosophy, the Basic Program advocates the strengthening of small and medium-sized enterprises in competition with big business. Public enterprise is considered necessary only when vital economic functions cannot be performed on a private competitive basis. The key idea of the Basic Program lies perhaps in this conclusion: "Every concentration of economic power, even in the hands of the state, harbors dangers." This is the final Socialist programmatic recognition that the political issue of diffusion of power and of personal freedom is more important than the economic or legal issue of ownership of the means of production.

This apparently new trend in Socialist thinking is in fact a return to the original impulse of socialism, which aimed at greater freedom—political, economic, and cultural—for the working class. When public ownership was first accepted by Socialist parties, it was thought of primarily as a means to accomplish ends. But gradually, the means became for many Socialists an end in itself, and finally the end froze into an unchallengeable dogma. The recent abandonment of the concept of public ownership by democratic Socialist parties is an admission that socialism, if it is to remain democratic, must find means other than public ownership to bring about the better society they hope for.

In developing nations, Socialist parties have not gone as far in their abandonment of the concept of public ownership as have Socialist parties in the economically more advanced nations. Being more in a hurry, people in developing nations look to state action and considerable planning as necessary prerequisites of rapid economic growth, but such measures do not necessarily imply preponderant public ownership. In India, for example, with its strong commitment to democracy and socialism, there has been no head-on rush into state ownership of the economy. Shortly before his death, India's Prime Minister Nehru stated that the mixed Indian economy "in which private enterprise is greater than state enterprise" could be regarded as permanent rather than as a mere transitional stage. He also went on to define socialism as "equal opportunity for all and the gradual elimination of differences between rich and poor, to be achieved by peaceful means."[4] Other developing nations that enjoy constitutional government, such as the Philippines or Colombia, have also refrained from large-scale measures of nationalization. By contrast we find that, where

[4] *New York Times*, October 17, 1963.

there is strong authoritarian government (as in Burma or Egypt), nationalization of property has taken place on a large scale. In every state—regardless of its degree of economic or political development—the determining issue is still who owns the government rather than who owns property.

⚕ SOCIALISM IN THE UNITED STATES

The first Socialist party in the United States, the Socialist Labor party, appeared in Chicago in 1877. At first, it was largely made up of Germans who fled to the United States because of the antisocialist laws of Bismarck in the 1870s. Its best known leader was Daniel de Leon, who, however, was a better theoretician and polemicist than a political organizer and administrator. The party polled 21,000 votes in the presidential election of 1892, and 36,000 votes in 1896. It was never an important influence in the United States except in a few localities, and among a few groups of immigrants.

Its successor was the Socialist party, founded in 1901. Its first major leader was Eugene Debs, later followed by Norman Thomas. In 1904, it polled 400,000 votes, and about the same number in 1908. In the presidential election of 1912, it received 897,000 votes. This was 6 percent of the total vote, the highest percentage ever polled by it in any election. It maintained its absolute voting strength of about 900,000 votes in the elections of 1920 and 1932, obtaining much fewer votes in the intervening years of prosperity.

The Great Depression of the 1930s seemed to hopeful American Socialists the ideal opportunity for the growth of the Socialist vote and party organization. Yet events proved otherwise. In 1932, Franklin D. Roosevelt was elected President, and after four years of vigorous New Deal policies, the Socialist party obtained only 187,000 votes. This decline continued under the subsequent Roosevelt and Truman administrations. In 1952, after 20 years of New and Fair Deal programs, the Socialist party obtained only 18,000 votes—a big drop from 903,000 votes in 1932. The New Deal and Fair Deal policies were frequently described as "creeping socialism." Yet the facts show that the welfare state policies under Roosevelt and Truman eliminated socialism from American politics.

The Decline of the Socialist Party in the United States

In 1956, after four more years of expanded welfare state policies under President Eisenhower, the Socialist party polled only a little over 2,000 votes—probably made up, largely, of friends and relatives of the presidential and vice-presidential candidates. This abysmally low figure was tantamount to the death certificate of the Socialist party, and consequently it decided not to run in the presidential elections of 1960 and 1964. It is unlikely that it will ever be a political force in the United States, even to the limited extent of the years 1912–1932.

Since 1960, the Socialist party of the United States has allowed its members to work for individual candidates of other parties whom they find least objectionable. However, Socialist party members who follow this tactic are to avow their Socialist allegiance openly because the party is opposed to the Communist technique of "boring from within." Such cooperation is encouraged particularly with respect to candidates of other parties who favor the welfare state. The intimate connection between the growth of social security in the United States and the decline of the Socialist party is acknowledged by Norman Thomas, its leader of many years, as follows: "The establishment of a kind of welfare state has changed the situation for socialism, its problems and the tactics it must use to solve them."[5]

What is often overlooked in the history of the Socialist party of the United States is that even in its heyday its greatest popularity was not, as in Europe, in industrial areas, but in the agricultural states of the Northwest. In the election of 1912, the most successful from the Socialist viewpoint, there were only seven states in which more than 10 percent of the voters voted Socialist: Arizona, California, Idaho, Oklahoma, Montana, Nevada, and Washington. In these agricultural states, the Socialist vote represented, not the outcry of the "oppressed industrial proletariat" against capitalism, but the protest of farmers against low prices for farm products, high interest rates, and corruption in government. Interestingly enough, the Socialist vote in these agricultural states was strongest in the areas in which the agrarian Populists, a completely non-Socialist minor party of the last quarter of the nineteenth century, had been strong. The western farmer who voted for the Populists in the late nineteenth century or for the Socialists in the early twentieth century, was not a Socialist but a radical—although even his radicalism was relatively mild, for he opposed, not the Constitution or the American economic system, but the monopoly of the major parties, unscrupulous bankers, and corrupt politicians.

Reasons for the Failure of Socialism in the United States

In view of this long failure of socialism in the United States, the question is often asked what the reasons are behind this failure. According to earlier Socialist writers, the United States, as the leading capitalist country in the world, was bound to develop the "internal contradictions" out of which Socialist mass movements would develop. Yet nothing of the sort has

[5] Norman Thomas, *Socialism Re-examined* (New York: Norton, 1963), p. 130.

happened. Is it because socialism is European? There are strong Socialist movements in Australia, New Zealand, Chile, Uruguay, Israel, and other countries outside of Europe. Why the failure in the United States?

The basic reason probably lies in the fact that American capitalism—more than any other economic system in the world—has given to the people *now* what socialism promises them for the future. Specifically, socialism bases its appeal on two basic promises: (1) social equality, and (2) the abolition of poverty. Although no one will argue that American capitalism has lived up to these two principles 100 percent, it must have done so to a large extent, for Socialist propaganda has had very little effect so far.

As to the Socialist principle of equality, the Constitution of the United States and the reality of American social and economic life provide opportunity for those who look for it. Because in public opinion polls, over 80 percent of the American people describe themselves as middle class, it is clear that, psychologically at least, there is *little class consciousness* in the United States. Social mobility is very great, mainly because the American tradition demands it and because higher education is available to more persons than anywhere else in the world. There are, for example, 35 times more college students in the United States than in Britain, although the American population is only about 3½ times larger than the British.

As we saw earlier, the Socialist movement originated and grew in Europe, not primarily to get higher wages and better living conditions for

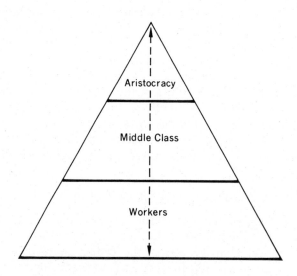

FIGURE 4–1. The European Social Pyramid.

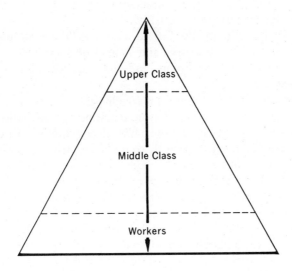

FIGURE 4–2. The American Social Pyramid.

workers, but to attain more *human dignity and equality* for them. The driving motivation behind the Socialist working-class movement in Europe was *human and political, not economic:* socialism was, and still is, a movement of protest against the *inequality of social classes* that Europe has inherited from its feudal past. The traditional social pyramid in Europe has been as shown in Figure 4–1.

By contrast, the American social pyramid has traditionally been as shown in Figure 4–2.

As can be seen from this figure, practically the whole American pyramid is middle class; moreover, the lines of demarcation between the middle and the other two classes are very fluid and the degree of upward and downward mobility is therefore very high. The frontier of open land and (later) of job opportunity has made it possible for workers on the land and in the cities to move upward into the middle class, and because there is no hereditary artistocracy, the composition of the upper class is also constantly changing. The European social pyramid shows the reverse: the barriers and classes are much more rigid than in the United States and the upward and downward mobility much weaker.

The key to the absence of socialism in the United States is thus to be found in the historical fact that the *United States,* unlike European and other countries (as in South America and Asia, for example) *is a nation without a feudal past.* It is therefore unnecessary today to fight the main residue of the feudal past: the inequality of classes.

Alexis de Tocqueville was the first to note that "the great advantage of the American is that he has arrived at a state of democracy without having to endure a democratic revolution; and that he is *born equal without having to become so.*"

As a result, whereas the demand for equality is a partisan one in Europe (or in other areas with a feudal past), requiring special political parties and movements to propagate it, the ideal of equality is inherent in the American creed. A French or British conservative may reject the ideal of equality as contrary to French or British traditions in the light of many centuries of inequality in the history of France or Britain.

The tables are turned in the United States: Whoever attacks equality can be condemned for harboring "un-American" sentiments, because the history and ideals of the United States are anchored in the principle of equality. American egalitarians therefore defend their position by invoking *national*, living symbols, such as the Declaration of Independence and the Constitution, whereas in Europe or Asia the egalitarian has to invoke *universal*, abstract ideals of socialism, liberalism, democracy, religion, and other ideological sources that are accepted by only part of his national community.

The Negroes' View Toward Socialism and Communism

There is one identifiable group left—the Negroes, constituting about 10 percent of the population—for which social equality is still a major problem, but even that particular group has never felt that socialism or communism is the solution. The Civil Rights Act of 1964, and the Voting Rights Act of 1965, combined with massive governmental programs for better education and job opportunities for Negroes, will greatly accelerate the process of assimilating the Negro to the general pattern of social and economic opportunity and equality.

Social Equality and the Gradual Reduction of Poverty

As to the reduction of poverty in the United States, there is no doubt that relatively fewer persons are poor in the United States than in any other country. Only the lowest fifth of families are considered to be poor for statistical purposes, because their income is below $3,000 per annum. However, this is poverty by American standards, and would be considered an acceptable level of living in most parts of the world, including some advanced Western nations. Moreover, the whole bias of the American economy is toward improving the relative lot of the lowest fifth as fast as possible. Looking at the change of family incomes in the years 1935–1962, one finds that the average family income (in constant dollars) doubled in those years. However, the lowest fifth improved its average income by 120 percent, whereas the highest fifth improved its average income by only 74 percent. The top 5 percent of income receivers improved their average income proportionately even less—by only 47 percent. Whereas in 1947, 32 percent of the American population were poor, the percentage dropped to 18 in 1964.

As the two major issues of traditional social concern—social equality and the abolition of poverty—are increasingly resolved in other societies with highly productive economies that are committed to the democratic ideal of equality, it is likely that in other countries, too, the socialism-capitalism controversy will lose its acerbity. Many will then discover that this controversy is irrelevant to basic problems of both domestic and foreign policy.

❦ THE MIXED ECONOMY

The historical encounter between socialism and capitalism in the context of democratic government has led to a growing *rapprochement* and interpenetration between the two ideologies. Capitalism has moved toward socialism with respect to the welfare state because the democratic ethos is incompatible with personal insecurity, want, and suffering where the means are available to remedy such conditions. Socialism, on the other hand, has moved in the direction of classical capitalism with respect to the issue of private ownership of productive property, because the democratic political value of diffusion of power and of personal liberty is incompatible with total ownership and management of the economy by the state.

In practical democratic politics, therefore, the difference between Socialist and non-Socialist parties has been reduced from an irreconcilable conflict of principle to a negotiable difference of quantity, particularly with respect to welfare policies. However, such differences exist not only between Socialist and non-Socialist parties: where (as in the United States, Canada, Mexico, and Colombia) Socialist parties are a minor political factor, non-Socialist parties still disagree among themselves as to how far and fast welfare policies should be followed. In such political systems, Conservative and Liberal parties used to be split in the nineteenth century over political issues, such as the suffrage, the relations of church and state, individual liberty, or problems of empire.

Today, the main area of disagreement between Conservative and Liberal parties is on social and economic policies. In both types of working democracies—that is, whether Socialist parties are a major factor or not—conflicts of social and economic interest and ideology are likely to be resolved peacefully and constitutionally in this century, just as the more politically colored conflicts of interest and ideology in the nineteenth century were generally resolved by peaceful means.

The evolving economy in non-Communist countries, whether governed by Socialist or non-Socialist parties, is neither capitalist nor Socialist, if capitalism means laissez-faire, and if socialism means public ownership. No generally agreed-upon name has so far been found for this type of economy because it has developed gradually and pragmatically rather than in pursuit of some preconceived ideology or master plan. Probably the most widely used term for economic systems operating within the framework of constitutional government is "mixed economy," indicating the mixture of predominantly private initiative and private property on the one hand and of predominantly public responsibility in social welfare on the other. In Continental Europe, the interesting term "social market economy" has frequently been used, emphasizing the nature of the economy as a market economy, but permeated with a sense of social responsibility.

PART II   CONSTITUTIONAL GOVERNMENT

CHAPTER 5

CONSTITUTIONAL GOVERNMENT

When we say that the American government is a constitutional government, what do we mean? The fact that a Constitution was written for the United States in Philadelphia in 1787 and adopted by the vote of the states in 1788 does not necessarily prove that the United States government is a constitutional government. After all, the Soviet Union adopted constitutions in 1918, 1924, and 1936. The 1936 constitution, which was adopted during the most intense period of terror and repression in the history of the USSR, was particularly noteworthy for the impressive list of civil rights which it purported to guarantee to citizens, including freedom of speech, press, and inviolability of the person. The Soviet constitutions have been only an elaborate façade behind which one-party rule and totalitarianism have been the reality of political life.

On the other hand, the fact that a country lacks a written constitution does not prove that its government is not a constitutional one. The English have one of the oldest and soundest constitutional systems in the world, but they have never tried to put their constitutional principles into a single written document. There *is* an English Constitution, but one cannot go into a library and ask for a copy of it. What serves the English as a constitution—and serves very well—is a combination of statutes, judicial decisions, customs, and conventions.

What, then, is constitutional government?

119

❧ THE NATURE OF CONSTITUTIONAL GOVERNMENT

Government is power. Constitutional government is power limited by law. It stands in contrast to government by fiat, government with unlimited power, government at the whim or uncontrolled discretion of the power holders, government which has no rules or rules subject to change without notice or regular procedure, government which does not undertake to recognize or assure any substantial body of liberties or rights for its citizens.

A constitution, it follows, is the general system of limitations—laws, customs, institutional patterns, rules—pertaining to the government of a country. A constitution is both the instrument for achieving limited government, and the product of a regime which recognizes that it is limited by law.

The distinction between a constitution and a government is fundamental. If the distinction is not observed, there is in fact no constitution, because the will of the government is unrestrained. A constitution is antecedent to a government, either in the sense that it brings the government into being or in the sense that it is superior to the government in character and in binding authority. Since a constitution imposes limits on a government, any exercise of authority by government beyond these limits is *unconstitutional*.

The reason why the Soviet Constitution of 1936 did not create a constitutional government, then, was because its fine language was utterly ineffective in creating a system of restraints on governmental action. Soviet officials did not regard it as a limitation on their powers, and Soviet citizens could not invoke its provisions for their protection. In England and the United States, on the other hand, public officials recognize that their authority is limited, and that they must keep their actions within boundaries prescribed either in a written document or by custom and usage.

As for the individual citizen in a constitutional system, he knows that he has rights which the government is obligated to observe, and the constitution provides methods for asserting and enforcing these rights against the government. But citizens are also restrained by the constitution. The rule of law governs both governors and the governed. Individuals in a constitutional system are bound by the rules, and can change them only by procedures specified in the constitution. There are Americans who wish the income tax amendment was not in the Constitution, but it is there and they are obliged to pay income taxes. There are always many Americans who oppose the President currently in the White House, but they are forced to recognize his authority, until his constitutional term expires or until he is removed by the constitutional process of impeachment (which has never happened).

One of the great merits of constitutional government, which is suggested by this latter example, is that it provides for the most dangerous incident in the life of a governmental system, the transfer of power from one individual or group to another. It foresees the inevitability that power holders will die or lose their bases of power, and so it arranges a peaceful and orderly system of succession instead of the murders or intrigues or coups d'état of a nonconstitutional system.

Constitutional government is not necessarily democratic government. There can be constitutional monarchies or constitutional aristocracies. (There could not, however, be a constitutional dictatorship, for the essence of dictatorship is the exercise of unlimited power.) But in the twentieth century constitutionalism and democracy go together and re-enforce each other. Under a constitutional system, individuals have freedom to read and to talk, to form groups, to become informed about public affairs. They will not for long accept restraints on their right to vote or limits on their areas of public concern.

This trend is evident in the history of the American constitutional system. Payment of property taxes as a prerequisite for voting was soon abolished. Suffrage, originally limited to males, was extended to women. The President, originally named by a process of indirect election, was soon chosen by popular vote. The United States Senate, originally elected by state legislatures, is now elected by the people of the states. The tendency in all constitutional systems is the same, toward constantly enlarging the basis for popular participation in government.

❧ THE MAKING OF THE AMERICAN CONSTITUTION

The Constitution of the United States was written between May 14 and September 17, 1787, by 55 men meeting in the city of Philadelphia. The parchment sheets on which it was transcribed are preserved as a patriotic shrine at the National Archives in Washington, and the document has come to be regarded with the awe and reverence usually reserved for religious objects.

The political unification necessary for adoption of the American Constitution was the product of the American Revolution. The thirteen colonies, though at first greatly diverse in status and character, had ultimately become in most cases royal provinces, each administered by a governor named by the English king. All had popularly elected legislatures, the same heritage of the English common law, and much the same judicial organization and procedure. There were, however, substantial geographical, economic, and political barriers among the colonies, and it took grave events to unite them in the loosest kind of joint endeavor.

The Articles of Confederation

What finally brought the colonies together was a common and increasingly intense dislike of British rule. The beginning of a system of intercolonial organization occurred in 1774, with the convening of the First Continental Congress in Philadelphia. This Congress was a completely irregular body representing dissatisfied elements in the colonies, but on the whole the instructions of the delegates were not revolutionary. They were willing to stay within the Empire, but they objected to the power of Parliament to tax them and legislate for them. However, the British government would not yield its power, and military preparations began on both sides. Before the Second Continental Congress met in May, 1775, the Battle of Lexington had occurred, where "the shot heard round the world" was fired. The Congress thus suddenly found itself busy with the task of managing a military operation, conducting foreign relations, and carrying on a *de facto* government.

Just exactly where the Continental Congress got its authority to function as a government was not too clear. The people of the states did not conceive that they had surrendered any of their rights of self-government to the Congress, and no state government felt bound by its decisions. Delegates to the Congress were appointed by the state legislatures and were subject to their instructions.

Clearly something more effective in the way of a central organization was required. On June 7, 1776, after Richard Henry Lee of Virginia had moved in Congress his resolution in favor of a Declaration of Independence, he offered a second one proposing a permanent confederation. The committee that was appointed quickly prepared a plan, but the Articles of Confederation were not adopted by the Congress and sent to the states for ratification until November, 1777. Approval by every state was required, and Maryland, the final state, held out until March 1, 1781, in protest against the western land claims of Virginia, Connecticut, and New York.

The Confederation thus belatedly inaugurated lasted for only eight years, and its experience proved increasingly unsatisfactory. The Articles provided for no executive, and virtually all functions were concentrated in a single legislative chamber. The Congress appointed such committees and civil officers as might be needed to carry on executive work. Courts could be provided only for the limited purposes of dealing with disputes between states, and captures and felonies on the high seas.

The authority of Congress did not rest on the people, but on the state legislatures that had ratified the Articles. Each state legislature chose and paid its delegates to Congress, and each state had one vote, just as in the United Nations today. A two-thirds vote of the state delegations was required for the adoption of important measures, and amendments to the Articles required the unanimous consent of the states.

The Confederation lacked most of the powers essential to an effective central government. Congress could not levy taxes; it could only make a requisition on each state for its share of the estimated monetary needs of the union. Congress could not regulate commerce between the states; and although it could make commerical treaties with foreign nations, the states felt little obligation to abide by them. Finally, Congress could not act directly on the citizens; it had to depend on the state governments for the execution of its measures. The Confederation could scarcely be called a government. As the Articles truthfully stated, it was a league of friendship entered into by sovereign states which remained sovereign.

In spite of its limited authority, the Confederation did achieve some successes. The Bank of North America was chartered by Congress in 1781. The Revolution was brought to a successful conclusion in 1783. Preparations for the government of the new lands to the west led to adoption of the famous Northwest Ordinance of 1787, applying to the areas between the Ohio and the Mississippi.

But in other respects the Congress was less successful at reaching solution for pressing problems. Attempts to negotiate commercial treaties with England, France, and Spain failed. As for internal trade, the rivalries of the states led to various forms of discriminatory taxation on each other's commerce. The situation of New Jersey, whose goods came in through New York on one side and Philadelphia on the other, led to Madison's well-known description of the state as a cask tapped at both ends.

The public finances were in a desperate situation. During the first two years under the Articles, Congress requisitioned $10 million from the states and received less than $1½ million. There were no funds to pay interest on the debt, which actually rose after the war was over. Redemption of the worthless Continental currency (memorialized in the famous expression, "not worth a Continental") was impossible.

With Congress incapable of correcting the economic ills of the country, pressure fell on the state legislatures. The most widespread demand was for relief from the burden of debts incurred during the Revolutionary inflation by state issuance of legal tender paper money and by various forms of moratoria on payment of debts. The paper money forces got a majority for their inflationary program in seven state legislatures.

Such events demonstrated that there were serious defects in the government, both of the states and the Confederation. The Revolutionary enthusiasm for the legislatures as the dominant branch of the government had diminished. Now responsible citizens were looking for some way of checking legislatures which, as Madison said, were drawing all power into their "impetuous vortex." The post of state governor was still too weak to restrain the assemblies. In a few states there were the beginnings of a system of judicial review of legislation. But the only effective method for controlling state irresponsibility appeared to be a strengthening of the central government.

This process took several years to achieve. In 1785 a meeting of representatives from Virginia and Maryland was held at Washington's home at Mt. Vernon for the purpose of discussing their joint navigation problems. James Madison saw the possibility of using this gathering to get a general meeting on commercial problems, which was held at Annapolis in 1786. It was this assembly which proposed that the states send delegates to Philadelphia in May, 1787, "to take into consideration the situation of the United States." Congress at first ignored this call, but in February, 1787, joined in and authorized a convention at the time and place already set, to meet for the "sole and express purpose of revising the Articles of Confederation."

The Constitutional Convention

The Convention met in Philadelphia on May 14, 1787, but a majority of the states were not represented until May 25. Some 74 delegates were appointed, but only 55 of them ever attended the sessions. Representatives from Rhode Island never did appear.

The members of the Convention were a notable group. They were comparatively young men; only 12 were over 54 years of age, and 6 were under 31. About half were college graduates. They were, almost without exception, men of substance and status in the new country—lawyers, physicians, planters, merchants. Most of them had risked their necks in prominent military or civilian posts during the Revolution. But the fact that only 8 of the 56 signers of the Declaration of Independence were in the Constitutional Convention was evidence that making a constitution enlisted different talents than making a revolution.

George Washington was the presiding officer. When he resigned his military commission in 1783, he had said that he was taking his leave of public life. But he reluctantly accepted designation as a delegate from Virginia, for he feared that if he did not attend, it would be taken as an indication that he had despaired of establishing a workable democratic government. He participated seldom in debates, but his influence and endorsement were essential to the adoption of the Constitution.

Benjamin Franklin, old and ill, was there, and his talents as a peace-maker helped the Convention past several danger points. The men who did the most talking and who were generally ranked as exercising the greatest influence on the decisions of the Convention were Gouverneur Morris and James Wilson of Pennsylvania, James Madison of Virginia, and Roger Sherman of Connecticut.

Under the Convention's rules, the deliberations were to be completely secret, and this undoubtedly encouraged freedom of discussion. The official journal was confined to the formal motions made and the votes taken. But Madison throughout the proceedings sat with his back to Washington, facing the other members and writing down everything that went on in his own version of shorthand. His notes were finally made public thirty years later, and they provide the principal information on the proceedings of the Convention.

✹ THE GREAT DEBATE

Almost immediately on assembling, the Convention proceeded to disregard the instructions it had received from Congress to confine its efforts to revising the Articles. It was apparent to the leaders that the Confederation, with its powerless Congress, could not provide what they felt the country needed—security for business development, protection against competitive state taxation, assurance of a sound currency, encouragement of foreign trade, and protection against foreign countries and Indians on the frontier.

The Virginia Plan

Consequently the Virginia delegation opened the proceedings by present-ing a series of resolutions providing for a new national government. The Virginia Plan called for a bicameral congress with representation based on population in both houses. The Congress was empowered "to legislate in all cases in which the separate states are incompetent, or in which the harmony of the United States may be interrupted by the exercise of indi-vidual legislation." Congress could also veto state laws that in its opinion violated the Constitution. A national executive was to be chosen by Congress, and there would also be national courts. The executive and the judiciary were to constitute a "council of revision" which could veto acts of Congress, but the vetoes could be overruled by a subsequent vote of both houses.

The New Jersey Plan and the Large State–Small State Controversy

The Virginia Plan, a radical departure from the Articles, was accepted unanimously as the basis for the initial discussions, but the prospect of a strong national government soon brought out the differing interests of the large and small states. Virginia, Pennsylvania, and Massachusetts headed the large state group, while New Jersey, Delaware, and Maryland spoke for the smaller states. The large states expected to dominate the new government, for under the Virginia Plan both houses were to represent population. The small states, seeing that they would be swamped by this arrangement, demanded equal representation in the second house.

When the small states were defeated on this point, they withdrew from the consensus that a strong government was needed, and proposed merely to revise the Articles. The recommendations they presented, commonly called the New Jersey Plan, would have retained a unicameral Congress in which the states would have equal representation. But the New Jersey Plan did give Congress the power to tax and to regulate interstate commerce, and made federal laws and treaties "the supreme law of the respective States." It also provided for a federal executive and judiciary.

On June 19 the Convention rejected the New Jersey Plan by a vote of 7 to 3. Madison stated the view of the majority when he argued that this proposal would correct none of the evils which had brought the delegates together. So the Convention agreed on the creation of a national government which would get its authority directly from the people and have the power to collect its own taxes, make laws, and enforce them in its own courts. Over each citizen there would be two governments, national and state, to both of which their citizens would owe obedience.

With the defeat of the New Jersey Plan, the small states took an adamant position on the issue of representation in Congress, insisting that in one house each state must have an equal voice. Differences on this issue were so fundamental that they almost broke up the Convention. Finally, on July 16 equal representation in the Senate was accepted by a vote of 5 to 4, with Massachusetts divided and New York not voting. Madison records that the next morning the large states held an indignation meeting to discuss what could be done, but that "the time was wasted in vague conversation." Thus the Convention surmounted its gravest crisis.

The North–South Controversy

A second major difference among the states was the contrast in their economic systems. The northern states were primarily engaged in commerce and shipping, and were on the threshold of an industrial economy.

The southern states were developing a large-scale plantation system of agriculture, manned with slave labor. They produced surpluses of agricultural commodities which they needed to exchange outside the South for manufactured products. Each region was concerned lest its economic interests suffer under a new national system.

The southern states were particularly determined to protect the slave system, and they secured the insertion of two provisions in the Constitution for that purpose. One was the guarantee that no ban should be imposed on the importation of slaves until 1808. A second was that three fifths of the slaves in each state should be counted in determining a state's quota of seats in the House of Representatives, and also its quota in any direct tax that might be levied by the central government.

Another provision dictated by the economic interests of the South was the absolute prohibition imposed on export taxes, so that Congress would not be able to tax the outflow of agricultural products from the South. The requirement that treaties be ratified by a two-thirds majority in the Senate was inserted on the demand of the southern states so that they would be in a position to veto commercial arrangements with other nations that might be detrimental to their interests.

Democratic Principles and the Executive Office

There were sharp differences among the delegates in their degree of enthusiasm about popular control of the government, which were brought out clearly in the debates on the executive office and the method of filling it. The choice before the delegates was between selection by Congress or by the people. The initial decision was 8 to 2 for congressional election. George Mason said that "it would be as unnatural to refer the choice of a proper character for Chief Magistrate to the people, as it would, to refer a trial of colours to a blind man."

The delegates were concerned, however, that congressional choice would lead to legislative intrigues and make the President subservient to Congress. Gouverneur Morris led the fight for popular election of presidential electors; he thought the people would not fail to elect a man of "continental reputation." By August 24 the Morris plan had the support of five states, and it won adoption in the final maneuverings. Each state was to choose electors equaling in number the senators and representatives from the state. They would meet in their respective states and cast ballots for two persons. If any one candidate received a majority, he was elected President, and the second highest would be Vice-President. If no candidate received a majority, the House would select the President from the five highest candidates, the delegation from each state casting only one vote.

With no political parties and no system for nominating candidates for the Presidency, this elector plan was as close as the Convention could come to popular election. In fact, the expectation was that, after Washington, no candidate would be likely to get a majority of the electoral vote, and that consequently the House would usually select the President. Giving each state only one vote for this purpose was another concession to the small states.

Ratification

The drafters of the Constitution realized that it would not be easy to secure ratification of the document. The Articles of Confederation provided that revisions could be made only by a favorable vote of Congress and approval of the legislatures in all thirteen states. Rhode Island had not even sent delegates to the Convention, and there were other states whose approval of the new Constitution was doubtful. Public opinion at the time was badly divided on the need for a stronger central government. In general, the rural areas were quite suspicious, as a Massachusetts farmer put it, of "these lawyers, and men of learning, and moneyed men, that talk so finely, and gloss over matters so smoothly, to make us poor illiterate people swallow down the pill."

The Convention faced this problem boldly. Ignoring the unanimity requirement in the Articles, the drafters provided that the Constitution should become effective on ratification by nine states. Moreover, they excluded both Congress and the state legislatures from the ratification process. The document would go directly to state conventions elected for the specific purpose of considering ratification. This use of state conventions instead of the legislatures could be justified as providing a more direct popular foundation for the new government, but it was also a practical means of bypassing hostile state legislators unlikely to vote to give up their powers. Moreover, the forces favorable to the Constitution sought to get the conventions elected as promptly as possible, before the opposition had a chance to organize.

The ratification campaign left as a legacy the most famous commentary on American government, *The Federalist*. These essays were newspaper articles written to influence the vote in the doubtful state of New York by Madison, Hamilton, and John Jay. Their discussions of the proposed Constitution were of considerable influence, and have been subsequently accepted as authoritative guides to constitutional interpretation.

As it turned out, the Constitution was ratified by wide majorities in seven of the state conventions, but in the important states of Massachusetts, Virginia, and New York the voting was close. North Carolina and Rhode Island were the last two states to ratify. If a unanimous vote had been required to make the Constitution effective, it is probable that they would have stayed out, thus frustrating the entire effort. The absence of a bill of rights was the feature most widely criticized in the ratifying conventions, and in several doubtful states, particularly New York and Massachusetts, the promise that a bill of rights would be added was instrumental in securing the votes needed for ratification.

⚘ KEY PRINCIPLES OF THE CONSTITUTION

The ideas embodied in the Constitution were not particularly new nor were they creative inventions of the founders. They were drawn from the entire European political heritage of the new nation. The genius of the Convention was in its practicality and willingness to compromise dogmatic principles in order to achieve a workable basis for union. The key principles of the document may be said to be four in number: (1) popular sovereignty; (2) federalism; (3) separation of powers; and (4) limited government.

Popular Sovereignty

The Declaration of Independence is generally accepted as the cornerstone of American ideas about government, and the most representative and influential statement of American political theory. The basic conceptions had come from the English philosopher, John Locke, but the doctrines were sharpened by the experience of resistance to British rule. These principles were so much a part of American thinking that the Declaration referred to them as "self-evident." In addition to the Declaration, the constitutions of the new American states that were adopted between 1776 and 1780 abound in statements of current political assumptions.

The basic premise of the political thought of the time was that men are by nature endowed with certain inalienable rights. This conception assumed that a state of nature existed before the establishment of civil government. In this primeval condition all men were free, in the sense that they were subject to no one, and equal in the right to rule themselves. As men they possessed a body of natural rights, including the right to "life, liberty, and the pursuit of happiness." These rights not only antedate the existence of government; they are superior to it in authority.

The exercise of coercive power by governments over men born free and equal can be justified, then, only by the consent of the governed. The process as expressed by the Massachusetts Bill of Rights was that "the body politic is formed by a voluntary association of individuals; it is a social compact by which the whole people covenants with each citizen, and each citizen with the whole people, that all shall be governed by certain laws for the common good."

The exact nature of this contract on which government was based, or the circumstances under which it was agreed upon, were not much discussed. But the concept was given a sense of reality by the numerous written compacts that had figured in American development, especially the Mayflower Compact of 1620 and the colonial charters. The slogan, "no taxation without representation," was a particular application of the consent theory, with roots deep in English constitutional history.

Government is created by contract to serve the welfare of the people. Quoting again from the Massachusetts document, the aim of government is "to secure the existence of the body politic, to protect it, and to furnish the individuals who compose it with the power of enjoying in safety and tranquillity their natural rights, and the blessings of life." A government which fails to serve the ends for which it was set up has breached the contract which brought it into existence and forfeited the loyalty of its citizens. Thus the right of revolution, obviously fundamental to legitimizing the American nation, was established. The Declaration of Independence stated the case as follows:

> Whenever any form of government becomes destructive of these ends, it is the right of the people to alter or to abolish it, and to institute new government, laying its foundation on such principles and organizing its powers in such forms, as to them shall seem most likely to effect their safety and happiness.

When the framers faced the problem of setting up a governmental system which would give effect to these basic principles, they turned out to be somewhat divided as to how far they were prepared to turn over the government to popular control. Direct election was provided for the House of Representatives, but the Senate was to be chosen by the state legislatures. Judges were not to be elected, and only a few of the delegates favored direct popular election of the President.

The Constitution clearly bases the government on the representative, or republican, principle, but the only time the term "republican" appears in the Constitution is in Article IV, which provides that the United States shall guarantee "a republican form of government" to every state in the Union. Some have argued that since the United States was created as a republic, it is a serious mistake to think about it as a "democracy." This position is usually taken by conservatives who treasure the aristocratic manifestations in the initial constitutional provisions, and who disapprove of modern trends toward egalitarianism, direct democracy, and mass society in general. Unquestionably an evolution has gone on which may be described as a change from a republic to representative democracy, but this development has taken place within the framework of constitutional principles. The transformation of presidential choice, for example, from indirect to direct election occurred without any change whatever in the language of the Constitution.

Federalism

The most novel feature of the Constitution was the federal structure of the government it created. American federalism is a form of political organization in which authority is divided between two levels of government, each possessing its powers as a matter of right, and each acting on the same citizen body. Midway between a confederation, or league of states, and a completely centralized, unitary government, the American federal pattern was a unique invention combining the principles of unity and diversity.

The powers of the new central government were taken from the existing state governments and "delegated" to the United States.[1] The most significant listing of powers delegated to Congress is found in Article I, Section 8; they range all the way from the punishment of counterfeiting to the declaration of war. These authorizations were typically stated rather broadly—for example, the power to regulate commerce or to levy taxes. Backing up these broad grants of specific powers, moreover, was the general authorization to Congress in the last clause of Article I, Section 8, "to make all laws which shall be necessary and proper for carrying into execution the foregoing powers. . . ."

In the Constitution as originally drafted, no effort was made to state any general formula reserving to the states the powers not delegated to Congress. That these undelegated powers remained with the states was regarded as so obvious that it did not need to be spelled out. However, specific reassurances were demanded during the ratification debates, which were met by the Tenth Amendment: "The powers not delegated to the United States by the Constitution, nor prohibited by it to the States, are reserved to the States respectively, or to the people."

The Constitution thus set up ground rules for the federal system by an allocation of authority between two levels of government. But this was not enough. Conflicts between the states and the nation over the division of functions were bound to occur. To make the federal system work, there needed to be rules for deciding such contests, and an umpire to apply those rules. The principal rule supplied by the Constitution is the "supremacy clause" of Article VI: "This Constitution, and the laws of the United

---

[1] Except for the power to conduct foreign relations. The Supreme Court held in *United States* v. *Curtiss-Wright Export Corp.* (1936) that the individual states had never possessed any competence in foreign relations, and that at the time of the Revolution this power passed directly from Britain to the Continental Congress and then to the Confederation.

States which shall be made in pursuance thereof, and all treaties made, or which shall be made, under the authority of the United States, shall be the supreme law of the land; and the judges in every state shall be bound thereby, any thing in the Constitution or laws of any State to the contrary notwithstanding."

This meant that no state was to have any power to retard, impede, or burden the operations of any constitutional powers exercised by Congress. When Congress entered a field in which it was authorized by the Constitution to act, its legislation would void all incompatible state regulations. Enforcement of the supremacy clause was entrusted in the first instance to "the judges in every state," but in the Judiciary Act of 1789 the First Congress provided for review of state court decisions by the Supreme Court, which has ever since functioned as the umpire of the federal system.

Separation of Powers

The Constitution set up American governmental institutions on the

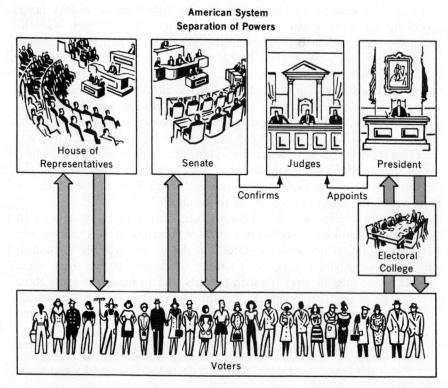

FIGURES 5–1 and 5–2. Comparison of Presidential and Parliamentary Systems.

separation of powers principle, with legislative, executive, and judicial functions entrusted to three separate branches of government (see Figure 5–1). The executive and the legislative are independent of each other in that each is elected by separate electoral processes for assured terms of office. The President cannot dissolve Congress or shorten its term or remove any of its members. The Congress, even though it may have a majority which does not support the President, cannot remove him from office except by the difficult process of impeachment, which has never been accomplished. The federal judiciary, though appointed by the President and confirmed by the Senate, is independent in the sense that the judges have tenure for life, and judicial authority to enforce constitutional requirements on both the President and Congress is universally acknowledged.

By way of contrast, the English Constitution concentrates authority in the legislature (see Figure 5–2). The English executive is a Cabinet or Council of ministers, headed by the Prime Minister, which is in effect a committee of the majority party in the House of Commons. The Cabinet remains in power only so long as it retains the confidence of the House. The English judiciary has great prestige and security, but it cannot

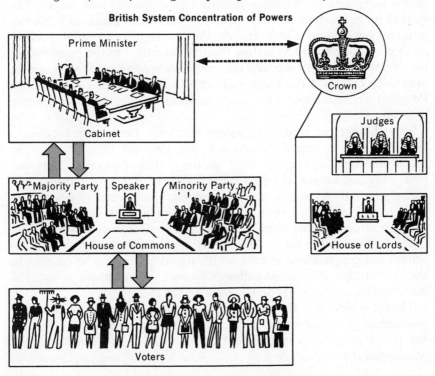

FIGURES 5–1 and 5–2 (*Continued*)

challenge the legitimacy of parliamentary action. So the English system is one of legislative supremacy.

Although the phrase "separation of powers" has a measure of accuracy in describing American constitutional arrangements, it is in many respects a most misleading description. It is more accurate to say that the American Constitution, through a system of "checks and balances," provides for a government of separated institutions sharing powers. The great task of American government is to get these separate institutions to work together with some measure of effectiveness.

The Constitution vests "the executive power" in the President, but many of his most important executive functions involve congressional participation. The Senate must confirm all important appointments. The organization of and allocation of powers to executive departments depend on congressional legislation. The President has great independent power in the field of military and foreign affairs, but he must secure the approval of two thirds of the Senate for the ratification of treaties, and all presidential programs, both foreign and domestic, depend upon congressional appropriations of the necessary funds.

Congress, for its part, is granted "all legislative powers," but the President is authorized to "recommend to their consideration such measures as he shall judge necessary and expedient." In fact, the initiation of legislative programs has become almost entirely the President's responsibility. After passage by Congress, all legislation must be submitted to the President for his signature before it becomes effective, and a presidential veto can be overridden only by a two-thirds majority of each house of Congress. The President has thus become the major architect of congressional legislative programs.

Federal judges are completely independent once they are on the bench, and their salaries cannot be reduced, but they get their positions by presidential appointment, and must run the gantlet of senatorial confirmation. They are subject to impeachment, and, in fact, impeachment proceedings have been brought against nine federal judges, four of whom were convicted. Congress can change the number of justices on the Supreme Court, and can exercise some measure of control over its power to hear cases. In their turn, the federal courts can invalidate any presidential actions and congressional statutes which the judges find to be contrary to the Constitution. No specific authority for such judicial review is stated in the Constitution, but it has been exercised since 1803.

Thus it is clear that there is no rigid separation of powers in American government. The President is chief executive, chief legislator, and through the power of judicial appointment, a major force in determining the constitutional positions taken by the judicial branch. Congress, through its powers of appropriation, investigation, and confirmation, goes far beyond a mere legislative role to intervene in the administrative side of government. The courts through their authority to interpret the Constitution and federal statutes can exercise a major role in the formulation of policy. This may look like a blueprint for confusion, and in fact the separation of powers has been responsible for much deadlock, frustration, lack of direction, and working at cross-purposes in American government. Successful operation of these complicated checks and balances requires both goodwill and good luck. But occasional confusion is better than disaster, which would certainly have been the result if the goal of separation of powers had been sought by attempting to divide the executive, legislature, and judiciary into separate water-tight compartments.

Limited Government

Basic to the entire idea of constitutionalism is the concept of limited government. Under a constitution, governmental power is both authorized and limited by undertakings arrived at in advance, consented to by those affected, and given continuing validity by appropriate enforcement processes. The rule of law and of representative institutions with defined authority stands under the American Constitution as a guarantee of individual liberty against the exercise of arbitrary power.

In part the idea of limited government is implemented by constitutional provisions that specifically deny certain powers to the government. Thus the Constitution prohibits the suspension of the writ of habeas corpus or the passing of laws impairing the obligation of contracts. More important are the prohibitions which were added to the Constitution by the Bill of Rights, particularly the First Amendment, which guarantees the freedoms of speech, press, assembly, and religion against congressional restraint. The Fourteenth Amendment, added to the Constitution after the Civil War, forbids the states to deprive any person of life, liberty, or property without due process of law, or to deny the equal protection of the laws.

In part, also, the goal of limiting government power is achieved through the system of checks and balances just discussed. The executive and the legislative are the major power centers; Hamilton symbolized their roles as those of the sword and the purse. It is largely to offset and restrain their power that the Supreme Court has been permitted to develop its unusual role of judicial review. The fact that judicial determinations can occasionally override executive and legislative action has led some commentators to refer, rather immoderately, to the American system as one of judicial supremacy. Admittedly the courts do play a significant role in making a reality out of the paper limitations of a written constitution. But even courts would be helpless without the support of a tradition which makes freedom a value of the highest order, and unless there are the resources, the opportunities, and the will to protect the principles of an open society from attack or frustration. As Judge Learned Hand has said, "in a society which evades its responsibility by thrusting upon the courts the nurture of [the spirit of moderation], that spirit in the end will perish."[2]

There may be some risk that, in stressing the limitations on governmental power, one may forget that the purpose of those limits is not to produce a weak government. A government that is unable to deal effectively with the cataclysmic challenges of the modern world is as dangerous for its citizens as one that bears too heavily on them. The American Constitution, it has been well said, is both an instrument of power and a symbol of restraint. The lesson of the Articles of Confederation—that governmental weakness and incompetence will not safeguard liberty or foster the good life—had been well learned by 1787. The founders at Philadelphia sought to establish a government strong enough for protection against foreign enemies, preservation of the peace internally, and fostering of commercial development and the general welfare. At the same time, they wanted a national government limited so as not to obliterate the states or threaten individual rights of liberty and property. This balance they well achieved in the American Constitution.

[2] Irving Dilliard, ed., *The Spirit of Liberty: Papers and Addresses of Learned Hand* (New York: Knopf, 1959), p. 125.

CHAPTER 6

THE VITALITY
AND ADAPTABILITY
OF THE CONSTITUTION

The American Constitution is now by far the oldest and pre-eminently the most successful national written constitution in the modern history of man. In the period since 1789 scores of constitutions have been drawn up for states or nations that have subsequently been outgrown or abandoned or destroyed by peaceful or violent change. France, for example, has had fourteen constitutions since 1789. In many countries constitutions have been mere paper documents, exerting no substantial direction or control over the public affairs of the state.

Why has the American Constitution proved so effective and so enduring? How has a nation of 200 million people, of continental proportions and worldwide responsibilities, with a government that spends well over $100 billion annually, been accommodated within the confines of a document drafted more than 175 years earlier for a handful of people in thirteen isolated states along the Atlantic seaboard? Before we attempt to answer this question, it might be well to look at the experience of the only other major power that rivals the United States in the longevity of its political institutions and the persistence of its constitutional system.

⅍ THE ENGLISH UNWRITTEN CONSTITUTION

It has been easier for the English to achieve vitality and adaptability in their Constitution because they have never taken the risk of sitting down and trying to put their principles of government into a single document. For England, its constitutional convention has been one thousand years of history. Whenever Parliament enacts an important statute granting authority, establishing an institution, or limiting the powers of an office, it is creating part of the Constitution. Magna Carta (1215), the Petition of Right (1628), and the Bill of Rights (1689) are constitutional landmarks in bringing the power of the Crown under parliamentary control. The Act of Settlement (1701) regulated succession to the throne and established the irremovability of judges. The Parliament Acts of 1911 and 1949 reduced the power of the House of Lords and limited the duration of Parliaments to five years. The Representation of the People Act (1949) was the latest of a series of statutes dealing with voting and elections.

The decisions of the superior courts have supplied another important section of the English Constitution. Principles of the common law, deduced from the decisions in countless individual cases, control many relations between the individual and the state. Whenever Parliament speaks on a subject, it supersedes any conflicting judicial rules, but even then there is considerable room for judicial interpretation.

Custom and convention have great weight in supplying principles for the English Constitution. Custom controls much of the procedure in Parliament, such as the status of the impartial Speaker of the House of Commons, questions by members to ministers, the protection of the rights of the legislative minority, and the allocation of time for parliamentary business. Conventions establish many of the basic operating conditions of the parliamentary system—for example, that a government outvoted in the House of Commons may dissolve the House and appeal to the electorate; that if the electorate returns a majority against the Government, it must resign; that the Prime Minister, on his resignation, advises the Crown who should be his successor; that the Cabinet is collectively responsible for general policy; and that there must be at least one session of Parliament each year.

The Case for an Unwritten Constitution

Why have the English never gathered these scattered statutes, judicial principles, customs, and conventions into a single constitutional document?

The answer is that they have never found it imperative or even desirable to do so. Unlike the United States, England never had to go through the experience of overthrowing a foreign ruler and setting up a new system of self-government. For the past four hundred years they have had a Parliament with both the power and the ability to meet the nation's various crises with appropriate legislation.

Instead of one concise written constitutional document, the English now have hundreds of statutes and declarations in Parliament of basic constitutional character, and thousands of decisions in cases before the courts bearing on fundamental liberties and powers. These are all written. Even the various usages and conventions are recorded in documents of the Cabinet and the Crown or in constitutional treatises. So in a sense it is not really true to say that the English Constitution is unwritten.

The English would not want to try to condense all these constitutional principles into a single document. Writing a constitution is not easy, as the founders of the American Constitution found out in Philadelphia. It is much more feasible to take up one constitutional issue at a time, rather than throw open to controversy the entire governmental framework. Moreover, as soon as a constitution is written down, it begins to get out of date and to require revision. So written constitutions must provide for the possibility of amendment. But amendment is typically a more difficult process than the enactment of ordinary legislation, and often desirable amendments are delayed or defeated by the complications. The English can respond to any need for constitutional change by ordinary legislative procedures.

Protection Under an Unwritten Constitution

But how much protection is there in a constitution which is subject to change by any passing parliamentary majority? Most Americans would feel uneasy if our Constitution could be changed anytime a majority in Congress felt like doing so. In England, however, the freedom to make constitutional changes has not been used rashly or irresponsibly.

Constitutional reforms in England have generally occurred only after thorough discussion and the securing of a mandate from the electorate. For example, the reform of the House of Lords in 1911, which largely stripped that body of its powers, was preceded by two general elections in 1910 in which the status of the Lords was the paramount issue. On such major issues as extension of the franchise, all changes since 1918 have been preceded by an all-party conference under the chairmanship of the non-partisan Speaker of the House of Commons. It has also been the custom for important legislative proposals to be investigated by royal commissions of inquiry, which include distinguished private citizens and experts as well as members of Parliament. Thus the unwritten English Constitution has resulted in no special problems of instability or uncertainty

At the same time, the English Constitution has exercised a definite restraining influence on governmental power. In theory Parliament is omnipotent; it was once said that "Parliament can do everything but make a woman a man, and a man a woman." But in fact Parliament is limited. The limits are not the American limits of a written Constitution enforced by the Supreme Court. They are the limits of usages, of conventions, of understandings, of attitudes of mind. Moreover, Parliament is not a monolith; it is an amalgam of Crown, Cabinet, Commons, and Lords. The Crown will not let the Cabinet abuse its powers of resignation and dissolution. The Cabinet is limited to policies that it can get the Commons to accept. The House of Lords, even with its reduced powers, can still force the Cabinet and the Commons to take a second look at a proposed constitutional change.

A final explanation of the English unwritten constitution is that Englishmen tend to have greater trust in government than Americans do. The United States was born in rebellion against an unpopular government, and even though that was long ago, an element of suspicion of *all* government has always been part of the American outlook. In this respect, American political feeling resembles more that of the French than of the British.

The aristocratic origins of English government are perhaps another factor. Among gentlemen, written pledges are unnecessary and almost cast aspersion on the parties to an agreement. Under Cromwell, when the gentlemen were temporarily out of power, a written constitution was made. After Cromwell, there has never been a revolutionary break with the past, and therefore there has been no need for a comprehensive constitutional document.

❧ THE AMERICAN UNWRITTEN CONSTITUTION

Actually, there is a sense in which the American Constitution is also unwritten. Fundamentally the written system relies on and is supported by an unwritten consensus on democratic goals and values. There has been a will to make the Constitution work which does much to account for its persistence when so many other written constitutions have failed to survive.

More specifically, the American Constitution is more than a written document because some of its language is so broad that it has meaning only when made precise by statutes or judicial decisions. There are gaps in the Constitution sufficiently wide so that political institutions can grow within them largely free of constitutional restrictions. The American Constitution has developed in part by custom and convention just like the English Constitution.

The framers of the Constitution were wise enough to avoid the evil of too great specificity in drafting key provisions of the document. Their general intent was to stick to the fundamentals and leave the implementation to subsequent legislative decisions. Thus no departmental organization for the executive branch was provided in the Constitution. The question of a system of lower federal courts was left to Congress, as was the matter of presidential succession beyond the Vice-President.

Parties and the Constitution

Other areas were not touched on at all in the Constitution. One of our most important political institutions, the political party, is completely unknown to the Constitution. There were no political parties when the Constitution was drafted. Parties were regarded as dangerous; they were called "factions," and the framers took some pains to try to prevent the rise of a party system. But the struggle over adoption of the Constitution led to a division between Federalists and Anti-Federalists. Washington had expected to govern on a nonparty basis and he placed both Alexander Hamilton and Thomas Jefferson in his Cabinet. Soon there were two distinct factions, the Federalists led by John Adams and Hamilton, and the Republicans under Jefferson and Madison.[1]

This development was inconsistent with the constitutional plan of presidential election, which called for all electors to cast two votes, and gave the candidate with the most votes the Presidency and the runner-up the Vice-Presidency. The 1796 balloting gave the Presidency and Vice-Presidency to different parties, Adams and Jefferson ranking first and second in the electoral voting.

Further complications arose in the election of 1800, when each party chose candidates for both President and Vice-President. The Republicans secured a majority in the electoral college, but because every Republican elector voted for both Jefferson and Aaron Burr, who was their vice-

[1] The present Democratic Party started out under Jefferson as the Republican Party, later was called the Democratic-Republican Party, and finally the Democratic Party.

presidential nominee, the result was a tie. Consequently, the election was thrown into the House of Representatives, which still had a Federalist majority and was tempted to elect Burr over Jefferson. Fortunately, wiser heads prevailed, but this experience demonstrated how the growth of parties had made the original constitutional provisions for election of the President unworkable. The Twelfth Amendment had to be adopted, requiring electors to ballot separately for President and Vice-President. While the consequences of a party system were thus recognized, there was still no mention of parties in the Constitution, nor is there to the present day.

Nominating procedures were of course unknown when the Constitution was adopted. Initially the new parties chose their national candidates by a caucus of their members in Congress. Since the 1830s nominating conventions have been held to name the candidates for President and Vice-President, but the arrangements and procedures of these conventions are not controlled by the Constitution.

The Permissive Constitution

With respect to elections and the suffrage, the tone of the Constitution was generally quite permissive. The times, places, and manner of holding federal elections were left to the states, though Congress was authorized to make or alter such regulations. Persons qualified to vote in state elections were also made eligible to vote for federal officials. However, this is one area where additions to the written Constitution—specifically, the Fourteenth, Fifteenth, and Nineteenth Amendments—have been found necessary to reduce the scope of state discretion in determining eligibility to vote.

The Constitution makes no provision for the Cabinet as an institution. Article II does, to be sure, authorize the President to require the opinion in writing of the heads of departments, but it says nothing about an executive or advisory council for the President. Washington established the practice of meeting with his department heads—there were only four then—and so the institution of the Cabinet arose. Who will attend, how often it will meet, and what use will be made of it, are entirely up to each holder of the presidential office to decide. The American Cabinet is not, of course, anything like the English Cabinet, which likewise functioned on a *de facto* basis for about two centuries before the law took formal cognizance of it in the 1930s.

Custom and convention, then, have controlled the development of many American constitutional arrangements. The tradition that no President should serve for more than two terms, based on the example of Washington and Jefferson, was thought to be a part of the unwritten Constitution until Franklin Roosevelt breached it by running successfully for a third and fourth term. The key to the effective functioning of Congress is the committee system, but all the aspects of committee operation, including the selection of chairmen on the basis of seniority, depend on custom. The rule that representatives in Congress must be residents of the district they represent—which is contrary to the English practice—is again not found in the Constitution.

☙ CONSTITUTIONAL AMENDMENT

The most obvious and formal method of keeping a written constitution abreast of the times is by amendment. Since 1789 the American Constitution has been amended 25 times, under procedures authorized by Article V.

Amendments to the Constitution

The First Ten Amendments were drafted by the First Congress to meet the widespread protests against the absence of a bill of rights in the original Constitution, and were ratified in 1791. A second group of amendments— the Thirteenth (1865), Fourteenth (1868), and Fifteenth (1870)—were adopted after the Civil War to abolish slavery and protect the rights of the newly freed Negroes.

The remaining amendments have had a variety of purposes. In two cases they were adopted to reverse decisions of the Supreme Court. The Eleventh Amendment (1795) overrode a 1793 decision which allowed states to be sued in federal courts by citizens of other states. The Sixteenth (1913) authorized the federal government to levy an income tax, which the Court had held unconstitutional in 1895.

Three amendments have dealt with presidential elections and terms of office. The original language on presidential election soon proved faulty, as just noted, and the Twelfth Amendment (1804) made some necessary corrections. The Twentieth (1933) changed the beginning of presidential terms from March 4 to January 20, and the Twenty-second (1951) limited the President to two terms. The Twenty-fifth Amendment (1967) provides improved arrangements for presidential disability and succession.

❧ THE TWENTY-FIVE AMENDMENTS ❧

THE BILL OF RIGHTS (1791)

1. Freedom of religion, speech, press, assembly, and petition.
2. Right to bear arms.
3. Regulation of quartering of soldiers.
4. Prohibition of unreasonable searches and seizures.
5. Protection of the rights of accused persons and of the privilege against self-incrimination; prohibition of the taking of life, liberty, and property without due process of law.
6. Right to a speedy, public, and fair trial.
7. Right to a trial by jury in civil cases.
8. Prohibition of excessive bail and cruel and unusual punishment.
9. Rights retained by people.
10. Powers reserved to the states or to the people.

LATER AMENDMENTS

11. Prohibition of lawsuits in federal courts by citizens of one state against another state (1795).
12. Separate election of President and Vice-President by electoral college (1804).
13. Prohibition of slavery (1865).
14. Privileges and immunities of citizens, due process, equal protection of the laws (1868).
15. Guarantee of the right to vote irrespective of race or color (1870).
16. Power of Congress to levy taxes on incomes (1913).
17. Direct popular election of Senators (1913).
18. Prohibition of intoxicating liquors (1919).
19. Guarantee of the right to vote irrespective of sex (1920).
20. Presidential term of office to begin January 20; congressional to begin January 3 (1933).
21. Eighteenth Amendment repealed (1933).
22. Limitation of presidential tenure to two terms (1951).
23. Guarantee of the right to vote in presidential elections to residents of the District of Columbia (1961).
24. Guarantee of the right to vote in federal elections without payment of poll or other taxes (1964).
25. Regulation of presidential succession (1967).

The Nineteenth Amendment (1920) gave women the vote, the Twenty-third (1961) allowed residents of the District of Columbia to vote in presidential elections, and the Twenty-fourth (1964) forbade the poll tax as a prerequisite for voting in federal elections. Finally, there was the ill-starred Eighteenth Amendment (1919), authorizing the federal government to prohibit intoxicating liquor, which was repealed in 1933 by the Twenty-first Amendment.

The Amending Process

Article V provides two methods for proposing amendments: (a) by a two-thirds majority of each house of Congress, or (b) by a convention summoned by Congress at the request of the legislatures of two thirds of the states. Only the first of these methods has so far been employed. There are likewise two ways by which amendments may be ratified: (a) by three fourths of the state legislatures, or (b) by ratifying conventions in three fourths of the states. (See Figure 6–1.) In only one of the amendments thus far adopted, the Twenty-first, did Congress specify the use of conventions. The reason for this exception was the fear in Congress that over-representation in the state legislatures of rural areas, which tended to be "dry," might imperil adoption of the amendment repealing prohibition, whereas conventions would more equitably represent the views of the urban areas.

Failure of Attempts to Use the Convention Method

Since a constitutional convention has never been called under Article V to propose amendments to the Constitution, there is no agreement as to how it would operate. In calling the convention into existence, Congress would

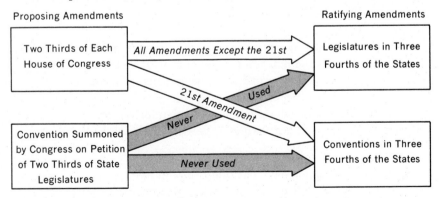

FIGURE 6–1. Four Methods of Amending the Constitution.

have to determine how delegates were to be elected, the mandate of the convention, the majority necessary to propose amendments, and such other matters as it felt were important to safeguard national interests. Presumably Congress would wish to allocate delegates to the states in proportion to population, to guard against gerrymandering if delegates were chosen by districts, and to insure that constitutional standards for voting were enforced to prevent racial or other types of discrimination.

There might be some expectation that voting in the convention should be by states, since that was the procedure in the original convention. However, Congress could certainly choose to require that the delegates vote as individuals. It might also wish to require a two-thirds majority to propose amendments. The possibility always exists that a convention, once assembled, would depart from the instructions it had received from Congress, as the Constitutional Convention did in 1787. But it seems clear that Congress was intended by the Constitution to have continuing control of the whole amendment process, since Article V gives Congress the option between modes of ratification, no matter what the method of proposal.

There have been two principal efforts to secure amendments to the Constitution by the convention route. Following World War II a national organization propagandized the state legislatures to petition for a convention to propose an amendment limiting national income taxes to 25 percent of incomes, and it succeeded in getting petitions adopted in as many as 27 states by 1952. Then in 1962 the Council of State Governments developed a package of three "states' rights" amendments for which they asked the legislatures to petition. One provided for a Court of the Union, composed of all fifty state chief justices, to meet on extraordinary occasions to review judgments of the U.S. Supreme Court. A second, aimed at overruling the Supreme Court's decision in *Baker* v. *Carr* (1962), would have freed state legislative apportionment from any federal constitutional restrictions.

The third proposed amendment, the most important for our present purposes, dealt with the amending process itself. It would have abolished the convention method of proposing amendments (after using it to get these three amendments proposed), and would have put in its place a new plan which would bring the proposing of amendments completely under the control of the state legislatures. The text of the amendment was as follows:

Whenever applications from the Legislatures of two-thirds of the total number of States shall contain identical texts of an amendment to be proposed, the President of the Senate and the Speaker of the House of

Representatives shall so certify, and the amendment as contained in the application shall be deemed to have been proposed, without further action by Congress.

The dangers in rendering the Constitution subject to amendment without any participation by Congress became obvious as soon as this extreme proposal got into the focus of public attention. If an amendment is adopted by a two-thirds vote in both House and Senate, there can be some assurance that the national implications of the amendment have been considered and that there is some degree of national consensus on the issue. There is no such assurance when the sole consideration is in the scattered forums of the 50 state legislatures, as was amply demonstrated by the consideration of these three amendments. Within one year, by the end of 1963, they had been considered by the legislatures of half the states. Though they made radical changes in the American federal system, and though there had been no general public consideration of the amendments, the proposal to change the amending procedure was adopted by 12 state legislatures; the apportionment amendment received 13 adoptions, and the Court of the Union proposal was accepted by 5 states. Once a general understanding of the purpose of the amendments was achieved, however, the movement was dead.

Time Limitation on Ratification

Only five amendments proposed by Congress have failed of ratification by the states, and two of these came from the First Congress. The most recent was the child labor amendment, proposed in 1924 to give Congress the authority to regulate or prohibit child labor which had been denied by Supreme Court decisions in 1918 and 1922. It is now customary for Congress, in proposing amendments, to impose a seven-year time limitation on ratification. This was not done in the case of the child labor amendment, and some states were still ratifying it in 1937. The Supreme Court was asked to rule that because of the lapse of time since the amendment had been proposed, it was no longer open for ratification, but in *Coleman* v. *Miller* (1939) the Court refused, holding that the amending procedure is political in nature, to be controlled by Congress and not by the courts.

Decline in Pressure for Amendments

Perhaps the most striking fact about the amending procedure is the relative infrequency with which it has been used. Excluding the First Ten Amendments, which must be considered as almost part of the original Constitution, amendments have been adopted at a rate of less than one per decade. Following the Civil War amendments, there was a period of over 40 years during which the Constitution appeared unamendable. This was an era of agrarian discontent, industrial unrest, and growing pressure for political and economic reforms. The conservatism of the Supreme Court, symbolized by its invalidation of the income tax in 1895, made constitutional amendment seem a necessary step toward achieving liberal legislative goals, but no amendments could be secured.

In 1913, however, the long liberal campaigns for the income tax and direct election of Senators succeeded, and the women's suffrage amendment followed shortly thereafter. Moreover, adoption of the Eighteenth Amendment revealed the possibility that a small but dedicated pressure group could exploit the amending machinery for its own purposes. With six amendments added to the Constitution between 1913 and 1933, the difficulties of the amending process no longer seemed so formidable. In addition, the liberalization of the Supreme Court's views by President Franklin Roosevelt's appointments substantially eliminated liberal interest in further amendments.

After the 1930s, pressure for amendments to the Constitution came almost entirely from conservative and reactionary sources. The increase in executive power and congressional expenditures, the acceptance of new welfare functions internally and new responsibilities internationally by the federal government, and the reduced role of the states were all trends which stimulated the resistance of various conservative groups. Lacking the power to block these developments through the regular political processes, they fell back on the strategy of constitutional amendment. During the 1950s the Bricker Amendment to limit the federal government's power to enter into international agreements, various proposals for revising the presidential election process so as to reduce the importance of the large industrial states, as well as the proposal to place a ceiling on federal income taxation already mentioned, were conservative measures which failed of adoption. In the 1960s the three states' rights amendments of the Council of State Governments were supported by the far right in the political spectrum.

The only amendment secured by this drive from the right was the Twenty-second, adopted in 1951. The limitation of the President to two terms was initially proposed as a Republican measure after that party had suffered four defeats at the hands of President Roosevelt, but was subsequently supported by conservatives of both parties who feared strong executive leadership. Ironically, the first President to feel the effect of the amendment was a Republican, President Eisenhower.

CONSTITUTIONAL INTERPRETATION

Almost as important as the amending process in adapting the Constitution to changing conditions is the device of constitutional interpretation. In fact, it has been the possibility of gradual modification of constitutional meanings over the years to meet new times and new necessities which has permitted resort to formal amendment to be relatively infrequent.

Interpretation by Congress and the President

In a sense, Congress interprets its powers under the Constitution every time it passes a law or holds a hearing. There are always in Congress a substantial number of members who pride themselves on their knowledge of the Constitution, and whenever new legislative programs are being considered, much of the congressional debate will be concerned with the constitutional justification for the new program.

In the same way the President construes the Constitution whenever he makes a decision, issues an executive order, or signs a bill into law. The Constitution is manifested in the historic crises that Presidents have met— Lincoln facing the disintegration of the Union, Roosevelt facing the collapse of the national economy. Their actions were based on explicit or implicit interpretations of executive power. When the President has any doubt about the sufficiency of his constitutional authority, or when he wishes to provide the firmest possible basis for his action, he will ask the Attorney General for a legal opinion covering his proposed action.

Judicial Interpretation

The most highly rationalized type of constitutional interpretation, however, is that engaged in by judges, and particularly the Supreme Court. No matter how great the prestige of the President or Congress, there is a general assumption that until the Supreme Court has spoken, the Constitution has not been officially interpreted. And almost invariably the President and Congress, even when they hold opposite views, yield to the Court's position. Thus judicial interpretation is in most areas of constitutional meaning the final arbiter.

The Constitution contains many broad phrases such as "due process of law" or "freedom of speech." How does the Supreme Court decide what these words mean? One test that is often suggested is the *intention of the framers*. It does seem logical that, where the language of the Constitution is vague or subject to diverse interpretations, the Court should try to resolve the uncertainties by seeking guidance from the understandings of the men who wrote the document.

However, there are more difficulties than one might imagine in determining the intent of the framers of the Constitution. Fifty-five delegates were present at one or more sessions of the Convention, but some took little or no part in the proceedings. Some propositions on which they voted were carried by narrow majorities. What was said, and the reasons given for votes cast, are known almost entirely through the necessarily incomplete notes which Madison took. On no issues did all members speak; on few did a majority speak. Many decisions must have been compromises which fully pleased no one.

If the intention of the 55 men at Philadelphia cannot be discovered with assurance, what chance is there of determining the intention of the delegates to the state ratifying conventions whose votes put the Constitution into operation? And the ultimate in uncertainty is reached if we seek to discover the intention of the people who elected the delegates to the state conventions. The members of the First Congress, who drafted the First Ten Amendments to the Constitution, also must rate as founders.

In spite of these complications, there are some areas where the purpose of the drafters may seem reasonably clear, and where legitimate use can be made of historical data in discovering these purposes. Thus in *Barron* v. *Baltimore* (1833), the Supreme Court had to decide whether the First Ten Amendments applied to the states as well as Congress. Chief Justice John Marshall held that they did not, relying primarily on the historical fact that the Bill of Rights had been drafted to meet the objections of those who were afraid of the power of the new central government.

All too often, however, persons who seek to settle constitutional arguments by appealing to the intention of the framers are simply reading their own policy preferences into the language of the Constitution. When the Supreme Court was trying to decide in *School District* v. *Schempp* (1963) whether the First Amendment makes it unconstitutional to read the Bible in public schools, Justice Brennan expressed his opinion that it would be "futile and misdirected" to ask what the Founding Fathers had intended on this point.

First, Brennan said, "the historical record is at best ambiguous, and statements can readily be found to support either side of the proposition. . . . Second, the structure of American education has greatly changed since the First Amendment was adopted." Justice Brennan thought it would be a more fruitful inquiry for the Court to ask "whether the practices here challenged threaten those consequences which the Framers deeply feared; whether, in short, they tend to promote that type of interdependence between religion and state which the First Amendment was designed to prevent."

Another major issue for the Court is what degree of responsibility it can assume in modifying previous constitutional interpretations to meet new situations and new needs. Once the meaning of a particular constitutional provision is authoritatively determined, is the Court bound to that interpretation for all time? Some members of the Court have thought so. Chief Justice Roger B. Taney said, in the famous *Dred Scott* case in 1857:

> [The Constitution] speaks not only in the same words, but with the same meaning and intent with which it spoke when it came from the hands of its framers, and was voted on and adopted by the people of the United States. Any other rule of construction would abrogate the judicial character of this court, and make it the mere reflex of the popular opinion or passion of the day.

More recently Justice Frankfurter took this same position in *Ullmann* v. *United States* (1955): "Nothing new can be put into the Constitution except through the amendatory process. Nothing old can be taken out without the same process."

The Supreme Court has generally rejected this rigid view, which would make the nation a prisoner of its past and deny the legitimacy of amendment by consensus and usage. It was such narrow textualism that Chief Justice Marshall was warning against in *McCulloch* v. *Maryland* (1819) when he said: "We must never forget, that it is a constitution we are expounding . . . a constitution intended to endure for ages to come, and, consequently, to be adapted to the various crises of human affairs."

⚓ CONSTITUTIONAL CHANGE AT WORK

The fact that the Constitution permits change makes some people uneasy. They think of the Constitution as a straitjacket, and whenever a change occurs they are sure that the Constitution has been violated. When the Supreme Court in 1935 upheld the constitutionality of congressional action in reducing the gold content of the dollar so far as private contracts were concerned, Justice McReynolds, dissenting, ejaculated in Court: "As for the Constitution, it does not seem too much to say that it is gone." Others are sure that the Constitution has been violated because the President has become a "dictator," or because Congress has become a "rubber stamp," or because the Supreme Court has become a "super-legislature," or because states' rights have been lost to an all-powerful "octopus" of central government in Washington. They do not understand that the Constitution, as Justice Frankfurter said, is "not a literary composition, but a way of ordering society" which defies understanding outside the context of politics and political change.

Certainly there have been developments tending in the directions indicated by such criticisms, but these changes have taken place within the boundaries of a flexible constitutional system and have been based upon reasonable interpretations of the written text. It is precisely because the Constitution does permit change that it has persisted. The only constant thing is change, said Heraclitus, the Greek philosopher (6th–5th century B.C.), and if the Constitution could not change with the country, it would have had to be discarded long ago.

Change in the Executive

The American Presidency has evolved by the process of constitutional change into the most powerful executive in the democratic world. But the foundation for this development was consciously laid by the founders of the Constitution, who overcame their doubts about strong executives in inventing this new office. They equipped it with tremendous authority— the power to appoint, to recommend legislation, to supervise the executive departments, to act as Commander in Chief, to assume control of foreign relations. These powers have from the beginning been available to any President who knew how to use them.

The one great modification in the original plan for the Presidency—the method of selection—occurred without any significant change in the language of the Constitution. Indirect election, through the electoral college, was soon replaced by what is in fact direct election by the people. As the choice of the national electorate the President can now claim, even more than Congress, to represent the national will, and this direct link to the electorate has supplied the one element needed for the full development of the presidential office.

The Vice-Presidency has also been substantially modified by practice, though this is a much more recent constitutional development. This office, created at a late stage in the Constitutional Convention, was given the task of presiding over the Senate, even though this seemed an infraction of the principle of separation of powers, largely because it was feared the Vice-President would otherwise have nothing to do. In fact it worked out that way for a century and a half, and the list of utter unknowns who have served as Vice-President is lengthy. The risks of a functionless Vice-President were dramatically illustrated when Harry Truman succeeded to the Presidency in 1945 in ignorance of the fact that the atomic bomb had been developed and was almost ready for use. Since President Eisenhower's terms, the office of Vice-President has acquired new stature and significance in the American political scene.

Change in Congress

As for Congress, while it is far from being a "rubber stamp," it is true that many of the developments to which the constitutional system has adapted have reduced its status, particularly in relation to the President. Originally the constitutional position of Congress had such potentialities that something like the legislative supremacy of a parliamentary system might have developed. During the first part of the nineteenth century the President generally owed his position to the decision of the congressional caucus, and after the elections of 1800 and 1824 the House of Representatives had the constitutional responsibility of selecting the President because no candidate had a majority in the electoral college. After the Civil War, Congress again achieved dominance, and if the impeachment of President Johnson had not failed by one vote, the pattern of congressional supremacy might have been firmly established.

The decline of legislatures vis-à-vis the executive has been general in the twentieth century. For one thing, the relative clumsiness and poor organization of large representative bodies puts them at a disadvantage. The executive is always in session, capable of moving quickly to formulate programs and meet emergencies. Nor does the American Congress any longer have a monopoly on the representative function. Not only has the President, as just noted, become the representative of the whole people. Representative functions have also been assumed by interest groups which are quite unknown to the Constitution, but which citizens may find speak for them far more effectively in Washington than their elected congressmen. Even offices and bureaus in the executive branch often take on representative functions, and the laws as passed may be much less significant than the laws as administered.

If the stature of Congress is perhaps less than was contemplated when the Constitution was adopted, its range of legislative responsibilities is much greater. From the limited, laissez-faire goals of eighteenth-century legislation, we have moved to the twentieth-century welfare state where Congress accepts responsibility for assuring full employment, education, medical care, social security, public health, recreation, and a hundred other imperatives of modern American life. The constitutional foundation for this tremendous expansion in activities has readily been found in existing language of the Constitution, particularly the commerce and taxing powers. For a short time, between 1935 and 1937, the Supreme Court blocked such programs by a narrow interpretation of congressional powers, but that threat soon passed. The only actual change in the Constitution required to facilitate this vast expansion of federal activities was the income tax amendment, which made possible the financing of government at its present level. The barrier against the income tax, however, had been erected, not by the Constitution, but by a highly questionable Supreme Court interpretation.

The Stature of the Supreme Court

The Supreme Court, like Congress and the Presidency, has had its ups and downs, but in general it has much exceeded the expectations of 1787. Alexander Hamilton in No. 78 of *The Federalist* spoke of the Court as the "least dangerous" of the branches, possessing "neither force nor will, but merely judgment." However, the role of ultimate interpreter of the Constitution earned such prestige for the Court that it has always emerged eventually unscathed from its numerous controversies with the President and Congress. The Court's wounds, as Charles Evans Hughes once said— thinking of such decisions as *Dred Scott* and its 1895 ruling that the income tax was unconstitutional—have been largely self-inflicted. Since 1954, when the decision banning racial segregation in the public schools was handed down, the Court has assumed on an unparalleled scale the role of moral leadership in the political drive for equality and civil rights.

Increase in Powers of the Federal Government

Finally, constitutional evolution has changed the balance of functions between the federal government and the states. Looked at over the long reaches of American history, there has been an obvious trend toward increasing the powers and functions of the federal government. The central-local relationship has been the product of political conflict, compromise, and consensus. Of course the adoption of the Constitution was in itself a major victory of those forces favoring a strong national government, a victory which the Federalist party consolidated during the succeeding years under the astute guidance of Alexander Hamilton. But the anti-Federalist, states' rights forces were quickly rallied by Jefferson into a coalition strong enough to win the Presidency in 1800 and ultimately to destroy the Federalist party. Once in office, however, Jefferson's party by no means moved to dismantle the federal establishment. In fact, Jefferson is particularly remembered for his bold move in purchasing the Louisiana Territory, in spite of his own expressed doubts about the constitutionality of such federal action.

After the defeat of 1800, Federalist and nationalist ideology was kept alive by Chief Justice John Marshall on the Supreme Court. From 1801 to 1835 he devoted his immense judicial skill to broadening the constitutional interpretations of federal power. His successor, Roger B. Taney, was of the opposite persuasion, and the years up to the Civil War saw the pendulum swing back toward state powers.

Out of the Civil War the Republican party emerged as the nationalist voice of the industrial East and Midwest, and the Democratic party as the states' rights spokesman of the South. But the responsibility of government which came to the Democratic party with Woodrow Wilson's election in 1912, and the necessities of wartime organization, laid the foundation for a reversal of party positions which was fully consolidated by Franklin Roosevelt's New Deal. From 1932 to 1952 the general Republican position was critical of the centralization attending the government's depression, war, and cold war programs. In 1952 a Republican President took office pledged to reverse these centralizing tides. Although President Eisenhower did largely succeed in halting further increases in federal functions, his efforts to find services which could be discontinued or returned to the states were completely without result.

What this experience suggests is that shifts of power toward the central government are not the result of political ideologies or conspiracies or Supreme Court decisions, but are rather caused by the inexorable pressures of wars, depressions, new means of communication, urbanization, industrialization, technology, and all the other factors that have shrunk the size of our world and created problems so large and so urgent that of necessity they are pushed up to the national level for handling. Finally, it must be stressed that this process of centralization has not required the granting of any new constitutional powers to the federal government. The central-local relationship has been the product of political conflict, compromise, and consensus within the long-established boundaries of the federal system.

℣ WORLD SIGNIFICANCE OF THE AMERICAN CONSTITUTION

The era of the written Constitution was ushered in by the American and French Revolutions. Up to that time the dominant conception of a constitution was the English evolutionary idea stated by the English statesman and thinker Lord Bolingbroke in 1793:

> By constitution we mean, whenever we speak with propriety and exactness, that assemblage of laws, institutions and customs, derived from certain fixed principles of reason, directed to certain fixed objects of public good, that compose the general system, according to which the community hath agreed to be governed.

But the Americans and the French were dealing with a revolutionary, not an evolutionary situation. They meant to break with the past, to make a new start, and so they sat down and thought out a government. They put down in writing a framework of administration and an allocation of powers and a system of restraints on power. Their invention of the written constitution has been subsequently adopted by every nation that faces the problem of making a new start and operating under the rule of law.

The fact that the French have had 14 constitutions since 1789 suggests some of the problems in thinking out a government. A constitution in and of itself does not bring stability to a country if it is split by religious or racial or class conflicts or is threatened by powerful foreign neighbors or has a tradition of violence in its public life. There must be some correspondence between constitutional goals and political realities.

The fact that the American Constitution of 1789 is still in operation is certainly due in part to the favorable circumstances of its national setting. This was a new country, still malleable, protected by two oceans from foreign conquest, without sharp class distinctions, with great natural resources and wide-open spaces to absorb the discontented and disadvantaged, and with considerable experience in self-government. But these features must not be allowed to deprive the founders of due credit for the wisdom of their basic decisions.

The American Constitution has had tremendous impact on world opinion and unusual value for the framers of other constitutional systems, particularly during the nineteenth century, when the struggling American nation was a symbol of freedom to much of the world. The French and American constitutions started what has been called a "constitutional cult." Even Tsar Alexander of Russia corresponded with Thomas Jefferson to learn how the American Constitution functioned, and the abortive Russian constitution of 1820 was the first constitutional attempt by a European ruler to combine the federal and monarchial principles.

The revolutionary movements of the mid-nineteenth century in Europe got much of their inspiration from America. This was especially true in Germany, where the revolutionists of 1848–1849 constantly referred to the American example and wanted to create a free Germany "like America." The Frankfurt Constitution of 1849 borrowed from the American Constitution both in broad matters of principle and in matters of drafting and detail. Key articles were drawn almost textually from the American document, which had been translated into German and widely circulated.

For the Latin American countries which gained their independence in the nineteenth century, it was the federal character of the American Constitution and the strong independent executive that were most attractive. The highly centralized, bureaucratic organization which Napoleon had developed in France was of course familiar to Latin America, and might have seemed better adapted to the conditions prevailing there. But centralism was associated with conservatism, whereas federalism had a liberal image and was favored regardless of its appropriateness to local political or geographic conditions. When the Brazilian monarchy was overthrown in 1889, a federal republic, with a constitution modeled after that of the United States, took its place.

The American federal pattern was more successfully followed by the Swiss constitution of 1848, and by two countries in the British Commonwealth, Canada (1867) and Australia (1900). Decisions by the United States Supreme Court regulating relations between the federal government and the states are cited and often followed by the courts of Canada, Australia, and other federal countries.

In the twentieth century, as the United States has become rich, powerful, and conservative, its example has become less attractive to developing nations, which find it hard to identify with the American colossus. To the extent that the American Constitution has remained a model, it is two of its liberal features—the Bill of Rights and judicial protection for the individual—that have been influential. The institution of a strong Supreme Court, with power to enforce constitutional restrictions on the executive and the legislature, was adopted in several of the post-World War II constitutions, notably those of West Germany, Italy, and India. The American Bill of Rights has symbolized in many lands the goal of individual freedom and the right to resist governmental oppression.

CHAPTER 7

FEDERALISM

One of the serious reservations which the framers had in setting up a new Constitution was whether a large country under a strong central government would be a threat to the freedom of its citizens. The delegates who opposed the Virginia Plan for a strong central government had a picture in their minds, drawn in part at least from the experience of the Greek city-states, of the "small republic" as the ideal form of government. Roger Sherman of Connecticut put it this way: "The people are more happy in small than large States."

The problem of course, was that small republics were too weak, standing alone, to protect their independence and their economies, and so they had to associate in some common organization for mutual protection. But Sherman and other supporters of the New Jersey Plan believed that a confederation limited to the functions of keeping the peace among the states and defending them against foreign enemies was all that was needed.

It was James Madison's role to answer the small republic argument. He contended that from antiquity to the current American states, small republics had been beset by conflicts between classes which were fatal to liberty. A large republic would be preferable, for there, he argued, liberty would be protected by "the great variety of interests, parties, and sects which it embraces." An "extended republic of the United States" would be divided into many groups, no single one amounting to a majority. Only as smaller groups associated together could majorities be formed, a process which would force each group to moderate its position and protect the liberties of all.

The Convention was persuaded by Madison's argument, and even more by realization that their goals of security, peace, and economic development could be achieved only through a strong central government. But this created a coexistence problem. How could this new power center be accommodated within the same governmental structure with the existing and powerful state establishments? The framers found a brilliant solution. They invented the federal system.

We now think of the threefold distinction between a *confederation,* a *federal* system, and a *unitary* government as routine and obvious. (See Figure 7–1.)But in 1787 only two forms, the confederal and the national (unitary), were recognized. The opening words of the resolution proposing the Virginia Plan stated these two alternatives: a "merely federal" Union or "a National Government." "Merely federal" meant a confederation such as was then in existence. It was because this "merely federal" plan had failed that the Virginia delegation proposed a truly "national" government. But what actually emerged from the Convention was the blueprint for a large republic intended to achieve both liberty and security by a division of responsibilities and functions which has come to be considered as the true form of federalism.

It should be noted that there are still problems with respect to use of the term "federal." Strictly speaking, "the federal government" includes both the national and the state governments, which together make up the federal system. However, it is common practice to refer to the national government in Washington as the federal government, and that practice is followed in this work.

❦ THE CASE FOR FEDERALISM

Since 1787 the federal system has been adopted in many other countries in addition to the United States, including Canada, Australia, Switzerland, India, Germany, Russia, and Mexico. By contrast, well-established democracies such as England, France, and Italy operate on the unitary system where all governmental power is vested in the central government, and local districts are used only as administrative areas for carrying out national programs under central direction.

Advantages of the Federal System over the Unitary System

Federal systems have the following advantages over the unitary plan.

1. Federalism tends to offer a more effective plan of government for big countries. Switzerland is a distinct exception to the rule that large size and federalism go together. The difficulty of governing a country with the area

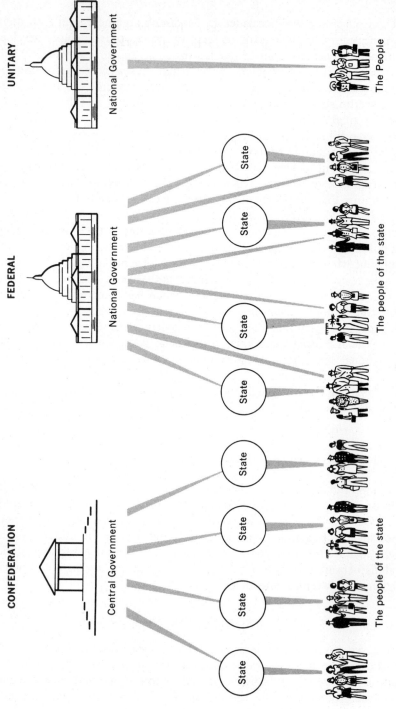

FIGURE 7–1. Comparison of Confederation, Federal, and Unitary Types of Government.

and population of the United States or India from one capital is obvious. Under federalism many public functions are performed at the state or provincial level and need never concern the central authorities.

2. Federalism is well adapted to a country with strong regional differences. Diversities of race, language, tribe, or religion are accommodated by federal systems in Switzerland, India, Canada, Sudan, and Nigeria. There is of course always the possibility that loyalties to a region may be so strong as to conflict with loyalty to the federal union, as is illustrated by the separatist movement in Quebec and the bitter language conflicts in India. The success of American federalism is due in part to the fortunate fact that its federal units are not based on differences of race, national origin, religion, or language, but merely on geography.

3. The states or provinces in a federal system bring government closer to the people. Important centers of influence and decision are near enough, so that popular participation in elections and other political activities is encouraged.

4. The state level is an important training ground for national politics. Woodrow Wilson, Franklin Roosevelt, Adlai Stevenson, and George Romney are among those who got their first significant political experience as governors of important states. State legislators and state judges often move up into corresponding positions in the national government.

5. The states are political laboratories where new ideas can be tried out without committing the whole country. Wisconsin first experimented with unemployment compensation. Georgia was the first state to reduce the voting age to 18. Prohibition on a national scale in the United States was a disaster, but if individual states wish to try to make it work they are free to do so. Nevada can legalize gambling; New Hampshire can start a state lottery, without involving national consequences.

6. A federal system permits more effective forms of administrative decentralization to be developed. In a unitary system the central government uses the local districts as administrative areas, but in a federal system the states can be treated as partners and share the responsibility for initiating and directing important programs. Thus the United States pays 90 percent of the cost of the interstate highway program, but the initial planning and the construction of the system fall to the states.

A federal system also has its costs, of course, some of which will become clear in the following discussion. There are bound to be disputes between the states and the national government over the allocation of functions and resources, as well as competition and conflict among the states themselves. Where the population is highly mobile, as in the United States, different systems of criminal, family, business, or tax laws in the various states can create many problems. For example, in 1966 North Carolina was causing considerable trouble for her sister states because she had no cigarette tax, and a large-scale cigarette smuggling operation had developed in which cigarettes bought in North Carolina were bootlegged in other states with high taxes. The obvious solution was for North Carolina to levy a cigarette tax also, but there was no authority to compel the state to take such action. The autonomy, flexibility, and adaptability of a federal system have their consequences in overlapping, conflict, and confusion.

✳ STRUCTURE OF AMERICAN FEDERALISM

In a federal system there must be an initial agreement on a distribution of functions between the two levels of government. The pattern of allocation which emerged from the Constitutional Convention was fairly complex.

1. Some powers were exclusively delegated to the national government. The conduct of foreign relations and the power to coin money are good examples.

2. Some powers were exclusively reserved to the states. This was done, not by specifically naming any such powers, but by the general language added in 1791 by the Tenth Amendment which provided: "The powers not delegated to the United States by the Constitution, nor prohibited by it to the states, are reserved to the states respectively, or to the people."

3. Some powers were to be exercised by nation and states concurrently—the taxing power, for instance.

4. Some powers were prohibited to the national government, such as those against the levying of direct taxes or suspending the writ of habeas corpus. Of course, since the federal government had only those powers delegated to it in the Constitution, any powers not delegated were in that sense prohibited.

5. Some powers were forbidden to the states. Article I, Section 10, states a whole group of such prohibited powers, intended primarily to enforce the federal government's control over foreign relations, the monetary system, and foreign commerce.

6. Some powers are forbidden to both the nation and the states. These include the ban on bills of attainder (legislative punishment), *ex post facto* laws (making an act unlawful which was not illegal when it was performed), and titles of nobility.

Enforcing the Division of Functions

Since functions and powers are divided between and shared by the two levels in this rather intricate fashion, controversies are bound to occur. A federal system requires rules to apply in cases of dispute, and an umpire to apply and enforce those rules. In the American Constitution the rule for settling controversies is the "supremacy clause" of Article VI:

> This Constitution, and the laws of the United States which shall be made in pursuance thereof; and all treaties made, or which shall be made, under the authority of the United States, shall be the supreme law of the land; and the judges in every state shall be bound thereby, any thing in the Constitution or laws of any state to the contrary notwithstanding.

The umpire is the Supreme Court.

The effectiveness of the supremacy clause was first demonstrated in the great case of *McCulloch* v. *Maryland* (1819). In 1818 the Maryland legislature levied a tax on the politically unpopular Bank of the United States, which had been chartered by the national government. The cashier of the Baltimore branch of the Bank refused to pay the tax and was convicted of violating the law by the state courts. The Supreme Court, however, unanimously upheld the Bank's position, Chief Justice Marshall basing his opinion squarely on the supremacy clause. "If any one proposition could command the universal assent of mankind," he wrote, "we might expect it would be this: that the government of the Union, though limited in its powers, is supreme within its sphere of action." Consequently, no state had any power "to retard, impede, burden, or in any manner control, the operations of the constitutional laws enacted by congress."

When Congress enters a field in which it is authorized to act, then, its legislation voids all incompatible state regulations. In practical terms, however, the question whether Congress has pre-empted a given area is a difficult one, since federal statutes seldom state whether all local rules on the matter are suspended. It falls ultimately to the Supreme Court to determine the relation of federal and state statutes. In *Pennsylvania* v. *Nelson* (1956), Chief Justice Warren attempted to codify the tests which the Court has used to guide such decisions. First, is the scheme of federal regulation so pervasive as to make it a reasonable inference that Congress has left no room for the states? Second, do the federal statutes touch a field in which the interest of the national government is so dominant that it must be assumed to preclude state action on the same subject? Third, does enforcement of the state act present a serious danger of conflict with the administration of the federal program?

In the *Nelson* case, a conviction for violation of the Pennsylvania sedition act had been reversed by the state supreme court on the ground that a federal sedition law (the Smith Act of 1940) had occupied the field and superseded the state law. The United States Supreme Court agreed. Using the three criteria just suggested, the Court concluded that Congress had taken over the entire task of protecting the country from seditious conduct when it passed the Smith Act, even though no express intention to exclude the states was indicated in that statute.

Crises Points in the Federal System

The Union established by adoption of the Constitution has undergone many crises, including the bloodiest civil war in history. When national power was used in ways detrimental to state or regional interests, interpretations of the federal relationship were quickly developed to justify resistance to national authority.

Interposition. The Federalists initially controlled Congress, and as they began to lose ground to Jefferson's new Republican party, they reacted by passing in 1798 the Alien Enemies Act aimed at Jefferson's French supporters, and the Sedition Act punishing any criticism of the national government. The Jeffersonians, outraged by what they regarded as an unconstitutional abuse of congressional power, drafted in protest the famous Kentucky and Virginia Resolutions (so-called because of their adoption by the legislatures of those two states). These resolutions argued that under the Constitution the states, which were "integral parties" to the compact, had the right to judge when the federal government exercised powers which had not been granted by the compact, and could "interpose" state authority "for arresting the progress of the evil, and for maintaining within their respective limits, the authorities, rights, and liberties" guaranteed by the Constitution.

The resolutions were not clear as to how interposition was to be carried out. One suggestion was to call for the submission to the states of an amendment to the Constitution authorizing the alleged improper assertion of federal power. If such an amendment failed of ratification by three fourths of the states, then the federal action would be nullified as an act of usurpation not warranted by the Constitution.

Jefferson's victory over the Federalists in the elections of 1800, due in no small part to popular resentment over the Alien and Sedition Acts, terminated this episode. But the concept of interposition has periodically been rediscovered. During the War of 1812 the New England states, suffering because of the disruption of their trade with England, were seriously disaffected. They joined in the Hartford Convention of 1814–1815 to recommend to the legislatures of the states that they pass measures to protect their citizens from the operation of unconstitutional national acts. But before the resolutions were even delivered, the war was over, the complaints were forgotten, and the only result of the Convention was to annihilate the Federalist party.

In 1956 the long-slumbering doctrine of interposition was revived by southern opponents of the Supreme Court's decision banning racial segregation in the public schools. Almost 100 congressmen from 11 southern states issued a manifesto charging the Court with a clear abuse of judicial power encroaching on the reserved rights of the states and the people, and commending those states "which have declared the intention to resist forced integration by any lawful means." Legislatures of most of the southern states proceeded to draft declarations of interposition purporting to relieve their states from the necessity of enforcing the Court decision. When the governor and legislature of Arkansas argued in the 1958 Little Rock case, *Cooper* v. *Aaron,* that they were not bound by the segregation decision, the Supreme Court sharply and decisively restated the principles of federal supremacy which make the claims for interposition incompatible with the American federal system.

Nullification. Nullification was originally a part of the interposition doctrine, but it also had a history of its own, particularly as developed by John C. Calhoun in the pre-Civil War period. The theory of nullification originated with Jefferson's statement in the Kentucky Resolutions of 1798 that "where powers are assumed which have not been delegated, a nullification of the act is the rightful remedy." The idea was later developed as a rationalization for southern opposition to the constant increase in tariff rates between 1816 and 1828. Calhoun was alarmed at the open talk of secession in the South, and offered the doctrine of nullification as a substitute, contending that it was a logical extension of the Virginia and Kentucky Resolutions.

A South Carolina convention then declared the federal tariff acts null and void and forbade federal agents to collect them in the state. President Jackson immediately challenged this action, saying that the power of nullification was "incompatible with the existence of the Union," and sent gunboats into Charleston Harbor to enforce the tariff. The nullification statute was eventually repealed by the state after Congress had worked out a compromise measure on the tariff rates.

Secession. As the slavery issue increased in intensity, southern statesmen shifted their ground from nullification to secession as the means to preserve their economic life and social institutions. For Calhoun, secession was justified as a final remedy to preserve a state's rights. If the character of the Constitution was radically changed (as by the abolition of slavery), even if this was done through the amending process, Calhoun contended that any state, "acting in the same capacity in which it ratified the constitution," would have the right to depart from the Union.

Lincoln's decision to use force to keep the southern states in the Union and the victory of the North in the Civil War closed the debate over the legality of secession. The final decision was rendered at Appomattox Courthouse. In *Texas* v. *White* (1869) the Supreme Court summed up the principle which it had taken a bloody civil war to establish: "The Constitution, in all its provisions, looks to an indestructible Union, composed of indestructible States."

Admission of New States

Article IV, Section 3, provides for the admission of new states into the Union by Congress. The only stated limitations on congressional discretion are that "no new state shall be formed or erected within the jurisdiction of any other state; nor any state be formed by the junction of two or more states, or parts of states, without the consent of the legislatures of the states concerned as well as of the Congress."

Thirty-five new states were admitted to the Union between 1791 and 1912. (See Figure 7–2.) Five were carved out of the territory of older states—Vermont, Kentucky, Tennessee, Maine, and West Virginia. In the first four cases, the legislature of the older state gave its consent. But West Virginia was formed from the western counties of Virginia during the Civil

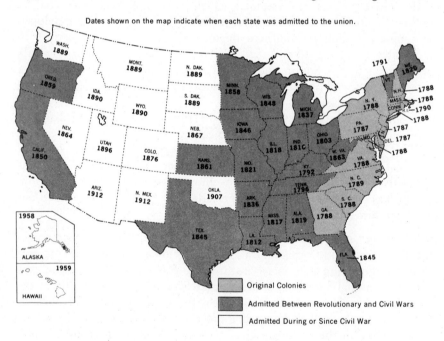

FIGURE 7–2. Admission of States to the Union. (Adapted from *Statistical Abstract of the United States 1965*.)

War when Virginia was in military opposition to the Union. However, after the war, Virginia formally consented to the dismemberment.

Of the remaining thirty states, all but two went through a probationary status as organized territories before they were admitted as states. The exceptions were Texas, which, upon its admission in 1845, was an independent republic, and California, which was formed out of a region ceded by Mexico in 1848.

The normal procedure by which a territory becomes a state calls for Congress to pass an enabling act allowing the territorial government to convene a popular convention to propose a state constitution. If the voters ratify this constitution, it is submitted to Congress for approval. Congress then may pass a resolution admitting the new state. A statehood resolution, like other legislation, is subject to presidential veto, but unlike other statutes, it cannot be repealed.

Congress may grant or withhold statehood for any reasons it chooses. Before the Civil War the primary motive in admission was to maintain a balance between slave and free states. Nevada was admitted, in spite of its sparse population, to provide a necessary ratifying vote for the Thirteenth Amendment. Hawaii and Alaska were strong candidates for admission from at least 1944, when the platforms of both political parties recommended statehood, but various political considerations delayed action by Congress. Alaska finally won admission in 1958, and Hawaii in 1959, the first states to join the Union since 1912. Recently suggestions have been made that California be divided into two states.

Each state admitted to the Union enters on an equal footing with the other states. There is no such requirement in the Constitution; in fact, the Constitutional Convention specifically voted down an "equal footing" proposal. The delegates from the original states apparently had difficulty conceiving that the territories to the west could ever be entitled to rank with the founding members of the Union. But as Congress came to admit the first new states, it specified that they should have full equality. The Supreme Court has firmly followed this precedent, even when Congress has not. For example, under the enabling act admitting Oklahoma as a state, Congress specified that the state capital should be located at Guthrie for at least seven years. After four years, the state legislature moved the capital to Oklahoma City. The Supreme Court in *Coyle v. Smith* (1911) held that the state was not obliged to obey the congressional directive, for if Congress could impose restrictions on the states in the process of admission, then the nation might become a union of states unequal in power and status.

Another application of the equal footing doctrine, this time to the disadvantage of a state, came in the case of *United States v. Texas* (1950).

In 1947 the Court had ruled, in cases involving California and Louisiana, that the soil beneath the 3-mile marginal belt along the Atlantic Ocean had not belonged to the original states, and consequently that the states later admitted to the Union did not own the 3-mile belt along their coasts either. But Texas had been an independent nation prior to admission, and was conceded to have owned its coastal belt of land during that period. The Supreme Court held, however, that Texas had surrendered its dominion and sovereignty over its coastal shelf when it entered the Union on terms of equality with the existing states.

Congress subsequently reversed the effect of this holding by passing the Submerged Lands Act of 1953 which ceded to the states ownership of land and resources under adjoining seas to a distance of 3 miles from shore or to the state's "historic boundaries." The Supreme Court has interpreted this statute to grant Florida and Texas jurisdiction 10 miles into the Gulf, since their historic boundaries were 3 marine leagues, whereas the other Gulf states have only 3 miles. To this extent the equal footing rule has been disregarded by Congress and the Court.

⁂ FEDERAL RELATIONS TO THE STATES

The Constitution imposes several obligations upon the national government with respect to the states. Under Article V no state may be denied equal representation in the Senate without its consent. Again, the government must respect the territorial integrity of the existing states in forming new states, as already noted. Certain other obligations, all appearing in Article IV, Section 4, deserve more extended discussion.

Guarantees Against Invasion and Domestic Violence

The protection against foreign invasion owed by the national government to the states is simply a corollary of national self-defense. During the War of 1812 and the Civil War, it was for a time beyond the power of the federal government to repel invasions.

On application of a state legislature, or of the state executive if the legislature cannot be convened, the United States must guarantee a state against "domestic violence." A request from a state is not necessary, however, where domestic violence threatens the enforcement of national laws. Article I, Section 8, authorizes Congress to provide for calling forth the militia to execute the laws of the Union, suppress insurrections, and repel invasions. Congress adopted legislation in 1792 and 1795 authorizing the President to take such action "whenever the laws of the United States shall be opposed, or the execution thereof obstructed, in any state, by combinations too powerful to be suppressed by the ordinary course of judicial proceedings."

In 1894 President Cleveland sent troops into Illinois, against the strong protest of the state's governor, to prevent violence in connection with a strike against the Pullman Company and to keep the trains moving. Again, in 1957 President Eisenhower found it necessary to use federal troops to control violence in Little Rock, Arkansas, and enforce court orders seeking to accomplish gradual desegregation of the local high school.

Guarantee of a Republican Form of Government

Article IV, Section 4, provides that "The United States shall guarantee to every State in this Union a republican form of government. . . ." This is the only limitation in the Constitution on the internal governmental organization of a state. No definition is provided of a republican form of government, but the language may be interpreted as requiring a form somewhere between a monarchy or oligarchy on the one hand, and a pure or direct democracy on the other.

In designating the "United States" as responsible for this guarantee, the Constitution does not specify which branch has the responsibility for its enforcement. The President, in case of need, could employ the armed forces to preserve a state's republican government, and the Congress could refuse to seat Representatives from a state which had departed from the republican principle. But the Supreme Court has on several occasions declined to attempt a judicial interpretation and enforcement of the clause. For example, in *Pacific States Telephone & Telegraph Co.* v. *Oregon* (1912), it was alleged that the insertion in the Oregon constitution of a provision for direct legislation by way of the initiative and referendum deprived the state of a republican form of government and made it a pure democracy. The Court's reply was that, in the absence of any determination on this point by the political branches of the government, it would refuse to consider such charges. Thus the republican form of government clause appears to be judicially unenforceable.

Control over Territories

Jefferson's doubts about the authority of the national government to acquire new territory are well known. In making the Louisiana Purchase he felt he had been justified in seizing the opportunity to protect American rights to the Mississippi waterway, but he requested Congress to propose a formal amendment to justify future acquisitions of territory. No such action has ever been taken, and few have thought this course necessary.

In contrast, the power of Congress to "dispose" of territory is explicitly written into Article IV, Section 3. The principal exercise of this power occurred in granting independence to the Philippine Islands.

Incorporated Territories. The same section gives Congress power to "make all needful rules and regulations" respecting territories of the United States. For well over a century, this was a major responsibility, as Congress provided territorial governments to keep up with the westward expansion of the United States. These were what the Supreme Court came to call "incorporated territories"—that is, territories which were in preparation for statehood, and in which the inhabitants enjoyed the full protection of the Constitution. Alaska and Hawaii were the last of the territories in this status.

Puerto Rico. Puerto Rico has the unique position of an American "commonwealth" rather than an incorporated territory. Acquired from Spain by the Spanish-American War, Puerto Rico is an island inhabited by over 2 million Spanish-speaking people with a Latin cultural background. This makes their position in the American Union quite anomalous.

The present relationship of Puerto Rico to the United States is based on a statute adopted by Congress in 1950, Public Law 600, authorizing the Puerto Ricans to draw up their own constitution, with a requirement that it include provisons for a republican form of government and that it contain a bill of rights. After this constitution was adopted, Congress approved it with only minor changes.

The form of government in Puerto Rico is much like that of an American state. There is an elective governor and legislature and an appointive supreme court. Puerto Rico may change its constitution without submitting the amendments for congressional approval, but it is bound by the United States Constitution. Most federal laws do not apply in Puerto Rico, but Congress can pass legislation specifically applicable to it. Puerto Ricans do not pay federal income tax, and Congress has given the island certain tax advantages. Puerto Ricans are, of course, American citizens and can move freely anywhere in the United States.

Theoretically Congress could at any time revoke the compact entered into with Puerto Rico under Public Law 600 and resume direct rule over the island, but such action is most unlikely. While continuation in Commonwealth status appears to be acceptable to the great majority of Puerto Ricans, two other alternatives have considerable support there— independence or statehood. In 1964 Congress set up a commission to consider these alternatives and report on the future state of the island's government.

District of Columbia. The District of Columbia likewise has a distinctive and unique status. By Article I, Section 8, Congress has power of "exclusive legislation" in the District, and it is completely without power over its governmental affairs. The District is to all intents and purposes governed by the House and Senate Committees on the District of Columbia. Three commissioners appointed by the President with Senate consent head the local government, and the judges for the District's local courts are appointed in the same way.

The District did have home rule power prior to 1874. Since that time efforts to restore to the District's residents the right to elect their own governmental officials have been uniformly defeated in Congress, but pressure for home rule is increasing and is almost certain to be successful in the near future. A large federal subsidy to the District will always be necessary, however, because of the great amount of tax-exempt government property in the District, and this will ensure some continuing congressional responsibility for District affairs. The Twenty-third Amendment, adopted in 1961, did grant the voters of the District the right to vote in presidential elections.

Other Territories. Finally, there are certain other territories in the possession of the United States. The Virgin Islands and Guam have a large measure of self-government, though their governors are appointed from Washington, and their residents have full rights of American citizenship. The residents of Samoa, however, are classed as American *nationals*, a condition less than full citizenship but involving allegiance to the United States and the obligation of protection by the national government. Certain former Japanese islands in the Pacific—the Marianas, Marshalls, and Carolines—are held by the United States under the supervision of the United Nations. The Panama Canal Zone is a strip of land on either side of the Canal which the United States controls under treaty with Panama.

⅍ INTERSTATE RELATIONS

Federalism is characterized not only by vertical relationships between nation and state, but also by horizontal contacts between state and state. The Constitution foresaw five kinds of interstate problems and adopted provisions for handling them.

Disputes Between States

As quasi-sovereign authorities with wide powers for independent action, the states were bound to have disputes with each other over such matters as boundaries or water resources. For settling such controversies the federal courts are available. By Article III, Section 2, federal judicial power was extended to "controversies between two or more states." Moreover, the

Supreme Court could assume original jurisdiction over any case in which a state was a party.

In controversies between states the Supreme Court has tended to apply strictly its usual standards of what constitutes sufficient injury to bring about a real "case or controversy." On several occasions, the Court has gone out of its judicial way to discourage litigation and to suggest that the disputing states settle their controversies by negotiation or compact. On the other hand, the Court has accepted cases where serious and irreparable injury was allegedly threatened by such hazards as sewage pollution of large rivers or by the diversion of vitally necessary water from interstate streams.

In adjudicating disputes between states, the Supreme Court uses federal, state, or international law as the situation may demand. In *Kansas* v. *Colorado* (1907) the Court suggested that it was building up a body of "what may not improperly be called interstate common law."

There has never been a serious issue of state refusal to obey a Supreme Court decision in a suit between states. The closest approach was in the long controversy between Virginia and West Virginia over payment of the debt which the latter state assumed when it split off from Virginia during the Civil War. After West Virginia made no move to pay the judgment against her handed down by the Court in 1915, a 1918 decision warned the state that enforcement of the decree would be forthcoming, though the means of collection was not specified. Fortunately the state paid up, thus relieving the Court of the problem of determining how it would get the money from the state treasury.

Interstate Compacts

Of course, states can agree as well as disagree. The Constitution authorizes compacts between states, through the rather negative device of forbidding such compacts unless Congress consents to them. In fact, Congress has given its consent to a great number of compacts, covering such diverse matters as conservation of natural resources, mutual sharing of water in interstate streams, flood and pollution control, and provision of educational or health facilities.

One of the most famous compacts was that between New York and New Jersey which established the Port of New York Authority to develop and operate harbor and transportation facilities in the bistate area. In 1953 the same states signed another compact regulating labor practices in the New York port. Because of evidence of crime and racketeering on the waterfront, the states agreed on a comprehensive set of regulations for employment on the docks, enforced by a bistate waterfront commission.

Interstate Privileges and Immunities

According to Article IV, Section 2, "the citizens of each state shall be entitled to all privileges and immunities of citizens in the several states." Such privileges and immunities include the right to pass through or reside in another state, to institute or maintain court actions in any state, and to be exempt from higher taxes than are paid by the state's own citizens.

But a state is not obliged to treat out-of-state citizens equally with its own if there are acceptable reasons for placing them on different footings. State universities may charge a higher tuition for out-of-state students than for their own residents. Persons licensed by one state to practice law, medicine, or other professions involving the public interest must prove their competence and secure licenses in any other state in which they propose to practice. Higher fees for hunting or fishing may be charged to outsiders on the ground that local citizens pay taxes which are used in part for the upkeep of the public domain. However, if the fees are exorbitantly discriminatory, they will be held invalid. Of course, a state can limit the right to vote to its own citizens, and impose a reasonable residence requirement before allowing new residents to vote in the state elections.

Full Faith and Credit

Under Article IV, Section 1, each state must accord full faith and credit to three types of official acts of sister states: public records, statutes, and court decisions. Public records create no problem, but the effect of state statutes and court decisions in other states requires some explanation.

As for statutes, no state is obliged to enforce the criminal laws of another state. For other types of statutes, the general principle is that the full faith and credit clause does not necessarily require a state to subordinate its own policy to that of another state in case of conflict. The matter must be settled by appraising the respective interests of each state. For example, a resident of Massachusetts normally employed in that state by a Massachusetts corporation was injured while working temporarily in California. The Massachusetts compensation act provided an "exclusive" remedy for industrial accidents, even those occurring outside its borders. But California also had a compensation act fixing liability for all accidents occurring in that state. The Supreme Court in *Pacific Employers Insurance Co.* v. *Industrial Accident Commission* (1939) held that the claim of the Massachusetts law was obnoxious to California policy and so refused to enforce it.

So far as judicial proceedings are concerned, the full faith and credit clause requires judgments conclusive in one state to be recognized as final in all states. This conclusiveness is not automatic. A litigant who has secured a court order in one state and wants to have it enforced against a person who has since gone to another state must bring a new legal action in the latter state. The court there will accept the original decree, examine it, and if it finds the order to be properly authenticated, will issue an enforcement order of its own. The defendant may appear in court and contest the order, but he may not reargue the merits of the case.

Because of the lenient divorce laws in some states, major problems have arisen as to whether other states are required to give full faith and credit to "quickie" divorces granted in those states. In the cases of *Williams* v. *North Carolina* (1942, 1945) two residents of North Carolina, which has relatively rigid divorce laws, went to Nevada, lived in a tourist court for six weeks, shed their respective spouses, married each other, and then returned to North Carolina. That state refused to recognize the validity of the Nevada decrees and brought bigamy charges against the couple, contending that six weeks residence in Nevada was not enough to establish domicile there or give that state claim to jurisdiction over North Carolina residents. The Supreme Court in its 1945 decision accepted this contention and upheld the right of North Carolina courts to decide for themselves, before giving full faith and credit to out-of-state divorce decrees, whether or not residents of the state had established a bona fide domicile outside the state.

The *Williams* decision has not been overruled, but the chaos which this doctrine might cause if widely followed is so obvious that it is now generally agreed that "quickie" divorces operate to terminate the marriage in all states. However, some states have refused to accept quick divorces as altering rights to property, alimony, or the custody of children of their residents.

Extradition

As just noted, the full faith and credit clause does not require a state to enforce the criminal laws of another state. The only obligation here is in the provision of Article IV, Section 2, that a person charged with a crime who flees to another state "shall on demand of the executive authority of the state from which he fled, be delivered up. . . ." Congress in 1793 passed a statute implementing this provision. But in *Kentucky* v. *Dennison* (1861), the Supreme Court held that Congress had not provided any means to compel the execution of this duty, and that the federal government could not constitutionally force a state official to take such action. Thus governors can, and occasionally do, refuse to honor a request for extradition. However, most of the states have adopted a uniform criminal extradition act. Also, Congress has helped out by adopting a law making it a federal offense for a person to go from one state to another with the intent of avoiding prosecution or imprisonment.

⚹ THE TIDE OF CENTRALIZATION

A strong tide appears to be flowing toward centralization of functions in the federal government. As pointed out in the preceding chapter, this is not a new development. Throughout our history there have been complaints that states' rights were being lost to the national government. But it is probably true that in the 1960s the trend toward federal assumption of new responsibilities is more marked than ever before in our history.

The reasons for this tendency are rather clear, and can be illustrated by the current urban problem. Everyone knows that America's great cities are sick. Much of the housing is bad. Streets are clogged with automobile traffic. Those residents who can afford it flee to the suburbs, leaving the central city to the poor and the minority groups. Crime and juvenile delinquency present a policing problem of tremendous difficulty. Water supplies are inadequate. These problems are too big for the cities to handle alone. They need help.

When the cities turn to the states in which they are located, what do they find? All too often, they find that the state's financial resources are already strained and that it cannot spare additional funds on the scale that the cities require. They find that the state legislature is dominated by rural representatives who do not understand or care about the problems of the metropolis. They find that the state government has few staff members who are competent to advise or assist the cities in handling questions of education, transportation, urban renewal, policing, public health, and delinquency.

When the cities turn to the federal government, what do they find? First, Washington has the tremendous financial resources yielded by the federal income tax. Second, they find a President who owes his election primarily to urban voters and who must of necessity be sensitive to their needs. Third, they find federal departments staffed with persons well-trained and knowledgable in the fields of health, education, policing, transportation, social welfare, and housing. In short, they find in Washington the money, the interest, and the skill they need to a much greater degree than in the states.

The combination of federal strength and state weakness can be illustrated by the general field of commercial regulation and control. The

Constitution gives the federal government broad powers to regulate commerce among the states. The Supreme Court early interpreted this to mean that the federal government could regulate interstate commerce, leaving intrastate commerce to the states. But with the growth of national transportation and communication systems, interstate gas pipelines, and electric grids, the area of intrastate commerce has progressively diminished. Except for a brief period in 1935 and 1936, the Supreme Court has interpreted the federal commerce power broadly enough to uphold almost every congressional regulatory statute, and such federal agencies as the Interstate Commerce Commission, the Federal Trade Commission, and the National Labor Relations Board have exercised authority over a wide area. Agriculture even in its most local manifestations was held subject to federal legislation by the Supreme Court in *Wickard* v. *Filburn* (1942).

Even in the areas of commercial regulation which remain with the states, they have failed to distinguish themselves. State public utility commissions are usually rather poorly financed and staffed. When they attempt to challenge the intrastate telephone or electric rates of the giant utilities, they are no match for the expert and well-paid engineers and accountants of the companies. State failure is perhaps most obvious in one area of commercial regulation where the states retain almost full responsibility—insurance regulation. The states collect millions of dollars in taxes and fees from the insurance companies which they incorporate and are supposed to regulate, but not one state spends more than eight cents on the dollar of this income for regulation. In 1966 a Senate inquiry showed that nine states, which had chartered 811 insurance companies, had no insurance examiners at all. Scandals in state insurance departments and failures of insurance companies—58 from 1960 to 1965—have created demands for federal regulation, at least in the auto insurance field.

All too often, then, the states have lost functions to the federal government or have been subjected to federal controls because of their failure to meet their own obligations properly. Most states are not raising the revenues they need to carry on their own functions and provide assistance for their hard-pressed local governments. Until 1966 New Jersey was operating without either a sales tax or an income tax. Refusal to give urban areas the representation in state legislatures to which their population entitled them eventually led to imposition of the federal rule of "one man, one vote" by the Supreme Court in *Reynolds* v. *Sims* (1964).

Better than anything else, however, the civil rights struggle of the 1950s and 1960s demonstrates how state autonomy has been lost because of state failure to meet their constitutional obligations. Segregation in the public schools, denial of the right to vote or access to public accommodations because of race, were practices long-established which in most cases the states were not moving to correct. The Supreme Court's 1954 decision branding racial discrimination in the schools unconstitutional had very little effect. It was necessary for Congress to impose federal power, through a series of civil rights acts beginning in 1957, to compel state acceptance of federal constitutional standards.

These controls finally took the severe form of the Voting Rights Act of 1965. In states where the registration or voting record established a prima facie case that racial discrimination was being practiced, this statute denied the state's right to establish any qualifications at all for voters. Although the Constitution guarantees to the states the right to decide who can vote, it also forbids denial of the franchise on grounds of race, and the states which had for so long refused to enforce the Fifteenth Amendment had little reason to complain when Congress and federal registrars took over this vital state function.

‽ FEDERAL GRANTS-IN-AID

Another manifestation of the centralizing tendency is the increased use of federal grants-in-aid to the states. By 1967 there were no less than 170 programs under which federal financial assistance was available to the states, and the sums involved had increased from $3.1 billion in 1955 to $14.6 billion in 1967.

The original federal grants were of public land, and what are still referred to as the state "land-grant colleges" were established under the terms of the Morrill Act of 1862. The first cash grants came in 1887 for the maintenance of agricultural experiment stations, followed by grants for forestry in 1911, highways in 1916, vocational education in 1917, health in 1918, the social security system in 1935, public housing in 1937, airports and hospitals in 1946, and libraries in 1956. In 1965 federal grants amounted to an estimated 15 percent of all state-local income.

The federal government makes grants available to the states in order to promote activities regarded by Congress as beneficial to the public welfare, which the states might not undertake without federal stimulus or be able to afford without federal financial support. One of the arguments for the grant-in-aid system is that federal funds, which are distributed among the states according to a formula specified by Congress in each grant statute, can perform an equalizing function and enable the poorer states to bring their services up to an acceptable national minimum.

Another effect of the grant-in-aid system has been to revitalize some areas of state activity and enable the states to retain certain activities which might otherwise have gone to the federal government by default. When federal grants are made available to the states, there are accompanying federal regulations and requirements which ensure that state administration of the program will meet federally established standards. The states, of course, are required to match the federal funds in some degree. For the interstate highway program, the federal contribution is a high 90 percent to the states' 10 percent. (See Tables 7–1 to 7–3.)

TABLE 7–1. *Federal Grants to State and Local Governments, by Purpose:*
1935 to 1964

In millions of dollars, except per capita. Includes Alaska, Hawaii, Puerto Rico, Guam, and Virgin Islands. On basis of checks issued for years ending June 30. Does not represent programs for all years; starts with all existing programs in 1935, adds new programs as instituted, and drops programs as terminated.

	Total			Social Welfare						
Year	Amount	Per Capita[a]	Total	Public Assist-ance[b]	Employ-ment Security Adminis-tration[c]	Health Serv-ices[d]	Other Welfare Serv-ices[e]	Educa-tion[f]	High-way Con-struc-tion[g]	All Other
1935	2,197	$17.26	24	(X)	1	(X)	2	21	275	1,898
1940	967	7.20	524	271	120	22	68	44	165	278
1945	917	6.76	693	410	34	79	74	96	87	137
1950	2,208	14.33	1,715	1,123	215	124	184	70	429	64
1955	3,094	18.49	2,382	1,427	189	119	369	278	597	115
1959	6,314	35.75	3,459	1,966	297	247	597	351	2,614	240
1960	6,837	38.08	3,625	2,059	317	255	576	418	2,942	270
1961	6,920	37.90	3,968	2,167	359	284	723	436	2,623	329
1962	7,702	41.48	4,550	2,432	449	305	898	465	2,783	369
1963	8,313	44.09	4,836	2,730	330	343	911	522	3,023	454
1964 (prel.)	9,758	50.99	5,370	2,944	405	389	1,093	540	3,644	744

X Not applicable.

a Based on estimates of total population, excluding Armed Forces abroad, as of July 1.

b Old-age assistance, medical assistance for the aged, aid to families with dependent children, aid to the blind, and aid to permanently and totally disabled.

c Administration of unemployment insurance service, employment service, and veterans' unemployment allowances, and the distribution of certain tax collections to State accounts in unemployment trust fund, when applicable.

d Maternal and child health services, services for crippled children, and other public health service and construction programs.

e Vocational rehabilitation; State and territorial homes for disabled soldiers and sailors; child welfare services; national school lunch program; and others.

f Colleges of agriculture and mechanic arts, agricultural extension work, vocational education, education of the blind, Office of Education emergency grants, maintenance and operation of schools, school survey and construction, defense educational activities, library services, training for education of mentally retarded, and others.

g Federal-aid highways, including regular and emergency, prewar and postwar; and trust fund activities, including restoration of roads and bridges, flood relief, secondary and feeder roads, grade crossing elimination, public land highways, and others.

Data from Dept. of Health, Education, and Welfare, Social Security Administration; *Social Security Bulletin,* June 1965. (Based on *Annual Report of the Secretary of the Treasury.*) Table adapted from *Statistical Abstract of the United States, 1965.*

Arguments against the grant system are that it limits state discretion in the spending of funds, and forces the states to undertake activities that will bring in federal money. It is also contended that grants from Washington merely return to the states tax receipts taken from them, and that this is unnecessary and costly centralization. However, the grant principle has proved to be an effective method of achieving national purposes without direct federal assumption of new functions.

A most important new grant-in-aid program was adopted in 1965 with the passage of the Elementary and Secondary Education Act, which for the first time made federal funds available through the states for general educational purposes. Previous efforts to pass an aid to education act had always failed because of controversy over the exclusion of religious schools from the aid program. But the 1965 act avoided this source of opposition by concentrating aid in poverty-impacted areas and by approving programs broad enough to benefit the students in parochial as well as public schools. The first year's authorization for funds amounted to $1.3 billion, and future expenditures for this program are bound to increase rapidly.

An interesting new proposal made under the Johnson administration was that the federal government should make general financial grants to the states, which they would be free to use for any purpose in support of their general budgets. The theory of this proposal is that the federal income tax in an expanding economy will yield revenues beyond the needs of the federal government, and that the states will otherwise lack the resources to maintain their operations on an effective level.

The widespread use of grants-in-aid calls attention to the fact that there is much more cooperation among the three levels of government than is generally realized. It is highly misleading to talk about federal centralization as though everything the federal government does must be taken away from the states, or as though the only choice to be made in administering a new program is between federal and state activity. In fact, a great many of the functions of our present federal system are performed jointly by two or all three levels of government. Nor is this a twentieth-century development. Early examples of federal-state administrative cooperation occurred in operation of the militia, law enforcement, court practices, conduct of elections, public health measures, pilot laws, and numerous other fields.

Today the list of cooperative federal-state-local activities is almost endless. A dramatic example is in police work. The Federal Bureau of Investigation operates an active training program for state and local police officers, and assists them in crime solution with its fingerprint files and scientific detection laboratories. In the public health field federal, state, and local programs are so intertwined that it may be difficult for an official to know in what capacity he is operating at a particular time. The social security

TABLE 7-2. *Federal Grants, Shared Revenues and Commodities Distributed as Related to State General Expenditure and Total Personal Income (by Percent)*

	Federal Grants-in-Aid, Shared Revenues and Commodities Distributed, Fiscal 1962 (thousands)	Grants, Shared Revenues and Commodities Distributed as Percent of Expenditures	Grants, Shared Revenues and Commodities Distributed as Percent of Personal Income
Alabama	$194,811	35.3	4.0
Alaska	49,289	47.3	7.8
Arizona	84,634	27.3	2.9
Arkansas	110,658	39.1	4.3
California	730,282	19.7	1.6
Colorado	108,644	29.7	2.5
Connecticut	88,195	18.6	1.2
Delaware	15,599	13.5	1.1
Florida	158,666	21.4	1.5
Georgia	194,439	30.4	3.0
Hawaii	40,071	18.4	2.6
Idaho	49,308	37.5	4.0
Illinois	359,619	27.0	1.3
Indiana	134,516	19.7	1.3
Iowa	102,824	23.0	1.7
Kansas	93,864	26.4	2.0
Kentucky	160,631	24.9	3.3
Louisiana	227,614	27.2	4.2
Maine	41,605	25.5	2.3
Maryland	113,860	19.9	1.4
Massachusetts	200,020	24.4	1.5
Michigan	275,906	17.6	1.5
Minnesota	141,631	22.3	1.9
Mississippi	120,797	31.9	4.4
Missouri	223,761	36.6	2.3
Montana	56,048	40.2	4.2
Nebraska	61,191	32.9	2.0
Nevada	28,545	30.8	3.2
New Hampshire	32,273	33.7	2.4
New Jersey	169,675	24.6	1.0
New Mexico	72,959	30.0	4.1
New York	548,354	17.9	1.1
North Carolina	166,414	22.3	2.2
North Dakota	38,560	28.0	3.9
Ohio	367,039	27.9	1.6
Oklahoma	177,527	35.6	4.0
Oregon	122,330	29.7	3.0
Pennsylvania	359,404	21.7	1.4
Rhode Island	35,123	23.9	1.8
South Carolina	89,832	26.0	2.6
South Dakota	59,436	44.8	4.6
Tennessee	178,071	34.3	3.1
Texas	384,260	27.7	2.0
Utah	57,051	28.3	3.1
Vermont	40,979	41.2	5.5
Virginia	159,018	26.9	2.1
Washington	148,307	19.8	2.1
West Virginia	100,361	31.3	3.2
Wisconsin	126,561	18.3	1.4
Wyoming	51,128	49.4	6.7
Total, all states	7,651,740	24.5	1.9

SOURCE: Adapted from *The Book of the States, 1964-65*, Chicago, Ill., The Council of State Governments, pp. 298-299.

TABLE 7–3. *How States Rank in Federal Grants Received*

The redistributive effect of federal grants is shown by dividing each state's share of total grants (Column 1) by its share of the 1963 federal tax burden (Column 2), yielding a "benefit-to-burden" ratio or index (Column 3) according to which 34 states (and the District of Columbia) received *relatively* more in grants than they paid in taxes, while 16 states received *relatively* less. States are ranked according to this index.

Rank		(1) Federal Grants Received (by Percent)	(2) Federal Taxes Paid (by Percent)	(3) Ratio of Benefit-to-Burden (1) ÷ (2)
1.	Alaska	.57	.12	4.75
2.	Wyoming	.65	.16	4.06
3.	North Dakota	.71	.19	3.73
4.	South Dakota	.68	.22	3.09
5.	Mississippi	1.46	.48	3.04
6.	Montana	.77	.27	2.85
7.	Arkansas	1.33	.47	2.82
8.	New Mexico	.99	.36	2.75
9.	Idaho	.63	.26	2.42
10.	Louisiana	2.65	1.16	2.28
11.	Oklahoma	2.09	.94	2.22
12.	Utah	.83	.39	2.12
13.	Vermont	.35	.17	2.05
14.	Alabama	1.98	.98	2.02
15.	Tennessee	2.30	1.21	1.90
16.	Kentucky	1.85	1.04	1.77
17.	Georgia	2.30	1.36	1.69
18.	Oregon	1.51	.91	1.65
19.	Hawaii	.60	.37	1.62
20.	South Carolina	1.04	.64	1.62
21.	Arizona	.98	.65	1.50
22.	West Virginia	1.01	.68	1.48
23.	Colorado	1.49	1.01	1.47
24.	D.C.	.98	.69	1.42
25.	Nebraska	.91	.67	1.35
26.	Maine	.55	.41	1.34
27.	Nevada	.31	.23	1.34
28.	North Carolina	1.91	1.47	1.29
29.	Washington	1.88	1.58	1.18
30.	Kansas	1.16	1.00	1.16
31.	Minnesota	1.94	1.68	1.15
32.	Texas	5.01	4.37	1.14
33.	Missouri	2.46	2.31	1.06
34.	Iowa	1.29	1.23	1.04
35.	Virginia	1.87	1.79	1.04
36.	New Hampshire	.32	.34	0.94
37.	Rhode Island	.47	.50	0.94
38.	Florida	2.31	2.48	0.93
39.	California	9.08	11.23	0.80
40.	Wisconsin	1.69	2.09	0.80
41.	Massachusetts	2.79	3.57	0.78
42.	Michigan	3.36	4.39	0.76
43.	Maryland	1.45	1.97	0.73
44.	Indiana	1.68	2.33	0.72
45.	Pennsylvania	4.78	6.55	0.72
46.	Ohio	4.03	5.64	0.71
47.	Illinois	4.36	7.04	0.61
48.	Delaware	.29	.50	0.58
49.	New York	7.12	13.39	0.53
50.	Connecticut	1.11	2.21	0.50
51.	New Jersey	1.94	4.30	0.45

SOURCE: Adapted from *Congress and the Nation, 1945–1964*, Washington, D.C., Congressional Quarterly Service, 1965, p. 1387.

system, Selective Service, the National Guard—these and many other examples of cooperative federalism demonstrate how the levels of government work together.

The federal government has even experimented with a regional approach to problems that concern more than one state but not the entire country. A notable example is the Tennessee Valley Authority, established by Congress in 1933 to develop the resources of the Tennessee River basin. The TVA is headed by an independent three-man board based in the area and entirely outside the Washington bureaucracy, and the organization has worked unusually closely with the states on the problems of the region. In 1965 Congress authorized a $1.1 billion program for development of the economically depressed Appalachian Mountain region, covering West Virginia and parts of ten other states.

⚕ THE FUTURE OF THE STATES

While many gloomy predictions are heard that the states are threatened with a complete loss of function and are heading for extinction, nothing could be further from the truth. For all their troubles, the states continue to be active, essential, and in many respects, successful partners in American federalism.

For one thing, the American party system is still completely based on the states. No movement for centralizing control over either major party has had the slightest success. The national parties are merely federations of state and local parties, which join every four years, more or less loosely, to elect a President, and then go their separate ways for another four years. So long as the power bases of the state parties remain untouched, so long as the states have equal representation in the Senate, so long as the members of the House must live in the districts they represent and rely on local support to get elected, the political foundation of the states will be impregnable.

Actually, the comparative figures on public employment and public expenditures suggest that the role of the states is increasing, not decreasing. The great increase in the number of public employees since World War II has been at the state and local level, not the national. Federal employees in 1965 numbered 2.6 million, 100,000 fewer than in 1946, whereas during the same period state and local government employees increased from 3.3 million to 8 million. The states accounted for over 2 million of the 1965 total.

This great increase in state and local employment has been the result of the population explosion and the physical and social problems stemming from urbanization and suburbanization. Between 1957 and 1965, increases of the following magnitude occurred in specific categories of state and local employment: highways, 24 percent; police, 30 percent; public health and hospitals, 41 percent; schools, 60 percent; and public welfare, 62 percent.

The data on governmental expenditures show the same situation. Excluding the costs of wars and war-induced obligations, which are inevitably national, and considering only direct domestic expenditures, the federal share of such expenditures actually declined from 1938 to 1962, whereas both the state and local shares increased. Judged by comparative expenditures, the principal federal centralization which occurred was in the 1930s, when the federal government under the New Deal emerged into the modern era considerably in advance of the states.

The states, it seems clear, are not obsolescent. Though they have their problems, they will survive, for they have an essential role to play in American federalism. They are valuable laboratories in which new kinds of legislation can be tested, and new administrative techniques devised. They retain the loyalties of the great majority of their citizens. The reapportionment of state legislatures in accordance with the principle of one man, one vote that the Supreme Court ordered in 1964 was resented in some quarters, but its effect can only be to strengthen state government by making state legislatures more representative and more sensitive to the problems of their urban areas. The states will continue to require massive federal financial support. But vigorous and dynamic state governments are needed to relieve the centralizing pressures on Washington and to provide healthy balance in the federal system.

CHAPTER 8

LAW AND THE COURTS

Article III of the Constitution begins: "The judicial power of the United States, shall be vested in one supreme court, and in such inferior courts as the Congress may from time to time ordain and establish." The Constitution does not attempt to define "judicial power" any more than it defines "legislative powers" in Article I or "the executive power" in Article II. When we are forced to try to distinguish among these three basic governmental powers, we usually fall back on generalities such as that the legislature makes the laws, the executive enforces the laws, and the courts apply the laws in settling disputes. Inadequate and even misleading as these characterizations may be, we can get considerable insight into the judicial function by focusing on the two concepts: that of law and of disputes.

❧ LAW

In the broadest sense, a law is a norm for conduct, backed up by some form of sanction so that adherence to that norm can be compelled, or failure to conform can be punished. Law embodies the agreements that a political society has made about how life in that community is to be lived. Law is a method for promoting whatever values a community wishes to achieve—monogamy, protection of property, assurance of personal safety, clean streets, equal treatment of all races, abatement of nuisances, enforcement of contracts.

The Purpose of Law

The purpose of law is to bring some measure of order, of predictability, of "settledness" into what would otherwise be the chaos of community living. It gives protection to property "lawfully" acquired and "lawfully" used. It ensures that individuals will have certain rights, which are guaranteed by rules laid down in advance. In a "lawless" community, persons must protect their own lives and property. But law takes over the task of protection by forbidding acts which are socially disapproved, and punishing those acts when they are committed.

Sources and Classifications of Law

There are many sources of law, and many ways of classifying law. There are the *moral codes* of the great religions which, while usually not directly enforced by governmental sanction, nevertheless profoundly influence the secular legal standards of nations. There is *natural law*, a body of fundamental principles which may be drawn either from divine sources or from rationally developed standards of right and wrong, and which are presumed to have an authority superior to that of any man-made law. Our concern here, however, is with what may be called *positive law*—that is, law commanded and enforced by the political authority of the state.

American positive law, strongly influenced by its English background, has four main sources—*common law, equity, constitutions,* and *statutes.*

Common Law

The common law was a creation of English judges in centuries of deciding disputes after the Norman Conquest. Operating without written legal codes or statutes, they made their decisions on the basis of custom or common sense or prejudice or personal codes of ethics or conceptions of what would best serve the interest of the king, the nobles, the church, or the nation. Once a decision had been made, there was a tendency to decide subsequent cases involving the same problem in the same way. Thus arose the rule of *stare decisis*, meaning "adhere to the decisions" or "let the decided cases stand." The general principles of law established in this way came to be called the common law because, in contrast to the law or custom of particular localities, it was "common" to the whole of England. The common law comprised the wisdom and experience of many generations of judges and laid down many important principles protective of individual rights of person and property.

Equity

Over the years, however, the common law tended to become rigid, both in its principles and its remedies. Writs (court orders) were developed for certain specific purposes, and if a litigant needed relief that could not be supplied by one of those writs, the common law courts could not help him. Basically the remedy they were prepared to supply was money damages to compensate for a wrong. They were unable to prevent or abate the wrong itself. If Smith was threatening to cut down trees belonging to Jones, Jones could do nothing at common law except wait until the trees were cut down and then sue Smith for the value of the trees. But what Jones really needed was some legal method of preventing Smith from destroying the trees.

In such situations, where the regular courts were unable to sit, suitors began to appeal to a member of the King's Council, called the Chancellor. Gradually the Chancellor's office, the Chancery, took on the status of a court with its own body of law, known as *equity*, and its own remedies, principally the writ of *injunction*. The function of this writ was typically to prevent, or enjoin, action from being taken. Thus an equity court, in a dispute over the ownership of trees, could enjoin action by both parties to the dispute until the matter of ownership was settled.

The English common law judges resented the rise of the competitive equity courts, and for a long time there was hostility between the two sets of judicial institutions. But eventually the two systems of jurisprudence were correlated, and in the United States equity jurisdiction was merged into that of the regular courts.

Constitutions and Statutes

In contrast to these two forms of judge-made law are two varieties of "legislative" law—constitutions and statutes. Judge-made law is *inductive*; on the basis of a number of individual decisions a general rule is constructed. Legislative law is *deductive*; a general principle is stated by a constitutional convention or a legislature and then is given meaning as it is applied in deciding a series of individual controversies.

The special problems of constitutions as sources of law have already been noted. Constitutions tend to state very general principles, and they are hard to amend, so they require or permit great latitude in interpretation. Statutes are typically more limited in their scope and language; they aim to solve particular problems or lay down rules covering defined situations. Nevertheless, statutes also require interpretation when they are applied.

During the past century judge-made law proved increasingly unable to deal with the problems of an industrialized society. Legislatures responded to the challenge with an enormous output of regulatory and social welfare legislation. Just as the common law courts initially resisted the rise of equity, so judges in the United States initially resented statute law replacing the standards of the common law, and they restricted the impact of the new legislation by narrow and hostile interpretation. But this was a tactic which could not long prevail. Today statutes are by far the most substantial source of the law which American courts apply.

⚹ THE COURTS

Disputes and the Courts

In primitive societies an individual who is wronged resorts to personal vengeance and retribution. A civilized society socializes this do-it-yourself kind of law enforcement and sets up courts with coercive power to rectify private wrongs. This socialization extends to the furnishing of public prosecuting officers who take on the responsibility of bringing suit against wrongdoers under the criminal law, thus relieving the victim of the necessity of seeing that some punishment comes to lawbreakers.

Initially English courts could offer redress only against unlawful private action. They could not undertake to grant relief against wrongs committed by the king or his officers. In fact, the law assumed that the king could do no wrong—that is, he was not legally accountable for his acts. But the idea of the rule of law is a persistent one, and hard to limit. The great English judge, Lord Coke, in 1615 invented the writ of *mandamus* (Latin for "we order") so that the jurisdiction of the courts would be wide enough to cover both public and private wrongs. The equity writ of injunction was also available for use in the control of public officers. American courts have inherited these same responsibilities and the same instruments for enforcing the law against public and private lawbreakers.

Both the police and the courts are law enforcement agencies, but they are quite dissimilar in their operations and functions. The police endeavor to promote obedience to law and to prevent lawbreaking by active programs of patrolling, public information, collecting of information, and surveillance. When crimes have been committed, they are responsible for solving them and arresting the guilty parties. But of course they have no right to make the final determination of guilt or to punish. That power is reserved to the courts.

Judges, unlike the police, cannot undertake law enforcement activities on their own initiative. They begin to function only when "a case" is filed.

in court, either by a private citizen with a dispute over (for example) money or property or marital status, or by a public official bringing a civil or criminal suit against an individual accused of law violation. Of course many cases filed in court are never tried. Litigation is expensive and time consuming, and there is much pressure to settle civil suits out of court. The threat of a court proceeding may be enough to lead disputants to compromise their claims.

Article III of the Constitution limits the federal courts to dealing with "cases" and "controversies." What are the characteristics of a case or controversy?

First, there must be two parties with interests adverse to each other, so that each side will be fully motivated to bring out all the facts supporting its claims. The court does no independent research on the facts of the case (though it may take "judicial notice" of facts that are so well known as to be matters of common knowledge). It relies on the self-interest of the parties to ensure that the case will be fully presented. In a collusive or friendly suit, where the parties have the same interests, the court is unlikely to be given a full view of the facts.

Second, the party bringing the suit must have a substantial legal interest at stake. He must be able to claim that one of his legal rights has been invaded or denied. This must be a right which he possesses personally, deriving from common law or constitutional or statutory provisions, a legal claim which gives him "standing to sue" and obliges the court to hear his complaint.

Third, the dispute must arise out of a real set of facts; it cannot be a mere hypothetical or feigned controversy. The federal courts do not exist to settle points of law in the abstract or to give advisory opinions. They apply the law only when necessary to resolve an actual dispute between real people.

Fourth, the case must be one in which there can be an enforceable determination of the rights of the parties. The courts will not waste their time with complaints about situations that could not be remedied by powers of relief available to them.

The parties in a legal proceeding are usually represented by counsel. In all criminal prosecutions, whether federal or state, the Supreme Court has ruled that counsel must be supplied to any defendant who cannot himself afford to hire a lawyer (*Gideon* v. *Wainwright* [1963]). Under the supervision of the judge, counsel for the opposing parties attempt to establish through the testimony of witnesses and the presentation of evidence, facts which will support the position of their client, and by cross-examination of witnesses of the opposing side to discredit or rebut testimony damaging to their own case.

There is a right to trial by jury in all criminal and some civil proceedings. The jury, under appropriate instructions from the judge, finds the facts and renders a verdict on the facts. The judge determines questions of law and, in cases tried without a jury, also makes the findings of fact.

Judicial Organization: The Dual Court System

The judicial function is performed in the United States under rather complex and confusing organizational arrangements. There is a complete system of state courts in each state, from the lowest trial courts to a state supreme court. But superimposed thereon is another complete system of federal courts, which draw their jurisdiction from the federal Constitution. (See Figure 8-1.) The relations of these two sets of courts, whose jurisdiction is to a certain extent overlapping, have created numerous problems.

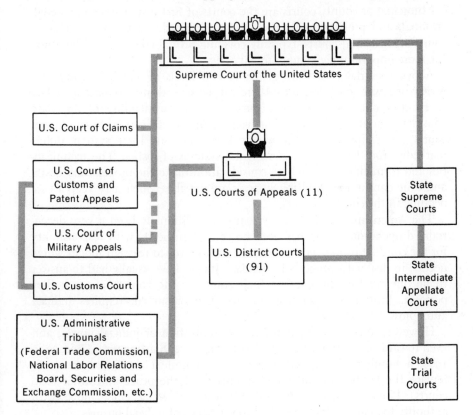

FIGURE 8-1. Organization of the Judicial System of the United States.

State Courts. The American pattern of judicial organization has been strongly localistic. When the country was sparsely settled and methods of communication and transportation were primitive, courts needed to be close to be convenient. The result was the widespread adoption of the justice-of-the-peace system to provide courts on a neighborhood basis. At the next higher level, courts tended to be established with reference to the distance a man could travel in a day on horseback. These local courts and judicial districts, once set up, proved very difficult to modify.

State courts are organized in hierarchies, often with overlapping jurisdiction. Justices of the peace or other part-time magistrates, where they still exist, constitute the lowest level of trial court. They typically are authorized to grant small money judgments, and as criminal courts to try minor offenses. They are not courts of record (that is, their proceedings are not recorded), and if their decisions are appealed, a new trial must be held in the next highest court.

Municipal or county courts are the courts of first instance for most civil, criminal, and probate (wills and estates) proceedings. Circuit or district courts are also trial courts, typically covering several counties and handling the more important civil and criminal cases.

Above the trial courts are generally two levels of appellate courts for review of lower court decisions; there will be several intermediate appellate courts and one state supreme court. The easy availability of appellate consideration and the tremendous volume of appeals carried to the higher courts are characteristics in which the American legal system differs markedly from English and continental systems of justice. The technicalities and formalities of appellate consideration make the process very costly and time consuming. Multiple appeals are possible which may keep a case pending in the courts for years.

The American state judicial system has traditionally been a very decentralized operation. There has been no central authority with responsibility for the conduct of judicial business, or with power to reassign judges where needed to deal with congested calendars. Judges have usually had to answer to no one for the efficiency of their courts or the volume of work they perform. Judicial independence, it has been assumed, requires judicial autonomy.

However, some movement toward centralization of judicial power, and even toward unification of courts, has taken place. Starting with Chicago in 1906, a number of large cities have set up unified municipal courts to replace the haphazard collection of justices of the peace and other local courts. These unified courts are administered by a chief judge with authority to assign judges according to the needs of judicial business.

At the state level New Jersey took the lead in 1948 by setting up a completely integrated judicial system, with all judges except those on the state supreme court subject to interchange and assignment by the chief justice of the supreme court. A number of other states have followed suit, at least to the extent of setting up an office of judicial administration or administrative chief judge. Much remains to be done to bring effective administrative direction and unification to state judicial hierarchies, but the trends are definitely in that direction.

Federal Courts. The federal courts are organized in a three-level hierarchy. The district courts, one or more of which is located in every state and in the District of Columbia, are the trial courts of the federal system. There are 91 district courts, with more than 300 district judges. Trials are held in the district courts before a single judge, except that, when the constitutionality of a federal statute is questioned, and in certain other situations, three judges must sit in the trial of a case. Juries are frequently employed, in both civil and criminal cases.

Appeals from the district courts go to the federal courts of appeals. The 50 states are divided into ten judicial circuits, with an appeals court for each circuit, plus an additional appeals court for the District of Columbia. (See Figure 8–2.) There are some 80 judges for these courts, and appeals are usually heard by a panel of three judges. The courts of appeals also review orders of certain administrative agencies, such as the Federal Trade Commission and the National Labor Relations Board.

At the apex of the federal judicial hierarchy stands the U.S. Supreme Court. Created directly by the Constitution, the Supreme Court is primarily an appellate court, but the Constitution does define two categories of cases which can be heard in the Courts' *original jurisdiction*, that is, without prior consideration by any other court. These are cases in which a state is a party, and those affecting ambassadors, public ministers, and consuls. However, the Court generally does not accept a suit invoking its original jurisdiction unless it feels that there is a compelling reason of public policy for doing so.

All the remaining business of the Supreme Court comes to it in its *appellate jurisdiction*, which it exercises, as the Constitution says, "with such exceptions, and under such regulations as the Congress shall make." The number of cases filed with the Supreme Court every year (over 2,000) is so great that of necessity it can consider and decide only a small proportion. It is true that Congress has provided for an *appeal* as of right to the Supreme Court in certain classes of cases—for example, where a state court has upheld a state law against a claim that it violates the federal Constitution. In theory the Supreme Court is obligated to accept all such appeals, but in fact it dismisses many of them on the ground that they do not present a substantial federal question.

In all other cases review is sought from the Supreme Court by filing with

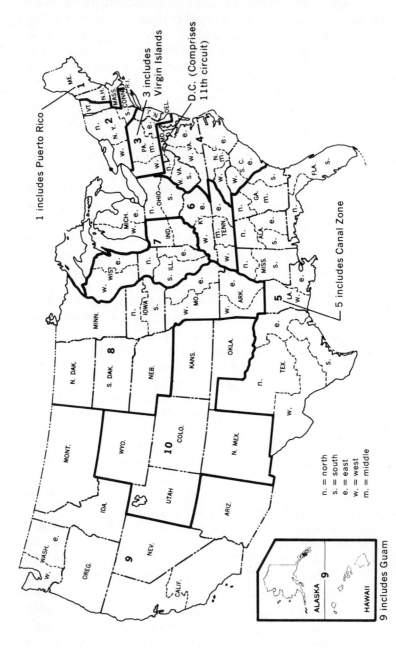

FIGURE 8–2. Federal Judicial Districts and Circuits. The numerals indicate the courts of appeals areas. The heavy lines show the jurisdictional boundaries of each circuit. The broken lines show the district court areas in states having several districts.

1 includes Puerto Rico

3 includes Virgin Islands

D.C. (Comprises 11th circuit)

5 includes Canal Zone

9 includes Guam

n. = north
s. = south
e. = east
w. = west
m. = middle

ALASKA 9

HAWAII

the court a petition for writ of *certiorari* (Latin for "to make more certain"). Granting of this writ is completely at the discretion of the Court, and in fact less than 10 percent of the petitions are usually granted. The effect of the writ, if granted, is to direct the lower court to send up the record in the case for review. Petitions for certiorari are examined by all members of the Court, and are granted if four justices vote in the affirmative. Usually no reason is given when petitions are denied, but in general the Court accepts only cases which present substantial issues of law or policy.

Relations of Federal and State Courts

The Constitutional Convention created the Supreme Court, but left to Congress the decision whether there should be a system of lower federal courts. In the First Congress the Anti-Federalists argued that one federal court (that is, the Supreme Court) was enough, and that the responsibility of enforcing federal law should be mainly entrusted to the existing state courts. But this view was defeated, and the Judiciary Act of 1789 provided for a complete set of federal trial and appellate courts. This was a decision of tremendous consequences for the strength of the central government. If state courts alone had been charged with the responsibility of trying cases involving federal law, they could hardly have been expected to be generous in their interpretations of federal power, and the Supreme Court as the sole federal court would have faced a hopeless task in trying to correct the errors of fifty state supreme courts.

The jurisdiction of the federal courts is defined by Article III on two different bases: (a) subject matter, and (b) nature of the parties involved. The subject matter classifications are:

1. *All cases in law and equity arising under the Constitution;*
2. *All cases in law and equity arising under the laws of the United States;*
3. *All cases in law and equity arising under treaties made under the authority of the United States; and*
4. *All cases of admiralty and maritime jurisdiction.*[1]

Any case falling in these four fields can be brought in the federal courts, regardless of who the parties to the controversy may be.

Issues arising under the first three of these headings are referred to generally as "federal questions." A plaintiff seeking to bring a case in the federal courts on one of these grounds must set forth on the face of his complaint a substantial claim as to the federal question involved, showing

[1] This provision was included in the Constitution to promote uniform regulation of commerce.

that an interpretation or application of the Constitution or a federal statute or treaty is essential to judicial decision of his case.

The second basis for federal court jurisdiction is in terms of the parties involved. Article III extends federal jurisdiction to:

1. *Controversies to which the United States is a party;*
2. *Controversies between two or more states;*
3. *Controversies between a state and citizens of another state;*
4. *Controversies between citizens of different states;*
5. *Controversies between a state, or the citizens thereof, and foreign states, citizens, or subjects; and*
6. *All cases affecting ambassadors, other public ministers, and consuls.*

Cases involving these classes of parties can be brought in the federal courts, regardless of the subject matter of their controversy.

Of these six classes, the first and the fourth are by far the most important in the generation of litigation. The United States enters federal courts as a party plaintiff in a great number of civil and criminal suits every year. The government can also be brought into federal court as a defendant in situations where it has waived its sovereign immunity and consented to be sued. If the government is not liable to suit, it may be possible to sue officials acting for the government, particularly if they are alleged to be going beyond their authority under an unconstitutional statute.

Suits in the fourth category, between citizens of different states, are commonly referred to as *diversity of citizenship* cases. The original purpose of opening the federal courts to these cases was to provide a neutral forum for the determination of such disputes, because the state courts might be biased in favor of their own citizens and against "foreigners" from other states. Today there is less likelihood of such bias, and many persons have urged the abolition of this class of federal jurisdiction, which imposes a very great burden on the federal courts. In 1958 Congress undertook to reduce the number of diversity suits by limiting them to disputes involving more than $10,000.

The fact that a legal dispute meets the test of federal jurisdiction does not mean that it must be filed in a federal court. It is true that Congress has given the federal courts exclusive jurisdiction in some areas, notably in federal criminal, admiralty, patent, and bankruptcy cases. But in all other areas the state and federal courts enjoy *concurrent* jurisdiction over Article III cases, and the plaintiff can choose whether he wishes to file his suit in a state or a federal court. Where such a suit is filed in a state court, however, the defendant can, if he prefers, by appropriate and timely action have the case transferred to a federal court for trial.

Where state courts do try cases involving the application of federal law, they are bound by the *supremacy clause* of the Constitution. Article VI, after making the Constitution, laws, and treaties of the United States "the supreme law of the land," continues: "And the judges in every state shall be bound thereby, anything in the Constitution or laws of any state to the contrary notwithstanding."

The U.S. Supreme Court is the final appellate tribunal for both the federal and the state courts. Any decision of a state supreme court which involves a substantial federal question (that is, application of the Constitution or the validity of federal laws or treaties) is subject to review by the Supreme Court. This power was not established without some resistance, however. Initially many states could not reconcile themselves to the idea that their supreme courts could be checked by any higher authority, and there were some historic confrontations on this issue.[2]

Challenges to the power of the Supreme Court over state courts have been repeated occasionally during crisis periods, most recently after the Supreme Court's decision in *Brown* v. *Board of Education* (1954) holding racial segregation in the public schools unconstitutional. Several southern states adopted statutes of interposition or nullification, purporting to release the courts of their states from obedience to the *Brown* decision. In *Cooper* v. *Aaron* (1958) the Supreme Court was faced with the claim by the governor and legislature of Arkansas that they were not bound by the *Brown* holding. In rejecting this claim, the Supreme Court pointed out that "the principle that the federal judiciary is supreme in the exposition of the law of the Constitution" had been established as early as 1803 in the great case of *Marbury* v. *Madison,* and that this principle "has ever since been respected by this Court and the Country as a permanent and indispensable feature of our constitutional system."

Even when the authority of the Supreme Court is fully recognized, there are numerous opportunities for conflict between the two systems of courts—state and federal. In general, neither state nor federal courts may interfere with each other's proceedings or judgments by issuing writs of injunction. However, federal courts enjoin state officials from enforcing unconstitutional state statutes, and can also issue the writ of habeas corpus to test the constitutionality of state court convictions for violations of state criminal laws.

Where conflicts arise between federal and state courts, the federal courts have the superior power position. For example, in the fall of 1964 the legislature of New York adopted four alternative plans for redistricting the state legislature, hoping that the courts would find at least one of them constitutional. However, all were declared in violation of the state constitution by the state courts. But the federal district court in New York,

---

[2] The principal Supreme Court decision was *Martin* v. *Hunter's Lessee* (1816).

which also had jurisdiction of a suit concerned with the districting of the New York legislature, ordered an election to be held in the fall of 1965 on the basis of one of the four plans that it found least objectionable. The New York supreme court then ordered cancellation of this election because it was to be held on the basis of a plan declared unconstitutional under state law. Thus challenged, the federal district court immediately issued an injunction against any interference with the election. The New York secretary of state decided that he must obey the federal court order and proceeded with arrangements for the election.

Selection and Status of Judges

Judges are selected by two principal methods. One is the pattern which prevails on the European continent and generally in the countries with the French civil law tradition. There the judiciary is a distinct professional career, separate from the practice of law. Young men intending to become judges take a special set of examinations after their law training is completed. The successful candidates become career civil servants in the ministry of justice. They are assigned first to minor positions, and then by the process of promotion they may rise to the more important posts in the judicial hierarchy.

This system guarantees judges who are able and well trained. On the other hand, it leads to bureaucratization of the judiciary and some limitation on judicial independence, since advancement depends upon pleasing one's superiors in the ministry.

By contrast, the Anglo-American pattern is to select judges from the practicing bar. There is no special training or internship for judges in England or America. In both countries it is assumed that men who have achieved distinction or recognition in the practice of law will have the qualities needed to be a good judge. The two countries differ, however, in that all English judges are appointed, whereas in the United States both appointment and election are used.

The Federal Judiciary. All federal judges are appointed by the President, with Senate confirmation. The process is frankly and entirely a political one. With few exceptions the President limits his choice to members of his own party. During the eight most recent presidential terms, from 1933 to 1965, there were only two exceptions to this rule in Supreme Court appointments—President Truman's appointment of Republican Harold Burton, with whom he had been associated in the Senate, and President Eisenhower's naming of Democrat William Brennan, Jr. In the lower federal courts, during the present century over 90 percent of all judicial appointments have gone to members of the President's party. Specifically, President Eisenhower appointed 158 Republicans and 12 Democrats to the district and appeals courts. President Kennedy named 113 Democrats, 10 Republicans, and 1 liberal.[3]

District judgeships are filled primarily on the recommendation of the state party organization and the senator from the state, if there is one of the President's party. The nominees thus suggested are given a thorough check by the Department of Justice, the FBI, and the American Bar Association's committee on the federal judiciary. Of the 228 district judges appointed by Presidents Eisenhower and Kennedy, 124 (54 percent) were practicing lawyers at the time of appointment, while 53 (23 percent) were state judges, 24 (11 percent) were lawyers in government positions, and 20 (9 percent) held other government or political positions.

For appointments to the federal courts of appeals, again the recommendations of the appropriate senators and state party organizations are of primary importance. Since the appellate circuits cover more than one state, vacancies must be allocated to the various states on some basis satisfactory to the party organizations. Positions on the courts of appeals are much more likely to go to men with previous judicial experience than in the case of district judgeships. Among the 66 courts of appeals judges named by Presidents Eisenhower and Kennedy, 35 (53 percent) were either state or federal district judges at the time of their appointment, while 17 (26 percent) were in private law practice, 7 (11 percent) were government lawyers, and 3 (5 percent) were in other government positions.

Vacancies on the Supreme Court present major policy problems for the President. He receives suggestions from many sources, and particularly from his Attorney General, but he makes his own decisions, and often he has his own ideas on the subject, either as to specific candidates, or as to the qualifications he wants. Presidents are usually interested in the political viewpoint of a possible nominee, and the line he is likely to take in deciding cases. Of course, predicting the future decisions of a man to be placed in a lifetime position on the bench is risky business. Theodore Roosevelt was unusually careful in picking men who could be expected to vote right on the big issues, and he was very angry when Justice Oliver Wendell Holmes, soon after his appointment to the Court, disappointed his expectations in an important antitrust case. President Taft felt that the most significant thing he had done during his administration was to

[3] These and subsequent data are taken from Sheldon Goldman, "Characteristics of Eisenhower and Kennedy Appointees to the Lower Federal Courts," *Western Political Quarterly*, Vol. 18 (1965), pp. 755–762.

appoint six justices who shared his conservative views. "And I have said to them," Taft chuckled to newspapermen when his term was expiring, "Damn you, if any of you die, I'll disown you."

The Senate must confirm all judicial appointees, and this gives senators their control over judicial selection. If the President should name a man who is opposed by the senator from the state concerned, the senator has only to notify the Senate that the nominee is "personally obnoxious" to him, and the rule of "senatorial courtesy" will ensure his rejection. Occasionally the Senate declines to confirm a nominee for the lower federal courts on other grounds. In 1965 an interesting case occurred when Senate concern about the fitness of a nominee sponsored by Senator Edward Kennedy led to withdrawal of the nomination.

For Supreme Court appointments the Senate confirmation stage affords an opportunity to consider the political views of the nominee. Perhaps the most famous instance was the violent opposition to Louis D. Brandeis when he was nominated by President Wilson in 1916. Brandeis was attacked by conservatives because of his alleged lack of "judicial temperament," but won confirmation on a straight party vote. Charles Evans Hughes was also unsuccessfully opposed in 1931, some liberal Democrats and agrarian Republicans picturing him as a "corporation lawyer." The nomination of John J. Parker was actually defeated in 1930—the only instance of this sort in the present century—because of allegations that he was antilabor and anti-Negro. His distinguished career on the federal court of appeals subsequently made it clear that he would have been more liberal than the justice who got the position, Owen J. Roberts.

Although judicial appointments go almost entirely to members of the party in power, the character of American parties guarantees that the appointees will represent various shades of opinion on political issues. Neither the Democrats nor the Republicans are ideologically pure parties; Democratic appointees are not all liberals and Republican appointees are not all conservatives. President Eisenhower's four Republican appointees to the Court could be categorized as one liberal (Warren), two moderates (Harlan and Stewart), and one conservative (Whittaker). He also appointed Brennan, a liberal Democrat. On the other hand, President Kennedy, under pressure from conservative southern Democratic senators, named several segregationist judges in southern states.

It is sometimes argued that only men with previous judicial experience should be given federal judicial appointments. In fact, this already happens in many instances. Almost 30 percent of the district judges named by Presidents Eisenhower and Kennedy had had prior judicial experience, while 60 percent of their appointees to the courts of appeals were former judges. But it would be unfortunate for presidential freedom of selection to be limited by a judicial experience requirement, particularly at the Supreme Court level. The major questions with which the Supreme Court deals require political judgment more than technical proficiency in private law. If judicial experience had been a prerequisite in the past, most of the greatest Supreme Court justices would have been ineligible for appointment, including Marshall, Story, Taney, Miller, Bradley, Hughes (at his first appointment), Brandeis, Stone, Black, Frankfurter, and Warren. In spite of all criticisms, it should be recognized that the present system of appointing judges has resulted in a federal bench of high prestige and unquestioned honesty.

The State Judiciary. In the states, judges are both appointed and elected. The practice of electing judges was one of the bequests of Jacksonian democracy to the American system of government. Prior to 1832 only one state elected all its judges, but every state admitted to the Union from 1846 to 1959 provided for election of most or all of its judiciary. In spite of great current dissatisfaction with elective judges, in 1960 two thirds of the states still used election as a principal means of choosing their judges.

One problem with elections is that voters generally can have no basis for judgment as to the relative merits of judicial candidates. Usually all they can do is to vote blindly for the candidates put up by their party; this means that the judges are not really elected at all, but are in effect appointed by the party leaders who make up the ticket. The local bar associations usually poll their members on the relative merits of the candidates, and although even these results are not necessarily reliable, they are about all the independent voter has to go on in making his decisions.

Another objection is that judges who have to win elections are necessarily obligated to their political sponsors and supporters. Where judges run on a party ticket, they are expected to make a substantial contribution to the party campaign fund. Where judges are elected for a long term, the assessment may be one year's salary or more. Many lawyers who would make excellent judges refuse to submit themselves to the pressures, costs, and obligations of a political campaign.

Appointment of state and local judges by responsible political executives—governors or mayors—has generally come to be regarded as preferable to election. Although there is no guarantee that undesirable political influences will not be at work, the responsibility for bad selections is focused directly upon the official who made the appointment.

The bar associations have urged that they be given greater responsibility for the selection of judges, on the plea that this would take the process "out of politics." They propose that commissions of lawyers and other responsible citizens be set up to name men who would be suitable for judicial positions, and that the appointments would then have to be made from among these nominees. This idea was incorporated into a combined system of appointment and election adopted by Missouri in 1940. Under this plan, commissions are established to nominate judges at the various court levels. For the higher courts the commission consists of seven members: the chief justice of the state supreme court, three lawyers elected by the state bar association, and three persons appointed by the governor, none of whom can hold public office or be a party official. This commission nominates three men for each judicial vacancy, and the governor must appoint one of the three.

The elective feature of the Missouri Plan is that at the next election after the new judge has served for one year, his name is put on the ballot and the voters are asked to decide whether he should be retained in office. If the vote is favorable, he then serves out a specified term of years, and is eligible for re-election. A number of states have now adopted the Missouri Plan or some variation of it.

Tenure of Judges. Judicial independence and guaranteed tenure are among the most important criteria of how democratic a political system is. The independence of judges was established in England by 1689, long before broadly based political democracy had developed, and this was an important feature of the American heritage.

Recent experience in the Union of South Africa and Ghana has shown how the disintegration of a democratic system is signaled by attacks on the independence of the judges. Conversely, the courage and stature achieved by judges in West Germany and India after World War II constituted hopeful signs of the political maturity of those countries. If a general liberalizing political trend should continue in the Russian system, one of the most positive indications should be the development of greater independence in the judiciary.

In the United States, most state judges serve for specified terms of years, but federal judges hold office during "good behavior," which in practice means life tenure. They can be removed only by impeachment; only four federal judges have ever been impeached. Because some federal judges have insisted on remaining in office after their mental powers had failed, Congress has encouraged the withdrawal of older judges by setting up attractive retirement arrangements. Life tenure, plus the constitutional provision that a judge's compensation may not be reduced while he is in office, constitute a strong guarantee of independence for the federal judiciary.

CHAPTER 9

THE SUPREME COURT
AND JUDICIAL REVIEW

The Supreme Court was created directly by Article III of the Constitution. Compared with the other two major institutions deriving directly from the Constitution, the Presidency and the Congress, the Supreme Court might have appeared to rank as a very junior partner in the governmental enterprise. Alexander Hamilton made a prospective estimate of the Court's potentialities to this effect in No. 78 of *The Federalist*:

> *The Executive not only dispenses the honors, but holds the sword of the community. The legislature not only commands the purse, but prescribes the rules by which the duties and rights of every citizen are to be regulated. The judiciary, on the contrary, has no influence over either the sword or the purse; no direction either of the strength or of the wealth of the society; and can take no active resolution whatever. It may truly be said to have neither FORCE nor WILL, but merely judgment....*

However, equipped only with the power of judgment, the Supreme Court has so utilized its moral and intellectual resources as to earn respect and authority equal to, if not in some respects greater than, that of the executive and Congress. It has come to occupy the position of official constitutional interpreter, philosopher, and umpire of the federal system. In its application of the Bill of Rights it has functioned as the nation's principal forum for consideration of the operating conditions of a free society. Sometimes it has appeared to be a brake on progress. Its decisions have often been unpopular. But always the Court has been entitled to respect for its efforts to reason its way through to an understanding of the principles and intentions of the Constitution.

⚞ THE SUPREME COURT

Membership of the Court

The Supreme Court is composed of the Chief Justice and eight Associate Justices. Initially the Court had six members, but Congress later increased its size five times and reduced it twice. Since 1869 the membership of the Court has been stabilized at nine. In 1937 President Roosevelt's "Court-packing" plan would have authorized appointment of one new justice for each sitting justice who remained on the Court after reaching the age of 70, up to a maximum of 15. The plan failed to win general support, and was defeated in Congress.

How the Court Operates

The Supreme Court meets annually in October, and remains in session, though with periodic recesses, until the following June. The Court formerly sat in the old Senate chamber in the basement of the Capitol. By contrast, the Court now occupies a palace of white marble so elegant that when it was completed in 1935, one justice suggested that the members of the Court ought to ride in on elephants.

The Court sits for four hours daily, Monday through Thursday, in an impressive high-ceilinged courtroom, with enormous pillars and red velvet hangings. The visitors' benches are nearly always occupied, for aside from special occasions like presidential inaugurations, this is the most impressive show in Washington. The justices meet in the robing room behind the drapes shortly before 10:00 o'clock. By tradition, each justice shakes hands with every one of his colleagues. Promptly at 10 the court crier raps his gavel, spectators rise, the velvet curtains part, and the justices come through to take their places behind the long bench as the crier chants:

> The Honorable, the Chief Justice and Associate Justices of the Supreme Court of the United States! Oyez, Oyez, Oyez! All persons having business before the Honorable the Supreme Court of the United States are admonished to draw near and give their attention, for the Court is now sitting. God save the United States and this Honorable Court.

During the 16 hours of its public sessions each week the Court hears oral arguments in scheduled cases and announces its decisions. For every case on the docket, the record of the proceedings in the lower courts and briefs stating the arguments for each side are filed with the Court. The justices study these materials before the case comes up for hearing. The time for oral argument is strictly limited; except in the most important cases, counsel for each side will have one hour or less to address the Court. When time is up, a red light goes on at the lectern where the counsel stands facing the Court, and he must stop immediately. Legend has it that Chief Justice Hughes once called time on a lawyer in the middle of the word *if*.

Counsel seldom have an opportunity to make their arguments without interruption. The justices frequently break in with questions, comments, or requests for clarification. From the questions asked, it is often possible to predict how the individual justices are likely to vote in deciding the case. Probably their minds are not often changed by the oral argument, but it does give counsel a chance to emphasize what they feel are the main points for their side. In the old days, when the Court was less hurried and cases could run on for days, lawyers often delivered long and impassioned orations to the Court. But now oral argument is calm and businesslike, with occasional flashes of wit or asperity in the repartee.

On Friday of each week when the Court has been sitting, the justices meet in conference to decide the cases heard that week. The proceedings are absolutely secret. No one other than the justices is present. The Chief Justice presents each case that is ready for decision, making such comments and offering such opinions as he chooses. Discussion then goes down the table, each Associate Justice speaking in order of seniority. When all have given their views on the case, voting begins. Now the order is reversed, the most junior justice voting first and the Chief Justice last. This procedure maximizes the role of the Chief Justice, because he has the chance to formulate the issues initially, and to break the tie if the Associate Justices are evenly divided.

Following the vote, the Chief Justice assigns the writing of the "opinion of the Court" to himself or one of his colleagues. However, if there is a divided vote and the Chief Justice is in the minority, then the senior Associate Justice who voted in the majority controls the assigning of the majority opinion. Drafts of opinions are circulated among the justices, and the author may revise the final opinion on the basis of comments by his colleagues. Justice Holmes once commented that this process amounted to taking out all the raisins and leaving the dough.

Concurring and Dissenting Opinions

In the early years of the Court it was customary for all justices to give their opinions seriatim in a case, and there was no single opinion "of the

Court." However, when Marshall became Chief Justice, he wrote the opinion for the Court in almost all important cases. Justices were still free to write *concurring* or *dissenting* opinions, but there was a tendency for them to go along with the Court unless their disagreement was sharp. The fame of Justices Holmes and Brandeis as dissenters was based on the quality rather than the quantity of their dissents. Beginning about 1935, however, dissenting opinions became more frequent, and for the past two decades or so, nonunanimous opinions have far outnumbered unanimous opinions.

It is often argued that dissenting opinions detract from the effectiveness of a Court decision. When the Court divides 5 to 4 on a constitutional issue it is obvious that the Constitution is not "self-applying," that the law is not entirely clear and plain, but rather is open to differences of opinion.

"You're sure you've got it straight? Five ham and Swiss on rye *with* mustard, and four ham and Swiss on rye *without* mustard." Drawing by Robt. Day;
© 1963 The New Yorker Magazine, Inc.

On the European continent, judges are not allowed to express dissent. There the court must speak with one voice, and disagreements on a bench of judges are concealed behind the veil of official unanimity.

The Anglo-American common law tradition has given more freedom to the judge, however. The possibility of registering dissents from the bench encourages and protects the independence of the judiciary, and permits the development or maturing of alternative legal theories which, though held by a minority today, may in time prove their greater vitality and become the accepted view. Chief Justice Hughes made this point:

> A dissent in a court of last resort is an appeal to the brooding spirit of the law, to the intelligence of a future day, when a later decision may possibly correct the error into which the dissenting judge believes the court to have been betrayed.[1]

Concurring opinions are written by justices who agree with the result reached by the Court but not entirely with the reasons given in the opinion for the Court. The number of concurring opinions written by Supreme Court justices has also increased markedly in the past three decades. As an example of judicial output, during the 1964 term of the Court, Justice Harlan wrote 10 opinions for the Court, 11 concurring opinions, and 16 dissenting opinions.

Until 1965 decisions were normally announced only on Mondays, but now they may be given at the beginning of any session. The justice who wrote the opinion for the Court summarizes the main points of his opinion in a few minutes. Dissenters may also outline their disagreement if they wish. No advance notice is ever given as to when a decision in a particular case will be ready, and the opinions are distributed to newsmen only after the decision has been announced from the bench. In the printing operation, each opinion is divided among several printers so that they will not know what case they are working on.

The Role of the Chief Justice

The role of the Chief Justice is extremely important, for he can develop a substantial position of leadership on the Court. His formal authority stems primarily from his role as presiding officer at Court sessions and in the conference, and from his power to assign the writing of opinions. But he is also the symbolic head of the Court, and if he has the skill and tact and prestige of a Hughes or a Warren, he can use his position to guide the decision-making process toward consensus and to keep discussion from bogging down in quibbling and personalities.

[1] *The Supreme Court of the United States* (New York: Columbia University Press, 1928), p. 68.

The most famous Chief Justice in Supreme Court history was John Marshall, the third Chief Justice (1801–1835), who used his influence so effectively that he must rate as one of the founders of the Republic. For 35 years he dominated the Court and was second only to Washington in determining the initial character of the federal constitutional system.

It was Marshall, who in *Marbury* v. *Madison* (1803) successfully asserted the Court's power to declare acts of Congress unconstitutional. It was Marshall, who in *McCulloch* v. *Maryland* (1819) established the authority of Congress to achieve national purposes under the "necessary and proper" clause and other broad grants of constitutional power. It was Marshall, who in *Gibbons* v. *Ogden* (1824) first construed the commerce clause and struck down state regulations which conflicted with national interests. It was Marshall, who in *Dartmouth College* v. *Woodward* (1819) expanded the coverage of the contract clause and encouraged the judicial protection of vested rights which was to be a theme of continuing significance throughout much of the Court's history. It was Marshall, who by his courage, his convictions, and his intellectual vigor raised the Supreme Court from a third-rate status to a position of equality with the President and Congress.

⅍ THE POWER OF JUDICIAL REVIEW

The Supreme Court's power of judicial review falls into two categories. First is the power to declare acts of Congress unconstitutional, which Marshall claimed for his Court in *Marbury* v. *Madison* in 1803, and which also came to include the power to review the constitutionality of presidential actions. Second, the Supreme Court has the power of judicial review over the constitutionality of state legislation. (See Figure 9–1.)

Review of Congressional and Presidential Acts

It is primarily the authority of the Supreme Court to judge the constitutionality of congressional and presidential acts that has made it the world's most powerful judicial institution. Surprisingly enough, this power was not specifically authorized by the Constitution, and this has led to endless arguments as to whether the framers intended the Supreme Court to have such authority.

Two of the most eminent constitutional scholars, Charles A. Beard and Edward S. Corwin, have concluded that they did, but for different reasons. Beard contended that 25 of the 55 members of the Convention expressed their approval of some form of judicial control of legislation. Corwin drew

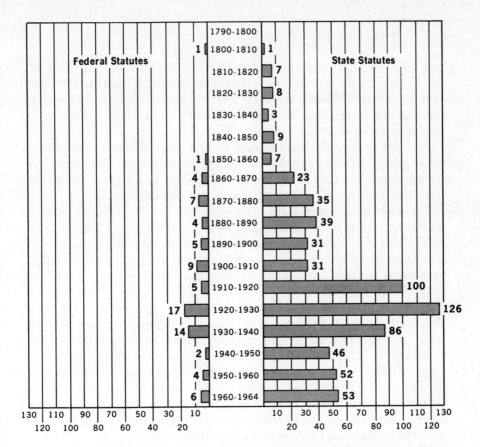

Federal Statutes		State Statutes
	1790-1800	
1	1800-1810	1
	1810-1820	7
	1820-1830	8
	1830-1840	3
	1840-1850	9
1	1850-1860	7
4	1860-1870	23
7	1870-1880	35
4	1880-1890	39
5	1890-1900	31
9	1900-1910	31
5	1910-1920	100
17	1920-1930	126
14	1930-1940	86
2	1940-1950	46
4	1950-1960	52
6	1960-1964	53

FIGURE 9-1. Supreme Court Decisions Holding Federal and State Statutes Unconstitutional, 1790–1964, by Decades. (Based on data from *The Constitution of the United States of America: Analysis and Interpretation*, Senate Doc. No. 39, 88th Cong., 1964, pp. 1387–1522.)

his evidence from the popular desire at the time to check the abuses of legislative power, and the logic of the kind of government that the Constitution created. More recently Judge Learned Hand has denied that judicial review was a "logical deduction from the structure of the Constitution," but it was, he agrees, "a practical condition upon its successful operation."[2]

The case of *Marbury* v. *Madison* arose in the following way. Marbury had been appointed a justice of the peace for the District of Columbia by President Adams before he went out of office in 1801. The commission was signed, and sealed, but the Federalist Secretary of State, none other than John Marshall, failed to deliver it on March 3. When President Jefferson

[2] Learned Hand, *The Bill of Rights* (Cambridge, Mass.: Harvard University Press, 1958), p. 15.

took office on March 4, he instructed Madison, the new Secretary of State, not to deliver the commission. Marbury then filed a petition for mandamus to compel Madison to deliver the commission. He filed it directly in the Supreme Court, thus invoking the Court's original jurisdiction under the Judiciary Act of 1789.

As Chief Justice,[3] Marshall seemed to have two alternatives—the Court could grant Marbury's petition or deny it. It seemed that Marshall was bound to lose the contest for power and prestige to his great antagonist, Jefferson, whichever he did. If the writ was issued, Madison, with Jefferson's support, would refuse to obey it, and the Court would have no practicable means of compelling him to do so. If the Court refused relief to Marbury, it would be admitting officially that it was powerless to control the executive. In either event, the judiciary and the Federalists would be humiliated and the triumph of Jefferson and the Democrats would be complete and obvious.

In this situation Marshall's decision was a masterful stroke. He ruled that the Judiciary Act of 1789, in authorizing the Supreme Court to grant writs of mandamus in its original jurisdiction, had unconstitutionally extended the Court's original jurisdiction beyond that provided for in the Constitution. The Court consequently declined to issue the writ, leaving Madison and Jefferson with nothing to deny or resist. But the writ was refused, not because the Court lacked power to give relief against executive officers, but because the Court asserted and exercised the much greater power of finding an act of Congress unconstitutional.

There were three steps in Marshall's argument as to why the Court should not enforce a statute that was contrary to the Constitution. First, the written Constitution is the fundamental law, superior to common and statute law, and subject to change only by the amending process. Second, the powers of the various branches of government are limited by the terms of the Constitution, and their actions are valid only when in conformity with those limits. Third, the judges have sworn to enforce the provisions of the Constitution as the superior law, and are therefore obligated to refuse to enforce any legislative act or executive order which is in conflict therewith.

This is a powerful argument, but it is not without its flaws. The President, also, takes an oath to support the Constitution. Does this give him the right to refuse to enforce a duly adopted act of Congress that he regards as unconstitutional? Marshall's argument rested on a basic, but unstated, assumption that the Supreme Court is better qualified to

---

[3] Marshall had been appointed Chief Justice by President Adams on January 20, 1801, and had been confirmed by the Senate on January 27, so he was Chief Justice and Secretary of State at the same time for more than a month.

interpret and to apply the Constitution than the other two branches. This is not necessarily true, but it has now been accepted as true for over a century and a half, and it constitutes a fundamental premise of judicial review.

Clearly there are many advantages in having one authoritative interpreter of the Constitution. It was proposed as an alternative to Marshall's position that each of the three branches should be the final interpreter of its own powers under the Constitution. Actually this principle would have been adequate to sustain the *Marbury* decision, for the Court was there passing on the issue of its own original jurisdiction. But recognition of three final interpreters of the Constitution would have led to great confusion in the many constitutional areas where there is no strict separation of functions.

The importance of this role as sole authoritative interpreter of the Constitution was not simply that it justified the Court in declaring acts of Congress unconstitutional. It enabled the Court to exert a continuing influence on the development of the nation, and to operate as a major participant in American political life. The Court could check not only Congress, but also the President, as was demonstrated when it undertook to declare President Roosevelt's New Deal unconstitutional by declaring its most important legislative enactments invalid in 1935 and 1936. It could also serve as umpire in disputes between the President and Congress, such as occurred in 1952 when President Truman seized the steel mills to prevent a strike that might have cut off needed munitions for American troops in Korea. The Court appreciated the President's motives, but concluded that Congress had made clear its intention that the President should not possess the seizure power, and so ordered the mills returned to their owners.

Review of the Constitutionality of State Legislation

The second aspect of judicial review is the Supreme Court's authority to pass on the constitutionality of state legislation. As explained in the preceding chapter, any decision of a state supreme court involving a "federal question," that is, one arising under the Constitution, laws, or treaties of the United States, can be appealed to the Supreme Court. Only in this way can constitutional provisions be given uniform interpretation and effective application throughout the United States.

The Supreme Court is also by this power over state legislation enabled to serve as umpire in disputes between the nation and the states. Every federal system requires an allocation of authority between the two levels of government, and conflicts over the division of functions are bound to occur. To make the federal system work, there need to be rules for deciding such contests, and an umpire to apply these rules. In all the successful federal systems—Canada, Australia, Switzerland, West Germany, as well as the United States—the highest court performs this function.

As umpire of the American federal system, the Supreme Court must necessarily have power to declare invalid any state legislation or other state action that infringes on the constitutional authority of the central government or the other states in the federal Union. Unlike the power to declare acts of Congress unconstitutional, there was no doubt that the Constitution intended the Supreme Court to review *state* legislation. The First Congress passed the Judiciary Act of 1789 in which it made provision for the Supreme Court to hear cases where it was alleged that state laws conflicted with the federal Constitution. By 1964 the Court had held unconstitutional, provisions of 656 state constitutions or statutes and 84 municipal ordinances. Justice Holmes thought it was more important for the Supreme Court to have the power to review state legislation than acts of Congress. He said:

> I do not think the United States would come to an end if we lost our power to declare an act of Congress void. I do think the Union would be imperilled if we could not make that declaration as to the laws of the several States. For one in my place sees how often a local policy prevails with those who are not trained to national views. . . . [4]

In its role as umpire of the federal system the Supreme Court enforces three kinds of restrictions on the states.

First, it measures state legislation by constitutional standards. The original Constitution contained certain provisions aimed directly at the states. Article I, Section 10, is entirely devoted to prohibitions on the states; for example, they are forbidden to "pass any bill of attainder, *ex post facto* law, or law impairing the obligation of contracts."

But by far the most important constitutional limitations on the states are those imposed by the Fourteenth Amendment, which forbids the states to deprive any person of life, liberty, or property without due process of law, or to deny to any person within its jurisdiction the equal protection of the laws. It was on the basis of the equal protection clause that the Supreme Court declared racial segregation in the public schools unconstitutional in 1954. Ten years later the Court ruled that equal protection of the laws required that the members in both houses of the state legislatures must be elected from districts roughly equal in population.

[4] "Law and the Court," *Speeches* (Boston: Little, Brown, 1934), p. 102.

The concept of due process has had even greater importance over the years. Soon after adoption of the Fourteenth Amendment, the due process clause was expanded by a conservative Supreme Court into an instrument for striking down state legislation regulating business and economic life. For example, a New York state 10-hour law for bakers was declared unconstitutional as a denial of due process in 1905 by the Court, on the ground that it deprived employers and employees of the freedom to contract with each other. The Court finally abandoned this concept, called *substantive due process*, in the 1930s.

By that time, however, the Court had laid the foundation for a new expansion of the due process clause in a different direction. In the 1925 case of *Gitlow* v. *New York*, the Court held that the "liberty" protected against infringement by the due process clause of the Fourteenth Amendment included the "freedom" of speech, press, and assembly protected against congressional denial by the First Amendment. Later the Court added the religion clauses of the First Amendment and most of the limitations on criminal trials covered in the Fourth through the Eighth Amendments to the list of rights which it would guarantee against state action. As a result, the Court has been projected into some of the most controversial problems of its entire history as it has sought to determine the constitutionality of Bible reading and prayers in the public schools, civil rights demonstrations, failure to provide counsel to defendants in state criminal proceedings, and hundreds of other dilemmas.

Second, as umpire of the federal system the Court must determine whether state legislation conflicts with congressional legislation. While state statutes may infringe on acts of Congress in many areas, the most persistent problems arise in connection with the regulation of commerce. The first case the Supreme Court ever decided involving the commerce clause, *Gibbons* v. *Ogden* (1824), concerned New York's effort to establish a monopoly on steamboat transportation in its waters. The states do possess considerable power to regulate commerce, but they must yield if Congress has "pre-empted" the field by adopting regulations of its own. Since Congress often does not make clear in passing a regulatory statute whether it intends to exclude state regulation, the Supreme Court may have to use its own judgment as to whether enforcement of the state law would be harmful to national interests. In this field the Supreme Court has performed one of its most important functions by protecting the national economy from discriminatory local regulation and taxation.

Third, the Supreme Court acts as arbiter of the federal system by settling disputes among the states. Litigation between states is handled by the Court in its original jurisdiction. Typical subjects of controversy are boundaries, water rights, and monetary obligations. In 1963 the Supreme Court finally settled in favor of Arizona a 40-year contest between that state and California over water rights in the Colorado River and its tributaries (*Arizona* v. *California* [1963]).

Interpretation of Congressional Statutes

The Supreme Court has another function which, though less dramatic than reviewing the constitutionality of acts of Congress or serving as umpire of the federal system, is very important in its total impact. This is the function of interpreting congressional legislation as it is applied in lawsuits decided by the Court. Whereas the Court held only 9 acts of Congress unconstitutional between 1937 and 1964, during that period it determined the meaning of federal statutes in hundreds of cases, and often the results were more significant than those occasioned by a ruling of unconstitutionality. For example, in 1957 the Court practically knocked out the Smith Act as a weapon for jailing Communists by the interpretation it gave to the word "organize" in that statute (*Yates* v. *United States* [1957]). Again in 1958 the Court held that the State Department could not refuse to grant passports to Communists, because the statute on which it was relying did not grant that authority (*Kent* v. *Dulles* [1958]).

For businessmen, the most important function of the Supreme Court is to interpret federal regulatory, tax, and labor relations statutes. These statutes are generally interpreted initially by the government agencies charged with their enforcement. Thus tax laws are interpreted by the Bureau of Internal Revenue and the Tax Court. The Taft-Hartley Act is interpreted by the National Labor Relations Board. The Natural Gas Act is interpreted by the Federal Power Commission. But eventually the more important or controversial of these interpretations will come up to the Supreme Court, and although it will give great weight to the views of the agency administering the statute, it has full power to make its own interpretation.

Of course it is always possible for anyone who dislikes the Supreme Court's interpretation of a statute to appeal to Congress and ask that the offending interpretation be reversed by new language. In 1958, after the passport decision, the State Department and President Eisenhower made an urgent appeal to Congress for statutory authorization to deny passports to Communists, but Congress, taking a less serious view of the problem, failed to act and hence let the Supreme Court interpretation stand. On many occasions business interests have gone to Congress seeking reversal of unfavorable Supreme Court statutory interpretations, and often these efforts are successful. One example concerned the Supreme Court ruling that the DuPont Company must dispose of its vast holdings of General Motors stock. Congress passed a law confirming that the stock must be disposed of, but under more favorable conditions than the Court had imposed.

Controversy over Judicial Review

The Supreme Court, because of the great powers it wields, has been the center of controversy throughout much of our history. The first interest with which the Court collided was that of the states. In the case of *Chisholm* v. *Georgia* (1793), the Court ruled that a state could be sued in the federal courts by a citizen of another state. The irate states quickly secured adoption of the Eleventh Amendment to nullify the effect of this decision.

President Jefferson was the Court's next antagonist. After his election in 1800, the Supreme Court under Chief Justice Marshall remained a Federalist bastion. The Democratic Congress under Jefferson shut the Court down for 14 months by postponing its next term, and brought impeachment proceedings, which failed, against the most virulent of the Federalist justices. Nevertheless, as we have already seen, Chief Justice Marshall was able to maintain control of the Court and to use it to establish strong nationalist doctrines.

Roger B. Taney, Marshall's successor as Chief Justice (1835–1864), brought the spirit of Jacksonian democracy onto the Court. States' rights and state police power were emphasized more, and central authority less. Like Marshall, Taney was concerned to protect property rights, but now it was agrarian property—land and slaves—rather than the commercial-creditor classes that won judicial favor. In fact, the Taney Court's attachment to the slave interest proved its undoing. The *Dred Scott* decision in 1857, which helped to bring on the Civil War, plunged the reputation of the Court to its lowest depths. Congress showed its contempt for the Court after this decision by changing its size three times in seven years for obvious political purposes. When the Court seemed about to declare some of the Civil War Reconstruction legislation unconstitutional in 1868, Congress withdrew the Court's jurisdiction to decide the case (*Ex parte McCardle*).

Gradually the Court regained its prestige by re-establishing contact with the dominant trends of the times. The post-Civil War period was one of raw and rapid industrial expansion. A continent was being harnessed with railroads, resources were being exploited, great fortunes built. At first the Court was reluctant to legitimize the economic freedom that business enterprise demanded. But the pressures were too strong to resist. The due process clause of the Fourteenth Amendment was readily available to protect the property and status of business corporations. The high point in the Court's dedication to the new capitalism came in 1895, with three important decisions. One declared the income tax unconstitutional (*Pollock* v. *Farmers' Loan and Trust Company*). Another held that the sugar trust did not violate the Sherman Act (*United States* v. *E. C. Knight Company*). The third upheld the jailing of the Socialist leader, Eugene V. Debs, for violating a court injunction against a strike by the railway workers' union (*Debs* v. *United States*).

A property-oriented, laissez-faire philosophy continued to dominate the Court for the first third of the twentieth century, symbolized by such decisions as *Lochner* v. *New York* (1905), holding the 10-hour law for bakers unconstitutional, and *Adkins* v. *Children's Hospital* (1923), striking down a minimum wage law for women. But there was now a strong minority position on the Court, stated first by Justice Oliver Wendell Holmes, who was appointed by President Theodore Roosevelt in 1903, and later joined by Justice Louis Brandeis (1916) and Harland F. Stone (1925). They opposed the doctrinaire conservatism of the Court majority, arguing for the right of legislatures to seek new social and economic remedies for the evils of an industrial civilization.

Throughout this entire period the Supreme Court was under severe attack by the liberal and agrarian forces in the nation. The Republican Progressive Party under Theodore Roosevelt and the La Follette third party in 1924 were strongly anti-Court. But the Court was supported by all the substantial conservative and propertied interests. The Supreme Court was "their" branch of the government—"guardian of the dollar, defender of private property, enemy of spoliation, sheet anchor of the Republic." It was the Court they relied upon to protect their interests against undependable Congresses and liberal Presidents like Woodrow Wilson and the two Roosevelts. Various proposals during this period to limit the power of the Court to declare acts of Congress unconstitutional uniformly failed.

The conservative Court was finally defeated by the depression of the 1930s and President Roosevelt's legislative program for restoring prosperity. Ignoring the changed temper and economic conditions in the country, the Court in 1935 and 1936 declared unconstitutional a whole series of New Deal recovery statutes, usually by votes of 5 to 4 or 6 to 3. After his overwhelming electoral triumph in 1936, President Roosevelt, who had had no Court vacancies to fill during his first term, undertook to eliminate the judicial barrier to his program by the Court-packing plan already mentioned.

In spite of President Roosevelt's popularity and the general public conviction that the Court was wrong, the addition of members to the

Court was widely regarded as an unjustified assault on the principle of judicial independence, and was defeated in Congress. However, in several key cases in the spring of 1937 the Court upheld New Deal legislation by a vote of 5 to 4, and the crisis was over. This was "the switch in time that saved nine." Then vacancies began to open up, and within a few years the Court was composed almost entirely of Roosevelt appointees.

These men were all economic liberals, and the Roosevelt Court quickly legitimized state and federal use of regulatory powers, particularly the commerce power. It supported labor's right to organize under the Wagner Act. It abandoned "substantive due process" as a limitation on state regulatory power. And it was at this point that a remarkable change began to occur in the relation of the Court to American politics and in the character of its public support. Up to 1937 the Court had generally lagged behind the dominant opinion trends in the country. It had been a brake on the social mechanism. Robert H. Jackson, before he became a member of the Court in 1941, wrote that "never in its entire history can the Supreme Court be said to have been for a single hour representative of anything except the relatively conservative forces of its day."[5]

As a result of the Roosevelt revolution this situation changed, and the Court became more liberal than Congress. No longer interested in trying to prevent Congress or the states from adopting economic reform legislation, the Court turned its attention very largely to the area of civil liberties and political rights. The important problems for the new Court were those involving the Bill of Rights—issues of censorship, limits on freedom of speech, press, and assembly, compulsory flag salutes in the public schools, abusive use of congressional investigatory power, jailing of Communists under the Smith Act, and denial of due process in criminal prosecutions.

The new Court, which had been unanimous in withdrawing from supervision over economic legislation, soon split wide open over the nature of its obligation to protect civil liberties. The beginning of what came to be a classic confrontation on the Court occurred as Justice Hugo Black and Felix Frankfurter, representing the contrasting positions of judicial activism and judicial restraint, disagreed on the extent to which the Court should intervene to support libertarian values.

Justice Black believed that the First Amendment freedoms occupied a *preferred position* among American liberties, for a free and democratic society could not exist without freedom of speech, press, and assembly. He tended to be an absolutist in the enforcement of these freedoms. When the First Amendment says "Congress shall make no law," he insisted that it meant what it said, and the Court should not hesitate to strike down

[5] Robert H. Jackson, *The Struggle for Judicial Supremacy* (New York: Knopf, 1941), p. 187.

legislation that violated this command. The Court's highest responsibility was to protect these basic freedoms against infringement from whatever source for all persons or groups, no matter how unpopular they might be. He said: "Our Constitution assumes that the common sense of the people and their attachment to our country will enable them, after free discussion, to withstand ideas that are wrong" (*Barenblatt* v. *United States* [1959]).

Justice Frankfurter on the other hand was reluctant to declare legislation unconstitutional, for he regarded legislatures as the most democratic branch of government and thought judges should defer to their decisions except in highly unusual cases. He insisted that the values of liberty and freedom were not absolutes; they must be balanced against the claims of authority and order. Justice Jackson put this view very well in a case where both he and Frankfurter dissented:

> The choice is not between order and liberty. It is between liberty with order and anarchy without either. There is danger that, if the Court does not temper its doctrinaire logic with a little practical wisdom, it will convert the constitutional Bill of Rights into a suicide pact.[6]

In 1954, however, both the activists and the apostles of judicial self-restraint united in the Court's portentous ruling that racial segregation in the public schools was unconstitutional, and this unanimity was maintained in every subsequent decision touching on the segregation issue. The *Brown* decision (*Brown* v. *Board of Education of Topeka*) inaugurated a period of almost continual controversy for the Court. Opposition to the ruling was in part reasoned, but also in part vituperative in the extreme, calling into question not only the ability but also the motives and the patriotism of the justices.

The bitterness of these attacks was self-defeating, and the Court's opponents could expect no general success in the country at large on the issue of maintaining segregation. But in 1957 the Court raised up additional enemies when it handed down decisions limiting the investigation of Communists by congressional committees and their criminal prosecution under the Smith Act (*Watkins* v. *United States; Yates* v. *United States*).

In some quarters these decisions were regarded as a threat to national security, and in the 1958 session of Congress these forces joined with opponents of the *Brown* decision to support a number of measures intended to "curb" the Court. With one minor exception, all of these bills were defeated, some very narrowly. Court-curbing was no more acceptable in 1958 than Court-packing had been in 1937.

These episodes demonstrate the respect that is so widely felt for the

---

[6] *Terminiello* v. *Chicago* (1949).

judicial institution in the United States. Many who opposed the conservatism of the Court in 1937 and who thought it was mistaken in its national security decisions in 1957, nonetheless concluded it would be an even greater mistake to try to correct judicial errors by means that would weaken the judicial institution.

The Court's next difficulties were caused by two 1962 decisions. In the first, *Engel* v. *Vitale*, the Court held that state-required prayer in the public schools was unconstitutional because it amounted to an establishment of religion, a joinder of state and church forbidden by the First Amendment. The following year the Court reached the same conclusion concerning Bible reading and recitation of the Lord's Prayer in public schools (*School District* v. *Schempp* [1963]). These decisions were almost unanimous, only a single justice dissenting in each case.

Again there was an immediate outburst of indignation, and numerous constitutional amendments were introduced in Congress to validate religious exercises in the schools. But as the first emotional flurry passed, the basis for the Court's decision became better understood and the leaders of many, if not indeed a majority, of the religious groups in the country expressed approval of the Court's position. The proposed constitutional amendments to reverse the Court made no progress.

The other famous 1962 decision was *Baker* v. *Carr*, in which the Court asserted that the practices of the states in districting for election to state legislatures were subject to judicial review. Most of the state legislatures in the nation were in fact unrepresentative because of discrimination against populous urban and suburban areas, but up until 1962 the Supreme Court had denied there was any judicial responsibility for correction of these inequalities. But *Baker* v. *Carr* opened up the possibility of appeal to the courts against the "rotten boroughs" in the states.

This decision was generally a popular one, and in almost every state, suits were filed to compel more equitable redistricting. In 1964 the Supreme Court brought the movement to a climax by affirming that the principle of equal population districts—the so-called "one man, one vote" principle—was required by the equal protection clause in both houses of all state legislatures (*Reynolds* v. *Sims*).

Although many suggestions for resistance to the *Baker* v. *Carr* line of decisions were heard, the only effort that came close to success was the proposal by Senator Dirksen of Illinois for a constitutional amendment, which failed by only seven votes to secure the necessary two-thirds majority in the Senate in 1965. The Dirksen amendment would have accepted the Court's standard of equal population districts in one house of bicameral state legislatures, but would permit districting for the other house to take into account factors other than population.

Is Judicial Review Compatible with Democracy?

Throughout its history opponents of the Supreme Court, from Jefferson to the John Birch Society, have complained that it was exercising political power, and that the justices were misusing their judicial authority to make policy decisions which, in a democratic system, belong to the elected branches of the government. Recent actions of the Court, particularly *Brown* v. *Board of Education of Topeka* in 1954 and *Baker* v. *Carr* in 1962, have demonstrated how in fact the judges can seize the leadership in dealing with problems vital to the public welfare. The issue is whether American democracy is stronger or weaker because of the possibility of judicial participation in national policy-making.

The case against a strongly activist Court has been soberly stated by members of the Court itself. During the 1920s and 1930s, when the conservative majority on the Court was declaring liberal legislation unconstitutional, Justice Holmes was constantly telling his colleagues that they must not prevent the enforcement of laws that reasonable men could regard as helpful in solving society's problems. When the Court's interference with the legislative will reached its climax in 1936, Justice Stone warned the Court that "the only check upon our own exercise of power is our own sense of self-restraint," and he added: "For the removal of unwise laws from the statute books appeal lies not to the courts but to the ballot and to the processes of democratic government" (*United States* v. *Butler*).

As the Court of the 1950s and 1960s actively intervened to promote civil and political rights, it heard similar warnings about the dangers of political involvements. Justice Frankfurter questioned the credentials of the Court for making policy judgments: "Courts are not representative bodies. They are not designed to be a good reflex of a democratic society" (*Dennis* v. *United States* [1951]). Justice Harlan, objecting to the Court's getting involved in the "political thicket" of legislative apportionment, protested the "current mistaken view . . . that this Court should 'take the lead' when other branches of the government fail to act." The Supreme Court, he said, is "a judicial body," not "a general haven for reform movements" (*Reynolds* v. *Sims* [1964]).

The opposing view, that an activist Court is not incompatible with democracy, stresses two main considerations. First, the Court, though not elected, is dependent in many ways on the elected branches of the government, and so is not free from popular control. For example, the Court may need help from the executive or legislature to get its decrees enforced. President Jackson is reported to have said, concerning one of the Supreme Court's rulings: "John Marshall has made his decision. Now let him enforce it." The Supreme Court handed down its ruling that racial segregation in the public schools was unconstitutional in 1954, but it was not until Presidents Kennedy and Johnson took an interest in the problem and Congress put on the pressure in the Civil Rights Act of 1964 and the Education Act of 1965 that compliance with the ruling began to be achieved in the more recalcitrant states.

Of course the President's greatest impact on the Court is through the power of appointment. Given a normal rate of turnover on the Court, a President can make its membership representative of current political ideas. If he is unhappy with the trends of decision on the Court, he can let the Court know about it, as President Roosevelt did.

As for the Congress, the senatorial power of confirmation, though employed successfully to defeat a Supreme Court nominee only once during the twentieth century, can at least be the occasion for flashing warnings of legislative displeasure to the Court. Judicial decisions based on statutory interpretation can be appealed to Congress by a request for new legislation. If it ever became sufficiently aroused, the Congress could completely abolish the Court's appellate jurisdiction. In fact, Congress can pass any legislation it likes concerning the Court short of reducing the salaries of sitting justices, taking away its original jurisdiction, or abolishing the Court entirely.

Second, it can be argued that when the Supreme Court's activism takes the form of protecting individual rights against infringement by federal or state governments, it is performing a most valuable democratic function. Perhaps more important than any other feature of the judicial process for democratic theory is its accessibility to individuals and minorities. Executives and legislatures are responsible to mass constituencies. Only large interests and effective pressure groups have the chips to get into the game of politics today.

The courts, however, are open to anyone with a valid case or controversy. America's largest racial minority, even after it had begun to organize through such groups as the NAACP, lacked the political power to secure an effective hearing from a series of Presidents and Congresses. It was only in the courts that its constitutional claims to equal protection could be registered. Even an ignorant convict in a state penitentiary who claims he has been denied due process of law can have his case considered by the Supreme Court by mailing it a handwritten petition.

The American system is admittedly unusual in the degree to which it permits a lifetime judiciary to participate in making basic policy decisions. Even in countries which have followed the American example since World War II by setting up strong supreme courts—particularly India and West Germany—the power to declare legislative acts unconstitutional has been sparingly employed, usually in connection with issues of federal-state relations. In democratic countries generally the tendency is to regard constitutional provisions more as guidelines for legislative acts, statements of fundamental principles of government, rather than as strict rules of law to be authoritatively interpreted and applied by the judiciary. However, the American practice of judicial review has won general acceptance because it has been exercised with considerable responsibility and because it provides an effective method of enforcing constitutional principles and guaranteeing individual rights.

CHAPTER 10

LIBERTY

Liberty has meant widely different things to different people and in different times. In the Declaration of Independence the liberty at issue was freedom from English rule for the American colonies, the liberty that comes with self-government. In 1863, when Lincoln issued the Emancipation Proclamation liberating the slaves in rebellious territory, liberty meant the termination of a legal status of involuntary servitude. In 1936, to the conservative organizers of the Liberty League, liberty meant repeal of the New Deal laws regulating the stock exchanges and promoting the growth of labor unions. To the American Civil Liberties Union (ACLU), liberty means the right to form organizations, to picket, to speak freely, to hold unpopular views.

In every sense in which it is used, however, liberty has a basic connotation of *freedom from control*—whether control by a foreign power, control by a human master, or control by laws or government agencies that are conceived to be unduly restrictive of individual expression or initiative. Liberty is in constant rebellion against authority. Yet it is the great paradox of liberty that it cannot exist except within a framework of authority. A system of unlimited liberty, where anyone is free to do anything he likes at any time, would constitute a condition of anarchy. It would be that "war of each against all" which Hobbes described, a state of nature in which life would be "solitary, poor, nasty, brutish, and short." As the Declaration of Independence goes on to say in the next sentence after its praise of liberty, "governments are instituted among men" precisely with the intent "to secure these rights."

And so the American colonies which rebelled against English authority set up a new government with more authority to tax and to regulate commerce than the English king had exercised. The Negroes who emerged from the Civil War as freedmen needed, and for a long time did not get, the vigorous support of governmental authority to help them emerge from the shadow of bondage. The Liberty Leaguers who objected to the National Labor Relations Act and the National Recovery Act of the New Deal saw nothing wrong with the Old Deal under which federal authority was used to levy protective tariffs and enjoin labor unions from striking or picketing. The ACLU does not want cities to censor motion pictures, but it expects the police to protect the street meetings of unpopular groups.

The tension between liberty and authority, then, is an absolutely necessary one for the existence of men in communities, and the larger the community the greater the tension. The question is never one or the other, but how much of each.

⚒ CONSTITUTIONAL BACKGROUND

Considering the great concern of the founders for liberty, it is surprising that the original Constitution contained so few indications of this interest. The theory of the Constitutional Convention was that traditional American liberties did not need much in the way of specific constitutional protection. The basic concept of limited national government was to be achieved by division of functions, separation of powers, checks and balances, calculated to frustrate any drive toward abuse of power. The drafters of the Constitution relied on the open spaces of the American continent to guarantee escape from confining situations. They saw the boundless resources of the country as insurance of economic opportunity. They conceived that the broad expanse of the republic would encompass such a variety of interests as to make combination into a domineering majority difficult. Thus individual liberty did not need to be planned. It would come automatically as the by-product of a system of economic opportunity, social mobility, and political responsibility.

But when the proposed Constitution went to the states for ratification, it quickly became apparent that the framers' view of civil liberties as needing no special protection was not widely shared. In several of the important states, ratification was secured only on the understanding that amendments protecting individual rights would be immediately added. James Madison took the lead in bringing together the various suggestions for amendments in the First Congress. Twelve were presented to the states and ten were ratified by 1791, constituting what soon came to be known as the Bill of Rights.

Only six of these amendments are of direct importance in our present discussion. The First, justly the most famous, covers freedom of speech, press, assembly, and religion. The Fourth through the Eighth deal primarily with procedural protections in criminal trials, but certain other matters are also covered, such as the prohibition on taking of private property for public use without just compensation.

For the most part the restraints imposed by these amendments are stated in general language. Only two are by their terms applicable to the federal government—the First, which specifically mentions "Congress," and the Seventh, which refers in one clause to "any court of the United States." However, the general understanding was that the amendments were being drafted to impose limitations on the new government set up by the Constitution, and the Supreme Court confirmed this understanding when in *Barron* v. *Baltimore* (1833) it held that the due process clause of the Fifth Amendment did not apply to the states.

This meant that the states were left free, so far as the Federal Constitution was concerned, to deny freedoms protected by the Bill of Rights. But the post-Civil War amendments, and particularly the due process and equal protection clauses of the Fourteenth, brought the states finally within the federal constitutional controls. As for the freedoms of the First Amendment, with which this chapter is particularly concerned, the Supreme Court held in *Gitlow* v. *New York* (1925) that the freedoms of speech and press guaranteed against congressional infringement by the First Amendment were also among the fundamental personal rights and "liberties" protected by the Fourteenth against impairment by the states. In 1940 the Court similarly brought the religion clauses of the First Amendment into effect against the states. Thus the libertarian principles of the First Amendment apply at all levels of American government.

✹ FREEDOM OF EXPRESSION

Apart from voting, there are three principal ways by which citizens in a free community express themselves on public issues.

First, they can talk—talk to their friends, their relatives, their neighbors, even to total strangers. They can talk at meetings, and if they are not invited to be on the platform, they can ask questions from the floor or heckle the speakers.

Second, they can get their views into print. Most people, of course, do not own newspapers, but they can write letters to the editor. They can print up a handbill or leaflet and distribute it on street corners or send it out by mail. A few can even write books.

Third, they can organize or assemble with other like-minded persons and make their views known by carrying signs in a parade, by marching in a picket line around city hall, by signing petitions addressed to the government, or by volunteer work in the office of a propaganda organization or political party.

All three of these types of expression are protected by the First Amendment, which provides that "Congress shall make no law . . . abridging the freedom of speech, or of the press; or the right of the people peaceably to assemble, and to petition the Government for a redress of grievances." (See Figure 10–1.) But in fact the amount of freedom of expression one

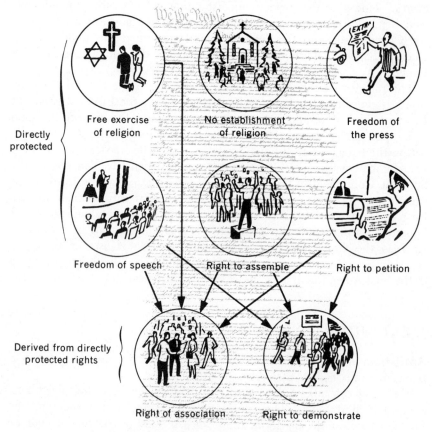

FIGURE 10–1. Rights Protected Under the First Amendment.

has depends a great deal upon the manner of the expression. This is so because, in spite of the flat statement in the First Amendment, there is no absolute right to freedom of expression at all times and in all places.

For example, we are all familiar with situations where speech is abridged or restrained, with common consent. One may not talk freely in a library reading room, or during a church service, or while a court is in session. There are rules of order governing legislative assemblies or public meetings, which restrain people from talking at the same time, or which prevent speech irrelevant to the issue under discussion. Clearly, the extent of one's right to self-expression depends upon what other rights may be competing for consideration. There is a right to speak, but there is also a right to privacy. There is a right to parade in the streets, but there is also a right to use the streets for transportation.

Methods of Restraint on Freedom of Expression

It is also relevant to distinguish the two methods by which government may seek to restrain freedom of expression. One is by legal limitations, imposed in advance, which prohibit or otherwise effectively restrain speaking or publishing or assembling. The other is by legal proceedings to punish persons for speech or publication or assembly that has allegedly violated statutory standards. To put it more simply, this is the difference between *prior restraint* and *subsequent punishment*. It is the difference between officials banning a meeting or silencing a newspaper, and prosecuting individuals for what they have said or done.

Prior restraint is generally regarded as more dangerous to freedom of expression than subsequent punishment. The great vice in censorship is that it throttles the expression of opinion; it prevents communications from ever reaching the marketplace of ideas. Prior restraint is aimed at what *may* be said or done if the meeting is held; it is justified by probabilities; it anticipates that abuses are going to occur. Moreover, prior restraint is dangerous because it is relatively easy to impose. It requires only a decision by the police or some other public official, which can often be taken behind a screen of informality and partial concealment.

In contrast, a system of subsequent punishment does not operate until after the communication has occurred. For whatever it may be worth, the people involved have been able to get their message before the public. If their communication has resulted in a violation of the law, that must be established by a criminal prosecution in which they will have all the safeguards of due process of law. The court will be dealing, not with hypothetical possibilities, but with what actually happened.

"But what happens if we take a licking in the marketplace of ideas?"
Handelsman; in *Saturday Review*, 1966.

✻ FREEDOM OF THE PRESS

Among the three forms of expression described above, print has the
greatest claim to freedom because its social setting makes the likelihood of
conflict with other rights the least. Communication by way of the printed
page is essentially a solitary process. Even in a crowded subway car, the
newspaper readers as readers are isolated from each other. Even those who
are reading the same paper are engaged in no collective experience. The
reader makes no noise; he creates no disturbance; he causes no problems.
Consequently the right to print and to publish is least likely to be limited
by the claims of competing rights. Of course the reader after finishing his
paper may throw it on the ground and be arrested for littering. He may
become so angered by what he reads that he throws a brick at the mayor.
But that is action, and of course unlawful action can be punished. It is the
communication process that is protected by the First Amendment.

Censorship of Print

There can be no censorship of print under the First Amendment. The
federal and state governments cannot prevent a book or newspaper from

being published; they cannot require that publishers secure a license in order to operate; they cannot levy special taxes that discriminate against publishing as compared with other businesses.

The outstanding anticensorship decision of the Supreme Court is *Near v. Minnesota* (1931). A state statute provided that "malicious, scandalous, and defamatory" newspapers could be treated as a public nuisance and enjoined from publication by court order. The Supreme Court by a vote of 5 to 4 held that this was "the essence of censorship." In *Mills* v. *Alabama* (1966) the Supreme Court held unconstitutional a state corrupt practices law prohibiting electioneering on election day under which an editor who published a political editorial in his newspaper on election day had been convicted.

But it is not only newspapers, periodicals, and books that are exempt from censorship. Anyone with a hand printing press is a publisher for the purposes of the First Amendment, with full rights not to be hampered by public officials. Circulation of handbills dealing with public issues cannot be prevented by the police or by city ordinance, the Supreme Court has ruled (*Lovell* v. *Griffin* [1938]).

Obviously it does little good to print if the printed matter cannot be circulated. There are several ways in which that prime medium of circulation, the Post Office, has attempted to use its strategic position to limit the freedom to print. One relates to the granting of second class mailing privileges, which amount to a subsidy, since the rates are much below the cost of service. During both World Wars I and II, various radical or antiwar publications were denied second class privileges. But when the Postmaster General attempted to withdraw second class privileges from *Esquire* magazine on the ground that it was not published "for the public welfare and the public good," the Supreme Court unanimously reversed him in *Hannegan* v. *Esquire* (1946).

Congress has barred certain kinds of material from the mails, including lottery tickets, obscene literature (to be considered shortly), and foreign political propaganda. The Post Office first began to confiscate foreign propaganda about 1940, though it had no statutory authority to do so at that time. In 1962 Congress passed a statute specifically authorizing the Postmaster General to detain "communist political propaganda" and to deliver it only upon the addressee's request. In *Lamont* v. *Postmaster General* (1965) the Supreme Court unanimously declared this statute unconstitutional, holding that to force an addressee to request in writing that his mail be delivered was an abridgment of First Amendment rights.

An aspect of press freedom currently under considerable pressure is the right of the press to print information about pending criminal prosecutions or trials in progress. In England restraints on press comments about criminal trials are very strict; only the barest facts of the case can be published. But the American tradition, with its great reliance on elected judges, has been much more permissive toward outside comment on judicial proceedings, and the Supreme Court has generally accepted this freedom (*Bridges* v. *California* [1941]).

There is, however, currently widespread concern that the right to fair criminal trials is being undermined by the freedom with which police and prosecutors make public, and the communications media circulate, evidence against suspects before their trials are held, thus making the task of securing an unbiased jury very difficult. In *Sheppard* v. *Maxwell* (1966) the Supreme Court reversed the second-degree murder conviction of Dr. Samuel H. Sheppard on the ground that "massive" and "virulent" publicity generated by a Cleveland newspaper had denied him a fair trial. The Court held that the trial judge had permitted a "carnival atmosphere" and even "bedlam" resulting from activity of newsmen in the courtroom, and had failed to isolate the jury from the publicity that attended this notorious prosecution.

There is as yet no consensus on methods of preventing such publicity without interfering with free press rights. It would presumably be unconstitutional for a judge to attempt to prevent prejudicial publicity by ordering a newspaper to curb its publications. But in the *Sheppard* case the Court pointed out that the trial judge could have controlled newsmen in the courtroom, limiting their number, location, and demeanor so that their presence would not disrupt the trial. Also, in view of the systematic misrepresentation of the testimony by the offending newspaper, the judge "should have at least warned the newspapers to check the accuracy of their accounts." Other suggestions made by the Supreme Court were (1) the jurors should have been locked up after the publicity got out of hand, and not been permitted to become press celebrities; (2) witnesses should not have been permitted to make out-of-court statements to the press; (3) counsel and law enforcement officers should have been subject to discipline for revealing prejudicial information to the press. The *Sheppard* ruling seems likely to have a great impact on the conduct of all future criminal trials.

Libel

Libel is the defamation of character by print or other visual presentation such as television. It has long been understood that false and malicious statements about an individual damage him in his legal rights and lay the publisher open to prosecution for libel. Such private defamation suits generally create no substantial First Amendment problems.

Some states have laws for the criminal punishment of libels aimed, not at private individuals, but at groups. Group libel laws are directed at those who make false, abusive, hatemongering attacks on racial, religious, or other groups in our society. Proponents of group libel laws argue that they are needed because the ordinary law of libel will not reach defamers of a group, and that individual members of the group may suffer severely because of defamatory comments about their group. It is noteworthy that England, which had never known racial problems until recent years, in 1965 adopted a Race Relations Act making racial defamation and incitement to race hatred a crime.

In 1952 the Supreme Court upheld the constitutionality of a group libel law in *Beauharnais* v. *Illinois* by a vote of 5 to 4. Beauharnais, who headed an anti-Negro organization, stood on a Chicago street corner and handed out petitions to the city council, asking the use of the police to protect white citizens from the "rapes, robberies, knives, guns and marijuana" of the Negro. The Supreme Court upheld his conviction for violation of the group libel statute, Justice Frankfurter holding that libelous utterances, affecting either private individuals or groups, are not within the scope of "constitutionally protected speech." But Justice Black, dissenting, thought that "no legislature is charged with the duty or vested with the power to decide what public issues Americans can discuss." If the question were brought before the Court again, it seems almost certain that the *Beauharnais* decision would be regarded as a mistake and that group libel laws would be declared unconstitutional, because they punish statements pertaining to social and political issues of public importance. Even if the views are offensive or hateful, the individuals who hold them are entitled to state them, at least so long as public order is not threatened.

The Supreme Court's more recent and more considered position on libel prosecutions was announced in the 1964 case of *New York Times* v. *Sullivan*. Here the problem was not libel of private individuals or groups, but alleged libel of a public official by a newspaper. The *New York Times* had printed as a paid advertisement a criticism of the treatment of Negroes in Montgomery, Alabama. The ad was submitted by reputable persons, but it was later discovered that it contained some factual errors.

The police commissioner of Montgomery, though not mentioned in the ad either by name or specific reference to his office, contended that criticism of the Montgomery "police" constituted libels of him, and an Alabama jury awarded him damages of $500,000. Another commissioner who sued on the basis of the same ad also got a $500,000 judgment, eleven additional libel suits were filed against the *Times* seeking a total of $5,600,000, and five suits asking $1,700,000 were brought at the same time against the Columbia Broadcasting System based on its coverage of Alabama civil rights controversies.

Clearly libel judgments of this magnitude, secured with such ease, could effectively silence all comment or reporting by the communications media in controversial situations. Such a result, the Supreme Court held, would be in conflict with "the principle that debate on public issues should be uninhibited, robust, and wide-open. . . ." At times public discussion "may well include vehement, caustic, and sometimes unpleasantly sharp attacks on government and public officials." Sometimes, the Court granted, there may even be false statements, damaging to official reputations. That is inevitable in free debate, the Court said. But "erroneous statements honestly made" cannot be punished as libel. If critics of official conduct had to guarantee the truth of every factual assertion, and face enormous libel judgments in case they made a mistake, who would run the risk of public comment?

So the Court's conclusion in the *New York Times* case was that a public official cannot recover damages for a defamatory falsehood relating to his official conduct unless he proves that the statement was made with "actual malice"—that is, "with knowledge that it was false or with reckless disregard of whether it was false or not."

Obscenity

Obscenity, like libel, has long been punishable under state laws, and there is also a federal obscenity statute applying to the mails. It was not until 1957 that the Supreme Court gave serious attention to the obscenity problem. Then in *Roth* v. *United States* it upheld laws punishing obscenity on the ground that obscenity was completely outside the area of "constitutionally protected speech." The First Amendment, the Court recognized, extends to "all ideas having even the slightest redeeming social importance—unorthodox ideas, controversial ideas, even ideas hateful to the prevailing climate of opinion." But obscenity, the Court went on, is "utterly without redeeming social importance," and so it does not share in the protection of the First Amendment.

This holding, however, still left the Court with the task of deciding what *was* obscene. In the *Roth* case the Court's test for obscenity was whether "to the average person, applying contemporary community standards, the dominant theme of the material taken as a whole appeals to prurient interest." Later, in *Manual Enterprises* v. *Day* (1962), Justice Harlan added a second test: the material must be "patently offensive," its indecency "self-demonstrating." Then, in *Jacobellis* v. *Ohio* (1964), the Court made its *Roth* rationalization that obscenity was utterly without redeeming social importance into a third test: anything *with* redeeming social importance could not be obscene.

In the 1966 *Fanny Hill* case (*A Book* v. *Attorney General of Massa-*

chusetts) the Court held that a book must fail all three of these tests before it could be regarded legally as obscene. Since the trial court admitted that *Fanny Hill* had "a modicum of social value," it could not be branded obscene. In fact, almost the only class of material likely to be regarded as obscene under these tests is "hard-core pornography." Even that is difficult to define, as Justice Stewart said in the *Jacobellis* case, which concerned a movie, "The Lovers." But, he added, "I know it when I see it, and the motion picture involved in this case is not that."

The Supreme Court, however, departed from its liberal policy on obscenity in *Ginzburg* v. *United States* (1966), where it upheld a criminal conviction and five-year sentence for violation of the federal obscenity law. The Court conceded that the materials published by Ginzburg, standing alone, might not have been obscene under the three original tests, but they now held that the "context" and "setting" in which the publications were presented could be considered as relevant to a determination of obscenity. The Court found that Ginzburg had been engaged in "commercial exploitation of erotica solely for the sake of their prurient appeal" and in the "sordid business of pandering"; consequently these transactions were "sales of illicit merchandise, not sales of constitutionally protected matter."

American limits on obscenity, which formerly were much more strict than in France or England, now tend to be more lenient than in those countries. Under the earlier standards, books that could not be published in the United States, such as James Joyce's *Ulysses*, were published in France. Now the situation has been reversed.

England has had a law for the censorship of stage plays since 1737, under which the Lord Chamberlain forces the removal of passages he considers obscene, sacrilegious, or otherwise offensive. The United States has had motion picture censorship in several states and cities, but in *Freedman* v. *Maryland* (1965) the Supreme Court imposed such strict procedural safeguards on movie censorship systems as to make them practically unworkable. Instead, attention has shifted to the possibility of a compulsory labeling system for movies, such as is used in England, where some films are given a universal license, and others are limited to adults.

❧ FREEDOM OF SPEECH

Speech by its nature is more likely than print to result in a conflict of rights. For speech by definition involves the interaction of at least two persons. Here is the beginning of a community interest in the speech process. Suppose two persons are discussing politics in a private house. The case for any imposition of government control here is as minute as it could possibly be. But that does not mean that there is no case at all. What if the discussion becomes an argument, and voices are raised to the annoyance of the neighbors? Suppose one of the discussants uses offensive language to the other, who resents it and starts a brawl? Suppose a weapon is drawn? At some point along the way a speech situation in which the public had no interest may turn into a matter justifying government intervention—and all this with only two participants.

An increase in the number of discussants or the use of public rather than private facilities multiplies the concerns that might necessitate governmental intervention. A large crowd attending an advertised meeting in a private hall is entitled to a maximum of protection, for the listeners are in voluntary attendance, and anyone who does not like the announced subject or speakers can simply stay away.

But suppose an unpopular group has asked to meet in a public school auditorium. Or suppose this group meets in a public park and persons unsympathetic to them happen by and take offense at what is being said. Or suppose that loudspeakers being used at an outdoor meeting in a public place annoy others by their noise, regardless of the words used. Clearly there is no end to the complications that can arise in a speech situation. Justice Jackson (in *Kunz* v. *New York* [1951]) has well contrasted the social settings of printing and speaking:

> Written words are less apt to incite or provoke mass action than spoken words, speech being the primitive and direct communication with the emotions. Few are the riots caused by publication alone, few are the mobs that have not had their immediate origin in harangue.

Prior Restraint of Speech and Assembly

Censorship of speech is just as bad in principle as censorship of the press, and it is only in unusual situations, where the social setting of the speech is such as to threaten danger to the public order, that controls over speech may be constitutionally imposed. The use of public streets, sidewalks, or parks for speech purposes may of course create traffic problems or the potentiality of disturbances. Consequently municipalities often require some system of advance notification of meetings in public places and the issuance of permits covering speaking there.

Such permit systems have been held constitutional by the Supreme Court, provided they are administered under standards that prevent discrimination or discretion in the granting of applications. If permits are issued to some groups and not to others, this is not only interference with freedom of assembly but also a denial of equal protection of the laws. Thus in *Niemotko* v. *Maryland* (1951) the Court invalidated as arbitrary and discriminatory the refusal of a city council to allow Jehovah's Witnesses to hold a meeting in a public park because the councilmen did not like the sect's views on saluting the flag.

The Supreme Court's insistence on strict standards for permit systems is illustrated by *Kunz* v. *New York* (1951). Here the Court reversed the action of New York City in removing a bigoted preacher from the public streets by revoking his permit for street preaching. The Court's objection to the permit ordinance was that it gave to an administrative official "discretionary power to control in advance the right of citizens to speak on religious matters on the streets of New York," with "no appropriate standards to guide his action."

Sound amplification creates a different problem, and may make speech liable to control as a public nuisance and an invasion of privacy (*Kovacs* v. *Cooper* [1949]). Local ordinances may also protect privacy by forbidding commercial canvassers of salesmen to sell from door to door (*Breard* v. *Alexandria* [1951]), but of course such limitations could not be imposed on persons going from door to door on public policy or religious errands (*Martin* v. *Struthers* [1943]).

Speech and Breach of the Peace

The freedom to speak, then, is generally protected from advance restrictions, but if speech results in unlawful action of some kind, the speaker may be liable to punishment. One of the most common problems is that speech may inflame tempers and lead to violence. Preservation of order is a prime responsibility of every community, and in all states there are statutes punishing breach of the peace, disorderly conduct, inciting to riot, and like offenses. Where speech is an element in these offenses, serious questions arise in balancing the right to speak against the necessity of maintaining public order.

The Supreme Court has worked out three tests to be applied in passing on the constitutionality of punishment for speech.

First, is the speech of a type entitled to constitutional protection? In *Chaplinsky* v. *New Hampshire* (1942), a member of Jehovah's Witnesses had cursed a city marshal, calling him a "damned racketeer" and "a damned Fascist," and he was convicted for calling the marshal "offensive and derisive" names in public. The Supreme Court upheld the conviction, on the ground that such language is not constitutionally protected. Insults and "fighting" words are "no essential part of any exposition of ideas, and are of such slight social value as a step to truth that any benefit that may be derived from them is clearly outweighed by the social interest in order and morality."

Second, does the ordinance or statute for violation of which the speaker is being punished validly recognize the constitutional necessity for protection of speech? The case of *Terminiello* v. *Chicago* (1949) arose when an unfrocked Catholic priest made an incendiary, Fascist-type speech under riotous conditions in a Chicago hall. Following the speech he was convicted of disorderly conduct and breach of the peace under an ordinance that appeared to make it unlawful to "stir the public to anger, invite dispute, bring about a condition of unrest, or create a disturbance." The Supreme Court held this ordinance invalid. A man could not be convicted just because his speech has created "public inconvenience, annoyance, or unrest." The evils had to be greater than that to justify a speech conviction.

Third, did a clear and present danger of actual breach of the peace result from the speech? In answering this question, a reviewing court of necessity has the difficult task of evaluating the correctness of the judgment of the police officers or others on the scene as to the potentialities for violence. In *Feiner* v. *New York* (1951) a university student was making a hotheaded speech on a street corner. A small crowd gathered, that became restless as the speech went on. One man said to two policemen who had stopped to survey the traffic problem being created that if they did not take that "son of a bitch" off the box, he would. The police then arrested the speaker, and he was convicted of disorderly conduct. The Supreme Court upheld this conviction, saying that the police and the trial court were best able to judge whether a riotous situation was developing. But Justice Douglas, dissenting, thought the record showed no likelihood of riot, and that this decision would permit the police to become "the new censors of speech."

❧ FREEDOM TO DEMONSTRATE

The organized demonstration is a form of communication that almost necessarily involves serious impact on other community interests. Demonstrations nearly always take place in public areas—the streets, the sidewalks, the parks. Demonstrators use public places because they want to make contact with the public. They want to bring their views to the attention of people who do not know about them, who have not asked to be informed concerning them, and who may very well object to them. An organized demonstration on public streets or sidewalks is bound to interfere to some degree with the normal use of these public facilities. A parade or a picket line, with songs, slogans, and signs, is "speech," but it is also action. As the Supreme Court has put it, it is "speech *plus.*"

Because of these facts, it is clear that the community is justified in requiring advance notification and permits for demonstrations. The Supreme Court so held in *Cox* v. *New Hampshire* (1941), where a group of

Jehovah's Witnesses had marched single file along city streets carrying placards to advertise a meeting, without securing the license required by state law for "parades or processions" in public streets. The Court upheld this statute as a reasonable police regulation, administered under proper safeguards.

Picketing initially came to the Court's attention in connection with labor disputes. In the nineteenth century, labor picketing was unlawful, but judicial attitudes gradually changed. In the 1940 case of *Thornhill* v. *Alabama* the Supreme Court finally brought picketing within the protection of the free speech clause, saying: "In the circumstances of our times the dissemination of information concerning the facts of a labor dispute must be regarded as within that area of free discussion that is guaranteed by the Constitution." However, the Court quickly made clear that it realized labor picketing was more than discussion. It was also economic coercion, which could lead to violence or be exercised for unlawful ends. So in an important series of cases from 1941 to 1957 the Court uniformly upheld various legislative and judicial restrictions on picketing.

The constitutional aspects of demonstrations and picketing in connection with the civil rights movement of the 1960s presented difficult problems for the courts. The starting point, of course, is that a demonstration is conduct as well as speech, and as conduct it is subject to regulation. As Justice Goldberg said in *Cox* v. *Louisiana* (1965):

> We emphatically reject the notion ... that the First and Fourteenth Amendments afford the same kind of freedom to those who would communicate ideas by conduct such as patrolling, marching, and picketing on streets and highways, as these amendments afford to those who communicate ideas by pure speech.

Although demonstrations are not entitled to the *same* protection as "pure speech," clearly the speech element present entitles them to *some* constitutional standing. How far this protection goes is not certain. Could a city bar all demonstrations on its streets? The Supreme Court has not so held, and it seems unlikely that it would do so. But picketing and demonstrating around courthouses can be prohibited. In 1949, after some unpleasant incidents where pickets had paraded around federal court buildings to express their views concerning trials that were under way inside, Congress passed a statute making it illegal to picket a building housing a federal court, with the intention of interfering with the administration of justice or influencing judges or jurors. An identical Louisiana statute was upheld by the Supreme Court in *Cox* v. *Louisiana*.

The public interest in keeping streets and sidewalks open for movement can be protected by legislation forbidding the obstruction of public passages. Such a law was also involved in the *Cox* case, and the Court impliedly granted that it was constitutional, although its enforcement was refused in this case because of the particular circumstances. In *Shuttles-worth* v. *City of Birmingham* (1965) the conviction of a civil rights leader for blocking the sidewalk while picketing a department store to protest its segregation policies was reversed by the Court because there was no evidence in the record that the sidewalk was actually blocked.

If the police undertake to arrest demonstrators for breach of the peace or other unlawful acts, they must be prepared to justify the arrests. Of course, if demonstrators obstruct traffic by lying down in the streets or if they physically attack the arresting officers, their conduct is clearly illegal. But more difficult problems arise when picketers simply disobey police orders to discontinue their demonstration. In *Brown* v. *Louisiana* (1966) five Negroes walked into a segregated library, asked for a book, and remained after the librarian had requested them to leave. No one else was in the library, and they stood quietly until the sheriff arrived and arrested them for breach of the peace. The Supreme Court by a vote of 5 to 4 held that their action did not amount to a violation of the breach of the peace law.

Where a hostile crowd has formed around the demonstrators and violence seems likely, the police have a more difficult problem. Should they seek to preserve order by ending the demonstration and, if necessary, arresting the demonstrators? Or should they let the demonstration continue and seek to control the crowd, arresting the principal troublemakers if necessary?

Obviously the police have to make their decision on their judgment of the facts in each specific situation. As we have seen, in the *Feiner* case the police arrested the speaker, and the Supreme Court approved. But in *Edwards* v. *South Carolina* (1963), involving a demonstration by some 200 Negro students on the grounds of the state capitol which seemed much more likely to lead to violence than the *Feiner* situation, the Court reversed the convictions of the demonstrators who had defied police orders to disband. The Court said: "The Fourteenth Amendment does not permit a State to make criminal the peaceful expression of unpopular views."

✤ FREEDOM OF ASSOCIATION

Freedom of association is not mentioned in the Constitution, but it is an important civil liberty derived from the right of assembly and the freedom of speech, press, and religion. One of the most effective methods of expression is to associate one's self with other like-minded persons for the achievement of common goals. Americans are inveterate "joiners," and the right to belong to groups is so universally assumed that it is seldom

challenged. However, groups that are unpopular or are regarded as dangerous—the Communist party, the Ku Klux Klan, the National Association
for the Advancement of Colored People (NAACP), the John Birch
Society—may find their associational freedom subject to attack. The
Communist party is a special problem to be considered later. Among other
organizations the experience of the NAACP has been the most important
in stimulating judicial statements on freedom of association.

After the *Brown* decision in 1954, the activities of the NAACP in
seeking to promote school desegregation aroused bitter hostility in most of
the southern states. Its members were subjected to economic coercion and
often to physical abuse. There were also efforts through legislation and
court action to hamper or terminate the work of the organization.

In Alabama the attorney general sought to enjoin the NAACP from
operating in the state on the pretext that as an out-of-state corporation it
had not filed the necessary papers to qualify it to carry on activities in
Alabama. As a part of this action the attorney general demanded a list of
all the NAACP members in the state, but the organization refused on the
ground that making the list public would subject members to harassment
and unconstitutionally restrain their freedom of association. The Supreme
Court upheld this refusal in *NAACP* v. *Alabama* (1958).

The NAACP concentrated much of its efforts on court suits to compel
desegregation, and here also it was subjected to pressure. A Virginia law,
typical of those in many other states, forbade the stirring up of litigation or
the improper solicitation of legal business. This legislation was aimed at
"ambulance chasing" and other unethical legal practices, but because the
NAACP admittedly seeks out test cases on which it can go to court, it was
accused of violating the statute in Virginia.

In *NAACP* v. *Button* (1963) the Supreme Court upheld the Association's litigation procedures, and in the decision recognized litigation as "a
form of political expression." The Court said that "in the context of
NAACP objectives, litigation is not a technique of resolving private
differences; it is a means for achieving the lawful objectives of equality of
treatment by all government, federal, state, and local, for the members of
the Negro community in this country." Indeed, "for such a group,
association for litigation may be the most effective form of political
association."

✴ RELIGIOUS LIBERTY

The First Amendment guarantees freedom of religion, and forbids establishment of religion. Of these two principles, religious freedom or tolera-

tion was the older and more firmly grounded when the First Amendment was adopted in 1791. The tragic results of religious discrimination and persecution, of punishment because of belief or conscience, had long been demonstrated in England and on the continent of Europe by the time the American nation was founded, and the theoretical and practical case for toleration was well developed in English writing.

The establishment provision, on the other hand, was in flat contradiction to the English practice of an official established church, and some variety of establishment prevailed in several of the American states at the time the Constitution was adopted. Thus the principle of separation of church and state was an American invention, whose application remained to be worked out in practice.

Freedom of Religion

The basic demands of the "free exercise" clause are that government must not force or influence a person to go to or remain away from church. The government must not require anyone to profess a belief or disbelief in any religion, or punish anyone for entertaining or professing religious beliefs or disbeliefs. These principles seem clear enough, but in application difficult problems of interpretation may arise. The following illustrations will indicate how the Supreme Court has reacted to certain claims of religious freedom.

1. Parents cannot be forced by state law to send their children to public schools if they prefer to have them receive a religious education in parochial schools which meet state standards. This ruling, in *Pierce* v. *Society of Sisters* (1925), did not actually rely on the religious freedom clause, but the result was the same as if it had done so.

2. The children of Jehovah's Witnesses, who believe that saluting the flag is forbidden by the Bible because it is equivalent to "bowing down before a graven image," cannot be compelled to join in the flag salute ceremony in the public schools. In fact, in *West Virginia State Board of Education* v. *Barnette* (1943), the Court decided that no child, regardless of his religious beliefs, could be compelled to salute the flag as a condition of attending the public schools.

3. A state cannot make it a crime for a person to solicit for religious or philanthropic causes without securing the prior certification of a public official that the cause is a bona fide religious one. The Court said in *Cantwell* v. *Connecticut* (1940) that requirement of prior state approval for solicitation of funds amounted to "a censorship of religion as the means of determining its right to survive."

4. A city which imposes a tax on door-to-door merchants cannot levy

this tax on individuals who go from door to door offering religious publications for sale, as is the practice of Jehovah's Witnesses. In *Murdock* v. *Pennsylvania* (1943) the Court said that incidental collection of small sums for religious tracts did not make this type of evangelism commercial, any more than passing the collection plate makes a church service commercial.

5. Actions or practices which are made criminal by law or are outrageously offensive to public morals are not rendered immune from punishment because of alleged religious motivation. In 1879 the Supreme Court upheld a congressional statute making the Mormon practice of polygamy in the Utah territory a crime (*Reynolds* v. *United States*).

6. One way that Jehovah's Witnesses practice their religion is by distribution of their literature. A member of this sect took her nine-year-old niece with her to sell literature on downtown street corners at night. Massachusetts law forbids girls under 18 to sell newspapers or other merchandise on the streets, and the aunt was found guilty of violating the statute. The Supreme Court in *Prince* v. *Massachusetts* (1944) held that the statute was a reasonable police regulation designed to protect the welfare of children, taking precedence over the competing claims of religious freedom.

7. Sunday closing laws do not violate the religious freedom of Jewish merchants and others whose religions require them to close their stores on a different day. In *Braunfeld* v. *Brown* (1961) the Court ruled that Sunday observance, while originally religiously motivated, had now become purely a secular device for providing a uniform day of rest.

One issue the Supreme Court has not had to face is whether it would be a violation of the religious freedom of conscientious objectors to war if they were forced to serve in the armed forces. This problem has not arisen because all American draft laws have granted exemption from military service to religious objectors to war. The statutes currently grant exemption to persons whose opposition to war is based on "religious training and belief," which is defined as "an individual's belief in a relation to a Supreme Being involving duties superior to those arising from any human relation, but [not including] essentially political, sociological, or philosophical views or a merely personal moral code." In *United States* v. *Seeger* (1965) the Supreme Court interpreted this language broadly enough to cover quite unorthodox religious beliefs.

Many difficult issues remain. Can a cult leader who solicits money through the mail on representations that he has divine healing powers be prosecuted for mail fraud? The Supreme Court had such a case in *United States* v. *Ballard* (1944), and the majority of the Court was so sensitive to possible claims of religious persecution that they managed to avoid making a decision. What about persons who have religious scruples against medical treatment? There have been many cases where courts have ordered treatment of children against the wishes of their parents. But in 1965 the Illinois supreme court ruled that an adult woman who had refused a blood transfusion on religious grounds, and whose life had been saved by a court-ordered transfusion, had a valid claim against the state for violation of her religious freedom.

Religion and the Establishment Clause

There are two general views as to the meaning of the establishment clause. The first holds that it outlaws only the kind of establishment that existed in Europe in 1791, namely, one official tax-supported church. This view contends that what the framers wanted to prevent was *preference* for one religion over others. State contacts with religion or state support of religion would be proper unless discrimination between religions is involved.

The second view contends that the establishment rule outlaws *any* government support of, or connection with, religion. Complete separation of church and state is demanded, and no public financial support to religious institutions is permissible, even if made available on a nonpreferential basis. The Supreme Court has consistently supported this second position.

Establishment issues have been raised on many occasions in American history—the official designation of Thanksgiving Day, the provision of chaplains for Congress and in the armed services, compulsory chapel services at West Point and Annapolis. The Supreme Court's first important consideration of the issue came in the 1947 New Jersey bus case, *Everson* v. *Board of Education.* Justice Black there summarized the Court's understanding of the establishment clause as follows:

> Neither a state nor the Federal Government can set up a church. Neither can pass laws which aid one religion, aid all religions, or prefer one religion over another.... No tax in any amount, large or small, can be levied to support any religious activities or institutions, whatever they may be called, or whatever form they may adopt to teach or practice religion. ...In the words of Jefferson, the clause against establishment of religion by law was intended to erect "a wall of separation between church and State."

In the *Everson* case public funds were being used to pay the bus fare of children to parochial as well as public schools, but the majority of the Court held that these payments were for the benefit of the child, and so did not constitute financial assistance to religious schools.

"Released time" programs of religious education, where children are excused from regular public school classes to take religious instruction from teachers supplied by local religious groups, are constitutional, provided the classes are held off the school premises. This was the Court's holding in *Zorach* v. *Clauson* (1952), though three members of the Court charged that the use of the public school machinery to provide students for these classes made the program an unconstitutional joinder of church and state.

Religious observances in the public schools—the saying of prayers and the reading of the Bible—were held unconstitutional by the Supreme Court in 1962 and 1963 (*Engel* v. *Vitale; School District* v. *Schempp*). These decisions created a great public furore, and an effort to amend the Constitution to permit prayers in the public schools was begun. However, many religious leaders supported the decisions as wise steps toward keeping the divisive influence of religion out of the public schools. The wilder charges by the Court's opponents that it would logically have to proceed to root out all religious manifestations in public life, such as the offering of prayers at the opening of legislative sessions or the words "In God We Trust" on coins, were refuted by the Court itself in 1964 when it

6/18/63
"What do they expect us to do—listen to the kids pray at *home?*"
From *Straight Herblock* (Simon & Schuster, 1964).

refused to review a New York state court ruling upholding the use of the words "under God" in the pledge of allegiance by public school pupils.

A serious new establishment problem was raised by the passage of the Elementary and Secondary Education Act of 1965. Previous efforts to give federal financial aid to education had always foundered on the issue of inclusion of the parochial schools. President Johnson successfully bypassed this problem by proposing assistance primarily to schools serving children of low-income families, and the act as passed made funds available in various ways for improving the education of students in both religious and public schools.

Most of the funds go to public school districts in "poverty impacted" areas, to be used to meet the special educational needs of educationally deprived children, but through "shared-time" or "dual enrollment" programs, eligible children attending nonpublic schools will also participate in these benefits. The act also provides funds for the purchase of textbooks and library materials. The title to these books remains in the public school district, but in fact they will be used by the pupils of both public and nonpublic schools. Finally, the act provides for supplemental education centers where remedial instruction, laboratories, specialized teachers and counselors would be available for both public and nonpublic school students.

The legislation is carefully designed so that all the funds are channeled to public sources, and no financial aid goes for the teaching of religious subjects. On the other hand, federal funds are used to bear part of the cost of educating pupils in religious schools, and decisions of public school boards may be affected by the necessity of accommodating their programs to those of religious schools. Because the costs of education for nonpublic schools will be reduced by public assumption of such expensive items as science laboratories and gymnasia, more religious groups may find it feasible to set up their own schools, and the present dominant position of the public schools could conceivably be undermined.

Such considerations, however, are unlikely to cause the Supreme Court to regard the 1965 act as violative of the establishment clause. In the 1963 Bible-reading case, *School District* v. *Schempp*, the Court said that "to withstand the strictures of the Establishment Clause there must be a secular legislative purpose and a primary effect that neither advances nor inhibits religion." Certainly the 1965 statute has a secular legislative purpose—improving the education of children from poor families and in poverty-impacted areas. And while some encouragement may be offered by the operation of the act to the spread of religious schools, that effect can well be regarded as incidental rather than primary.

❧ THE RIGHT TO PRIVACY

There is no general language in the Constitution protecting the right to privacy, and yet such a right is one of the underlying conditions of a free society. Justice Brandeis once referred to "the right to be let alone" as "the most comprehensive of rights and the right most valued by civilized men." The Constitution comes closest to spelling out this right in the Fourth Amendment provision against "unreasonable searches and seizures," which protects the privacy of one's home from invasion by the police unless they have sufficient evidence of commission of a crime to secure a search warrant from a court.

The more interesting and difficult problems of privacy have occurred in recent decades with the development of means of surveillance which can invade privacy without any physical incursion into a home. Tapping of telephone lines was one of the first of these methods, and the Supreme Court decided in *Olmstead* v. *United States* (1928) that wiretapping was not forbidden by the Constitution because the government agents listened to conversations without ever actually physically entering the suspect's living quarters. However, Congress has provided by statute that evidence secured by wiretapping cannot be used in federal prosecutions.

Scientific advances have now provided even more effective forms of surveillance, so that government agents or anyone else can penetrate easily and effectively the privacy of houses, offices, and vehicles, or monitor the basic channels of communication. In the area of psychological surveillance, techniques such as the polygraph (lie detector test) and personality testing that probe into the interior thought processes of their subjects have come into wide use since World War II. Use of "truth drugs" and brain-wave analysis can carry these incursions ever farther. Computers have made possible the collection and instant availability of masses of information, so that "data surveillance" of individuals, businesses, and groups has become possible on a scale hitherto unknown.

What will remain of the right to privacy under this technological assault is not clear. However, it is interesting that at this precise time the Supreme Court has for the first time asserted the existence of a general right to privacy under the Constitution. This occurred in *Griswold* v. *Connecticut* (1965), where the Court held unconstitutional a state statute forbidding the use of birth control devices. In this case a doctor who had given birth control information to married couples had been convicted of violation of the law. Justice Douglas for the Court recognized "zones of privacy" contained in the "penumbra" of various provisions in the Constitution, including the First, Third, Fourth, Fifth, and Ninth Amendments. In the marriage relationship, he concluded, "we deal with a right of privacy older than the Bill of Rights. . . ."

✻ INDIVIDUAL FREEDOM AND NATIONAL SECURITY

The severest test of constitutional freedom occurs in periods of war and civil emergency, when danger or disorder threatens, passions become inflamed, and there is no longer toleration of the unorthodox and the extremists who are accepted in less tense times. The favorable geographical position of the United States, protected by two oceans, for a long period minimized any threat of foreign involvement. To be sure, this was not true during the early period of the nation, and in the bitter conflict between the partisans of England and France, the Federalist majority in Congress sought reprisals against the Jeffersonians by passing the Alien and Sedition Acts. At the time there was no constitutional test of the Sedition Act, but in the 1964 *New York Times* case the law was declared unconstitutional retrospectively by the Supreme Court.

After more than a century of freedom from serious foreign involvements, the United States was not psychologically prepared for the strains of World War I, and reacted hysterically, first to the German threat and then, after the Bolshevist revolution in Russia, to the specter of communism. Congress adopted the Espionage Act in 1917 and the Sedition Act in 1918, under which many persons were jailed for criticizing the war effort.

Justice Holmes was the spokesman for the Court in its first encounters with these World War I cases, and he developed the famous "clear and present danger" test to measure the extent of the government's power to punish the spoken or written word because of its connection with illegal action.

> The question in every case is whether the words used are used in such circumstances and are of such a nature as to create a clear and present danger that they will bring about the substantive evils that Congress has a right to prevent. It is a question of proximity and degree.

During wartime, Holmes added, many things that might be said in time of peace cannot be endured. So he argued in *Schenck* v. *United States* (1919) that persons mailing circulars to men urging them not to register for the draft could be punished. But in *Abrams* v. *United States* (1919) he thought the clear and present danger test should protect Communists who printed up leaflets urging munitions workers to strike to show their disapproval of American armed action against the Russian revolution.

The Status of the Communist Party

After World War II the American Communist party came under intensive pressure. Prosecution of its national leaders was begun in 1948 under the Smith Act, which makes it unlawful knowingly to advocate the overthrow of any government in the United States by force or violence, or to organize or knowingly become a member of any group which so advocates. The Supreme Court upheld the conviction of the party leaders in *Dennis* v. *United States* (1951). Although they were not charged with having taken any action for the immediate purpose of initiating a revolution, the Court majority, applying the clear and present danger test, decided that the Communist party constituted an evil of sufficient gravity to justify punishing its leaders for their advocacy of revolutionary principles. Later, in *Scales* v. *United States* (1961), the Court upheld the provision of the Smith Act making active and knowing membership in the Communist party a crime.

The Supreme Court has thus accepted the position that the Communist party is not a "legitimate political party," and that it and its members are not entitled to the normal constitutional protections of speech and association. The party has been forced off the ballot in all states, and its members have been subjected to many kinds of legal harassment.

On the other hand, it has not been government policy to outlaw the party completely, and it has continued to exist, well-infiltrated by FBI agents, in a curious half-world, neither legal nor illegal. The Internal Security Act of 1950 requiring all Communist-action organizations to register with the government was held constitutional by the Supreme Court (*Communist Party* v. *Subversive Activities Control Board* [1961]), but the government was unable to force the Communist party to register because such action would constitute self-incrimination (*United States* v. *Communist Party* [1964]). Provisions in the same law forbidding all Communists from applying for passports were declared unconstitutional (*Aptheker* v. *United States* [1964]) because of their sweeping application to all members of the party, regardless of their degree of activity or the purpose of their travel.

Loyalty Programs

As the cold war against communism developed after World War II, concern about the loyalty of public employees resulted in the adoption of a variety of legislative programs. Perhaps the most common was to require public employees to take an oath that they were not members of the Communist party. The Supreme Court upheld such a requirement in *Garner* v. *Board of Public Works* (1951), Justice Frankfurter saying: "In the context of our time, such membership is sufficiently relevant to effective and dependable government, and to the confidence of the electorate in its government."

A congressional statute forbids employment by the government of members of organizations advocating overthrow of "our constitutional forms of government." A federal loyalty review program was set up in 1947. All federal employees and applicants were required to undergo a loyalty check. Hearings were held by loyalty review boards when damaging information was received, but some of the customary protections of the hearing procedure, particularly the right to be informed of the source of the charges and to confront the person making the accusations, were not present in these proceedings.

The Supreme Court avoided a direct ruling on the constitutionality of the loyalty review program, though in *Cole* v. *Young* (1956) it did hold that only employees in "sensitive" positions (that is, where national security might be involved) should be subjected to the loyalty procedures. On the issue of fair hearing procedures, the Court, finally, in *Greene* v. *McElroy* (1959) ruled that failure to inform a person of the source of the charges against him or to permit him to confront his accusers was contrary to "our traditional ideas of fair procedure."

Legislative Investigations

Congress has broad power to investigate as an aid to its legislative function, and to punish for contempt persons who refuse to testify before its committees. Although this authority is used to secure information on every aspect of congressional activity, since World War II the most publicized investigations have dealt with suspected subversive activities and organizations.

The investigations conducted by the House Committee on Un-American Activities and Senator Joseph McCarthy were particularly controversial. Many persons contended that these committees were not interested in securing information for legislative purposes, but only in exposing individual Communists and forcing witnesses to take the Fifth Amendment to avoid self-incrimination. The Supreme Court warned in *Watkins* v. *United States* (1957) that there is no power to expose for the sake of exposure. But, since the Court accepts the position that the Communist party is not a legitimate political party, it has upheld legislative inquiries into Communist activity as fulfilling a proper legislative purpose, and has ruled that

4/5/61

"They're ALL Communists except thee and me—" From *Straight Herblock*
(Simon & Schuster, 1964).

individuals, unless they take the Fifth Amendment, can be required to reveal whether they are members of the Communist party. However, the Court does insist that congressional committees give witnesses procedural protections and not ask questions outside their authorized area of investigation. Since 1961 the Court has reversed a substantial number of contempt convictions on these grounds.

The English Policy on Totalitarian Parties

The English policy of dealing with the Communist party and Fascist groups has been quite different from the American. While the government does concern itself with any underground or conspiratorial activities of such parties, no effort has been made in England to deprive them of their freedom openly to organize and carry on propaganda activities. The British concept, in which all the democratic parties—Conservative, Labour, and Liberal—concur, is that if the totalitarian parties are given enough rope they will hang themselves. Although the Communist party of Britain has contested a number of seats in Parliament without any harassment or governmental curbs, it has not since 1950 been able to elect a single member to Parliament. In effect, therefore, the freedom granted to totalitarian parties in Britain has been a disadvantage to them, for it has forced them to reveal their impotence and the unattractiveness of their doctrine, and has deprived them of a chance to pose as martyrs.

✌ ECONOMIC LIBERTY AND HUMAN RIGHTS

Finally, the relationship between human rights and economic liberty should be recognized. The struggle for human rights has often been presented in terms of a conflict between economic and political liberty, between property and people. There is, of course, a sense in which such conflicts are very real. The crudest sort of confrontation of this kind was presented by the slavery issue. Property rights had to be destroyed if slavery was to be ended. Though President Lincoln hoped to work out a system of compensation for slaveholders as slavery was abolished, his temperate approach proved impossible of fullfilment.

There have been other classic confrontations of economic and human rights—the employment of young children in textile mills, the insistence of the steel companies that they could not operate profitably unless their employees worked a 12-hour day, the argument that a minimum wage for women was immoral because it forced an employer to pay more for services than they might be worth to him. Some claims for economic liberty have been so extreme that they would deny to the government any right to exercise an ameliorating influence in economic and industrial affairs. But there is no such guarantee of laissez-faire in the Constitution, though in some periods of our history the Supreme Court seemed to think there was.

There *is* in the Constitution, however, a full recognition of the importance of economic liberty to a free society, as a number of specific provisions illustrate. It is a striking fact that, while the Declaration of Independence is concerned with "life, liberty, and the pursuit of happiness," the Fifth and Fourteenth Amendments guarantee against the deprivation of "life, liberty, or *property*" without due process of law. The government has the power of eminent domain—that is, to take private property when it is needed for a public purpose—but the Fifth Amendment requires Congress to give "just compensation" for property so taken. The states are forbidden to pass any law "impairing the obligation of contracts."

But these guarantees of property rights do not exist in a vacuum. They are limited in application by the broad powers of Congress to regulate commerce and to levy taxes and spend money for the "general welfare." Hence, economic liberty is always subject to some measure of restriction in the public interest when sentiment for such limitation is sufficiently strong. Efforts to interpose the Constitution as an absolute barrier to legislative adjustments have, in the end, always failed.

Chief Justice Marshall succeeded for a time in the early nineteenth century in interpreting the clause forbidding the impairment of contracts as a bar to government regulation of corporations, but it is now more than a century since that clause had much significance. Later, corporations were found by the Supreme Court to be "persons" under the protection of the Fourteenth Amendment, and from about 1880 to the 1930s the due process clause was utilized by the Court to strike down much economic reform legislation of the states, such as limitation on hours of employment, minimum wages for women, and price control laws. However, in 1934 the Court admitted that the states could regulate the price of milk (*Nebbia* v. *New York*), and in 1937 state minimum wage laws were approved (*West Coast Hotel Co.* v. *Parrish*). Since that time the Court has almost never invalidated economic regulatory legislation, state or federal, on due process grounds.

Business and property owners generally operate today under a maze of federal, state, and local governmental controls—taxation, inspection, zoning, public health and safety, fair employment, depreciation standards and accounting requirements, minimum wages, maximum hours. Entry into some trades and professions is surrounded by restrictions that may be more concerned with protecting the guild from competition than with assuring competence of performance. Public utilities have their rates fixed and may be subject to government competition. But the private sector is still by far the greater part of the American economy, and Americans are free to invest their capital and skills as they choose. The system of economic liberty is guaranteed not so much by the specific language of the Constitution as by the general recognition that a substantial measure of economic liberty is essential to the development of individual freedom and political liberty.

CHAPTER 11

EQUALITY AND
CIVIL RIGHTS

The Declaration of Independence affirmed that "all men are created equal," yet there was no language in the Constitution reflecting this concern. There were, to be sure, provisions protecting various civil rights, particularly the guarantees of uniform standards of criminal justice in the Fourth through the Eighth Amendments. But there was nothing specifically affirming the equality of all persons under law. On the contrary, there were several provisions accepting and guaranteeing the institution of human slavery. It must be noted that Jefferson's condemnation of the slave trade in his original draft of the Declaration of Independence was cut out of the final version.

All this was changed by the Civil War and the passion for equality that it unloosed. Slavery was abolished by the Thirteenth Amendment, and the Fourteenth undertook to guarantee that the freedmen would enter fully into the privileges of their new status. However, the equal protection of the laws promised to Negroes by the Fourteenth Amendment remained a promise only. Neither the country, the Congress, nor the Court was prepared to translate these fine words into deeds. Ironically enough, the original beneficiaries of the equal protection clause were not Negroes but business corporations, which in case after case were able to avoid tax or regulatory statutes on the grounds of inequality of treatment. The constitutional standing of the equal protection clause fell so low that in 1927

Justice Holmes deprecated it as the "usual last resort of constitutional arguments" (*Buck* v. *Bell*). But a change was finally at hand. Within a few years the equal protection clause became the foundation of a massive mid-century drive for civil rights and equality of opportunity.

＊ EQUALITY OF OPPORTUNITY

Equality of opportunity has been one of the great boasts of American democracy. Our folklore is full of Horatio Algers who have risen from poverty to wealth and power by their hard work and winning personalities. Being born in a log cabin was a positive advantage in running for the Presidency during the nineteenth century. Yet at the same time no one could help recognizing the grievous inequalities of opportunity in American life. One reaction to this conflict of dream and reality is the cynicism of George Orwell: "All men are created equal, but some are more equal than others." Abraham Lincoln thought there was a better way to regard the idealism of the Declaration of Independence.

> [It] meant to set up a standard maxim for free society which could be familiar to all, and revered by all; constantly looked to, constantly labored for, and even though never perfectly attained, constantly approximated, and thereby constantly spreading and deepening its influence, and augmenting the happiness and value of life to all people of all colors everywhere.

In fact the process which Lincoln described has been enormously successful. American society has been remarkably open and has offered tremendous opportunity for recognition of individual merit and imposed comparatively few arbitrary barriers to personal fulfillment. There have been many reasons for this favorable situation. In the beginning the American settlers were relatively homogeneous in social status, language, and religion. The rich natural resources of the new country offered great opportunity to anyone with industry and initiative. The frontier was always just over the horizon for those who felt hemmed in by the more settled communities. Of course, classes developed, based, as in Europe, on birth and wealth, but class lines were not as rigid or taken as seriously as in England, and upward mobility was constantly possible. It was not Utopia, but there was room and opportunity was real.

The inequalities of opportunity that have marred American society in the past century have their basis in social, economic, or legal disadvantage or some combination of these factors. The *immigrants* who came to America in a swelling tide from 1850 to the 1920s often encountered social and economic discrimination. The Irish, for example, were initially despised and given the meanest jobs to do, but they quickly made their way into political life and used their political skills to improve their economic and social position.

The *poor*, whether native or foreign-born, have never shared fully in American opportunities. Although subject to no actual legal disabilities, they have generally lacked the motivation or the resources to secure an adequate education, and so have been deprived of the most important requisite for individual advancement. Until fairly recently only the children of middle- and upper-class parents went to college.

Women as a class have had to struggle against many kinds of discrimination. They were less likely to go to college, they were barred or discouraged from entering most professions and many types of employment, their pay scales were generally lower than those for men, and their legal situation subordinated them in various respects to their husbands.

Some inequalities stemmed from *geographic location*. Americans living in regions that lacked natural resources or industrial development tended to suffer from malnutrition and ill-health and lack of education and opportunities for employment because of the poverty of their surroundings. The sickness of the coal industry meant the decline of opportunity for residents in Kentucky and West Virginia. The cutover forest lands of Wisconsin and Michigan, the exhausted iron ore quarries of Minnesota, the overcropped dust bowls of the Great Plains—these regional catastrophes created economic inequalities that had great human impact.

In the programs of the New Deal the federal government made the first concerted attack on inequality of opportunity. President Roosevelt inaugurated a series of emergency programs to relieve unemployment, to restore confidence in the private enterprise system, and to start up the machinery of a stalled economy. Unemployment compensation and the social security system met some of the basic social and human needs. A fascinating experiment in reducing regional inequalities was conducted by the Tennessee Valley Authority. The major lesson of the New Deal was that never again could the government permit a nationwide depression to occur, and Keynesian economics made this a feasible goal.

World War II brought full employment and job opportunities for all previously disadvantaged groups, including women. At the close of the war, fear of a postwar depression led the government to assume further responsibilities for the health of the economy by adoption of the Full Employment Act of 1946. In spite of the Republican philosophy of reducing the sphere of the federal government, President Eisenhower did not find it desirable to dismantle any of the machinery intended to create the economic base for greater equality of opportunity.

The innovative spirit of the New Deal was revived again under Presidents Kennedy and Johnson. The most ambitious and comprehensive program ever undertaken in the United States for remedying inequalities included such features as area redevelopment programs like that for the Appalachian region; a federal equal pay act for women; improvement of educational opportunities for the children of poor families by an extensive program of federal financial grants to elementary and secondary schools; fellowships for needy college students; a recent subsidy program which would permit poor families to live in private rather than public housing; and a wide-ranging "poverty program" aiming to train the dropouts, the illiterates, and the unemployables for useful jobs and re-entry into society.

The most important target of these new efforts was the Negro. From the time of emancipation, the plight of the Negro had been by all odds the most glaring and persistent contradiction of the American claim of equality of opportunity. For a few years after the Civil War the federal government gave some attention to improving the lot of the newly freed slaves, but the efforts were soon abandoned. Concentrated largely in the southern states, deprived of the vote, offered a segregated education of the most primitive kind, limited in employment opportunities to manual and domestic labor, kept in their "place" by a rigid code enforced by sanctions ranging from insult and economic pressure to lynching, Negroes lived as a lower caste almost completely excluded from sharing in the American heritage.

Only after the century was half over did the tide begin to turn. Although many factors were at work, by all odds the most important was the Supreme Court's electrifying decision on May 17, 1954, in *Brown* v. *Board of Education of Topeka*, holding racial segregation in the public schools unconstitutional. While the civil rights revolution can be dated from this event, it is desirable first to fill in some of the background for this ruling.

The Right to Vote

One of the major factors in Negro inequality was denial of the right to vote. The states determine who is eligible to vote in state and local elections, and, as will be explained more fully in the next chapter, the Constitution also permits the states to determine the federal electorate. However, racial discrimination is forbidden by the Constitution, both by the equal protection clause of the Fourteenth Amendment and by the Fifteenth Amendment, which specifically guarantees that the right to vote shall not be abridged on account of race, color, or previous condition of servitude. Unfortunately, these provisions are not self-enforcing, and aside from certain civil rights statutes after the Civil War, the federal government for almost a century gave no attention to the problem of Negro voting.

Denial of the franchise to Negroes was accomplished in large part by intimidation and violence, but the southern states also sought to discover "legal" methods of accomplishing their purpose. The most successful devices were tests for literacy and "understanding the Constitution," which could be manipulated with great effectiveness to disfranchise Negroes. A Mississippi law requiring voters to be able to read, understand, or interpret any section of the Constitution was upheld in *Williams* v. *Mississippi* (1898), because on its face it did not discriminate against Negroes.

However, another type of restriction, the so-called "grandfather clause," was declared unconstitutional. An Oklahoma law imposed a literacy test for voting, but gave exemption for persons whose ancestors had been entitled to vote in 1866. The Supreme Court in *Guinn* v. *United States* (1915) held this provision to be an obvious attempt to evade the Fifteenth Amendment.

Another device for achieving Negro discrimination was to bar them from primary elections. The Supreme Court abetted this tactic when in *Newberry* v. *United States* (1921) it ruled that party primaries were not part of the election process, and consequently constitutional protections on voting did not apply to them. When the Texas Democratic party by action of its party convention confined party membership to white citizens, the Supreme Court upheld this action in *Grovey* v. *Townsend* (1935).

However, the propositions that primaries are not elections and that political parties are private clubs which can choose their own members were both so absurd that the Supreme Court could not long maintain them. Primaries were declared to be part of the election process in *United States* v. *Classic* (1941), and *Smith* v. *Allwright* (1944) reversed the private club rule. But this was about as far as the Supreme Court could go. Intimidation, coercion, and inertia still prevented most Negroes from voting in the South, and this situation could be changed only by intervention on the part of the federal government to enforce constitutional rights.

The first step was taken by the Civil Rights Act of 1957, the first civil rights legislation since the post-Civil War period. The act set up a Civil Rights Commission to gather evidence on denial of the right to vote and other civil rights. It also empowered the Attorney General to seek injunctions against state officials or groups conspiring to deny the right to vote. Some injunctions were secured under this act—10 under Eisenhower and 60 from 1961 to 1965 under Kennedy and Johnson—and no suits were lost, but the results were not spectacular. Something more effective was obviously needed.

The next step was the Civil Rights Act of 1960. It empowered federal judges to appoint referees to register, for voting in federal and state elections, qualified Negroes who had been refused registration in areas where a pattern of discrimination had been established by suits under the 1957 statute. This act placed too great reliance on federal district judges in the South, who were themselves white southerners subject to all the pressures and prejudices of their localities, and in fact no referees were appointed under this act.

The Civil Rights Act of 1964 was primarily a statute to guarantee access to public accommodations, but it also had some voting provisions in Section I which began to deal positively with the main instrument of legal disfranchisement—literacy and "understanding" tests. Literacy tests had been held constitutional by the Supreme Court as recently as 1959 (*Lassiter* v. *Northampton County Board of Elections*), but this was only on the condition that they were bona fide tests of literacy and not instruments of racial discrimination. In fact, studies by the Civil Rights Commission and others had fully established that voting registrars in southern states were selecting easy questions for white applicants and registering them even when they gave wrong answers and failed to demonstrate literacy, whereas Negro applicants were given the hardest questions and Negro college graduates were being certified as illiterate. The Act of 1964 provided that state registration officials must apply their standards equally, disregard minor errors, and administer the tests in writing so that review of their decisions would be possible.

One year later Congress, under President Johnson's urging, was prepared to go much further, and to take over as a federal responsibility registration of voters in areas where discrimination against Negroes was evident. The Voting Rights Act of 1965 suspended the use of literacy tests or similar voter qualification devices in states and voting districts that had less than 50 percent of voting age residents registered in 1964 or actually voting in the 1964 presidential election, and authorized the appointment of federal voting examiners who would go into these areas and register Negroes. With the passage of the 1965 Act, the machinery was finally available to achieve the registration of Negroes despite any state resistance.

The Act of 1965 had an immediate impact in adding thousands of Negroes to the voting rolls. In Alabama local elections in the spring of 1966, a substantial number of Negroes filed as candidates for office, and several were successful. For the first time white candidates campaigned among Negroes for their votes, and racist appeals were less frequent in public election statements.

The poll tax, which was an additional bar to Negro voting, and which in 1965 was still a requisite for voting in five states, was also a congressional target. In 1964 the Twenty-fourth Amendment was adopted barring the poll tax as a voting requirement in federal elections. While the 1965 Act was before Congress, the House proposed to insert a provision barring the poll tax in state and local elections as well. However, because of uncertainty whether this provision would be constitutional, the act as passed simply expressed the sense of Congress that the use of poll taxes abridged the right to vote and directed the Attorney General to institute court action against enforcement of poll taxes. In *Harper* v. *Virginia State Board of Elections* (1966) the Supreme Court held that the requirement to pay a fee as a condition of obtaining a ballot was an invidious discrimination contrary to the equal protection clause. Thus all the remaining poll tax systems were rendered unconstitutional.

Equal Access to Public Accommodations

One of the abortive efforts which Congress made after the Civil War to protect the civil rights of Negroes was passage of the Civil Rights Act of 1875, which forbade racial separation or discrimination in public conveyances, hotels, and theaters. The Supreme Court declared this law unconstitutional in the *Civil Rights Cases* (1883), on the ground that the Fourteenth Amendment forbade only *state* action, not discrimination by private individuals or corporations. This decision stripped Congress of any power to prevent racial discrimination by railroads, bus lines, restaurants, hotels, and other privately owned facilities of public accommodation. And so Jim Crow flourished for three quarters of a century.

It was not until 1946 that the Supreme Court took the first step toward breaking this impasse by finding segregation of the races on interstate buses to be an unconstitutional burden on commerce (*Morgan* v. *Virginia*). The Interstate Commerce Commission followed with a 1955 order banning racial segregation on all interstate facilities. In 1956 the Court struck down Jim Crow rules for local transportation as a denial of equal protection (*Gayle* v. *Browder*).

Discrimination continued to be the rule, however, in many hotels and eating places. Beginning in 1960, the "sit-in" was widely employed against segregated restaurants. Negroes would take seats at "white only" lunch counters and, after being refused service, continue to sit there until arrested or ousted by force. They were customarily charged with breach of the peace or criminal trespass (that is, remaining on private property after being requested to leave).

While the Supreme Court decided a number of sit-in cases between 1961 and 1964, it never found a case that would require it to pass squarely on the constitutional situation of trespassers. If such a case had arisen, the Court would probably have had to rule that trespass on private property is punishable, even if the purpose of the trespass is an expression of protest against racial discrimination by the owner.

However, the legal situation was changed when Congress passed the Civil Rights Act of 1964, making unlawful racial discrimination in access to public accommodations such as restaurants, hotels, and motels. Under the

1964 Act it is the owner of the restaurant who refuses service for racial reasons who is guilty of unlawful conduct, not the person who enters the restaurant demanding service. The statute, which is based on the power of Congress to regulate interstate commerce and facilities used by travelers in interstate commerce, was upheld by the Supreme Court in *Heart of Atlanta Motel* v. *United States* (1964).

Segregation in Education

The practice of racial segregation in the public schools was so firmly established in the South, as well as in certain northern states and cities, that it was not even challenged in the courts until the 1930s. Constitutional support for segregated schools was supplied by the famous Supreme Court decision in *Plessy* v. *Ferguson* (1896), which announced the doctrine of "separate but equal"—that is, it was not unconstitutional to provide separate public transportation facilities for the two races if the facilities were equal. Justice Brown wrote in that decision:

> The object of the (Fourteenth) amendment was undoubtedly to enforce the absolute equality of the two races before the law, but in the nature of things it could not have been intended to abolish distinctions based upon color, or to enforce social, as distinguished from political equality, or a commingling of the two races upon terms unsatisfactory to either.

Actually, of course, facilities in the segregated Negro schools were never "equal," but the Supreme Court for years avoided recognizing that fact. It was not until a 1938 decision (*Missouri ex rel. Gaines* v. *Canada*) that the Court finally began to enforce the equality requirement for separate educational facilities. This and subsequent decisions stimulated many school districts to start programs for raising the level of their segregated schools.

But it was too late for such half measures. The time of "separate but equal" was running out. The Supreme Court was moving swiftly towards its epoch-making decision day of May 17, 1954. In *Brown* v. *Board of Education of Topeka* and four other cases the Court held that "segregation of children in public schools solely on the basis of race, even though the physical facilities and other 'tangible' factors may be equal, deprive[s] the children of the minority group of equal educational opportunities. . . ." Separating children in grade and high schools "from others of similar age and qualifications solely because of their race generates a feeling of inferiority as to their status in the community that may affect their hearts and minds in a way unlikely ever to be undone."

This was the reply of the 1954 Supreme Court to the 1896 Court, which had denied in *Plessy* v. *Ferguson* that separation of the races stamped Negroes with a "badge of inferiority," and had asserted that "if this be so, it is not by reason of anything found in the act, but solely because the colored race choose to put that construction upon it."

By its decision in the *Brown* case the Supreme Court assumed the most stupendous task in its entire history—to enforce and to supervise the changing of social habits and customs amounting to a way of life in many sections of the country. Obviously no judicial fiat could overnight change men's minds or wipe out the consequences of decades of inequality, poverty, and neglect.

The Supreme Court fully appreciated the enormity of the task it had undertaken. Its plan of action was to remand the cases to the courts where they had originated, which were to work out decrees of enforcement on equitable principles and with regard for "varied local school problems." The local courts would consider whether the actions or proposals of the various school authorities constituted good faith implementation and progress toward full compliance with the *Brown* ruling "with all deliberate speed."

At first it seemed that the prestige of the Supreme Court might substantially temper the expected resistance to the decree. The Court may have expected that it would receive some support from Congress and the President in winning acceptance for its ruling, but no such aid was forthcoming. On the contrary, 96 southern congressmen signed a manifesto in 1956 challenging the legality of the Court's decision, and President Eisenhower, while declaring that he would enforce the law, persistently declined to attempt any organization of popular support for the desegregation ruling. Thus the responsibility for effecting this tremendous social revolution was left primarily to some 58 federal judges in the southern states, many of whom were personally opposed to the principle of the *Brown* decision.

Under these circumstances it was not surprising that progress toward the goal of desegregation of the schools was slow and uneven. In the border states a considerable measure of integration was soon achieved, but in the "Old South" almost complete frustration was accomplished by a variety of methods. The most publicized resistance was that organized by legislation in Virginia, and the violence associated with integration of the Little Rock, Arkansas, high school in 1957. President Eisenhower was forced to send federal troops to control the riotous situation there and to enforce federal court orders aimed at accomplishing gradual desegregation of the high school.

The role of the different actors in this enormously difficult and complex movement toward racial equality in the schools can be summarized briefly.

First, there are the local pressure groups which raise the issue of segregation in local school systems and file suits to bring the matter into court. Often the National Association for the Advancement of Colored

People (NAACP) performed this function, though more recently other civil rights groups of a more activist temper have been involved. In some sections of the South, reprisals against those active in civil rights organizations were so severe and effective that initially no one would speak up to protest segregated schools.

Second, there are the local school boards and officials who, acting on their own initiative or under the compulsion of a district court order, must prepare a desegregation plan. School officials, even when they were willing to act, usually preferred to wait for the pressure of a court order to justify themselves to the segregationists of the community.

Third, there are the state legislatures. Their initial contribution in the southern states was to pass, usually under the governor's leadership, a bewildering mass of laws aimed to prevent or punish steps toward integration. They adopted legislation purporting to nullify the Supreme Court's *Brown* decision and to "interpose" state authority to protect state rights; to withdraw state consent to be sued on matters relating to public school operation; to invoke the state police power against the threat that integration would lead to disorder; to authorize school authorities to exercise their discretion in assigning pupils to schools; to turn the public schools into private schools by leasing them to private groups; and to pay from state funds the tuition of pupils going to private schools.

Most of the laws passed were generally recognized even by their sponsors to be unconstitutional, but the process of litigation takes time and delays the progress of desegregation programs. The only one of these types of laws that received any support from the Supreme Court was the Alabama pupil placement law, authorizing education authorities to place pupils in schools on the basis of various criteria, among which race was not mentioned. Although there could be no doubt that the statute was intended to defeat integration, the Supreme Court held in *Shuttlesworth* v. *Birmingham Board of Education* (1958) that the law was not unconstitutional on its face, and that consequently it would not be voided until evidence was presented of its use for illegal purposes.

Fourth, the federal district court judges occupied a central strategic position in achieving integration "with all deliberate speed." They could order school boards to act, or they could sabotage the Supreme Court order by employing all the delays that the technicalities of the law afford. Of equal importance were the judges of the federal courts of appeals, principally of the Fifth Circuit, which covers the states of Alabama, Florida, Georgia, Louisiana, Mississippi, and Texas, who reviewed the decisions of the district courts in those states. Generally the appellate court justices, somewhat further removed from the pressures of local situations than the district judges, took a conscientious view of their obligation to enforce the Supreme Court's ruling.

Fifth, there is the Supreme Court itself. After handing down the enforcement plan in 1955, the Supreme Court for a time deliberately sought to stay above the battle and let the lower courts work out the problems. But in 1958, when a federal district judge ordered a 30-month delay in the modest Little Rock integration program, the Supreme Court met in an unusual special summer session and upheld the court of appeals reversal of this order in *Cooper* v. *Aaron*. The Court flatly charged that the governor and legislature of Arkansas had caused the violent resistance in that state, and reaffirmed the constitutional obligations of the states to obey the Court's mandate.

Another noteworthy enforcement decision was *Griffin* v. *County School Board of Prince Edward County* (1964). This Virginia county, which was involved in the original 1954 litigation, had closed its public schools in 1959 rather than integrate them. A private foundation built its own schools, and the state and county provided tuition for pupils attending them. From 1959 to 1963 no public education was available for Negro children in the county. The Supreme Court held that closing the public schools of one county while they were maintained in all other counties was a denial of equal protection, and added: "There has been entirely too much deliberation and not enough speed in enforcing the constitutional rights [of] Prince Edward County Negro children."

Finally, there is the major role of the President and Congress, who belatedly assumed their responsibilities for carrying through on the revolution the Supreme Court had begun. In the fall of 1962 President Kennedy had to send federal marshals and troops to enforce a court order to admit a Negro student to the University of Mississippi. After police dogs, cattle prods, and fire hoses had been used against demonstrating Negroes in Birmingham in 1963, President Kennedy proposed new federal civil rights legislation. Following his assassination President Johnson made adoption of the Kennedy civil rights bill one of his primary purposes, and with his persuasive leadership a bipartisan majority in Congress passed the Civil Rights Act of 1964. So far as education is concerned, this statute authorized the Attorney General to bring school desegregation suits in the name of the United States, a power which Congress had refused to provide in the Civil Rights Act of 1957.

The 1964 Act also included a general provision prohibiting racial discrimination in any local program receiving federal financial assistance. This sanction became of very great importance in 1965, when Congress adopted President Johnson's plan for federal financial assistance to elementary and secondary schools. To become eligible for these grants in the fall of 1965, all public schools had to certify that they were integrated or file acceptable plans for achieving complete integration by the fall of 1967.

The combination of financial and judicial pressure seems certain to achieve within the foreseeable future the goal the Supreme Court set in the *Brown* decision. It is true that much of the progress in the hard-core segregation areas has thus far been token compliance. Moreover, this is by no means simply a southern problem. Increasingly, civil rights groups have been publicizing *de facto* segregation in northern cities such as Boston, New York, and Chicago. In such cities segregated schools exist because neighborhood schools in all-Negro neighborhoods produce all-Negro schools. (See Figure 11–1.)

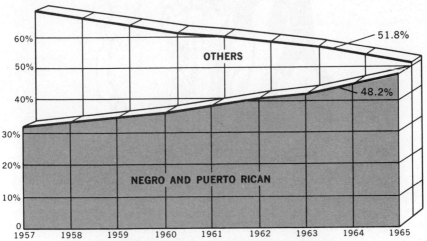

The percentage of Negro and Puerto Rican enrollment in New York City's public schools is rising while the percentage of "other" students, mostly white, declines.

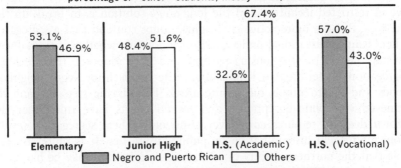

The percentage of Negro and Puerto Rican enrollment, higher than that of "others" in the elementary schools, declines in upper grades except vocational high schools because of the greater drop-out rate of those two groups.

FIGURE 11–1. Negro and Puerto Rican Enrollment in New York City Public Schools. (Adapted from *The New York Times.* © 1964, 65, 66 by The New York Times Company. Reprinted by permission.)

May 19, 1963
"Up North we sort of nibble 'em to death." Drawing by Bill Mauldin. From
I've Decided I Want My Seat Back by Bill Mauldin. Copyright
1962, 1963, 1964 by Bill Mauldin. Reprinted by permission
of the author and Harper & Row, Publishers.

The primary fault here is with the housing barriers that force Negroes to
live in restricted localities, and the long-range solution is to break up the
ghettoes. But the more active civil rights groups contend that a segregated
school is unconstitutional under the *Brown* doctrine whether it is produced
by state law or by the housing pattern, and have proposed that *de facto*
segregation be terminated by bussing white pupils into Negro neighborhoods and Negro pupils into white areas. This drastic step has not yet
achieved very wide acceptance, and several courts have ruled that the
Brown decision requires corrective action only where segregation results
from intentional discrimination by public authorities. It is quite conceivable that the northern variety of educational segregation may be harder to
correct than the southern.

Equal Access to Housing

Equal access of Negro families to housing, as just noted, remains a goal for
the future. The Supreme Court has done what it can to invalidate dis-

crimination in housing. In 1917 a Louisville segregation ordinance which prevented Negroes from buying property in certain sections of the city was declared unconstitutional by the Court (*Buchanan* v. *Warley*). Then the "restrictive convenant" was adopted, under which property owners bound themselves not to sell or lease their property to Negroes or certain other groups. But in 1948 the Court held that such convenants were not judicially enforceable (*Shelley* v. *Kraemer*).

These rulings did little to break the housing barriers, however. Positive legislation at the city and state levels was required that would require owners of property and real estate agents to offer housing for rent or sale without racial restrictions. Many such "open occupancy" laws have been passed, usually after bitter political resistance by organized property owners and real estate interests. In California a state open occupancy law passed by the legislature was repealed in 1964 by a popular referendum, but in 1966 the State Supreme Court declared the referendum measure unconstitutional as a denial of equal protection of the laws. In 1966 a federal open housing measure proposed by President Johnson failed of enactment in the Senate.

✻ EQUAL JUSTICE UNDER LAW

Equality is also a key concept in the establishment of justice, which the Preamble to the Constitution rates second only to the formation of a more perfect union. "Equal justice under law" is the motto that is carved above the portal of the massive marble palace which houses the Supreme Court in Washington. Justice is rendered "under law" when it follows regularized procedures and decides individual cases in the light of authoritative general principles set down in advance. Justice is "equal" when it applies the same principles to everyone alike and disregards all extraneous considerations of class, race, color, wealth, or influence.

The formula adopted in the Fifth and Fourteenth Amendments for guaranteeing that justice will be done under the American Constitution is to require that no person be deprived of life, liberty, or property without due process of law. In general, "due process" means by the judgment of a court. Courts are the custodians of the internal coercive powers of the state. They are trusted to make these important decisions because they *judge*. Judging is a special way of thinking. It involves, first, an ascertainment of the facts in dispute by a carefully controlled process in which all the parties to the controversy participate. The second stage is to determine the appropriate rule of law applicable to these facts by examination of statutes and constitutional provisions, comparison with previous judicial decisions on comparable controversies, and deductions from general moral principles or other authoritative sources.

The goal of equal justice under law guides courts in all their proceedings, both civil and criminal. But it is in the enforcement of the criminal law, where liberty or even life may be at stake, that concern for proper judicial standards is greatest. Most of the specific provisions with respect to judicial procedure found in the Constitution relate to criminal prosecutions.

American practices were strongly influenced by those of English justice, and certain assumptions were such a basic part of the American heritage that they are not specifically mentioned in the Constitution. For example, it is a fundamental tenet of Anglo-Saxon justice that an accused person is regarded as innocent until proved guilty in a court of law. Moreover, the burden of proof in a criminal proceeding rests upon the prosecution, and guilt must be established beyond a reasonable doubt. As we have already seen, guilt is personal, and no one can be punished because of the acts of others for which he had no responsibility. In addition to these underlying assumptions, there are a number of procedural requirements for the system of American criminal justice specifically stated in the Constitution.

The Federalism Problem

The principal provisions regarding judicial procedure are found in the Bill of Rights, in the Fourth through the Eighth Amendments. (See Figure 11–2.) The Fourth guarantees protection from unreasonable searches and seizures. The Fifth contains not only the due process clause, but also provides trial by jury and freedom from double jeopardy and self-incrimination. The Sixth specifies the essential features of a fair trial, including full notice to the defendant of the accusation against him, confrontation with witnesses, and impartiality of the jury. The Eighth forbids excessive bail, excessive fines, and cruel and unusual punishment.

However, the Bill of Rights, as we saw in Chapter 10, applies directly only to the federal government and its institutions. Consequently the procedural protections of the Fourth through the Eighth Amendments were applicable only in the federal courts. Not until the Fourteenth Amendment was adopted in 1868 was there any constitutional basis for federal concern about the standards and processes of state criminal justice. And even then, state courts were controlled only by the general standard of due process of law.

An interesting problem was thus created for the federal system, and for the Supreme Court, which was ultimately responsible for determining the constitutional standards for both federal and state courts. For a long time the Supreme Court held that the *state* courts, bound only by the need to

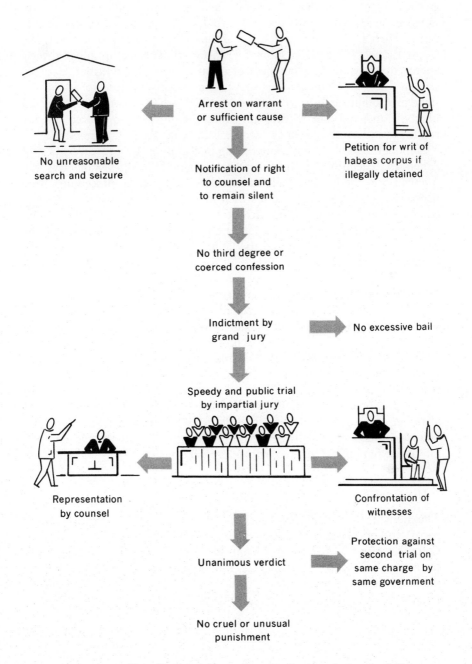

No unreasonable
search and seizure

Arrest on warrant
or sufficient cause

Petition for writ of
habeas corpus if
illegally detained

Notification of right
to counsel and
to remain silent

No third degree or
coerced confession

Indictment by
grand jury

No excessive bail

Speedy and public trial
by impartial jury

Representation
by counsel

Confrontation of
witnesses

Unanimous verdict

Protection against
second trial on
same charge by
same government

No cruel or unusual
punishment

FIGURE 11–2. Constitutional Protection for Persons Accused of Crime.

give due process, were free to adopt practices which would be unconstitutional in the *federal* courts because forbidden by specific provisions in the Bill of Rights. "Due process" was a comparatively loose requirement, the Court thought. It left the states free to experiment and to adopt diverse approaches toward their practices of criminal justice. As Justice Cardozo said in *Palko* v. *Connecticut* (1937), the states were free to adopt any standards so long as they were not in conflict with "the concept of ordered liberty," and did not violate principles of justice "so rooted in the traditions and conscience of our people as to be ranked as fundamental."

Although this rule gave interesting recognition to the diversities of American federalism, it did create two major difficulties. One was the problem for the Court itself of deciding just which procedures were necessary to ordered liberty and which might be ignored without denying equal justice under law. The members of the Court often disagreed on what was essential and what nonessential; Justice Black charged that the "ordered liberty" test permitted the Court to substitute "its own concepts of decency and fundamental justice for the language of the Bill of Rights."

The second difficulty was the one of explaining to ordinary citizens, untrained in the intricacies of constitutional law, how it was that the American Constitution did not equally protect defendants in state and federal courts. How could one explain why a federal court had to appoint counsel for a defendant too poor to hire one, whereas a state court did not? How could it be justified that a defendant could be convicted in a state court on evidence that could not have been legally presented in a federal court?

The pressure of such anomalies eventually led the Court very largely to abandon the effort to apply differing constitutional tests to state and federal courts, as we shall see in the following review of the more important procedural protections recognized by the Constitution

Unreasonable Searches and Seizures

The Fourth Amendment protects the people "in their persons, houses, papers and effects, against unreasonable searches and seizures." This provision gives effect to the ancient English maxim that a man's home is his castle. As the test of reasonableness, the amendment relies primarily upon requirement of a search warrant, issued "upon probable cause, supported by oath or affirmation, and particularly describing the place to be searched, and the persons or things to be seized." Warrants must be obtained from judicial officers, who are expected to prevent overzealous or unjustified police action. Searches and seizures may be made without search warrants in connection with lawful arrests, but evidence of crime that is seized without warrant and without justification by law enforcement officers cannot be used as evidence in a judicial prosecution. This is the so-called exclusionary rule, adopted by the Supreme Court for federal prosecutions in a 1914 decision.

The Supreme Court had no occasion to decide whether the state courts were bound by the unreasonable search and seizure rule until 1949. The case of *Wolf* v. *Colorado* involved an abortionist who had been convicted on the basis of records seized by the police in an unauthorized search of his office. The Supreme Court held that "the security of one's privacy against arbitrary intrusion by the police" was an essential element in the concept of "ordered liberty," and so entitled to Fourteenth Amendment protection against state action. But the Court majority then illogically went on to hold that the exclusionary rule did not apply in state courts, and that consequently illegally secured evidence could still be used to send a man to jail.

During the next decade the Supreme Court was confronted with some shocking cases of local police methods; in one instance the police secured evidence to convict a man for possessing drugs by having his stomach pumped to bring up morphine tablets he had swallowed (*Rochin* v. *California* [1952]). After a few experiences like this the Court concluded in the 1961 case of *Mapp* v. *Ohio* that the exclusionary rule should also be applied to the states. Thus for both federal and state courts evidence secured by unreasonable search and seizure is now inadmissible in court.

Self-incrimination and Coerced Confessions

One of the important provisions of the Fifth Amendment is that no one "shall be compelled in any criminal case to be a witness against himself." This protection has been interpreted to cover witnesses before congressional committees and grand juries as well as defendants in criminal cases. There has been sharp difference of opinion about the desirability of the self-incrimination rule, but it embodies a basic principle of Anglo-Saxon jurisprudence that no individual is obliged to help the government prove that he committed a crime. It is up to the prosecutor to prove his case by adducing evidence against the defendant; for this reason the American system of criminal procedure is referred to as "accusatorial" in comparison with the European "inquisitorial" system.

The most obvious effect of the Fifth Amendment is that the defendant in a criminal trial cannot be compelled to take the witness stand, and opposing counsel cannot call attention to the failure of a defendant to take the stand in his own defense. Before a grand jury or legislative committee, because there is no indictment for crime, a person from whom evidence is sought cannot refuse to be a witness; but once he is on the stand he can decline to answer particular questions on the ground of self-incrimination. If the prosecuting officers or the legislative committee want a certain person's testimony badly enough, they can, under several federal statutes, grant the witness immunity from prosecution for any criminal action he may reveal and thus compel him to talk (*Ullmann* v. *United States* [1956]).

The Supreme Court initially held that the privilege against self-incrimination was not applicable at the state level (*Twining* v. *New Jersey* [1908]; *Adamson* v. *California* [1947]). However, here again the Court has reversed itself. In *Malloy* v. *Hogan* (1964), a majority ruled that protection against self-incrimination was an "essential mainstay" of the American accusatorial system, and that it would be "incongruous to have different standards determine the validity of a claim of privilege . . . depending on whether the claim was asserted in a state or federal court."

Confessions extorted by force or violence (the "third degree") are of course forbidden in the federal courts by the Fifth Amendment, for in such cases the defendant would obviously have been under compulsion to testify against himself. The same rule was first applied in state courts under the due process clause in 1936 (*Brown* v. *Mississippi*). Subsequently the Court extended the ban to confessions secured by nonviolent means where there is mental or psychological pressure of an "inherently coercive" character. Convictions founded in whole or in part on involuntary confessions are a denial of due process of law, without regard for the truth or falsity of the confession, even though there is evidence aside from the confession to support the conviction.

More recently the Supreme Court has sought to bar even voluntary confessions if they are secured in violation of constitutional rights. The Court first moved in this direction in the famous case of *Escobedo* v. *Illinois* (1964), where a suspect was refused the right to see his lawyer while he was being held and questioned in the police station as a murder suspect. The Court ruled that whenever a police investigation ceased to be general and focused on a specific suspect, he was entitled to the assistance of counsel, and a subsequent conviction would be invalid if he was denied access to counsel.

Two years later, in *Miranda* v. *Arizona* (1966), the Court went further and in a 5 to 4 decision laid down a stiff code of conduct for police interrogation, including the following requirements:

1. *If a person is held in custody for interrogation, he must first be informed in clear and unequivocal terms that he has the right to remain silent.*

2. He must be warned that anything he says can and will be used against him in court.
3. He must be given the right to consult with counsel prior to questioning, and to have counsel present during questioning if he desires.
4. Failure to request counsel does not constitute a waiver of the right to have counsel.
5. If the accused is unable to secure a lawyer, one must be appointed for him.

The Court recognized that a lawyer would probably advise the suspect not to talk to police until he had investigated the case, and said this would be merely good professional judgment on the attorney's part. The Court warned that if interrogation went on without the presence of counsel and a confession was secured, a heavy burden would rest on the state to demonstrate that the defendant knowingly and intelligently waived his privilege against self-incrimination and his right to retained or appointed counsel.

The dissenters in *Miranda* argued that the Court was really expressing a distrust of all confessions and saying that it was inherently wrong to secure

GRIN AND BEAR IT   By Lichty

"The Supreme Court decision spells it out, Roscoe! If a motorcycle officer asks where the fire is, you don't have to tell him!"

Lichty; in *Chicago Sun-Times*, 1966. Used by permission of Publishers Newspaper Syndicate.

evidence from the accused himself. They thought that society's interest in the detection and prevention of crime was being downgraded in preference to the rights of criminal suspects. But the Court replied that the rules announced were already followed by the FBI, in American courts martial, and under English and Scottish law.

The *Miranda* decision set off a nationwide debate. Many law enforcement officers contended that the new rules would make it impossible any longer to solve crimes by securing confessions. On the other hand, it was argued that police now concentrate on confessions because that is easier than going out looking for evidence, and that *Miranda* would force them to do a more creative job. Also, several studies purported to show that confessions are not presently involved in the great majority of convictions.

Indictment by Grand Jury

The Fifth Amendment provides: "No person shall be held to answer for a capital, or otherwise infamous crime, unless on a presentment or indictment of a grand jury. . . ." The purpose of the grand jury provision is to require prosecuting officers to prove to a body of laymen that there is a prima facie case of criminal violation so that citizens will not be subjected to the expense and indignity of a criminal trial without reasonable cause. If the grand jury finds the evidence sufficiently strong, it votes an indictment or a "true bill."

This is one area where the states are not required to follow federal standards. In about half of the states a prosecuting officer may bring a person to trial by filing an "information" against him. The Supreme Court upheld this practice in 1884 (*Hurtado* v. *California*) and has never reversed this decision.

Trial by Jury

The Constitution provides for jury trials in criminal cases by the Sixth Amendment (and also by Article III, Section 2, of the original Constitution), and in civil cases "where the value in controversy shall exceed twenty dollars" by the Seventh Amendment. The Supreme Court has held that "jury trial" means the common law jury of twelve men, with a unanimous verdict required. However, Congress has provided for the trial of petty crimes without a jury, and in a criminal case the accused can waive a jury and be tried by the judge.

The Sixth Amendment requires juries to be "impartial." Intentional exclusion of any group in the population from jury lists, or any system of weighting or preference which will render any group in the community more or less likely to be represented on juries, will create constitutional questions. In 1946 the Supreme Court held it was unconstitutional to exclude women from federal juries (*Ballard* v. *United States*). The 1949 Smith Act trial of Communist party leaders in New York was bogged down for seven weeks by defense efforts to establish that poor people, manual workers, Negroes, Jews, women, and members of the Communist and American Labor parties were deliberately excluded from federal jury panels in New York, in favor of "rich, propertied, and well-to-do," but the trial judge found there had been no such purposeful discrimination.

States are under no federal constitutional obligation to grant jury trials, though in fact they all do so for serious criminal cases. State juries need not follow the common law pattern; they can have fewer than twelve members, and depart from the unanimous verdict requirement. But both the due process and equal protection clauses forbid racial discrimination in jury selection. The Supreme Court has moved against Negro discrimination in impanelling juries in a whole series of cases, the most important being *Norris* v. *Alabama* (the Second Scottsboro Case) in 1935. In 1954 the Court reversed a conviction in a Texas county court because of systematic exclusion of persons of Mexican descent from jury service in that county (*Hernandez* v. *Texas*). However, the Court does not require proportional representation of different races and groups on juries. That would be completely impractical.

The Right to Counsel

The Sixth Amendment specifies certain rights essential to an adequate defense in criminal cases, including: "to be informed of the nature and cause of the accusations; to be confronted with witnesses against him; to have compulsory process for obtaining witnesses in his favor. . . ." The only Sixth Amendment right that has caused much controversy is the last one—"to have the assistance of counsel for his defense."

The principal problem that arises is in situations where the defendant is too poor to hire a lawyer to defend him. In 1938 the Supreme Court ruled that defendants must be represented by counsel in all federal criminal proceedings (*Johnson* v. *Zerbst*). Consequently the trial court would have to assign counsel for any defendants who came to court without legal representation.

At the state level the Court first dealt with this problem in the famous First Scottsboro Case, *Powell* v. *Alabama* (1932). The case involved seven Negro boys, ignorant and illiterate, who were charged with the rape of two white girls on a freight train passing through Alabama. They were brought to trial under conditions of extreme public hostility with only the most nominal kind of representation by counsel, and quickly sentenced to death. The Supreme Court reversed the convictions on the ground that "in a capital case, where the defendant is unable to employ counsel, and is incapable adequately of making his own defense because of ignorance, feeblemindedness, illiteracy, or the like, it is the duty of the court . . . to assign counsel for him as a necessary requisite of due process of law."

It was not clear from this decision whether in a noncapital case, where the defendant did not suffer from the disabilities of the Scottsboro boys, the requirement of counsel would also apply. The Supreme Court had such a case ten years later. In *Betts* v. *Brady* (1942) the defendant, who was white, of ordinary intelligence, and charged with robbery, requested the court to appoint counsel for him, because he was financially unable to secure a lawyer. The trial court refused on the ground that in that Maryland county it was the practice to appoint counsel only in murder and rape prosecutions. The Supreme Court upheld this practice, holding that historical research showed "appointment of counsel is not a fundamental right, essential to a fair trial." Counsel had been necessary in the Scottsboro case only because of the "special circumstances" of those defendants.

For the next twenty years a stream of denial-of-counsel cases came before the Court in which it had to decide whether the circumstances were "special" enough so that counsel was a constitutional necessity. In many of these cases the Court did find that counsel had to be supplied. This was generally the holding, for example, where the offense was a capital one; where the conduct of the trial judge appeared to be questionable; where the defendant was young or ignorant or otherwise handicapped; or where technical points of law were involved. In fact, after 1950 the Supreme Court never affirmed a state criminal conviction where denial of counsel was claimed.

Clearly the Court was moving toward a firmer position on the necessity for counsel. Finally, in the celebrated case of *Gideon* v. *Wainwright* (1963), the Court overruled *Betts* v. *Brady* and held that representation by counsel was a constitutional necessity in criminal cases.[1] The decision was generally well received in the legal profession, and programs for supplying counsel to indigent defendants were promptly inaugurated or improved throughout most of the states.

The *Gideon* decision did raise some important problems for future decision. It was not clear whether the requirement of counsel applied only in the trial of serious crimes or in all cases, even petty crimes and misdemeanors. Again, would the Supreme Court apply the *Gideon* rule retroactively, to invalidate all past convictions where counsel had been

---

[1] An extraordinarily interesting account of this decision is the book by Anthony Lewis, *Gideon's Trumpet* (New York: Random House, 1964).

denied? And at what stage in the criminal procedure does the requirement of counsel begin to apply? This latter question was answered in *Escobedo v. Illinois* (1964) and *Miranda v. Arizona* (1966). As was already noted, the Court in these cases ruled that the right to counsel extended back to the stage where the police began to interrogate a suspect.

Double Jeopardy

The Fifth Amendment in archaic language forbids the government to place any person twice "in jeopardy of life or limb" for the same offense. The underlying idea, as Justice Black said in *Green v. United States* (1957), "is that the State with all its resources and power should not be allowed to make repeated attempts to convict an individual for an alleged offense, thereby subjecting him to embarrassment, expense and ordeal and compelling him to live in a continuing state of anxiety and insecurity, as well as enhancing the possibility that even though innocent he may be found guilty."

The double jeopardy provision means that after an accused has been acquitted in a federal court, the government cannot appeal the decision or try him again for the same offense. But where a jury fails to agree on a verdict and is discharged, a second trial is permissible. An accused waives his immunity against double jeopardy when he requests a new trial or appeals from a verdict of guilty. If a conviction is set aside on appeal, the defendant may be tried a second time for the same offense, and he assumes the risk of a heavier penalty than was given in the first trial. But according to *Green v. United States* (1957) he cannot be subjected to the risk of being convicted on a more serious charge than in the first trial.

In *Palko v. Connecticut* (1937) the Supreme Court held that the double jeopardy rule does not apply to the states. More recently, the Court has been willing to concede that it may apply, but has not yet found a case where the rule was violated. A macabre situation arose when the state of Louisiana proposed to take a condemned man to the electric chair for the second time, after mechanical failure had prevented electrocution from being effective on the first trip. The Supreme Court held that this was not double jeopardy in the constitutional sense (*Louisiana ex rel. Francis v. Resweber* [1947]).

Under our federal system the same action may be made a crime by both federal and state law—for example, robbing a national bank. The Supreme Court has ruled that both federal and state prosecution in such cases is not double jeopardy (*Abbate v. United States* [1959]; *Bartkus v. Illinois* [1959]).

Cruel and Unusual Punishment

The Eighth Amendment's ban on "cruel and unusual punishment" under current moral standards does not interfere with execution by hanging, shooting, electrocution, or lethal gas. It would forbid torture, maiming, lingering death, and possibly flogging. It is conceivable that sentiment may some day develop to the point where capital punishment will be generally regarded as "cruel."

In *Trop* v. *Dulles* (1958) the Supreme Court held that taking away the citizenship of a member of the armed forces convicted of wartime desertion was a cruel and unusual punishment. Denationalization, Chief Justice Warren said, involves "no physical mistreatment, no primitive torture. There is instead the total destruction of the individual's status in organized society. It is a form of punishment more primitive than torture, for it destroys for the individual the political existence that was centuries in the development." In another interesting case, *Robinson* v. *California* (1962), a state law making narcotics addiction a crime to be punished rather than an illness to be treated was held to constitute cruel and unusual punishment.

Habeas Corpus

The purpose of the writ of habeas corpus (Latin for "have the body [in court]") is to provide a judicial remedy for arbitrary arrest or unlawful punishment. The writ, when issued by a court on petition of a person who is imprisoned or being held by police, requires the officers involved to bring the prisoner before the court and show that there is just cause for depriving him of his liberty. If the court is not satisfied, it can order the prisoner's immediate release.

Initially habeas corpus was not available to prisoners who had been duly convicted and sentenced by a court. But in 1867 Congress passed a law authorizing the federal courts to issue writs of habeas corpus to prisoners in custody "in violation of the Constitution or of any treaty or law of the United States." Under this provision, persons convicted of crime in state courts who claim that their constitutional rights were denied in the trial can, after failing to get redress in the state courts, have their charges reviewed by a federal court through writ of habeas corpus, and this is very often done.

Article I, Section 9, of the Constitution provides that the writ of habeas corpus "shall not be suspended, unless when in cases of rebellion or invasion the public safety may require it." The Constitution does not say who is to suspend the writ, but since this provision is in the legislative article of the Constitution, it was generally assumed that the power belonged to Congress. However, early in the Civil War, President Lincoln ordered the writ suspended in various parts of the country. While Chief Justice Taney vigorously criticized this action, Congress subsequently passed a statute authorizing the President to suspend the writ when in his judgment such action was necessary.

After the Civil War was over, the Supreme Court in *Ex parte Milligan* (1866) held that the President had no power to suspend the writ in areas outside an actual theater of war. Again, after World War II, the Court in *Duncan v. Kahanomoku* (1946) ruled that the declaration of martial law in Hawaii and the suspension of habeas corpus until 1944, long after the threat of invasion was over, was unjustified on the ground that the supension had not been authorized by the Hawaii Organic Act of 1900.

Military Justice

The armed forces maintain a system of courts-martial for punishment of offenses by their members, under regulations prescribed by Congress. The right to indictment by grand jury is specifically made inapplicable by the Fifth Amendment to "cases arising in the land and naval forces." Congress has by statute provided that other constitutional protections, except for jury trial, shall prevail in court-martial proceedings.

In general, courts-martial constitute a system of justice completely separate from the civilian courts. The decision of a court-martial must be affirmed by the appropriate command officers, and a final appeal may be taken on matters of law to the Court of Military Appeals, a bench of three civilian judges set up by Congress in 1950. Appeal from this court to the Supreme Court is specifically prohibited by the 1950 law.

However, the writ of habeas corpus supplies a method whereby detention resulting from a court-martial decision can be reviewed by the civil courts. Such review is strictly limited, but it does permit the conformity of court-martial procedures to constitutional standards to be examined.

It is clear that in recent years the Supreme Court has been much concerned with strengthening the constitutional rights of persons accused of crime, and particularly in upgrading the standards of state and local law enforcement. In fact, the Court has been sharply criticized by law enforcement officers and others who charge it with giving too much protection to the criminal and unduly handicapping society's efforts to bring lawlessness under control.

Unfortunately the facts are at present largely lacking to support or refute these charges, and it will be necessary to await further experience to determine whether the new level of protection for persons accused of crime will substantially handicap the successful prosecution of criminals. But it is important to remember, as Justice Frankfurter once said, that the constitutional protections of the criminal law are provided "not out of tenderness for the accused but because we have reached a certain stage of civilization"—a civilization which, Justice Douglas added, "by respecting the dignity even of the least worthy citizen, raises the stature of all of us."

PART III 🌿 THE POLITICS OF
AMERICAN DEMOCRACY

CHAPTER 12

PUBLIC OPINION
AND ELECTORAL
BEHAVIOR

Politics is commonly defined as a struggle for power. "Politics," wrote Max
Weber, "means striving to share power or striving to influence the
distribution of power, either among states or among groups within a
state."[1] While this definition applies equally to politics in the United
States and in other countries, the manner in which the struggle for power
takes place and the people who participate differ greatly from one country
to another. For instance, in a country ruled by a military junta, the striving
for power may be limited primarily to the officers of the armed forces. In a
Communist country, the struggle is principally among the upper echelon
of leaders in the Communist party. In the United States there is a place for
every citizen to take part in the political process, and the means by which
citizens may participate are varied, including running for office or seeking
appointment to an administrative position, becoming leaders in a political
party or political interest groups, attempting to influence public opinion,
and voting.

[1] H. H. Gerth and C. Wright Mills, eds., *From Max Weber: Essays in Sociology*
(New York: Oxford University Press, 1946), p. 78.

ꙮ PUBLIC OPINION

The concept of *government based on public opinion* is relatively new in history. It developed simultaneously with the evolution of democratic government and the extension of the suffrage, and even today it is not accepted by the rulers of authoritarian regimes. Thus the attitude toward public opinion as a political force differs greatly in countries such as the United States and Great Britain on the one hand, and the Soviet Union and Saudi Arabia on the other.

Every government, regardless of its organizational structure, must be concerned, to some extent, with public opinion. Government officials in modern democracies, realizing that their tenure in office may be brief if they are indifferent to the views of the majority of the people, employ a variety of methods to assess the opinions of their constituents. Officials in totalitarian regimes, although less concerned with losing office, also realize that if their governments are to function effectively, they must have the support of a substantial number of citizens. They, too, attempt to learn the attitudes of their people, if for no other reason than to anticipate subtle or passive resistance to new policies.

The different approaches of democracies and dictatorships toward the opinions of their citizens reveal a fundamental distinction between the two types of governments. In democracies, freedom of speech and press is guaranteed; methods are devised for exchange of information and ideas between public officials and the people; the belief is held that public officials have the responsibility to translate into public policy the wishes of the people; dissent may be expressed without fear of reprisal; and the right to dissent implies freedom to join with others to vote the government out of power. In dictatorships, the opposite is true on virtually every point. There is no freedom of speech or press; officials are more interested in molding public opinion than in responding to it; public opinion has little positive effect on governmental activities; and individuals who express dissenting views may expect swift and certain punishment.

What Is Public Opinion?

When writers first began to reflect on the influence of public opinion on the governmental process, the political regimes they observed were less complex than most present-day democracies. In that age—prior to the airplane, radio, and television and when the literacy rate was much lower and the suffrage was more limited—public opinion was considered to be primarily the opinions held by the upper and upper-middle classes on political issues, which were generally less complicated and changed more slowly than those of today. Early scholars who observed the influence of these people on governmental policies often regarded public opinion as a type of organic entity or mystical force. For instance, James Bryce, a brilliant British scholar, writing at the beginning of this century, described public opinion as "a real force, impalpable as the wind, yet a force which all are trying to discover and nearly all to obey."

In recent decades, through the research of political scientists, social psychologists, and sociologists much has been learned about public opinion, but no universally acceptable definition has yet been devised. V. O. Key suggested what is perhaps the most useful definition of public opinion: "those opinions held by private persons which governments find it prudent to heed."[2] Many other scholars approach the problem by defining separately the two words *public* and *opinion*. They insist that for the term to have any tangible meaning it must apply to a particular public and to opinions regarding some specific issue or issues.

General and Special Publics. Although on some broad topics there is sufficient interest on the part of the entire citizenry to have a general public opinion, surveys have shown that only a small proportion of the population has sufficient information and interest to form an opinion on many political issues. When one is considering most political questions, therefore, it is useful to think of those with opinions as special or "attentive" publics, and those who do not, as "inattentive" publics. For instance, the attentive public on the question of the nation's entry into a war would be virtually the entire populace or the general public. If the issue were the level of price support for farm commodities, the attentive or special public might be limited primarily to the farmers and the processors of farm commodities. If the question were the acquisition of property for a city park, the attentive public would be the interested local citizens. It is apparent that the issue determines the "public."

As the political issues change, the relationship of the attentive and inattentive publics may shift, with an attentive public becoming inattentive and vice versa. In actuality, often one issue will elicit the attention of one group or groups, a different problem may interest a second element of the citizenry, and a third might attract the attention of still another public. Thus the publics group and regroup depending on the particular issue or controversies.

The inattentive public should not be considered unimportant. Although

2 V. O. Key, Jr., *Public Opinion and American Democracy* (New York: Knopf, 1961), p. 14.

they may make little effort to be informed, and what knowledge they have is usually superficial, from the standpoint of policy formation they are important for two reasons: there are many of them, and they share the basic attitudes and values of other Americans. If they are activated, they become part of the attentive public and may assist in establishing the limits within which the government must act.

On some political questions there may be no sharp distinction between the attentive public and the inattentive; instead, the population could figuratively be placed on a spectrum, with the highly attentive public at one end, the inattentive at the other end, and the remainder of the population spaced along the spectrum according to their interest and opinions on the specific question. For instance, in 1966 the opinions of the American people probably could have been viewed in this fashion on the question of American policy in Vietnam.

The Role of Opinion Leaders. From the standpoint of the process by which opinions are formed, it is also useful to conceive of the attentive publics as being composed of two groups—the formal and informal opinion leaders and those who are informed but take a more passive role. Of these, the opinion leaders, and in particular, the formal opinion leaders, are the most important. The primary relevance of public opinion in the governmental process must be considered from the standpoint of the existence of this elite of political activists. These are the individuals who are most active in originating new policies, in suggesting changes in existing policies, and in activating and converting other individuals to their views. As Gabriel Almond has remarked, "Who mobilizes elites, mobilizes the public."[3]

It is difficult to say precisely who should be included in the group of opinion leaders, for the membership is indefinite and changes. Undoubtedly the number one formal opinion leader is the President, whose pronouncements and activities are daily reported on television, radio, and in the press. Also included among the formal opinion leaders are many of the other elected public officials; leaders of economic, religious, ethnic, and other interest groups; syndicated columnists, journalists, and news commentators; political party leaders; and numerous other political activists who function in a variety of middle and top-level capacities. These political elites are tremendously important in the opinion formation process. Whereas most of the formal opinion leaders are from the the upper and upper-middle strata of the population, informal opinion leaders are found at all levels in society. The latter include persons who hold no official

[3] Gabriel Almond, *The American People and American Foreign Policy* (New York: Harcourt, Brace & World, 1950), p. 138.

positions in the government or political parties, but who are well informed politically and discuss political issues with numerous friends, acquaintances, and even casual contacts.

Some political observers believe that to a large extent the character and quality of the nation's political opinions and policies are dependent upon the nature and behavior of these opinion leaders. In the words of Professor Key:

> The longer one frets with the puzzle of how democratic regimes manage to function, the more plausible it appears that a substantial part of the explanation is to be found in the . . . leadership echelon. . . . Focus of attention on this sector of the opinion system . . . does not deny the importance of mass attitudes. It rather emphasizes that the pieces of the puzzle are different in form and function and that for the existence of a democratic opinion-oriented system each piece must possess the characteristics necessary for it to fit together with the others in a working whole.[4]

In addition to opinion leaders, the attentive publics include those who are aware of the political issues of the day—or at least those issues that relate directly to them—but who are comparatively passive. Many members of political interest groups would fall into this category. While not originators of opinions, these individuals often discuss public affairs, make some attempt to keep informed, and help to modify and mold political attitudes. For many of these individuals, opinion formation is a two-step process, or multistep, with much of their information being received directly or indirectly from opinion leaders. Aware of the significance of political decisions, the persons in this second category may be stimulated to take actions that shape public policies. They, therefore, play an important role in the development of public opinion and in bringing it to bear on public policy.

The Function of Public Opinion

Observers of democratic government have long pondered the relationship of public opinion to governmental actions. Although it is no doubt correct to say, as did James Bryce, that "public opinion is the real ruler of America," such statements tell us very little about the actual role of public opinion in the American system of government.

Obviously, the impact of public opinion on public policy will vary according to different circumstances and political problems. Depending upon the particular issue and set of conditions, public opinion may be

[4] Key, *Public Opinion and American Democracy, op. cit.*, p. 537.

considered to perform any one of at least three different functions—supportive, directive, or permissive.[5]

Supportive Function. For most continuing programs general public opinion performs a supportive function. From the adoption of the Constitution—which was originally opposed by a large segment of the population —to the present, most programs after being established have been undergirded by an opinion consensus. Public support for existing programs is so customary that it is commonly taken for granted, and its significance is usually overlooked until proposals are made for changing such approved programs. Reactions to suggestions to change the federal postal system and the social security program serve as illustrations. A proposal in the 1950s that the government contract with a private corporation for carrying the mail met swift adverse reaction and was not pursued. Senator Barry Goldwater, early in the 1964 presidential campaign, found his suggestions for making the social security system optional so unpopular that he hastened to endorse the existing program. The importance of the supportive role of public opinion is further illustrated by noting changes that have occurred in public policies that lacked such support. Over a century ago the absence of an opinion consensus regarding slavery resulted in the Civil War and the abolition of slavery. Another example was the lack of public sentiment favoring prohibition, which made it virtually impossible to enforce prohibition laws and led to the repeal of the Eighteenth Amendment.

Directive Function. Under some circumstances the public may be so united in their opinions about an issue that public opinion may be said to be directive. Undoubtedly there are fewer instances of public opinion performing a directive than either supportive or permissive functions, but there are occasions when mass opinions have appeared so closely correlated with public policy as to appear directive or decisive in the adoption of that policy. For example, the step-by-step involvement of the United States in World War II paralleled so closely the development of an opinion consensus that it may be said to have been directive. Public opinion polls in 1940 and early 1941, for example, showed that the people were more willing to aid Britain at the risk of war than was Congress at that time.

Permissive Function. In the formation and enactment of governmental policy, public opinion commonly performs a permissive function. On most public problems the political attitudes of the general populace do not require the adoption of a specific policy, but allow the elected officials wide

[5] This concept of the role of public opinion is based on the discussion by V. O. Key, *ibid.*, pp. 29–37.

latitude in working out solutions. Often, because of the low intensity of opinion of many individuals and the apathy or ignorance of others, public opinion permits the policy-makers to select any one of a number of alternatives, including doing nothing, without having to fear reprisals at the polls. Indeed, on some questions, actions favored by a majority who do not hold strong views may be defeated or delayed by an organized and active minority. For example, shortly after President Truman in 1949 presented his government health insurance proposal, correspondence to congressmen indicated general approval. Yet due to the efforts of the American Medical Association the proposal was then defeated and it was not until 1965 that a modification of it, the medicare program, was enacted. Another example of the permissive function of public opinion is the admission of Hawaii as a state, which opinion surveys show was approved by a sizable majority of Americans for over fifteen years prior to the date of admission to the Union. As neither issue was of major importance to most of the electorate, Congress had considerable discretion in deciding what action to take and when.

We know that public officials and government agencies make extraordinary efforts to assess public attitudes; yet we find instances in which opinion surveys show a majority favoring a particular proposal, but no action occurs. On the other hand Congress adopts a measure urged by a small special public, but one in which the majority of the people have no interest. The relationship between governmental policy and public sentiment thus may appear ambiguous at times; nevertheless, astute public officials seldom question the importance of the permissive role of public opinion.

In the following explanation of President Johnson's decision-making process regarding Vietnam, note the efforts to prepare the public—"the jury"—for new decisions:

> ... The intricate choreography of Presidential decision-making seemed a familiar ritual—the initial, relatively circumspect statements, the supporting testimony of diplomatic and military advisors, the White House briefing for Congressional leaders, the round of telephone calls from the big oval office to influential private citizens around the country, the polls, the word-pictures evoking an unruffled President moving toward a painful but inescapable decision. ... There were those in Washington who were certain that the verdict was in even before Mr. Johnson began his long address to the jury.[6]

The longer one contemplates the function of public opinion in democratic government, the more one is impressed with the importance of

[6] *Newsweek*, February 7, 1966.

responsible leadership in the development of policy proposals and the presentation of political alternatives. Democracy is based on the ability of the average citizen to reach intelligent decisions; but he must be provided information and guidance in making those decisions. General public opinion in a representative democracy might thus be conceived in most instances as establishing the boundaries within which public officials acting as representatives of the people make decisions.

Assessing Public Opinion

Government officials have the responsibility of both informing the people regarding political questions and heeding their opinions in the formulation of public policies. They inform the public in a variety of ways, including public addresses, press conferences and press releases, meetings with private citizens and organized groups, and appearances on television programs.

But how do public officials learn the views of the general and specialized publics so that they may reflect those opinions in their decisions? In considering this question, it is well to remember the distinction between general public opinion and specialized opinions held by attentive publics. On broad issues of public policy, it is essential that the government have the support of the general public, but it is not necessary to seek their concurrence on the detailed application of those policies. As the majority of the people probably will have no opinions on more specialized issues, the views officials will seek are usually those of political interest groups or the attentive publics.

The Mass Media as a Means of Assessing Public Opinion.   Most public officials attempt to keep abreast of public events through the mass media of communication—in particular, newspapers and periodicals. Aware that opinions are shaped by interpretations of events as well as by the events themselves, many top officials read several daily newspapers and one or more weekly newsmagazines. For years it has been customary for certain members of the White House staff and also staff members of other government offices to devote full time to reading and analyzing sources of expressed opinion. These staff members then pass on to the President and other officials summary accounts of the news and editorial columns. For example, the State Department once announced that it had a staff that analyzes "editorials from 90 daily newspapers, the output of 62 columnists, plus articles by special writers for particular newspapers or wire services, about 60 magazines, regular reports from 60 major private organizations, results of public opinion polls . . . and news stories and letters to the editor revealing opinions of important groups and prominent individuals."

Political Interest Groups.   Reference was made earlier to the role played by political interest groups as attentive or special publics. As will be explained in Chapter 15, these groups utilize a variety of means for informing public officials of their views. On many issues the opinions held by the public are largely shaped by political interest groups. These groups tend to equate their interests with the public welfare and to exaggerate the extent to which the general public shares their opinions. Hence, while such groups provide one means of assessing public attitudes, experienced political officials usually check the statements of interest-group leaders and lobbyists with other sources to determine the degree to which the general public concurs with the goals of a specific group.

Communications with Private Citizens.   Officials learn much regarding mass opinions from direct communications with private citizens. Letters, telegrams, telephone calls, and personal conversations provide a means for assessing opinions. Public officials soon learn to distinguish between such communications that are initiated by personal interest and those that are stimulated by pressure groups. In order to be cognizant of their constituents' views, most congressmen visit their districts to consult individual opinion leaders and to talk to rank-and-file voters.

"*My* mail seems to be running about three to one against *everything!*"
Drawing by D. Fradon; © 1965 The New Yorker Magazine, Inc.

Elections.   In democracies, elections not only perform the function of determining who will hold public office but also serve as a measurement of public opinion. Presidential elections have been the primary means by which the American citizenry has voiced a collective opinion. In actuality, the extent to which an election measures public opinion varies from one election to another. Because Americans reach their individual voting decisions for a variety of reasons, often an election proves little more than who is to hold office, and it is difficult to determine what mandate was received by the winning candidate. But most presidential elections provide a crude measurement of the direction the electorate wishes the government to move, and in some presidential elections—such as 1932 and 1964—the voters appear to speak with a clear and forceful voice, at least on general social policies if not on administrative and legislative details.

In a number of states, in addition to selecting public officials, the electorate may vote to recall officials and may participate directly in the legislative process through the initiative and referendum.[7] Through the recall, a public official may be removed from office prior to the expiration of his term. The initiative permits a specified number of voters to propose a statute or constitutional amendment by petition and have it submitted for approval or rejection by the electorate. Through the referendum, a bill or a constitutional amendment that has been adopted by the legislature is submitted to the voters for their approval. These elections provide a more precise measurement of opinion on specific issues than do most general elections. Opinion is divided concerning the relative merits of the recall, initiative, and referendum. However, proponents argue that these three governmental devices increase the influence of the individual voter, serve as checks on elected officials, and provide an additional means by which mass opinions may influence public policy. Opponents point out that these devices tend to lengthen the ballot and place more burden on the voter, and that in most instances the actions are initiated by special interest groups.

Public Opinion Surveys.   Public opinion polls or surveys provide the most effective means for assessing the opinions of large numbers of individuals on a variety of topics. By combining a knowledge of social psychology with mathematical probability, the polling organizations are able to ascertain with a high degree of accuracy the opinions of the entire American public through interviews with a carefully selected sample of 1,500 to 6,000 persons. Although efforts at sampling opinion and predicting election results have been made for more than a century, modern public opinion polling may be said to date to the 1930s when Dr. George Gallup organized the American Institute of Public Opinion (AIPO) and Elmo

---

[7] Twenty-one states make provision for the initiative or referendum, twelve states authorize the recall of state officials, and approximately three fourths of the states provide for the recall in some or all cities.

Roper established his Roper Survey. Today more than 1,000 organizations are engaged in opinion surveys; however, most are engaged in marketing research and do not conduct polls on political issues or attempt to predict election results. In addition to the Roper and Gallup polls, other well-known organizations that conduct surveys of political opinions include the Survey Research Center of the University of Michigan, which has been publishing survey results since 1948, and the Harris Survey, which was established by Louis Harris in 1954.

Even though opinion polling is now a well-established occupation, it is still the subject of several criticisms, two of which should be mentioned here. Several critics of the polling organizations believe that most commercial pollsters have not emphasized sufficiently that within the total process —drafting a questionnaire, selecting the sample, conducting the interviews, tabulating and analyzing the results—decisions must be made that make possible errors in the final results. A second criticism is that the surveys in general have neglected the impact of opinion leaders on political attitudes. Most opinion surveys have ignored the fact that while one man's vote counts the same as another's, one man's opinion may be more important than another's in the determination of mass attitudes.

Predicting election results is at once the activity which attracts the most interest in opinion surveys and the endeavor in which pollsters are most reluctant to engage. According to the pollsters, public opinion surveys are no more than a measurement of opinion at the time of the survey, and should not be used to predict behavior at a later date. They explain that because at least a week is usually required to tabulate and process the results of nationwide interviews, any number of events might occur between the time of the interviews and the election that might invalidate a prediction based on a projection of survey data. A second reason—and one not always admitted—why polling organizations are reluctant to predict election results is that not uncommonly the votes for the two presidential candidates have been very close, often within a few percentage points, and nationwide opinion surveys cannot always obtain that degree of accuracy. For example, in 1948 all of the better-known polls predicted that Harry Truman would lose, but he polled 49.5 percent of the popular votes and was the victor. In that election the Gallup poll underestimated Truman's vote by 5 percent and the Roper poll by 12 percent. Since 1948 the major polling organizations have made improvements in their procedures, but one should not expect absolute accuracy. For instance, in 1964 both the Gallup and Harris polls missed the final results by three percentage points. Polling organizations naturally feel on safer grounds in conducting surveys on questions where an error of a few percentage points is of little practical significance. For example, in marketing a new product, a manufacturer is satisfied if a marketing survey errs by only a few percent. In a political election, these few percent usually mean the difference between victory and defeat.

Sample surveys provide a valuable supplement to the other means of assessing political opinions. Opinion polls may indicate the extent to which the views expressed by the press, the personal communications to public officials, and the opinions of interest group leaders are shared by the general public. Recent Presidents and many members of Congress have closely watched the opinion surveys published in the press in order to determine both general opinion on particular issues and changes in the support for policies. During the extended controversy over American policy regarding Vietnam, President Johnson is said to have carried with him reports of recent polls which showed the extent to which the public supported his policies.

Opinion surveys may help illuminate the significance of election returns; from such surveys one may learn what specific political forces and issues contributed to the victory of the winning candidate. For instance, an opinion survey might show that a victorious candidate won because of his stand on issues A, D, and F, despite the unpopularity of his views on issues B, C, and E. Opinion polls have revealed much information on public attitudes between elections, and variations of opinion among the various segments of the population. Sample surveys have shown not only the proportions of the population favoring a given proposal but also the areas of apathy, ignorance, and misinformation. Efforts have been made to probe such properties of mass opinion as the intensity or the strength with which views are held and the stability of opinions or the likelihood that opinions will change.

The Impact of the Mass Media on Public Opinion

Adlai Stevenson once remarked: "I believe that in 99 cases out of 100, the American people will make the right decision—if and when they are in possession of the essential facts." The primary means by which the people receive these "facts" is through the mass media of communications. Without these means of disseminating information and ideas, there could scarcely be a democratic government. Indeed, free elections and a free press are basic to democracy. Viewed broadly, the mass communications media include all of the means by which vast audiences may be informed— newspapers, magazines, books, radio, television, brochures, handbills, posters, billboards, and public lectures. Essential for the function of self-government is the free flow of ideas and information through these various media.

Patterns of Government Control.   The extent to which the communications media are controlled or regulated by governments ranges from the
complete control which characterizes totalitarian regimes to virtually no
control and a minimum of regulation in the United States and other
democracies. The practices followed by governments fall into four general
categories.

First, customarily in totalitarian states all of the mass media are strictly
controlled by the government. In such countries as the Soviet Union
virtually all newspapers, periodicals, and other publications are published
by the government or under government supervision; the radio and
television are state operated, and the motion pictures are government
produced. Even the novelists, poets, and artists have been instructed by the
government regarding permissible themes and content.

Second, in certain other dictatorships, such as Spain or Egypt under
Nasser, the government operates the radio and television stations, often
publishes one or more newspapers, but permits privately owned newspapers and periodicals to be published under rigid censorship regulations.
Any privately owned press that criticizes the government or prints any
prohibited information or ideas may expect to lose the right to publish.

A third pattern prevails in a number of democracies, including France,
Great Britain, West Germany, and the Scandinavian countries. In these
countries the press is free from government control and censorship, but
governmental agencies operate all or most of the radio and television
stations. In these countries the view is held that the airways are a public
resource and as such should not be granted to a relatively small number of
individuals to be used for their personal economic gain.

In the United States, a fourth pattern of relationship between the government and the mass media has been followed. All elements of the
mass media are privately owned, and any type of censorship over the
opinions or information disseminated by the communications media is
prohibited by the Constitution. Since the days of the Alien and Sedition
Acts, enacted during the administration of the second President, the only
occasions on which the government has become involved in censorship of
the press have been during wartime, and primarily during the Civil War
and World War I. If, from time to time, a public official refuses to divulge
information, reporters quickly charge the government with censorship. But
withholding information—which often is subsequently made available—
hardly resembles the censorship practices in dictatorial regimes, where a
newspaper may be banned and the editor imprisoned merely for criticizing
the government. The Federal Communications Commission (FCC) grants
licenses to radio and television stations in accordance with the "public
interest, convenience, and necessity"—terms never adequately defined by

Congress or the FCC. The Commission exercises a degree of control over the operations of the licensees but not the content of the programs.

The Performance of the Mass Media. Throughout America's history it has been apparent that a free press is essential to the functioning of a democratic society. The communications media rival the family, the school, and religious institutions in molding general attitudes and values, and are no doubt most important in shaping opinions on current political issues. Because of their importance, considerable attention has been directed to the manner in which the mass media—in particular the newspapers, radio, and television—perform their function of providing the people an intelligible and intelligent account of political events and issues. With freedom of speech and press guaranteed, with eight out of ten Americans having access to daily newspapers, and with nine out of ten being exposed to television, one might assume that the people are amply informed regarding political issues. Yet a number of professional journalists and other students of the mass media have called attention to disturbing shortcomings in the functioning of the mass media.

Despite the daily torrents of words, it is asserted, the people are not provided an account of significant political events and issues in a context which explains their meaning. Much of the reporting in the press and on television and radio is either of trivial events or "spot" news, with very little, if any, interpretive material. Often superficial reports are given of major political issues with little background information, whereas detailed accounts will be presented of crimes, scandals, athletic events, and the private lives of celebrities. Many newspapers, in addition to emphasizing trivial and sensational rather than significant news, stimulate few discussions of current problems, and do little to educate the people on political issues.

Television has been criticized even more strongly than the newspapers for failing to inform and educate the people. The charge has been made that television is neither an educational nor an entertainment medium, but that it is primarily an advertising medium operated largely for the benefit of the network and station owners, the pitchmen who perform, and the advertisers. Though this criticism may appear to some to be too harsh, many will agree that the violence, sentimentality, and banality of the westerns, "soap operas," and many other television programs help to document the statement of a former chairman of the FCC that television has become a "vast wasteland." Lester Markel, an editor of the *New York Times*, has written: "The newspapers in general are not doing their assigned job, the only job that justifies their existence—the news. Too much of their space is devoted to entertainment and too little to information. As for television, potentially the most powerful of the mass media, it is almost entirely big and brassy business."[8]

The trend toward increased concentration of ownership of the mass media has been a source of concern to a number of individuals. Fear has been expressed that such concentration will create inordinate power in the hands of a relatively few individuals and will reduce the free flow of ideas and opinions. In 1945, newspaper chains (two or more dailies under common ownership) owned 368 dailies; twenty years later, of the 1,750 dailies in the nation, 750 were owned by chains, and the number so owned was increasing each year. In addition, more than 30 percent of the television stations were affiliated with newspapers and thus were under the same overall management. Although the owners of some communication chains assert that they permit the editorial policy of each paper to be determined by the local editor, other owners admit that they establish the editorial and news policies for all of their newspapers. For example, the *Wall Street Journal*, December 15, 1965, quoted William Randolph Hearst, Jr., editor-in-chief of the Hearst chain, as stating: "I don't want someone running off with his own national or international policy; then it would be his paper and not ours." Even within those chains where the policies are locally determined, all newspapers usually share the same sources of national and international news. Hence the growth of chains reduces the opportunity for the presentation of diverse opinions and viewpoints.

The trend toward monopoly conditions is further illustrated by the decline in the number of cities with competing dailies. Between 1930 and 1965 the number of cities with two or more newspapers declined from approximately 300 to less than 50, and the sole newspaper in many of these cities is owned by a chain. In New York City, for example, the number of general daily newspapers shrank from 12 in the 1930s to its current figure of 4.

The extent to which the communications industry has been permeated with a conservative business bias has disturbed individuals who believe that the mass media should be a means of projecting the opinions and attitudes of all major segments of society. Many owners consider their newspapers or broadcasting stations not as social institutions with public responsibilities, but as business enterprises to be managed as the owner desires. To them, operating newspapers or broadcasting stations is a business run primarily for profit. As businessmen, they often share a conservative political outlook. Those views are sometimes reflected in the news columns of papers as well as on the editorial pages. Controversial issues, especially liberal ones,

[8] *The New York Times Magazine*, August 8, 1965, p. 68.

are sometimes avoided for fear of alienating advertisers or certain interest groups and reducing the profits.

As in the case of other business groups, most newspaper publishers usually support Republican candidates. During this century, only in 1964 have a majority of the nation's newspapers supported the Democratic candidate for President. For instance, in 1960 while 65 percent of the press supported Nixon, only 15 percent favored Kennedy, and the rest professed to be neutral. The fact that Democratic presidential candidates were elected from 1932 through 1948 and again in 1960 with little press support might lead one to the erroneous conclusion that newspaper support is unimportant in campaigns. A recent study of newspapers in California indicates that although the influence of a newspaper in an election is dependent upon several factors, including the other sources of information available to the voter, many voters follow the recommendations of the newspaper they read. For example, 39 percent of the readers of one newspaper who were interviewed stated that they "always" or "occasionally" took to the polls a sample ballot printed by the paper with its recommendations for each office. According to this study, press endorsements of candidates are more influential in local elections than in state and have greater impact in state elections than in national elections.

The charge of "managed news" has been made frequently in recent years. While most misgivings regarding the mass media relate to the operation of the press, the criticism of "managed news" has been made by journalists who assert that government officials—through emphasizing certain information and withholding other—have attempted to "manage" the news. An assessment of this charge illustrates a dilemma in government-press relations. It is true that some public officials have tried to create in the minds of the people illusions regarding public policies. It is also true that all phases of government cannot be conducted effectively in the headlines. Some information, if prematurely divulged, would seriously interfere with the solution of domestic and international problems. Our international commitments add an extra dimension to the problem. Public officials assert that "national security" requires withholding particular information, and most individuals are not qualified to judge whether they are correct. Douglass Cater, a well-known journalist and presidential assistant, succinctly set forth the problem, and possibly the solution, when he wrote: "A free press and a purposeful government are destined to be involved in war of sorts. What the protagonists should always be seeking is not total disarmament but a measure of understanding on weapons control."[9]

[9] Douglass Cater, "Public Opinion," in *American Government and Politics*, ed. Stephen K. Bailey (New York: Basic Books, 1965), p. 165.

For many years political observers have pointed out that it is more difficult to develop a national opinion in the United States than in Great Britain. In addition to the vastly larger territory and the less homogeneous population, there are no national newspapers comparable with those in Britain. For instance, *The Times* is read by opinion leaders throughout Great Britain, but the *New York Times*, which is the most influential newspaper in the United States, is read by relatively few individuals in the South, Midwest, or West. While there are no national newspapers in the United States, developments in mass communication in recent decades make it possible for Americans throughout the nation to be similarly informed. Through the news magazines, syndicated columns, the national news services, and television and radio network newscasts, people in Atlanta or Albuquerque may receive the same accounts of international and national events as those in Chicago or New York.

Although the current performance of the American press leaves much to be desired, it compares favorably with that of any earlier period in the United States and with the mass media of other countries today. Reporting in the American press is undoubtedly less biased, and more objective and responsible than in previous eras. While some publishers, editors, and reporters may lack the desired dedication to truth and objectivity, others have taken their responsibilities seriously. Although there is less competition among newspapers than formerly, the news reports on radio and television supplement those in the press, and tend to counteract deliberately distorted accounts that may occur in one-paper areas. The paradox of concentration of ownership should be mentioned. On the one hand, in such concentration there is always a potential abuse of power. Yet, in practice national magazines or network radio and television broadcasts are in many communities the major voices of moderate and relatively unbiased opinion, where previously the biased opinions of the local "establishment" as expressed in the local paper reigned supreme. Possibly now more than in any previous period, the newspapers, radio, and television have a vital role to play in providing the information necessary if the people are to reach valid conclusions regarding the great issues of our time.

☙ ELECTORAL BEHAVIOR

Voting is both a manifestation of public opinion and a means of granting political power. Considering the significance of elections in the American governmental system, it is natural that efforts should be made to determine what variables are associated with voting. The following factors influence both voting behavior and public opinion.

Social Factors and Voting

Obviously a variety of social and psychological factors and forces influence both electoral behavior and the development of political attitudes in general. Some of these forces are at work in an individual's life from childhood; others are more immediate to the voting decisions. Of the various forces in an individual's social and physical environment the most important is the family.

The Family. The family serves as the principal early determinant of information and ideas regarding political parties, government, social problems, religion, ethnic groups, and other matters. The ideas and concepts gained directly from parents are usually reinforced by the newspapers, periodicals, and books in the home, by friends and occupational associates of the parents, and by the community or neighborhood.

The impact of the family on the development of early attitudes is difficult to overstate. Consider the differences in political perspectives of the son of a corporation executive who reads his father's *Wall Street Journal* and hears discussions of "oppressive" governmental regulations of business, and the son of a factory worker who reads his father's union newspaper and listens to discussions of strikes and lockouts. In the early formative years, individuals develop various political attitudes, some of which are retained much if not all of their lives. These attitudes often lead to specific types of overt political behavior—such as voting a straight party ticket or nonvoting; they also condition a person's political outlook, so that later in life he may be inclined to accept or reject certain kinds of information, depending on whether it conforms or conflicts with his pre-established political orientation.

Voting is essentially a group phenomenon, and the family is the most important and influential group to which a person ever belongs. Professor Lazarsfeld found in his Erie County, Ohio, survey that disagreement regarding presidential candidates occurred between husband and wife in only one couple out of twenty-two. Other studies have shown that among voters whose parents had the same party affiliation, approximately eight out of ten stated that their first vote was for that party and more than two out of three retain throughout their adult years the same party attachment as their parents.[10] The degree of political interest which a person has is often closely related to the attitudes of his parents, with the children of party activists or weak partisans adopting the orientation of their parents.

[10] See Key, *Public Opinion and American Democracy, op. cit.*, p. 296.

Moreover, the children of political independents tend also to become politically independent.

Since parental influences are so strong, how does one account for those individuals—nearly one third of the voters—whose party affiliations are dissimilar from their parents? To a considerable degree the answer is mobility—occupational, economic, and geographic mobility. While it is easy to overemphasize economic mobility within our society, the American educational and economic systems present vast opportunities for individuals to change their socioeconomic status. The impact of the American family upon political and social attitudes is undoubtedly less than in more static societies, or than it was in the past. In the United States today, young people frequently do not follow the vocation of their parents and many enter occupations that place them in different strata of society and different geographic regions. In their new situations and associations they may encounter new political perspectives and information that may erode parental influences.

Occupation. Considering the proportion of a person's time devoted to his occupation and its influence on his socioeconomic status, where he lives, his choice of friends, and the use of his leisure time, it is not surprising that the way one earns his livelihood is an important determinant of political behavior. Table 12–1 shows the percentage of different occupational groups voting for Democratic presidential candidates from 1948 through 1964. As would be expected, the strongest support for Republican candidates came from the professional and managerial class, followed by the other white-collar workers and the farmers. Union members are the most consistent Democratic supporters. As the percentages indicate, the farmers have the most unstable voting pattern. As a group, Midwestern farmers have often switched from one party to the other, and the percent-

TABLE 12–1. *Vote for Democratic Candidate for President, 1948–1964*

	1948 Percent	1952 Percent	1956 Percent	1960 Percent	1964 Percent
Professional and managerial	19	31	31	44	57
White-collar workers	47	35	39	48	63
Skilled workers	72	51	44	57	76
Unskilled workers	67	67	47	59	80
Union members	76	55	51	62	83
Farm operators	59	37	46	33	63

SOURCE: Survey Research Center, University of Michigan.

age who go to the polls varies widely from one election to another. One explanation of this voting behavior is that, living and working more in isolation than most other people, the farmer is less likely to be swayed by membership in organized groups, by co-workers, or by party activists. Many farmers also apparently vote for the party which offers the most satisfactory farm program.

Although these data are useful, much of significance is lost in broad analytical categories. The gross percentages presented in this table fail to illustrate fully cleavages within these categories and the importance of group influences on electoral behavior.

For example, within the "professional and managerial" classification are corporation executives, private entrepreneurs, attorneys, doctors, college professors, and several other subgroupings. While the aggregate figures indicate that historically the group as a whole supports the Republicans, some within the group have voted overwhelmingly for Republican candidates and others have supported Democrats by equally large margins. For example, the proportion of top-level business executives and northern doctors voting the Republican ticket during the 1950s was undoubtedly higher than these figures indicate, for large proportions of other groups in this broad category supported Democratic candidates.

A study of subgroups within the academic profession indicates both the fallacy of using broad categories in classifying individuals and the importance of a person's occupation on his partisan attachments. A survey of more than 2,500 professors teaching in nine different subject-matter areas in American colleges revealed that the proportion of Democrats to Republicans depends upon the area of specialization. While more than 70 percent of the social scientists classified themselves as Democrat, less than 30 percent of the mathematicians and engineers so categorized themselves. This research suggests that for these individuals the information gained in their profession and contacts with colleagues may be more important than the persistence of parental influences in determining their political preferences. As shown in Table 12-2, six of the nine groups surveyed favored the Democratic party, but only two groups reported more Democratic than Republican parents and in each instance the difference was slight.

Socioeconomic Status. In addition to occupation, other socioeconomic voting variables include income, education, and where a person lives. In virtually every category, the more income a person has the greater the likelihood that he will be a Republican voter. This is true of occupational categories, individuals living in different regions and urban and rural communities, all educational and age groups, and all racial and religious groups. This does not mean, of course, that there are not many wealthy

TABLE 12–2. *Party Preferences of Academically Affiliated Professional Groups*

	Dem. Percent	Rep. Percent	Ind. (or other) Percent	Both Parents Dem. Percent	Both Parents Rep. Percent
Philosophy	78.7	13.7	7.5	30.4	37.5
Sociology	77.9	10.4	11.7	36.2	35.9
Political Science	73.7	16.4	9.9	30.0	35.7
History	72.4	20.4	7.2	32.6	40.7
Psychology	70.2	20.6	9.2	38.9	35.7
Botany	50.0	39.7	10.3	27.3	45.6
Geology	35.3	51.5	13.2	25.7	47.7
Mathematics	29.1	55.6	15.3	27.5	43.9
Engineering	27.2	61.9	10.9	25.1	44.9

SOURCE: Adapted from Henry A. Turner, Charles G. McClintock, and C. B. Spaulding, "The Political Party Affiliation of American Political Scientists," *The Western Political Quarterly*, Vol. XVI, No. 3 (September, 1963), 650–665. Reprinted by permission of University of Utah, copyright owners.

Democrats. Both John Kennedy and Lyndon Johnson were millionaires when they became presidential candidates, and Adlai Stevenson, while less affluent, had considerable inherited wealth.

Opinion surveys have indicated a correlation between education and voting. Various studies have shown that college graduates vote Republican in higher proportions than high school graduates, who in turn cast their ballots for Republicans in larger percentages than those with only a grade school education. Undoubtedly the tendency of those with higher educations to vote Republican may be attributed in part to their economic status and occupations. As was shown by the preceding chart, among those with graduate degrees the field of specialization apparently has an influence on partisan preference, with a large proportion of those in the social sciences supporting the Democratic party.

Regional and Residential Influences.   Due in part to historical reasons, the people in certain regions of the nation are predominantly Republican, while in others most of the voters are Democrats. As will be explained in Chapter 13, in some states one party is so dominant that they are virtually one-party states. Within regions and states there are pockets or communities in which the great majority of the voters are affiliated with the smaller party in the state or region. After the Civil War the states below the Mason-Dixon line so consistently supported the Democratic party that this area came to be known as "the Solid South." Regardless of religion or ancestry most southerners—whether lawyers, merchants, doctors, bankers, factory workers, or tenant farmers—have been Democrats. The strongest and most consistent support for the Republicans has been found in Maine and Vermont in the northeast, and the tier of four states consisting of North Dakota, South Dakota, Nebraska, and Kansas. During the seven presidential contests starting with 1940 these states were in the Republican column every election except 1964. Regional influences on party identification have thus contributed to the multigroup character of each party; if it were not for regional influences, the voters would tend to divide throughout the entire nation between the two parties more along class and economic lines. Regional influences on party politics are less strong today than formerly, and as the nation becomes more homogeneous they may be expected to decline further.

Divergences in political attitudes also exist between communities when compared in terms of size—that is, large cities, suburbs, small cities, and rural areas. Samuel Lubell found that in every presidential election since 1928 a majority of the voters in the twelve largest northern cities have voted Democratic, whereas in the nearby suburbs a majority have voted Republican each time except 1936 and 1964. In each of these elections, regardless of the candidates or the issues, the suburbs voted 14 to 17 percent more Republican than the central city.[11] This does not mean that all suburbs are Republican strongholds. There are all types of suburbs and in many the majority of voters are Democrats.

Generally in small cities outside the South the voters tend to support the Republican party in larger proportions than they do in large cities. In cities of 10,000 to 50,000 population the business community—functioning through the local Chamber of Commerce, service clubs, and other organizations—often exerts a more pervasive influence on the entire community than in larger cities, where labor unions and other groups are more likely to operate as competing political forces. Thus in small cities, laborers, government employees, and others are more likely to vote the Republican ticket than in major cities.

Religion and Race. In a number of countries—such as Italy, France, Germany, Ireland, Sudan—religion has served as the basis for organizing some parties. In the United States, Protestants, Catholics, and Jews are found in both parties, but not in the same proportions. Northern Protestants tend to support the Republican party, Catholics tend to be Democrats, and since the 1930s the great majority of Jews have voted the Democratic ticket. Historical factors account in part for this alignment of voters. Protestant groups generally came to the United States first, became

[11] *Los Angeles Times*, February 7, 1966.

TABLE 12–3. *Religious Groups Voting for Democratic Candidates*

	1948 Percent	1952 Percent	1956 Percent	1960 Percent	1964 Percent
Protestant	43	36	35	36	61
Catholic	62	51	45	82	79
Jewish	(a)	71	77	89	89

(a) Too few cases to compute.

SOURCE: Survey Research Center, University of Michigan.

established and often prospered. Most Catholics and Jews came later, often were considered by the now-established earlier arrivals to be minority groups, and customarily moved to cities where Democratic party organizations aided them to become citizens and voters. Franklin Roosevelt and his New Deal, with its emphasis on social reforms, helped to cement the ties of most minority groups to the Democratic party.

As in the case of other voting variables, the candidates and the issues may alter the voting patterns of each group. Note the variations in the percentage of each group voting for Democratic candidates in the presidential elections of 1948 through 1964 as shown in Table 12–3. The candidacy in 1960 of John F. Kennedy, the first Catholic to be elected President, illustrates the salience of religion to electoral behavior. As the table indicates, numerous Catholic Democrats who had voted for Truman in 1948 supported Eisenhower in 1952 and 1956, but returned to the Democratic fold in 1960. Of the Catholics who voted for Eisenhower in 1956, nearly six out of ten supported Kennedy in 1960. Although Kennedy received the votes of many Catholic Republicans, a sufficient number of Protestant Democrats supported his opponent so that—according to estimates of the Survey Research Center—his religion resulted in a net loss of approximately 2 million votes. Apparently because of Kennedy's election and Presidency, the importance of religion as a factor in voting behavior is declining. Of those interviewed, the proportion who stated they would vote for a Catholic increased from 71 percent in 1960 to 84 percent three years later.

The importance of ethnic or racial background as a determinant of voting behavior no doubt declines with each generation. For millions of immigrants and their descendants, America has truly been a great "melting pot." Yet, in certain areas—in particular, a number of cities east of the Mississippi and north of the Ohio River—ethnic voting is a fact of political life. In New York City, for example, each party appeals for the votes of the major ethnic and racial groups in the city by nominating persons from each of these groups. However, not uncommonly their efforts are in vain. For example, in 1961 the Republican candidate for mayor was a Jew, yet the majority of the Jewish voters supported the Democratic candidate.

The Negroes today constitute the single most important racial minority group in the United States. From the Civil War until the administration of Franklin Roosevelt most northern Negroes voted the Republican ticket, largely out of gratitude to Lincoln for the abolition of slavery. In recent elections Negroes have voted for Democratic candidates in constantly increasing proportions until 1964 when approximately 95 percent voted for the Democratic presidential nominee. A major factor in this exceptionally large Negro Democratic vote in 1964 was candidate Goldwater's vote against the Civil Rights Act in the Senate in 1964.

Influence of Age on Voting. Election studies have correlated age with party preference and voting. During recent decades the Republican party has attracted a higher proportion of older voters and the Democratic party more of the younger voters than the national average (see Table 12-4).

TABLE 12-4. *The Vote Among Population Groups for Republican Presidential Candidates*

	1952 Percent	1956 Percent	1960 Percent	1964 Percent
National	55.4	57.8	49.9	38.7
Men	53	55	48	40
Women	58	61	51	38
White	57	59	51	41
Non-white	21	39	32	6
College	66	69	61	48
High school	55	58	48	38
Grade school	48	50	45	34
21–29 years	49	57	46	36
30–49 years	53	55	46	37
50 years and older	61	61	54	41
East	55	60	47	32
Midwest	58	59	52	39
South	49	51	49	48
West	58	57	51	40
Republicans	92	96	95	80
Democrats	23	15	16	13
Independents	65	70	57	44

SOURCE: The Gallup Poll.

The reasons for this phenomenon are not fully known, but it has been suggested that as people grow older they receive higher incomes, acquire more property, become more conservative, and are more disposed to support the Republican party. On the other hand, many young voters, in comparison to the senior citizens, are less interested in politics, do not have such strong party attachments, are more inclined to be swayed by political events and the personality of the Chief Executive. As Democrats have been in the White House all but eight years since 1932, that party has had more opportunity to appeal to new voters both through the personality and leadership of the President and through the enactment of new programs.

The foregoing analysis has focused largely on why some persons consider themselves Democrats and others Republicans. It is no doubt true that classifying voters according to social characteristics may explain little regarding factors influencing voting unless those factors are related in some fashion to political decisions made by public officials. Being a businessman, doctor, Negro, or Catholic may influence a person's electoral decision only if he believes that the victory of a party is relevant to him as a businessman, doctor, Negro, or Catholic. Thus when a large proportion of a given category of voters support a party, it is not due merely to the impulse of social forces, but to what appears to be a rational decision based on the best available information. As noted, the various factors that influence political behavior are interrelated. For many individuals their social and psychological environments are harmonious. For others, when conflict occurs between family, socioeconomic status, or other factors, the individual may retain his partisan attachments, move to the opposite party, or become a political independent.

Influence of Parties, Candidates, and Issues

An analysis of the economic and demographic bases of partisan preferences implies a static quality of electoral behavior and may lead one to the erroneous conclusion that the act of voting is simply an unthinking response to social forces. The sociological factors related to voting, of course, are not static; they change over a period of time, and help to produce new electoral patterns. Yet in order to understand the dynamism that characterizes the American electoral process and the extent to which voters make rational, purposive decisions, one must examine the voters' perceptions of the political parties, candidates, and issues. As has been indicated, a person's perception of these will be influenced by the information he receives through the mass media, his friends, occupational associates, family, and other social forces.

Party Affiliation. The great majority of the electorate identify them-selves with one of the two major parties. For many individuals the party is an important "reference group," that is, a group with which the individual significantly identifies, and from which he derives some basic values and goals. The influence of party attachments tends to be in proportion to the strength of those attachments. For instance, the Survey Research Center found that in the 1964 election, 90 percent of the individuals classified as "strong Republicans" but only 56 percent of the individuals classified as "weak Republicans" voted for Goldwater, and 95 percent of the "strong Democrats" but only 81 percent of the "weak Democrats" voted for John-son. See Table 12–5 for a breakdown of voters according to partisan at-tachments.

Political party affiliation provides a stabilizing force in American politics. Most Americans choose their party early in life and do not change. Regard-less of the candidates or the issues, millions of voters can be counted on by each party. The Survey Research Center reported in 1960 that 56 percent of the voters interviewed stated that they had never voted for a presidential candidate of the opposite party. While there is a continuous movement of voters from one party to the other and many voters will cast ballots for candidates of the opposite party, major shifts in party affiliation have occurred only as a result of some national crisis such as the Civil War or the Great Depression (see Chapter 13). Individuals who change their party affiliations at other times usually do so because of some marked change in their own lives such as marriage, moving, a new job, or a change in economic status.

From the standpoint of the stabilizing role of parties, it is significant that more than half of the electorate always vote for their party's presiden-tial candidate; from the standpoint of political dynamism, it is equally

TABLE 12–5. *Distribution of Party Identification, 1952–1964 (by Percent)*

Identification	1952	1954	1956	1958	1960	1962	1964
Strong Democrat	22	22	21	23	21	23	26
Weak Democrat	25	25	23	24	25	23	25
Independent Dem.	10	9	7	7	8	8	9
Independent	5	7	9	8	8	8	8
Independent Rep.	7	6	8	4	7	6	6
Weak Republican	14	14	14	16	13	16	13
Strong Republican	13	13	15	13	14	12	11
Apolitical	4	4	3	5	4	4	2
TOTAL PERCENT	100	100	100	100	100	100	100

SOURCE: Survey Research Center, University of Michigan.

noteworthy that more than four out of ten persons have voted or are willing to vote for presidential candidates of the other party. Thus while partisan psychological attachments are not changed lightly, many voters will cross party lines in elections.

The voter's perceptions of candidates and issues and the looseness of partisan attachments, all help to account for the dynamic character of American elections. This characteristic is dramatically illustrated by recent election returns. For instance, the Republican percentage of the two-party vote dropped from 57.8 percent in 1956 to 49.9 percent in 1960, and to 38.7 percent in 1964. Although the amount of the decline in the Republican vote is important, equally significant is the fact that Republicans received fewer votes from virtually every socioeconomic category of voters. This decline cannot be attributed to a change in the social bases of Republican support but to a general loss of support from the public at large.

The Impact of Candidates and Issues. While social forces and partisan affiliation influence electoral decisions, the candidates and the issues may be the most important factors in determining the success of a party in a particular election. The ability of a party to retain control of the Presidency in several successive elections and the practice of analyzing voters according to social characteristics have led to the mistaken conclusion that parties draw their support from relatively unchanging blocs of voters. Recent research has indicated that in every election the victorious party receives the votes of millions of individuals who either voted for the opposite party in the preceding election or did not vote. Thus even though a party is returned to office, the composition of its electoral majority may be considerably different from that of the preceding election. Many of these new supporters undoubtedly have been swayed by the candidate or the policies espoused by the party.

The term "candidate orientation" refers to interest in candidates separate from their party affiliations and the political issues. From this standpoint candidates are viewed on the basis of both their presumed effectiveness in office and their personality characteristics. Each candidate is judged on the basis of his past record and his personal appearance and style. The impact of a candidate on the outcome of an election can easily be illustrated. For example, in 1952 and 1956, millions of Democrats crossed party lines and voted for Eisenhower. The fact that the Democrats in 1956 carried both houses of Congress while Eisenhower won the Presidency indicates that many voters were casting their ballots on the basis of candidate orientation rather than because of their partisan affiliations or the issues.

For issue-oriented individuals, public policies provide the strongest norm according to which they make their electoral decisions. While most candidates conduct their campaigns largely on promises of future action, voters tend to judge the parties retrospectively; they respond more to events they have experienced and to policies enacted by a party than to new proposals. Parties are rewarded for enacting policies considered beneficial, and many voters react emphatically if they believe favored policies might be jeopardized by the election of a particular candidate. For instance, the Survey Research Center found that in the 1964 election the Democrats benefited more from having sponsored social security legislation than in previous elections when it appeared less likely that the opposition candidate, if elected, would alter the program.[12]

Independents and Vote Switchers. Before the days of sample surveys, according to American folklore the independent voter was considered to be the more interested, well-informed, judicious person who reached his voting decision after considering all issues and the qualifications of the candidates. Opinion surveys have indicated otherwise, if the term "independent" is applied to those individuals who do not identify themselves with any party. These "independents"—comprising only 5 to 10 percent of the electorate—in general have little interest, information, or concern with politics and often do not vote.[13] Most reach their voting decision late in campaigns, usually because of lack of interest and involvement. As a group they tend to have a volatile voting record, first supporting one party and then the other.

In any presidential election the voters might be considered to be composed of three groups: the standpatters, the new voters, and the switchers. The standpatters are those who voted for the same party as in the preceding election. The new voters are the ones who, because they were too young or for other reasons, did not vote in the previous election. The switchers are those persons who voted for a different party than in the preceding election. While the standpatters are most numerous, recent research indicates that there are more switchers and new voters than previously thought. For instance, in 1960, of those who voted for Kennedy, there were approximately 19.1 million standpatters, 10.3 million switchers, and 4.8 million new voters. The distribution of Nixon's vote was approximately as follows: 26.6 million standpatters, 2.7 million switchers, and 4.8 million new voters. In the presidential elections of the 1940–1960 period

[12] Donald E. Stokes, "Some Dynamic Elements of Contests for the Presidency: The Goldwater Disaster in Context," a paper delivered at the annual meeting of the American Political Science Association, September 8–11, 1965.

[13] Bernard R. Berelson, Paul F. Lazarsfeld, and William N. McPhee, *Voting* (Chicago: University of Chicago Press, 1954), pp. 314–322.

the number of switchers is believed to range from one eighth to one fifth of those who voted in two successive elections.[14]

Whereas the standpatters add stability to the political system, the new voters and the switchers—and in particular the latter—provide flexibility and contribute to the dynamic nature of American politics. Although more research on the switchers is needed, present information indicates that they are not dissimilar in interest, involvement, or education from the standpatters. Most of the switch voters consider themselves to be affiliated with one of the parties, but have voted for the opposite party in order to support a candidate or policies. These voters would, therefore, be considered as candidate-oriented or issue-oriented voters. Hence the switchers apparently do differ from the standpatters in being more open to persuasion and more willing to support the candidate of the opposite party if they believe he is better qualified or will implement desired policies.

℀ SUFFRAGE QUALIFICATIONS AND NONVOTING

Obviously an important factor affecting the outcome of elections is the extent to which all elements of the population have the suffrage. Universal suffrage is today so commonplace among Western democracies that one often forgets that it is a recent phenomenon. In Great Britain, where modern democratic government first developed, at the turn of this century no more than two thirds of the adult males had the vote. All women were not given the suffrage in the United States until 1920, in Britain until 1928, in France and Italy until 1946; and in most countries women are still disfranchised.

In the United States, due largely to the inability of the Founding Fathers to agree on specific requirements, the Constitution left to the states the establishment of voting qualifications. When George Washington was elected President, probably not more than one man out of fifteen could vote. Gradually the suffrage was granted to others. The first struggle over the expansion of the electorate occurred during the early part of the nineteenth century when the states one by one removed the tax-paying and property-owning requirements for voting, and universal white manhood suffrage was achieved. The second effort to extend voting rights followed the Civil War with the adoption of the Fifteenth Amendment, which was intended to grant the vote to male Negroes. The third extension of the right to vote came at the close of World War I with the adoption of the

[14] V. O. Key, Jr., *The Responsible Electorate* (Cambridge, Mass.: Harvard University Press, 1966), pp. 16–25.

Nineteenth Amendment, which established women's suffrage. The fourth major move toward a full realization of universal suffrage occurred in the post–World War II period when federal legislation was adopted aimed at guaranteeing to the Negro the right to register and vote in all states.

Voting Requirements

In every state a voter must be a citizen of the United States and meet age and residential requirements. The minimum age for voting is 18 in Georgia and Kentucky, 19 in Alaska, 20 in Hawaii, and 21 in the other forty-six states. Three southern states—Louisiana, Mississippi, and South Carolina—require two years of residence; eleven middle western and western states require six months; in all others a person must live for a year in the state, and lesser periods in the county, town, or precinct. Approximately two fifths of the states have some form of literacy test for voting. Most states specifically disqualify from voting those who are classified as mentally incompetent and those who have been convicted of a felony.

In the United States, registration is generally a prerequisite for voting. In some places, such as North Dakota and in rural areas of several states, registration is not required, but elsewhere prospective voters must register personally in advance in order to vote. Registration is required in order that the election officials in each precinct will have a list of the qualified voters. In most European countries, the local government officials compile the register of voters; hence, each voter's name appears on the list without any effort on his part, and no one is disqualified by failing to register.

Two types of registration systems—periodic and permanent—are employed by the various states. In fourteen states a voter must register periodically, usually every two or four years. The other states employ permanent registration. In these states, once a person is registered he need not reregister unless he moves, changes his name, wishes to change his party affiliation (in states with closed primaries), or has failed to vote.

Negro Suffrage

Despite the fact that the Fifteenth Amendment, ratified in 1870, specifies that no person could be disqualified from voting because of race or color, the southern Negroes have constituted the largest group of disfranchised citizens in the United States. The elimination of restrictions on their rights has been one of the great social problems of recent years. In 1965 the Department of Justice in filing a suit against Mississippi charged that the state " . . . and its officials for the past three-quarters of a century have been writing and adopting constitutional provisions, statutes, rules and regulations, and have been engaging in discriminatory practices, all designed to keep the number of white voters at the highest possible figure and the number of colored voters at the lowest." The same charge could be made against several other southern states.

Possibly the most effective methods used to keep Negroes from voting have been intimidation and violence. Negroes have been threatened with economic sanctions or bodily harm if they attempted to register or vote, and some who failed to heed the threats have lost their jobs, been forced to move from tenant farms, have had their homes, churches, and businesses bombed, and have been beaten or even killed. The *Wall Street Journal* of November 6, 1964, reported that "acts of violence and harassment" during the 4-month period that year—June 21 to October 21—against civil rights workers and Negroes in Mississippi "included nine unsolved killings, among them the widely publicized murder of the three civil rights workers in Neshoba County; the beating of 80 persons; the burning of 33 churches; 31 bombings; 35 shooting incidents resulting in the wounding of three persons; and the arrest of over 1,000 persons, mostly while engaged in

5/19/63
"Those Alabama stories are sickening. Why can't they be like us and find some nice, refined way to keep the Negroes out?" From *Straight Herblock*
(Simon & Schuster, 1964).

September 16, 1962
"See you in church." Drawing by Bill Mauldin. From *I've Decided I Want My Seat Back* by Bill Mauldin. Copyright 1962, 1963, 1964 by Bill Mauldin. Reprinted by permission of the author and Harper & Row, Publishers.

registration attempts and on petty charges such as failing to move on when ordered by a policeman." Although these incidents occurred at the peak of the civil rights and voter registration drive in the state, they nevertheless give some indication of the extent to which intimidation and violence have been used to prevent Negroes from voting in the South. Other methods and stratagems are discussed in Chapter 11.

Nonvoting

Much has been written regarding the large proportion of nonvoters in the United States in comparison with other democracies. For example, in recent elections in Italy and Austria 90 percent or more of the qualified voters have participated; over the past two decades voter turnout in West Germany has ranged from 78 to 88 percent of those of voting age; and approximately 80 percent of the Canadian electorate may be expected to cast ballots in a national election. By comparison, in presidential elections in the United States during the preceding two decades the percentage of voting-age persons going to the polls has been as low as the 51.6 percent who voted in 1948, and no higher than the 63.8 percent who elected Kennedy over Nixon in 1960. (See Figure 12–1.) Two questions are raised by these figures: first, why does a smaller proportion of eligible persons vote in the United States than in several other democracies; and, second, what factors are related to nonvoting in the United States?

The lower proportion of persons voting in the United States may be explained in part by legal and administrative obstacles to registering and voting. In the record turnout year of 1960, approximately 35 million persons of voting age did not vote. According to the American Heritage Foundation, of that number an estimated 8 million were disqualified because they had moved prior to the election and could not meet residential requirements. Two and a half million others were traveling, 2 million were in the armed forces, and 500,000 were living abroad and did not obtain absentee ballots. Others of voting age who did not vote included an estimated: 2.5 million aliens; 5 million persons who were sick; 115,000 who were opposed to voting for religious reasons; and approximately 3½ million southern Negroes, who for various reasons did not vote in 1960. Also the failure to register disqualified a large number who could have voted if the American states employed automatic registration by government officials

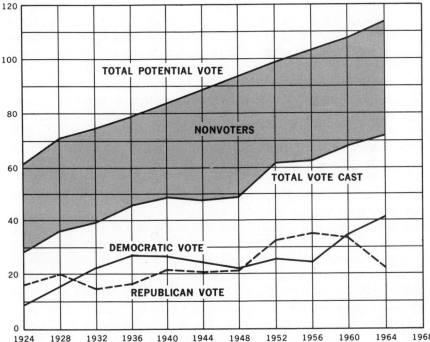

FIGURE 12–1. The Vote Cast in Presidential Elections Since 1924. (Based on data from *Congress and the Nation*, Washington, D.C., Congressional Quarterly Service, 1965, p. 1532.)

similar to that of most western European countries and Canada. It is of interest to note that in 1960 of those who registered, 81.5 percent voted, a figure comparable with the percentage voting in Canadian elections.

Psychological factors are important in determining the level of voter participation. Many fail to vote because of indifference or noninvolvement. Indeed, of those who are qualified, the likelihood that a person will vote is related to his personal interest and involvement in politics. Voter turnout usually is highest in national elections because of the greater interest in them than in state or local elections. The importance a person attributes to voting will help determine whether he votes: some are impelled by a sense of civic duty to vote; others, questioning the political efficacy of their vote, may not make the effort. In areas where there is little two-party competition, voting tends to be lower than in areas where there is strong competition. One reason for the relatively low level of electoral participation in the United States may be the similarity of the two parties. A study of voters in the United States and four other countries—Great Britain, West Germany, Italy, and Mexico—revealed that a smaller proportion of the people in the United States than in the other countries were fearful of the possible victory of an opposition party.[15]

Opinion surveys have shown that nonvoters are to be found in virtually every social and economic grouping in the nation, but some groups vote in larger proportions than others. The voting participation of women is about 10 percent lower than that of men, but the gap is gradually narrowing. The higher the income and the more education a person has, the more likely he is to vote. Often the two go together; if they do not, a person with high income and a grade school education is more likely to vote than one with a college education but a low income. Protestants are less likely to vote than are Catholics, and Catholics are less likely to vote than are Jews. People who have strong party affiliations are more likely to vote than those with weak party attachments or those who consider themselves to be political independents. People over 35 years of age are more inclined to vote than those younger, but after age 65, voting drops off due to old age and declining physical activity. As is true in the case of forces influencing partisan affiliation, the factors helping to determine voter participation tend to be interrelated. Undoubtedly the most important factor causing a person to vote or not vote is his personal interest and involvement in politics. Hence, the data relating to nonvoting tend to serve as a crude index of political interest.

Finally, in many cases nonvoting may be considered a form of voting. The voter who feels satisfied with his lot in life may decide that the victory

[15] Robert E. Lane, "The Politics of Consensus in an Age of Affluence," *American Political Science Review*, LIX, No. 4 (December, 1965), 890.

of either party would not make much difference to him personally. Before Hitler came into power in 1933, voter participation in German elections was often over 90 percent of the electorate; but as subsequent events proved, this did not represent high democratic maturity. This does not mean that low voter participation is in itself desirable, but that no irrefutable conclusion may be drawn from the mere fact of high or low percentages of voters. The quality of the candidates and policies that voters support is more important than the quantity of the people who go to the polls.

CHAPTER 13

THE AMERICAN
PARTY SYSTEM

Government in the modern world is party government. In most countries today governmental power is vested in the leaders of political parties. From a historical standpoint party government is a fairly recent development. Political parties, often considered the greatest political invention of the British people, originated in England in the late seventeenth century as a necessary element in the evolution of representative government; as government became more representative, the influence of parties increased proportionately. Political parties developed in the United States near the end of the eighteenth century, were not established elsewhere until the nineteenth or twentieth centuries, and in certain new states have existed no longer than one or two decades.

During the thousands of years prior to the development of parties, political authority was held by individuals because of particular circumstances—royal birth, military leadership, religious position, wealth, or specialized knowledge or training. In these earlier regimes, short-lived oligarchies or factions occasionally arose which resembled certain political parties of today. These groupings were basically different from present-day parties, however, because they were extraconstitutional or even anticonstitutional organizations. Political parties today, either through legal provisions or custom and practice, have acquired a constitutional status. (See Figure 13-1 showing the United States political spectrum.) In brief, in

314

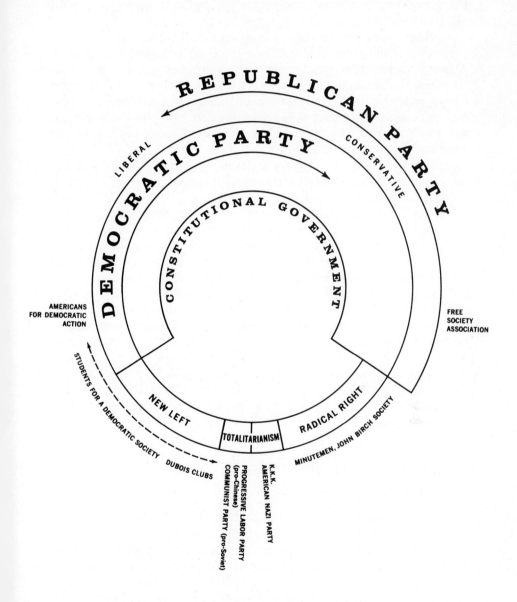

FIGURE 13–1. The United States Political Spectrum.

most modern countries the only legitimate means by which persons now acquire political authority is through political parties. As a consequence, parties have become semigovernmental organizations and are as essential to the functioning of the governments as are legislative bodies or judicial agencies.

A political party may be defined as an organization that has as its basic purpose controlling the choice of governmental personnel and policies. Although parties differ greatly from country to country and even within countries, this definition applies to all true political parties. Unorganized cliques and other types of organizations, such as political interest groups, may be found that attempt to influence the choice of public officials and policies, but only a political party has as its *raison d'être* the selection of governmental personnel and policies.

Political party systems are generally classified according to the number of parties competing effectively for control of the government: as one-party, two-party, and multiparty systems.

If a single party monopolizes governmental power, the country is said to have a *one-party system*. In some countries, only one party is allowed; these include Communist countries such as the Soviet Union, and other regimes such as Egypt. In other countries, such as Mexico, there are no constitutional restrictions on the number of parties, but one party has been able to exercise virtually complete control over the government, and the lesser parties wield little influence. If two parties customarily have a chance to win control of the government, the country is commonly considered to have a *two-party system* even though one or more minor parties may also nominate candidates. The United States, Great Britain, and New Zealand are examples of nation-states with two-party systems. If *more than two parties* share governmental power, the country is considered to have a *multiparty system*. Italy and France are two well-known examples of multiparty countries.

✹ THE DEVELOPMENT OF
AMERICAN PARTIES

The history of political parties in the United States is almost as long as the history of the country itself. The Democrats trace their origin to Thomas Jefferson, who was elected President in 1800, and the Republicans to 1854. Because American parties have developed in a pragmatic fashion and are shaped by past customs and practices as well as by influential party leaders, one cannot fully appreciate and understand politics today without some knowledge of the past.

In order to provide a perspective for studying present-day parties in the United States, a brief survey will be presented of the origins and development of the American party system. This account will focus primarily on the two major parties and their efforts to capture the Presidency, the highest electoral prize. Such an analysis must omit many facts and events and oversimplify others. But by concentrating on the broad panorama of party history, one can gain an appreciation of features of the American party system, sometimes overlooked, and an understanding of the basic factors underlying the organization and functioning of American political parties today.

No provision was made in the Constitution for political parties. The fact that both the British Whig and Tory parties were run by aristocratic leaders undoubtedly did not endear the British party system to the framers of the Constitution, who failed to see a need for parties in the United States. To provide for the selection of the President and Vice-President, the Founding Fathers devised the electoral college system, which fulfilled the function of both nominating and electing these officials. Nominations for other offices were by self-announcement or by caucuses of local leaders. The Founding Fathers, like the leaders of many recently created nations, hoped to see the country move ahead as one united citizenry rather than divided into opposing factions or parties. President George Washington undoubtedly reflected the opinion of many of his contemporaries when, in his Farewell Address, he warned of "the baneful effects of the spirit of party."

The First American Parties

Washington, who was unanimously elected President by the electors, sought to direct the government in a nonpartisan fashion, but political parties developed during his administration. The formation of the first two parties may be attributed to Alexander Hamilton, the first Secretary of the Treasury, and Thomas Jefferson, the first Secretary of State. Hamilton, who lived in New York City, was the founder and acknowledged leader of the Federalist party. An exponent of the principle that "the rich, the well-born, and the good" should rule, Hamilton advocated a government based on strong executive leadership, centralized power, and policies beneficial to the business and commercial community. Although Washington attempted to be nonpartisan, he came to accept the policies of his Secretary of State.

Jefferson, a Virginia plantation owner, led the opposition to Hamilton. Basically equalitarian, he favored a limited and decentralized government, a strong legislature, and policies that would benefit the small shopkeepers,

❧ POLITICAL ERAS ❧

FIRST DEMOCRATIC ERA

	Federalist, Whig	Jeffersonian-Republican, Democrat
1801		Jefferson
1805		Jefferson
1809		Madison
1813		Madison
1817		Monroe
1821		Monroe
1825		J. Q. Adams
1829		Jackson
1833		Jackson
1837		Van Buren
1841	Harrison-Tyler	
1845		Polk
1849	Taylor-Fillmore	
1853		Pierce
1857		Buchanan

REPUBLICAN ERA

	Republican	Democrat
1861	Lincoln	
1865	Lincoln-Johnson	
1869	Grant	
1873	Grant	
1877	Hayes	
1881	Garfield-Arthur	
1885		Cleveland
1889	Harrison	
1893		Cleveland
1897	McKinley	
1901	McKinley-T. Roosevelt	
1905	T. Roosevelt	
1909	Taft	
1913		Wilson
1917		Wilson
1921	Harding-Coolidge	
1925	Coolidge	
1929	Hoover	

SECOND DEMOCRATIC ERA

	Republican	Democrat
1933		F. Roosevelt
1937		F. Roosevelt
1941		F. Roosevelt
1945		F. Roosevelt-Truman
1949		Truman
1953	Eisenhower	
1957	Eisenhower	
1961		Kennedy-Johnson
1965		Johnson

workers, farmers, and planters. Shortly after Washington's second inauguration, Jefferson left the Cabinet to organize and lead his party which, first known as the Anti-Federalists, then as the Jeffersonian-Republicans, later became the Democratic party. The first electoral contest between the two parties occurred in 1796 when John Adams, the Federalist candidate for President, defeated Jefferson by the narrow margin of 3 electoral votes. Four years later Jefferson was elected President, and the Federalist control of the national government was ended.

Eras of One-Party Control

One of the popular misconceptions of American politics is that the control of the national government alternates at short intervals between the two major parties. A critical examination of the past reveals that this is not an accurate interpretation of the manner in which our party system has functioned. If considered from the standpoint of the Presidency, political party history since 1800 may be divided into three periods, each of which saw one of the major parties virtually monopolize the office of the President and consequently the direction of national affairs.[1]

First Period: The Election of Jefferson, 1800. The first of these three periods was from the election of Jefferson in 1800 until the Civil War. During these sixty years the party founded by Jefferson and reorganized by Jackson lost only two presidential elections.

Jefferson realized, as did later successful party leaders, that to win national elections a party must appeal to a broad cross section of the major segments of the population and that this can be accomplished only by advocating policies that represent the interests of these individuals and

[1] See Henry A. Turner, "National Politics: Eras of One-Party Control," *Social Science*, Vol. 28, No. 3 (June, 1953), 137–143.

groups. In his inaugural address in 1801, Jefferson announced that his administration favored not only the "encouragement of agriculture," but also "commerce as its handmaid." Thus, while recognizing the primacy of agriculture in his time, he understood the importance of gaining support from the commercial interests.

After eight years as President, Jefferson was succeeded by his Secretary of State, James Madison, who, after two terms, was followed by his Secretary of State, James Monroe, who after a similar period was replaced by his Secretary of State, John Quincy Adams. During these years the Federalist party declined, and 1816 was the last time the party nominated a candidate for the Presidency. For a short interval the United States became a one-party nation. Because of the lack of partisan conflict, these years have been mistakenly called the Era of Good Feeling.

The demise of the Federalists was due to several factors, the principal one being the lack of broad popular support. Failing to win general support, the Federalist-controlled Congress in 1798 enacted the oppressive Alien and Sedition Acts which were intended to silence the most outspoken critics of the party's policies and leaders. Finally, during the War of 1812, the Hartford Convention, called by party leaders to oppose the war and to propose amendments to the Constitution, placed the stigma of treason on the party.

The "Era of Good Feeling" was short-lived and in 1824 the party of Jefferson split into four factions, each of which supported a different presidential aspirant. As no candidate received a majority of the electoral votes, the House of Representatives elected John Quincy Adams as President even though Andrew Jackson had received the largest popular vote. Four years later the various factions had combined into two groups, the Democratic-Republicans led by Jackson, and the National-Republicans led by Adams. Jackson, who represented more accurately the Jeffersonian program and tradition, was elected President. A short time later Jackson and his supporters dropped the last half of their party name and began calling themselves Democrats. His opponents, who felt he was assuming too much power, began caricaturing him as King Andrew I and referring to themselves as "Whigs," the name of the British party that opposed the King.

The 1828 election ushered in a period known as "Jacksonian democracy." Previously the political leaders had come largely from the eastern states and from the gentry. As new states were admitted to the Union and as suffrage restrictions were gradually removed, there was a shifting of political power from the seaboard states to the western and southern states and from the upper to the middle and lower classes. The election of Jackson, the first "man of the people" to occupy the White House, illustrates this shift in political power.

Only by nominating military heroes were the Whigs able to capture the Presidency. In 1840 they were led to victory by General William Henry Harrison, hero of the battle of Tippecanoe, and in 1848 they elected General Zachary Taylor of Mexican War fame. Failing to win elections, plagued by the slavery issue, and lacking a long tradition and program to unite them, the Whigs nominated their last presidential candidate in 1852 and shortly thereafter disappeared from the political scene.

In the three decades prior to the Civil War, the parties underwent a number of changes, and several developments occurred that had a lasting impact on American politics. With the expansion of the suffrage there occurred a notable increase in popular participation in the government, more elaborate political organizations developed, the party boss appeared in many cities, and the patronage system became the order of the day. Ballots grew longer as more officials were elected to offices and terms of office were often reduced. Certain practices of the parties today date from these years. These include the convention demonstrations for presidential candidates and the drafting of party platforms. The first national committee was established in 1848, and it became standard practice for all the electoral votes in a given state to be cast for the one candidate receiving the plurality of the popular votes. From the standpoint of American politics, possibly the most important contribution of these decades was the firm entrenchment of the two-party system. Although a single party has been able to win most presidential elections for long periods, in every election since 1824, two parties have competed seriously and vigorously and usually on fairly even terms.

Second Period: The Election of Lincoln, 1860. The Civil War, a major landmark in American politics, introduced a new political era. In 1860 the Democratic party split into northern and southern wings, each nominating a separate presidential candidate. With the Democrats divided, the Republican party—founded in 1854 by Whigs, dissident Democrats, and former third party members—elected Abraham Lincoln even though he received less than 40 percent of the popular votes. This first Republican victory was followed by the secession of the South and the Civil War.

The Civil War and Reconstruction period profoundly affected party history in the United States. One result was the "Solid South"—a one-party region in which the Democratic party was supreme. Another result, largely attributable to the war and its aftermath, was the virtual monopolization of the Presidency by the Republicans for nearly three quarters of a century. From the election of Lincoln until the election of Franklin Roosevelt seventy-two years later, the Democrats were able to elect only two men to the Presidency: Grover Cleveland in 1884 and 1892 and Woodrow Wilson in 1912 and 1916. It would be incorrect, however, to assume that the Democrats were completely submerged. With a solid core of votes in the South and considerable support in much of the North, the Democrats continued as the chief opposition party. In addition to the Democratic presidential victories, the party in two other elections, 1876 and 1888, polled more popular votes than the victorious Republicans and on several occasions the Democrats had majorities in one or both houses of Congress. But the fact remains that for fifty-six of these seventy-two years Republicans occupied the White House and directed national affairs.

The phenomenal success of the Republicans was due to a number of factors. First, the Republicans who had been in power during the war were able to take credit for saving the Union and to stigmatize the Democrats as the party of rebellion. For at least two decades after the war, Republican campaign orators "waved the bloody shirt" and accused the Democrats of being responsible for the war. But the early Republican leaders, realizing that a purely negative approach would not be successful, presented policies aimed at eliciting support from every sizable sector of the electorate. They rallied commerce and industry to their standard by a program of high tariffs, direct subsidies, and generous land grants. To supplement the support of the business community, they granted homesteads to the western farmers and pensions to the northern war veterans. Campaigning as the party of "free labor" and advocating "liberal wages for workingmen and mechanics" the Grand Old Party won the support of many wage earners. The Negroes were reminded that the Republican party was their emancipator and that the Democrats had favored slavery.

During the last part of the nineteenth century and the early twentieth century, the two parties offered the voters little choice from the standpoint of concrete policies. As the Democrats differed little in most respects from the Republicans, Cleveland's two terms in office did not essentially disrupt the period of Republican control of the government. Near the turn of the century, it appeared that the West might be breaking away from the Republican coalition of the industrial North and agrarian West, but Theodore Roosevelt, one of the most skilled political leaders in American history, reunited the North-West sectional alliance. Realizing that changing conditions required a realignment in party policies, the Republican Roosevelt was able to shift the policies of the party decidedly to the left.

In 1912, when Taft was nominated for a second term, Roosevelt, who desired the nomination, led his supporters out of the Republican national convention and organized his Progressive Party. With the Republican voters divided between Taft and Roosevelt, the Democratic nominee, Woodrow Wilson, was elected President. Four years later, while Europe was at war, Wilson was re-elected by a very narrow margin.

During his administration Wilson, through his legislative program and the precedents he established for strong presidential leadership, brought about a reversal of the positions of the two parties regarding states' rights versus federal power. Previously the Democrats from the days of Jefferson had traditionally stood for states' rights and limited government, whereas the Republicans had favored a strong central government and the use of federal power to promote national interests. Wilson led the Democrats away from its states' right, laissez-faire position, and helped forge it into the party that advocates a strong national government and the utilization of that government to solve social and economic problems. The Republicans, in turn, have come to be known as the party favoring more power for the states and limited action by the national government.

Wilson's administration proved to be only a brief interruption in the era of Republican dominance, and in 1920 the GOP returned to power by electing as President Warren Harding, who was followed by Calvin Coolidge and Herbert Hoover.

Third Period: The Election of Franklin D. Roosevelt, 1932. The period of Republican domination of national politics came to an end with the election of Franklin D. Roosevelt in 1932, which, like the election of 1860, is one of the landmark elections in American history. Following his victories in 1932 and 1936, Roosevelt ended the no-third-term tradition in 1940, and in 1944 was elected to a fourth term. Roosevelt's death in the spring of 1945 elevated Harry Truman to the Presidency, and in 1948, much to the chagrin of the public opinion pollsters who predicted his defeat, Truman was returned to the White House.

Since Roosevelt's first election as President, the Democrats have dominated national politics in a fashion reminiscent of the earlier period of Democratic rule and the subsequent interval of Republican hegemony. Although there is evidence that a realignment of the parties had started with the 1928 election, the Great Depression was the fundamental reason for the abrupt transfer of electoral power from the Republicans to the Democrats. Public opinion surveys have shown that voters in every major socioeconomic group moved from the Republican to the Democratic camp between 1928 and 1932. In the subsequent Democratic victories, the exact composition of the majorities changed from election to election, but a number of persons who had previously considered themselves Republicans transferred their allegiance permanently to the party in power.

In the years since 1932, the Republicans, like the Whigs before them, have been able to gain control of the Presidency only by nominating a military hero. In 1952 and 1956, under the banner of General Dwight Eisenhower, the Republicans gained the White House, but they were able to control Congress only two of those years, 1952–1954. The Democrats reoccupied the White House with the narrow victory of John Kennedy over Richard Nixon in 1960, which placed the first Catholic in the office of the Chief Executive. This was followed by a second precedent-breaking election in 1964 when Lyndon Johnson, who had been elevated to the Presidency upon the assassination of Kennedy, became the first resident of a southern state to be elected since the Civil War. (See Figure 13–2, which shows the trends in the last seven presidential elections.) These and other events indicate that American politics is in a state of flux and that other new developments of major proportions may be forthcoming.

Reasons for Periods of One-Party Dominance

A number of reasons may be given to explain the fact that for as long as seven decades one party has been able consistently to win national elections. First, of course, is the obvious one that the party in power simply espoused policies which appealed to more voters than did the opposition party. In the past the party in control of the government has often been alert to changing conditions and has adjusted its policies to meet the new problems. Moreover, as the party in power is in the position of recommending programs, it has first choice among available policies, and its less successful opponents then have the unfortunate alternatives of supporting the same policies or merely opposing them or proposing other policies they hope will be appealing to the voters but which, in fact, will probably be less popular.

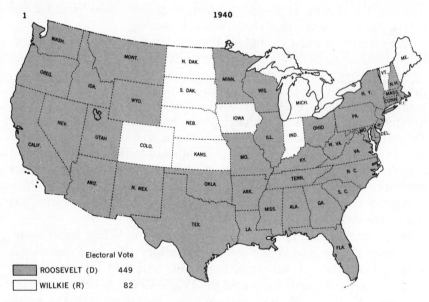

	Electoral Vote
ROOSEVELT (D)	449
WILLKIE (R)	82

FIGURE 13–2. The Voting Trends in Presidential Elections from 1940 to 1964. (Adapted from *The New York Times.* © 1964, 65, 66 by The New York Times Company. Reprinted by permission.)

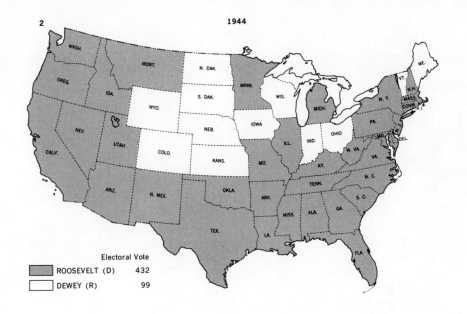

2   1944

Electoral Vote

ROOSEVELT (D)   432
DEWEY (R)   99

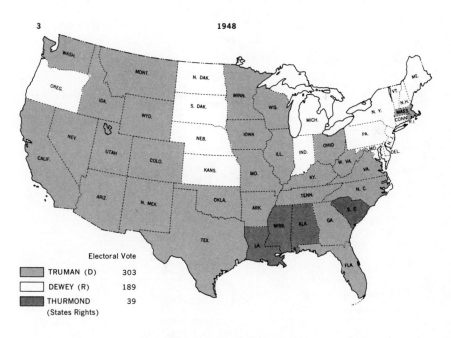

3   1948

Electoral Vote

TRUMAN (D)   303
DEWEY (R)   189
THURMOND   39
(States Rights)

FIGURE 13–2. (*Continued*)

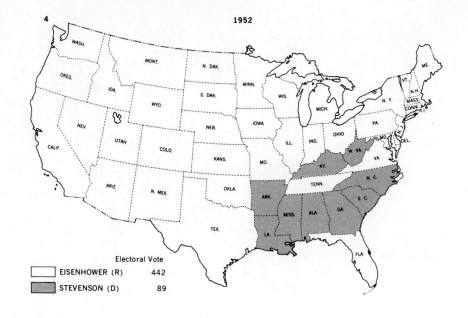

1952

4

Electoral Vote

☐ EISENHOWER (R) 442
▨ STEVENSON (D) 89

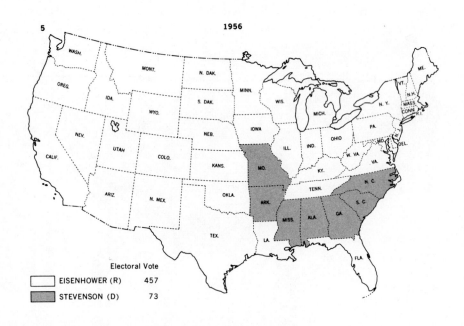

1956

5

Electoral Vote

☐ EISENHOWER (R) 457
▨ STEVENSON (D) 73

FIGURE 13–2. (*Continued*)

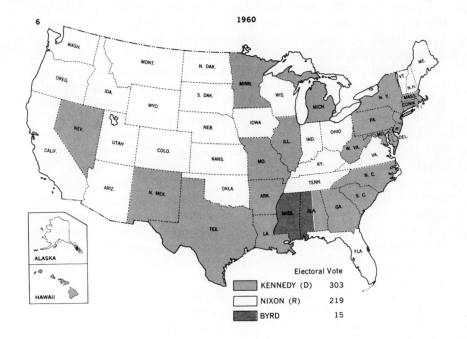

6   1960

Electoral Vote

KENNEDY (D)   303
NIXON (R)   219
BYRD   15

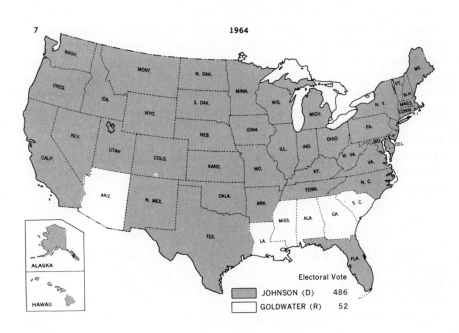

7   1964

Electoral Vote

JOHNSON (D)   486
GOLDWATER (R)   52

FIGURE 13–2. (*Continued*)

The old adage that success breeds success applies in politics, and the very fact of its position of leadership brings other advantages to the party in power. It has, for instance, certain perquisites—honors, favors, and preferments; it can award appointive offices, grant contracts, select locations for governmental facilities; it can provide its younger men with the experience and publicity essential for aspirants seeking higher elective office, and this knowledge may encourage able party members to enter politics and induce ambitious persons in the opposition to change party affiliation. Furthermore, as Americans have the tendency to vote for incumbents, the party with the largest number of officeholders may expect to benefit at the polls in subsequent elections.

In each period after a party has been in office for a number of years, it has been able continually to attract more partisan supporters until it has gained an appreciable majority over the opposition. In subsequent elections when there has been little choice between the program or candidates of the two parties, this preponderance of traditional party voters may have meant the difference between victory and defeat. Before the Civil War the Democrats had this advantage, whereas after the election of Lincoln the Republicans gained increasing favor and by 1896 clearly outnumbered the Democrats. After the Great Depression the tide reversed, and the results in recent elections indicate that a majority of the voters have formed the habit of voting the Democratic ticket.

Other factors have been, in part, responsible for these extended intervals of one-party dominance. In the past it has been at a time of national crisis that a major change of political orientation has taken place. At the beginning of each of the three periods cited above, the party that was recently evicted from power was forced to labor under an opprobrium that placed it at a disadvantage. In the years following 1800 the Federalist party was discredited by the Hartford Convention and the Alien and Sedition Acts; after the Civil War the Democrats were stigmatized as the party of rebellion; and for at least two decades after 1929 the Republicans were criticized as being responsible for the depression. Regardless of the relevance of the accusations, the party in power in each instance missed few opportunities to exploit them to their advantage.

The Republicans and Democrats Today

Although the two major American parties are more similar than are the parties of Great Britain or of any other major power, an analysis of the Republican and Democratic parties today reveals differences regarding both their concepts of the proper function of government and their chief sources of electoral support. Any comparison of the Republicans and

Democrats, however, should be prefaced with the observation that there are greater divergences of viewpoints within each party than between the two parties.

Although there is danger of overgeneralization, it may be said that history and circumstances have placed the present-day Democratic party in the role of exponent of positive governmental programs, whereas the Republican party occupies the position of advocate for less governmental action and more individual responsibility. While Republicans controlled the Presidency, the United States became industrialized; under Democratic leadership, the United States has adjusted to the effects of industrialization. As has been explained, first Woodrow Wilson and later Franklin D. Roosevelt reversed the traditional approach of the Democrats regarding states' rights and the role of the federal government. Subsequent Democratic Presidents have followed their lead, and the Democratic party has gained a reputation of being more willing than the Republicans to utilize government to attack social and economic problems. Today the Democratic party is given credit—or blamed—for initiating such legislative measures as old-age pensions, unemployment insurance, medical care programs, labor and farm programs, federal aid to education, antipoverty programs, civil rights legislation, tariff reforms, and foreign aid programs. Although in some states—in particular, industrial states in the East and on the West coast—Republican governors and legislators have initiated similar measures, the Republican party nationally has gained the image of reluctantly accepting such programs while urging a reduction in government expenditures, lower taxes, less government regulation, and more responsibility on the part of the individual citizen for handling social and economic problems. (See Tables 13–1A and 13–1B.)

TABLE 13–1A. *Vote Tests for Federal Role* (*Average Percent Scores*)

| | 1965 | | 88th Congress | |
	Dem.	GOP	Dem.	GOP
Larger Federal Role:				
Both chambers	80	36	75	40
Senate	72	46	79	47
House	79	33	74	40
Smaller Federal Role:				
Both chambers	18	61	20	56
Senate	15	52	18	50
House	18	63	21	57

SOURCE: Adapted from CQ *Fact Sheet* (December 3, 1965), p. 2417. Washington, D.C., Congressional Quarterly, Inc.

TABLE 13–1B. *Vote Tests for Federal Role, by Party and by Region in both Senate and House (by Percent)*

	Senate		House	
	Dem.	GOP	Dem.	GOP
For Larger Role:				
Eastern	98	73	97	54
Southern	54	27	50	16
Midwestern	94	31	92	27
Western	93	41	93	27
Against Larger Role				
Eastern	2	26	2	41
Southern	39	71	46	80
Midwestern	4	66	6	71
Western	3	58	6	69

SOURCE: Adapted from *CQ Fact Sheet* (December 3, 1965), p. 2418. Washington, D.C., Congressional Quarterly, Inc.

Theoretically and actually the role of the opposition party tends to be a negative one. The fact that the Republican party has been out of power much of the time for the past 40 years, undoubtedly accounts in part for its lack of a record of positive accomplishments. Thomas Dewey, twice the Republican presidential nominee, once observed that a party must be in office to establish a record. A second reason for the differing reputations of the two parties regarding the proper function of the federal government is that the composition of the two parties is dissimilar. It is true that each party contains some voters from virtually every socioeconomic group in the nation, and the composition of each party changes slightly from election to election. But the fact remains that the most solid block of support for each of the two parties differs. As the topic of voting behavior was discussed in Chapter 12, only a brief sketch will be presented here of the principal groups affiliated with each party.

From the election of Lincoln "the center of gravity of wealth" has been in the Republican party. The GOP dominated national politics during the period of spectacular business growth, and since that time business generally has been associated with the Republican party. President Eisenhower, after leaving office, once remarked that the Republicans have been referred to as the "party of business" and he personally was "proud of the label." His Secretary of Defense, Charles E. Wilson, former head of General Motors, made a statement that drew fire from many quarters— "what is good for General Motors is good for the nation." Public opinion surveys have shown that a majority of those in the upper-income groups have consistently voted the Republican ticket. Many business executives, independent entrepreneurs, and members of certain professional groups—including physicians, dentists, attorneys, engineers, and others—have durable psychological attachments for the Republican party. Independent American farmers and businessmen in small communities have been traditional Republican supporters; as these two groups of our economy have declined in proportionate significance, the Republican party has declined politically.

Although there are numerous wealthy individuals in the Democratic party and in recent years it has won the affiliation of many intellectuals, the party finds, as it did in the days of Jefferson and Jackson, that its most solid core of support is in the ranks of the middle and lower classes, labor, minority groups, and the South. Most of these groups are more interested in the enactment of welfare and regulatory programs than are the more affluent groups usually associated with the Republican party.

⚓ FUNCTIONS OF AMERICAN PARTIES

Providing Personnel for Government

The primary function of political parties is to provide personnel for government. In the United States and in other democratic countries, this function is accomplished principally by the recruitment, nomination, and election of public officials. This electing function is the one activity that distinguishes American parties most effectively from other organizations. To understand the significance of this activity, one might ask how the thousands of elective officials in the United States would be selected if there were no parties.

In addition to presenting a choice of candidates for public office, political parties in a democracy provide a peaceful means for succession to office, whereas in authoritarian regimes, often the only method for removing public officials is through the use of force. American parties concentrate more on the electing function and place less emphasis on other activities than do parties in most other countries.

Organizing and Conducting the Government

A second purpose of political parties is to organize and conduct the government. If one party controls the Presidency and Congress, it organizes both branches and attempts to secure the enactment and execution of its program. The party thus serves to bridge the gap between the two branches created by the separation of powers. Because of the nature of American politics, members of the President's party in Congress will not necessarily support him on every issue, but—if for no other reason—the common desire to establish a record that will attract votes in future elections provides an incentive for cooperation between the President and Congress. Even if the opposition party controls the legislature, responsibility for administering the government is still centered in the Chief Executive and the party he represents. When one party controls the Presidency and the other Congress, the party system may, of course, create obstacles to the smooth operation of the government.

Serving as a Countercheck to the Party in Power

The opposition party serves a useful function in American politics. In a two-party system the opposition party helps to insure that the government will be responsible, by checking on and criticizing the party in power. In the United States the concept of the "loyal opposition" has not been institutionalized to the extent that it has in Great Britain; nonetheless, it is considered the role of the defeated party to scrutinize and point out defects in governmental policies and present alternative proposals. Although the criticism is often not entirely constructive and at times appears to be intended merely to harass the party in power, the opposition role of checking and criticizing is an important party function and helps to prevent the adoption of unwise policies and to lessen inefficiency and malfeasance in government.

Representing Group Interest

A fourth function of the parties in America is the important representative one. Political parties and legislative bodies together serve as the two principal representative agencies of popular power. In the process of developing and promoting party platforms and programs, political parties perform the function of articulating and aggregating the interests and demands of many political interest groups, which often find they must obtain party support in order to achieve their goals. From the myriad of interests and desires asserted by groups, political parties reject some issues and select others that they articulate, explain, debate, and promote. The parties thus serve as "political brokers," modifying and compromising the proposals of various groups as they develop party programs. In this process, the parties add a semblance of order and coherence to American politics and contribute to the stability of the nation.

Educating and Informing the Electorate

Fifth, political parties participate in the process of educating and informing the electorate regarding political issues. It is true that parties in the
United States place less emphasis on their educational role than do their
European counterparts. This is because the United States has no "ideological parties" such as Socialists or Christian Democrats that are based on a
well-defined general philosophy. Even in Britain there are Labour party
organizations of physicians, lawyers, students, and others. Although such
party organizations do not exist in the United States, American parties do
help to educate and inform the voters in a variety of ways. Parties, in
articulating group interests, are, of course, helping to inform the people,
but the educational function encompasses more than merely explaining
and advocating specific policies. Political leaders, through public addresses,
campaign communications, legislative debates, news conferences, and press
releases, inform the citizenry on a variety of issues of concern to the
majority of the population.

The educational role of parties also includes participating in the political
socialization of the electorate. The term "political socialization" refers to
the process by which individuals gain the attitudes, values, interest, and
information that influence their political decisions and actions and lead
them to perceive political events in a particular manner. Political parties
share with the family, other groups, and the media of communications in
the socialization of the populace. Research on attitude formation reveals
that for many dedicated partisans the party to which they belong serves as
an important reference group and is one of the most influential determi-
nants of attitudes on political issues and candidates. By accepting the
position of the foremost party spokesmen, these individuals are able to
simplify and clarify the confusing array of domestic and foreign problems
that confront them. Thus, depending upon a person's point of reference—
his party—a proposed policy may be "right" or "wrong" and a public
official may be a public-spirited statesman or a venal politician.

Unifying the Nation

Sixth, the major political parties in the United States have helped to
unify and nationalize the country. Because they usually adopt moderate,
middle-of-the-road policies, the parties unify rather than divide the people.
Today, regardless of where one lives, the great majority of Americans
consider themselves to be Republicans or Democrats. Common membership in the two parties throughout the fifty states has assisted in drawing

together the most heterogeneous population of any country of the world. The national nominating conventions, meetings of national party committees, and the party organizations in Congress have aided in the creation of a unified populace. Thus the parties have not only united the people within the several states, but have also helped to transform a federation of states into a unified nation.

An activity of parties in an earlier age that aided in this unification process was their assistance in the "Americanization" of immigrants. This acceleration of the process of nationalization was a function obviously not performed by parties in any other country. Parties were not motivated by idealistic reasons alone; encouraging and helping an immigrant to become a citizen meant a possible new vote for the party. Aside from the school, the party was perhaps the most important influence in the Americanization of the 43 million immigrants who have come to the United States since 1820.

⚘ CHARACTERISTICS OF THE AMERICAN PARTY SYSTEM

The party system of any country has distinguishing characteristics that are largely the result of certain underlying factors and circumstances, including the history of the people, the constitutional system, the geography, the religious and ethnic composition of the population, and the level of economic and technological development. It is these factors that are primarily responsible for the characteristics of the American party system described below.

A Two-Party System

The most apparent and fundamental feature of the American party system is that it is a two-party system. Even though in virtually every national election more than two parties have nominated candidates, with rare exceptions the real contest for control of the national government has been between two major parties. Other features of American parties result from this basic fact—that the United States has a two-party system.

American Parties Are Multigroup Organizations

Because the electorate in the United States is a heterogeneous mixture of many social, economic, ethnic, and religious groups spread through fifty states, any party that obtains a majority of the vote must of necessity be composed of different groups. In an effort to achieve a majority coalition,

both parties make some appeal to every major segment of the population—
business, labor, farmers, the professions, and others. A party program is
thus determined both by the desire to attract new voters and by the need
to retain the support of groups within the party. As a result, party
programs tend to be compromises negotiated by party leaders between the
often conflicting policies advocated by different groups.

American Parties Are Pragmatic, Nonideological Organizations

The British statesman, Edmund Burke, once defined a political party as "a
body of men united for promoting . . . the national interest upon some
particular principle in which they are all agreed." Major parties in the
United States do not conform to this definition. Because of their histories,
traditions, leaders, and membership, each of the two parties takes fairly
consistent stands on certain issues. But within each party, disagreement
may be found on virtually any question. Neither of the two parties is fully
united on any principle, and both are largely uninterested in doctrine or
ideology. As each party is composed of groups with varying opinions, party
programs are often expressed in broad, general terms. Such programs are
usually adopted in order to win votes and to maintain coalitions, and both
parties attempt to avoid issues that will repel voters and divide their party.
Most party leaders realize that extreme or radical policies are adopted at
the risk of alienating blocs of voters and losing elections—as the Republicans found in 1964. Hence, party programs tend to be moderate and
pragmatic. Republican Senator Jacob Javits of New York was expressing
this view when he told a gathering of party members that "the house we
build must be big enough for all: conservatives, moderates and progressives." He added, "This is the course which Abraham Lincoln and
Theodore Roosevelt charted for us in telling terms."

Some individuals have criticized American parties because they do not
provide the voters meaningful choices on public policies. They argue that
the parties should draft party platforms containing specific and differing
policies. According to this view, parties should be programmatic organizations, and party members should be united in support of a general
philosophy of government. They argue that once a party espouses a policy,
all elected officials should be obligated to support it. Although many
European parties conform to this pattern, American parties have not and
undoubtedly will not in the foreseeable future.

American Parties Are Decentralized

Because of the federal form of government, political parties in the
United States are decentralized. The national parties, in addition to being

coalitions of a variety of socioeconomic groups, are confederations, or alliances, of state and local party organizations. Actual control of the parties resides at the state and county levels rather than at the national. As the state and local party organizations are largely autonomous units, the national leaders seldom have sanctions that may be employed to discipline them.

A comparison with the British system is instructive. Great Britain has a unitary form of government, and British parties are highly centralized. Once a British party adopts a policy, all party members in Parliament may be required to vote for that policy. In Great Britain the national party leaders may determine who may "stand" for Parliament in an electoral district. In the United States, anyone with the necessary legal requirements may "run" for Congress, regardless of his philosophy of government or the wishes of the national party leaders. A candidate once elected may consistently oppose the policies of his party and still be returned to office as long as a majority of his constituents vote for him. Moreover, a Democratic congressman from California and one from Mississippi may regularly take opposing positions on important partisan issues, and the same may apply to Republican senators from New York and Arizona.

Variations in the States' Party Systems

The two-party system is firmly entrenched in the nation, but not in all fifty states. If the party systems in the states were plotted on a political spectrum, they would range from those with two equally balanced parties through modified two-party and modified one-party systems to one-party systems. In approximately one third of the states, the two parties compete on nearly even terms. In several other states, there is vigorous competition between the two parties for presidential electoral votes, Senate seats, and the governorship, but one party customarily wins most other offices. In a number of modified one-party states one party predominates, but the other party may receive as much as one third of the votes and will elect a few candidates.

The remaining one third of the states may be classified as one-party states, for the opposing party seldom provides serious competition for the party in power. In those states the smaller party is often so weak and poorly organized that the only real struggle for political power is within the ranks of the larger party. In some of these one-party states, the second party may even fail to nominate candidates for most local and congressional positions. One point should be noted regarding the state party systems: while there are constant changes in the pattern of competition, the overall trend appears to be toward more interparty competition.

❦ WHY THE TWO-PARTY SYSTEM?

Because most countries do not operate under a two-party system, the question naturally arises: Why does the United States, with the most diverse population of any country in the world, have a two-party system?

Of the factors contributing to the two-party system, undoubtedly the most significant is the method used to elect members of Congress and the President. Members of Congress are elected from single-member districts—that is, the one candidate in each geographic district with the largest number of votes is elected. This "winner take all" system works to the disadvantage of all except the two leading parties. A third party cannot anticipate victory unless it either joins a major party or draws support from one. Faced with these prospects, most third-party adherents, or groups that might otherwise form minor parties, join a major party. If a system of proportional representation with multiple-member districts were used, each party would gain seats in the legislature proportionate to the number of popular votes it received. With an opportunity to participate in electoral victories, minor parties would have less incentive to merge with other parties, and some groups now within the two major parties might break away and form their own parties.

The separate election of the President, which, in effect, takes place in a "single member district" consisting of the fifty states, also helps to create and to maintain the two-party system. Under the prevailing arrangement, one nominee customarily receives the entire electoral vote of a state, and the candidate who receives the highest number of electoral votes becomes President. Political leaders and party organizations in the various states know that in order to participate in this, the ultimate victory, they must join one of the two leading parties. If the United States had a parliamentary form of government, it is possible that there would be two parties in each state, but not the same two parties throughout the nation, as is the case in Canada. In a few instances, third parties—such as the Farmer-Labor party of Minnesota, the Progressive party of Wisconsin—have elected governors, other state officers, and national legislators, but they subsequently merged with a major party or disappeared. In a parliamentary system, if no major party has a decisive majority, a minor party by winning a few seats may hold the balance of power and determine what policies will be enacted, as did the British Liberal party after the 1964 election. Undoubtedly the knowledge that a third party cannot expect to elect a President or gain a balance of power has contributed to the demise of third parties in the United States.

Other factors—historical, legal, and psychological—have been influential in the establishment or maintenance of the biparty system. The United States inherited many political institutions and practices from the British, and the early American leaders, although reluctant to form political parties, were influenced by the British bipartisan practices.[2] Once the two-party system was firmly entrenched, legal provisions and practices militated against third parties. Congress is organized along bipartisan lines, hence members of minor parties cannot expect to be appointed to important committees or to become committee chairmen. Statutes provide for bipartisan appointments to a variety of committees, commissions, and boards. Legal impediments in a number of states make it difficult for persons wishing to organize a new party to obtain a place on the ballot. The loyalty of voters to the party of their choice strengthens the present two-party alignment. As was explained in Chapter 12, many people accept the party affiliation of their parents as well as their religion, and are only slightly less inclined to change their religion than their partisan allegiance.

In explaining the reasons for the two-party system in the United States, it has been suggested that certain problems dividing other countries into three or more parties have been avoided and that most troubling American problems have been of a bimodal character. Regarding the first point, it is correct that the United States—with its lack of class consciousness, its freedom from the problem of a royal family or pretender agitating or hoping to be placed on a throne, and its adherence to the doctrine of separation of church and state—has avoided some problems that have encouraged the development of a multiplicity of parties in other countries.

The inherent dualism of American political issues is another matter. Those who assert this position call attention to such dichotomous issues as the early question of the "strict" versus the "loose" interpretation of the Constitution, the issue of property rights versus the rights of people, the division of the nation along sectional lines, and the separation of the citizenry into conservative and liberal camps. In brief, it has been argued that these issues have divided the American electorate naturally into two parties, whereas the political questions confronting the French or Italian voters have been responsible for their multiparty systems. One may ask, however, whether the dualism of political issues has been a *cause* or a *result* of the party system. One characteristic of the biparty system is that it

[2] It has been suggested that the British aristocrats who originated the two-party system were influenced by their interest in sports or games which were played by two competing individuals or teams. The early ideal of political behavior in English party politics was "fair play" such as is found in a game played by gentlemen. Even today only in English-speaking countries does one hear references to the "rules of the game" in talking about politics.

forces individuals to compromise their demands and unite with others in order to share political power. Hence, if the United States had a multi-party system, political issues might appear in a different form.

⚘ MINOR PARTIES

The monopolization of the electoral process by the Republicans and Democrats during the past one hundred years tends to obscure the fact that in virtually every national election a number of minor or third parties nominate candidates. The variety of these parties makes it difficult to classify them. For instance, some parties have limited their activity to one state, some to one geographic area, and others have sought votes throughout the nation. Most minor parties have short histories, but a few have existed for several decades. Some minor parties promote a single issue or doctrine, but others have broader, more practical programs.

Although no means of classifying these myriad parties is entirely satisfactory, an examination reveals that minor parties with long histories have characteristics different from those of transient third parties. Minor parties that have existed several decades tend to be doctrinal or ideologically oriented, whereas short-lived third parties often are protest movements of voters who have disassociated themselves from one of the major parties.

The long-range doctrinal parties do not exist to elect candidates, but to propagate a particular ideology or to advocate a specific cause. Examples of such parties are the Prohibition, the Socialist, and the Socialist-Labor parties, each of which originated prior to the turn of the century. These parties, not expecting or hoping to win elections are essentially different from the major parties. In a sense, they operate outside the two-party system, for they have little or no influence on the outcome of elections or on the programs of the major parties. Although they call themselves parties and nominate candidates, they consider the ballot primarily as an inexpensive means of propagandizing their program. From the standpoint of their basic purpose, these organizations might correctly be considered as pressure groups and not as parties.

Splinter, or Secessionist Parties

Of the transient parties, two general types may be identified. First, there have been several splinter, or secessionist, parties, each consisting of a specific segment of a major party that has temporarily broken away from the older organization. Recent examples of splinter parties include the

Progressive party of 1912, which was formed when Theodore Roosevelt failed to receive the Republican presidential nomination, and the States' Rights or Dixiecrat movement of 1948, which consisted of disaffected southern Democrats who broke away because of disagreement over the party's stand on civil rights. In 1912 Roosevelt, the candidate of the Progressives, actually polled more votes than the Republican nominee, but the party dissolved after the election. Some of its adherents supported the re-election of a Democrat, Woodrow Wilson, in 1916, but most of them returned to the Republican fold. In the 1948 election the Dixiecrats carried several southern states, but realizing that they could not hope to elect a President and that as Dixiecrats their members in Congress would lose their committee chairmanships, they shortly rejoined the Democratic party.

Independent Short-Term Parties

In addition to the splinter parties, there have been a number of short-term parties, which developed because of dissatisfaction with the programs of the major parties. Until recent years most of these parties have been of a reformist nature, advocating social and economic reforms that were ignored by the major parties. For example, in the decades prior to the Civil War, the Abolitionist and the Liberty parties were formed because of the slavery issue, which neither the Democrats nor Whigs met forthrightly. In the years before 1900 several minor parties appeared that advocated reforms desired by farmers and laborers. Of these, the most successful was the Populist party, which in 1892 polled over 1 million votes for its presidential nominee and elected several members of Congress. Four years later the Democrats adopted most of the planks of the Populist platforms, with the result that the Populists lost most of their appeal. In recent years, several small parties have appeared that have favored such policies as repealing the income tax, and the withdrawal of the United States from the United Nations. These groups, taking such names as the Constitution Party and the National States' Rights Party, usually appear on the ballots of very few states—often only one or two—and receive miniscule electoral support. Like the more liberal third parties mentioned above, they are protesting the programs of the major parties; but, unlike those reformist third parties, these groups provide no constructive alternative program.

Minor parties have been of little importance in recent elections. The Liberal party exercises some influence in New York either by nominating candidates of its own or endorsing candidates of the major parties. But since 1948 no other minor party has played a significant role in a national election. Although minor parties will no doubt continue to nominate candidates, it is unlikely that they will play as important a role in American politics as they have in the past. For one reason, most groups wishing the adoption of specific policies have learned that pressure group activity is more effective than working through a minor party. Then, too, the direct primaries provide dissident groups within the major parties a means of protesting existing conditions and of securing candidates acceptable to themselves. Due in part to the increased activities of political interest groups and the direct primaries, the programs of the major parties have undergone an almost continual adjustment and tend to keep more in tune with the times than formerly.

❧ THE TWO-PARTY VERSUS THE MULTIPARTY SYSTEM

A comparison of the two-party system with the multiparty system provides an additional perspective for viewing American political parties. Multiparty systems exist in a number of countries, including most western European countries and Argentina, Brazil, Chile, Israel, and Japan. Because of the differences between the party systems in the various multiparty states, it is difficult not to overgeneralize. For instance, the Scandinavian countries where a Labor party generally predominates, have fairly stable four-party systems, whereas in countries like Israel and France there have been as many as ten or twelve parties competing for votes at one time.

The principal argument offered in favor of the multiparty system is that it provides more accurate representation for different political viewpoints. In some countries the several parties represent virtually every shade of the political spectrum, ranging from the extreme left to the extreme right. In France, for example, in the past the voters have been able to choose between candidates advocating communism, socialism, a moderate democratic system, extreme authoritarianism, or even the re-establishment of a monarchical regime. We have observed that various viewpoints are represented in each major party in the United States, but such a variety of choice obviously is not available to the electorate. Proponents of multiparty systems argue that in the United States, not only are the voters limited to candidates of two parties, but also these choices are relatively meaningless because both parties have similar programs.

Advocates of the dual party system assert that a comparison should be made on the basis of how the government actually operates under each type of party system and not on the theoretical grounds of the variety of choice offered the voters. In the two-party system, majorities in the legislature are produced automatically by elections. When the votes are counted, one party has won and has received a mandate for organizing and conducting the government. The other party stands in opposition and has the responsibility for criticizing those in power and offering an alternative program. Moreover, the victorious party will be in power until the next regularly scheduled election, which means that it is assured time to implement its program. If the voters become dissatisfied, they may at the next election vote into office the opposition party. Thus, while the voters have a limited choice from the standpoint of who is to represent them, they have an "either-or" choice from the standpoint of selecting the party that will have responsibility for the enactment and execution of public policies.

By comparison, as governments in multiparty systems are composed of combinations or coalitions of parties, there is seldom a clear division between the government and the opposition, and no one party may be held responsible. Moreover, there is no alternative party to whom the voters may turn if they become displeased with those in power. If one coalition is replaced by another, the new governing combination may contain some of the parties in the previous government.

There is widespread agreement that multiparty government generally lacks the vigor and stability of two-party government. In countries where electoral support is fragmented among a number of parties, majority coalitions may be in a constant state of flux. In such countries, when legislative measures are proposed to meet some critical social or economic problem, a party opposing the program may withdraw from the coalition, causing the government to fall. In these countries much time and effort is expended merely in forming governments. For instance, in France during 1951–1956, under the Fourth Republic, the average life of a cabinet was seven months. In some instances, parties nominate candidates and seek positions in cabinets not so much to promote positive programs as to block opponents or to prevent action. Such behavior accounts for much of the ineffectiveness and lack of vigor of some multiparty governments. Although the instability of multiparty states is sometimes attributed to the national character of the people, there are reasons to ascribe it to the number of parties.

The two-party and the multiparty systems should also be compared from the standpoint of their effectiveness in moderating group conflicts and unifying the people. In the United States, Great Britain, and other countries with two-party systems, the parties perform a moderating and unifying function. Groups espousing extreme causes learn that they must modify their proposals in order to have them adopted in party platforms, and individuals seeking high political offices soon realize that they must take a middle-of-the-road stance if they are to be elected.

In a multiparty system the parties make little effort to moderate the conflicting demands of different groups and to unite the citizenry. Indeed, in some multiparty systems the parties often do the opposite. For instance, groups that in the United States would feel constrained to work within the major parties might in a multiparty state form their own party. Leaders of such organizations may reason that they will gain more support by advocating radical rather than moderate programs. Moreover, if the leaders of a party know they cannot obtain a majority, they may make extreme promises and advocate radical programs, confident that after the election they will not be in a position to implement such a program.

Although the type of party system a country has is not necessarily the result of a reasoned decision, perhaps an understanding of a nation's underlying approach to government may be gained by noting its type of party system. If the goal of government is to provide a faithful mirroring of all shades of opinion, the multiparty system is more logical. Conversely, a two-party system is more logical if the citizenry holds the view that the main function of government is to govern. The French multiparty system compared with the British and American two-party systems may illustrate contrasting views of government held in these democracies.

⚕ ONE-PARTY GOVERNMENTS: COMPATIBLE WITH DEMOCRACY?

Americans have a tendency to equate one-party systems with totalitarian regimes, although, in fact, the one-party systems found in various nation-states may be grouped into several categories. The question of whether one-party states are compatible with democratic government must be answered separately for each category.

First, there are the Communist and Fascist totalitarian states, in which all parties are prohibited except the single official state party. Obviously these party systems are not compatible with democratic government.

The second category includes those one-party states in Asia and Africa, such as Pakistan, Egypt, and Guinea, that are not totalitarian, but that allow only one political party. In such cases, the official party is not ideological, as are Communist or Fascist parties, but is generally tailor-made for the needs of the current dictator. Such single-party states tend to be authoritarian rather than totalitarian, and therefore less extreme than Communist or Fascist systems with respect to either aims or methods. For instance, the typical penalty for the political dissenter in such a regime is imprisonment or exile rather than death. Given educational and economic advancements, such one-party systems may develop in the direction of multiparty or two-party states.

Mexico exemplifies a different situation. Here we have a country in which numerous parties freely exist—from Communists to near-Fascists. All parties are permitted freedom of expression, the press, assembly, and association, but only the official government party, the *Partido Revolucionario Institucional,* is allowed to win elections. In congressional elections, the government party decides how many seats are to be allocated to opposition parties, and in presidential elections its candidate is always elected.

A fourth category is exemplified by India, where, since independence in 1947, the Congress party has been dominant on the national level and in nearly all state governments. In every election since then, the Congress party has won at least three quarters of the seats in the Parliament with the other seats divided among a number of small parties. No party in the United States or Great Britain has had the kind of political influence possessed in India by the Congress party, which holds its dominant position largely because it is the party that fought for and won Indian independence. However, it is by no means certain whether the Congress party will continue indefinitely to occupy this position of pre-eminence with the Indian electorate.

The most important point in appraising one-party, or nearly one-party, states is the direction in which the country is moving. There is no doubt that Mexico has steadily moved toward a more mature democracy in the last thirty years under the guidance of a dominant party that is genuinely committed to democracy. Conversely, Ghana, under its one-party system led by Kwame Nkrumah, was steadily moving toward more repressive dictatorship prior to his removal from power in 1966.

CHAPTER 14

POLITICAL PARTIES
IN ACTION

American political parties are dissimilar from political parties of other countries—in the way they are organized, in the functions they perform, and in the manner in which they operate. Like certain other governmental institutions, the political parties have evolved over a long time, and have developed because of the particular needs and circumstances of our nation and its citizenry. The fundamental purpose of American political parties is the election of public officials. In order to carry out that function the parties must be organized; and they must nominate candidates, conduct campaigns, and raise funds.

❧ PARTY ORGANIZATION

Political parties in the United States have two general types of formal organizations, each of which is directly related to a major function of political parties—winning elections and conducting the government. The term "party organization," as commonly used, refers to the party machinery that has been constituted for the purpose of nominating and electing candidates for public office. As this chapter focuses on the electoral process, this kind of party organization will be described here. The other kind of party organization—that which is concerned with running the government

—will be discussed in subsequent chapters on Congress (see Chapters 16 and 17). Both of these types of party machinery contribute to the success of a party, but they operate more or less independently.

National Party Organization

The National Convention. At the national level, political parties are organized primarily for the purpose of electing the President and Vice-President and members of Congress. The national convention, composed of delegates from the fifty states and the territories, convenes quadrennially to nominate candidates for the Presidency and Vice-Presidency and to adopt a platform. The convention has no other major functions. Unlike the conventions of European parties, the national conventions in the United States exercise no control over candidates for legislative offices.

The National Committee. During the four-year interval between meetings of the national convention, the national committee and the national chairman, in theory, direct and guide the party. The national committees of both parties formerly consisted of one man and one woman from each state and territory. In 1952 the Republicans added as an *ex officio* member the state chairman of the party in the states carried by the Republicans in the preceding election. In most states the committee members are selected by the delegates to the national convention, but in some states they are chosen by state conventions, committees, or in direct primaries.

The national committee selects the site and makes the plans for the national convention. Individual members of the committee serve in a liaison capacity with their state party organization, may handle some patronage matters when their party controls the Presidency, and assist with the presidential campaign in their states. The committee, however, does not direct the party affairs in the sense that similar party committees do in Great Britain, Germany, and other countries. The reason lies in the decentralized character of American parties. The fact that each state, regardless of its population, has the same representation on the national committee lends support to the view that the national parties might be considered as alliances or confederations of state and local party organizations; and that the national committee, instead of being considered as a governing body, should be viewed as a gathering of representatives from autonomous or semiautonomous organizations.

The National Chairman. According to custom the national chairman is appointed by the presidential nominee and then is formally elected by the national committee. Usually his initial task is to direct the presidential campaign. If his party's nominee is elected President, the national chairman will probably continue in that capacity but only as long as the President desires his services. Although he holds the highest position in his party, he remains the agent of the President. Concerned with strengthening the party throughout the nation, he delivers addresses, keeps in touch with state and local party organizations, and assists in various fund-raising activities. He shares with the House and Senate campaign committees the responsibility of assisting in the off-year congressional campaigns.

The national chairman supervises the work of a permanent secretariat, referred to as the "National Committee Staff." The size of the secretariat fluctuates widely, diminishing between elections to as few as sixty employees and expanding during election years to several hundred. The permanent staff performs such tasks as writing speeches, checking registration and voting trends, conducting research on political issues, maintaining liaison with state and local party units, and other housekeeping duties. The basic purpose of the staff is to prepare for, and assist in, presidential campaigns. In recent years, however, the national committee staff has given considerable assistance in congressional campaigns. In 1965 the Democratic national chairman announced that additional writers and publicists had been employed to assist congressmen prepare newsletters and speeches, and to advise them on public relations techniques.

Campaign Committees. Each party has separate Senate and House campaign committees to assist candidates seeking election to Congress. These committees, responsible to the legislators and not to the national committee or chairman, illustrate the influence of the separation of powers. In brief, realizing that the national committee and chairman are primarily concerned with the election of the President, the national legislators have formed their own committees which are in no respect subordinate to the national chairman or the national committee. Each committee employs a small permanent staff which performs such tasks as compiling voting records on members of Congress, preparing campaign literature, drafting speeches or press releases, and distributing campaign funds to candidates. Although organized independently, within each party the three committees—national, congressional, and Senate—and their staffs exchange information, work together in raising campaign funds, and cooperate in various other ways.

State and Local Party Organizations

Unlike the national party organization, which is not established or regulated by Congress, the state party organizations have been prescribed by each of the state legislatures, which often have set forth in considerable detail how the parties are to be organized and what functions they are to

AMERICAN DEMOCRACY

perform. Although all states provide for similar party organizations, the detailed party structures vary widely from state to state. Specifically, all states provide for two levels of organizations—state and county or local. Commonly, the most important organizational units are the state central committee and the county central committees. In addition, there are usually a state convention, and district committees created to assist candidates whose constituencies are not statewide but are larger than one county. There are, often, also city, ward, and precinct organizations. (See Figure 14-1.)

State Party Organization. The state central committee has the responsibility for directing and coordinating party activities throughout the state, assisting in statewide campaigns, supervising fund-raising activities, and calling the state convention. Methods of selection of committee members

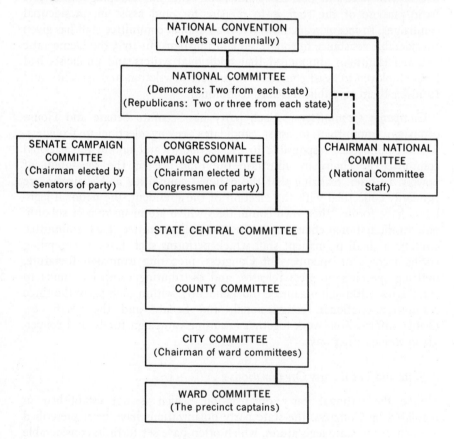

FIGURE 14-1. Organization of the Political Parties.

vary from state to state and include indirect election by county or congressional district committees, appointment by officeholders and nominees, and election in direct primaries. State committees range in size from only a few in some states to more than 900 in California. The larger committees commonly select an executive committee which, in conjunction with the chairman, will perform most of the committee's duties. Although the chairman may be an influential party leader, more often he is the spokesman for the governor or perhaps a group of powerful individuals who themselves remain in the background.

The state party conventions, which were formerly important party gatherings because of their role in the nomination of candidates, are now generally of little consequence. In a few states candidates for statewide offices are selected by the state convention, but in most states such nominees are chosen by direct primaries. The state convention engages in such activities as drafting the state party platform, serving as a forum for political speakers, and selecting party officials, and in some states, delegates to the national convention.

Local Party Organization. The county central committee is usually the basic organizational unit below the state level. County committees perform such tasks as coordinating the work of other local party units, organizing and conducting campaigns, securing candidates for local offices, helping raise funds, and making recommendations on patronage appointments. County committee members in some states are elected in party primaries, but more commonly they are the party leaders of county subdivisions—usually precincts or townships. The approximately 3,000 county chairmen of each party might be considered, in the words of V. O. Key, as "the second lieutenants, or perhaps the noncoms, of the political army and have under their immediate direction and leadership the troops—the party workers who get out the vote."[1]

Urban communities often have party committees for each city ward. The ward leaders together may form a city committee which will conduct and coordinate citywide party activities. The individual ward committeemen may supervise the work of the precinct committeemen or captains. The precincts, which are the smallest units in the party organization, usually range in size from 100 to 600 voters. The precinct committeeman is the party's representative in his district and has the responsibility to see that the voters are registered and go to the polls on election day. In many cities the parties have active precinct captains only during campaigns, if at all. But in the more highly organized cities one or both parties will attempt

[1] V. O. Key, Jr., *Politics, Parties, and Pressure Groups*, 5th ed. (New York: Crowell, 1964), p. 327.

to have a captain or committeeman active in most precincts throughout the year. Precinct captains may be appointed by party leaders, or chosen in a party caucus, or elected in a party primary.

Although a chart outlining the structure of a party would indicate that it is organized in a hierarchical pattern similar to a business corporation or a military unit, there is little similarity from the standpoint of the manner in which they actually function. In a political party there is no top authority comparable to a corporation president or an army general. Effective power in the parties is at the state and local levels rather than at the top of the party structure. Moreover, each level of party organization is primarily concerned with its own problems and usually functions independently of the others.

In the past there have been party bosses, governors, and others who have been able to exercise sufficient control over the party throughout a state to insure a high degree of unified and coordinated action, but such examples have been rare in recent years. There have also been instances when, due to the strong charismatic leadership of a presidential nominee or the efforts of a particularly able national chairman, a party has conducted a well-coordinated nationwide campaign with considerable cooperation from all levels of the party, but this is not normally the fashion in which American parties have operated.

NOMINATIONS

One of the basic purposes of political parties is to nominate candidates for public office. The method by which this is done varies considerably from one political system to another. In the United States the nominating process differs in two respects from that of most other countries. First, the rank-and-file American voters may participate more directly in the making of nominations than voters elsewhere; and second, nominations are regulated more by law in the United States than in other countries. In the Soviet Union and other totalitarian regimes the leaders of the government party make the nominations by preparing a list of candidates, who will be unopposed in the election. In most democracies other than the United States candidates are commonly selected by a caucus or committee of dues-paying members in accordance with the rules drawn up and enforced by the party. In those countries few if any governmental regulations exist regarding the nominating procedures, and the general membership of the parties normally does not take part. In the United States almost every phase of the nominating process, with the exception of the national nominating convention, is regulated by legislation so that the will of the voters may prevail.

The nominating process in the United States also illustrates dramatically the decentralized character of American parties. As Professor E. E. Schattschneider has observed: "The nature of the nominating procedure determines the nature of the party; he who can make nominations is the owner of the party."[2] In the United States the parties are "owned" primarily by the local and state party members, for nominations are made at those levels. In each electoral district complete autonomy is exercised by the local party members over the choice of candidates. While a President may encourage an individual to run for office, neither he nor any other national party official has authority over the designation of candidates. In Great Britain, by comparison, both the Conservative and the Labour party executives have authority to approve candidates for public office. Although the power is not often used, the British national party organizations may veto any local choice for nomination and deny him the use of the party name. Moreover, as there are no local residence requirements for holding office in Great Britain, the national party organization may have a person nominated (with the approval of the local party) in a "safe" district even though he lives elsewhere.

During early American history nominations were made in caucuses of party leaders. By the 1830s the convention system began to replace the party caucuses and soon became the most widely used method for making nominations. During the second half of the nineteenth century, conventions fell into disrepute due to the commonly held belief that they were controlled by party bosses and well-financed pressure groups. In an effort to make the nominating process more democratic, reformers began advocating the direct primary which would permit the voters to make the final decision regarding the party nominees. Wisconsin in 1903 became the first state to adopt a mandatory direct primary law.

Although all states have now adopted the direct primary, limited use is still made of the caucus and the convention for making nominations. In some New England and middle western states caucuses open to all party members are held in certain areas for making nominations for local offices. Some states—New York, Connecticut, Delaware, Indiana—hold conventions for nominating candidates for the important statewide positions. The great majority of candidates today, however, are nominated in direct primaries.

The Direct Primary

From the standpoint of procedure the direct primary resembles the general election. The state prepares the ballots, provides for them to be counted,

2 E. E. Schattschneider, *Party Government* (New York: Holt, Rinehart and Winston, 1942), p. 64.

and certifies the results. From the standpoint of purpose they are different: direct primaries are held *to nominate candidates;* general elections are held *to elect public officials.*

Two types of primaries are used—the closed and the open. Approximately forty states have closed primaries, which means that only those voters who have registered with a party may participate in the selection of that party's nominees. In states using open primaries a voter need not declare his party affiliation, but may participate in the nomination of candidates of either party. The state of Washington has a unique variation of the open primary called the "blanket type," in which a voter is permitted to split his ticket and vote for candidates of both parties in the primary the same as a voter may do in any state in a general election.

In five states—Colorado, Connecticut, Massachusetts, Rhode Island, and Utah—provision is made for preprimary conventions in which the convention delegates may endorse candidates. In these conventions party activists may indicate which of the aspirants they believe are most highly qualified for the nominations, but the final decision is left to the general membership. For instance, in Colorado the name of each candidate receiving at least 20 percent of the vote in the preprimary conventions appears on the primary ballot as an endorsed candidate. Other candidates may have their names placed on the primary ballot by filing for nomination. In a few other states unofficial party organizations have been formed which endorse candidates prior to the primary. For instance, in California the Republican Assembly and the Democratic Council have made preprimary endorsements, the former for approximately three decades.

In some electoral districts, winning the nomination of the majority party virtually assures victory in the general election. As was explained in Chapter 13 within the nation there are a number of one-party states. Also in states in which the voter strength is evenly divided between the two parties, there are regions in which one party predominates. In addition, in certain metropolitan areas some electoral districts have been gerrymandered so that the nominee of the larger party in the district will consistently be elected. Because winning the nomination is tantamount to being elected in so many electoral districts, the nominating process assumes greater importance than it would if two-party competition existed in elections throughout the nation.

Eleven southern states, recognizing that winning the Democratic nomination virtually assures victory in the general election, have provided that if no candidate receives a majority of the vote in the first primary election, a runoff primary will be held between the two candidates who received the most votes in the first primary.

Nonpartisan primaries are used to nominate state legislators in Minnesota and Nebraska, and in several states for the nomination of judicial and local officials. In nonpartisan primaries no party labels appear on the ballots and the individuals receiving the highest and second highest number of votes become the candidates. Frequently if one candidate receives a majority he is declared elected.

Recruitment and Nomination of Candidates

While nominating candidates is a basic function of political parties, in the United States the activity is not monopolized by the parties. Many candidates are self-recruited; they secure a place on the ballot by circulating their own petitions and they conduct their own campaigns without support from party organizations. Also it is well known that there have been examples of political interest groups recruiting candidates and assisting in their nomination campaigns. Undoubtedly, however, most candidates for public office are recruited, assisted, or at least encouraged, by party officials.

Although the direct primary was adopted to further democratize the nominating process, the extent to which the voters participate in the actual designation of candidates varies considerably from one electoral district to another. In some constituencies the primaries are usually hotly contested and the party members may choose between two or more prospective nominees for most offices. At the other extreme are those localities in which the party leaders prepare a slate that will seldom be opposed in the primary, and the typical party member has little more influence, if any, in the selection of party nominees than he would have under a convention system. But if the latter condition exists, the direct primary still provides a method by which the organization's slate may be opposed and other individuals nominated.

❧ NOMINATING AND ELECTING THE PRESIDENT

The national nominating convention is a peculiarly American institution. The chief executive of no other major power is nominated by a comparable procedure. In most modern democracies the person who becomes the nation's chief executive must first be selected the leader of his party, a position usually achieved only after years of parliamentary and party experience. Then, if his party gains a majority in parliament, he becomes the chief executive.

In the United States a person generally becomes the acknowledged leader of his party only after being nominated for the Presidency. The national convention makes it possible for an individual to follow a variety of routes for advancement to this, the highest elective office. In recent decades, while several presidential nominees have had experience in Congress, others have found a lack of such experience not an insurmountable obstacle, and have been nominated after careers as governors, in the military, or in business. Indeed, more governors than senators and congressmen have been nominated for the Presidency. In brief, the national convention opens the Presidency to people with a variety of backgrounds and makes it possible for individuals to achieve that position who would be precluded if the choice were limited, as in most countries, to national legislative leaders.

The National Convention

The national convention illustrates how political institutions in a free society evolve to meet the needs and temperament of the people. The Constitution provided for the President and Vice-President to be chosen by the electors, who after being elected in a manner to be determined by the individual state legislatures, would meet in their respective states and each vote for two persons. The ballots would be counted in the presence of the two houses of Congress and the individual receiving the largest vote would be elected President, providing it was a majority of the vote; and the one receiving the second number of votes would be the Vice-President. If no person received a majority, the House of Representatives, with the delegation from each state casting one collective vote, would choose the President from the five contenders having the largest number of votes. The framers of the Constitution apparently believed that in most instances no person would obtain a majority of the electoral vote and the House of Representatives would often make the choice. Thus, in effect, the electoral college would nominate as many as five candidates, one of whom would be elected President by the House of Representatives. However, the entire process of nominating and electing the President and Vice-President was soon assumed by the parties, and the electoral college has not functioned as anticipated by the Founding Fathers. The parties through custom and practice have amended the Constitution and have changed the process by which the President is elected.

The first procedure developed by the parties for selecting presidential nominees was the congressional caucus, but opposition developed to "king caucus" because too much power was vested in the congressmen and senators and because it denied representation to party members living in electoral districts where the opposition party had won the election. In 1832 the Democrats became the first major party to hold a national convention, and since that time presidential candidates of major parties have been nominated by national conventions.

Selecting the Delegates. The only governmental regulation of the national conventions are the state laws which prescribe how the delegates are to be chosen. The parties themselves establish the rules for allocating delegates among the states and for all other matters relating to the convention. The state legislatures have provided for delegates to be selected by three means: (1) less than one third of the states and the District of Columbia choose the delegates in presidential primaries; (2) three states permit party committees to designate the delegates; and (3) most states have provided that delegates be chosen by state conventions.

Presidential Primaries.   Wisconsin in 1905 was the first state to adopt the presidential primary and within the next ten years, half of the states had followed suit. But since that time the number of such states has gradually decreased so that by 1964 only sixteen states and the District of Columbia used some form of the presidential primary.

Various criticisms have been voiced regarding the presidential preferential primaries. Due to defects in certain primaries and to the failure of every leading presidential contender to enter each primary, preferential primaries are meaningful in no more than five or six states. As presidential hopefuls commonly enter only those primaries they believe they can win, in only a few states are the voters able to indicate a choice among the leading contenders in either party. For instance, in 1964 only in three states were Republican voters able to choose among the leading aspirants, and Johnson had no serious opposition in any state. Among other criticisms of the preferential primaries are the following: they are expensive and give an advantage to individuals with large funds; they exhaust prospective candidates; they may be decided on local and not on national issues; and a defeat in an early primary may eliminate a potential presidential nominee.

On the positive side it should be noted that presidential primaries provide the opportunity for individuals, like Dwight Eisenhower and John Kennedy, who are not necessarily the choice of the party leaders, to prove their popularity with the voters. Hence, presidential primaries have been instrumental in the nomination of candidates who might not otherwise have been nominated.

Allocation of Delegates.   Both parties have followed the general rule of allocating delegates to the national convention according to the number of representatives each state has in Congress. Republicans and Democrats use different formulas, and there have been minor rule changes through the years allowing differing numbers of delegates. In the 1964 Democratic presidential convention there were 3,052 delegates; and in the Republican conventions of 1956–1964, the number of delegates ranged from 1,308 to 1,331.

Convention Procedure. The conventions of the two parties follow remarkably similar procedures considering that they have developed independently and are not regulated by legal provisions. Certain features of the conventions—such as the keynote and nominating speeches, the floor demonstrations for prospective nominees, and the method of balloting—developed more than a century ago and have continued largely by tradition. Both parties have made some changes because of television. For instance, nominating speeches have been shortened, the principal addresses and other events are scheduled to permit them to be viewed by the maximum television audience, and motion picture and television stars are placed on the program to attract a larger audience. Complete convention coverage by the networks provides the political parties hours of free television time, which would cost millions of dollars to purchase.

Next to the nomination of the President and Vice-President, the most important function of the convention is the drafting of the party platform. The resolutions or platform committee, composed of one man and one woman from each state and territory, usually holds hearings prior to the opening of the convention. Customarily most of the platform has been drafted in advance; and if the President is planning to run for a second term, it may have been prepared under his personal direction. Occasionally a dispute will erupt on the floor of the convention over some provision, but, commonly, platforms are adopted with little opposition. Much has been written regarding the similarities of platforms of the two parties. Although the platforms are similar, a careful reading will reveal important differences in the platforms and some indication of the different orientation of the two parties. Moreover, as party platforms serve the purpose of uniting the party as well as helping to elect the President, they must necessarily avoid some issues and be vague and ambiguous on others.

The nomination of the presidential candidate, which is the basic reason for the convention, follows the adoption of the platform and usually occurs on the third or fourth day of the convention. Presidential nominations generally may be classified in three categories. First, if a President is seeking a second term, he will generally be nominated by acclamation. Second, in conventions at which a President is not seeking renomination often the strongest candidate has been nominated on the first ballot because he had obtained sufficient delegate support prior to the convention. During the preceding half century in each party two thirds or more of the nominees have been nominated on the first ballot. Third, in a number of instances two or more ballots have been required to make a nomination. Prior to 1936 the Democrats required a two-thirds majority for nomination, and on one occasion, 1924, 103 ballots were required before the delegates gave John W. Davis the necessary two-thirds majority.

Vice-presidential Nominations. The nomination of the vice-presidential candidate, occuring on the day following the presidential nomination, tends to come as an anticlimax. By tradition, the presidential nominee is permitted to choose his running mate. In 1956 Adlai Stevenson deviated from the customary practice and left the choice of the vice-presidential nominee to the delegates, but all other recent presidential candidates have personally made the selection. Formerly vice-presidential candidates were usually selected primarily "to balance the ticket," both from the standpoint of factions within the party and of geography, and their qualifications for the Presidency were considered only secondarily. But in recent years, owing to the death in office of Presidents Roosevelt and Kennedy and the illnesses of other Presidents, qualification for the Presidency has been given more consideration in selecting vice-presidential candidates, and undoubtedly was a major factor in the choice of such vice-presidential nominees as Cabot Lodge and Lyndon Johnson in 1960 and Hubert Humphrey in 1964.

Presidential Campaigns and Elections

Presidential campaigns are the most elaborate, spectacular, and expensive feature of American politics, and they differ sharply from election campaigns anywhere else. In no other country do so many people expend so much effort over such a vast expanse of territory and over so long a time soliciting the votes of such a large electorate. In most Western democracies the chief executive is a member of parliament and, like all other national legislators, is not voted on by the entire electorate of the country, but is elected by the voters of one constituency. In other countries where a president is elected by the general electorate, as in France and the Philippines, campaigns are much shorter, the distances to be traveled are less, the electorate is smaller, and the electronics communications media are used considerably less than they are in the United States. As the first presidential primary in the United States is held in March, American presidential candidates must usually plan for a campaign of at least nine months. By comparison, Italian campaigns are restricted by law to six weeks, and British campaigns are customarily limited to three weeks, as was the 1965 French presidential campaign during which each of the candidates was permitted only two hours of television time.

Winning the Nomination. One of the popular myths regarding the American Presidency is that the office customarily seeks the man; whereas, in reality, few Presidents have been elected who have not actively sought the office. Most presidential candidates must conduct two campaigns—the first to obtain the nomination and the second to win the election. Each of the campaigns requires careful and detailed planning, a personal campaign organization, and ample funds. Often presidential aspirants lay the groundwork for their presidential campaigns several years prior to actually seeking the nomination and election.

One of the first steps in the campaign for the nomination is the "build-up," through which the aspirant hopes to gain sufficient national prominence and stature that he will be considered "presidential timber." If the aspirant holds a major office such as United States senator or as governor of a populous state, the publicity ordinarily received in such an office helps him gain national prominence. In addition, prospective candidates solicit invitations to appear on television programs, to deliver addresses to the national conventions of powerful interest groups and to political rallies or to fund-raising dinners. Not uncommonly, a prospective candidate will travel abroad, hoping to gain a reputation for being well informed regarding foreign affairs. By noting the individuals engaging in activities of these types in the year or two prior to the conventions, one can compile a fairly accurate list of those persons who hope they might be nominated as presidential candidates. Those whose efforts are successful become national celebrities and will be listed on public opinion polls with others considered as potential presidential nominees.

An individual wishing the presidential nomination must win the support of delegates who will attend his party's convention. Two approaches are commonly employed for gaining delegate support. One, referred to as the "outside" strategy, is to concentrate on winning delegates selected in presidential primaries. The other, known as the "inside" approach, is to work primarily for the support of delegates elected by party conventions and committees.[3] The specific strategy adopted will depend on a variety of factors, including the personality and financial resources of the candidate, the other persons seeking the nomination, and the individual's relationship with other party leaders. John Kennedy in 1960 decided on the "outside" approach, believing that he must rely on his popular appeal and win major victories in presidential primaries, both to gain the votes of delegates thus chosen and to impress leaders of delegations from other states. By way of

[3] Charles O. Jones, "The 1964 Presidential Election—Further Adventures in Wonderland," *American Government Annual, 1965–1966* (New York: Holt, Rinehart and Winston, 1965), p. 3.

contrast, Barry Goldwater in 1964 chose the "inside" strategy; he won only one major presidential primary, and although public opinion surveys showed he was not the choice of the majority of the Republican voters, he was nominated because of support he had acquired from state and local party leaders.

In the months prior to the final presidential campaign most potential presidential nominees, one by one, are eliminated. Some fail to be re-elected to other public offices—Richard Nixon's defeat in the 1962 California gubernatorial election, for example, virtually removed him from the 1964 presidential race. Others who appear to have the desired qualifications fail in their television or other public appearances to project an image of presidential stature. Still others are defeated in key presidential primaries. Finally, in the national conventions all but two are eliminated.

Campaign Strategy. After winning the presidential nomination, one of the first tasks of the candidate is to plan the grand strategy of his election campaign. Among the factors to consider are the campaign themes and issues, specific geographic and group targets, the myriad organizations participating in the campaign, the timing of campaign output, the employment of public relations personnel, and the use of the communications media.

The general themes will be selected in an effort to establish a favorable tone for the campaign. Experienced political practitioners, noting that "you can't win defensively," generally advise candidates to conduct a positive campaign. Often the principal theme will be expressed in a slogan, or a phrase, and will relate to domestic conditions and world affairs. For instance, in 1924 the Republicans urged the voters to "keep cool with Coolidge," in 1932 Roosevelt offered the nation a "New Deal," in 1952 Eisenhower campaigned on "cleaning up the mess in Washington," and eight years later Kennedy promised to get the nation "moving again."

Presidential campaigns are seldom conducted with the view to appealing equally to all voters. Instead, the electorate is usually considered as groups of voters and greater efforts are made to influence some groups than others. Customarily much of the campaign output is directed toward specific geographic and group targets. The aim of each candidate is to win states with electoral votes totaling 270 or more. As the candidate who carries a state receives its entire electoral vote, candidates concentrate their efforts on the large doubtful states and spend relatively little time in the less populous states and those considered "safe" for either nominee. In 1960, although Nixon campaigned in all fifty states and Kennedy campaigned in forty-three, each spent more than half of his time campaigning in the seven largest pivotal states. Goldwater in 1964, believing he could not carry those particular states, concentrated his efforts in less populous southern, mid-western, and southwestern areas.

In addition to geographic targets, campaigns are usually waged with the view of attracting the votes of certain socioeconomic groups. Programs are developed which appeal to voters as businessmen, laborers, farmers, physicians, members of ethnic minorities and other groups. Candidates, in employing group appeals, run the risk of alienating some groups by appealing for the support of others. For instance, in 1964 Johnson un-doubtedly realized that by emphasizing civil rights as a campaign issue, he would gain support from Negro voters, certain ethnic groups, and most liberals, but that he might lose certain southern states and support among some conservatives in the North.

Among the target groups are the members of the candidate's party. Research on voting behavior has verified what practical politicans have long believed—that individual voting decisions are generally based on the voters' perceptions of three factors—the parties, the issues, and the candi-dates (see Chapter 12). Campaigns are usually designed to win votes on the basis of each of these variables. From the standpoint of party affiliation, voters are viewed as strong partisans, weak partisans, independents, and members of the opposite party, and each group is considered as a specific target. Issues are formulated with the view toward activating strong partisans, to strengthening the party ties of weak partisans, and to convert-ing independents and members of the opposite party. In terms of these three principles of activation, reinforcement, and conversion, Johnson in 1964 conducted a near model campaign.

Campaign Organizations. A bewildering number of organizations par-ticipate in presidential campaigns. These organizations may be grouped into four categories. First, there are the official party organizations, which are active between campaigns and whose staffs are greatly expanded in the months prior to the election. Second, often a candidate for the Presidency or other major office establishes a personal organization that will work directly with him. Many times these organizations are formed to help the candidate win the nomination and will be continued until after the election, when they are dissolved. Third, various *ad hoc* groups are estab-lished and subsidiary party organizations are activated. Each party creates temporary organizations, such as the Volunteers for Goldwater-Miller and the Independent Citizens for Johnson-Humphrey, to attract the active support of individuals who might not want to work with the regular party organizations. Uniquely American are the organizations of registered voters of one party for the candidate of the opposite party—such as "Democrats for Goldwater," and "Republicans for Johnson." Fourth, special interest groups have political action committees which participate in election campaigns. Well-known examples of such groups include the AFL–CIO Committee on Political Education and the American Medical Association Political Action Committee.

Professional Campaign Management and Opinion Surveys. In recent years the charge has been made that "Madison Avenue" has taken over political campaigns. In this context "Madison Avenue" refers to public relations and advertising firms, many of which have their New York offices on that street. The fear has been expressed that political candidates are being "packaged and sold" to the voters in much the same fashion as advertising agencies sell soap, cereal, or automobiles.

It is true that in recent years there has been a considerable increase in the employment of public relations personnel in political campaigns. With the increased use of television and the decline in the old-style political machine there has developed a new type of professionalism—the political public relations and campaign management firms. For a handsome fee, such firms will take the responsibility for virtually every aspect of a campaign. They will plan the general strategy, raise funds, recruit campaign workers, write speeches, prepare campaign literature, handle press conferences, make arrangements for the candidate's public appearances, and prepare advertising copy and film used in the press or on television. A few candidates for Congress and state elective offices have used public relations personnel to manage all aspects of their campaigns. In presidential campaigns public relations and advertising personnel are commonly employed to advise on the use of the mass media, to help prepare campaign literature and filmstrips, and to arrange for the desired space in the press and time on radio and television, but they have not managed the presidential campaigns. In this age of specialization professional assistance is sometimes needed, but there is little evidence to support the charge that "Madison Avenue has taken over."

Another example of the new professionalism in campaigns is the extensive use of public opinion surveys. Most candidates for major offices carefully analyze the opinion polls appearing in the press and employ private polling organizations to conduct more specialized surveys, the results of which are often used in planning campaign strategy, in deciding what questions to discuss, and in determining how to handle specific problems. Such recent presidential contenders as Rockefeller, Nixon, Kennedy, and Johnson have made extensive and effective use of opinion surveys. For example, Kennedy's victory in the 1960 West Virginia primary (which was instrumental in his winning the Democratic nomination) has been credited to a change in his campaign strategy which he made because of information produced by a polling organization working for him.

Campaigns have been greatly affected by developments in public opinion polling, motivational research, propaganda techniques, professional campaign management, and advertising as well as by revolutionary developments in communication and transportation. Today a candidate traveling by jetliner in a single day may address a group at breakfast in New York, attend a luncheon meeting in Chicago, and deliver a dinner address in Los Angeles or San Francisco, which via television could be seen and heard in nine out of ten homes in the nation. It has been estimated that at least 100 million Americans saw one or more of the television "debates" between Nixon and Kennedy in 1960.

Campaigns and Election Results.   Does the campaign make a difference in who wins a presidential election? Some individuals insist that they do not, but most candidates behave as if the outcome of the election depended solely on their campaign. In some elections the victorious candidates would undoubtedly have won, and with approximately the same margin, even if there had been no campaign. For example, in 1964 Lyndon Johnson's percentage of the popular vote was approximately the same as the percent of the electorate who indicated a preference for him to public opinion pollsters at the time of his nomination.

In some elections the campaign has obviously made a difference in the outcome. Most observers believe that neither Truman in 1948 nor Kennedy in 1960 would have won had there been no campaigns. In 1960 Kennedy's plurality was less than one vote per precinct, and in each of these elections a shift of a few thousand votes in key states would have elected the opposing candidate. Moreover, although many voters make their voting decision by the time the candidates are nominated, many do not; opinion surveys have shown that in recent presidential elections from one fifth to one third of the electorate have said they reached their decision during the campaign, and approximately one tenth of the voters have stated that they decided during the final two weeks of the campaign.

Presidential Elections Classified.   After the parades, the rallies, the informal speeches to small crowds, the television addresses to millions of viewers—after the campaigns have ended and the electorate has voted, what do the results mean? Presidential elections have often been interpreted as great collective decisions, and different systems have been devised for classifying the individual elections. The following classification based on the partisan affiliations of the electorate suggested by Professor Angus Campbell and his associates is possibly the most useful.[4]

MAINTAINING ELECTIONS.   In maintaining elections, the prevailing pattern of partisan identification has continued and the party holding office has been returned to power. During the past century most elections have been of this type. Recent examples include the elections of 1936, 1940, 1948, and 1964.

DEVIATING ELECTIONS.   In deviating elections due to some event, set of circumstances, or candidate, the second largest party replaces the party which, during that era, has the support of the majority of the voters. These elections deviate from the normal pattern in that the basic division of partisan support remains unchanged, but the majority party is defeated. Examples are 1912 and 1916—when Wilson won during the period of Republican hegemony—and 1952 and 1956 when Eisenhower was victorious even though the majority of the electorate retained their affiliation with the Democratic party.

REINSTATING ELECTIONS.   In reinstating elections the dominant party is returned to office after being out of power. The elections of 1920 and 1960 are examples.

REALIGNING ELECTIONS.   In realigning elections are included those rare instances when a significant number of voters make a lasting change in their partisan identification. Since the formation of the present two parties, this type of election has occurred only twice—in 1860 and in 1932—and both were associated with major crises—the Civil War and the Great Depression.

℀ CONGRESSIONAL CAMPAIGNS AND ELECTIONS

Every two years campaigns are waged for the 435 seats in the House of Representatives and one third of the seats in the Senate. Many of these campaigns are miniatures of presidential campaigns. The candidate establishes a personal campaign organization, coordinates his efforts with those of other candidates and organizations, solicits support from influential interest groups, prepares campaign literature, purchases radio and television time and space in the press, and addresses organized groups and political rallies. Some candidates—in particular, those seeking to represent heavily populated states in the Senate—have employed private polling

[4] Angus Campbell, Philip E. Converse, Warren E. Miller, and Donald E. Stokes, *The American Voter* (New York: Wiley, 1960), pp. 531–538.

"I have never stooped, my friends, nor will I stoop, to the kind of vicious false-hoods, mud-slinging, and personal vilification indulged in by my opponent and his Commie pals." Drawing by Whitney Darrow, Jr.; Copr. © 1956
The New Yorker Magazine, Inc.

organizations and public relations personnel to assist them in their campaigns.

For a number of senatorial aspirants and more than one half of the candidates for the House of Representatives the direct primary is the crucial test. Those candidates residing in a "safe" district or state are virtually assured election once they have their party's nomination. Moreover, after holding office for a term or two their renomination becomes less difficult; in an election year seldom are more than eight to twelve representatives defeated for renomination, and only rarely does a senator fail in his efforts to be renominated.

Most congressional candidates seeking nomination through the direct primaries tend to base their campaigns largely on their personal qualifications and to discuss few political issues. Unlike their counterparts in Great Britain, Scandinavia, and other democracies, those wishing to be nominated to the national legislature in the United States are not required to receive the endorsement of the national party organization or to support the party program. Any individual with the legal qualifications may enter a direct primary; and if he wins, he becomes the candidate of the party. After winning the nomination, if he has sufficient local prestige and support, he may be elected even though he might be opposed by the national leadership of the party.

The general election campaigns of candidates seeking seats in Congress in presidential election years tend to differ from those of off-election years. In presidential election years if the party's candidate for Chief Executive is likely to win, most congressional candidates gear their campaigns to his and attempt to ride into office "on his coattails." However, if the presidential candidate is unpopular, some congressional candidates ignore the national ticket and others publicly disassociate themselves from it, as several Republicans did in 1964. In midterm congressional elections a different situation prevails; without the influence of the presidential election, candidates tend to conduct individual campaigns often based on local issues or personalities. In recent presidential elections, only in 1956, when President Eisenhower was elected to a second term, has the President's party failed to gain control of Congress. Since the Civil War the party in power has lost congressional seats in every midterm election except one, 1934.

✹ POLITICAL FINANCE

Although more information is available regarding campaign contributions and expenditures in recent elections than for any previous period, political finance remains "the dark continent" of American politics. The numerous electoral contests, the many official and unofficial organizations involved in political campaigns, and the inadequacy of financial reports filed by candidates and political organizations render the task of compiling an accurate tabulation of political spending extremely difficult

What Campaigns Cost

The available information indicates that the costs of election campaigns are constantly mounting. This is due principally to the growth in the electorate, the gradual rise in the general price structure, and the increase in the use of television in campaigns. According to the most reliable estimates, campaign expenditures for candidacies at all levels of government during presidential election years were $140,000,000 in 1952;

$155,000,000 in 1956; $175,000,000 in 1960; and $200,000,000 in 1964.[5] Although, if computed on the basis of cost per vote per office, these sums are not extraordinarily high in comparison to costs in other countries, the fact remains that it is a vast amount of money, and the expenses are rising steadily.

What does it cost to be elected to public office in the United States? Because several campaigns are customarily conducted in one area simultaneously, it is difficult to apportion among the various candidates precisely what is spent electing one official. The reports filed by candidates, however, do give some indication of the high cost of running for major office. In 1965 John Lindsay reportedly spent more than $2½ million being elected mayor of New York City. In their 1962 gubernatorial campaigns Nelson Rockefeller in New York and Edmund G. Brown and Richard Nixon in California, each reported expenditures of approximately $2 million.

The expense of seeking election to Congress varies greatly. If only token opposition exists, a candidate's expenditures will naturally be much less than if he has vigorous opposition. The cost of senatorial campaigns ranges from only a few thousand dollars in thinly populated states to as much as $2 million—the amount reportedly spent by Robert Kennedy in the 1964 New York election. The cost of election to the House of Representatives also varies according to numerous factors, but the typical candidate probably spends about $50,000, or almost the amount of his salary for his two years of office.

Political committees functioning at the national level in 1964 reported total expenses of $48 million. Table 14–1 summarizes the total campaign costs of these committees that spent funds primarily to elect a President and Vice-President. Other national committees concentrating on electing members of Congress spent approximately $9 million. As the table shows, the Republican expenditures in 1964 surpassed the combined disbursements of Democratic and labor organizations, thus re-establishing the pattern of all recent presidential elections except 1960, when combined Democratic and labor spending equaled that of the Republicans.

The fact that the Democrats have won most of the presidential and congressional elections during the past three decades while spending less than their opponents disproves the commonly held belief that the party or candidate with the most money always wins. Candidates for Congress with the most money often win, but not merely because they have more money.

[5] In addition, candidates and campaign organizations are given hours of volunteer labor and the use of automobiles, airplanes, office space, and other items of value without charge. Alexander Heard, *The Costs of Democracy* (Chapel Hill, N.C.: University of North Carolina Press, 1960), pp. 7–8; Herbert E. Alexander, *Financing the 1964 Election* (Princeton: Citizens' Research Foundation, 1966), p. 13.

TABLE 14–1. *National Spending in the Presidential Election, 1964*

Committees	Total Campaign Costs
41 Republican	$19,314,796
49 Democratic	13,348,791
40 Labor	3,816,242
34 Miscellaneous	2,121,172
	$38,601,001

SOURCE: Adapted from *Congressional Quarterly*, Special Supplement, January 21, 1966, p. 56.

Often the candidate most likely to win receives more funds as well as other types of support, principally because individuals like to support a winner. It is not uncommon, however, for the victorious candidate to have less funds than his opponent. The lack of money may be offset by other political resources such as newspaper support, enthusiastic volunteer workers, and the backing of powerful interest groups. The primary purpose of campaign funds is to permit the candidate to gain access to the voters in his appeal for votes, and beyond a certain point, additional funds may make little difference in determining the winner.

How the Money Is Spent

The specific campaign expenditures, of course, vary according to the office sought, the candidate, his campaign strategy, and the availability of funds. However, in presidential campaigns, the amount paid for publicity dwarfs all other types of expenses. The largest single publicity expenditure is for television. In every presidential election since 1952—the first election in which television was used extensively—the cost for television and radio time has sharply risen from that of preceding years. According to the Federal Communications Commission the total charges for political broadcasting in campaigns at all levels in 1964 were approximately $34.6 million. Another major expenditure in recent years has been for public opinion polls. It has been estimated that in the same year political candidates and committees at all levels of government paid at least $5 million for public opinion surveys.[6]

Sources of Campaign Funds

A vast amount of money obviously must be obtained to pay legitimate campaign costs. What are the sources of these funds? During recent years

[6] Herbert E. Alexander, *Financing the 1964 Election* (Princeton: Citizens' Research Foundation, 1966), p. 60.

TABLE 14–2. *Total Contributions of $500 or Over to National Committees*

Party	1948 Percent	1952 Percent	1956 Percent	1960 Percent	1964 Percent
Democratic	69	63	44	59	69
Republican	74	68	74	58	28

SOURCE: Adapted from *Congressional Quarterly*, Special Supplement, January 21, 1966, p. 58.

the means of financing campaigns have undergone a change, and today political funds come primarily from five sources.

First, there are contributions by the candidates, their relatives, and friends. Customarily candidates contribute to their own campaigns. If a candidate has the personal and family resources of a Nelson Rockefeller or of a John Kennedy, he and his family may contribute a large proportion of his expenses. For example, of the estimated $3.5 million to $5 million spent by Nelson Rockefeller in his unsuccessful bid for the Republican presidential nomination in 1964, all but $100,000 was provided by the candidate and his family.[7]

Second, both parties solicit and receive numerous large and small gifts. Public opinion surveys show that approximately 10 to 12 percent of the electorate contributed to national, state, or local campaigns in 1960 and 1964. The Republicans tend to be more systematic in their appeals for funds and make their solicitations in a fashion similar to the United Fund drives. Both parties appeal for funds to the rank-and-file voter, but in recent presidential election years about two thirds of the amount received by each party has been in sums of $500 or more (see Table 14–2). In 1964 the Goldwater forces, through television and direct mail solicitations, obtained a much larger proportion of their funds in small sums than in any previous recent elections. Traditionally the Republicans have received considerably more from the business community than have the Democrats. The Democrats, however, received larger amounts from business in 1960 and 1964 than previously. After Kennedy entered the White House, the Democrats created the President's Club, consisting of persons who contributed $1,000 or more annually, and by the time of the 1964 election, Johnson had expanded the membership of the "club" to about 4,000 persons.

Third, a major source of party funds has been derived from fund-raising activities. President Kennedy during his first two years in office attended twenty fund-raising functions which grossed more than $9,000,000. These included two $1,000 per person dinners, one $1,000 per person cocktail

[7] *Ibid.*, pp. 23–24.

party, and a number of $100 dinners. In 1960 the Republicans received $7,700,000 from two sets of banquets held simultaneously in different cities and connected by closed circuit television. Individual candidates also hold fund-raising dinners.[8] Herbert Alexander estimated that in 1964 at least $36,600,000 was paid for attendance at fund-raising activities ranging from one dollar rallies to $5,000 cocktail parties. Among fund-raising activities were the sale of advertising to corporations and others in political programs and books. By charging $15,000 per page, it is believed that the Democrats received $1,500,000 for advertising in the 1964 national convention program. In 1966 Congress adopted an amendment to a taxation measure which prohibited corporations from deducting such advertising expenditures or the cost of tickets to political dinners or programs as a business expense.

Fourth, as is true in most Western democracies, political interest groups both directly and indirectly make important contributions to political parties and candidates. Congress has enacted legislation prohibiting corporations and labor unions from contributing directly to candidates or political parties; however, it is well known that both types of organizations have found methods for making contributions to campaigns. Some corporations aid the party and candidates of their choice by such means as paying the salaries of officers and employees who are engaged in political activities, granting bonuses to executives with the understanding that the money will be given to a candidate or a party committee, publishing and circulating political opinions at the expense of the corporation, and purchasing radio and television time or newspaper space for presenting political opinions. A congressional committee reported that in the 1956 election the officers and directors of the 225 largest corporations in the nation contributed $1,816,597 in individual gifts of $500 and more to the Republicans and $103,725 to the Democrats.[9]

Labor unions have also used most of the above methods of assisting candidates and party committees. As noted previously, the AFL–CIO has created a subsidiary organization, the Committee on Political Education, which collects and spends funds to aid political parties and candidates. Also it is not uncommon for unions to collect voluntary contributions from members to be used in campaigns, to spend "educational funds" promoting political views and candidates, and to endorse candidates in their publications. Of the amount spent by national level labor committees in

[8] Apparently all funds raised by candidates are not used for campaign purposes. In 1966 a senator was charged with having diverted to his personal accounts more than $100,000 obtained from fund-raising dinners.

[9] 1956 General Election Campaigns, Report of the Subcommittee on Privileges and Elections of the Committee on Rules and Administration, U.S. Senate, 84th Congress, 2d Session (Washington, D.C.: Government Printing Office, 1957), pp. 13–15, 24.

the 1964 campaigns nearly $900,000 was transferred to political candidates and committees.

Fifth, government employees, while a less important source of campaign funds than formerly, still make political donations. Federal and state civil service employees generally feel under no compulsion to contribute, but they may if they wish. Public employees who do not have civil service status often are solicited for donations, and many make contributions. Not uncommonly, specific amounts are suggested as suitable contributions.

Regulation of Party Finance

The problem of regulating campaign funds is complicated by a variety of factors including certain competing American values. For instance, most Americans agree that (1) money should not be the deciding factor in an election, and (2) a few persons or groups should not be permitted to gain control of the political processes through contributions. On the other hand, there is widespread agreement that (1) each person should be permitted to spend his money as he wishes, and (2) each person should be allowed to support the candidate of his choice—and if he desires—through campaign contributions.

The federal nature of our government has also made the regulation of party finance difficult. The national government and the states have concurrent control over presidential and congressional elections, while the states have jurisdiction over state and local elections. As a result, certain types of contributions prohibited by federal corrupt practices legislation—such as contributions by corporations to political campaigns—are prohibited by some states but are permitted by others.

Legislative regulations of political finance are of four types. First, the national government and all states have legislation outlawing the bribery of voters and similar expenditures. In more than half of the states the legislatures have enumerated permissible campaign expenditures and have prohibited all others. Other regulations of party finance are aimed at three general objectives: publicity of income and expenditures, limitations on groups which may contribute, and limitations on the size of contributions and expenditures.

Publicity of Income and Expenditures. The principle of public disclosure of the sources of funds is well established. Since 1910 the national government has required candidates for Congress and political committees under federal jurisdiction to file at given intervals financial statements with the Clerk of the House of Representatives. Committees covered by the law include nationally organized committees, those assisting candidates in two or more states, and those that are branches of a national committee. The information required includes the names and addresses of the persons who contributed $100 or more and those to whom payments of $10 or more have been made. Most states have similar legislation. The underlying assumption of this legislation is that by publicizing the names of the donors and the purposes for which funds are spent the candidates will be more circumspect regarding the solicitation and use of funds, and the voters will be able to make more intelligent decisions regarding candidates.

Considerable information is derived from the reports which would otherwise not be available, but the expectation of those who sponsored the legislation has not been fully realized. Although the permanently organized national committees usually file accurate reports, other committees and some losing candidates often file incomplete reports or fail to file. Moreover, data that are filed often are not analyzed and published in the press or otherwise made readily available to the electorate. Hence, the information has been useful primarily to the political parties and to students of American politics.

Limitations on Groups That May Contribute. Congress has enacted legislation forbidding contributions by corporations, national banks, individuals or firms with government contracts, and labor unions. As has been explained, there are many loopholes in these laws that permit these groups to make contributions. Federal employees are also forbidden from soliciting contributions from other employees, but such employees may make contributions if they wish. Some, but not all, states have similar legislation.

Limitations on Size of Contributions and Expenditures. The Hatch Act of 1940 limits to $5,000 the amount any individual may give in a calendar year to a national party organization or to any candidate for federal office. This statute also limits expenditures of a national committee to a maximum of $3 million a year. The Corrupt Practices Act of 1925 placed limitations on spending by candidates for Congress. Candidates for the House of Representatives may spend either up to $2,500 or 3 cents per voter with a maximum expenditure of $5,000. Senatorial candidates are limited to either $10,000 or 3 cents per voter with a maximum expenditure of $25,000.

There is virtually unanimous agreement that legal limitations on campaign spending serve no useful purpose, tend to decentralize further campaign expenditures, and make it more difficult to control and account for funds. Soon after the Hatch Act was adopted, both parties were advised by their attorneys that they could bypass the $3 million limitation merely by creating additional party organizations, each of which could spend up to the legal limit. Nor has the legal limit on candidate spending reduced the amount of money involved in congressional elections. As the limitation applies only to expenditures made with the "knowledge and consent" of the candidate, congressional nominees customarily provide for funds to be collected and disbursed by committees that are not required to file reports under federal statutes if they work within a single state.

The $5,000 ceiling on individual contributions obviously does not restrict the total amount that one person may give in an election. A person wishing to give more may make separate gifts of $5,000 to numerous party and candidate committees. Or, if he wishes to make a larger contribution to one candidate, he may make contributions in the names of his wife, children, and other relatives. For instance, in 1956 twelve families gave a total of $1,040,526 to Republican candidates and committees and $107,109 to Democrats. In 1960 members of the DuPont family gave $136,585 to Republican committees; and in 1964 Henry Ford II contributed $40,000 to the Democratic presidential campaign through fourteen committees.[10]

To this date the legislative efforts to regulate party finance have not been entirely successful in producing the desired results, and additional reforms are needed. Yet the efforts at regulation have not been entirely futile. No serious student of politics would advocate removing the regulations and reverting to the days when Republican National Chairman Mark Hanna literally assessed corporations and banks according to each one's "share in the general prosperity" for William McKinley's campaign. Thus, at least the extreme abuses of earlier days are now impossible.

Proposals for Improving Political Finance

The basic problem of political finance is how the political parties and candidates can obtain the funds for necessary expenditures without becoming dependent upon a relatively small number of individuals or interest groups. This problem has been investigated by congressional committees, a presidential commission, and private groups and individuals. A number of recommendations have been suggested both for providing financial and other assistance to political candidates and committees and for providing more effective regulation of political finance.

Among the former are recommendations that political parties be granted a limited amount of free radio and television time, as they are in most European countries, Canada, and Australia; that candidates be permitted to mail some literature free through a restricted use of the franking privilege, as candidates may in Japan; that the government provide direct subsidies to political parties, as is done in West Germany; and that more citizens be encouraged to contribute to campaigns by making tax deductible, contributions up to a total of $500 or $1,000 annually.

[10] Herbert E. Alexander and Harold B. Meyers, "The Switch in Campaign Giving," *Fortune* (November, 1965), p. 171.

Among the recommendations for improving federal regulation of political finance are proposals for removing the $3 million limit on spending by individual political committees, for removing or increasing the limitation on spending by congressional candidates, for a more strict enforcement of existing statutes which forbid or restrict certain types of contributions and expenditures, and for extending the federal legislation to include the direct primaries as well as the general elections. Since some candidates spend more in the primary than in the general election campaign, the failure of federal legislation to include primary campaigns is a glaring omission. The President's Commission on Campaign Costs, created by President Kennedy, recommended the establishment of a Registry of Election Finance which would have the responsibility for a more effective system of public disclosure.

The experience of the British in regulating campaign expenditures is instructive. Under British law, strictly enforced, all expenditures for a candidate for Parliament during an election campaign must be channeled through his agent who alone is authorized to spend money on his behalf. The law limits campaign expenditures to 450 pounds with an additional one and a half to two pence per voter in the district, or about $2,400 per candidate. This system has two major loopholes. First, it covers only expenditures for candidates and does not include expenditures for campaigns on principles or issues which may greatly affect the outcome of the election. Second, British law does not cover expenditures between elections. However, to the extent that the election campaign itself influences the final decision of many voters, strict regulation of campaign expenditures is a major step toward regulating the role of money in politics. In the United States, Florida has followed the British pattern by requiring all campaign expenditures to be channeled through the candidate's treasurer, who can be held accountable for all funds received and spent. Unlike the British system, Florida has no limit on the amount that a candidate may spend. The only restriction is on campaign donors, who are allowed to contribute no more than $1,000 to any one candidate in a primary or general election.

A number of bills incorporating some of the above proposals have been introduced into Congress, but none has been enacted. It has been suggested that one reason for the lack of congressional action is the fact that the legislators, having succeeded in being elected under the present system, are reluctant to enact different legislation. Most political observers, however, share the sentiments expressed by President Kennedy in 1961 when he said: "It is not healthy for the democratic process—or for the ethical standards in our Government—to keep our national candidates in [the present] condition of dependence."

CHAPTER 15

POLITICAL
INTEREST GROUPS

People with a common interest frequently join together in order to further that interest. If they believe their interest might be affected by governmental action, they may direct their combined efforts toward influencing government. For many people, group action has proved to be the key to success in the modern political world. From the time that individuals first had access to government, such groups have attempted to persuade public officials to adopt the policies they desired. The types of organized groups and the extent of their political activities have varied greatly, depending primarily on the level of social and economic development and the governmental system.

In the United States one of the first statements regarding political interest groups was written by James Madison in 1788 during the struggle over the adoption of the Constitution. In No. 10 of *The Federalist* Madison observed that ". . . a landed interest, a manufacturing interest, a mercantile interest, a moneyed interest, with many lesser interests, grow up of necessity in civilized nations, and divide them into different classes, actuated by different sentiments and views. The regulation of these various and interfering interests forms the principal task of modern legislation."

Various terms or phrases have been employed to describe the private organizations or groups that attempt to influence government. In the past the most commonly used term was *pressure groups*, but a number of writers have contended that this is misleading, for it implies that such groups necessarily use questionable methods and have objectionable goals, which, as a matter of fact, is not the case. The tendency in recent years is to refer to these organizations as *political interest groups,* or *interest groups.* Other terms employed include *organized interest groups* and *special interest groups.* In practical politics, the differences in terminology often become the distinction between one's own group as an "interest group" and the opponents' as a "pressure group." By definition, such a group is any private, nonpartisan group of people who seek to influence some phase of public policy. Hence legislative bodies or political parties are not political interest groups even though they influence public policies.

Although political interest groups and political parties are similar, if only the two major political parties are compared with interest groups, a distinction may readily be seen. Although the major parties have as their fundamental purpose gaining control of the personnel and politics of the government, they tend to concentrate on the nomination and election of public officials rather than on the choice of policies. Political interest groups are also interested in the personnel and policies of government, but they are primarily interested in public policies and are concerned with the selection of public officials only secondarily. Political interest groups do not wish—and are not prepared—to take over and operate the entire government. Such groups do not periodically submit their program to the voters in an election; if they participate in the electoral process, it is customarily by supporting party candidates whose views are similar to theirs.

Only in democratic systems, where freedom of association and free speech and press are guaranteed, can interest groups as we know them, organize and promote their interests. In democratic philosophy no single individual or group has a monopoly on understanding and developing policies that are in "the public interest." Democratic doctrine frankly concedes that people with divergent backgrounds, experiences, and ideological commitments have different social and economic interests. The entire democratic process is designed to encourage all interests to compete openly with other interests.

By contrast, totalitarian doctrine holds that only one interest may be promoted—the interest of the state—and that the ruling party has the right and duty to determine and enforce authoritatively that single interest. Hence a basic difference exists between interest groups in democracies and those in totalitarian regimes. The purpose of interest groups in a totalitarian state is to transmit government policies to the group and its members. The purpose of interest groups in a democracy is the reverse: to translate group interests into government policy. Democracies welcome organized groups, for they articulate the heterogeneous interests of the citizenry and add strength and stability to the political system. In totalitarian states the government and the official party attempt to encompass or control all phases of group interests. Those in power determine what groups may organize, and either provide their leadership or rigidly supervise their activities. Other voluntary associations are prohibited and all media of communication are strictly controlled to insure support for the official policies and to prevent dissent. In short, in a totalitarian system political interest groups comparable to those in the United States and other democratic countries are not permitted.

☙ FUNCTIONS OF POLITICAL INTEREST GROUPS

In the United States and other Western democracies, political interest groups perform several functions, among which are the following:

First, political interest groups help to crystallize opinion and to stimulate discussion of political issues. Numerous amorphous ideas may be suggested as solutions to problems in any area of public concern. Many interest groups sift, study, and debate the various ideas and then develop concrete proposals. This process crystallizes opinion on issues and makes for a clearer statement of public policy. By advocating the policies they have developed, groups stimulate discussion of political issues and help educate the people.

Second, organized interest groups provide a type of group representation. Because of the great diversity and complexity of many electoral districts, it is impossible for elected representatives to know the problems and opinions of all their constituents. Moreover, the primary interests of many individuals today are related more to occupational, fraternal, or ideological associations than to the specific problems of the geographic electoral district in which they live. As is commonly known, the word "lobby" refers to interest groups seeking the enactment or defeat of legislation. The representative role of interest groups is indicated by the popular reference to the lobby as the "third house."

Third, political interest groups provide a channel of communication between their members and public officials. In this age, in which government is involved in numerous and complicated matters, many legislative and administrative officials readily admit that organized interests are a valuable source of much specialized and detailed information. John F. Kennedy, when serving in the Senate, once stated: "Lobbyists . . . because of their familiarity with the problems of the interests they represent, and because of their ability to accumulate and supply information frequently not available from any other source . . . can be extremely useful. In many instances they . . . provide an important link between Congress and the particular economic or other special interest that they represent." "Lobbyists" or leaders of interest groups also inform public officials regarding the anticipated effects of proposed policies. The communication process, however, is not a one-way street, for often they obtain information from government agencies which they transmit to their members.

Fourth, political interest groups help check on the activities of other interest groups and public officials. If an interest group makes extreme or unreasonable demands, it may be opposed by other groups. Interest groups also scrutinize the activities of public officials and help insure that they perform their tasks in a responsible fashion.

⅊ GROUP TACTICS AND TECHNIQUES

Interest groups are pragmatic organizations; aware of the crucial decision-making points in the political process, they generally follow the principle of taking whatever action will produce the maximum results for their members with the minimum expenditure of time and energy. Methods used by organized interest groups in Great Britain, France, or Switzerland might be different from those used by similar groups in the United States. Moreover, actions that might be effective for one group in the United States might not succeed with another. The tactics and techniques employed would depend on such factors as the goals of the group, the cohesion of its members, its financial resources, the prestige position of the organization, the quality of its leadership, the size and geographic dispersion of its members, and its relations with the political parties and other interest groups. The complexity of modern government renders the representation of group interests a highly specialized task.

Where, then, do organized interest groups attempt to exert influence? Depending on the goals and characteristics of the particular group, it may attempt to influence its own members, other organized interest groups, the public at large, legislators, executive and administrative personnel, and the courts.

Influencing the Membership and Other Groups

Scholars have noted for many years that in most large organizations an active minority customarily effectively controls the group. This tendency is referred to as the "iron law of oligarchy." In many large interest groups the leaders, officers, and paid staff form a small elite who run the organization and who, from the viewpoint of the initiation and adoption of policies, in effect become the organization.

The officers and staffs of many different organizations often spend much time attempting to influence group members and potential members. Efforts are made to increase the cohesion of the group and to retain and enlarge the membership. In group publications, in national and state conventions, and in local meetings the leadership often attempts to get the members to accept and support the policies of the organization, and to engage in political activity which will promote the aims of the organization.

The efforts of political interest groups to influence public officials have tended to cause political observers to overlook the extent to which groups seek the cooperation of other organized groups. Pressure groups attempt to obtain the assistance of their allies and potential allies, the endorsement of groups not directly interested, and the neutralization of opposing forces. Such cooperation may be accomplished by merely activating others, by promising reciprocal assistance in the future, or by making compromises on proposed programs. A congressional committee investigating lobbying activities once commented on the "growing joint effort in lobbying" and added that "the general theme of combination rather than conflict grows bolder and more insistent every year."

Interest Groups and the Public

One of the noteworthy features of pressure group activity in recent years has been the continual increase in the efforts of groups in the United States to gain support for their programs by using the mass media of communication to influence public attitudes. Research on public opinion formation indicates that all segments of the population are not equally interested in every political problem. Instead some special or attentive "publics" are interested in one issue and different "publics" are interested in others. Public relations campaigns are directed primarily to the special publics likely to become concerned with the particular proposal and to other individuals referred to as "opinion leaders." If opinion leaders become interested in a program, they will probably influence many who might otherwise be uninterested in the issue.

Today many organizations employ public relations counsels to advise them and to direct propaganda campaigns. The use of these public relations experts is a distinguishing characteristic of modern propaganda. The rise of the public relations counsel has occurred concomitantly with the growth of pressure groups and the extraordinary development of the communications media.

Basically the aim of political interest groups in employing propaganda, either for short-term or long-range goals, is to make their program appear synonymous with the "general welfare." From a short-range viewpoint, a public relations campaign either may give the impression that there is such widespread support for a proposal that the campaign itself will provide the momentum necessary to secure the acceptance of the policy, or it may stimulate a sufficient number of persons to urge public officials to adopt the desired program.

The long-range or strategic aim of propaganda campaigns tends to be ideological, usually urging on the public a particular philosophy of government. In brief, the purpose of such campaigns is to condition the attitudes of the people so that they will respond almost automatically with favor toward programs desired by the group and reject those opposed by it. The National Association of Manufacturers has developed a strategic concept of propaganda, which they refer to as their "bank account theory." In one of their publications they explain that it requires making "regular and frequent deposits in the Bank of Public Good-Will" in order that "valid checks can be drawn on this account," on the proper occasions.

Some corporations employ institutional advertising, which may be defined as the use of paid space or time in the communications media to promote or oppose ideas. Such advertising, which regularly appears in some periodicals and newspapers, and occasionally on television, does not promote products but expounds a general philosophy such as "free enterprise" or the virtues of individualism. Business groups enjoy an advantage over other groups in this area, for the expense of such advertising may be deducted as an operating expense the same as other advertising expenses.

A number of the larger pressure groups disseminate press releases, clipsheets, and prepared editorials to the press. The effectiveness of this type of propaganda is largely due to the fact that when used, it gives the impression of straight reporting or editorials prepared by the staff of the local press.

In their efforts to influence public attitudes, political interest groups have not overlooked the educational system. Some groups, including the National Association of Manufacturers, have prepared and distributed books, booklets, posters, film strips, and other "teaching aids" to the schools. At one time the NAM announced that it distributed "at least two million booklets" free to the schools every year.

A method that has recently come into widespread use to influence public attitudes toward a general problem is the mass demonstration. These have been used extensively by civil rights groups and pacifist movements. Through mass demonstrations such groups as the Southern Christian Leadership Conference, the Congress of Racial Equality (CORE), the National Urban League, the National Association for the Advancement of Colored

People (NAACP), and the Student Non-Violent Coordinating Committee have focused attention on the extent to which Negroes have not been granted equal rights. These demonstrations have undoubtedly been more effective than any other available method in impressing on the public the plight of the Negroes.

Interest Groups and Political Parties

Group leaders, realizing that much of their success in achieving their political goals may depend on the support they receive from one or both political parties, usually take one of two approaches toward political parties. Many groups—especially the smaller organized interest groups—avoid too close an identification with either party but attempt to secure the support of both parties. Other groups have tended to align themselves with one party, but still attempt to work with the other party.

Political interest groups use a variety of methods to influence political parties. Several organizations urge their members to work actively in a party and, if possible, to be elected to a position in the party organization. The John Birch Society, for instance, has urged its members to infiltrate and take over party organizations. Most of the larger groups appear before the resolutions committees of the parties to urge the adoption of their groups' programs as planks in the parties' platforms. Often they attempt to obtain the endorsement of both parties and thus remove their proposals from the arena of partisan controversy. Although interest groups do not in their own name nominate candidates for public office, they often work for the nomination and election of certain candidates.

Interest groups that participate in election campaigns will usually support a candidate of either party if his general outlook is similar to that of the group. Organized labor has followed the policy, first prescribed by Samuel Gompers, of "rewarding friends and punishing enemies" by support or opposition in campaigns and at the polls, regardless of their party affiliation. But as noted above, some organizations have found most of their "friends" in one party and most of their "enemies" in the other.

Pressures on Legislators

In the past, organized groups in the United States concentrated most of their efforts on promoting and opposing legislative proposals. Although in recent years interest group activities have expanded in other areas, the most obvious actions of pressure associations are still those in which they attempt to influence legislative decisions.

POLITICAL INTEREST GROUPS 381

The principal organized interests maintain permanent staffs of professional lobbyists, press agents, research personnel, and secretaries in Washington, and have staffs in state capitals during legislative sessions. Organizations that have only an incidental interest in legislative proposals do not usually have a full-time lobby staff, but may employ a lobbyist to represent them on occasions when legislative issues of interest arise. Some interest associations have "stables" of legislators who will work closely with them because either the legislators are members of those groups or they owe their election primarily to them. Interest groups with like-minded spokesmen in the legislature, or "inside lobbyists," have an advantage over other organizations.

Lobbying consists basically of communicating with the legislators, and political interest groups utilize every opportunity to inform legislators of their wishes. Available information indicates that political interest groups originate a large proportion of the bills introduced in Congress and the state legislatures. Committee hearings on bills provide the opportunity for pressure groups to present information and arguments and also to show how strongly the members of the group favor or oppose a given proposal. Officers of organizations, their lobbyists, or lay members will testify before committees. Occasionally delegations will be organized to attend committee hearings. At crucial times—such as when a committee is considering a bill or when the measure is being debated by one of the houses of the legislature—political interest groups may have their members write, telegraph, or telephone their legislators. Some organizations attempt to flood the legislators with messages, whereas others concentrate on having communications sent by the principal supporters of individual legislators and other influential persons in each district.

Influencing the Executive Branch

In Great Britain, with its parliamentary form of government and centralized parties, interest groups have directed more attention to the Cabinet and less to individual legislators than have interest groups in the United States. In recent years, however, in the United States, too, political interest groups have increased their efforts to influence the executive branch of the government. Aware of the expanded role of the Chief Executive as the chief legislator, pressure groups have importuned the President and governors to incorporate or omit particular proposals from their legislative programs and to increase or decrease specific budgetary requests. After the legislature enacts a controversial bill, it is not uncommon for political interest groups to inundate the Chief Executive with letters, telegrams, and personal calls urging him to veto or sign the measure.

The growth of governmental regulations of business and industry and the tendency of legislatures to invest administrative officials with broad discretionary powers have caused organized groups in recent years to indicate more interest than formerly in administrative agencies. Such agencies, which have been given quasi-legislative powers, find that representatives of organized interests often appear before them to support or oppose changes in rules and regulations. The Administrative Procedure Act requires most federal administrative agencies to permit interested individuals to request the issuance, repeal, or amendment of rules and to conduct public hearings on such matters. Political interest groups have availed themselves of these rights and lobby the administrators in much the same fashion as they lobby Congress and the state legislatures.

As groups are aware that administrators may forcibly execute or virtually nullify a statute, it is understandable that organizations often seek the appointment of their members or of persons friendly to their group to administrative positions of concern to them. Pressure groups with friends in high administrative posts sometimes find that they have advantages not available to others in securing subsidies, contracts, permits, licenses, favorable adjustments of tax problems and antitrust suits, and other favors and privileges.

Pressure groups may also seek to influence administrative actions by working through legislators. Groups may urge the legislature to amend the statutes under which an agency functions, and they may urge increases or decreases in an agency's budget in order to expand or curtail its operations. In rare instances, organized interest groups have succeeded in getting legislators to investigate administrative agencies in an effort to punish uncooperative administrators. However, it is not correct to assume that the relationship between political interest groups and administrative agencies is typically one of hostility. On the contrary, it is not unusual to find political interest groups, governmental organizations, and legislators working together harmoniously.

Interest Groups and the Courts

Although political interest groups devote less effort toward influencing policy through the courts than through the legislative or executive branches, a number of organizations—acknowledging the importance of the judiciary in the political process—have turned their attention to the courts. Many groups realize that they may be affected by judicial actions: decisions that result from the power of judicial review, the interpretation of the Constitution, statutes, or treaties; the issuance of injunctions and other court orders; or decisions in civil or criminal cases affecting personal and property rights. Hence, whether judges are elected or appointed, various organizations scrutinize the records of prospective judges and oppose those believed to be biased against their group.

Various groups have sought to advance their interests by testing the constitutionality or interpretation of legislation or the actions of public officials. Organizations with small memberships or those representing minority groups may find that they are more successful in taking their causes to the courts than to the legislative or executive branches. A noteworthy example is the National Association for the Advancement of Colored People, which has for years employed litigation as a principal means for upholding Negro rights. In winning court cases such as *Brown* v. *Board of Education of Topeka* (1954), in which school segregation was outlawed, the NAACP won political victories fully as important as any gained in the halls of Congress. Some organizations intervene in suits as *amici curiae,* or "friends of the court," which permits them to file briefs in a case in which they are not a party, and in this way to support other groups involved in litigation. There are also examples of articles being prepared for publication in law reviews with the expectation that they will be used in briefs or may be read by judges and possibly influence later decisions.

For some interest groups, attempting to influence government is virtually an endless process; if the legislature enacts and the Chief Executive signs a measure considered undesirable, pressure organizations may seek to have it nullified, or at least amended, by judicial action. A classic illustration occurred when the United States Supreme Court in 1911—after several years of urging by corporation attorneys—applied the "rule of reason" to the Sherman Anti-Trust Act and decreed that the measure did not apply to all monopolies, but only to the "unreasonable" ones. In other instances interest groups have succeeded in having the executive and legislative branches nullify court decisions. The "tidelands" oil controversies is an example: after the United States Supreme Court ruled in 1947 that the federal government and not the states had jurisdiction over the "tidelands" (the submerged land along the coast), oil interests succeeded in 1953 in getting Congress and the President to approve an act granting the land to the states, an action deemed favorable to the oil interests.

⚵ THE VARIETY OF INTEREST GROUPS

Although political interest groups have been studied and analyzed for many years, we still have only an approximate idea of how many groups seek to press their claims on government. Even less is known regarding the cost of interest group activities. The Federal Regulation of Lobbying Act requires the registration of lobbyists and the filing of reports of group expenditures. A total of 7,000 lobbyist registrations were filed between 1946 and 1965, and group expenditures of more than $10 million a year on activities relating to national legislation have been recorded. The aggregate of group legislative expenditures in the states probably exceeds the national figures. In California alone more than 400 lobbying groups have reported expenditures in excess of $3 million during a single legislative session, and this amount includes only those costs related to the employment of registered lobbyists.

It is customary to classify interest groups according to their membership or primary interests, such as business, labor, farm, professional, religious, ethnic, or others. The following discussion begins with the economic interest groups, which have the largest membership and which undoubtedly are the most influential in American politics.

Business Groups

In all modern democracies, business groups organize and are active in the determination of public policy. In the United States, business has obviously been influential from the early days of our history. As previously noted, Madison in 1788 referred to the various interests. John Randolph in 1829 commented on the relationship between the ownership of property and political power. "The moment you separate the two," Randolph explained, "that very moment property will go in search of power, and power in search of property."

Strictly speaking, the term "businessmen" applies to only a small minority in the United States. The Census Bureau in 1960 classified only 5 million people as businessmen, but obviously many individuals in such fields as law, accounting, real estate, public relations, investments, and insurance share the attitudes characteristic of organized business and many think of themselves as businessmen. If one adds the numerous stock owners—currently well over 20 million—who identify themselves through their stock ownership with business, it is apparent that organized business serves as a reference group to millions of individuals.

Although business is represented in the political arena by a variety of organizations, three types are most prevalent. First, there are the "peak" associations, each of which includes as members a number of other organizations. The two largest and most influential business organizations of this type are the National Association of Manufacturers and the United States Chamber of Commerce. Second, there are many trade associations that attempt to influence government, usually on the national or state levels. Third, some individual business corporations and firms are active in politics at all levels of government.

Organized in 1895, the National Association of Manufacturers in recent years has had a membership that has fluctuated from about 16,000 to 18,000 individuals, firms, and corporations engaged in manufacturing. The organization tends to reflect the more conservative business viewpoint of the larger manufacturing firms. For instance, its members comprise only about 8 percent of the manufacturing firms in the nation, but they produce approximately 75 percent of the industrial production. Representing a relatively small number of individuals and businesses, the NAM has relied heavily on public relations, spending as much as $2½ million in a single year. Over a four-year period this group distributed more than 18 million pamphlets. More recently, the NAM—like big business in general—has mellowed in its intransigent opposition to government in the economy, and has adopted a more positive attitude toward the solution of pressing social and economic problems. However, it still believes that such remedial reforms should be undertaken preferably by voluntary organizations, so as to make governmental intervention unnecessary.

The United States Chamber of Commerce was formed in 1912 after President Taft suggested that such an organization would help the government to "keep in closer touch with commercial affairs." The Chamber, a federation composed of 3,400 local and state chambers, has membership groups in every sizable community in the nation. Having a more diversified membership and interests than the NAM, the Chamber tends to take less specific stands on public issues and adopts policies which, in their words, "are general in application to business and industry." Like the NAM, the Chamber has opposed most legislative measures providing for social reforms and for benefits for organized labor. On some measure on which all elements of business are in general accord, such as the Labor-Management Reporting and Disclosure Act of 1959 (the Landrum-Griffin Act), the Chamber of Commerce, acting through its local chapters, can inundate Congress with literally thousands of letters, telegrams, and telephone calls.

A third association for businessmen that has attracted considerable attention has been the Committee for Economic Development, which was formed by a number of the more progressive business leaders during World War II. This organization has not attempted to represent any particular business interest and has limited its activities largely to conducting research and issuing reports on a number of public questions. These reports have been carefully reasoned and informative and have undoubtedly helped to shape some public policies.

From the standpoint of members of organizations and energy expended in influencing governmental decisions, the trade associations are the most

noteworthy form of business organization. Of the business groups registering under the Federal Regulation of Lobbying Act, a large proportion are
trade associations. These organizations are multipurpose groups, composed
of competing firms producing similar goods or rendering similar services.
According to the Department of Commerce there are some 14,000 trade
associations of which 1,700 are organized nationally. Most of the national
trade associations were established in this century, but some have their
origin in local or regional groups that started before the Civil War.
Although trade associations have been formed for a variety of reasons, most
of them serve as a channel of communications between the government
and their industry. They have provided the primary means by which many
business groups lobby public officials and obtain information from the
government.

The term "political interest group" is broad enough to include individual business concerns—primarily corporations—when they act politically, as many do. Throughout most of the nineteenth century and well
into the twentieth, the main actors in the politics of interest were the
owners, managers, and lobbyists of individual business concerns. During
the generation between the two World Wars, trade associations developed,
and although the activities of individual entrepreneurs did not cease, they
did at least relatively diminish. Starting in the 1950s a number of observers
have detected a growing tendency for major corporations to strike out on
their own, rather than to work through a trade association. Included
among the corporations that registered as employing lobbyists are such
firms as the American Express Company, the Bank of America, Johns-
Manville Company, Kaiser Steel Corporation, Shell Oil Company, Trans-
World Airlines, and the Western Union Telegraph Company.

Agricultural Groups

Since the formation of the Patrons of Husbandry (the Grange) in 1867,
groups representing diverse agricultural interests have been a powerful
factor in American government and politics. The Grange, along with the
National Farmers' Union, established in 1902, and the American Farm
Bureau Federation (Farm Bureau), organized in 1919, constitute the three
major farm organizations in the United States. These organizations bear a
number of striking resemblances to the major business associations such as
the NAM and the Chamber of Commerce. Like them, they are federated,
multipurpose organizations. Their concern is less with individual commodities or farm products than with the total economic condition of American
rural life.

The Farm Bureau, with 1,600,000 members, is the largest and most influential of the farm organizations. With most of its members in the middle western and southern states, the Farm Bureau is primarily concerned with the interests of the corn and cotton farmers. In recent years the organization has supported Republican policies more often than those of the Democratic party. During the Eisenhower administration the Farm Bureau worked closely with the Department of Agriculture, but since that time the relationship has been less cordial. The Farm Bureau is commonly considered to be the spokesman for the more affluent farmers, and its statements on public policy often parallel those of organized business.

Like their business counterparts, each major farm organization reflects the interests and outlook of somewhat different clienteles. The Grange, which originated as a Midwestern radical farm movement, is now a comparatively conservative organization with most of its membership living in New England, New York, Pennsylvania, Ohio, and on the Pacific coast. Today the Grange has a membership of 750,000 farm families. Founded as a fraternal order, it still claims to be the "only Farm Fraternity in the World." During the 1930s and 1940s the Grange viewed political and economic questions in much the same light as conservative business groups. Since then the Grange has shifted its position, but it still supports relatively conservative policies regarding international relations, the federal government, and organized labor.

The Farmers' Union, the second oldest and the smallest of the three general farm organizations, was organized in the semiarid farming lands of the great plains area. It has spread into other states and today it is the largest farm organization in six states—the Dakotas, Montana, Minnesota, Colorado, and Oklahoma—and has substantial support in Nebraska and Wisconsin. The Farmers' Union presents a paradox: it is a liberal organization with a conservative clientele, and much of its membership lives in states that have often voted Republican. The Farmers' Union has advocated the establishment of farm cooperatives and a larger role for the federal government in regulating and assisting agriculture. Unlike the other two major farm organizations, the Farmers' Union has supported most of the policies of Democratic administrations and has been willing to work with labor unions.

In addition to these major agricultural associations, there are literally hundreds of other farm organizations—producer associations, cooperatives, marketing groups, and others—actively involved in the political representation of agricultural interests. Many of these organizations are formed along farm commodity lines. Illustrative are the American Livestock Association, the National Apple Institute, the National Pork Producers Association, the

National Cooperative Milk Producers Federation, and the National Wool Growers Federation.

Labor Organizations

In the federal structure of organized labor the basic building blocks are the 75,000 to 80,000 local unions. These local unions, which might be compared with our local units of government, are organized into approximately 130 national craft or industrial unions. These are the constituent units of the AFL–CIO, just as the fifty states are the constituent units of our federal government. In some respects the national unions, which usually have authority over such matters as the calling of strikes and the establishment of wage policies and work rules, are more powerful than the AFL–CIO itself. Some of the national unions are titans in their own right. Such organizations as the Steel Workers, Automobile Workers, Carpenters, and Machinists have a membership of more than 750,000 each. By comparison a number of other national unions are quite small; 40 percent of the national unions in the AFL–CIO have fewer than 25,000 members.

The AFL–CIO resulted from the merger in 1955 of the American Federation of Labor (AFL), established in 1881, and the Congress of Industrial Organizations (CIO), created in 1938, when eight industrial unions, dissatisfied with the craft orientation and organizational conservatism of the Federation, broke away from the parent group. Membership of Americans in unions affiliated with the AFL–CIO in 1966 was approximately 13.5 million. Since the end of World War II, due largely to the relative decline of the number of blue-collar workers (who are easier to organize) and the greater proportionate increase of white-collar workers (who are very difficult to organize), the rate of growth of the AFL–CIO has steadily declined in proportion to the total labor force, and some unions have lost in terms of total members. The AFL–CIO has established the Committee on Political Education (COPE), which has engaged in a variety of political activity, including endorsing candidates and assisting in campaigns.

In addition to the unions affiliated with the AFL–CIO, there are some fifty national unions that are independent of that organization. These include the railroad brotherhood; the Teamsters (the largest in the United States), which has flourished despite its ouster from the AFL–CIO in 1957; and the United Mine Workers, which was an early pillar of the CIO. According to Department of Labor statistics, total membership of Americans in unions in 1964 was 16.8 millions, which represents less than 29 percent of nonagricultural workers and less than 22 percent of the total labor force.

The Professions

Strictly speaking, the "professions" have traditionally been considered to be those callings which regulate themselves on at least a semiofficial basis, and for which the principal condition of entry is the completion of a prescribed course of higher education. As the licensing of professions falls within the jurisdiction of the states, professional associations generally are more concerned with state governments than the national government. However, as the latter has expanded its activities, professional associations have found more reason to turn their attention to the national level. Of the various professional associations the medical and legal groups have been most active in national politics.

Since 1948 the American Medical Association has been more deeply and continuously involved in politics than any other professional group. Organized nationally in 1901 by local medical associations, some of which were established a century earlier, the AMA in 1965 had a membership of 206,000, or approximately 75 percent of all licensed physicians in the country. The AMA has its national headquarters in Chicago, where nearly 900 staff members are employed in its nine-story, block-long building. In Washington the AMA maintains a full-time staff of more than 20 persons, including 4 or more registered lobbyists. One favorite lobbying tactic is to activate local doctors to get in touch with their congressmen or senators. State and county medical societies also lobby. Direct political action in elections is the responsibility of the American Medical Political Action Committee (AMPAC), which is patterned after the AFL–CIO Committee on Political Education. ·

Much of the political activity of the AMA during the past two decades was stimulated by the introduction of bills in Congress which would provide for government participation in meeting the mounting costs of medical care. The AMA labeled such measures "socialized medicine" and attempted to organize its members as political workers in the campaign to defeat the proposals. In one 3½-year period the cost of the campaign came to $4,678,000 and in a single year (1949) 54,233,915 booklets, pamphlets, leaflets, and other pieces of literature were distributed. The *Wall Street Journal* (February 8, 1965) estimated that AMPAC and its constituent committees poured between $2 million and $3 million into approximately 100 congressional elections in 1964. During the first three months of 1965, while the Medicare bill was being considered by Congress, the AMA reported spending $951,590 for lobbying activities. Of this amount more than $900,000 went for radio, television, and newspaper advertising.

In a society where "the rule of law" has deep institutional roots, it was inevitable that members of the legal profession should play a prominent part in government. By contrast with the AMA, the American Bar Association (ABA)—the major professional group for lawyers—has engaged in few highly controversial political issues. The historic role of the lawyer in American politics has been to represent interests other than his own. Hence, his primary identification has been with his clients rather than with his professional associations. The ABA has ordinarily confined its activities to such professionally relevant problems as legal aid, defendants' rights, administrative procedures, and judicial personnel and jurisdiction. Since 1945 the ABA has assisted the Senate Judiciary Committee and the Department of Justice by reviewing the qualifications of prospective federal judges. With more than half of Congress numbered among its members, the ABA exercises considerable influence on such matters. The diffusion of interest of attorneys and the somewhat limited range of activities of the ABA undoubtedly help to explain the relatively small membership of the ABA. Barely one third of the nearly 300,000 practicing attorneys in the United States are members of the ABA. Aggregate memberships in local, county, and state bar associations are more inclusive, and it is at these levels that the influence of the organized bar weighs most heavily on the political process.

Other Interest Groups

Some foreign governments have employed American professional lobbyists, and have sought to influence governmental decisions in the United States in a fashion similar to that of American interest groups. In recent years some 400 such "foreign agents" have been registered with the State Department. These countries apparently have reason to believe that such lobbyists might secure more favorable decisions from some officials than would their own representatives. For instance, it was reported in 1965 that the Agriculture Committee of the House of Representatives gave Venezuela, which employed a well-known American lobbyist, a higher quota on sugar that could be sold in the United States than had been given to Argentina and other countries that did not have American lobbyists representing them.

Shared attitudes rather than property, occupation, or income constitute the group "interest." Therefore, the range of political interest groups is virtually as wide and diverse as society itself. For instance, many groups have shared attitudes due to common experiences, religious affiliations, or ethnic backgrounds. Examples of such organizations include the American Legion, the National Council of Churches, the National Catholic Welfare Conference, the National Jewish Welfare Board, and the National Association for the Advancement of Colored People.

Some scholars have suggested that a distinction be made between the groups that are organized to advance the personal interest of their members and those that advocate other causes. It has been proposed that the latter category be called "promotional," or "opinion," or "ideological" groups. While there is the obvious problem of classifying groups that advocate other causes as well as programs for their own personal benefit, the concept of the promotional or opinion group is useful. The variety of such shared attitude groups may be seen by noting such examples as the American Civil Liberties Union, the American Association for the United Nations, the National Council for the Prevention of War, and the Women's Christian Temperance Union. The proliferation of interest groups has produced a reaction among individuals who are concerned that government may favor the special interests to the disadvantage of the general citizenry. As a result, citizens have organized groups to defend the general interest. Examples of such "anti-special interest groups" are the League of Women Voters and the National Committee for an Effective Congress. While such groups lack the financial resources of many special interest groups, they have been influential in promoting the cause of good government.

The Radical Left and the Radical Right

The radical left and the radical right groups comprise a particular type of political interest group in the United States. While some such groups have formed minor parties, others have not; and regardless of their names and forms of organization, they resemble the more typical political interest groups more than they do major political parties. Such groups also exist in Europe and elsewhere, and in a multiparty system they often form political parties. These groups in the United States illustrate the problem of distinguishing precisely between political interest groups and political parties. In a democracy characterized by a highly heterogeneous population one should not be surprised to find radical groups on the left and the right with views deviating sharply from those of the great majority of the population.

In speaking of radical groups of either the left or the right, a distinction must be drawn between radicalism in the sense of extreme programs on the one hand and radicalism in the sense of commitment to revolution and violence on the other. For example, on the left any one of the Socialist parties in the United States may be called radical because their programs of public ownership of the means of production are totally opposed to the existing private ownership system. Yet, when speaking of the Communist party of the United States as radical, we refer to its official commitment to revolution as the means of bringing about its objectives. Similarly, on the radical right, a group which seeks to abolish the income tax and social security system is radical in the sense that it proposes what seem to nearly all Americans fundamental changes. This kind of radicalism is to be distinguished from that of groups that oppose the democratic process itself.

The Radical Left.   The radical left in the United States historically has consisted principally of Marxists and Socialists and has been organized as minor parties, some of which have existed for several decades. The most widely known of these organizations are the Communists, Socialist Workers, Socialist Labor, and Socialist parties. The influence of these organizations, while never of major significance, has diminished in the post-World War II period. The decline of the Communists in the United States may be attributed in part to the association, in the minds of many Americans, of the Communists with the nation's two principal adversaries, the USSR and Communist China. The decline in support of democratic socialism in the United States is no doubt due partly to the high level of economic prosperity in this country and the failure of British socialism to produce any startling economic results.

During the early 1960s a number of new radical left organizations appeared. As they derived much of their support from college students and attracted relatively few who were past the age of 30, these groups have been referred to as the "Young Radicals," or the "New Left." While some of their leaders are avowed Marxists, these organizations have attracted many young people whose primary concern was to do something personally regarding social and political problems. These organizations have differed from the older Socialist and Communist organizations in that their members have been less involved in discussing political and economic theories than in taking personal political action. As a leader of one of the groups explained: "We are interested in direct action and specific issues." He added that they did not "spend endless hours debating the nature of the Soviet Union."

Among the new leftist groups are the Progressive Labor party (a pro-Chinese Communist group), the Young Socialist Alliance, the Student Peace Union, the W. E. B. DuBois Clubs (which are Marxist), and the Students for a Democratic Society. There is considerable variation among the groups from the standpoint of their membership, leadership, orientation, and goals. Undoubtedly many of their members initially became interested in these groups through their participation in demonstrations for equal rights for Negroes. In the international area, many leaders of these groups have tended to support the position of the Soviet Union and Communist China, and have urged that the United States cease opposing revolutionary change in underdeveloped countries. Young leftist groups have organized mass demonstrations protesting American military action in Vietnam, the draft, and even decisions of university administrators.

Within the United States they have advocated the extension of socialism, and have denounced the "power structure" or "the establishment," which for many apparently was epitomized by university administrators as fully as by corporation executives or government officials. There has been both positive and negative reaction to the New Left. Those who view it favorably regard it as a healthy sign for young Americans, particularly in colleges, to show a deep personal interest in problems of poverty, racial inequality, and international relations. On the other hand, the undeniably communistic and Marxist tinge to some of these groups has called forth a negative response to the entire New Left movement.

The Radical Right.   There have been radical right groups in the United States for more than a century. During the 1840s and 1850s the Native American and Know Nothing parties were active, and the Ku Klux Klan was first organized shortly after the Civil War. Both radical left and radical right groups appear to proliferate during times of severe social and political tension and change. The post-World War II period—characterized by revolutionary technological innovations, major social transformations, and continual international crises—has spawned an unprecedented number of radical right organizations.

As in earlier periods, some of the recent radical right groups have formed political parties. In 1960 a National States' Rights party, two Constitutional parties, two Conservative parties, and a Tax-Cut party appeared on ballots in one or more states. The total vote of these six parties was less than 80,000. Possibly because most of the extreme right supported the candidacy of Barry Goldwater, only two radical right parties, the National States' Rights and a Constitutional party, nominated candidates in 1964, and their combined vote barely reached 12,000.

Most radical right groups have organized and functioned as political interest groups rather than as political parties. Estimates of the number of such extreme right groups have ranged to more than 1,000, of which only about 25 have gained a substantial membership. The variety of far right groups may be seen by noting a few types. Several groups, such as Reverend Billy James Hargis's "Christian Crusade," have borrowed from the techniques of evangelistic crusades. The Minutemen, by way of comparison, is a secret federation of guerrilla units that have organized and armed for the ostensible purpose of resisting a Communist invasion. Some leaders of the radical right, such as Dan Smoot and Clarence E. Manion, have relied primarily on sponsored radio and television programs and newsletters to carry their messages to the people. Others have established affiliated units across the nation. For instance, Robert Welch announced that the John Birch Society planned to have by the time of the 1966 election 50 chapters, each with 20 members, in at least 325 of the congressional districts.

Anticommunism is the avowed *raison d'être* of most radical right groups, and they view most problems only in the light of the internal "Communist menace." Looking back to a mythical golden age, the extreme right couples its fear of communism with support of states' rights politics and laissez-faire economics. Both social security programs and government regulation are denounced by ultraconservatives, some of whom "equate the growth of the Welfare State with Socialism and Socialism with Communism."

From *Hold Me*, by Jules Feiffer. © Copyright 1960, 1961, 1962 by Jules Feiffer, reprinted by permission of Random House, Inc.

Ultranationalistic, the radical right, while possessed with their fear of internal communism, oppose efforts at international cooperation to combat communism abroad. Hence, their slogan: "Get the United Nations out of the United States and the United States out of the United Nations." Some of them are basically authoritarian; unable to convert a majority to their views, they denounce democracy, which, in Robert Welch's words, "is merely a deceptive phrase, a weapon of demagoguery, and a perennial fraud." Radical right groups have conducted campaigns against such programs as the income tax, civil rights legislation, urban renewal, civil defense, the fluoridation of drinking water, the Supreme Court, foreign aid, and the United Nations.

According to the leaders of the radical right, an evil conspiracy has gained control of much of the country—public schools, colleges, churches, labor unions, government, and even business. This conspiratorial theory of history, for them, accounts for the problems confronting the United States and justifies their own political tactics.

Radical right groups have employed three general approaches in their efforts to influence public policy. First, members have been urged to infiltrate the parent-teachers associations, civic organizations, and the political parties; to run for election to school boards, city councils, and state and national offices; and to establish "front" groups patterned after Communist and Fascist organizations. Several Republican leaders have denounced the John Birch Society for attempting to infiltrate their party organizations. Second, propaganda has been used extensively, and the radical right has employed all media of mass communications. Third, asserting that one must "fight fire with fire," rightist leaders have exhorted their followers to harass public officials and others through tactics commonly associated with Communists and Fascists but not widely employed previously by others in the United States. Such groups have also resorted to character assassination as a political weapon. The best-known example is Robert Welch's calling Dwight Eisenhower a "conscious agent of the Communist conspiracy," and labeling all Presidents from Woodrow Wilson's day to the present as disloyal.

As long as interest groups use constitutional means, they should be encouraged, for a complete and vigorous expression of the maximum number of viewpoints is a source of strength in a democratic society. Unfortunately, as we have seen, some of the groups on both the radical left and the radical right do not believe in democracy, and have resorted to slander, misrepresentation, and intimidation in pursuing their goals.

On the whole, Americans have been fortunate that the antidemocratic groups have not been strong and have failed to become a factor in the regular political processes in the United States. Typically one does not find in Congress or the state legislatures Communists or Fascists or other extremists of this type as can be found in many of the other successful democracies of the world. While there is no need to inflate the importance of such extremist groups in the United States, their potential harm should not be underestimated. They serve as a perpetual reminder that side by side with those Americans whose basic commitment is to democratic ideals and practices is a group of people in the United States who are opposed to the moderation and tolerance of democracy.

❧ GROUPS AND DEMOCRACY: THE DILEMMA OF REGULATION

In the American pluralist society, interest groups have developed in large numbers, and have played an important role in the struggle for political power, adding vitality and strength to the body politic. The Founding Fathers, with considerable wisdom, provided a constitutional basis for interest group activity in the First Amendment which guarantees freedom of speech and press, and the right to assemble and to petition government.

Although recognizing the value of interest groups and the useful functions they perform, various scholars have called attention to problems that might arise from interest group activity. First, there is the possibility that some groups will exert influence and obtain benefits from government out of proportion to their numbers or to their contributions to society. It is well known, of course, that not all individuals are organized, and that of those who are organized, some groups have more resources and advantages not possessed by others. Second, it is sometimes difficult to know who is represented by an organized group. An organization may have a name that indicates that it represents hundreds of individuals, when it actually is a "front" group for others who do not want their identity known. Third, groups may employ methods and tactics—such as gifts to officials, bribery, or intimidation—which, if used on a wide scale, would tend to undermine our political system.

Political interest groups thus constitute a dilemma for democratic government. In order for a free society to flourish, individuals must be permitted to organize and take joint political action, and the Constitution guarantees this right; yet, if unrestrained, interest groups might subvert the political system.

As a partial effort to solve the dilemma, laws have been enacted to require certain interest groups and their lobbyists to register with the government. The chief statute is the Federal Regulation of Lobbying Act, passed in 1946, which provides that paid lobbyists and organizations that solicit, collect, and spend money for the "principal purpose" of influencing federal legislation must register with the Clerk of the House of Representatives and the secretary of the Senate, and they must file quarterly reports listing all persons who have contributed $500 or more and all persons to whom payments of $10 or more have been made. Lobbying Registration laws, some based on the federal statute, have been passed by most states. In addition, other federal statutes require particular types of interest groups to register with the Securities and Exchange Commission or the Secretary of Commerce; and certain lobbyists, or agents, of foreign powers are required to register with the Department of State.

The theory behind these statutes is that by disclosing information regarding those who are attempting to influence public policies, governmental decisions might be made more on the merits of the issues rather than on the amount of influence applied.

Because of defects in the phraseology of lobbying legislation and the absence of agencies specifically charged with enforcing their provisions, some groups that lobby have not registered. In actuality, the principal safeguards regarding interest group activity are not to be found in statutory regulations but in the total functioning of the political system. In any governmental system, as long as people are free to organize and the channels of communication remain open, one major safeguard against any specialized interest exercising too much influence is the countervailing power of other interests. Confronted with such organized opposition, groups often modify their political aims. On occasions when special interests believe that no organized groups are aligned against them, they find that their demands, if too far-reaching, may activate a potential interest group and hence bring into existence a new organization. However, the counterbalancing power of opposing organizations or potential groups will not always suffice, for in some areas opposition forces are weak or do not exist.

As was explained in Chapter 13, political parties and elected officials commonly perform the function of effecting a balance among the competing demands of the various interests and thus compel individual groups to moderate their goals. Moreover, many administrative officials, whether politically appointed or selected through the civil service, often oppose the special interests and support what they consider to be the "public interest." Finally, the American democratic system is founded on the premise that the citizenry, if given sufficient information, will make the proper decisions and insist that the "rules of the game" be followed. In general, the public is not well informed regarding political interest groups. One problem, then, is to provide the people with more adequate information regarding special interest groups. In the words of a congressional committee investigating lobbying activities, "an informed and vigilant public is the only lasting guaranty that pressure groups will operate in an open and aboveboard manner."

CHAPTER 16

CONGRESS: MIRROR
OF THE NATION

The existence of a vital, representative assembly is perhaps the most obvious characteristic of a democratic system of government. Virtually all regimes have elected assemblies of some kind, but many are mere façades behind which the decisions are made by a powerful elite. All of the trappings of the democratic process may exist, but approval by the representative assembly may be taken as a foregone conclusion. Thus, the Supreme Soviet in the Soviet Union is in no sense a deliberative body, but meets only to listen and approve without dissent.

As a general proposition, then, a legislative assembly is effective to the extent that its approval is *required* for the undertaking by government of new programs and policies, to the extent that it is free to *consider* and *debate* the issues, and to the extent to which the members of the legislature freely *represent* groups of voters who are responsible for their presence in the legislature.

❧ THE ROLE OF CONGRESS IN THE POLITICAL SYSTEM

In his defense of the Constitution in *The Federalist* James Madison contended that the legislature would always be the dominant institution in a republican form of government because it drew its support directly from the people, had access directly to their pocketbooks through the power to tax, and had broad authority to extend its influence into the other branches of the government. For Madison, "it is against the enterprising ambition of this department that the people ought to indulge all their jealousy and exhaust all their precautions."

And yet in the middle of the twentieth century, a committee of the Congress itself has arrived at the following judgment:

> To any student of government, it is eminently clear that the role of the Congress in determining national policy, defense or otherwise, has deteriorated over the years. More and more the role of Congress has come to be that of a sometimes querulous but essentially kindly uncle who complains while furiously puffing on his pipe but who finally, as everyone expects, gives in and hands over the allowance, grants the permission, or raises his hand in blessing, and then returns to the rocking chair for another year of somnolence broken only by an occasional anxious glance down the avenue [meaning Pennsylvania Avenue] and a muttered doubt as to whether he has done the right thing.[1]

Congress, in the picturesque phrase of Senator Joseph Clark, has become the "sapless branch."

Madison's prediction and Congress' self-judgment reflect both the circumstances and times under which the judgments were made and the differing conceptions of the role that the legislature should play in a democratic system of government. Madison saw the role of Congress in the light of colonial experience and experience under the Articles of Confederation when legislatures were indeed dominant and even irresponsible. Congress today laments what appears to be the decline of its role in policy-making, owing to the pre-eminent position of the President as a kind of Tribune of the People.

Legislative-Executive Struggle

The study of Congress must be undertaken in the context of the historic struggle with the executive branch and occasionally with the judicial branch over the right to govern. In one student's perceptive phrase, the Constitution of 1787 "is supposed to have created a government of 'separated powers.' It did nothing of the sort. Rather, it created a government of separated institutions *sharing* powers."[2] Thus the President and Congress have challenged each other in virtually all areas of policy-making and execution, with each in the ascendancy at various periods of our history.

There has been something of a cyclical pattern in the history of legislative-executive relations, the most important variables of which have been

[1] *House Report 1406*, Eighty-seventh Congress, Second Session (1962), p. 7.
[2] Richard Neustadt, *Presidential Power* (New York: Wiley, 1960), p. 42.

the President himself, his conception of the role he should play in the constitutional system, and the circumstances under which he served. Washington, with Hamilton's assistance, established the prototype of forthright presidential leadership, relying heavily on Washington's great personal prestige. Jefferson proved to be a dynamic, forceful President, dominating Congress more subtly through his control of his party. Subsequently, presidential leadership declined, notwithstanding the occasional flashes demonstrated by Jackson, and later by Lincoln during the Civil War. The Whigs and later the Radical Republicans so dominated the government that Woodrow Wilson could write in 1885 that Congress was "the central and predominant power of the system" and that the U.S. government was "government by the Standing Committees of Congress."[3]

The turn of the twentieth century really marked the watershed in this historic struggle for predominance. The transformation of the United States into an important world power and its involvement in two World Wars gave to the executive branch the initiative in policy-making that far transcended diplomacy, reaching into the farthest recesses of domestic politics as well. The increasing reliance of the American people on the national government to mediate group conflict and provide protection against the consequences of a complex economic system led directly to executive leadership. Congress was not equipped to deal with the complexities of either problem, owing partly to its own disintegrative nature, but perhaps more significantly to the increasing expertise required in formulating solutions to problems of a highly technical character.

The administrations of Theodore Roosevelt, Woodrow Wilson, and Franklin Roosevelt clearly demonstrated the progress that could be made under strong executive leadership. And the periods of presidential dormancy under Harding and Coolidge only served to emphasize the need for strong leadership to provide focus for congressional action. Not only has the country looked for such leadership, but Congress has come to *expect* it. Even Dwight D. Eisenhower, who was severely criticized throughout his administration for failure to provide direction to Congress, differed not in recognition of the *need* for such leadership, but in the unwillingness to *use* the weapons that previous Presidents had fashioned and wielded in influencing Congress.[4]

This struggle between the legislative and executive branches of government is not unique to the United States, although elsewhere it takes on a quite different character. In the parliamentary systems of Europe the executive branch owes its power to its control of the majority in the

[3] Woodrow Wilson, *Congressional Government* (New York: Meridian Books, 1956), p. 23.

[4] See Emmet John Hughes, *The Ordeal of Power* (New York: Atheneum Publishers, 1962), pp. 107–116.

representative assembly. With a strong two-party system, England has established strong executive leadership through its Cabinet. But where the parties are more numerous and coalitions are required to elect a Cabinet, the executive is weaker. This was the situation, for example, that typically occurred in France before de Gaulle.

The Office of the Member of Congress

The basic facts regarding the office of a member of Congress can be quickly summarized. Senators are elected for six-year terms, with one third of the membership running for re-election each two years. They must be 30 years of age and nine years a citizen. Members of the House of Representatives are elected for two-year terms. They must be 25 years of age and a citizen for seven years. Both senators and representatives must live in the states from which they are elected.

These simple facts, however, contain a wealth of meaning. The briefer term for representatives results in their constant running for re-election. They must expend a high percentage of their energy and time in running for office, diverting them from their principal task, the consideration of policy. This constant reminder of the power of the electorate has its salutary effect, of course, in making the representative mindful of constituent needs, but there are many who feel the term is unduly brief. The two-year term also makes representatives envious of the greater security of senators, and thus willing to take the chance of moving up to the six-year term when opportunity permits.

The proposal by President Johnson in 1966 of a constitutional amendment to extend the term of office of members of the House to four years received a very mixed response, especially since the President proposed that the terms of members of the House run concurrently with his own. Opposition centered not only on the basic issue of the length of the term, but also on the greater influence of the President on the election of members of the House if they all ran during a presidential election year. Moreover, senators were not likely to look kindly on a change that would allow House members to challenge them for their seats in the Senate, without having to risk their own House seats in the process.

The longer term for senators has the effect of reducing the intimate relationship between the senator and his state. He may be a statesman for five years and a politician for one, hoping to curry favor with the electorate by more constituent-minded behavior as the election approaches, and depending on the lack of interest in legislative actions by the electorate to protect him against criticism for past actions.

The customary local residence requirements for elected representatives has the obvious impact of making the member of Congress the product of his own community, sharing the same experiences, values and concerns. He feels them deeply long before arriving in Congress, making it unnecessary that he be "pressured" into taking certain courses of action. The more long-range impact relates to his attitudes toward policy matters and his responsiveness to party discipline. The local party organization has often granted his nomination, or at least permitted it, and the representative may therefore be responsive to local party as well as local community forces. When these conflict with positions taken by the national party, he may defy the national party, secure in the protection afforded him by the local political structure.[5]

The Perquisites of Office

Senators and representatives today receive annual salaries of $30,000 per year, having received a pay increase of $7,500 beginning in 1965. In addition they are given certain allowances for expenses and staff. The average congressman employs 7 members on his personal staff, and often has the services of other employees of the House, such as the staff of the committees. He receives allowances for stationery, telephones and telegrams, travel, and office rent in his home district or state. He has the privilege of sending ("franking") free mail to his constituents, exclusive of campaign literature. In 1962 members of Congress sent out 111 million pieces of franked mail. The average senator has a staff of about twenty. Senator Robert F. Kennedy's staff of eighty in 1966 was probably an all-time high for any senator.

As a corporate body, Congress is not starved for personnel either. It employs about 24,000 people, ranging from highly skilled professional staffs of the members and the committees to clerical and maintenance personnel. Moreover, their offices are relatively well appointed and their buildings—massive, if not architecturally notable—are showplaces in Washington. No legislative assembly in the world is so generously endowed.

The perquisites of office for a congressman may seem more than ample, but in fact are hardly sufficient to allow him to maintain his family adequately. He has numerous financial burdens, including the necessity of maintaining two residences, contributing to numerous worthy causes, extra travel, and other expenses. In less complicated times, a congressman could

[5] The election of Senator Robert Kennedy in New York in 1964 was a significant exception to this rule, although he endeavored to identify himself with New York as best as he could.

live on less because he had time to earn outside income; today, his is a full-time job and his compensation should reflect his full-time duties.

The position of legislator has a widely varying character throughout the democratic world. In England, the member of the House of Commons is paid an annual salary of about $5,000, hardly enough to compensate him fully, and forcing him to seek other part-time employment or depend on private income. He has extremely limited allowances for mail and tele-phone service, no individual office space, and no secretarial assistance. As the job becomes increasingly complex, the member of Parliament is demanding more pay and better services, so far without much luck. The British attitude is permeated with the fear of the "professional politician," and compensation is therefore deliberately kept at a low level. In France, the member of Parliament is paid a substantial salary, equal to that of the average of the highest civil service class, even though he is expected to spend only five and one-half months in session. In both countries, the legislator is more a functionary of his national party than he is a delegate from a local constituency. In England, the party may even assign a candidate a constituency in which to "stand" for election.

⚐ HOW REPRESENTATIVE IS CONGRESS?

Method of Representation

The Great Compromise of the Constitutional Convention concerned the nature of representation in the Congress, basically providing equal repre-sentation for each state in one chamber and representation based on the proportion of the total population found in each state in the other. Each state, however, was entitled to at least one member of the House of Representatives regardless of population. This system has continued un-changed to the present time, based on the federal nature of the republic. New states, such as Alaska and Hawaii, entered the Union on a completely equal basis, each receiving two senators and its proportional number of representatives. The result is that a state such as Alaska, having a popula-tion in 1964 of 250,000, has equal representation in the Senate with the state of California, which had a population of 18,084,000.

Representation in the House of Representatives is apportioned among the states after each decennial census of the population, thus reflecting the shifts in population from one region to another. California, which had only 30 representatives during the decade of the 1950s was granted 38 repre-sentatives for the 1960s. New York, although gaining in population, lost in its proportionate share of the total population, falling from 43 to 41 members in the House.

Malapportionment and Gerrymandering

State legislatures historically have had the responsibility for creating congressional districts, although under present law some or all representatives may be elected at large within a state. In the 88th Congress (1963–1964) only 17 members of Congress were so elected. Under earlier federal laws, the state legislatures were required to create congressional districts containing "as nearly as practicable an equal number of inhabitants." This standard was not in force, however, until the Supreme Court's decision in *Wesberry* v. *Sanders* (1964), where it established the constitutionality of the doctrine "one man, one vote," and decreed the substantial equality of the population of districts.

The failure to retain this requirement had resulted in the creation, either by positive action or by default, of districts drastically unequal in size. Thus, according to the 1960 census, the 16th Congressional District in Michigan had a population of 802,994, whereas the 12th District had a population of 177,431. Each elected one representative to Congress. In effect, the value of the vote in the 12th District was 4.5 times the value of the vote in the 16th District in that state. Similar situations were found throughout the United States. These imbalances were the result of deliberate efforts of rurally dominated legislatures to favor the voters in the rural areas, or of failure to redistrict when population movements required it, often in violation of specific provisions in state constitutions which required reapportionment.

The practical result was that the membership of the House of Representatives tended strongly to overrepresent the rural areas of the United States. These rural districts, being relatively homogeneous in population make-up, tended to be "safe" districts, that is, districts in which one party tended to dominate from election to election. Representatives from these districts, already overrepresented, thus could build up seniority in the House and add to their influence year by year. The strictly urban districts in the core of the larger cities of the country were adequately represented, simply because they began to lose population to the suburbs. It was in the latter category that the severest discrimination took place. Well over half of these districts were seriously underrepresented, having far over the state average of population per congressional district. These were the districts where party competition tended to be more intense, where either party might win a given election. Already disadvantaged by the malapportionment, their representatives did not have the opportunity to develop long years of seniority.

Urban and suburban dwellers complained bitterly over this discrimination, but were unable to persuade state legislatures to correct the situation. In 1964, however, the Supreme Court interpreted the constitutional provision that representatives should be chosen "by the people of the several states" to mean that every citizen's vote was to be of equal value, and thus opened the way for reapportionment (*Wesberry* v. *Sanders*). The result of this decision, as it is applied by the lower federal courts in suits to force reapportionment of congressional districts, will be relatively equitable representation for citizens, whatever their geographical location.

State legislatures still can engage in the practice of gerrymandering districts, which means to draw the district lines in such a way as to favor one party over another in a more or less permanent fashion in given districts. By carefully distributing voters of the minority party in a state among various districts, and concentrating them heavily in a few, it may be possible for the majority party to take a disproportionate share of the districts in spite of a relatively modest advantage over the minority party on a statewide basis. But the practice will be more difficult as the discretion of the state legislature in forming districts is reduced.

Impact on the System of Representation

Whether the House will become more "liberal" as a result of population equalization in congressional districts is not clear. The House districts will probably include more heterogeneous populations, and therefore be less dominated by single groups. There is some evidence, however, that the real gainer in the situation will be the Republican party, which tends to have the advantage in suburban districts. Outside the South, the suburban Republicans tend to vote with their rural brethren, thus fragmenting the so-called urban vote. The House may indeed remain as relatively conservative as before.

The Senate has in fact become the "liberal" body in Congress, that is, more disposed to approve legislation providing for increased social welfare benefits and to use government as an instrument for regulating the economy. The reason for this difference essentially lies in the fact that House members tend to come from more homogeneous and safe districts. Because of malapportionment of congressional districts by state legislatures, the rural areas have received far more than their fair share of congressional districts. Thus, the safe, rural districts, relatively less touched by the powerful currents of modern, urban, industrial society have had inordinate strength in the House. Senators represent entire states and therefore find within their constituencies a large assortment of conflicting interests, among which the senator must seek to strike a balance. In most states, urban interests, led by highly vocal groups, which have the power of bloc voting, may be extremely influential. Organized labor and Negroes in recent years have held this power and have used it effectively.

The Senate also can be looked to for assistance by interests in states that are more notable for their space than for their population. Thus, the western states, relatively sparsely populated, have disproportionate strength owing to their equal representation in the Senate. They can use this strength to bargain for favors for such interests as mining, livestock, and agricultural products like sugar beets.

Many nations avoid the problems of apportionment and districting by adopting a totally different electoral system. Systems of proportional representation utilized in most continental European countries do not require the establishment of districts because the candidates usually run at large on party lists within a given electoral subdivision. The seats for each party are distributed roughly on the basis of the proportion of the total vote that each party received in that subdivision. Opportunities for discriminatory apportionment and gerrymandering are thereby minimized.

The Membership of Congress

Congress is rightly considered a representative institution, but this does not mean that the members themselves reflect in their personal background and experience the occupational or cultural characteristics of the people they represent. For politicians are a peculiar breed, selected through a rigorous recruitment system, and advanced by passing certain difficult political tests.

In the 1965 session, the members of Congress ranged in age from 25 to 87, whereas the average age of members of Congress was 52 years. The members of the House were a trifle younger, but senators averaged nearly 6 years older. Protestantism is the predominant faith in Congress, accounting for 76 percent of the membership in 1965. Twenty percent were Roman Catholics, and 4 percent were of the Jewish faith. These percentages roughly reflect the religious make-up of the population.

Since members of Congress have considerably higher levels of education than the average of the population, they are bound to have a different professional and vocational make-up. It would hardly be beneficial to the welfare of the nation if the leaders were nothing but an exact replica of the people in intelligence, education, and vocational accomplishment.

In 1965, the single most prominent profession represented in Congress was that of the lawyer, 58 percent identifying themselves with the legal profession. This strong position of lawyers has prevailed throughout American history, and was even true of legislative bodies in colonial times. Following—but far behind—were those who were engaged in business and banking, accounting for 28 percent of the membership. There was a scattering of labor union leaders, ministers, and physicians. The groups most severely underrepresented were women and Negroes; only 12 were women and 6 were Negroes. All of the latter were serving in the House of Representatives. Approximately two thirds of the members were war veterans.

Perhaps more indicative of the background of congressmen is the fact that 465—87 percent—had previous service as government employees and elected politicians. They therefore were hardly novices in government when they came to Congress; rather they had served apprenticeships in state government, on city councils, as district attorneys, and in many other forms of government service. They came to Congress, therefore, with a keen interest in public problems. And they were acquainted with the environment of conflict and pressure in which public issues are decided. Introduction into the House or Senate, although requiring considerable orientation to the institutions, was not the shock of the neophyte plunging into the political maelstrom for the first time.

The number of lawyers indicates also the self-selection process on which American politics depends. The legal profession draws to it individuals who have an interest in public affairs. Their stock-in-trade is controversy and they quickly develop skills as brokers among parties in conflict, skills which are highly useful in legislative life. Their professions allow them freedom to participate in politics, freedom that is not available to the salaried employee. There is no evidence that the predominance of lawyers makes Congress more conservative—an allegation frequently heard—for lawyers who differ widely in ideological position are found in both parties.

In contrast with earlier periods of American history, the typical congressman is a veteran of many years' service. Turnover—either forcible or voluntary—seldom exceeds 10 percent in any election, thus reducing to a minimum "new blood" in the legislative bodies, but also ensuring that there will be a maximum of experienced men. In 1957, for example, nearly half of the members of the House had served five terms or more and in 1961, 66 percent of the senators were serving in their second six-year term. Increasingly, membership in the House is becoming a career rather than a temporary period of service. For some this is a cause for concern, for it is argued that longer tenure tends to isolate congressmen from the rapidly changing forces in American life.

Background and Role of the Members of Congress

The background of the legislators is closely related to the roles they play in Congress. In a perceptive study of the Senate, it was found that there were four basic types of senators.[6] The *patrician* is well-born and comes from a highly political family, enters politics at an early age, and is a seasoned veteran by the time he reaches the Senate. The *professional*, by far the largest number and usually a lawyer, rises to the Senate from relatively modest circumstances, passing through a long apprenticeship in a variety of lesser offices. These two classes of senators tend to be highly respectful of the rules of the game in the Senate, become part of its inner ruling "club," occupying positions of both formal and informal leadership. The *amateur* makes his mark in life in some other occupation and enters politics late in life, often at a high level such as the governor's office. He tends to be less tolerant of existing rules and less in awe of the institution, perhaps because he has less time to make his presence felt. Finally, the *agitator* is a senator who is elected almost by accident, often appealing to the electorate on the basis of some ephemeral—and perhaps demagogic—issue. He is a maverick in the Senate, irreverent and disrespectful, and seldom stays more than one term. Senator Joseph McCarthy was an agitator par excellence.

⁜ THE LAWMAKING FUNCTION

Recognition should be given to the fact that representative assemblies did not begin as *legislatures* but as assemblies or *parliaments* consisting of representatives of the several privileged orders of medieval societies. They were convoked for the purpose of giving advice and for approval of the king's proposals, particularly with regard to the laying of taxes. They were therefore places of discussion and consent, but not of law*making* in the more direct and positive sense. These antecedents were carried forward in a more or less consistent fashion in the English political system, in that the English Parliament today is still not primarily a lawmaking body but is rather a "grand inquest of the nation," a chamber for debate and discussion, especially with reference to the propositions laid before it by the Cabinet. Realistically, its prerogatives are limited to approval or disapproval of the ruling party's proposals, but this seldom involves amendment or positive assertion of the right to formulate legislation.

The American tradition diverged markedly from this pattern. In their

[6] Donald Matthews, *U.S. Senators and Their World* (New York: Vintage Books, 1960), ch. III.

contests with the royal governors, the colonial legislatures early asserted their supremacy over the executive and made their assertion effective in practice. The Board of Trade in England could report with considerable justification in 1754 that the New York Assembly "have wrested from Your Majesty's governor, the nomination of all offices of government, the custody and direction of the public military stores, the mustering and direction of troops raised for Your Majesty's service, and in short almost every other part of executive government." This colonial experience established a strong tradition of legislative initiative, which has been an important element in the history of legislative-executive relations in this country.

Article I of the Constitution begins by stating "All legislative powers herein granted shall be vested in a Congress of the United States." After enumerating an extensive list of subjects on which Congress was empowered to act, Section 8 concludes by stating that Congress has the power to "make all laws which shall be necessary and proper for carrying into execution the foregoing powers. . . ." Although it appears to grant all legislative power to the Congress, the Constitution subsequently involves the President in the lawmaking function through his obligation to send to Congress annually a message on the State of the Union and through his power to veto bills approved by Congress. Thus from the very beginning the President has been involved in the legislative process. But the Constitution provided only the *opportunity* for influence, not the *substance* of influence itself. The substance would come when the circumstances required it.

Throughout most of the nineteenth century, the chief issues before Congress were highly political—the nature of the federal union, the level of the tariff, the amounts of money to be spent on internal improvements, and the conditions under which public land in the West would be distributed. While they were not entirely self-executing, these policies required only modest administrative machinery to implement them. Under these conditions congressional supremacy was not only understandable but tolerable, and the Presidency was indeed overshadowed in the lawmaking field.

Growth of Presidential Influence

Presidential influence in legislation arose when the Presidency was transformed into an instrument of popular representation through his election by a majority of the voters. The national political parties mobilized the voters into support of his candidacy and transformed the President himself into the spokesman for a national majority. The President was no longer only the Chief Executive of the nation, but he was also the only representative of the national will. Whereas others reflected the interests and aspirations of local constituents, his constituency was the nation. Others might speak for local majority interests; he alone spoke for the broad interests of the nation as a whole.

A second important basis for influence was derived from the nature of modern lawmaking, and the resources available for the formulation of solutions to social and economic problems. While most decisions that require the attention of lawmakers today still involve delicate political judgments—that is, judgments about the allocations of benefits to some individuals and groups and impositions of burdens upon other individuals and groups—they also require a very heavy amount of hard, technical data. For example, the decision of Congress to undertake programs for controlling the pollution of streams requires an assessment of the extent of the sources, and of the consequences of pollution as well as examination of the alternative solutions that might be adopted. All phases of this policy issue require detailed investigation by experts on these questions. Many private groups may make contributions to these investigations, but the integration of these data and examination of the policy alternatives in the light of these data require the unified consideration by executive agencies whose principal responsibilities are to deal with problems in this subject-matter area.

The result has been that virtually all legislation of lasting and general significance during this century has either started or become *presidential* legislation. The few instances of congressional initiative since World War II—the Taft-Hartley Act, the McCarran Immigration Act, the Kerr-Mills medical care bill—only highlight the dependence on presidential initiative. The problem for Congress is to find its proper role under these quite different circumstances.

Congressional Role in Policy-Making

There are those who argue that the legislature deals too much in details of policy, without allowing itself sufficient time and energy to examine broad outlines of policy and their meaning in American life. Former Secretary of State Dean Acheson, drawing on his vast experience with Congress, alleges that Congress attempts to intrude into foreign policy questions that are really the realm of experts, much the same as nuclear physics is the realm of the expert. The role of Congress, in his view, is to challenge the President on the main thrust of his proposals, examining them in the light of the values of the constituencies the members represent and the needs of the United States as they perceive them, avoiding concern for the specifics of the proposals which they are not competent to challenge.[7] The role of Congress would be to debate, to delay, and even to modify, but not to *make* general policy.

Consensus-Building and Legitimation

It is generally agreed that Congress can usefully perform the function of conciliating the wide variety of interests that have a stake in the outcome of policy disputes. Although the President and his administration may indeed represent a national majority, that is, a *numerical* majority, there are virtually limitless numbers of individuals and groups whose more limited interests must be considered in the process of policy-making. No administration, no matter how noble its aims, how broad its experience or deep its knowledge, can appreciate the complexity of the interests of every segment of the American public. The function of Congress may be to supply the representation of these interests.

In this sense, lawmaking is an effort to achieve *consensus* or something approaching consensus, among the groups whose interests are at stake. The administration proposals, which may reflect the wishes of a national majority as expressed in party platforms, in presidential appeals, or even in public opinion polls, are filtered through the legislative process, during which the varied groups are given an opportunity to *modify* the administration proposals, making them more acceptable to all concerned. The final package tends to reduce tensions among the conflicting groups in our society, and distribute the burdens and rewards in such a manner that no one group feels itself to be permanently disadvantaged. This is an intensely *political* function, involving less abstract wisdom in the philosophical sense, and more of a practical concern for the maintenance of allegiance and respect for the democratic institutions themselves.

The modern function of Congress is more that of *legitimation* than of creativity. This is seen most clearly in congressional resolutions approving presidential actions in the foreign field, such as approving the defense of Formosa or of Vietnam after the President has taken definite steps to do so. By its action, Congress provides authoritative approval by the community for these actions, and thus gives them legitimacy, that is, a sense that such actions are not only legal but also right. The substantive contribution of the Congress may then be relatively small, but its contribution in assuring that all interests have been heard and considered provides the decision with legitimacy even among those who are severely critical of the decision.

[7] Dean Acheson, *A Citizen Looks at Congress* (New York: Harper & Row, 1956).

There are, of course, those who reject the notion that members of Congress are incompetent amateurs attempting to be experts in fields beyond their ken. Ernest Griffith, formerly Director of the Legislative Reference Service of the Library of Congress, points to the marked improvement in congressional staffing that has allowed Congressmen to develop their independent judgment on important issues.[8] Many members of Congress, through longevity and acquaintance in depth with policy in given areas, can develop more informed opinions on these issues than can many "birds of passage" at the political level in the executive branch. Moreover, through having roots deep in their constituencies, they perform the extremely important role of evaluating the measures that involve changes in the nature of the federal system.

Providing Funds

An integral part of the lawmaking function of Congress is its authority to determine the levels of spending of the national government. Annually, Congress is required to finance the operations for the next fiscal year. This it does through a series of appropriations bills which are handled by the Appropriations Committees of the two houses.

Here again the President and his aides have tremendous influence, both in law and practice. The Budget and Accounting Act of 1921 imposed on the President the responsibility to deliver to Congress his estimates of the funds required to operate the government during the next year. The President therefore determines the *basis* for discussion of expenditures in Congress. The Appropriations Committees employ relatively large staffs to examine the budget, but there are serious practical problems in attempting to understand and criticize a document running thousands of pages in length, containing great detail on specific expenses, involving over 100 billion dollars, within a period of six months. Congress occasionally increases some amounts, but it usually cuts the budget, particularly in the case of relatively unpopular programs such as foreign aid. The overall budget seldom is much different than what the President asks for.

☙ THE REPRESENTATIVE FUNCTION

Perhaps the most readily agreed-upon function attributed to members of legislatures is that of "representing" the interests of the people who elected them. But the concept of representation is a complicated one, involving

[8] Ernest Griffith, *Congress, Its Contemporary Role*, 3d ed. (New York: New York University Press, 1961), p. 67 ff.

both the attitudes and expectations of those who represent and those who are represented.

Relationships to the Electorate

In the election of a legislator the voters may consider him to be a *delegate*, sent to undertake the accomplishment of certain objectives dear to their hearts. But the capacity to ascertain his policy views and hold him accountable depends on the interest the electorate manifests and the channels through which they inform themselves. The available evidence indicates that the electorate is not well informed regarding the candidate or the positions he has taken on the issues. In a 1958 study of the voters in several constituencies where a Republican candidate sought a congressional seat held by a Democrat, less than 1 in 5 had heard something about both candidates and more than half had heard nothing of either. Only 3 in 100 were able to make any reference whatsoever to legislative issues. The usual comments about the candidates were such vague evaluations as "He is a good man," or, "He understands our problems." It is for this reason that one congressman stated:

> The people back home don't know what's going on. Issues are not most important so far as the average voter is concerned. The image of the candidate plays a much greater role. If voters feel the candidate is conscientious and is trying hard to serve them, then that man has a good chance of coming back. Some people in marginal districts are able to hang on just because the public has this view of them.[9]

Moreover, few voters are informed about the legislative issues that are relevant at a given time. Those with a direct interest in a legislative issue will have more precise opinions, but the voters in general apparently have only limited information on specific issues of public policy. Their formulations are in terms of general aims of government and how far government should go in achieving certain goals.

Furthermore, in polls conducted on the question of whether the congressman should vote in accordance with the view of a majority of voters within his district or according to his own judgment, three out of five stated that a congressman should vote on the basis of his own judgment. In a sense, he is considered a *trustee* for their interests.

Even when the legislator makes a positive effort to know what his constituents desire, it is not always feasible to discover it. National opinion polls may have little relevance to his district. Only those who have some

[9] Charles Clapp, *The Congressman: His Work as He Sees It* (Washington, D.C.: The Brookings Institution, 1963), p. 421.

axe to grind may volunteer their views. There may be large numbers directly or indirectly affected by a given legislative issue, but who may not have perceived any direct involvement and therefore fail to register their opinions. The representative will read his mail attentively, visit with various opinion leaders in his district, read his district's newspapers avidly, and still be unable to discern clearly the nature of constituent opinion. On the reciprocal trade extension legislation of 1955, for example, even in districts where the issue should have been a matter of lively concern, such as in New England mill towns, no clear opinion was discernible.

Obviously on some votes the legislator performs as a delegate for the dominant opinions of his district. It is hard to conceive, for example, of a representative from Harlem not voting for civil rights legislation, and it is equally hard to conceive of a "black belt" congressman from Mississippi voting for it. But in such cases, the voting behavior of the representative is less the result of pressure than it is of conviction born of common experience with the people of his district. As amply demonstrated by Stephen Bailey in his classic study, Congress Makes a Law,[10] the attitude of the senator from Delaware was not the result of pressure *on* him by the DuPont interests, but the pressure *in* him from his aristocratic upbringing.

Determinants of Congressional Voting

This does not mean that there are no patterns of voting behavior that reveal the direction in which a congressman will go when faced with that ultimate decision. Voting studies about congressmen suggest that much depends on the nature of the constituencies. In highly competitive districts—where either party stands a good chance of having his candidate elected—there is a tendency for the representative to take moderate positions on the issues. He "hedges his bets" by avoiding extremes, since his constituency tends to be relatively heterogeneous, consisting of highly diverse groupings of individuals with widely differing values and interests. He may accomplish this "safe" voting pattern by either voting with his party or by voting his own personal convictions. On the other hand, the congressman from the "safe" district usually tends to represent a relatively homogeneous constituency and tends to vote its dominant interests, partly because its interests are more easily knowable.

The most reliable index of congressional voting is the party affiliation of the representative. In large part, the voters selected him because of the party label he wore during the campaign. He selected his party out of sympathy with its general orientation and ran for office under its banner.

[10] Stephen K. Bailey, Congress Makes a Law (New York: Columbia University Press, 1950), p. 192.

TABLE 16–1. *Voting by the 88th Congress,*
1963–1964 (by Percent)[a]

	Dem.	Rep.
Party unity		
Both chambers	69	71
Senate	64	66
House	71	72
Opposition to party		
Both chambers	16	17
Senate	20	20
House	14	16

[a] Failure to vote lowered both party unity and opposition to party scores.

SOURCE: Adapted from *Congressional Quarterly, Weekly Report*, Vol. XXIII, No. 45 (November 5, 1965), 224.

In Congress, he identifies himself with his partisan colleagues, receives the benefit of their political and personal support, and fears the withdrawal of that support if he fails to "play ball." All of these factors propel him in the direction of his party's position. As noted in earlier chapters, American parties are not highly disciplined either outside or inside the legislature, so they cannot *compel* acceptance of the party position. The fact that Senator Jacob Javits (Republican, New York) finds his voting record corresponding to the voting record of a middle-of-the-road Democrat, and that Senator John Stennis (Democrat, Mississippi) finds his voting record corresponding to the voting record of a middle-of-the-road Republican indicates the divergence that is tolerated in the two parties. Nevertheless, there are strong *central tendencies* around which most partisan members cluster.

Table 16–1 indicates the extent to which parties tend to vote together. In the 1963–1964 term of Congress, Democrats and Republicans tended by a margin of better than 2 to 1 to vote with their partisan colleagues on issues on which a majority of one party opposed a majority of the other. In only less than one out of five cases did they vote in opposition to a majority of their own party.

Methods of Representation: Advancing the Interests of Constituents

All that has been said up to this point concerns the "style" of the legislator's representation. But we are equally concerned with his methods of representation. How does he attempt to advance the interests of the people who elected him? One approach is to find a strategic position in the legislature where he may be influential. He may obtain a suitable committee assignment, since most of the critical decisions about the legislative proposals are made at the committee stage. A congressman from a rural district will try to obtain a place on the Agriculture Committee; a representative from an urban, working-class district may look for a place on the labor and education committees. He will try to locate a spot for himself on some of the more prestigious committees having broad legislative authority, such as the Ways and Means Committee in the House of Representatives or the Appropriations Committees in either house.

By careful preparation, by "doing his homework," by winning re-election several times, he may become recognized as a leader on given types of legislation affecting his district and thus be able to promote its interests markedly. The large number of military bases in Georgia is not attributable solely to its favorable climate and topography, because for many years the Armed Services Committees of both Senate and House were chaired by Georgians.

Errand-Boy Function

Much of the representative's time and effort will be spent on more mundane tasks. The American voter has converted his representative largely into his "errand boy" in Washington, ready at his beck and call to promote his individual and collective interests in a host of ways, ranging from contacts with administrative agencies to arranging hotel reservations for him in Washington. The average congressman and his staff spend more than half their time in such activities.

The voters base their requests on the correct assumption that the congressman speaks with a louder voice than does the individual citizen who seeks some favor or redress from an administrative agency. Most executive agencies maintain offices specifically for liaison with congressional offices in order to provide expeditious action on some inquiry or request for action emanating from the congressman. Thus, when the citizen writes, complaining that he has not received his social security check for two months, the congressman is likely to find out the reason for the delay in relatively short order. And if discretionary authority is involved in whether the citizen is entitled to those checks, he has a "friend in court" to plead his case.

These types of cases are handled routinely by staffs that have developed considerable skill in processing them. Less routine are statewide or district-wide matters that involve decisions which can affect the welfare of thousands of people. A typical example is the decision of the Department of Defense to close military establishments in various parts of the country. The existence of these bases means income and livelihood to many citizens and their closing is a matter of vital interest. The congressman is called upon to make representations before the proper officials in the Defense Department—the higher the better—and to demonstrate the importance of the specific base to the country's defense effort. Seldom would the congressman threaten reprisals for failure to give favorable consideration to the plight of the people in his district, but the executive official may not be unaware of the weapons available to the congressman if a sympathetic ear is not turned. And there may be room for negotiation, through such devices as "phasing out" a base rather than shutting it down fully at one time. Similar requests may come with regard to location of an interstate highway, applications for federal loans for the construction of sewage disposal or water supply facilities, or for the granting of a contract to an important company within the district.

Members of Congress undertake most services with alacrity and conviction because they recognize that they are performing a service for individuals and groups who may have legitimate grievances with administrative agencies whose labyrinthian procedures may leave them dumbfounded. Congressmen also recognize that the performance of these chores creates goodwill back home, and identifies them as someone who "can get something done in Washington." Presumably, this pays off at election time.

On the other hand, they also recognize that such demands on their time and attention mean that they cannot be as effective legislators as they would like to be. They are unable to dedicate sufficient time to informing themselves about the nation's problems. Some, such as Congressman Henry Reuss of Wisconsin, have suggested that Congress should adopt a Scandinavian device known as the "ombudsman," who would handle constituent complaints when referred to him by the members of Congress. As in Scandinavia, he would be an agent of the legislature who would specialize in grievances and have the full power of Congress to back him up in obtaining information. The presumption is that citizens' complaints would be handled more effectively by these experts, and the congressman and his staff would have more time for legislative business.

✤ THE OVERSIGHT FUNCTION

Closely related to its legislative and its representative functions is the function of checking on and exercising control over the administrative agencies that carry out the will of Congress as expressed in legislation or resolution. Each congressional committee has the responsibility to exercise "oversight" or to maintain close surveillance over the activities of agencies subject to its legislative jurisdiction. And Congress reserves the right to establish special investigating committees to highlight administrative practices called into question.

Two concurrent trends have made this function increasingly important. The first has already been alluded to: the relatively diminished role of Congress in the initiating of legislation. To compensate for this loss, Congress has sought to increase its role in holding the administration accountable. The second trend has been the increasing delegation of lawmaking to the administrative agencies. The increasing involvement of the federal government in regulating the economy made it clear that Congress could not foresee all of the contingencies that might arise in the execution of the law. It was therefore necessary to grant to the administrative agencies discretionary authority to be exercised when certain criteria were satisfied. The responsibility of Congress, then, was to determine the purposes, to establish standards to guide the administrators, to create the organization, and to appropriate the necessary funds.

Congress spelled out its intentions in law, in hearings, in committee reports, in debate, and in private conversations with administrators. Having granted discretionary authority, it determined to preserve the means of holding the administrators accountable for following the guidelines laid down.

Several recent inquiries conducted by congressional committees illustrate this role. In 1965, the Subcommittee on Intergovernmental Operations of the House Committee on Government Operations undertook an investigation of the Food and Drug Administration to assess its performance in regulating the marketing of new drugs—a matter of considerable interest owing to charges that the FDA had permitted the sale of some drugs without adequate testing. When the Federal Reserve Board raised the discount rate to its member banks at the end of 1965, the House Banking and Currency Committee immediately convoked hearings at which the members of the "Fed" had to defend their action. The inquiry was highly charged politically, involving significant questions of fiscal coordination, monetary policy, and the role of an independent agency such as the Federal Reserve Board in the constitutional system. It also permitted the Chairman of the Banking and Currency Committee, Congressman Wright Patman, once again to mount an attack on his favorite target, alleging that the "Fed" acquiesced to the pressure of the big banks for higher interest rates.

For the most part, these inquiries are conducted quietly, the purpose being to achieve significant improvements in administrative methods, and to obtain additional information that provides the basis for remedial legislation when required. The performance by administrative officials, especially before appropriations subcommittees, establishes a kind of rough "rating" on the agency and its chief personnel. Future legislative action may be based on the confidence the executive officials have been able to stimulate through their testimony and their attitude.

Perhaps the most intimate and accepted oversight relationships are found between the Joint Committee on Atomic Energy and the Atomic Energy Commission. There is some validity to the argument that the Joint Committee has become a part of the administrative apparatus of the Commission, involving itself not only in an examination of past administrative actions, but asking for and receiving the right to pass judgment on current administrative decisions. To a very considerable extent this intimacy vitiates the concept of a separation of powers, but exemplifies the very real tendency that is created under this oversight relationship for the Congressional Committee to become more the spokesman for, and the defender of, the administrative agency than to be its critic and political auditor.

The effectiveness of Congress in the performance of this function is much debated. To the executive officials, much of this kind of activity is simple "harassment," requiring interminable hours of explaining and re-explaining the same situations before innumerable committees. It is understandable, for example, that the executives of the Eisenhower administration (some of whom came from big business) would look with disdain on congressional oversight in view of the attacks by the Democrats in 1954 on the contract between the Atomic Energy Commission and a private utility combine known as Dixon-Yates to construct a plant to supply power to the Memphis, Tennessee, area. The investigation centered on alleged conflicts-of-interest of individuals who were working for both the government and financial institutions underwriting the enterprise, but really involved major policy issues regarding public and private production of energy in the United States. Under the severe attack launched in the Senate, the Eisenhower administration finally revoked the contract, and the power plant was constructed by the city of Memphis itself. To quote one close observer of the case, the President's adviser "saw a dastardly plot to discredit its private power policy, a tactic so vile as to deserve no notice from honest and wise men. . . ."[11] On the other hand, to the public power interests associated with the Democratic senators this represented an effective use of the congressional oversight function.

The consequences of the utilization of this power are varied. In some instances, such as in the investigations of alleged Communist infiltration in the Department of State from 1949 through 1954, the result was demorali-

[11] Aaron Wildavsky, *Dixon-Yates: A Study in Power Politics* (New Haven: Yale University Press, 1962), p. 306

zation of personnel in that agency. The objective of the Chairman of the Senate Committee, Joseph McCarthy, was to try to convict individuals for alleged subversive activities rather than to examine general administrative conditions or to propose new policies. On the other hand, the investigation by a special Senate Committee of the circumstances surrounding the dismissal of General MacArthur in 1951 from his command as Supreme Commander of United States forces in the Far East led to greater confidence in the conduct of the war, and to a lessening of the sharp political controversy that his firing had excited.

Advise and Consent

Congressional control of administration is strengthened in another way: through the powers granted to the Senate to advise on, and consent to, treaties and appointments of officers of the government. In each case, the power of the Senate generally lies, not in any open, formal exercise of this power, but in the threat of its use unless the administration consults on matters that are likely to be controversial.

With regard to treaties—which require the approval of two thirds of the Senators present—much of what might formerly have been handled by treaty is now dealt with by means of executive agreements and through legislative actions implementing foreign economic policy. These actions require authorization by a regular legislative bill and appropriations through the normal funding procedures. Furthermore, the President is frequently given blanket authorization to take certain actions in foreign policy, such as the Vietnam resolution of 1964, which authorized the President to "take all necessary measures to repel any armed attack against the forces of the United States and to prevent further aggression. . . ." and "to assist any member or protocol state of the Southeast Asia Collective Defense Treaty requesting assistance in defense of its freedom." The existence of such treaties as that involving the nations of Southeast Asia and the North Atlantic Alliance, however, indicate the continuing importance of this reserve power. In the 1965 session of Congress, for example, the Senate approved by a 71–0 vote certain changes in the United Nations Charter which were designed to reflect the increasing number of members in the UN.

The dramatic failure of Woodrow Wilson to obtain approval of the Treaty of Versailles, with its League of Nations Covenant, is usually cited as an indication of senatorial power. Wilson's failure to use senatorial advisers in the fashioning of the treaty, his unwillingness to countenance any alterations to assuage their wounded dignities or meet their objections, have been object lessons for all future Presidents. The presence of senators at the San Francisco conference to create the United Nations is a testament to this experience.

Appointments require the approval of a simple majority of the senators, but senatorial influence relates to the nominating rather than to the approval phase. Those who are nominated usually have advance senatorial approval, and if nominations are seriously contested, the usefulness of the candidates may be seriously diminished in the combat. Thus when Clare Boothe Luce was nominated as Ambassador to Brazil in 1959, she was finally approved after a bitter floor debate which partly centered on her remarks about the mental condition of one of the Democratic senators. She immediately resigned the post in recognition that her usefulness had been impaired.

But few nominations raise such political ire. Senators recognize it as a presidential prerogative to select his own team of officials, even while pressing upon him and his advisers the credentials of some individual whom they would want appointed. Most Presidents are not averse to acceding to senatorial recommendations, for they recognize them as coin of the political realm that can be called upon when he needs some credit. But there is neither a legal nor traditional basis for deferring to their recommendations. Such is not the case, however, with regard to certain categories of federal offices over whom senators of the President's party do claim some control. Specifically, these are such offices as district court judges, marshals, district attorneys, and in some instances heads of federal field offices. In these cases, the senators of the President's party demand deference, and if not granted, they may call upon the support of their Senate colleagues in rejecting the presidential candidates according to the custom of "senatorial courtesy." This custom dictates that senators will decline to approve a candidate who is "personally obnoxious" to the senator from the candidate's state. In doing so, each senator is protecting his colleague against the possibility of contrary factional elements developing within his own state.

The methods of congressional oversight stress committee action; little is done along these lines through open debate or challenges of administrative action on the floor of either house of Congress. In some European countries considerable use is made of committees for such oversight purposes, although nowhere to the extent of their use in the United States. In England and in many continental European countries the scrutiny of administrative behavior occurs principally through question periods in Parliament or the practice of *interpellation*. In each case the Cabinet minister appears before the entire chamber for questioning on matters relating to the conduct of business in his department. Under interpellation a debate may ensue, even to the point of taking votes on the chamber's support of the policy in question. Although repeatedly recommended by various observers for adoption in the United States, it has never found favor.

⚥ THE INFORMING FUNCTION

Most critics of Congress are quick to seize on the obvious lack of interest that members of Congress display toward formal debate as evidence of the decline of the legislative body or its failure to perform the informational function the country requires. The ordinary observer who visits either the Senate or House is indeed likely to be disillusioned by the small number of the members in the chamber, by the desultory manner in which a given legislator will deliver his immortal oration, and the almost perfunctory manner in which business is transacted. Perhaps recalling the stirring debates of Webster and Hayne—which undoubtedly were exceptional even in their own day—he wishes for more spark, for more content, for confrontation.

Press reaction is likely to be equally as deadening. Unless the debate is truly exceptional, unless the thoughts are uniquely original, or the issue so critical to political or national interests, it may be reported in the inside pages, if at all.

But the generalization glosses over a sufficient number of exceptions to make it worthy of qualification. Particularly in the Senate, the almost interminable debates—which sometimes are in fact filibusters—have illuminated important questions and sharpened the issues before final decisions have been made. And they have been widely reported in the press as well. The so-called "great debate" in 1951 over the President's power to station American troops in Europe under the North Atlantic Treaty Organization (NATO) without congressional approval raised many serious practical and constitutional issues. The creation of the Communications Satellite Corporation in 1962 called forth objections by numerous senators regarding the alleged "giving away" of public resources, and the debate was widely reported in the press. And throughout the 1960s a major speech by Senator J. William Fulbright, chairman of the Senate Foreign Relations Committee, was certain to stimulate widespread comment both in the Senate and in the national news media, particularly when it questioned administration policies.

Formal debates in England and in most Commonwealth countries are given considerably more publicity and therefore help to stimulate the debate itself. In Australia, for example, debates in the national legislature are broadcast. The serious press in England reports the parliamentary debates in considerable detail and provides the focus of political discussion in that country. *The Times* (London) reports daily the important statements made in Parliament while it is in session. By contrast, even the *New York Times* does not perform a similar service in the United States. The reason for the difference may be found in the fact that the Prime Minister and Cabinet sit in Parliament and thus force debate, and that the attention of the British citizen is not distracted by state politics.

Following the typical American pattern, development of the informing function has fallen to the committees of the two houses. And contrary to the parliamentary pattern elsewhere, the control over the process of obtaining and disseminating information is not necessarily in the hands of the government party—that of the President—but it may well be in the hands of a determined opposition. Owing to the decentralized character of power in the Congress and the impact of the seniority system, a committee may be hostile to the administration even though nominally controlled by its own party colleagues. When the President is of a different party than both houses of Congress, the committees are, of course, controlled politically by the opposition as well.

Congressional Studies by Means of Committees

The main function of Congress is to develop a body of information that provides the basis for further legislative action. Congressional committees hold hearings that serve as the basis for exploring certain legislative possibilities, even for the distant future. For example, the Senate Subcommittee on Foreign Aid Expenditures of the Government Operations Committee held hearings in 1965 on population issues, whose general focus was on the question of establishing offices of Population Problems in both the State Department and the Department of Health, Education and Welfare. Those who were called to testify included representatives of the Population Council, Princeton University's Office of Population Research, the Ford Foundation, a gynecologist who had developed a very simple and inexpensive mechanical contraceptive device, and many others. The purposes of the hearings far transcended the immediate question of the creation of these offices; they were designed to provide a forum for individuals who are concerned with population problems to expound their views. Their audience was necessarily restricted, since the hearings did not receive widespread attention, but the hope would be to reach certain opinion leaders—including the members of Congress themselves—in order to create a concern for problems of overpopulation. Legislative action might come in 1965 or 1966 or later, but the groundwork was being laid.

Some committees in fact have no purpose other than studies and recommendations with regard to a given policy area. Notable in this respect is the Joint Economic Committee, consisting of 16 members of the House and the Senate who devote themselves to the examination of far-ranging questions about the economy. In addition to an annual Report, it periodically publishes weighty tomes on such matters as monetary policy, federal expenditures, and employment. In a body geared for action on a piecemeal basis, it has sharpened the awareness of long-term problems, and has helped to elevate the tone of the discussion.

Congressional Investigations

As an instrument of "informing," Congress has yet to find a method equal to the congressional investigation. The reason may be found in the almost inherent tendency of investigating committees to search for "good guys" and "bad guys" in an affair under scrutiny. In effect, these investigations at times take on more the characteristics of trials than of legislative inquiries, and excite all of the interest that normally attaches to a trial when an individual's life, liberty, or property may be at stake. The involvement of a specific individual permits the dramatization of the issue in a personal way, at the risk of damaging the individual's reputation.

Perhaps the most famous of all of the investigating committees is the House Un-American Activities Committee. This committee has existed since 1938, first as a special committee, and then as a permanent committee since 1946. Since its inception it has been primarily concerned with investigation of Communist influence in various phases of American life. Its most famous inquiry concerned the allegations of Whittaker Chambers in 1948 regarding espionage activities, which ultimately led to the conviction of Alger Hiss for perjury. More recently the Committee concerned itself with an investigation of the Ku Klux Klan.

The chief techniques of the Committee have been to subpoena officials of organizations alleged to be subversive or individuals who have been named by others as having been associated with Communist organizations and causes, and to interrogate them on these associations. Often, the purpose of these interrogations is to punish the individual by exposure of his participation in these organizations, even though it may have occurred years, even decades, earlier. The justification of these exposés is that by revealing the activities of these individuals the Committee is making the nation aware of the menacing nature of the Communists or Ku Klux Klan and the techniques they use. Barring a few exceptions, the individuals who appear take refuge in the Fifth Amendment.

It is generally conceded that Congress has, and should have, the power to investigate in order to inform itself and the nation regarding problems possibly requiring legislative action. The reservations held by many concern the extent of congressional authority when it threatens, through exposure for the sake of exposure, the rights guaranteed to the individual by the First, Fourth, and Fifth Amendments to the Constitution.

Given the Court's reluctance to intervene, it seems clear that the reform of investigative practices remains the responsibility of Congress itself. The House of Representatives took certain steps to rectify its earlier permissive attitude by requiring that there be present more than one member of the Committee, that witnesses be allowed to have counsel, and that under certain circumstances the testimony of witnesses might be heard in executive session.

In concluding this section it should be noted that other techniques of investigation are utilized elsewhere. The state of New York has set up impartial commissions appointed by the governor but responsible to the state legislature as a means of obtaining objective information on state problems. In England the Royal Commissions of Inquiry, appointed by the Crown and consisting of experts or prominent public men, study given problems and make reports. Their procedures are dignified and sober, and in sharp contrast with the conditions often prevailing in congressional investigations. Perhaps the closest the United States has come to the Royal Commission has been in the Hoover Commissions (Commission on Organization of the Executive Branch of the Government), which studied reorganization of the national government and reported in 1949 and 1955.

❧ THE ROLES OF CONGRESS AND CONGRESSMEN

The most important fact about Congress is that it tends to reflect the standards of ethics, the prejudices, the anxieties, and the social values of the American public. Its roots are deeply embedded in the soil of each constituency, and it draws its proficiency and its inefficiency, its conscience and its bigotries, its profligacy and its conservatism from the same source that its constituents draw upon. That it is open to criticism is patently true; that it has performed ably the task of reconciling the conflicting forces of a continental nation and met the challenge—thus far—of the technological revolution and the changes in the nation-state system is equally true. Its role has changed as the problems facing the nation have changed and as the pressures of immediate action have tended to overcome the older habits of slow-moving deliberation. It still remains an alternative source of policy-making in an age when the Executive has come to occupy center-stage. The procedures it uses in making policy are our next subject for discussion.

CHAPTER 17

CONGRESS: SOURCE
OF PUBLIC POLICY

Some observers have described Congress as essentially a referee in the contest of interest groups. But this approach fails to include the legislature as a dynamic element in the process of distributing benefits and burdens. For, in fact, the legislature is a social system through which outside pressures are refracted, and information is filtered. The final decisions are not simply the result of manipulation of the legislature by outside forces, but take the form Congress itself imposes on these pressures and the manner in which it marshals available information.

⚘ CONGRESSIONAL ORGANIZATION:
FORMAL AND INFORMAL

Informal Rules and Practices

Congress has developed informal rules and practices, through which conflicts can be settled within reasonable bounds. The ritualistic character of congressional procedure may be explained in part by the fact that each member has equal standing in the chamber. He is elected by his own constituency and owes his presence to the voters, not to his colleagues in Congress. Having independent political support, he therefore expects the

427

same deference from his colleagues that he is prepared to give to them. This deference, which usually grows into respect as the members of Congress come to recognize the merits of their colleagues through close contact, manifests itself in innumerable ways: in respect for the rights of the others in debate; accommodation in scheduling consideration of bills; and defense of a colleague under attack by a common opponent, such as the Executive. The florid language used in debate, in which one always refers to "my learned and illustrious colleague from ———" is therefore not empty rhetoric but a manifestation of the need to keep an atmosphere of courtesy and orderliness. Similar traditions prevail in other parliaments as well. In England, even with the sharpest and most biting criticism, a speaker conforms to the rule of outward respect for the institution and his colleagues.

Because serving in Congress tends to be a permanent career for many of its members, there is deep concern for the maintenance of the institution itself and the traditions it embodies. One tradition emphasizes hard *legislative* work and attention to the business of each chamber, for failure to do so imposes larger burdens on the rest. Another is respect for seniority and its reverse: patient service during a quiet apprenticeship. Since most members have no higher political ambitions—or seldom have opportunities to realize such ambitions—longevity becomes a basis for advancement and respect.

Like any social group, Congress has sanctions for those who fail to measure up to the standards that are imposed. At the very mildest level, these sanctions may involve simple withdrawal of fellowship: as one congressman expressed it with regard to some of his colleagues, "People feel like leaving when certain individuals get up to speak."[1] At a more serious level, the legislator may be denied certain perquisites, such as appointment to a committee when his credentials are matched by others who have not offended. In its most severe form, the sanction may mean failure to gain the favor of his colleagues on legislation of interest to his constituency, thus diminishing his effectiveness as its representative. Both admirers and critics of the Senate have claimed to see an inner club or "Establishment" that governs the affairs of Congress, and shapes the product emanating from it.[2] In the Senate, the members of this "Establishment" are reputedly the practical men, the dedicated *Senate* men to whom that chamber is a home and a way of life. But recognition that there are men of this type—the compromisers, the gradualists,

[1] Charles Clapp, *The Congressman: His Work as He Sees It* (Washington, D.C.: The Brookings Institution, 1963), p. 30.

[2] See William S. White, *Citadel* (New York: Harper & Row, 1956), and Joseph S. Clark, *The Senate Establishment* (New York: Harper & Row, 1964).

the "reasonable" ones—should not blind the observer to the utility of the "outsider," the maverick, the individualist who equally well reflects his own constituency, and who may make proportionate contributions to the legislative product through agitation and dissent. The contributions of men like Senator Richard B. Russell of Georgia and Senator Wayne Morse of Oregon are different, but who is to say which is more valuable? It should be noted also that membership in the "Establishment" is neither an automatic disqualification nor advantage in moving upward. Both John F. Kennedy, who was not a member, and Lyndon Johnson, who was, became Presidents.

Differential Access to Congressional Power

Equally important is an understanding of the fact that the formal organization of Congress, its internal distribution of power, its allocation of responsibility, and its procedures provide *differential access* to those groups and individuals who are vying for recognition and reward. The organization and procedures of Congress are not neutral, and either by design, by history, or even by pure accident, they provide preferential opportunities for certain groups, regions, and even some administrative agencies to exert influence. Those groups, regions, or agencies having relatively little access, therefore, begin the legislative struggle under serious disadvantages.

To illustrate, it may be useful to describe the membership of two parallel committees of the Congress. The Agriculture Committees of both the Senate and House have jurisdiction over legislation dealing with all phases of agriculture and forestry. The membership of these committees consists almost exclusively of representatives of the food- and fiber-producing areas of the United States, chiefly from the Midwest and the South. The Agriculture Committee in the House of Representatives subdivides its work among commodity subcommittees that specialize in certain crops. Given the fact that Congress does its real legislative work at the committee level, the crucial decisions on legislation are made by those who have a direct interest and stake in these matters. The legislative product is certain to be, at the very minimum, acceptable to the commodity interests because anything seriously objectionable will be blocked.

Agricultural policy, however, concerns not only the producers of farm products, but also the consumers, the processers, the distributors, and taxpayers, who are not represented at the committee stage and thus are seriously disadvantaged. If they find agricultural legislation not to their liking, they must make an effort to block it on the floor of the chamber, where the weight of tradition and of parliamentary procedure is very much against them. The most they can hope to do is reject the work of the committee, for the general debate is seldom a useful place to improve highly complex bills.

Differential access is provided in a variety of ways. The fact that the South has traditionally returned its elected representatives term after term has resulted in a disproportionate number of southerners occupying committee chairmanships when the Democrats control Congress. From these vantage points, southern interests have been advanced or protected whenever the Democrats were in power. The power of Senator James Eastland of Mississippi in obstructing, for a long time, consideration of civil rights legislation from his position as Chairman of the Senate Judiciary Committee is only a dramatic and recent example of a relatively common phenomenon. The fact that the Senate in recent years has shown a decidedly more liberal persuasion than the House of Representatives also suggests differential opportunities for liberal and conservative groups.

The very nature of complex organizations makes them relatively conservative simply because it is difficult to mobilize sufficiently widespread support for a novel idea or program. But the structure of Congress makes this phenomenon even more pronounced. The decentralization of power in Congress means that a promoter of something new must fashion alliances that will overcome the resistance of strategically located groups at various stages of the legislative process. Adoption by the majority party is not sufficient, because the majority party may not be able to persuade some of its own members who may occupy vital positions that stand athwart the path of the proposal. Even committee approval may not be sufficient, because procedural roadblocks or contrary forces in the other chamber may stand in the way. For this reason, those who are concerned about maintaining the *status quo* find the decentralization of power and the complexity of existing procedures much to their liking.

The Role of Party

The fundamental principle in the organization of the Congress is party, with the Democrats and Republicans uniformly lining up with their partisan colleagues in contesting for control. That party which gains a majority in the House of Representatives, for example, can rest assured that it will control the leadership positions, such as the Speaker of the House, the majority leadership, the Rules Committee, and the chairmanship of all the committees. Through control of these positions, the party has the means to manage effectively the machinery of the two houses for whatever purposes the majority party agrees upon. But there is the rub— getting agreement.

As was explained in Chapter 13, American political parties are characterized by their lack of internal discipline and their inability to bring together the many diverse factions that are within them. Thus, the majority party, although in nominal control of the machinery of the two houses, seldom can exhibit sufficient unity to agree on every program and implement it. Fortunately or unfortunately, the minority party normally manifests similar unseemly divisions in its ranks and thereby presents the perfect setting for "coalition politics": the minority of the majority party combining with the majority of the minority party to defeat the objectives of the majority party.

Essentially this means that the advancement of a piece of legislation is dependent upon the ability of those who sponsor these programs to weave together a numerical majority out of sympathetic elements in the two parties. Except when one party has extraordinary majorities, as was the case during the 1965 session of Congress, the leadership must bargain with potential supporters, using whatever enticements or threats seem suitable, in order to build its majority. This results in a practice that is much condemned but widely used, known as "back-scratching," in which members of the legislature trade votes on issues which are of vital interest to some but of lesser consequence to others. Seldom is this exchange explicit; rather the granting of favors in one instance creates the expectation of reciprocal assistance in time of need. And those who have much to give in the way of favors, such as the Majority Leader of the Senate, or the Speaker of the House, can be counted on to collect their debts when an issue of importance to the party arises.

To many, this concept of party is not only untidy, but also absolutely contrary to their conception of representative democracy. For them, the majority party should be responsible for the organization and management of the Congress. To allow its members to defy party leadership and the views expressed by a majority of the members of the party means that the party cannot function as a responsible agent of the community. Decisions are not made by open debate between the two parties but rather through covert "deals" among members. The electorate has no means of establishing responsibility for the legislative program, because in fact neither party can consistently retain the loyalty of its members.

The most enduring example of this factionalism is the southern wing of the Democratic party. Not only on issues of race but also on questions such as government spending, federal-state relations, and foreign trade the southern Democrats have often found themselves in opposition to their northern colleagues and in agreement with the majority of the Republicans. Because of the strategic positions which the southerners occupy in committee chairmanships owing to their longevity in the chambers, they have influence over policy decisions that far exceeds their numerical strength.

The tendency to follow party majority opinion is still the single most important force in Congress, given its organization and the ties to party that exist between the legislator and his constituency. He was elected in a partisan campaign, usually with formal party support, which normally involves some financial assistance; he probably identifies with his party because of some ideological affinity; when he arrives in Congress he is immediately introduced to members of his own party and he continues to associate with them; he is physically separated from the opposition on the floor of the chamber; and he is often subjected to partisan appeals by those with whom he works. If the White House is occupied by a President of his party, he may find himself the object of considerable persuasion if not outright arm-twisting by the Chief Executive and his emissaries. Given all of these pressures, it would be rather remarkable if he were to vote persistently with the other side.

All of this means that the party has an important, but not always decisive, role in Congress: for the individual member, party is relevant, usually influential, but not always the determining factor. Other "reference groups" are significant to him: large, national interests with which he may identify, or local groups in his own constituency. When the pull of the other groups is powerful, he may ignore the dominant opinion in his party and vote with the opposition. Under severe pressure, he may avoid this conflict of loyalties simply by absenting himself; or he may vote to eviscerate the bill, and failing to do so, vote for it; or vote to strengthen the bill, and failing to do so, vote against it. In this way he can justify his contention that he was for and against the bill at the same time.

Such laxity in party discipline is almost unheard of elsewhere, except in France. Failure to support the party position even once on a major issue might be sufficient grounds for expulsion from the party in most European countries. In part this is explained by the importance of ensuring parliamentary support for the government. If the government in England, for example, loses a vote in Parliament, there is almost automatically a call for a new election. And members of the majority are under heavy pressure to avoid such an occurrence. Only in exceptional cases dealing with private legislation or moral issues (such as marriage or divorce laws, relations of church and state, conscription) are they free to vote according to conscience. But an equally important explanation lies in the character of many of the parties themselves. In contrast to the conglomerate parties of the United States, European parties tend to emphasize ideological content to a much higher degree, thereby sharpening the distinctions among them. Moreover, many of these countries have systems of proportional representation that enhance the chances of small splinter parties, which, because they reflect narrower classes, can develop a higher sense of unity.

Whatever the merits of such systems, they are inconceivable in the American context. The continental nature of our Republic, the traditional alliances of region and party, the complex array of interest groups, and the lack of interdependence between the Chief Executive and the Congress— all militate against such a disciplined party system. Modest efforts to reform the system along more ideological or programmatic lines may prove successful, but it is more likely that increased party cohesion, if it comes to pass, will reflect more profound changes in the economic and social structure of the United States.[3]

The Agents of Leadership

The caucus of the majority party is theoretically the ruling body for each chamber. But in fact its functions are relatively few and seldom performed owing to the decentralization in each house. The caucus selects the Speaker of the House, the majority leaders and whips of each chamber, and the heads of such strictly party organs as the policy committees and the campaign committees. But the opportunities for such selections arise only periodically when vacancies occur. Elected leaders retain their positions through the years, barring the exceptional revolt. Thus, for example, Sam Rayburn occupied the Speaker's chair from 1940 to 1961, save only two terms when the Republicans were in control of the House.

The Speaker. At the apex of the power structure in the House of Representatives is the Speaker. During some periods he has been virtual dictator of its proceedings. Speaker Cannon had behaved so autocratically that in 1910–1911 the members denied him several of his traditional weapons: the power to appoint the members of the standing committees, the power to control the flow of legislation through his membership on the Rules Committee, and an untrammeled power to recognize members for purposes of making motions. At present the Speaker is powerful, but within the context of a system in which power is more widely shared with other individuals and subunits, notably the standing committees.

The leadership role of the Speaker is based in part on certain formal powers. He refers bills to committees, although rule and precedent govern his actions to a considerable degree. Similarly, he has the power of

---

[3] But there are limits to violation of party support, as two Democratic congressmen discovered in 1965. Both were from the South and both had openly supported the candidacy of Senator Barry Goldwater for the Presidency. The Democratic caucus voted to strip them of their seniority rights on their committees. One resigned and was immediately re-elected as a Republican.

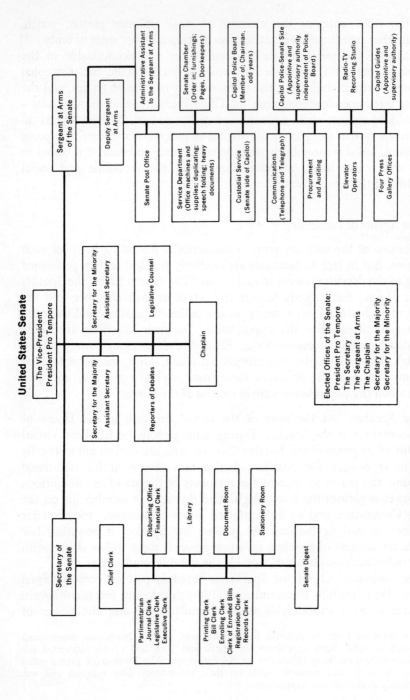

FIGURE 17–1. Organization of the United States Senate. (From *United States Government Organization Manual* 1965–66.)

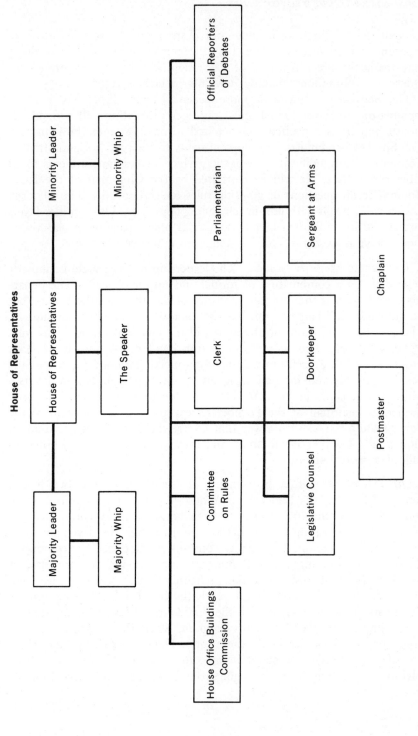

House of Representatives

FIGURE 17–2. Organization of the House of Representatives. (From *United States Government Organization Manual 1965–66.*)

recognition, but here again rule and custom dictate certain orders of procedure he is loath to violate. He interprets the rules, and in so doing may markedly affect the fate of legislation, but the precedents of the House are voluminous, making new interpretations risky.

The Speaker's influence is more personal than official. As a senior member of the House, he has great prestige both within and without the House, and he is consulted and deferred to on most important matters. The Speaker has influence on appointments to his party's Committee on Committees, a nonofficial party agency, which makes appointments to all other committees. He will be consulted by the Chairman of the Rules Committee on questions of granting rules for certain bills. The Majority Leader will consult with him in scheduling legislation. Other minor favors he may do for individual members, such as office space or special assignments, serve as levers for the expansion of his influence.

The Senate Majority Leader. The leadership in the Senate is similarly dependent on a combination of formal and informal power. The Senate Majority Leader is the managing director of the affairs of the Senate, but he must deal and bargain with the chairmen of the standing committees, who have powerful claims to the loyalty of the members owing to the rules of specialization. The success of Senator Lyndon Johnson as Majority Leader lay in his capacity to find common meeting ground for potentially hostile senators, and for bestowing favors—or failing to bestow favors—which put senators in his debt. He wove together his roles as Majority Leader, as chairman of the Democratic caucus, and as chairman of the Policy Committee in such a way that he was the center of negotiation on most policy and procedural issues, and thus was usually able to bring his colleagues to agreement.

Other Leaders. Other instruments of leadership in the two houses consist of the majority leader of the House, the assistant majority leaders, and whips. The majority leaders of both houses lead by controlling the lines of communication in the chambers and through the development of the legislative program. They are in constant contact with the committee chairmen, ascertaining their intentions, counseling urgency or delay, as they attempt to establish the working schedule for the chamber. They plan legislative strategy, in consultation with the Speaker and the committee chairmen. They work closely with the President and his agents in attempting to implement the President's program, when the Congress and the Presidency are controlled by the same party. The whips extend the reach of the Majority Leader by maintaining contact with individual members, advising of pending decisions, urging attendance, and corralling favorable votes.

Similar party organization is found on the minority side. The Minority Leader performs essentially the same functions for his membership, although having no formal responsibility for planning the program of the Senate or House. Nevertheless the minority leaders are vital cogs in the machinery of the two houses, owing to the fact that so much of the business of the two houses is carried on by unanimous consent. Particularly in the Senate, where there is no limitation on debate, either on motions to take up bills or on the bills themselves, acceptable arrangements with the minority must be made. The mutual respect which the leaders of both parties develop for each other over the years ensures that the legislative process will function with a minimum of acrimony and foot-dragging.

When the two parties are evenly divided, or when the votes of the minority are desperately needed to put over an administration program, the Minority Leader may be a crucial figure. A striking example of this was afforded by the passage of the Civil Rights Act of 1964, when Minority Leader Senator Everett McKinley Dirksen played a key role in formulating the necessary compromises to win the support of a group of Republicans.

Interest Groups and Legislators

As the national government has increasingly become involved in the economic and social life of the people of the United States, virtually every organization of any consequence has established an office in Washington to maintain a flow of information on what is happening in the nation's capital of interest to them, and to "represent" the interests of these organizations when legislation affecting their interests is being considered by Congress.

The difficulty in assessing the number who are so engaged is that the Lobby Registration Act has been so interpreted as to apply only to those whose principal purpose is to influence legislation and who are engaged in the "direct" activity of lobbying, that is, contacting congressmen or testifying before committees, not to mention such indirect activities as publicity campaigns through the newspapers, and stimulation of "grass roots" interest in congressional districts.

Lobbyists may often make useful contributions to the legislative process. Legislators are dependent on a flow of information from various sources in order to make rational and independent judgments. They are rightly suspicious of the evidence presented by the executive branch; they have limited information developed by their own staff, committee staffs, and the Legislative Reference Service of the Library of Congress. Lobbyists, then, provide important additional information—equally biased to be sure—from groups that are likely to be directly affected by the law.

A congressman who does not wish to be "brainwashed" by lobbyists, need not be. For every lobbying group urging him to act in one direction, there are probably several others urging quite contrary action. Thus he can weigh their arguments and evidence and arrive at his own conclusion. Moreover, testimony from congressmen and lobbyists alike indicates that a lobbyist who sets out to hoodwink or mislead a legislator will destroy his effectiveness and the influence of those he represents.

Not all groups have equal standing with members of Congress because they do not have equal standing with the general public either. Because of the respect afforded the doctor, the American Medical Association generally receives a respectful hearing. It may be doubted that the Teamsters' Union's access to the legislative chambers is as great as formerly, owing to charges made against its president, James Hoffa, and his final conviction in court for various criminal offenses. Other groups suffer not from a bad reputation but from having no reputation at all. They are unknown and therefore virtually ignored.

Lobbyists naturally rely to a considerable extent on personal contacts with the legislators and on direct communication with them through sending them reports and studies and through appearances of their clients at hearings. Much of what has been called the "social lobby"—the informal or perhaps formal meetings at cocktail parties or banquets—are designed to improve the chances of lobbyists obtaining a hearing from the congressman when he needs one. Personal contacts between congressmen and the lobbyist are frequent and usually involve an effort to present convincingly the cause the lobbyist represents. Open threats of reprisals for failure to accept his position would result in complete rejection of the lobbyist and very likely of the position espoused by him.

The contacts between the lobbyists and congressmen are frequently governed by the known attitudes of the congressmen. The lobbyists are unlikely to waste their time on someone known to be opposed to their position, because of both the apparent hopelessness of their cause and of the unpleasantness of such confrontation. Lobbyists tend to seek out those who are known sympathizers, supplying them with useful information and helping them to work effectively for their side through the development of strategy. They may also approach those who are undecided, although often contact through an intermediary—a congressional colleague or constituent —may be more effective.

The congressman himself is of course the key to the situation. He may in fact be the chief proponent of the interest of a particular economic group because of its importance in his district. There is no need to persuade him; he needs only adequate information to bolster his commitment. And by a process of bargaining with other members who are uncommitted, he may be able to bring together a majority that no outside group could manage to create.

The most effective lobbies are those that have electoral power, that is, large memberships that can be mobilized for voting purposes. These lobbies can encourage their members to impress upon their congressmen their interest in a given piece of legislation, leaving implicit the threat of reprisals for lack of sympathy. Lobbies with this kind of base to work on are likely to engage in indirect lobbying, although not ignoring the more direct approaches.

Few lobbies are really the well-heeled, slick operations described by the more sensationalist press. In fact, they range from one-man operations, dependent on fees, to large, general-purpose organizations like the Chamber of Commerce. Few have unlimited expense accounts or even highly qualified personnel. They frequently find it necessary to justify their very existence to their clients because of their inability to demonstrate concrete results. As much effort may be expended in finding the wherewithal to continue in operation as in lobbying itself.

Suffice it to say that the corrupting influence of lobbyists over members of Congress is exaggerated, if it is not simply a part of American folklore. If bribery was ever a major problem, it is not now. Legislators who respond to group influence do so because their constituencies generally favor aid to that group; in effect, they are the chief lobbyists. In general, the influence of lobbying in Congress ranks below the influence of party, constituency, the President, fellow congressmen, and even Cabinet officers.[4] The chief contribution of lobbying is positive: the supply of information on the effect of policy on interest groups, provision of technical information, and creation of a sense of participation in the political process for groups that may feel disadvantaged in other forms of political activity.

The Committee System of Congress

The fact that Congress remains today a *legislative* body and not only a debating society requires that it organize itself to deliberate over proposals. The nature of lawmaking is too exacting and complex to permit more than consideration of the major features of the legislation during debate on the floor of the chambers. The tedious, difficult struggle over the purposes of the legislation, the means to achieve those purposes, the language to express the purposes, must all be left to smaller bodies, which are the

[4] Lester Milbrath, *The Washington Lobbyists* (Chicago: Rand McNally, 1963), ch. XVII.

committees of Congress. As Woodrow Wilson commented, "Congress in session is Congress on public exhibition whilst Congress in its committee rooms is Congress at work."

The committees, then, are miniature legislatures to which their parent bodies delegate the responsibility for considering proposals that fall within given subject-matter areas. The delegation of this responsibility is based on the assumption that the members of the committees will develop expertise in those subject-matter areas and will therefore be in a position to make informed judgments on legislative proposals.

All the committees of Congress are not of equal importance. Some of them handle each year legislation of major consequence, whereas others have relatively restricted jurisdiction or "housekeeping" duties. Table 17–1 shows one observer's ranking of the committees in the two houses:

When legislative proposals are reported to the entire body of the Senate or the House of Representatives, there is a presumption that relevant alternatives have been examined, technical problems have been eliminated,

TABLE 17–1. *Standing Committees (Ranked in Groups, by Order of Importance)*

Senate	House of Representatives
I. Appropriations Foreign Relations Finance	Rules Appropriations Ways and Means
II. Armed Services Judiciary Agriculture and Forestry Interstate and Foreign Commerce	Armed Services Judiciary Agriculture Interstate and Foreign Commerce Foreign Affairs Government Operations
III. Banking and Currency Labor and Public Welfare Public Works Interior and Insular Affairs Aeronautical and Space Sciences	Banking and Currency Education and Labor Interior and Insular Affairs Space and Astronautics Public Works
IV. Post Office and Civil Service Government Operations	Post Office and Civil Service Merchant Marine and Fisheries Veterans Affairs Un-American Activities
V. District of Columbia Rules and Administration	District of Columbia House Administration

SOURCE: Ranking done by H. Douglas Price, in Stephen K. Bailey, *The New Congress*, pp. 54–55. © 1966 by St. Martin's Press, Inc.

and significant issues have been carefully examined. The entire membership is then prepared to make its decision on the desirability of that specific proposal, but is not prepared to rewrite the legislation on the floor.

The committees act as sifters of the huge number of legislative proposals that are introduced in Congress each year. In the mid-1960s the number approached 20,000 each two-year term. All of them had meaning and importance to someone, but varied in their importance to the national welfare and to the members of the legislative bodies. The committees are therefore faced with the burden of selecting from this flood of proposed measures a few that are thought to be worthy of consideration. In making these decisions, the members of the committees naturally respond to the pleas and pressure put upon them by various interested parties: the President, his department heads, other members of Congress, party officials, interest-group representatives. But the decision to forward bills to the membership of the entire chamber depends on the committees' judgment. And for most bills, in the words of Woodrow Wilson, "When it goes from the clerk's desk to a committee-room it crosses a parliamentary bridge of sighs to dim dungeons of silence whence it will never return."

Membership on the committees is allocated to the two parties in accordance, roughly, with the proportion of membership of each party in the entire chamber. Thus the majority party in each house controls every committee by the same margin that it controls the entire body. Appointments to these committees are handled by a committee on committees within each party. These membership committees attempt to meet both the demands of balanced representation on the committees and the wishes of the individual member to serve on committees that rank high in the hierarchy of committees in the chamber or that affect his district. The control over these appointments, usually well within the orbit of party leadership influence, provides the party leaders with great bargaining power over new members who are hoping to make Congress their careers.

Subcommittees. The reference of a bill to a committee usually results in its further reference to a subcommittee for detailed examination of its merits. These subcommittees are appointed by the chairmen; the subcommittee chairmen are usually the ranking members of the majority party. In some instances, a chairman may refuse to create subcommittees, either because he feels that the entire committee should handle consideration of legislation—as in the case of the Senate Finance Committee—or because the chairman wishes to avoid creation of subcommittees dominated by elements opposing him—as was the case of the House Banking and Currency Committee for a number of years.

When subcommittees are used, normally hearings take place before them, and their members then make recommendations to the full committee. Where confidence in the subcommittees is high, they are afforded great deference. Such is the case of the House Appropriations subcommittees; seldom does the full Committee overrule the judgment of its sub-units.

Committee Staff.   Perhaps the most important aides to congressmen are the professional staffs of the committees. Some of these staffs, such as those on the Appropriations committees and the Senate Foreign Relations Committee, are highly skilled, and are equally acceptable to both the majority and the minority. Others are made up of politicians who add little to the professional stature of the Congress. Where this occurs, the staff is likely to be divided between the majority and minority staffs. Unquestionably, the addition of these professional staffs has greatly increased the capability of Congress in grappling with the complex issues which come before it.

The Seniority Rule.   The broad grant of authority given the committees creates the most controversial feature of congressional organization and procedure: the rule of seniority. Respect for seniority is a hallowed tradition in all aspects of congressional life, but nowhere does it reach the sanctity achieved in the allocation of authority within committees. The rule of seniority provides that the chairmanship of the committee automatically goes to that member of the majority party who has served the longest continuous period on the committee. The status of each member is rigidly determined by the length of his continuous service, and one can hope to achieve chairmanship only by outlasting the other members of his party, provided one's party wins a majority in that chamber.

The chairmanship confers not only prestige but also power over both the members of his committee and the fate of legislation that is referred to it. It affords the chairman the opportunity to be an autocrat or a democrat, according to his own personal inclinations. And autocrats there are, as there are democrats in Congress. Specifically, the chairman controls the agenda of the committee, setting the order in which bills will be considered and the time that will be devoted to them. He generally controls the staff of the committee, making appointments and allocating responsibilities. He appoints chairmen and members of subcommittees, and thereby determines the extent to which individual members of the committee are given an opportunity to make their imprint felt on legislation, and their names known to the public. He chairs committee meetings, and can affect the fate of bills by his rulings on procedure. And his long experience, combined with these formal and informal powers, gives him status to which the other members necessarily defer. Outside the committee, the chairman negotiates with the leadership on scheduling bills, may manage the bill on the floor of the chamber, and is a member of the conference committee that resolves differences when bills are passed by the two houses in different forms.

The seniority rule favors those who have the highest likelihood of returning to Congress after each election, that is, those who come from basically one-party districts in which the possibility of the opposition winning is close to zero. Thus, when the Democrats control Congress, the chairmanships have tended to go to congressmen and senators from the southern states. When the Republicans are in control, the chairmanships have tended to fall into the hands of members from the Midwestern strongholds of rural Republicanism. In both cases, it is argued, the committees are dominated by men who are least responsive to the trends of contemporary political life. The liberal members of both parties therefore must struggle mightily to overcome a decided disadvantage in promoting legislation to their liking.

Evidence for the southern domination of committee chairmanships is found in the 1965 session of Congress in which the 11 states of the Deep South were represented by 105, or 24 percent, of the total membership but controlled 12, or 60 percent, of the 20 chairmanships in the House of Representatives. In the Senate, these states had 22 percent of the total membership, but controlled 56 percent of the chairmanships.

Defense of the seniority rule stresses the need for experienced men at the heads of these committees. By long acquaintance with the problems of the agencies with which they have to deal, with the rules of the Congress, and with the substantive issues that arise, they are in a position to give better direction to the efforts of the committee. Furthermore, it is argued that the automatic rule avoids divisive struggles over committee leadership that many other methods would invite. Finally, it is contended that the generalized description of chairmen as dictators and mossbacks misses the mark by far. Many of the chairmen are extremely permissive, allowing the committee members to work their will even over his opposition. And many of the chairmen from the South, far from being conservative and out of step, are progressives, like Senator Lister Hill of Alabama (chairman of the Senate Labor and Public Welfare Committee), or at least reasonable party men, like Congressman Wilbur Mills of Arkansas (chairman of the House Ways and Means Committee).

Seniority Versus Party Leadership. The seniority rule plus the decentralization of power among the committees has in effect set up a dual and conflicting system of leadership in the two chambers. On the one hand, there is the party leadership, which has control over the general machinery of the chambers and tends to be responsive to a majority of the members of the party in the House and Senate, and to the President when he is of the same political persuasion. This leadership tends to reflect greater concern for party fortunes with the electorate. On the other hand, the seniority leadership in the committees tends to respond to a "whirlpool" of power that consists of interest groups important to certain constituencies represented in the committee, and to administrative agencies that are beholden to the committee. This dual set of leaders frequently engages in very hard bargaining in order to avoid unseemly public battle. But when differences cannot be resolved, the individual member is forced to make a choice as to which leadership is more persuasive.

The Committee System of the British Parliament

The committee system of the British Parliament stands in sharp contrast to that of Congress. Committees in Parliament are not specialized, but deal with all types of legislation. They are simply called Committees A, B, C, D, and E. Members are appointed each session, but the membership may change as the issue changes in order to take advantage of the specialized knowledge of some members. The main function of the committee is to discuss legislation proposed by the Cabinet, and the minister carefully guides the committee in its deliberations. The British aim is a strong, unified leadership in Parliament, and their committee system is one of the many devices to make this aim a reality. Parliamentary committees *help* the Cabinet, but do not pretend to rival it. The American political system, by contrast, aims at dispersing power as much as possible, making unified leadership difficult and, at times, impossible.

❊ THE LEGISLATIVE PROCESS

Legislative Strategy

Success in legislative bodies, as in other organizations, depends not only on the intrinsic merits of the propositions considered, but also on the strategy utilized and the good fortunes that accidental circumstances provide. Those who expect favorable results from legislative action must therefore plan their approach, measure their resources, and mobilize their forces. At the same time they must retain sufficient flexibility to provide for making strategic retreats or for taking advantage of unforeseen opportunities as they arise.

The introduction of a bill does not necessarily signify real intent to obtain a legislative product. Members of Congress may introduce bills supported by constituents even though they doubt the merits of the bills and are certain of their rejection. The goal is to mollify rather than to promote. Legislators may introduce bills as educational devices for the purpose of bringing problems to the attention of fellow legislators and providing a focus for discussion among interested groups outside the legislature. Perennial bills that would establish a Department of Natural Resources would appear to be of this character, for concrete steps toward its implementation run afoul of the implacable opposition of both executive bureaus and private groups. Bills may also serve the purpose of threatening administrators who may be less responsive than is desired by a committee or an individual member. Threats to transfer functions, to revoke authorization for certain activities, indeed to scuttle an entire program, may be effective goads to administrative action.

Kinds of Legislative Action

The most important measures passed by Congress are public bills dealing with matters of general significance and application to the people of the country. Other forms of legislation, however, do occur. One is the private bill, dealing usually with claims of individuals against the government or special immigration cases. These are handled quite separately from general legislation and seldom require debate. Congress also passes joint, simple, and concurrent resolutions. Joint resolutions, in most respects, are like public bills, but concern directives to administrators or subordinate legislation; concurrent resolutions express the mutual conviction of the two houses on a given matter, whereas the simple resolution expresses the attitude of one house. The latter two do not have the force of law and are not signed by the President.

Origin of Legislation

The origin of most legislation is complex, usually resulting from long discussion, bargaining, and analysis by many people who have some stake, although not always the same stake, in its outcome. Recognition of a problem requiring public resolution may first occur in academic circles, in industry, in labor unions, or in administrative agencies. Along the way, certain solutions may be proposed and discarded as impractical, or impolitic. Eventually, some alternative is selected as the basis for formal consideration through introduction of legislation.

In a technical sense, congressmen are authors of all bills. Aiding them in the formulation of the precise language of a bill are legislative counsel in both houses who are experts in bill drafting. For assistance in the investigation of pertinent facts and figures, the individual congressman may call upon the resources of the Legislative Reference Service of the Library of Congress, which maintains a staff of experts in the various subject-matter fields for this purpose. In addition, he may call on the staffs of the legislative committees and on administrators who have practical experience in the area of his interest. Lobbyists, local public officials, university professors —all may have some hand in putting together a legislative package.

Illustrative of this process is the history of legislation dealing with medical care for the aged. Proposals for compulsory national health insurance were made as early as 1935, but no legislation was introduced until 1943. President Truman in 1949 made a determined but unsuccessful bid for passage of a prepaid medical insurance program for all persons. In 1954 President Eisenhower proposed to deal with medical care problems by having the federal government reinsure private insurance companies against unusually heavy losses on medical insurance. The origins of the law approved by Congress in 1965 may be found in a bill introduced by Congressman Aime Forand of Rhode Island in 1957, which provided that the social security taxes be raised to finance medical care for the needy recipients of old-age benefits. A determined effort by the Democrats, who controlled Congress in 1960, to implement this proposal failed when Congress approved in its stead the Kerr-Mills bill, which provided grants to participating states to help pay for medical care for persons who were "medically indigent," although not on public relief. The drive for the social security approach continued, however, meeting defeat again in 1962 and in 1964.

The origin of the legislation of 1965, then, may be found in the growing recognition of the medical problems of the aged and the increasing cost of medical care. Its origin may also be found in partial solutions and the combined pressure by the President, individual members of Congress, and organizations such as the National Council of Senior Citizens for Health Care Through Social Security, which was formed to maintain liaison among the various groups interested in promoting such legislation. The combination of these forces led to its final passage in 1965.

The choice of sponsors may be an important consideration in furthering the bill's chances. The names of some congressmen are anathema to most of their colleagues, whereas others are held in such high regard that the mere presence of their name on a bill assures serious consideration. If the chairman of the committee can be persuaded to sponsor the legislation, chances for passage are improved. Ideally, one might hope for bipartisan sponsorship, thus ensuring at least the claim of broad support regardless of political persuasion.

Reference of Bills

The Constitution provides that all revenue bills shall originate in the House of Representatives, and by tradition all appropriations bills, also, are first considered by that body.[5] With respect to all other bills, the supporters may choose whether to introduce and press for passage in one house first, or in both simultaneously. In most instances, administration bills are introduced in both houses at the same time, but likely favorable reception in one house may dictate making the effort there first in the hope of creating pressure on the other house for passage. (See Figure 17–3.)

Upon introduction, bills are given a number and are referred to the appropriate committee for study and investigation. The rules and precedents of each house generally dictate which committees are appropriate, based on their subject matter. The presiding officers have some discretion, however, and this may be used to advantage. In 1964, civil rights proposals were so framed that one of the constitutional underpinnings was the power of Congress to regulate commerce among the states. Thus, the Civil Rights bill was referred both to the Interstate Commerce Committee and the

[5] In Britain, only the government has the right to introduce money bills; this alone shows the enormous difference between the American and the British systems.

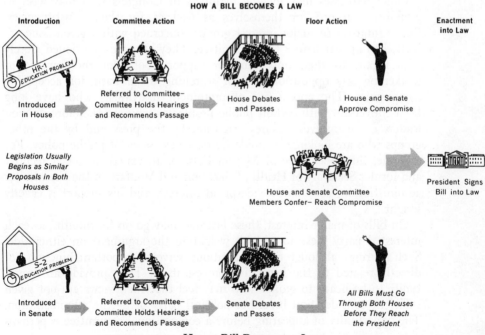

HOW A BILL BECOMES A LAW

Introduction	Committee Action	Floor Action	Enactment into Law
Introduced in House	Referred to Committee— Committee Holds Hearings and Recommends Passage	House Debates and Passes	House and Senate Approve Compromise

Legislation Usually Begins as Similar Proposals in Both Houses

House and Senate Committee Members Confer— Reach Compromise

President Signs Bill into Law

| Introduced in Senate | Referred to Committee— Committee Holds Hearings and Recommends Passage | Senate Debates and Passes | *All Bills Must Go Through Both Houses Before They Reach the President* |

FIGURE 17–3. How a Bill Becomes a Law.

Judiciary Committee of the Senate, which was traditionally the graveyard of civil rights legislation. Reference to the Interstate Commerce Committee made possible hearings and a favorable committee report.

Committee Hearings

Committee proceedings will normally be undertaken at two distinct levels: public hearings and staff investigation. The former are designed principally to establish a public record on the issue, and only secondarily to provide information to the members of the committee or other members of the house.

On major legislation the lead-off witness is normally the Cabinet officer who establishes the administration's position on the legislation. Other executive officials may offer more detailed substantiation of the Secretary's general position at a later time. The hearings on major bills are given considerable newspaper attention and thus are looked upon as welcome opportunities to create public support for the bill. An effective presentation of the administration's position may not change the minds of many members of Congress, but an ineffective performance or indications of weakness of provisions of the bill may provide ammunition for the opposition, who are looking for vulnerable points.

Other witnesses may include members of Congress who may wish to establish a record for themselves as well as for their constituencies. Representatives of major interest groups concerned with a given issue are invited to appear before the committee. They also are questioned closely with regard to their opposition or support, both for the purpose of weakening any opposition and of searching for a basis for acceptable compromise. The appearance of prominent individuals who have long been conversant with certain public problems—who are therefore opinion leaders in themselves—assures attention by the press and by the other groups who are looking for guidance on given issues of public policy. For example, the appearance of Marion Folsom, an expert on social security and former Secretary of Health, Education and Welfare in the Eisenhower administration, commands widespread interest, and his support is eagerly sought.

On bills of major interest, these hearings may go on for months, as each interested party seeks to add his weight to the argument on either side. Such hearings, although often repetitious, serve an important function not directly related to the legislative process itself. They provide an opportunity to be heard to groups who may feel that their views are not given sufficient consideration by either political party or by the administration. The opportunity of appearing before a congressional committee is perhaps the most valued aspect of freedom of speech for organized groups. Without this "safety valve," these groups might feel permanently disadvantaged in the competition for the attention of Congress.

Committee Deliberation

At the conclusion of public hearings, the committee then undertakes a careful examination of the legislation behind closed doors or in "executive session." At this point the bargaining that was characteristic of the formulation of the original proposals becomes even more intense. Individual members and staff aides are necessarily involved, but further consultation may be had with executive officials, with representatives of interest groups, and with academicians; all of these, however, participate at the sufferance of the committee. The procedure normally is relatively informal, with modifications made through the give-and-take of discussion and compromise. On hotly controversial legislation, however, all of the devices of parliamentary law may be wheeled out in promoting or impeding the approval of a bill.

The proceedings usually reflect the views of the chairman, and the result of this "mark-up" usually bears his firm imprint. He may dominate the committee, or he may act as mediator, trying to discover common ground on which the committee can present a relatively united front.

The careful examination of legislation at this phase reflects important tactical considerations. The committee must reach agreement on a product that will command support both in the committee and on the floor of the chamber. In many instances a simple majority of the committee may represent a minority in the entire chamber, and it is therefore necessary to reach a higher degree of agreement within the committee. Furthermore, a badly divided committee creates a lack of confidence in the chamber, whereas a unanimous report is almost unassailable. The success of the House Appropriations Committee may be attributed in part to the fact that its reports are almost always unanimous and therefore command great respect in the House. For the chairman, relative unanimity indicates that he has control of his committee and establishes his reputation for obtaining a defensible legislative product when it reaches the floor.

The result of committee deliberations may be a completely new or "clean" bill. The original proposal may have been transformed through the addition of wholly new provisions or the deletion of major parts of the original proposal. In the consideration of "Medicare" legislation by the House Ways and Means Committee, the Committee added an entirely new provision providing for a voluntary program of health insurance to cover doctors' bills, a provision not included in the original legislation.

Along with the bill, the committee prints a report, which conveys to the members of the house the intent, the general features, and the justification of the new legislation. These reports are carefully read by the members, and often provide the focus of debate on the floor if the matter is controversial. The minority may append its views and urge rejection of the bill or whatever modifications it thinks are necessary to make it acceptable. The reports may have additional significance: when a statute is challenged in the courts, the courts may use the committee reports as important material for guiding them in construing the statute.

The Calendars in the House of Representatives

Bills reported by the committees of the House of Representatives are placed on one of several "calendars," or schedules, which govern the order in which legislation is considered on the floor of the House. Appropriations bills and bills raising revenue are placed on the Union Calendar; public bills not appropriating money are placed on the House Calendar; noncontroversial, and therefore less consequential bills, are placed on the Consent Calendar; private bills providing relief in the form of claims against the United States or for immigration of individuals are put on the Private Calendar; motions to discharge a committee of further consideration of a bill are placed on the Discharge Calendar. Bills placed on the Consent and Private Calendars are routinely approved by voice vote unless special "watchdog" committees discover some weakness that would require more general consideration.

The House Rules Committee

The principal manner in which these bills come before the House is through the "rules" (or orders) of the House Rules Committee. The Rules Committee is one of the "leadership" committees of the House in that it is responsible for determining when and under what conditions major legislation will be considered. Usually the majority party has twice the number of the minority because the scheduling of the work of the House is considered to be a prerogative of the majority party. Normally, it works closely with the floor leadership of the House and with the committee leaders to bring bills to the floor expeditiously.

The power of the Rules Committee lies in its authority to decide whether a bill should be considered by the House at all. But even if its decision is in the affirmative, it may specify the length of time a bill will be considered, what motions may be made, and whether amendments may be proposed or not. In exercising this power, the Committee does not limit itself to controlling the "traffic" of bills, but discusses the merits of each piece of legislation and occasionally makes its decisions with regard to the granting of rules on whether it favors the bill or not. It may even bargain with the leaders of the legislative committees to ensure that certain objectionable features of bills are eliminated before it is willing to grant a rule.

Controversy has surrounded the Rules Committee for many years owing to its practice of substituting its judgment for that of the party leadership and the committee leadership. Dominated by a conservative coalition of Southern Democrats and Republicans, and led by Congressman Howard Smith of Virginia until his defeat in 1966, it placed roadblocks in the way of many pieces of legislation desired by liberals. In 1961, the Rules Committee was enlarged to permit the appointment of more Democrats who would vote with the party leadership, and in 1965 a rule was adopted providing for consideration of any bill which the Rules Committee has blocked for 21 days. This immediately made possible consideration on the floor of six measures that the Rules Committee had refused to report.

In spite of its frustration of majority will on important pieces of legislation, there is general agreement in the House that the Committee performs a useful function when it cooperates with the leadership. It prevents bills from reaching the floor that are not genuinely favored by the members but would be embarrassing to vote against if they were forced to vote. Veterans' pension legislation is a case in point. Moreover, by imposing restrictions on the manner in which bills may be considered, it prevents the worst excesses of logrolling, such as might occur on tariff and tax legislation.

Defenders of the Rules Committee correctly point out that there are other channels through which the majority may work its will. One of these is the discharge petition, by which a majority of the whole House may remove the jurisdiction over a bill from the Rules Committee. But members are reluctant to use this weapon, because it may bring reprisals against them and also their committees, and because such action violates one of the basic norms of the House: deference to its committees and their specialized roles. The discharge route is nevertheless followed, at least as often as one time per session. Passage by the House in 1965 of a Home Rule bill for the District of Columbia, bitterly opposed by the Southern Democrats and many Republicans, was accomplished through the discharge petition. The passage of the Civil Rights Acts of 1960 and 1964 was accomplished under the threat of the successful use of this petition.

Another frequently used device to bypass the Rules Committee is the suspension of the rules. It is used for bills having overwhelming support.

But debate on such measures is severely limited and no amendments are permitted, thus making it a take it or leave it proposition for the members of the House.

Consideration on the Floor of the House of Representatives

The House considers legislation in the Committee of the Whole, where the debate is controlled by a floor manager of the bill—a member and often the chairman of the committee—and a representative of the minority. Because of the severe limitations on debate in the House, the prolixity so characteristic of the Senate is absent. The speeches are concise explanations of the bill, criticisms of it, or enthusiastic outbursts of oratory. Debate is better attended in the House, at least in part because votes so closely follow upon debate, but it is doubtful that many minds are changed as a result of the oratory.

On the termination of debate, the bill is read for amendments and votes are taken either by (1) voice vote, (2) by a standing head count called a division, or (3) by a teller vote in which the members are counted as they pass by "tellers" who count those for and against the amendment. When the Committee of the Whole "rises" and reports to the House, the latter then may vote on any amendment adopted in the Committee of the Whole, or recommit the bill to the original committee that considered the bill, thus effectively killing it for that session. Final action then occurs, usually by roll-call vote. Approval requires a majority of those present and voting.

The Senate

As a second legislative chamber, the Senate of the United States is unique because of its equal standing with the House. There is no second chamber in any other democracy matching the influence and power of the Senate. In other countries, the power of the second chamber is usually one of delay only. In England, for example, the House of Lords has no jurisdiction whatever in financial legislation. Some democracies, like Norway and Israel, have no second chamber at all. In federal systems, such as the United States, Canada, Australia, and Switzerland, there has to be a second chamber to represent the interests of the territorial units of the federal union.

Much of what occurs in the Senate follows the pattern described in the House. Yet the general atmosphere of the Senate is so markedly different that some attention must be given to its distinctive features.

Because of its smaller size, the Senate is much less formal in its manner of operation. Many commentators refer to it as a "club" and the term fits the atmosphere. Rather than being ruled by disciplined majorities, it is governed by unanimous consent. Courtliness of manner is the traditional hallmark of senatorial behavior, not always adhered to, to be sure. Senators consider themselves the "upper house" and therefore patronize the House members, to the chagrin of the latter. Constantly sought out for their views on all manner of public issues, the senators are much more likely to consider themselves fountains of wisdom on a diverse range of topics. Because they represent many broad groups within their states, they are expected to be conversant with all legislative topics. Some of them are considered presidential "timber" and therefore have a national audience to speak to. Instead of serving on one or two committees, senators may serve on as many as four major committees, and must equip themselves to deal with widely diverse topics. Senator Javits of New York, for example, has served on over twenty Senate committees and subcommittees, including the committees on Government Operations, Judiciary, Labor and Public Welfare, Small Business, and the Joint Economic Committee.

Although the Senate is in most ways coequal with the House of Representatives, there are differences in their authority, which make for variations in their approach toward lawmaking. The fact that revenue measures constitutionally must, and appropriations traditionally do, originate in the House means that the Senate acts as a kind of appeal body with regard to decisions made in the House. This is particularly true with regard to appropriations, where the Senate often increases the amounts recommended by the House. This revising function often extends to other legislation, however, such as civil rights and education.

Its responsibility for giving advice and consent on treaties signed by the President has given to the Senate a pre-eminence generally in the field of foreign affairs. The major debates on foreign policy usually occur in the Senate, and these are given wide coverage by the communications media. The Senate Foreign Relations Committee has been recognized as the chief congressional instrument for consultation with the President on foreign policy, and for guidance of the Congress with regard to foreign policy. The inquiry by the Senate Foreign Relations Committee into the purposes and limits of the conflict in Vietnam in 1966 illustrates well the role that the Senate has played in this area. As foreign policy has required financial support, the House has acquired more influence than it used to have in the past. But in the public discussion of foreign policy issues, the Senate still retains its primacy.

Partisanship is characteristic of the Senate as it is of the House of

Representatives, but the operation of the Senate is much less a partisan affair. Whereas control of the agenda of the House is shared by the Majority Leader and the Rules Committee, the agenda of the Senate are controlled by the Majority Leader and the majority party policy committee. The difference lies in the fact that nearly everything done in the Senate is done by unanimous consent. This applies to bringing bills to the floor, scheduling debate, imposing limitations on debate, and virtually every other phase of Senate activity. There are no special "rules" governing debate nor any previous question to curtail debate; rather by a process of consultation the various groups in the Senate reach an agreement on procedure. Hence, the more effective the Majority Leader is in bringing together the leaders of these various interests, the more smoothly the Senate will run. It was in this regard that Senator Lyndon Johnson proved himself the master.

The Filibuster

This informal method of operation leaves the way open to the most famous feature of Senate procedure—the filibuster. The filibuster is, to use neutral language, extended debate. Traditionally opposed to curtailing debate until every individual who wishes to speak has done so, the Senate thereby permits an individual or determined minority to stall the Senate and prevent it from acting on the legislation under consideration. The justification of the practice is found in the power of such debate to inform the country of the issues involved in the legislation, but the intent is clearly to prevent action when a minority recognizes that it will be defeated. It is a last-ditch technique, and is relatively seldom utilized. In recent decades the filibuster has been used principally by southern senators to prevent the passage of civil rights legislation. It should be noted that the liberals have on occasion made use of the practice of unlimited debate also: they debated at length the 1954 amendments to the Atomic Energy Act, and in 1962 they engaged in a full-scale filibuster over the creation of the Communications Satellite Corporation.

Occasionally individual senators will speak for extended periods—the record is held by Senator Strom Thurmond, who spoke for 24 hours and 18 minutes in 1957—but these one-man oratorical displays are clearly to highlight an issue or gain publicity, or both. The effective filibusters are conducted by a band of senators who are determined to hold the floor until the majority despair of breaking their will and therefore move to consider other legislation. They are especially effective toward the end of the session of Congress, when there is much business to be done. As the Senate practices do not require that a speaker's address be relevant to the issue at hand, he may wander from reading the Bible to providing the senators recipes for "pot licker."

The Cloture Rule. Debate in the Senate may be limited only by the adoption of the cloture rule. In essence this rule permits a two-thirds majority of those present and voting to limit debate. Once adopted, debate continues, but each senator is allowed only one hour of speaking on all amendments and on final passage of the bill.

Cloture has been adopted very infrequently—only seven times—since its approval by the Senate in 1917. This record testifies both to the infrequent need for formal limitations on debate and to the inefficacy of the cloture rule for closing off debate. A determined minority opposed to some policy, plus those who revere the principle of unlimited debate, can usually combine to defeat a cloture motion. Thus, in 1966, when the Democratic leadership in the Senate, on the urging of President Johnson, sought limitation of debate on the motion to take up consideration of a proposal to delete the right-to-work provision of the Taft-Hartley Act, the Senate refused to do so by a margin of 51–48, far short of the needed two-thirds majority. There have been efforts to strengthen the cloture rule by allowing limitations of debate by three-fifths, absolute and simple majorities, but these have not gained much favor.

The filibuster has its share of critics and supporters. The critics (the liberal elements in both parties) argue that it prevents majorities from acting, makes a mockery of the legislative process in that it prevents decision on the *merits* of legislation, and denies the capacity of argument to persuade. The defenders of the filibuster (the conservatives in both parties) urge its retention in a vital form as a means of protecting minority rights against the tyranny of numbers, either to prevent action or to force some acceptable compromise; an intransigent minority can prevent the majority from acting irresponsibly under the influence of momentary passion or crisis. The Senate is the only legislative body in the world in which a minority is able to impose its will on the majority by means of the filibuster.

The Conference Committee

Important legislation seldom passes the two houses of Congress in identical form. If the differences are minor, the originating house may agree to the amendments proposed by the second chamber, thus obviating any further reconciliation of differences. Generally, however, it is necessary to reconcile such differences through the appointment of conference committees, which consist of the committee chairmen, the ranking minority leaders, and other seniority leaders on the committees in each house.

The conferees operate under rather special circumstances. The members are expected to defend the position assumed by each chamber in the passage of the bill in that chamber, but the overriding consideration is resolution of the conflict in a manner that will prove acceptable to the members of both houses. They are under considerable time pressure, especially as the session draws to an end and the members are anxious to clear the legislative decks. Their reports are usually accepted with little or no debate. Meeting in secret, they are in a position to determine the fate of the bills before them, without being subjected to the numerous outside pressures that normally are a part of the legislative process.

The usual result is a compromise between the positions taken in each house. On authorization or appropriations bills, this compromise is often made in rather exact terms, by halving the difference between the amounts authorized or appropriated by each house. On legislative matters, the representatives of each house will give in on some matters and stand firm on others, jockeying to protect those interests most dearly held by their colleagues.

There have been cases when the conference committees have adopted provisions rather startlingly different from those in dispute between the two houses. Studies of the work of these committees indicate, however, that instances of this kind are relatively few. The bargaining is hard, and the positions of the two houses are jealously guarded. In spite of the allegedly greater prestige of the Senate, the House members, because of their detailed knowledge of legislation, more often than not get their way.

The President Decides

Once majorities of the two houses have agreed on the legislation in identical form, the bill is sent to the President for his signature. At this point the Bureau of the Budget, acting for the President, circularizes the bill among the departments and agencies concerned with the subject matter, asking for their comments and views. Of necessity, this review must be brief because the President has only ten days within which to decide whether he will sign the bill or not.

If there is serious objection from the departments and the Bureau, the latter may prepare a draft of a veto message for the President and his aides to consider. If he decides to veto the bill, he must reckon with the extent of support the bill received in the two houses, for they may override his veto by a two-thirds majority of those present and voting. The President may normally count on a number of legislators of his party who will change their initial votes, recognizing his role as party leader. But a veto overridden may be interpreted as a sign of weakness in the Presidency and provide impetus for increasing rebellion even within the President's own party. There are, of course, other options open to him. He may refuse to sign the bill, allowing it to become law without his signature; he may refuse to sign a bill passed less than ten days from the end of the session, thus killing the bill by a "pocket" veto; or he may sign the bill, at the same time asking for revisions. Each of these softens the edge of the veto, and reduces the sharpness of the conflict between the two branches.

The few times each session that the President exercises this prerogative attests to the care with which Congress acts to avoid a veto. The possibility of such rejection is a specter that congressmen must constantly be aware of as they legislate. The infrequency of its use indicates also the desire of Congress to legislate rather than to create issues.

The Future Role of Congress

The critics of Congress are legion and its defenders are relatively few. Even among thoughtful and astute members of Congress, severe indictments are lodged against the present legislative system. Senator Joseph Clark calls Congress *The Sapless Branch*, and Congressman Richard Bolling refers to the House of Representatives as the *House Out of Order*. During the Van Buren administration, when such giants as Clay, Webster, Benton, Calhoun, and John Quincy Adams were serving in Congress, it was stated that "A more weak, bigoted, persecuting, and intolerant set of instruments of malice and every hateful passion, were never assembled in a legislative capacity in any age or any land." Mark Twain at one point said, "Suppose you were an idiot, and suppose you were a member of Congress; but I repeat myself."[6]

Chief among these indictments is the allegation that Congress consists of a congregation of "locals," that is, individuals whose base of power is in their local communities and whose vision of the public interest does not transcend the interests of their constituencies. In contrast, the President represents a broad national constituency and therefore maintains a perspective that is national in focus and responsive to the broad major interests of majorities within our society. The result is conflict between the pleaders for local self-interests and the representative of the general interest, which in turn means deadlock and inaction.

Second, it is argued that the Congress is irresponsible, that it is a large assembly of men whose actions are relatively uncontrolled and uncontrol-

[6] Alexander Wiley, *Laughing with Congress* (New York: Crown, 1947), p. 3.

lable by the people in whose interest they are purportedly acting. Because the political parties to which they nominally belong do not provide a firm rallying point for their actions, the individual voter cannot know to whom he should assign the credit or blame for past legislative action.

Third, it is alleged that Congress is relatively incompetent in dealing with the major policy issues of contemporary life. In spite of its efforts to improve its technical capacity through its committee system and through the employment of technical staffs, Congress remains woefully inadequate in the making of public policy in comparison with the expertise exhibited by the executive branch.

The remedies most frequently recommended for this allegedly sick institution usually involve a fundamental change in the political system itself. The most consistent recommendation calls for a revision of the party system, making the parties more highly centralized and capable of imposing discipline on their elected members. Members elected under the sponsorship of the parties would be required to support these positions rather than the parochial interests of their own areas. The parties and the individual members would thereby be more "responsible" to their voters. On the question of legislative competence, the critics argue that Congress must cease attempting to act as a legislative body; rather, it must restrict itself to debate, to the granting or withholding of consent, to scrutiny of executive actions. For the performance of these functions, Congress is presently admirably structured and staffed.

Recommendations such as these meet decided resistance from the American public as well as from many seasoned observers and practitioners of the legislative arts. For them, the fact that Congress is more locally oriented is its glory in that it permits the minority interest to be heard and to be counted. Instead of being submerged in an amalgam called a national party platform, these tenaciously held local interests can be protected by their strategic positions in the legislative process. Such protection for minorities is simple recognition that the public interest is not a national policy supported by large and powerful groups but is achieved by satisfying the interests of a wide variety of limited groups found in all parts of the country. The goal of these minorities is compromise, not obstruction, and this is what is achieved under the present circumstances. That Congress *can* act is demonstrated by the outpouring of basic legislation during the first years of the Johnson administration.

On the charge that it is irresponsible, the defender of Congress argues that party means more than the critics allege; indeed it is the single most important determinant of behavior in Congress. It is not the *sole* determinant, nor should it be. The parties reflect the basic coalition of forces through which the country is governed, and any effort to impose iron discipline would destroy the parties in some areas, making one-party representation virtually a certainty. Allowance must be made for regional and local differences even within the parties.

Finally, Congress cannot hope to challenge the executive in general expertise. But it can often provide reasonable alternatives, changes in focus, and different judgments on speed and direction of public policy. Its *political* judgment, as distinct from its technical competence, may be far superior to that of the President or his army of aides, administrators, and experts. Congress may operate on the margins of public policy-making, but these margins may be the elements that make public policies operative.

Dramatic changes in the legislative system in Congress are not likely to occur. The system is complex and frustrating for those who embark on legislative action. But respond it does, reflecting the pressures of both those who have something to gain or lose by legislative action and the moral and political convictions of the congressmen themselves.

CHAPTER 18

THE PRESIDENCY

Modern democracies may be broadly classified into two types: parliamentary and presidential. Of the two, parliamentary democracy has a longer history. Originating in Britain, it has evolved through several centuries to its present form in that country, has been transplanted to the Commonwealth nations, and has been adopted with variations by a number of countries in Europe and on other continents.

Under the parliamentary system, executive powers are divided between the titular chief of state, the political executive, and the Cabinet. The chief of state may be a hereditary monarch as in Britain, Belgium, or Japan, or he may be a president elected for a fixed term of office as he is in West Germany, Ireland, and Italy. In either instance he exercises very little political power; other than performing ceremonial functions, his primary responsibility is to designate the political executive who may be called prime minister, premier, or chancellor. The political executive holds office because he is the leader of the majority party or is able to organize a coalition Cabinet that has the support of a majority in parliament.

The presidential system originated in the Constitutional Convention in Philadelphia in 1787. The framers of the Constitution joined into one elective office the ceremonial duties and prestige of the king and the political power of the prime minister. The President of the United States, then, is both chief of state and chief of government, and the Presidency is one of America's principal political innovations. The presidential system has been adopted by a number of countries including Mexico, Colombia,

460

the Philippines, and Pakistan, but in no country does it operate as in the United States.

The records of the Constitutional Convention reveal that the vision of a chief executive who could act energetically, promptly and responsibly did not easily become reality. From their experience with the British monarch, George III, the Founding Fathers realized the danger inherent in a strong executive unless restrained by law and institutional checks. Yet, they recognized the weakness of government under the Articles of Confederation when there had been a legislature but no separate executive; as Thomas Jefferson noted, "173 despots could surely be as oppressive as one."

From the writings of political theorists, in particular, Locke and Montesquieu, and from their experiences with colonial and state governments, most of the delegates at the Constitutional Convention had come to favor a government based on the principle of separation of powers. A variety of proposals were suggested regarding the office of Chief Executive. Some delegates favored a plural executive of two or three persons with equal powers; others advocated a single executive. Some suggested that the executive be chosen for a six-year term and not be eligible for reelection; and others proposed that Congress select the Chief Executive. Finally the decision was made for the executive to be a single man—the President of the United States—separate from the legislature, elected by the electoral college for a four-year term with no prohibitions regarding reelection and having his powers granted by the Constitution. The men who drafted the Constitution preferred the safety of the separation of powers to the presumed efficiency of the fusion of powers which characterizes the parliamentary system.

☙ THE PRESIDENCY: QUALIFICATIONS AND PERQUISITES

The Constitution provides that the President must be at least 35 years of age, have resided in the United States for at least fourteen years, and be a "natural born citizen." Apparently included among "natural born citizens" are persons born abroad of American parents. Although Theodore Roosevelt succeeded to the office at age 42, John Kennedy at age 43 was the youngest elected President, and he followed Dwight Eisenhower, who, at age 70 when he left the White House, was the oldest person to hold that office. Since the adoption of the Twentieth Amendment in 1933, the President has taken office on January 20.

As is commonly known, the precedent of a President holding office for only two terms was established by George Washington, and was followed by Thomas Jefferson, Andrew Jackson, and others who, like Washington, could have been elected to a third term had they sought it. Both Ulysses S. Grant and Woodrow Wilson desired but did not receive the nomination for a third term; Theodore Roosevelt's nomination in 1912 is usually interpreted as a third term effort, even though he had succeeded to the Presidency upon William McKinley's death and had been elected only once previously. Franklin Roosevelt won election to a third term in 1940 and a fourth in 1944. The Twenty-second Amendment, which went into effect in 1951, limits any subsequent President to two elections and no more than ten years in office.

Congress establishes the salary and perquisites of the office, subject to the constitutional provision that the salary may not be increased or decreased during the term of the incumbent. The President now receives an annual salary of $100,000 plus an expense allowance of $50,000, both of which are taxable, and a $40,000 travel allowance which is tax free. In addition, he is provided a mansion, airplanes, helicopters, cabin cruisers, vacation retreats, and automobiles, as well as protection for himself and his family by the White House police and Secret Service staff. A separate budget provides allowances for entertainment, travel, maintenance of the White House, upkeep of equipment, and salaries of crews. Although it costs about $7,000,000 yearly to pay the President and operate the White House (as compared with $5½ million to maintain the British monarchy), some Presidents find it necessary to spend beyond the official salary out of their private income.

Presidential Succession

In a country with a parliamentary government, if the prime minister dies or is unable to continue in office, there is little danger of the country's remaining without a chief executive for long, because the parliament may select a new prime minister at any time. The separate election of the President for a fixed period of time led the Founding Fathers to provide for a reserve or stand-by President—the Vice-President. The Constitution provides that "in case of the removal of the President from office, or of his death, resignation, or inability to discharge the powers and duties of said office, the same shall devolve on the Vice-President. . . ."

This provision of the Constitution left three questions unanswered. First, when a President dies, does the Vice-President become President or merely assume the powers and responsibilities of the office? This question was answered, in effect, by John Tyler, the Vice-President at the time of the death of the first President to die in office; Tyler decided that the Constitution intended for the Vice-President to be President, and the seven other Vice-Presidents who have succeeded to the Presidency when a President died have accepted his precedent.

The second question is less easily answered, for it deals not with the finality of the death of the President, but with the indefinite "inability to discharge the powers and duties of said office." Who should decide if the President is disabled and the Vice-President should take over the duties of the office? President James A. Garfield clung to life for nearly three months after he was shot in 1886. After President Wilson's physical collapse and stroke in the fall of 1919, he was unable even to attend a Cabinet meeting for more than six months and was not able to perform all duties of his office for the remaining eleven months of his Presidency. In neither instance did the Vice-President assume presidential duties.

The third unanswered question is this: If the President dies and there is no Vice-President, who then becomes President? Congress at one time provided for the Secretary of State to be first in line of succession to be followed by the other Cabinet members. In 1947 Congress changed the law to provide that the Speaker of the House and the president pro tempore of the Senate be first in line of succession to the Presidency, to be followed by the Secretary of State and other Cabinet members.

The Twenty-fifth Amendment to the Constitution answers the questions regarding presidential succession and disability. Under this amendment if the President dies, resigns, or is removed from office, the Vice-President becomes President. Whenever the office of Vice-President becomes vacant, the President shall nominate a Vice-President, who takes office after a vote of confirmation by Congress. If the President believes he is unable to perform the duties of office, he informs Congress in writing, and the Vice-President serves as acting President until the President is ready to resume his duties. Should the President become disabled and unable to communicate this fact, the Vice-President with a majority of the Cabinet, notifies Congress, and the Vice-President serves as acting President until the President has recovered. In case of a disagreement regarding the President's disability or recovery, Congress has the power to decide whether the President or the Vice-President should carry out the duties of the office.

ഇ ROLES OF THE PRESIDENT

The Presidency has grown far beyond the expectations of even the most imaginative member of the Constitutional Convention. Article II of the Constitution, which states that the "Executive Power shall be vested in a

President of the United States," is one of the most indefinite of the Constitution. While setting forth certain powers and responsibilities of the office, the Constitution provides relatively little guidance for understanding the role of the nation's Chief Executive in this second half of the twentieth century. This lack of rigidity in the Constitution, however, has made it possible for the Presidency to expand or contract to meet conditions of changing times. Like the British Cabinet system, the powers and influence of the American Chief Executive result more from custom, practice, and the impact of personality than from the prescriptions set forth in a written document.

Calvin Coolidge once said that "the Presidency does not yield to definition," and Woodrow Wilson asserted that it was "one thing at one time, another at another." In attempting to understand this complex office, the Presidency today might be analyzed as seven offices in one. The President is at once the chief of state, chief legislator, chief administrator, leader of his party, commander in chief, chief diplomat, and national leader.

✻ THE PRESIDENT AS CHIEF OF STATE

As chief of state the President performs many of the functions of monarchs in such countries as Great Britain, Holland, Sweden, and Greece. The fact that these democracies retain their monarchs is evidence that in those countries the royal family is believed to fill a useful role. The President—and those monarchs—serve as symbols of the unity, continuity, and purpose of the country. They help to personalize what might otherwise appear as a distant and impersonal government. Presidents of such countries as West Germany, Italy, Switzerland, and India also serve as titular heads of state and perform similar ceremonial duties, but their positions are less prestigious.

Because of the relatively short history of the United States, the Presidency is more important as a national symbol than in nations with longer traditions and more settled national institutions. In the United States there is no institution other than the Presidency—with the possible exception of the Constitution—which serves as a focal point through which the people can identify not only with the state but with each other.

In countries where there is a monarchy, the royal family adds interest, glamor, and pageantry to the lives of the people. Lacking a royal family, the American people regard the President's family as the "first family" of the nation. The personal lives of the President, his wife, and children become, in effect, public lives, as the newspapers almost daily report on their social activities, habits, the way they dress, and their choice of friends.

Ceremonial Head of the Nation

As the ceremonial head of the nation, the President is expected to engage in a variety of activities. He greets and entertains visiting dignitaries from other countries. He receives delegations of businessmen, labor leaders, farmers, educators, and representatives of many other groups. He decorates astronauts, returning war heroes, and government employees. He addresses such groups as the United States Chamber of Commerce, AFL–CIO, and the American Legion. He throws out the first ball of the baseball season, buys the first Christmas seal, serves as the honorary president of the Boy Scouts, reviews parades, proclaims national holidays, and visits foreign countries as the chief of state. While he may delegate some of these responsibilities to the Vice-President, Cabinet members, or leaders of Congress, he personally performs most of these activities, for in their performance he is adding to his own stature, prestige, and influence. He thereby enhances all of his roles and powers, for he is seen as the representative of the entire nation, the symbol of our country.

The Founding Fathers obviously intended that the President be the nation's chief of state or chief magistrate. During Washington's first term a congressional committee sought a title suitable for the office of the President. They considered "His Excellency," "His Elective Majesty," and "His Highness, the President of the United States and Protector of Their Liberties." The fact that the President has come to be called, "Mr. President," dignifies the office and our democratic government in a manner more appropriate than the more regal titles first suggested.

Pardoning Power

The President's role as chief magistrate is also indicated by the judicial powers which were granted him. While creating a separate judicial branch of government, the Constitution authorized the President to appoint judges and "to grant reprieves and pardons for offenses against the United States except in cases of impeachment." Under this power he can temporarily postpone punishment, reduce a sentence, issue a pardon with certain restrictions, or grant a complete release from penalty. Annually the President, acting on the advice of the Attorney General, rules on thousands of requests for reprieves and pardons, and neither Congress nor the courts can overrule his decisions.

⚹ THE PRESIDENT AS CHIEF LEGISLATOR

While the President as chief of state performs functions similar to those of the British monarch, legislative responsibilities now cast him in a role somewhat comparable to that of the British prime minister. Most of our recent Presidents have developed legislative programs and worked for their enactment. Although originally indicating that he believed the separation of powers doctrine precluded the President from providing legislative leadership, Dwight Eisenhower later accurately analyzed the mid-twentieth-century legislative role of the President when he announced: "I am part of the legislative process."

The public has identified major legislative programs with the President and not with Congress. For example, Franklin Roosevelt, not the Seventy-third Congress, is properly given credit for the New Deal legislation; and Lyndon Johnson, not the Eighty-ninth Congress, is credited with civil rights and antipoverty legislation. Several Presidents, besides Franklin Roosevelt, have sought to dramatize their legislative programs by giving them descriptive labels. Theodore Roosevelt had the "Square Deal"; Woodrow Wilson, the "New Freedom"; Harry Truman, the "Fair Deal"; John Kennedy, the "New Frontier"; and Lyndon Johnson, the "Great Society."

The complexity of the times and the speed at which change occurs requires the President to serve as chief legislator. Prior to this century, when there was gradual social and economic change and the nation had few commitments abroad, presidential leadership of Congress was desirable but not essential. The revolutionary technological advances and changes of recent decades and America's worldwide international obligations require dynamic and imaginative leadership for Congress, leadership which only the President is capable of providing. In actuality, the role of legislative leader has devolved upon the President out of necessity: he is the only person who has the responsibility and the facilities to develop a comprehensive nationwide program, and whose position enables him to organize sufficient support from the public and the legislators to secure its adoption.

If Congress is to have effective leadership, it must be provided by the President, for there is no official or group of officials within Congress capable of providing continuous leadership for the 535 members of the House and Senate. Each member of Congress tends to think of himself as the representative of his congressional district or state; and most of them, in order to be re-elected, feel compelled to give precedence to local problems if they conflict with national issues. There are, of course, within each house certain individuals who, because of their positions or personality, can influence many of their colleagues. But within either house such leadership often is not enduring, and seldom is one individual or group able to bridge the gap separating the two houses.

The President's success in each of his roles is determined somewhat by his relations with Congress, for as chief of the administration, he must see that the needs of the departments and agencies are met, and that workable laws are enacted; as the chief diplomat and the commander in chief he must obtain congressional support for our foreign commitments and see that the requirements of our armed services are provided; and as head of his party, he attempts to secure the enactment of the party platform. The President has both constitutional and extraconstitutional powers that may be used in leading Congress, but their successful employment requires considerable political knowledge and skill, attributes with which all Presidents have not been equally endowed.

❊ THE PRESIDENT AS CHIEF ADMINISTRATOR

In accordance with the tripartite division of power, the President as head of the executive branch, is enjoined by the Constitution to "take care that the laws be faithfully executed." He is authorized to appoint public officials, and "he may require the opinion, in writing, of the principal officer in each of the executive departments, upon any subject relating to the duties of their respective offices." As the framers of the Constitution conceived the office, the President's primary role would be that of chief administrator. Based on these constitutional provisions and later congressional enactments, the President has the responsibility for overseeing the operations of the executive branch of government.

The President's role as chief administrator has been vastly expanded by congressional delegation of broad discretionary powers to administrators. This is largely a twentieth-century development. In our early history much legislation was self-executing—Congress passed laws and left the enforcement to individuals who brought action in court against offenders. As society has grown more complex and the activities of government have multiplied, Congress has created numerous administrative agencies to enforce public policies. Many statutes have been enacted that set forth general policies and the conditions under which certain actions may be taken. Congress has delegated to the President and other executive officers the responsibility of determining when these conditions exist, and for filling in the details of the laws through the issuance of executive directives—orders, rules, and regulations. These executive directives, known as "delegated legislation," have the force of law and are published in the Federal Register. Through the granting of such discretionary powers to the President and his top-level administrators, the responsibilities of the Chief Executive have been enlarged.

Although the President as chief administrator has the responsibility for directing and coordinating the governmental agencies, for several practical reasons, it is difficult for him to exercise effective control. First, because of his various other responsibilities, the President is able to devote very little time to supervising the myriad departments and offices; at best, he is a part-time administrator. Second, the sheer number of agencies and governmental personnel renders it virtually impossible for one individual to supervise their activities even if he could devote full time to the task. At present there are about 1,800 executive agencies with nearly 3 million employees. Third, the President shares with Congress control over the federal agencies. Congress creates them, defines their functions, appropriates funds for their operations, and often specifies their procedures and organization. Thus, as was explained previously, the Constitution provides for a system of *shared* powers rather than a clear-cut separation of powers. Fourth, several administrative units—including the Interstate Commerce Commission, Federal Reserve Board, and others—have an independent or semi-independent status; and some agencies, such as the Army Corps of Engineers, because of their particular relationship with members of Congress, are relatively free from presidential direction. Finally, other factors— such as the demands of political interest groups or bureaucratic inertia and tradition—may lead an executive agency to ignore the wishes of a President.

Means of Administrative Control

The principal means by which the President may exercise control over the administrative establishments are the executive budget, his power to reorganize, and his appointment and removal powers.

Budgetary Control. The functioning of the Bureau of the Budget, which has been made part of the Executive Office of the President, will be discussed in Chapter 20 but here it should be noted that the executive budget provides the President with an effective instrument of administrative control. Through the drafting of the budget the President passes on the plans and programs of the administrative agencies, determines how much money they may spend, and exercises some control over them. After Congress approves the budget, the Bureau of the Budget, having the responsibility for supervising its execution, maintains a continuous surveillance over expenditures to see that they are consistent with the President's entire program.

Administrative Reorganization.   Since the late 1930s Presidents have had greater power than formerly over the executive branch through their authority to reorganize the administrative agencies. Although Congress creates the agencies and prescribes their activities, it has been recognized that the President as the chief administrator should have the authority to transfer and regroup administrative units. Prior to 1939 the reorganization of administrative agencies usually required an act of Congress, a cumbersome and often time-consuming procedure. Since then, Congress, acting on the recommendations of the Committee on Administrative Management and the two Hoover Commissions (Commissions on Organization of the Executive Branch of the Government), adopted a different procedure and has renewed it several times. When a reorganization of an agency or agencies is desired, the President may submit the proposed reorganization to Congress. If within sixty days neither of the two houses rejects the plan, it goes into effect.

Appointment Powers.   The Constitution provides for the President to make two types of appointments. First, it states that the President "shall nominate, and by and with the advice and consent of the Senate, shall appoint ambassadors, other public ministers and consuls, judges of the Supreme Court and all other officers of the United States, whose appointments" are not otherwise provided by law. Second, Congress may authorize the President, or department heads, to appoint, without Senate confirmation, "inferior officers," and Congress may determine which officials are to be so classified.

Of the officials requiring confirmation, the Senate generally permits the President virtually complete freedom in choosing persons who will fill key positions in his official family—such as the United States Ambassador to the United Nations, the department Secretaries and the personnel of the Executive Office of the President. The rejection of Lewis L. Strauss as Secretary of Commerce in 1959 is the only example, since 1925, of a proposed Cabinet member being denied approval by the Senate. The Senate also usually approves, with little debate, the President's nominations for other top administrative positions, diplomatic posts abroad, and justices of the Supreme Court. However, in order to avoid possible difficulties, Presidents often inform Senate leaders regarding such proposed appointments prior to making the nominations.

"Senatorial courtesy" applies to most other positions requiring Senate confirmation. According to custom, the President, previous to sending such nominations to the Senate, consults the senators of his party from those states in which the appointments are to be made. Included among positions affected by senatorial courtesy are district court judges, postmasters, and federal marshals. If the President fails to consult with a senator of his party on such an appointment, the senator may declare the appointment "personally obnoxious" and request that confirmation be refused, and the Senate usually complies. In practice, senatorial courtesy places with the senators of the President's party the power to fill most federal positions in their states.

Although the great majority of the federal employees are selected through the Civil Service system, and many other positions are in effect filled by senators, the President through his appointments establishes to a large extent the tone and reputation of his administration. Most Presidents, having neither the time nor the staff to supervise the work of the multitudinous governmental agencies, have realized that the most effective means for ensuring that "the laws be faithfully executed" is through the appointment of able, courageous, and public-spirited individuals. As Presidents Grant, Harding, and others have found, the appointment of inefficient or dishonest individuals can do inestimable harm to the country and create scandals that will damage the reputation of the President and his administration.

Presidents have found recruiting able administrative personnel to be a difficult task. When a President takes office after his party has been out of power, as did Eisenhower in 1952 and John F. Kennedy in 1960, he customarily replaces most of the persons in the top administrative positions. Presidents usually request their friends and acquaintances to suggest names of possible appointees. President Johnson's staff developed a coded file of 20,000 prospective appointees, and with the use of an electronic computer, could swiftly select the names of several persons to present to the President when it was necessary to fill a position. Because of the relatively low salaries in government in comparison with private industry and with no assurance of a permanent position, many prospective appointees with executive experience in business have been reluctant to accept government positions. Salaries more comparable to those paid by industry would help solve the problem of recruiting able administrators.

Removal Powers. The Supreme Court ruled in 1926 (*Myers* v. *U.S.*) that the President could remove any appointive official who performs strictly executive functions and that Congress may not limit that power. In later decisions the Supreme Court announced that members of the independent regulatory agencies, such as the Interstate Commerce Commission and the Federal Communications Commission, who perform duties of a quasi-legislative or quasi-judicial nature could be removed only for such causes as neglect of duty, inefficiency, or malfeasance in office (*Humphrey's Executor* v. *U.S.*, 1935, and *Wiener* v. *U.S.*, 1958). Civil service employees can be removed from office only in accordance with civil service rules.

While the President has the authority to dismiss any appointive official exercising strictly executive powers, in some instances he may be unwilling to risk the consequences of such a removal. The dismissal of a department head or other high-level official, particularly those who are well known and have a national following, may create such a controversy that the President may prefer to allow him to continue in office even if he has not proved entirely satisfactory. Even officials with less prestige—such as an assistant secretary, an agency head, or a bureau chief—may have sufficient support from certain party leaders, members of Congress, or a political interest group that the President, although wishing to dismiss the person, may retain him rather than chance the political repercussion that might result from his dismissal.

The powers of the President as chief administrator are obviously not commensurate with his responsibilities. Although he wields influence and authority over the administrative agencies, it is not sufficient to guarantee a high degree of unity and coordination, or to insure that all agencies accede to his wishes. The President finds that his department heads are subjected to the influence of others, including Congress, their administrative subordinates, and the clientele of their departments.

In all large organizations—major corporations as well as governments— the principal executive power is the power of persuasion and not the power of command. The President's success as an administrative leader will depend largely on his ability to persuade those directly under him to support his policies, and he will find that giving an order will not necessarily assure that it is carried out. Harry Truman commented shortly before Dwight Eisenhower succeeded him in office: "He'll sit here, and he'll say, 'Do this! Do that!' *And nothing will happen.* Poor Ike—it won't be a bit like the Army."[1]

☆ THE PRESIDENT AS PARTY LEADER

Even individuals with little prior experience in partisan politics—such as college president Woodrow Wilson and generals Zachary Taylor and Dwight Eisenhower—have been elected as party men. Regardless of the

[1] Quoted in Richard E. Neustadt, *Presidential Power* (New York: Wiley, 1960), p. 26.

President's previous positions and experience, upon his nomination he becomes the leader of his party and he continues in that capacity as long as he is in the White House. As Clinton Rossiter has said, the President is the "Chief Republican" or the "Chief Democrat,"[2] and he must "put his hand firmly to the plow of politics." The President's statements become the most authoritative pronouncements on party policies. He is expected to carry out the party platform, which often he has helped to draft, and while in office he usually develops his own program, which then becomes the party program. The national party organization is closely identified with the President. The party national chairman, although formally elected by the national committee, is selected first by the President and serves as his agent (see Chapter 14). The national committee staff, in turn, is selected by the national chairman and works under his direction.

Because American national parties tend to be loose alliances of state and local party organizations and are not highly unified or disciplined, as they are in Great Britain, the President has relatively little control over his party. He cannot determine who should be nominated for positions in Congress or for state and local offices, and he cannot even require a state party organization to contribute its proportionate share of the national party budget.

The President and his party cooperate out of mutual need. The President must have the support of the party to be elected and to secure the adoption of his legislative program. Conversely, the success of the party and its candidates throughout the fifty states is dependent upon the popularity and program of the President, as the 1964 election unmistakably showed. As party leader, the President is expected to help raise campaign funds, to select most of his appointees from his party, to attend and address party meetings and rallies, and to assist in the election of at least some partisan candidates. The President may aid party members seeking election by endorsing them, posing for pictures with them, sending subordinates to assist in campaigns, and in some instances Presidents have even delivered campaign addresses for candidates. President Kennedy was on tour as party leader when he was assassinated.

The President's varied responsibilities as political and party leader require him to assume a dual personality. Most Presidents have been active in partisan politics prior to their election. After election each one is expected to lead his party and to work for its success. On the other hand, it is assumed that the President will adopt a nonpartisan role in many matters and be the political leader and spokesman for all the people. Furthermore, if his administration is to be successful, the President must

[2] Clinton Rossiter, *The American Presidency* (New York: New American Library, 1960), p. 29.

have the support of members of both parties. In short, the President is expected to be both a partisan and a nonpartisan political leader. Most Presidents have attempted to solve this apparent dilemma by performing many of their responsibilities in a nonpartisan fashion and at the same time performing those tasks expected of the leader of the party.

✻ THE PRESIDENT AS COMMANDER IN CHIEF

The President is designated by the Constitution as the "Commander in Chief of the Army and Navy of the United States, and the Militia of the several States, when called into the actual Service of the United States." Thus during peace and war the President is the supreme commander of the armed forces. The Founding Fathers, expecting that Washington would be elected President, intended for him to have the authority to take personal command of the troops. However, as one scholar has written, "The Napoleonic concept of the warrior-statesman has not taken root in the United States."[3] Although a number of Presidents—including Washington, Jackson, Grant, and Eisenhower—had had extensive military service, they, unlike President de Gaulle of France and political leaders of various other countries, chose not to wear their uniforms while serving as Chief Executive. In the United States the President serves as the living embodiment of the American belief in the "supremacy of civil over military authority."

Although the primary purpose of the military forces is to protect the security of the nation against external enemies, the President may utilize the regular armed forces and the National Guard for suppressing riots and internal disorders. Presidents, acting on their own authority as commander in chief, have sent troops to troubled areas. In recent years, to prevent defiance of federal laws and court orders in civil rights conflicts Eisenhower ordered troops to Little Rock, Arkansas; Kennedy, to the University of Mississippi; and Johnson, to Dallas County, Alabama. Also upon the request of state officials the President may direct units of the armed forces to assist state and local police in maintaining law and order.

As commander in chief, the President is responsible for training, equipping, and deploying the armed forces. His authority extends to commissioning the officers, deciding on promotions, selecting the officers for the top command and staff positions, and determining the relative strength and particular missions of each branch of the armed services. Naturally, the

[3] Joseph E. Kallenbach, *The American Chief Executive* (New York: Harper & Row, 1966), p. 527.

President delegates most of these tasks to his subordinates in the Department of Defense and to the top-ranking military officers.

The President shares with Congress power over the military. The Constitution authorizes Congress "to raise and support armies" and "to provide and maintain a navy." All appropriations for the military must be provided by the Legislature. Some members of the House and Senate Armed Services committees often take a personal interest in military matters. They not uncommonly attempt to influence such decisions as the selection of sites for military bases, the types of weapons to be developed, and the number and kinds of airplanes, ships, and other weapons to be procured for the armed forces.

While Congress, and not the President, is authorized by the Constitution to declare war, in actuality Congress tends to go along with the President in such declarations. Indeed, a President's recommendation that war be declared has never been denied. Events prior to the declaration of war in 1917 and in 1941 indicate that actions of foreign powers and decisions of the President had placed the United States and its antagonists on collision courses which led to inevitable declarations of war. In 1917 Congress declared war after German submarines had sunk ships with Americans aboard, and it appeared that Germany would dominate the Atlantic. In 1941 Congress declared war after Japanese planes bombed Hawaii.

Wartime Powers

During times of major wars, when the very survival of the nation has appeared to be at stake, the President's powers based on his role as commander in chief have expanded so greatly that this role overshadowed all others. Under war conditions all aspects of life must be geared to the war effort; thus Presidents have felt compelled to take whatever actions they considered essential for winning the war. During the Civil War, acting without authorization from Congress, Lincoln seized control of certain eastern railroads, suspended the writ of habeas corpus, and instituted a blockade of principal southern ports.

During World War II Franklin Roosevelt, learning from the experiences of both Lincoln and Wilson, assumed broader powers than any previous President. The following types of action taken by Roosevelt during World War II are illustrative of the vast powers and responsibilities he assumed, based entirely or in part on the commander in chief clause of the Constitution: 100,000 American citizens of Japanese descent were evacuated from the West Coast; more than sixty strike-bound or strike-threatened industries and plants were seized and operated; and a wide array of emergency boards and offices were created to control virtually every phase of economic life, from the allocation of raw materials needed for war production to the establishment of price control on consumer goods and the rationing of food, shoes, gasoline, and other items.

Most wartime Presidents have participated as commanders in chief in planning overall military strategy. This was true of Polk during the Mexican War and McKinley during the Spanish-American War, as it was of Lincoln during the Civil War and Franklin Roosevelt during World War II. Roosevelt, along with Winston Churchill, determined much of the allied strategy during World War II, including the decisions to win the war in Europe first and then concentrate all forces on the war in Asia.

Before the nuclear age, autonomy of field commanders was respected military doctrine, and it was commonly accepted that the President should not determine the tactics of individual battles. In 1964, for the first time, the question of whether the military commanders or the President should make decisions regarding the use of atomic weapons became an issue in a presidential campaign. Candidate Barry Goldwater took the position that commanders in the field should make decisions regarding the use of tactical atomic weapons, while Johnson believed that this should be the responsibility of the President.

Now, because of the gravity and complexity of the times, the President is often intimately involved with details of military tactics. President Kennedy is said to have followed the position of every ship during the Cuban missile crisis of 1962. During the Vietnam conflict President Johnson followed the military efforts closely. At times he reportedly participated in the decisions regarding targets to be bombed. There is widespread agreement that military decisions that may have far-reaching political implications should not be left to the generals.

The President's Role in the Nuclear Age

The most far-reaching strategic military decision made by any President as commander in chief was that of President Truman in 1945 to use the atomic bomb. This decision brought World War II to an end and ushered in a complex new era in which the President's role of commander in chief was altered by the frightening new power at his command. In earlier eras, the United States was freer to chart its own course. Now the President, in making decisions of international concern, must consider the opinions, safety, and welfare of the entire world. This greater power imposes greater responsibilities on the President than in the past.

Traditionally, there has been a distinction between the role of the President as commander in chief during peace and in time of war. The nuclear age and advanced military technology, however, have altered the meaning and conditions of peace and war. All-out war is unthinkable; true peace seems unattainable. When modern civilization can be destroyed in hours, the President of the United States is at all times responsible for the security of the nation and indeed of the world. It seems doubtful that there will ever again be a global war of long duration involving millions of armed men. In the nuclear age a nation must be in readiness at all times for a surprise attack. Therefore, the former peacetime role of the President as commander in chief has been enlarged to a continuing semiwar role. On the other hand, when a single decision by the President of the United States runs the risk of what Richard Neustadt terms "irreversibility become irreparable,"[4] the powers of the President as commander in chief are circumscribed. Having unprecedented power at his command, he is less free to use power.

Thus the nuclear age has both enlarged and limited the role of the President as commander in chief. At the same time, the changed role as commander in chief has sharpened and expanded his other roles, making him the most powerful person in the United States and the most influential in the world.

✻ THE PRESIDENT AS CHIEF DIPLOMAT

The Founding Fathers were aware that responsibility for conducting foreign relations must necessarily rest with the Chief Executive. The Constitution authorizes the President to appoint and to receive "ambassadors and other public ministers," and "to make treaties." These powers, however, are shared with Congress, especially with the Senate. Appointments to diplomatic positions must be approved by the Senate, and treaties require a two-thirds vote in the Senate. In addition, Congress, of course, has established the State Department and other agencies involved in foreign affairs and must appropriate funds for salaries and other expenditures.

Conducting Foreign Relations

Constitutionally, the President is the single official channel of communication between the United States and foreign powers. Any doubt regarding this point was answered in 1936 when the Supreme Court ruled that the

[4] Richard E. Neustadt, *Presidential Power* (New York: New American Library, 1964), p. 187.

President has "exclusive power ... as the sole organ of the Federal Government in the field of international relations." (*U.S.* v. *Curtiss-Wright Export Corporation,* 1936). Neither members of Congress nor private citizens may legally negotiate with foreign governments. Conducting foreign relations requires unified action, occasionally a considerable degree of secrecy, and often swift decisions. Congress obviously is not constituted to function in this manner. The Secretary of State, ambassadors, and other foreign service personnel are representatives of the President and not of Congress.

The President's pre-eminence in foreign affairs today stems in part from the staff, information, and facilities placed at his command. From American embassies, consulates, intelligence agencies, other governmental agencies, and even private citizens an overwhelming mass of information is collected regarding foreign developments. The State Department, White House staff, National Security Council, Central Intelligence Agency, and other government units assist the President in making decisions by sifting and analyzing these data. Thus the President has civilian agencies as well as military forces to help him plan and implement foreign policy.

From the days of Washington, the Secretary of State has been the ranking Cabinet officer and President's chief adviser and agent in foreign affairs. However, the role of the Secretary of State has varied from one administration to another. For instance, Dwight Eisenhower permitted John Foster Dulles broad discretionary powers in conducting foreign relations, but Woodrow Wilson (who sometimes typed his own diplomatic messages) was virtually his own Secretary of State. Under John Kennedy the Secretary of State apparently had less influence over foreign policy than did one of the President's assistants.

The long-term tendency undoubtedly is for a change in the relative position of the Secretary of State, with the President assuming more personal responsibility for conducting foreign relations. Improved communications make it possible for the President to be in touch personally with United States ambassadors abroad and the heads of foreign governments. The "hot line" connecting Washington and Moscow, for instance, is not between the State Department and the Soviet Ministry of Foreign Affairs but between the President and the Soviet Premier. Moreover, the possibility of an atomic war forces the President, as never before, to take responsibility for foreign affairs. At the present time the President's role as chief diplomat is one of the most important and demanding of his office.

One of the prerogatives of a sovereign nation is the right to recognize or to refuse recognition of foreign governments. The President's authority to receive ambassadors carries with it this power. By recognizing a new regime, the President may add to its prestige and domestic support. Conversely, by refusing recognition the President may hope to encourage opposition to a new government and lead to its demise. Recognition has also been withheld because of dislike for certain policies and practices of the government. The United States withheld recognition from the Soviet Union for sixteen years, and to this date has not recognized Red China. In such instances the President must decide whether more is to be gained by attempting to stigmatize the government by refusing recognition or by granting recognition and establishing means of communicating with the government and its people.

Treaties and Executive Agreements

As the United States has become increasingly involved in international politics, the government has entered numerous agreements with foreign countries. These are of two general types—treaties and executive agreements. Although the process of negotiating treaties is solely within the purview of the President, Wilson's experience in failing to secure the necessary two-thirds Senate approval for the Versailles Treaty and the League of Nations has led his successors to appoint influential senators to delegations negotiating treaties and to keep other senators informed of proposed treaties. The Constitution provides that treaties, along with federal statutes, are the "supreme law of the land." Thus, if a state law conflicts with a treaty, the latter takes precedence. If a conflict occurs between a treaty and a federal law, the Supreme Court has ruled that the one enacted or ratified first is overruled by the one of the later date.

Executive agreements, although not mentioned in the Constitution, have long been used by Presidents for reaching formal understandings with foreign governments. During this century far more executive agreements than treaties have been negotiated between the United States and other countries, largely because the former require no more than the approval of a simple majority in each house, while treaties require approval by a two-thirds vote in the Senate. Often executive agreements are based on authority previously delegated to the President by Congress. Examples include the reciprocal trade agreements that date to the 1930s, the lend-lease accords signed during World War II, and the numerous postwar foreign aid arrangements between the United States and other countries. A number of executive agreements have been negotiated by Presidents acting on their inherent authority over foreign relations and not under powers delegated by Congress and have not been submitted to Congress for its approval. An example of this type is the 1940 accord signed by President

Roosevelt and the British whereby the United States traded fifty overage destroyers for 99-year leases on some British naval bases in the Western Hemisphere.

World Leadership

Much of the recent expansion of the office of the President has resulted from the changes that have occurred in the position of the United States in world affairs. Until the beginning of this century American interest in foreign problems was sporadic and the nation's influence in international affairs was slight. After securing independence from England, the United States was primarily interested in settling the wilderness and expanding the nation's boundaries. By 1900 the land was settled, national boundaries were established, and the United States with a population then of approximately 60 million was gradually being recognized as a major world power.

The entry of the United States into World War I and the leadership of Woodrow Wilson at the peace conference projected the nation fully onto the world scene, but disillusionment with postwar developments caused many Americans to favor withdrawing behind the apparent security of the Atlantic and Pacific oceans. But the rise of Nazi Germany and World War II illustrated dramatically that the United States could never again isolate itself from world politics. At the conclusion of World War II the United States was the most powerful country on the globe, exercising initiative and leadership throughout the world. In 1910 Theodore Roosevelt sent the American Navy around the world to serve notice that the United States must henceforth be considered as a major power; today the United States has fleets *permanently stationed* in European and Asiatic waters!

The major crises that the Presidents have had to face in the last half century have been in foreign affairs. World wars overshadowed all other aspects of the administrations of Woodrow Wilson and Franklin Roosevelt; Truman was confronted with the possibilities of a Communist take-over in Greece and Turkey, the blockading of Berlin, and the Korean War. Eisenhower sent troops to the Middle East and was faced with the possibility of fighting over the islands of Matsu and Quemoy off the coast of China. Kennedy's confrontation with Russia regarding missile bases in Cuba was the major crisis of his administration. Johnson's problems regarding Vietnam outweighed all others. The domestic crisis situations—such as the violent resistance to school desegregation under Eisenhower and Kennedy—are not comparable in complexity or magnitude to these and other international problems.

In a century and a half the United States has been transformed from an insignificant group of English colonies into the most powerful nation in the world. But with power there are responsibilities, some of which all of the American people have not been fully prepared to assume. The President, while elected by the American electorate, today has responsibilities far broader than to his countrymen alone. As spokesman and leader of many friendly and allied nations, the President is expected to develop, articulate, and execute policies that will strengthen other countries and encourage them to support efforts toward expanding freedom and seeking peaceful solutions to international problems. In the future, presidential candidates must not be judged solely or even primarily on their ability to solve domestic problems, but they must be considered, in large part, on the basis of their qualifications for world leadership. The people of the entire world are deeply affected by the quality of the judgment of the President of the United States.

✻ THE PRESIDENT AS NATIONAL LEADER

Effective political leadership is essential to the successful operation of any government, and in the United States the mantle of leadership must necessarily fall upon the shoulders of the President. As the only official (along with the Vice-President) chosen by the entire electorate, the President is considered to be the spokesman and representative of all of the people. He is expected to represent the general interest against the divisive claims of the special interests, and to unite the nation against the centrifugal forces of geographic sectionalism and political factionalism. No one else can fill the role of national leader. As the conservative New Englander, Calvin Coolidge, explained, because " . . . Congress becomes subservient to the importunities of organized minorities . . . the President comes more and more to stand as the champion of the rights of the whole country."

As champion of all the people there are times when the President must be spokesman for the majority interest against pressure groups seeking special advantages. There are other times when the President is obligated to defend the interests of minority groups, as in the case of civil rights and liberties. Most definitely the responsibility of the President is not merely to represent or reflect majority attitudes. Indeed, when the President believes that the majority is unconcerned, uninformed, or wrong, it is his duty to attempt to change their attitudes. He cannot impose his opinions on the people, but as national leader he has the responsibility to educate and inform them on any matter of national concern. For instance, Franklin Roosevelt, although fully aware that the majority opposed the involvement of the United States in World War II, nevertheless tried to educate the people to the dangers of a victory by the totalitarian governments of Germany, Italy, and Japan.

Guardian of the National Interest

The President has always been the spokesman and guardian of the national interest. Traditionally he has been expected to respond instantly in times of natural disaster and send help any place in the nation where people suffer from earthquakes, fires, drought, or other disasters. In recent years, as the federal government has assumed greater responsibility for social and economic problems, the role of the President as guardian of the national interest has taken on new meaning.

As the ideal of equality for all persons has become more and more widely accepted, the President has come to stand as the conscience of the people. He has placed the prestige of his office on the side of the disadvantaged, and the nation has looked to him for leadership in the struggle for civil rights and liberties. As Franklin Roosevelt once remarked: "The Presidency . . . is pre-eminently a place of moral leadership."

As withholding civil rights from citizens deprives them of their share in the democratic process, depression and poverty deprive them of a share in the economic life of the country. Hoover's failure to utilize the power of the Presidency in the face of the Great Depression may have reflected the views of the citizenry regarding the Presidency at that time. Out of that depression and the post-World War II period, however, has come the belief that it is the duty of the President to act to prevent depressions before they occur and to work to eradicate poverty. The Council of Economic Advisers and the Office of Economic Opportunity, both located in the Executive Office of the President, assist him in these areas. As guardian of the general interest the President adjusts the nation's fiscal policies, intervenes in threatened strikes, and requests labor and business to follow guidelines in wage demands and price increases—all in an effort to maintain national prosperity and economic stability.

As the character of the United States has changed from rural to urban during this century, the problems of cities and metropolitan areas have made new demands on the President. The Departments of Labor and of Health, Education and Welfare have increasingly concerned themselves with the problems of the city. The recently established Department of Housing and Urban Development deals with such metropolitan problems as urban renewal, air pollution, waste disposal, and water supply; while the proposed Department of Transportation would attempt to solve urban transit problems. In the future the President may be expected to devote more time than in the past to these and related problems, for it is in the metropolitan areas where the greatest social and economic maladjustment exists.

✹ SEVEN OFFICES IN ONE

The President's various roles complement each other, but they also may conflict with one another. The President's success in one role, for instance as chief legislator or as national leader, may strengthen his position in another, such as chief administrator or commander in chief. At the same time, functions performed by the President as party leader may conflict with his efforts as chief diplomat or chief legislator.

The most obvious conflict occurs between the role of the President as chief of state and his other roles, all of which involve political leadership and decision-making. As chief of state, the President has great prestige, for in this role he is the symbol of the country. But in performing his various other responsibilities, he must make decisions which will lead to opposition and criticism. This combination of functions creates confusion and psychological tensions not experienced in parliamentary countries, where citizens may criticize the prime minister and at the same time show respect for the monarch as the chief of state. For instance, some Presidents have indicated that those who criticized their policies were lacking in patriotism. Franklin Roosevelt referred to the isolationists before World War II as "copperheads," with implications of disloyalty to the country; and Johnson in public statements permitted the inference that those who supported his policies in Vietnam were more patriotic than those who criticized them.

Some Presidents, such as Eisenhower, have emphasized their position as chief of state at a sacrifice to political leadership. Others, such as Truman, have taken stands on virtually all political issues, sometimes to the detriment of their prestige as chief of state. Although the times and the President's personality will influence his actions, most Presidents attempt to achieve a judicious blending of their functions of chief of state and political leadership.

In this chapter the office of the Presidency has been fragmented and discussed in parts. This classification of presidential responsibilities may result in an incorrect assumption: that all presidential duties can be neatly classified into one and only one of the seven categories and that the President is constantly taking off one "hat" and putting on another as he performs the duties of his office. In fact, most major presidential decisions and actions may relate to responsibilities in several areas. When the President makes decisions, he seldom conceives of himself as the chief administrator, or the chief of state, or commander in chief. Instead, he thinks of himself as *the President*.

In actuality, the Presidency is indivisible and it is more than the sum of its parts. It is an office which, broadly defined by the Constitution, has grown and developed; through changing times and under the influence of the Presidents, it has become an institution. The President, elected by the American people, supported by the Constitution and the precedents of the past, guided by a vision of the future, has the means to make a frontal attack on the problems of the present.

CHAPTER 19

PRESIDENTIAL
LEADERSHIP

The twentieth century has witnessed continual aggrandizement in the office of Chief Executive in Western democracies, with the most remarkable growth of executive power occurring during the mid-century decades. Since World War II the American President, the British Prime Minister, the West German Premier, and the French President have all wielded greater power than did their predecessors. This enlarged role of the executive has resulted from an extension of governmental responsibility on the domestic scene and continuing international crises and commitments. Only the chief executive can provide the leadership necessary to meet the problems and challenges of the age.

The duties of other chief executives have expanded, but as a result of America's unique position in the world and the organization of its governmental system, the responsibilities and burdens of the American President are undoubtedly greater than those of any other single official. Because of America's economic resources and military power the nation has greater obligations than any other country; and under our form of government the President stands alone as leader of the nation and performs tasks and has responsibilities which in other countries may be shared by other officials.

✻ THE PRESIDENT'S ASSISTANTS

Although the President does not share his leadership responsibilities, he, like the executive of any large enterprise, must have assistance. An important factor in determining the success of a President is his ability to

Jules Feiffer; in *The Village Voice*, 1965. Used by permission of Jules Feiffer.

recruit intelligent, knowledgeable, and conscientious assistants and to make the most effective use of their capabilities.

After a new President takes office, he may appoint as many as 1,000 to 1,500 persons to top- and middle-level executive positions. By comparison, when one party replaces the other in control of the British government, the only changes in personnel are ministers and their immediate parliamentary assistants, a total of some 70 individuals. Historically, one reason for the large turnover in the executive branch in the United States was the demand of political parties for patronage; but patronage pressures have greatly declined and today more important is the need for the President to have his administration staffed with loyal supporters. As the President, unlike the British Prime Minister, is not guaranteed control of the legislature or the united backing of his political party, he must establish a personal organization that will enable him to exercise the necessary leadership. In short, Presidents, lacking institutional controls and the support of a unified party, find that their best assurance of securing loyal cooperation and assistance is by appointing the optimum number of top- and middle-level executives.

The types of individuals selected for executive positions are influenced by the President's background and personality as well as by his party; and with a change of Presidents, the character of the administration is usually sharply altered. After Eisenhower took office there were more businessmen in the high governmental positions than at any time during the preceding twenty years. Under Kennedy, Washington was said to look like "an extension division of Harvard." Both Truman and Johnson, partly because they followed Presidents of their own party, appointed a large proportion of individuals with previous experience in government.[1] Change in personnel from one administration to the next helps to provide a dynamic quality to the government, a periodic infusion of new ideas, and a fresh look at domestic and world problems.

Actually, the tone or quality of an administration may be largely determined by as few as 200 to 300 of the most influential officials. Of these, the most important to the success of a President are the members of the Executive Office and the Cabinet. Hence attention will be directed here primarily to them. The President must rely on these officials for advice, information, and the performance of many tasks.

℣ THE EXECUTIVE OFFICE OF THE PRESIDENT

For a century and a half the American Presidents performed their duties with very little personal assistance. For instance, at the time of World War I, President Wilson had only 1 presidential secretary and approximately 45 clerks, stenographers, and messengers. The presidential secretary assisted with congressional relations, served as the press secretary, advised on appointments, and generally aided the President. Herbert Hoover added 2 presidential secretaries, but the organization of the President's office was largely unchanged until Franklin Roosevelt's administration.

In 1936 Roosevelt appointed the President's Committee on Administrative Management to investigate and make recommendations regarding the organization of the executive branch of the government. After studying the organization of the President's office, this committee tersely concluded: "The President needs help." As a result of the committee's recommendations, the Executive Office of the President was created in 1939. This is not a single organization as the name implies, but a title covering a group of individuals and agencies whose function it is to assist the President in the performance of duties that are strictly the President's responsibility. There are now approximately 2,000 people (not including the personnel of the Central Intelligence Agency) employed in these agencies and offices—more than forty times the number that assisted Wilson half a century earlier. Thus, in a few short decades the Presidency has been transformed

[1] Of the early appointments of Eisenhower, Kennedy, and Johnson, the following percentages came from government, business, and universities or foundations: Eisenhower—28, 36, 6; Kennedy—47, 6, 18; Johnson—59, 10, 13. Included among those from government are persons who held other government positions at the time of their appointments or who had previously served in government. See Seymour E. Harris, *The Economics of he Political Parties* (New York: Macmillan, 1962), p. 25; and *The New York Times* (December 26, 1965), p. 44.

from virtually a one-man operation to a well-organized and highly staffed institution. Today the chief executive of no other country has a comparable staff.

The White House Office

Of the several units of the Executive Office, the White House staff exercises the strongest influence on presidential policy and leadership. The character, size, and functioning of the staff vary according to the needs of the particular President and his method of working. President Eisenhower, no doubt due to his army background, increased the number of personnel and organized them in a manner somewhat similar to a military general staff. One of his staff members, Sherman Adams, who was given the title of Assistant to the President, presided over staff meetings, made assignments to other staff members, and served as the principal channel of communication and information to the President. When Kennedy took office he reduced the number of personnel, dropped the chief-of-staff approach, and worked more directly with all key members of the White House office. According to his biographers, Kennedy never held a general meeting of the entire White House staff. Johnson tended to combine the approaches of his two predecessors. Although under Johnson no presidential aide has had the authority of Sherman Adams, one individual—Bill D. Moyers—was recognized as having more influence than the others. Moyers often attended Cabinet and other meetings with the President, was given a number of major assignments, and had the authority to make many day-to-day decisions involving intra-administrative problems.

In recommending the appointment of several presidential assistants, the Committee on Administrative Management set forth the following qualifications: "They should be possessed of high competence, great physical vigor, and a passion for anonymity." An analysis of the functions performed by the President's personal staff of some 20 special assistants, administrative assistants, secretaries, and special counsels indicates that this is an accurate description of the qualities needed. The range of their tasks is as broad as the President's responsibilities.

Whereas some may be given a variety of general assignments, most White House staff members perform specialized functions. Aides are commonly assigned to direct the routine functioning of the office itself and to oversee the major areas of presidential responsibility—public opinion, national security, and relations with Congress and administrative agencies. The President has a personal secretary; customarily one White House staff member serves as appointments secretary determining who may see the President; and another is usually assigned the tasks of recommending persons to be appointed to governmental positions. Some staff members have such assignments as writing speeches, investigating or making studies of special problems, or coordinating programs. There is always a press secretary, who often has one or more assistants. Both Kennedy and Johnson appointed university professors to serve as special assistants for foreign affairs. Under recent Presidents from one to three White House aides have had as their chief responsibility serving as liaison with Congress. Usually one presidential assistant will be requested to coordinate the President's domestic program, one to work with the administrative agencies, and possibly another to serve as the secretary to the Cabinet. These aides and officials assist the President by providing him with advice on policies, alerting him to problems, and furnishing him ideas and information.

White House staff members are chosen because of their ability, knowledge, and loyalty to the President. Typically they are a diversified group and will include attorneys, journalists, university professors, businessmen, and former assistants to members of Congress. The key members of the White House staff have their offices near the President in the west wing of the White House. Today the members of the White House staff are indispensable to the President. Because the President trusts their judgment and is in daily contact with them, the staff members have a strong impact on his decisions. The Presidency has been greatly strengthened by the personnel of the White House staff, but the President still has the responsibility for decision-making. As John Kennedy once remarked, "The President bears the burden of the responsibility. . . . The advisers move on to new advice." Harry Truman stated it more briefly: "The buck stops here."

The Bureau of the Budget

This agency provides the President with a powerful instrument of administrative control and coordination as well as a means for exerting legislative leadership. Established by the Budget and Accounting Act of 1921, the Bureau was originally located in the Treasury Department, but in 1939 it was transferred to the Executive Office of the President. The Budget Director is one of the few top officials whom the President may appoint without Senate approval. Most of the other Bureau personnel are selected under civil service regulations.

The chief function of the Bureau of the Budget is to prepare the national budget. All federal agencies are required to submit to the Bureau detailed estimates of their proposed expenditures for the forthcoming fiscal year. Acting in accordance with the instructions of the President, the staff of the Bureau holds budget hearings, reviews the estimates, and revises the proposed expenditures so that the plans of the various government agencies conform with the President's general program. In establishing his budgetary policies the President makes important decisions regarding the relative importance of programs. For instance, he may decide that due to a reduction in world tension, military spending may be cut back making possible more expenditures for domestic purposes; and that among the domestic programs, funds are more badly needed for education or urban renewal than for building highways or dams.

Following congressional approval of the budget—usually after various downward and rare upward revisions—the Bureau has the responsibility for supervising its execution. The Bureau maintains continuous supervision over expenditures to see that they are consistent with the President's overall program, are authorized by law, and do not exceed amounts appropriated. The administrative agencies are required to obtain the Bureau's approval before transferring funds from one allocation to another and to submit to the Bureau reports that are digested and transmitted to the President. The Bureau thus assists the President in planning and coordinating the programs and expenditures of the various executive agencies.

The Bureau assists the President in other ways. One office of the Bureau has the responsibility for conducting management and organization surveys and for submitting proposals for improving the functioning of executive agencies. The recommendations resulting from these management surveys have assisted agencies in changing their internal operations and have resulted in proposals for reorganization.

The Bureau of the Budget is also the President's chief legislative clearinghouse. All legislative proposals originating with executive agencies, before being sent to Congress, must be submitted to the Legislative Reference Office of the Bureau to determine if they are in conformity with the President's general program and policies. Any enrolled bill—a bill passed by Congress but not yet acted on by the President—is also sent to this office, which in turn refers it to all interested agencies for their recommendations. The staff digests these recommendations and advises the President whether he should sign or veto the bill. If a veto is recommended, the Bureau prepares for the President a draft of a proposed veto message.

The Council of Economic Advisers

In 1946 Congress acknowledged the responsibility of the federal government for promoting prosperity and economic stability by passing the Employment Act, which created the Council of Economic Advisers

(CEA) and established it as a unit of the Executive Office. The CEA consists of three professional economists, usually selected from leading universities, who are appointed by the President with the consent of the Senate. The CEA, and its staff, undertake a continuing analysis of national economic trends and developments, appraise the economic programs and policies of the government, and advise the President regarding policies that will encourage economic growth and prevent recessions. The CEA prepares for the President an annual report on the national economy that the President transmits to Congress at the beginning of each session.

The National Security Council

Congress in 1947 passed the National Security Act, which created the National Security Council (NSC) and charged it with the responsibility for advising "the President with respect to the integration of domestic, foreign, and military policies relating to national security." The NSC is composed of the President who serves as the chairman, the Vice-President, the Secretary of State, the Secretary of Defense, and the Director of the Office of Emergency Planning. The President frequently invites other persons to attend meetings, including the U.S. Ambassador to the United Nations, the Chairman of the Joint Chiefs of Staff, the Secretary of the Treasury, and members of the White House staff.

The principal purposes of the NSC are to bring together the top officials who have responsibilities for national security and foreign policies, and to provide them information that will permit thorough analysis of all aspects of such policies. Information and analysis of relevant factors are provided by the staff of the NSC, governmental units represented on the NSC, and the Central Intelligence Agency, which functions under the direction of the NSC.

Some impression of the value of the NSC as an advisory body for the President may be gained from the following account by a former White House staff member, who explained:

> In a meeting representing different departments and diverse points of view, there is a greater likelihood of hearing alternatives, of exposing errors, and of challenging assumptions. ... That such meetings can sometimes be useful was proven by the deliberations of the NSC executive committee after the discovery of offensive weapons in Cuba. ... Every solution or combination of solutions was coldly examined, and its disadvantages weighed. The fact that we started out with a sharp divergence of views, the President has said, was "very valuable" in hammering out a policy.[2]

[2] Theodore C. Sorensen, *Decision-Making in the White House* (New York: New York University Press, 1964), pp. 59–60.

Other Executive Office Units

From the standpoint of assisting the President, the other five units of the Executive Office are less important. Three of these agencies have functions related to national security.

The National Aeronautics and Space Council, established in 1958, is composed of the Vice-President, who serves as chairman, the Secretary of State, the Secretary of National Defense, the Administrator of the National Aeronautics and Space Administration, and the Chairman of the Atomic Energy Commission. This body advises the President on space programs and policies and is authorized to establish the responsibilities of federal agencies, both civilian and military, engaged in space and aeronautical activities.

The Office of Emergency Planning was established in 1961 primarily to assist the President by planning and coordinating policies for the mobilization of civilian resources in case of a major war. Its activities include developing plans for civil defense, the emergency use of manpower and other resources, and the organization of the government in an emergency. As noted above, its Director is one of the statutory members of the National Security Council.

The Office of Science and Technology, created in 1962, advises the President in developing programs that will assure the most effective use of science and technological knowledge for national security and domestic purposes.

The other two units in the Executive Office are the Office of Special Representative for Trade Negotiations, which was established in 1963 to assist the President in carrying out the trade agreements program; and the Office of Economic Opportunity, created by Congress in 1964, to direct the battle against poverty. This latter office has the responsibility for such projects as the Work Experience Programs, Urban and Rural Community Action Programs, the Youth Corps, and the Work-Training and Work-Study Programs.

☙ THE CABINET

Many Americans, including some newspaper columnists, apparently believe that the American Cabinet should perform the same functions as the British. A comparison of the American and British Cabinets, however, illustrates a fact of political life—governmental institutions with the same name may in reality be quite different. Although the American Cabinet derived its name from the British institution, the two bodies are dissimilar. They differ from the standpoints of the basis for selecting members, their political powers, and their responsibilities. The British Cabinet is composed of leaders of the majority party in Parliament, each of whom has been elected by a constituency the same as the Prime Minister; and each member shares with the Prime Minister responsibility for developing and defending governmental policies and for running the government. By comparison, in the United States none of the Cabinet members is elected, and the President alone is politically and constitutionally responsible for developing public policies and administering the government. Whereas British policies are collective decisions of the entire Cabinet, the President may ignore the Cabinet; and if he does consult it he can say, as did Lincoln, "Seven nays, one aye, the ayes have it."

The Cabinet was instituted by Washington, who called meetings of his department heads to discuss governmental problems. It was not until 1907 that the Cabinet was referred to in a federal statute, and it was not mentioned in the Constitution prior to the Twenty-fifth Amendment. There are now eleven executive departments: State; Treasury; Defense; Justice; Post Office; Interior; Agriculture; Commerce; Labor; Health, Education and Welfare; and Housing and Urban Development. The three most recently organized are Defense, which resulted from the merging of the Departments of War and Navy in 1947; Health, Education and Welfare, which was created in 1953 by combining a number of established agencies; and Housing and Urban Development, which was created in 1965, also from existing agencies. Congress was also expected to accept a recommendation made by President Johnson in 1966 to organize several agencies into a new Department of Transportation.

Selection of Cabinet Members

In choosing his Cabinet a President must consider many factors. Although a number of early Presidents chose national party leaders for Cabinet posts, more recent Presidents have recalled accounts of Lincoln's difficulties with Seward and Chase, and Wilson's with Bryan, and have not selected presidential contenders or other national party leaders. Thus Kennedy appointed Adlai Stevenson, who had twice been his party's presidential nominee, as Ambassador to the United Nations and not as Secretary of State, a position which Stevenson apparently would have preferred.

The Cabinet traditionally has been chosen entirely from the President's party, but in recent decades opposition party members have been chosen during national emergencies or when a President wanted to remove the operation of a department from the arena of partisan conflict. During World War II Roosevelt appointed two well-known Republicans as heads of the War and Navy Departments; and Kennedy, after his extremely narrow victory, selected Republicans as Secretaries of the Defense and Treasury Departments, both of which often are focal points of political controversy.

Various other political considerations have helped to determine certain Cabinet appointments. Almost invariably, a President will appoint one or more of his department heads in order to repay political debts, to give representation to different factions in the party, or to utilize a person's political knowledge and presumed ability to work with Congress. For example, Johnson appointed as Postmaster General, Lawrence O'Brien, who had managed both his and Kennedy's election campaigns and had served in the White House Office as the chief liaison with Congress. Also for practical political reasons a President may attempt to select his department heads so that each geographic area will be represented and so that no major religious or ethnic group will believe its members have been excluded.

Executive experience, specialized knowledge of the work of a particular department, and acceptability to the clientele of a department have all been important factors in determining the choice of Cabinet members. Because of the huge budget and operations of the Defense Department, Eisenhower appointed the head of General Motors as his Secretary of Defense; and Kennedy, also desiring a person with top management experience, chose for the same post the chief executive of Ford Motor Company, who was retained in that position by Johnson. As heads of certain departments—including Agriculture, Commerce, and Labor— Presidents customarily appoint persons who have knowledge of those areas and who are acceptable to leading organized groups interested in the work of the department. For similar reasons the Secretary of the Interior usually is a westerner and is acquainted with conservation problems, which are the primary concern of that department.

In addition to selecting department heads because of political considerations and their qualifications for particular positions, Presidents have customarily made some selections for personal reasons. For example, most Presidents want to appoint as department Secretaries one or more persons whom they know well and have found personally compatible; John Kennedy's appointment of his brother Robert as Attorney General is a notable example.

The Role of the Cabinet

Not only is the American Cabinet different from those of other countries, through the years its own role has changed. Historically, the Cabinet members have been considered to have two principal functions: individually they served as the administrative heads of the departments; and, presumably, they collectively served as advisers to the President.

In reality, the part played by the Cabinet has depended largely on the President's conception of it, his personality, and the growth and organization of the government. Washington created the Cabinet to serve as an advisory body, and, by selecting both Jefferson and Hamilton for his first Cabinet, he gave representation to the opposing political views of the day. Many of the other early Presidents considered their Cabinets to be councils of party leaders, but most later Presidents have not. Some Presidents, notably Franklin Pierce and Warren Harding, conferred with their Cabinets on virtually every presidential decision and assiduously followed the advice received. Others, more self-confident and stronger political leaders, came to have little regard for the opinions of the several Secretaries on questions beyond the spheres of their respective departments, and sought political advice elsewhere. Jackson and Theodore Roosevelt, for instance, relied on a small group of unofficial advisers who were known as the "kitchen cabinet."

Changes in the organization and operation of the executive branch have had a greater impact on the role of the Cabinet than is generally understood. As all executive agencies were originally grouped within the departments, formerly the President in Cabinet meetings could obtain the views of the head of every agency, and he might give directives that could be transmitted to each unit in the executive branch. Toward the end of the nineteenth century, Congress began establishing agencies outside the departments, and today some of these—such as the Veterans Administration and the National Aeronautics and Space Administration—have more personnel than certain executive departments. Thus no longer do the heads of all executive agencies, or even the largest ones, have Cabinet status.

Franklin Roosevelt began the practice followed by his successors of inviting persons other than Cabinet members to Cabinet meetings. Among those often attending Cabinet meetings are the Ambassador to the United Nations, the Administrator of the National Aeronautics and Space Administration, the Chairman of the Atomic Energy Commission, the Director of the Bureau of the Budget, the Chairman of the Council of Economic Advisers, and various special assistants to the President and other members of the White House staff. During Johnson's administration as many as fifty officials have attended a single Cabinet meeting.

This increase in the number attending Cabinet meetings has diminished the potential usefulness of the Cabinet as an advisory body. A larger group reduces the effectiveness of discussion, multiplies the possibility that confidential information may be leaked to the press, and decreases whatever collegial relationship might develop from meetings of a smaller, well-defined group. Richard Fenno has accurately summarized the role of the Cabinet:

> In matters of prestige, partisan politics and legislative relations alike, the Cabinet collectively has only a symbolic value, a value which readily disappears when the need for action supersedes the need for a show window.... The political help which the President receives comes not from the group but from individual Cabinet members, who can and do augment the President's effectiveness in his leadership roles.[3]

Another governmental change that has tended to reduce the influence of the Cabinet was the establishment of the Executive Office of the President. Within the White House Office the President has a number of assistants who can advise him, and units of the Executive Office that cut across departmental lines, such as the National Security Council and the National Aeronautics and Space Council, have been created to offer advice on specialized problems.

In the past the Cabinet served for certain Presidents both as a political council and as an agency for coordinating administrative activities; today it performs neither function. The primary function of Cabinet members now is to serve as administrative heads of their departments. The diminished role of the Cabinet is seen in the decline in the frequency of Cabinet meetings. While some Presidents have held Cabinet meetings as often as twice a week, recent Presidents have held them infrequently, with Kennedy and Johnson seldom having more than one Cabinet meeting a month. Cabinet meetings will no doubt continue to serve as a sounding board for certain presidential ideas and proposals, as a means of communicating information to top officials, and as a method of establishing an *esprit de corps* within the administration, but it is unlikely that the Cabinet will again serve as a political council where collective decisions are reached on major policies.

❧ THE VICE-PRESIDENT AS PRESIDENTIAL ASSISTANT

The office of Vice-President is a paradox. It is the second highest in the nation and has been filled by many able individuals; yet Vice-Presidents have wielded little influence or power. The responsibilities and influence of the Vice-President have increased in recent decades, but even now congressional leaders, Cabinet officers, and White House staff members have greater influence on public policy than does the Vice-President.

[3] Richard F. Fenno, Jr., *The President's Cabinet* (Cambridge, Mass.: Harvard University Press, 1959), p. 247.

The Vice-Presidency provides an illustration of a deviation from a strict adherence to the separation of powers theory. Although the Vice-President is an executive official, he is also President of the Senate. His formal powers in that capacity are minimal: he votes only in case of a tie, and he has the customary powers of a presiding officer. Vice-Presidents—such as Alben Barkley, Richard Nixon, Lyndon Johnson, and Hubert Humphrey—who have previously served in the Senate may have some influence and help promote the President's program through their personal friendships and knowledge of the Senate, but even these individuals have found they had less influence in the Senate as Vice-President than they previously had as senators. Because the Vice-President's role of presiding officer may be temporarily filled by a senator, his attendance is not required throughout every session, and he consequently has time for other tasks.

In the past, Vice-Presidents were virtually ignored by the Presidents and members of their official families. For instance, during the half year that Wilson's illness rendered him unable to meet with his Cabinet, Vice-President Thomas Marshall was neither included in Cabinet meetings nor otherwise informed regarding governmental decisions. The first President to invite the Vice-President to Cabinet meetings was Franklin Roosevelt; but when he died, Harry Truman had little information regarding current activities of the government.

Both Truman and Eisenhower attempted to keep their Vice-Presidents informed and to utilize their services. In particular Eisenhower, more than other Presidents, encouraged his Vice-President to engage in a variety of activities. As the President's emissary, Richard Nixon traveled to Moscow and South America, addressed various organized groups, campaigned for political candidates, met with party leaders, and attended meetings of the Cabinet and the National Security Council and presided over these meetings when Eisenhower could not attend. Under both Kennedy and Johnson, the Vice-President engaged in similar activities, though to a lesser extent than under Eisenhower. As a result of the national recognition that Nixon received from such activities, he was nominated by his party for the Presidency, the first Vice-President since Van Buren (1836) to be nominated for this office without first having succeeded to the Presidency upon the death of the Chief Executive.

The questions naturally arise: Why does the Vice-President play such a minor role in the determination of public policy? Why does the President, so obviously overburdened, make such limited use of the Vice-President? First, political power tends to be positional—it is commonly associated with an office or position, and the office of Vice-President provides the incumbent with relatively little power. Second, as the Vice-President may have competed against the President for the presidential nomination—as had Johnson in 1960—the President may be reluctant to give him assignments that would possibly enhance the Vice-President's political stature and at the expense of his own.

Probably of more importance is the need for the President to have assistants who are directly accountable to him, who are amenable to his wishes, whose best interests are identical with the President's, and who may be dismissed at any time. The fact that the Vice-President usually has a considerable political following and is elected for a four-year term excludes him from that category of persons. Each President is aware that friction may develop between him and the Vice-President and that the latter may not give his complete support to the President's program. At the time Johnson selected Humphrey for his running mate, Humphrey reportedly agreed to support the administration's program, to clear public addresses with the White House, and to have no public disagreements with the President.

The role of any particular Vice-President is determined by the President. The expanded role of recent Vice-Presidents has been due entirely to decisions by the Presidents. Some Presidents encourage their top assistants, Cabinet members as well as the Vice-President, to engage in activities that would enhance their national reputations. Other Chief Executives have been primarily concerned with their own reputations and have so dominated and overshadowed the other top executive officers that they have had little opportunity to develop into public personalities.

☆ LEADING PUBLIC OPINION

The success of the President as a national leader depends in large measure upon his efforts and ability at guiding and directing public opinion. The more dynamic and influential twentieth-century Presidents have all understood, as did Lincoln, the importance of public opinion. In Lincoln's words: "Public sentiment is everything. With public sentiment nothing can fail; without it, nothing can succeed." The President is second to none in his ability to attract public notice and to focus the attention of the people on political issues and problems. More than any other person, the President determines what political issues will be reported in the mass media, debated in Congress, and discussed across the country.

The British statesman Benjamin Disraeli once commented that what "ideas . . . are correct no one can say; but with words we govern men." If it was true in Britain in Disraeli's day that men were governed with ideas and words, it is even more true in the United States today. Franklin Roosevelt was the first President to realize the possibilities for national leadership by talking directly to the people via the radio. In his "fireside chats" on radio he was able to explain and discuss the political issues confronting the country. Television further enhanced the opportunity of the President to fulfill his role as national leader. Prior to radio and television, relatively few persons heard the voice of the President. Today the President—his personality, mannerisms, and voice inflections—is more familiar to millions of Americans than their congressman or their mayor.

The Presidential Press Conference

The presidential press conference has evolved during this century to provide the President with a forum for expressing his views on national political issues. This is an uniquely American institution. In no other country does the Chief Executive meet the press so often or under similar conditions. Although the press conference has been compared with the question hour in the House of Commons and the interpellation in the French Parliament, it is not actually comparable, for the last two are means by which not the press but members of the legislature may question ministers.

The growth of the presidential press conference has paralleled the establishment of the modern Presidency. Although Theodore Roosevelt often talked to specially invited reporters in the White House, Woodrow Wilson is usually credited with initiating presidential press conferences, for he was the first President to hold regularly scheduled press conferences to which all accredited White House reporters were invited. Franklin Roosevelt, who held more press conferences than any other President, established it as a precedent that has been followed by all of his successors. Under them the presidential press conferences became more institutionalized and came to resemble semipublic mass meetings, with usually 200 to 300 reporters attending. Eisenhower permitted the meetings to be filmed on video tape for later telecast. Kennedy took the next step of allowing a number of his press conferences to be directly televised.

Early in his administration Lyndon Johnson indicated his intention to follow the practice of his predecessors, explaining the value of the presidential press conference as follows:

> For the President, the questions of the nation's curious journalists provide renewed insight into the concerns of the country, helping him to shape his program and give direction to his Administration. Even more importantly, the press conference adds dimension to the office of the Presidency itself. Through it, the President can communicate his views, his reflections and his reasons for decisions, helping to fulfill his special and high responsibility to inform and educate the people on great public questions.

Although he thus praised the presidential press conference, it soon became clear that Johnson preferred informal, unscheduled meetings with a small number of reporters to the general press conferences. In the summer of 1966 Johnson introduced what was referred to as a "double-header" news session. First, he held a news conference in his office without television or newsreel cameras. Then he went to the White House movie theater, which is used for television broadcasting and recording. There, before the television cameras, representatives of the major television networks asked him one question each from among those that had previously been discussed in his office.

Much of the value of press conferences, both for the President and the public, obviously depends upon the President. Franklin Roosevelt and John Kennedy thoroughly enjoyed press conferences, for these meetings with reporters gave them greater opportunity to express their wit and humor than on more formal occasions. Other Presidents, like Dwight Eisenhower and Lyndon Johnson, often gave the impression of enjoying less the spontaneous questioning of the reporters, and held press conferences only because they were established institutions.

That there are potential dangers in the presidential press conferences, particularly when televised, is apparent. The press generally has favored the practice of reporters being permitted to raise questions on virtually any issue and to expect an immediate answer. The President obviously should not be expected to know all the details regarding every highly complicated issue. Yet if he fails to answer questions or gives an incorrect answer, it may appear to millions of Americans watching on television that he is uninformed or is withholding information. Furthermore, if answers to questions regarding national security and foreign policy are hastily given without consideration for all possible ramifications, grave international misunderstandings may result. "Double-header" news sessions may generally avoid these problems in that, in effect, the President has a "dress rehearsal" before appearing on television.

Qualities of Opinion Leadership

Presidents have varied considerably in their efforts and talents for mobilizing public sentiment. Although opinion leadership obviously requires the ability to communicate with the people, it does not demand that the President be gifted at elocution. Of recent Presidents, Truman, Eisenhower, and Johnson were not accomplished orators, but nevertheless had the capacity to communicate effectively with the public. More important than oratory is the moral quality of a President's leadership, the extent to which his statements and actions generate confidence, and his capacity to perceive and to personify the temper of the times. More than a half century ago Woodrow Wilson correctly analyzed the President's role as national leader when he wrote:

His is the only national voice in affairs. Let him once win the admiration and confidence of the country, and no other single force can withstand him, no combination of forces will easily overpower him. His position takes the imagination of the country. . . . If he rightly interpret the national thought and boldly insist upon it, he is irresistible; and the country never feels the zest for action so much as when its President is of such insight and calibre.

The capacity for national leadership is evidenced by a President's ability to strike the proper balance between communicating sufficiently via television and other mass media and keeping his impact from being limited through overexposure, in his timing in presenting to the people information and arguments, and in the sense of urgency he attaches to a particular problem. An example of a President's use of timing and urgency to emphasize a problem occurred in March, 1965, when, after the nation had been shocked by the assassination of three civil rights workers in Alabama, President Johnson appeared on television before a joint session of Congress and announced that he would immediately send a voting rights bill to Congress. His address, broadcast during "prime" evening time over national television and radio networks, did much to accelerate the passage of the Voting Rights Act by Congress.

The more able Presidents have had the ability to select from various ideas and proposals those which most accurately reflect the unarticulated as well as the expressed aspirations of the majority of the population, and by calling them to the attention of the nation make those ideas the key political issues of the day. As Wilson noted, the President must not only "win the admiration and confidence" of the people, he must also "rightly interpret the national thought." In short, he cannot lead the people against the onrushing forces of history, but if he correctly interprets the spirit of his times, he may direct contemporary forces toward desired goals.

✻ LEADING CONGRESS

The present-day American President must provide leadership for Congress in the formation of public policy. Every recent President, regardless of his personal inclination, has found that he must serve as the leading legislator, and that much of his reputation as President is based on the legislation enacted during his administration. "The President," explained Clinton Rossiter, "who will not give his best thoughts to guiding Congress, more so the President who is temperamentally or politically unfitted to 'get along with Congress,' is now rightly considered a national liability."[4]

[4] Clinton Rossiter, "The Presidency—Focus on Leadership," *The New York Times Magazine* (November 11, 1956), p. 58.

Although there is general agreement that the President should be the chief legislator, a variety of circumstances have made it difficult for Presidents to exercise effective and continuous legislative leadership. The separation of powers complicates the President's leadership problems. As we have seen, the executive and legislature are coordinate branches of government, each receiving its authority from the Constitution and jealously guarding its prestige and independent status. Usually many members of Congress are older than the President, have been in public office longer, believe they know more about political problems, and are reluctant to accept his guidance. As the members of Congress and the President are elected by different constituencies, they view political issues from different perspectives; many members of Congress take a local, more provincial view of issues, whereas the President in reaching decisions must consider the broader national and even international aspects and ramifications. In addition, the Constitution provides the President few means for inducing Congress to follow his lead. Unlike the British Prime Minister, he cannot dissolve the legislature and call a new election, nor can he require the members of his party in the legislature to vote for his proposals.

Constitutional Powers

There has been a remarkable variation in the success of the several Chief Executives in obtaining the enactment of their legislative programs. The Constitution, which made few provisions for presidential direction in the formation of legislative policy, grants the President two relatively important legislative powers—the message and the veto powers—and one that is comparatively unimportant—the authority to call special sessions.

Legislative Messages and Recommendations. The Constitution enjoins the President to "give to the Congress information of the State of the Union, and recommend to their consideration such measures as he shall judge necessary and expedient." During the nineteenth century, Presidents tended to interpret this provision literally and limited themselves merely to calling the attention of Congress to current problems. Starting with Theodore Roosevelt and Woodrow Wilson, most Presidents have interpreted the message power as authorization to develop a legislative program and to work for its enactment.

In the weeks prior to the opening of a congressional session, the President and his assistants sift through the recommendations submitted by the executive agencies and presidential advisers and prepare the President's legislative program. These proposals will be outlined by the President in the "State of the Union" message. Beginning with Thomas Jefferson all

Presidents until Woodrow Wilson sent their messages to Congress to be read by a clerk. In order to focus public attention on his program, Wilson reinstated the practice of the first two Presidents—that of delivering his message in person before a joint session of Congress. This traditional message is usually followed by several other messages recommending particular policies that are often accompanied by drafts of bills. In 1965, for example, Johnson sent 30 messages to Congress requesting legislation, and in 1966 he requested action on more than 125 legislative measures. These presidential proposals usually constitute the principal agenda of legislative sessions.

The Veto Power. The President participates directly in the legislative process through his power to approve or veto legislation. (See Chapter 17.) Most Presidents prior to the Civil War took the view that they should veto only those bills they believed to be unconstitutional, and consequently they vetoed relatively few bills. More recent Chief Executives have used the veto as an instrument to exert legislative leadership and have vetoed bills they believed to be unwise and not in the national interest. The greater use of the veto in recent decades may be seen by noting that previous to Franklin Roosevelt, only Cleveland vetoed more than 100 measures, and many of these were private pension bills. By comparison Franklin Roosevelt vetoed 631 measures, Harry Truman 251, and Dwight Eisenhower 181. Because of the difficulty of obtaining the necessary two-thirds vote in each house of Congress, a vetoed bill seldom becomes law. Of their vetoes, Franklin Roosevelt had only 9 overriden, Truman 12, and Eisenhower— although faced with a Congress controlled by the opposite party for six years—had only two vetoes overruled.

The number of bills vetoed is not an accurate index of the significance of the veto power. Due to the difficulty of obtaining the two-thirds vote needed to enact a bill over a presidential veto, a President may be able to forestall the adoption of particular bills by simply announcing that they would be vetoed if enacted. Moreover, members of Congress knowing that modern-day Presidents show little hesitation in vetoing bills, have at times changed the content of legislative measures to meet presidential approval. Thus the veto, originally a negative weapon, has become an instrument for positive legislative leadership.

The President, unlike some forty state governors, does not have the item veto. Through the item veto a Chief Executive may strike out sections or parts of a bill, but approve the remaining sections, which become law. Knowing that the President is required to accept or reject the entire measure, Congress at times has attached riders that the President would probably veto if enacted separately, but that he will approve in order to secure the main provisions of the bill. The omnibus nature of many appropriation bills also argues for permitting the President to disapprove of certain items in a bill while approving others. However, Congress has evinced little interest in amending the Constitution to give the President this or other authority that would reduce its own prerogatives.

Control of Legislative Sessions. A third, and less consequential, constitutional provision authorizes the President to call special sessions of Congress and to adjourn the two houses "in case of disagreement between them with respect to time of adjournment." As the two houses of Congress have never disagreed regarding adjournment, the latter authority has never been exercised. Moreover, since the adoption of the Twentieth Amendment, providing for Congress to convene each year in January, Congress has usually been in session for eight or nine months each year, and there has been little reason for calling special sessions. However, Woodrow Wilson, Lyndon Johnson, and other Presidents have threatened to call special sessions of Congress if the two houses adjourned prior to adopting certain legislative measures. In 1948 Harry Truman, in what was considered to be an election stratagem, convened Congress in special session after the national nominating conventions and challenged the Republican-controlled Congress to enact the program advocated by the Republican platform.

Extraconstitutional Powers

Because the Constitution makes so few provisions for presidential leadership in the formation of legislative policy, the President's success as a national legislator is dependent upon his knowledge of extraconstitutional institutions and methods and his skill in utilizing them.

Public Opinion and Legislative Leadership. One of the President's principal sources of strength in working with Congress is his ability to influence public opinion. The President can focus attention on his legislative program through press conferences, in news releases, in messages to Congress, and in other public statements and addresses. Since the development of television, Presidents have often used this medium to appeal directly to the public for support for legislative measures. Lyndon Johnson explained his approach when he said, "You first get the basic support of the people and then you act." The great majority of the population do not have opinions on many issues and do not hold strong opinions on others. The President, by calling particular issues to public notice, is often able to increase the "attentive" public and bring the pressure of their opinions to bear on members of Congress. Woodrow Wilson expressed a similar thought when he said the President "has no means of compelling Congress except through public opinion." Wilson added, "if Congress is overcome" by the President, it will be "only because the President has the nation behind him and Congress has not."

The President's Party Leadership in Congress. Although American legislators, unlike their British counterparts, refuse to bind themselves to support their party's legislative proposals, American government is nevertheless party government. No President has achieved an enviable legislative record whose party did not control both houses of Congress and who did not energetically assert his role as party leader. Because all members of the President's party cannot be counted on to support his legislative measures, the President must seek support from both parties, but the principal support comes from his own party. Moreover, the likelihood of securing the enactment of a legislative program is greatest if the President's party has sizable majorities in each house and if a number of the legislators believe they owe their election to the President. Woodrow Wilson, Franklin Roosevelt, and Lyndon Johnson, all enjoyed this advantage when they were establishing their outstanding legislative records.

The President has relatively little influence over the selection of his party's leaders in the House and Senate, but he must work through them and secure their cooperation if his proposals are to be adopted. Before the opening of a legislative session the President usually discusses his proposed program with congressional party leaders and plans the general strategy to obtain its enactment. Throughout legislative sessions it is now customary for the President to meet with his party's congressional leaders weekly at the White House, often at breakfast, to discuss the progress of bills and the tactics to be employed. Presidents often emphasize that the enactment of particular proposals will enhance the chances of their party in succeeding elections.

Participation in the Legislative Process. Recent Presidents and their assistants have participated directly or indirectly in virtually every phase of the bill-passing process. It is now accepted practice for executive officials to draft the bills that comprise the President's legislative program. All recent Presidents have placed a high priority on cooperating with Congress, but the formalization of executive-legislative relations into a full-time staff activity developed during the administrations of Eisenhower, Kennedy, and Johnson. Previously liaison between the executive and Congress had been more informal and often on an *ad hoc* basis. Kennedy assigned the task of coordinating executive-legislative relations to a trusted assistant on the White House staff, who had years of practical political experience and counted among his personal acquaintances many members of Congress. He and two other presidential assistants devoted virtually full time to legislative liaison activities. When Johnson took office, he continued this arrangement.

In addition to White House staff members, under Kennedy and Johnson approximately 40 other congressional relations officers have been spread throughout the departments and agencies. In the State Department the official charged with congressional relations customarily has held the rank of assistant secretary. During Johnson's administration, every Monday each of the departments and agencies was required to submit to the White House reports of their activities on Capitol Hill during the previous week and their anticipated relations with Congress during the ensuing week.

Personal Persuasion. While key administration bills are under consideration by Congress, the President's congressional liaison officers spend much time on Capitol Hill performing such tasks as supplying information regarding bills, helping arrange for influential persons to testify at committee hearings, and attempting to persuade reluctant congressmen to vote as the administration wishes. Votes may be obtained on a *quid pro quo* basis. One of Johnson's White House staff members once explained: "Sometimes you have to offer a dam here, or a defense project there, to get a bill through. This is a tough game, and sometimes we do make deals."

The President may grant numerous minor favors that will add to the prestige and status of congressmen of both parties and increase their indebtedness to the President. Favors that may be dispensed by the President include accepting a congressman's recommendations on appointments; presidential support for a congressman's bill; assistance in a forthcoming election campaign; and invitations to White House dinners, bill signing ceremonies, or a weekend at a presidential retreat. Letters of congratulations signed by the President on White House stationery, or pictures taken with the President, often become valued mementos. After accepting invitations or other acts of friendliness, congressmen of either party often find it more difficult to oppose or criticize the President.

A President, such as the two Roosevelts and Lyndon Johnson, who has a special talent for personal relations, may gain support for a bill merely by discussing it with legislators in the President's office, at social events, or in a telephone call. Such efforts at personal persuasion are usually reserved for occasions when an informal poll of the House or Senate shows that a presidential measure may fail by a few votes to be enacted. A member of the influential House Committee on Rules reported the following reaction to such a call from President Johnson:

What do you say to the President of the United States? I told him I'd sleep on it. Then the next day I said to myself, "I've always been a party man, and if he really needed me of course I'd go along even if the bill wasn't set up exactly the way I wanted it." Probably I took half a dozen *guys with me. We won in the crunch by six votes. Now, I wouldn't have voted for it except for his telephone call.*[5]

In his relations with Congress the President has occasion to recall that politics is both "the art of the possible" and "a struggle for power." As members of Congress have political power in their own right, the President's power to persuade often becomes the power to negotiate, and not uncommonly, he is required to compromise—to accept half a loaf or nothing at all. A President's power to persuade members of Congress clearly depends on more than reasoned arguments, friendly gestures, and advantages that adhere to his office. In order to persuade some members of Congress, he must convince them that he has the political skill and the determination to use with maximum effectiveness the advantages that accrue to him because of his status and authority. This does not mean that the President should crudely bargain for support for his legislative program. However, the President patently should use all the influence and advantages of his office to obtain nationally desirable goals. He must, therefore, be prepared to give recognition to those who support his program and withhold favors from those who do not. As Richard Neustadt has written: "The essence of a President's persuasive task with Congressmen and everybody else, is to induce them to believe that what he wants of them is what their own appraisal of their own responsibilities requires them to do in their interest, not his."[6]

℀ PRESIDENTS–STRONG AND WEAK

Various efforts have been made to categorize the Presidents according to their comparative strength as Chief Executive. One of the more widely accepted classifications resulted from a 1962 survey of seventy-five distinguished students of American history, who grouped the Presidents into five categories: great, near-great, average, below average, and failures.[7] Five were ranked as great: Washington, Jefferson, Lincoln, Wilson, and Franklin Roosevelt. Six were placed in the near-great category: John Adams, Jackson, Polk, Cleveland, Theodore Roosevelt, and Truman. Only Grant and Harding were considered failures. All others were rated as average or below average. For the purpose of this discussion we will consider those classified as great or near-great as strong Presidents. What then are the qualities that set the strong Presidents apart from the others?

Each of the great and near-great Presidents has been so classified because of the character of his leadership, his influence on major events of the day,

[5] *Newsweek*, August 2, 1965, p. 22.
[6] Richard E. Neustadt, *Presidential Power* (New York, Wiley, 1960), p. 46.
[7] Arthur M. Schlesinger, "Our Presidents: A Rating by 75 Historians," *The New York Times Magazine* (July 29, 1962), p. 12.

and his lasting impact on American and world history. Consider briefly the contributions of the five "great" Presidents. Four successfully led the nation through a major war, but they also had other noteworthy achievements. Washington, during his administration, performed the important task of organizing the government and establishing it on a firm foundation, and bestowed prestige on the office of Chief Executive by his dignity and force of character. Jefferson is known for the Declaration of Independence, his democratic ideals which have a pervasive effect upon our government and philosophy, for founding the Democratic party, and for the Louisiana Purchase. Lincoln, in addition to preserving the Union, abolished slavery, and helped to establish the Republicans as the political party that dominated the government for seven decades. Even if Wilson had not led the nation during World War I and had not been instrumental in establishing the League of Nations, his legislative record would have assured his reputation as one of the more outstanding Presidents. Similarly, Franklin Roosevelt's New Deal would have secured him a place among the great Presidents even if our victory in World War II and the establishment of the United Nations were not associated with his name.

No doubt the time during which each President occupied the Presidency has influenced his conception of the office and his ranking as President. All of the "great" Presidents served during periods when momentous decisions were made, but had men of lesser ability, such as James Buchanan or Warren Harding, then been in office, they might have permitted the nation to drift. Nonetheless, during other times, forceful presidential leadership was not favored or considered essential. During the last third of the nineteenth century the nation had a succession of weak Presidents; only Cleveland exerted sufficient leadership to be ranked as a strong President. These were the early decades when laissez-faire was the prevailing social and economic thought and most people supported a negative role for government and the President. Later, as the United States became a major world power and as reaction to laissez-faire developed, Theodore Roosevelt and Wilson emerged as the first of the modern strong Presidents. Building on precedents they established, Franklin Roosevelt ushered in a new period of presidential leadership. Never again can a President assume a passive role, serving merely as the head of the administrative agencies.

Desired Characteristics of Presidential Leadership

The strong Presidents, in addition to possessing the obvious traits of intelligence and integrity, were endowed with an unusual amount of energy, determination, and fortitude. But more important, they were activists, and during the twentieth century at least, they have been liberal Presidents. They considered it their responsibility to provide leadership for Congress and the people. They employed the power and prestige of their office to guide the nation toward a more complete fulfillment of the ideals of American democracy. Other Presidents had forceful personalities and did not lack the capacity to lead, but they either accepted a literal interpretation of the separation of powers or were more willing to accept the *status quo*. By contrast, the strong Presidents, rather than permit themselves to be dominated by Congress and by events, attempted to direct and channel the social and economic forces of their times toward constructive national goals.

Strong Presidents were more concerned with their place in history than with current popularity. They had a sense of history that permitted them to place in proper perspective the events of their day. Most strong Presidents had many loyal supporters, but they incurred the powerful opposition, even wrath, of others who opposed their plans. Today Washington, Jefferson, and Lincoln are universally admired and respected, but during their lifetimes they were opposed and bitterly denounced by many of their countrymen. Men of lesser stature might have compromised their ideals and goals in order to achieve public approval, but the strong Presidents persisted in doing what they thought to be right, confident in their belief that history would verify their judgment.

In the final analysis, the strong Presidents have been distinguished from the others by their ability to guide public opinion and their effectiveness in their relations with other leaders in politics, including congressmen, executive officials, and representatives of foreign states. This skill is likely to be acquired only through practical political experience, or perhaps through a combination of experience and study. Woodrow Wilson is the only one of the strong Presidents who had not had considerable political experience before being elected to the Presidency, and he had devoted his adult life to study of government. A person who has served as a governor or congressman is more likely than an amateur to be a successful President.

⅍ A TWENTIETH-CENTURY PRESIDENCY

The tremendous responsibilities placed on the American Chief Executive pose questions regarding the organization and functioning of the Presidency. Is it true, as Harry Truman once remarked, that "no one man can really fill the Presidency"? Are there dangers inherent in concentrating in the hands of one person the responsibilities and powers the President now possesses? Is there a conflict between new demands for individual freedom and executive leadership?

Can One Man Fill the Presidency?

Whether one person can satisfactorily perform the duties of the Chief Executive has long been questioned. Starting during the latter part of the nineteenth century several plans have been proposed to institute changes that might provide stronger and more responsible executive leadership. Some have suggested establishing a Cabinet form of government somewhat similar to that in Britain, Canada, or Australia, arguing that by thus uniting the executive and legislative branches, the executive would have the power necessary to provide forceful leadership and at the same time the legislature could more effectively hold the executive accountable for its actions. Others have urged that efforts be made to achieve more energetic and responsible governmental action through stronger and more centralized political parties.

There are now fewer advocates of such proposals because events and personalities have themselves strengthened the Presidency. Due to the establishment of the Executive Office of the President and his unrivalled access to the mass media, the President now has the assistance and the facilities to be a strong leader.

Does the President Have Too Much Power?

From the beginning of our history fear has been expressed that a President might wish to establish himself as a monarch or a dictator. Beginning with Washington, every strong President has been accused of wanting to usurp powers belonging to the other branches of government or reserved to the people. In addition, in recent years some critics have argued that Congress has delegated to the President too much authority, and that he might use such authority improperly. These critics have overlooked the fact that "what Congress gives, Congress can take away." Indeed, in the domestic area the President can take no important action without the continued support and approval of Congress, which must provide the funds and personnel necessary for any government program. Moreover, if a President should develop a desire for dictatorial power, Congress, the courts, the state governments, political interest groups, the press, and public opinion, all can be counted on to check such aspirations.

These various checks do not guarantee that the President's policies will be wise or in the public interest. The best assurance that the public interest will be served is through an active opposition party that scrutinizes all presidential proposals, offers constructive criticisms, and submits an alternative program. Unfortunately, the opposition party in the United States has seldom functioned in this fashion. Although individual congressmen may criticize proposals, only rarely does the opposition party conduct a debate in Congress which clarifies the issues and educates the public regarding alternative programs or solutions. A well-organized and constructive opposition would be an invaluable improvement in the American governmental system. As President Kennedy once stated: "The men who create power make an indispensable contribution to the nation's greatness, but the men who question power make a contribution just as indispensable ... for they determine whether we use power or power uses us."

The principal potential danger in presidential government lies in the power that one man—the President—has to make decisions in the international sphere. Although Congress can limit the President's actions in domestic affairs, it does not serve as an adequate check in international relations. The President can be restrained only by his advisers, most of whom he has appointed. Decisions by the President can involve the country in war; and rash or irrational decisions could possibly lead to a war that might be avoided by a more restrained or intelligent Chief Executive. The problem is not due to new presidential power; for the President, acting on his authority as commander in chief, has always been able to commit the nation to policies that might result in armed conflict. The possibility of modern nuclear warfare inserts a new element of danger.

More than two decades ago Edward S. Corwin pointed out that one of the hazards of the presidential system is "that there is no governmental body which can be relied upon to give the President independent advice and which he is nevertheless bound to consult."[8] Congress created the National Security Council as an advisory body to the President on military and foreign policy. But the President is not required to act on the advice of the Council; moreover, a strong President may so dominate the Council, whose members are selected by him, that they may be reluctant to assert opposing views. Major presidential decisions on national security and foreign policy are, of course, customarily made only after the President has consulted with various political leaders and experts. The President can find many people who will support him in what he wants to do; what he needs are men who will not hesitate to oppose him when they feel he is wrong. A characteristic of the British Cabinet system that has recommended it to some American political scientists is the collegial nature of major political decisions.

[8] Edward S. Corwin, *The President: Office and Powers*, 2d ed. (New York: New York University Press, 1941), p. 316.

Is There a Conflict Between Individual
Freedom and Executive Leadership?

At the same time that domestic and international conditions require more government and stronger presidential leadership, there has developed a desire for more individual freedom, fewer restraints, and the expansion of civil rights and liberties. These two contemporary trends in American life have created tensions in the body politic. They do not represent conflict between two ideologies, between "the rulers" and "the people," or between authority and freedom, but rather a psychological conflict between the democratic impulse and the need for leadership. These two simultaneous developments illustrate an ambivalence in democracy: (1) Emotionally, individuals want maximum freedom, but (2) intellectually and rationally, they realize that in government as well as in business and other organized activities, there is need for leadership.

Possibly the United States is moving toward a pragmatic solution similar to that in Great Britain, where there is strong respect for individual liberty combined with forceful political leadership in the national government. In the United States greater freedom may be achieved for the citizenry by presidential leadership and governmental action—through expansion of civil rights, public education, increased recreational facilities, less censorship in literature and entertainment, and more freedom from want and fear because of expanded social security and medical care programs. With greater individual freedom, citizens may become more aware of the necessity to accept effective leadership in national affairs. Indeed, the President, who, it was feared at times, would become an autocrat unmindful of the wishes of the people, has instead become the chief champion for sustaining and expanding individual liberties.

CHAPTER 20

RUNNING THE
NATIONAL GOVERNMENT

Government, for most citizens, consists principally of the more publicized and dramatic activities in which public employees as well as private citizens take direct roles. Thus the average citizen thinks of government as the activities of Congress in making laws, the actions of the President in the conduct of foreign policy, and the decisions of the Supreme Court on issues of great constitutional importance. The primary functions of these institutions concern policy-making: the channeling of demands made by private individuals and groups through legitimate agents who convert these demands into authoritative policy.

Government also impinges directly on the individual through the application of general rules to specific situations, both those foreseen and unforeseen. In terms of the number of employees involved, the amounts of money spent, the individual contacts with citizens, the significance of decisions made by the public employees, or almost any other criteria, the multitude of administrative agencies erected to implement general policy—the bureaucracy[1]—constitute the heart of government.

[1] Throughout this discussion the term "bureaucracy" is used in a nonpejorative sense, i.e., as a neutral term referring to the federal public service.

ꙮ DIMENSIONS OF THE BUREAUCRACY: SIZE

To understand the operations of the bureaucracy, it is necessary first of all to have some conception of its dimensions and its principal characteristics. One dimension is sheer size. The United States government today employs almost 3 million civilian employees, approximately 4.5 percent of the total working force in the United States in 1966. By far the largest proportion of those employees perform their labors in field offices outside of Washington, D.C.; only about 10 percent are employed in the nation's capital.

ꙮ VARIETY OF THE ACTIVITIES

In addition to the dimension of size, we must be aware of the variety of activities and programs in which the federal government engages. These programs range from the operation of the Alaska Railroad to the management of medical research on major diseases, and to the more commonplace transportation and delivery of the mails. There is no citizen whose life is not touched in some way by some activity of the federal government, whether it be in the payment of taxes, in the observance of some federal statute with regard to safety, in the receipt of some service such as special school programs underwritten by the federal government, or in the construction of some facility such as the interstate highways.

Such varied activities require the services of every skill known to man. The nuclear physicist may be employed in the discovery of new radioactive isotopes that may be useful in medicine or in further scientific inquiry; the engineer may be working on the design of water delivery systems as a part of a hydroelectric power and water project; the economist may be involved in the assessment of the impact of American foreign aid programs on the developing economies of new nations.

ꙮ THE RISE OF THE ADMINISTRATIVE STATE

The growth in the size of the bureaucracy, the variety of its programs, and the frequency of its impact on the individual's life has been the subject of much lamentation. For some critics, the growth of the bureaucracy is a visible evidence of the moral degradation of the American people when compared with an earlier period when government was small and the individual was relatively untouched by its operations. Some perceive the growth of the bureaucracy as the product of a gigantic plot to destroy freedom and to regiment the public under controls exercised by power-hungry individuals who think they know what is good for everyone else.

Although each of these assertions may have a trace of truth, they fail to credit the transformation of the character of American society under the impact of the industrial revolution as the chief element in the changed and changing role of government. The farmer who sought protection for prices of his products sold in distant markets demanded the creation of an agency to regulate the railroads. He was rewarded with the Interstate Commerce Commission. Industry, faced with ruinous price wars and unfair methods of competition among holding companies representing gigantic combinations of capital, demanded the Sherman and Clayton Anti-Trust acts. With them, they were provided the services of the Anti-Trust division of the Department of Justice, and the Federal Trade Commission. Motorists who bought increasingly powerful cars in rapidly increasing numbers demanded improved highways to carry them. The highways improved under the supervision of the Bureau of Public Roads. The examples could be multiplied a thousandfold.

"... and, in return, I'd be happy to vote against any further centralization of power in the hands of federal agencies." Ruge; in *Saturday Review*, 1964.

In newly developing areas throughout the world, the bureaucracies are carrying the burden of modernization to a considerable degree. Lacking private capital, the state has become the primary instrument for economic betterment, and the civil servant has become the administrator of the national wealth. Since the civil service often constitutes the single largest concentration of educated and experienced personnel, they have an extraordinary influence over the direction and speed of development, far greater than that exercised by civil servants in the United States. Moreover, they play an important *political* role in inculcating a sense of national identity among peoples whose loyalties previously were exclusively local and tribal.

⚘ THE SPIRIT OF THE BUREAUCRACY

A classic discussion of bureaucracy by the German sociologist, Max Weber, described bureaucracy as a "pure type" when it had the characteristics of (1) specialization of roles, (2) selection on the basis of achievement, (3) advancement on the basis of established rules, (4) full-time salaried employees who are committed to the bureaucracy as a career, and (5) decision-making according to rules within a hierarchical set of relationships.

To a certain extent every bureaucratic system in the world satisfies these criteria. But the startling differences among the administrative patterns of various societies testify to the powerful impact of culture. For administrative relationships are not only relationships among people within the bureaucracy but are patterns of behavior between the administration and the public and the other institutions of government.

Illustrative of one administrative pattern is the French bureaucracy. The French administrative structure developed from the royal household, but was adapted to the purposes of the modern nation-state with the overthrow of the monarchical system. The civil service was already powerful and relatively professional; only its master had changed. The bureaucracy became the servant of an all-powerful, impersonal state. The top-ranking bureaucrats were often drawn from a narrow social class that had access to higher education. Because of political instability, the bureaucracy provided the necessary continuity in government and often made crucial political decisions that others were not prepared to make. The bureaucracy was fortified, moreover, by guarantees of security, adequate pay, and official rank, all of which contributed to high social status. Much of this remains applicable to France today.

The American administrative system may be distinguished for its *repre-*

sentative rather than its *class* character. Although representation is normally thought to be the exclusive prerogative of the elected representative, the American political system creates an expectation that the bureaucrat will also respond to the public's conception of the general interest. The administrator therefore faces serious political issues, not by simply looking for direction from elsewhere—the Congress or the President—but by grappling with them himself and contesting over them with other participants in the administrative process.

This suggests that all of the lines of influence in the American bureaucracy are not hierarchical according to the vertical lines normally found on organization charts. The bureaucrat is subject not only to immediate legal superiors in the government agencies but to the host of other individuals and groups that have a stake in the outcome of an administrative decision. Each recognizes in the bureaucrat the authority to make binding decisions affecting his welfare. The contests that take place in administrative settings may indeed appear to be almost as political as those that occur in Congress, where bargaining is the normal method of problem-solving. For example, a regional officer in the Bureau of Reclamation of the Department of the Interior may attempt to balance off—in effect represent—the wishes of the outdoor enthusiast, the municipal home dweller, the industrialist, and the ecologist in attempting to decide how to manage a given reservoir. Each has a vital stake in water management and can be highly vocal in support of his demands before the administrative unit involved.

The American bureaucracy is distinctive and representative also for the character of those who serve and the conditions under which they labor. Far from being a social, economic, or political elite, the American bureaucracy constitutes a reflection of the American public. Its personnel is recruited nationwide and from all classes of the population. There are no artificial barriers against internal advancement. In general, there is no established relationship, for example, between the "best" universities and the bureaucracy. No private elite groups have more or less ready access to the highest levels of the administrative service. Moreover, entry is permitted at all levels, making the infusion of new blood both a possibility and a practical reality.

This, however, does not imply that there are not differences. One major difference is the relatively high degree of professionalization of the federal executives. A much higher percentage in the federal service has had advanced professional training and has worked in professional capacities than is characteristic of other groups, such as business executives. Moreover, in comparison with business executives, governmental executives have a broader occupational experience and mobility, moving in and out of public life relatively freely.

❧ BUREAUCRACY AND POLICY-MAKING

By constitutional doctrine and by prevailing usage, the formulation of legislation was in the hands of the Congress and the President until the twentieth century. But the exigencies of life in modern American society have forced a revision in the role of the bureaucracy in the making of public policy. The complexity of the issues and the necessity of coordinating new policy with existing programs required that the bureaucracy become a full partner in virtually every phase of the policy-making process. No longer is it accurate to classify bureaucratic work as neutral and technical in character, as though the personnel of the bureaucracy were so many elements in a complex piece of machinery.

The constitutional-legal description of the role of bureaucracy also fails to deal with the real environment in which the bureaucracy pursues its labors. For the bureaucracy is a human institution, peopled by individuals with commitments to, and dependence on, their activities within their agencies. These commitments, in addition to their professional pride, tend to develop within agency personnel strong policy drives that in time become traditions and even dogma. These become "the way things are done," sacred against tampering by the uninitiated. Thus, the Federal Bureau of Investigation developed an *esprit* as well as a reputation that only the most intrepid critic might challenge. Similarly, the Forest Service personnel developed a virtually unassailable concept of the public interest in which they figure as guardians of the national forests.

The development of new programs in the federal government requires a nice integration of what exists, what is proposed, and what is possible. It requires the avoidance of measures that are obviously impractical or have failed in the past. It requires an awareness of all of the technical and procedural ramifications involved in inaugurating a new program. Finally, it demands an appreciation of the substantive values of existing programs and adeptness in improving the programs. The bureaucracy has collective experience and knowledge that must be consulted in any major effort to change policy.

Policy Implementation

The nature of public policy also requires the delegation of a broad range of discretion to the administrators in the application of general laws and guidelines to specific cases. Congressional legislation increasingly has the character of general statements of purposes to be achieved, of classes of individuals who are eligible or subject to the statute, and of conditions under which the provisions of the statute should be applied. Congress has neither the time nor the capacity to foresee every contingency that might arise under a statute, or every individual case that might develop. The burden of reading congressional intentions and applying them to given circumstances falls on the bureaucracy.

Although seldom officially admitted, this is essentially a policy-making function. For decisions in a group of cases with similar characteristics become the *rule* for the agency that is applied to all other cases as they arise. Officials as well as the public must therefore know not only the law but the regulations made pursuant to the law if they are to conform to their respective roles as law enforcer and law obeyer.

Thus, the Higher Education Act of 1965, which provided for the expenditure of over $800 million in support of various educational programs, in one section authorized the creation of a Community Service Program that was defined as

> an educational program, activity, or service, including a research program and a university extension or continuing education offering, which is designed to assist in the solution of community problems in rural, urban, or suburban areas, with particular emphasis on urban and suburban problems. . . .

What these programs would consist of was not made clear in the Act, but the Commissioner of Education was charged with the responsibility of receiving and *approving* plans submitted by state agencies in whatever detail the Commissioner might require.

The bureaucracy, although formally neutral, actively promotes the policy programs in which it believes, by various methods ranging from public relations campaigns to direct lobbying with the members of Congress. Public information officers provide reams of information about government programs to interested parties; operating personnel in the field discuss their activities before luncheon clubs and professional groups. Agencies develop close relationships with interested clientele groups who can be relied on to cooperate in promoting programs of mutual concern. By an infinitely complex web of relationships in Washington, D.C., experienced bureaucrats work with sympathetic congressmen, with lobbyists, with newspapermen, and with other executive officials in creating a favorable climate for consideration of their propositions.

The bureaucracy is of course subject to political control through the President and Congress, and must respond when the political winds change, as painful as such response is for people who have committed themselves to existing programs. In some instances its response may be lethargic, but this then requires more dynamic and forceful political leadership to overcome natural unwillingness to follow new paths. The resistance encountered in certain departments when the Eisenhower administration took office in 1953 after 20 years of Democratic control suggests the severity of this problem in some cases, but the political leadership finally managed to overcome it and redirect bureaucratic efforts toward the Eisenhower administration goals. The bureaucracy is also limited in that it cannot identify itself with either of the major political parties, whatever its private convictions.

❧ POLITICAL LEADERSHIP AND CONTROL

In the constitutional sense, the President is Chief Executive, with authority over virtually every official in the executive branch, and with responsibility for the activities in which the officials are engaged. In a formal sense, he makes his influence felt through the advisers he selects and the principal administrators who presumably reflect his views in their own areas of policy responsibility. Given presidential determination to effect some change in existing administrative practice or policy, and a clear statement of his wishes, undoubtedly he can have his way.

But the realities of big government make clear presidential leadership a seldom-encountered and sometimes vigorously avoided phenomenon. For the President is a single man, and though his reach is much extended through the White House Office, the Bureau of the Budget, the National Security Council, and the Cabinet, he cannot commit himself to more than a fraction of the business that is nominally under his jurisdiction. He must rely on the good judgment and the keen political sense of his associates to defend his interests and promote his general political philosophy even if they can only be guessed by intuition.

❧ CONGRESSIONAL INFLUENCE

Congress, moreover, is not willing to give the President unchallenged control of the executive establishment. The members and the committees of Congress perceive a very real stake in maintaining maximum influence in the decisions that are made, both because of a desire to protect the prerogatives of Congress and because those decisions may have direct and immediate effect on the welfare and interests of the people they represent.

The character of congressional control also contributes to the disintegrative structure of the executive branch, with many bureaus becoming almost autonomous entities. Their autonomy reflects in considerable part their special relationships with the congressional committees having jurisdiction over their affairs. These committees maintain close liaison with the bureaus, protecting them from "unwarranted" interference with congressional intent by the political leaders in their departments and even from presidential control. This protection may come in the form of legislation desired by the bureau but opposed by the administration, or funds in excess of recommendations by the Bureau of the Budget, or threats against those who may not accept the committee's thinking.

Congressional weapons in dealing with the bureaucracy are sufficient in number and in potency to give any President pause. The most powerful weapon is its power to cut the budget submitted by the President, or in some instances to increase the amounts he asked for. It may set personnel ceilings and establish the qualifications for people in various positions. It has the basic responsibility for designing the organization of the executive agencies, and may grant or withhold authorization for reorganization of his administration. Congressional committees may undertake investigations, and the General Accounting Office, which is considered the auditing agency of the Congress, makes periodic reports on alleged inefficiency and mismanagement in the executive departments.

✤ SUBGOVERNMENTS

Much of the machinery of government continues to operate on the basis of a momentum and a sense of direction developed through years of careful adjustments with the environment in which it is located. Career administrators, whose familiarity with their programs far exceeds that of any political executive appointed by the President, may have relative freedom in the realization of the goals their organizations have established. Unless controversy arises, the President and his aides may find it far more conducive to political peace and progress to allow the machinery to perpetuate itself.

The capacity of administrative agencies to make necessary adjustments often depends on the development of what Douglass Cater has called "subgovernments."[2] These are alliances of the principal public and private groups who have an interest in a given area of public policy-making. Such alliances may cut across the boundaries between the executive and legislative branches, between the two major political parties, and between major interest groups. The chairman of a committee, or the chairman of an

[2] *Power in Washington* (New York: Vintage Books, 1963), p. 2.

appropriations subcommittee, may be the key figure in this subgovernment, which may include bureau chiefs, lobbyists, and major economic groups doing business with or receiving services from the government.

One of these subgovernments to which Cater pointed is the military-industrial complex. The military services of the government are responsible for the development and maintenance of an arsenal capable of adequately defending United States interests throughout the world. The chief producers of the weaponry for this arsenal are private concerns that not only produce the weapons but engage in research and development of new weapons. Major industries in various parts of the country utterly depend on defense contracts, and the prosperity of these industries determines the economic well-being of numerous communities. Thus there develops an interlocking alliance among the industry, the military services, spokesmen for communities, and representatives in Congress, all of whom are urgently interested in promotion of some product, or some research possibility that will ensure jobs and profits. Far from engaging in debates over policy according to the classical concept of the separation of powers, members of Congress and executive officials collaborate in seeking appropriations from the federal treasury that can then be distributed among the various competitors for contracts. Other subgovernments—veterans' benefits, oil production—are so strong that the President may feel that efforts to influence them are futile.

It is notable that the political party appears to play no role in these subgovernments. By and large this is a realistic assessment, in spite of the occasional efforts to award contracts or authorize projects that may help the electoral chances of a given congressman. Partisanship is likely to be a much more important factor in *new* programs in which the party organizations are often invited to assist in staffing the agency and in which local party officials in areas in which the program operates feel a proprietary interest in granting favors to recipients of federal programs. Thus the "Anti-Poverty" program of the Johnson administration has suffered attacks both for its alleged partisan character and for its failure to clear everything with local Democratic politicians.

✤ ORGANIZATION OF THE EXECUTIVE BRANCH

Departments

The formal structure of the executive branch follows no single pattern. (See Figure 20–1.) The principal form of organization is the *department*, headed by a Secretary who is appointed by the President, confirmed by the

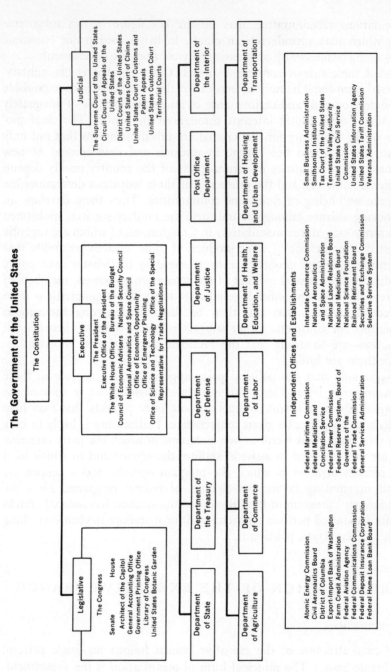

The Government of the United States

The Constitution

Legislative

The Congress

Senate
House
Architect of the Capitol
General Accounting Office
Government Printing Office
Library of Congress
United States Botanic Garden

Executive

The President

Executive Office of the President
The White House Office   Bureau of the Budget
Council of Economic Advisers   National Security Council
National Aeronautics and Space Council
Office of Economic Planning
Office of Emergency Planning
Office of Science and Technology   Office of the Special
Representative for Trade Negotiations

Judicial

The Supreme Court of the United States
Circuit Courts of Appeals of the
United States
District Courts of the United States
United States Court of Claims
United States Court of Customs and
Patent Appeals
United States Customs Court
Territorial Courts

Department of State

Department of the Treasury

Department of Defense

Department of Justice

Post Office Department

Department of the Interior

Department of Agriculture

Department of Commerce

Department of Labor

Department of Health, Education, and Welfare

Department of Housing and Urban Development

Department of Transportation

Independent Offices and Establishments

Atomic Energy Commission
Civil Aeronautics Board
District of Columbia
Export-Import Bank of Washington
Farm Credit Administration
Federal Aviation Agency
Federal Communications Commission
Federal Deposit Insurance Corporation
Federal Home Loan Bank Board

Federal Maritime Commission
Federal Mediation and
Conciliation Service
Federal Power Commission
Federal Reserve System, Board of
Governors of the
Federal Trade Commission
General Services Administration

Interstate Commerce Commission
National Aeronautics
and Space Administration
National Labor Relations Board
National Mediation Board
National Science Foundation
Railroad Retirement Board
Securities and Exchange Commission
Selective Service System

Small Business Administration
Smithsonian Institution
Tax Court of the United States
Tennessee Valley Authority
United States Civil Service
Commission
United States Information Agency
United States Tariff Commission
Veterans Administration

FIGURE 20–1. Organization of the Government of the United States. (Adapted from *United States Government Organization Manual 1965–66*.)

Senate, and who sits in the President's Cabinet. By far the largest number of federal employees are found in these departments.

But even though the general departmental structure has many similarities, it is incongruous to classify together such organizations as the Department of Defense, with its three constituent military services and its more than one million civilian employees (and nearly 3 million uniformed servicemen), and the Department of Labor, with its less than 10,000 employees. Both the size of these two organizations and their traditions and missions make them drastically different. Every Secretary of Defense has testified to the difficulty in exercising control and coordinating the efforts of the military departments, owing to the strong loyalties and professional commitments developed during their separate existence and to the tensions that exist between civilian and military leaders.

Independent Agencies

A second major type of governmental unit is the independent agency, which is headed by a single administrator who does not carry Cabinet rank. These agencies are usually more specialized than the major departments; typical agencies are the Federal Aviation Agency and the Veterans Administration.

The justification for the creation of agencies of this type is far more political than administrative. Proponents often argue that there is something unique about the programs they are engaged in, which necessitates separate organizational existence. In some instances this may have the ring of reality, as in the case of the National Aeronautics and Space Administration, which embarked on obviously novel efforts in space exploration. But this position is hardly tenable with regard to the Veterans Administration or the United States Information Service, both of which are engaged in programs closely related and in some instances identical with programs conducted in other departments. Most educational benefits are provided by the Office of Education in the Department of Health, Education and Welfare, and there seems to be no *administrative* justification of separate status for Veterans Administration programs.

The real justification is found in the desire of interested parties—sometimes interest groups, sometimes members of Congress, often both—to ensure administrative responsiveness to their wishes, and to preclude "interference" on the part of older departments which have more settled (and oftentimes more orderly) approaches toward administration. Sometimes separate status indicates a strong distrust of existing departments and an unwillingness to commit programs to the departments for that reason. It may even indicate distrust of a single individual. Thus, when Henry Wallace was appointed Secretary of Commerce in 1945, the price of his approval by the Senate was the separation of the Reconstruction Finance Corporation from his jurisdiction, owing to the intense animosity in the Senate toward Wallace. The independent status of the information agencies and the foreign aid organizations—with their various names and internal make-ups—reflected great distrust toward the State Department as a defender of American interests, and a desire to ensure greater independence of action by these agencies.

Finally, separate status may indicate a desire to launch new programs with new personnel outside the regular procedures for hiring, for program management, and for budgeting. Thus the Peace Corps and the Office of Economic Opportunity, both initially under Sargent Shriver, were granted independence in order to pioneer new territory in as rapid and imaginative a way as they could.

Independent Regulatory Commissions

A third organizational form is the independent regulatory commission, which, as its name implies, is an organization headed by a plural body and concerned principally with regulation of some essentially private economic activity. Among others, there are the Interstate Commerce Commission, which is concerned primarily with regulation of the railroads and trucking industry; the Securities and Exchange Commission, which regulates the stock exchanges and establishes rules governing the issuance of new securities; and the Federal Power Commission, which regulates the electric power and natural gas industries.

The term "independent," however, is more troublesome to define. Historically, the creation of these commissions reflected the desire of major public groups to ensure more equitable treatment by economic interests that had virtual monopoly power, that performed some essential service, or that utilized some form of property declared to be in the public domain. Because the issues were complex and regulations required frequent adjustment, Congress felt itself incapable of making the necessary decisions and therefore delegated the task to the regulatory commissions. Moreover, because the courts were incapable of mastering the complex, technical subject matter and of handling cases expeditiously, the commissions were charged with a "quasi-judicial" function, that of making judicial-like decisions among competing interests. In effect, the regulatory commissions were given legislative and judicial power under general guidelines laid down by Congress. The commission form of administration was designed to protect the agency against "politics" by representation of various groups on the commission and by isolating it from the influence of the President.

This was done by giving the commissioners specific and often lengthy terms of office (as long as 14 years), by staggering the terms, by requiring that they be bipartisan, and by denying the President the power of removal of the commissioners except for specific cause. The assumption was that the judgments to be made would involve technical rather than policy questions, and should therefore be insulated from partisan influences.

The results have proven otherwise. Relative independence from the President and partisan politics—and thus from the principal legitimate channel for holding government responsible—has been achieved. But independence of the commissions from the major industries they are supposed to regulate has not been accomplished. The common tendency of the commissions is to make some form of accommodation with which both the industry and the commission can live. In some instances the commissioners come from the industries they are to regulate and therefore may lack a crusading zeal to reform them. The opportunities for future employment in the industry may temper enthusiasm for strong control. The entrenched position of the industry and the tremendous investment in established ways of doing things make efforts to impose significant restrictions or standards extremely difficult. The industry may also count on powerful allies in Congress who have effective budgetary and legislative weapons against too vigorous efforts at regulation. The record of the Interstate Commerce Commission in regulating the nation's railroads is perhaps an extreme example of a fairly common phenomenon.

Corporations

A fourth organizational form is the government corporation. These are governmental bodies that are organized to operate more or less as business enterprises, freed from the normal budgetary and financial controls imposed on regular administrative agencies. Examples of such corporations are the Tennessee Valley Authority, which generates enormous quantities of hydroelectric power as well as manages a variety of resource-oriented activities in the Tennessee Valley; the Federal Deposit Insurance Corporation, which insures depositors of funds in member banks against loss; and the Export-Import Bank, which helps in the financing of export operations through guaranteeing credits and granting loans.

The independence of these enterprises is not found in the legal limitation on the powers of the President, but in the freedom they enjoy from annual appropriations and in their capacity to reinvest their funds as they deem wise. The President does appoint the heads of these agencies and may remove them as he sees fit. But once given an appropriation, the corporation, within certain limits, may operate as a business, having the advantages of flexibility and more immediate response to situations requiring speed and adaptation.

These corporations do not, however, escape entirely from normal governmental controls. The majority must follow federal personnel practices, must report and receive approval of administrative expenses, and submit reports of their operations to Congress and the President. Because most government corporations are not truly profit-making institutions, they must from time to time request appropriations to continue their operations, thus providing the President and Congress with an opportunity for review of their operations. As a practical matter, these corporations operate in areas overlapping other federal activities and cannot hope to accomplish their purposes without cooperation with other agencies.

Government Contracts

Since World War II a relatively new form of government program administration has developed that involves the granting of contracts with private companies to carry on some necessary governmental activity. These arrangements have been particularly important in the area of national defense, where the Department of Defense or one of its military departments has made grants to companies for research and development of a new weapons system or for studies of strategy involving novel military problems such as insurgency. The Rand Corporation and the Institute for Defense Analysis are two well-known government contractors engaged in such work. Major manufacturers also compete for such research and development awards because of the implications they have for future production contracts for the weapons systems once they are developed.

The growth of the government-by-contract approach has raised important questions of public administration. Part of the justification for this approach lies in the utilization of the resources of the private economy, thereby obviating the necessity of building public organizations to do the work. The private companies, it is argued, are freer from administrative routine and restrictions, and because of their necessity of making profits will strive to do the job efficiently. Available evidence indicates that such results are not always forthcoming. In some instances, it is evident that "contracting-out" is a way of avoiding the salary restrictions imposed on federal employees. The types of contracts, often of the "costs plus fixed fee" variety which preclude loss, do not always stimulate efficiency but may result in quite the opposite. Finally, unless the contracting agency has clearly in mind what it wants, and maintains vigilance over the development of the program, the contractor, a private firm, may in effect be wielding public authority without adequate public accountability.

Internal Organization

In the typical department the Secretary is accompanied by a relatively small number of aides and assistants who are appointed either by the President or the Secretary and are responsible to the Secretary. These constitute the political leadership of the department and they are responsible for the conduct of its operations. It is this corps of political leaders that change when a new administration takes office. A new group entering these positions assumes the burden of redirecting the efforts of the bureaucracy toward the goals of the new President, Secretary, and party.

The job of guiding the bureaucracy and of redirecting it is not an easy one. In the first place it requires sophisticated knowledge of the substantive work of the department, something not all political executives have. It requires persistence in overcoming lethargy, if not outright opposition. Many political executives do not remain long enough to see their jobs through. It demands a clear perception of the goals to be achieved, which hardly can be gleaned from the reading of partisan platforms.

The central offices of these bureaus are in Washington and it is there that general policy decisions are finally made. The headquarters staff usually includes specialists in budgeting, programming, personnel, and information, as well as experts in the various technical fields that constitute the work of the bureau. The large majority of the personnel of these operating units are found in field offices throughout the United States and throughout the world. Legally subject to the same laws and guided by the same directives, civil servants function in widely diverse circumstances and are subjected to pressures toward modification of accepted practice both from local interests as well as from their own recognition of difficulties of applying general policy to given situations. The result is strained relations between the central and field offices and accusations of overcentralization and "bureaucratic red-tape" from persons who rely on the bureau's service.

Decentralization of power is a cherished value in American society, and efforts toward that end are usually applauded. But equally cherished is the value of equal treatment of all citizens, regardless of their physical location. The central office therefore seeks adherence to its standards so that everyone will have equal access to the bureau's benefits. Thus, for example, the Federal Housing Administration determines what factors of income will be considered, and to what extent, in guaranteeing a loan made on a house. It would be manifestly unfair for the FHA to apply certain guidelines in one area, and others in another location. Guidelines are necessary to deal promptly with routine cases, reserving to the central office the more difficult ones. Frequent inspections and audits can assure adherence to standards.

Another aspect of internal organization concerns the relationships between the technical specialist and the administrator who must deal with specific cases. Both are vital to an enterprise and both contribute to the decisions that are made, but they tend to approach the same problems from quite different perspectives. The result often is conflict that can have serious political consequences. To illustrate, an economist, a land appraiser, an engineer, and an administrator each may have something to say about the location of a new interstate highway near a city or town. The economist may contribute his expert knowledge regarding the economic effects of the highway on the business life of the city; the land appraiser will tell how much the land will cost in various locations; the engineer will contribute his knowledge of the construction possibilities in various locations; and the administrator may be acutely aware of the community's attitudes with regard to the location of the highway. No decision-maker can ignore any of these factors, and a final decision may be a compromise of many of the positions taken by these "experts." The real "expert" may be the one who can reconcile these differences without alienating the technical specialists and the allies that they may come to represent in the community concerned.

❊ ADMINISTRATIVE MEASURES AND PROCEDURES

For the public, the major questions in dealing with an administration are whether it has been dealt with fairly, expeditiously, and in accordance with procedures that are understandable and predictable. Organization and control are important only insofar as they contribute to the realization of these goals and increase public confidence in the bureaucracy's capacity to achieve them. In general terms, administrative actions either regulate public behavior or provide services, and each calls forth distinctive procedures.

Regulatory and Enforcement Measures

The most direct and uncompromising form of administrative action is enforcement of the law, comparable in many ways to the actions of local policemen. Even in the field of criminal law, which is generally a preserve of the states, there are a significant number of federal statutes that are enforced by federal agents. The Lindbergh Act, an antikidnapping statute, the Mann Act, a statute making transportation of women across state boundaries for immoral purposes illegal, and narcotics statutes—all are enforced by federal agents through police-type activities. Federal narcotics agents, for example, are empowered to seize illegally possessed narcotics and to take into custody those who have them in their possession.

An extremely powerful weapon in the hands of the bureaucracy is the power to issue a license. The licensing power implies the prerogative of granting a privilege to engage in a form of activity that is otherwise proscribed by law. Thus no one may engage in the commercial transmission of messages by radio without a license from the Federal Communications Commission. Nor may an airline fly a plane nor a pilot navigate that plane without obtaining licenses for that purpose. To obtain the privilege to engage in those activities, it is necessary to satisfy the licensing authority that one has complied with the statutory requirements imposed by Congress and the regulations made pursuant to those statutes. There is no *right* to engage in these activities; one does so in many instances only under circumstances of "public convenience and necessity."

Another form of administrative activity concerns the issuance of orders to individuals or groups to desist in a given practice or to comply with a decision rendered by the agency. Thus the Post Office Department may issue an order refusing to transmit mail it believes to be calculated to defraud. The Federal Trade Commission may issue "cease and desist" orders to companies that make false or misleading claims in their advertising.

Less sweeping and general, but no less direct and binding, are other actions taken to secure compliance with the requirements of law. Typical would be the situation of the individual taxpayer, who is required to file an income tax return each year. Failure to report or to pay the amount justified by one's income, or intentional or unintentional errors in the return will result in personal contacts with the Internal Revenue Service agents. These officials will attempt to bring about a resolution of discrepancies and will order payment of taxes due. Failure to pay promptly may result in fines, and evidence of deliberate fraud may bring a criminal indictment for tax evasion.

In fact, much of the contact between the public and public officials is of this character. Rather than highly formalized proceedings, there are negotiations in which each side explains and justifies his actions, almost always with reference to a given statute or regulation. Thus a businessman will argue that a given expense is a legitimate business deduction, while the Internal Revenue Service agent may attempt to verify this claim. Or a farmer will discuss with the county Agricultural Conservation Committee his acreage allotment under various price support schemes, attempting to demonstrate why his allotment should be expanded. Sometimes the question is the meaning of the law or regulation, but often the question is the sufficiency of evidence, and weight of evidence is frequently difficult to assess.

Methods of Information-Gathering

To begin actions against alleged violators of the law it is obviously necessary to provide a basis in evidence. The means of obtaining evidence, however, varies widely. In some instances the federal agencies are active investigators and supervisors, while in others they are passive instruments, available to anybody who wishes to use their facilities for consideration of a grievance.

The most active effort by the federal government is found in the criminal law field, with the Federal Bureau of Investigation, federal attorneys and marshals, narcotics agents, and treasury agents investigating violations of federal criminal law. Less well-known, however, are the activities of such agencies as the Food and Drug Administration and the Bureau of Land Management, which maintain surveillance over individuals or groups who operate in their field of public policy. For example, the BLM inspects the ranges owned and managed by the federal government to ensure that cattle-owners are not running cattle on these lands in excess of the number permitted by the Bureau. Evidence of overstocking may result in warnings to the errant party, or possibly fines for repeated offenses. The Food and Drug Administration requires that drug manufacturers submit experimental evidence of the effectiveness and safety of the drug they propose to market, allowing the FDA to make its independent judgment on whether it should be licensed for public distribution.

In many instances the federal agencies are not equipped to investigate all of the possible violations that might occur. Resources are limited, and not all violations warrant inquiry. Sampling the behavior of several individuals or companies might be one approach, hoping that the evidence of a representative few will be indicative of the behavior of all. Another method is to rely on the registration of complaints by aggrieved parties who ask for government to intervene in their behalf. Thus, a labor union may appeal to the National Labor Relations Board for a ruling on a given action or procedure by an employer that the union feels constitutes an unfair labor practice. Or a state or a municipality may complain that the American Telephone and Telegraph Company is charging excessive rates for its interstate operations, and call for reductions in rates. Such appeals to these administrative agencies place them in the role of judge rather than of prosecutor and often entail the processing of the complaints through rather formal procedures. Perhaps the most highly formalized (or court-like) procedures, however, are those employed when the agency itself initiates the complaint. Formal procedures guard against the possibility of arbitrary judgments resulting from combined responsibilities for prosecution and adjudication.

≿ PROVIDING GOVERNMENT SERVICES

The federal government is engaged in providing an almost infinite variety of services to its citizens—medical services, educational programs, social security, recreational benefits. In addition, indirectly it aids its citizens through the subsidization of various activities, such as airlines, merchant ships, and through research carried out by federal employees and people working on federal contracts. In some instances, the government may even actively promote its services, as it did in advertising benefits under medicare.

The direct benefits are granted through individual application and a sometimes lengthy process of verification of qualifications. A veteran may apply to the Veterans Administration for admission to a VA hospital for treatment of an ailment that he claims was incurred during military service. Once decided favorably, the veteran is thereafter eligible for treatment under whatever restrictions apply. Similar procedures are followed for the applicant for an FHA mortgage guarantee, or for the applicant for educational assistance.

In many instances the applying entity is not an individual but a city, a university, or a corporation. A city may seek funds for redevelopment of its urban core under the Urban Renewal program of the Department of Housing and Urban Development. A university may seek federal funds for undertaking research or to support a new graduate program. A corporation may apply for a loan from the Small Business Administration or from the Department of Commerce under its program of aid to depressed areas. In many of these instances a demonstration of the applicant's willingness and ability to share some of the financial burden may be an important factor in deciding whether federal funds should be granted. Negotiations ensue during which there may be considerable competition for the federal funds from various applicants, each of which believes fervently in the program it proposes.

Except in cases of deliberate fraud, the only sanction against failure to abide by the standards established by the agency is withdrawal of funds. But this may be a powerful weapon when the recipients have depended on the service or the funds and have planned their programs on the basis of this assistance. The Office of Education, for example, has the authority to withhold funds under the 1965 federal aid to education program from school districts that fail to desegregate their facilities. Funds that otherwise might have gone to those districts may then be shifted elsewhere.

❦ THE PUBLIC SERVICE

Since the beginning of the Republic there has been dispute over the proper basis for staffing the federal government. The dispute has centered on the question of whether personnel for the public service should be selected on the basis of merit or on the basis of political inclination or party service. Often the issue has not been clear-cut because technical or professional merit might be admitted as important criteria but only in combination with party allegiance. Thus Thomas Jefferson, faced with an adminstration made up almost exclusively of Federalists who were little disposed to support him, could argue for "due participation" for Republicans, as the Democrats were first called, even at the expense of removing people who were otherwise qualified for office.

For the overwhelming preponderance of positions in the federal service, the merit principle has been the basis for recruitment and selection. Starting with the Pendleton Act of 1883 there has been a gradual extension of the classes of positions for which it is necessary to qualify through competitive examinations. From very modest beginnings—only 10 percent of all federal personnel were in the classified service in 1884—the merit system now covers very close to 90 percent of all personnel, including those who are in independent merit systems such as TVA and the Foreign Service. Not all of the remainder can really be classified as "spoils," because many of this remaining percent are in temporary positions for which no examining procedure fits, or are foreign nationals serving abroad.

The conflict between the two systems of recruitment and personnel management reflects enduring demands on the public service: competent performance and political responsiveness. The public service performs a wide variety of tasks that require professional and technical competence at least at the same level as that required in private businesses. The scientists and engineers, the administrators and accountants, the clerks and secretaries can perform their jobs adequately only if minimum qualifications are established and if stability of employment is assured.

On the other hand, the bureaucracy must be responsive to new emphases and even sharp departures in philosophy and program. Professional skills do not in themselves provide this responsiveness; in fact, they may impede it when associated with commitment to a previous program that is called into question. The infusion at the top of new personnel whose commitment is to the party's, the President's, or the Secretary's program for that agency may have a powerful impact in reorienting it in a new direction. The new recruits are usually less anxious over careers in the federal service, and more concerned with the promotion of an overall approach toward government in accord with that of the President.

⚵ THE ROLE OF THE POLITICAL EXECUTIVE

The second Hoover Commission (U.S. Commission on Organization of the Executive Branch of the Government) identified approximately 1,000 political executive positions in the federal government, consisting of heads of agencies, their deputies, and assistants, general managers of boards and commissions, noncivil service bureau chiefs, and various other subordinate executives. The Commission's Task Force on Personnel stressed the role of the political executives in providing political leadership:

> In the National Government, it is the function of political executives to represent within the administration the policy purposes of the President, to bring the general public's point of view to bear upon administrative decisions, to provide leadership in developing national policy, to exercise statutory powers vested in them as public officials, and to act for the Chief Executive in seeing that all of the laws are faithfully executed; in short, to take the responsibility for governing.[3]

In part, this leadership is internal: working with the career officials to design new programs, to modify old ones, to plan the budget, and to implement present programs. But in larger part, the role of the political executive concerns external relationships: the promotion of new programs or defense of old programs among groups that have an interest in what the department or agency does, negotiation with other agencies that operate in the same substantive field, bargaining with the Bureau of the Budget over how much money will be asked for from Congress, and satisfying Congress that funds will be spent to good purpose or that new departures will resolve a given problem.

The quality of the performance of political executives depends on their ability to operate at the proper levels in directing the bureaucracy. Their experience seldom will allow them to substitute their judgment for the technical knowledge of the staff of scientists, administrators, and advisers

[3] *Task Force Report on Personnel and Civil Service* (Washingon, D.C.: U.S. Government Printing Office, 1955), p. 1.

in their agencies. They must rely on this expertise, but use it as a means of exploring the policy alternatives their agencies confront. Thus the technicians of the Water Pollution Control Administration may measure the effluent entering streams, provide techniques for its removal or prevention, and estimate costs for doing so. All this is useful information, but in no way decides whether the treatment should be done at one point in the river or another, or whether the proper technique should be prevention or treatment, or who should pay the costs of prevention or treatment. These are political questions the political executive must deal with, across departmental boundaries, with Congress, and with the Bureau of the Budget and the President.

A relatively large number of political executives have held prior public office and are therefore acquainted with the stresses and strains of public life. Over three fourths of all political executives appointed from the Roosevelt to the Kennedy administrations had held some public office prior to their appointments, most of them at the federal level and in the executive branch. Moreover, in many instances their private careers have direct relevance to their executive positions. Labor lawyers, for example, such as Arthur Goldberg or Willard Wirtz, had long experience in the field over which they exercised jurisdiction as Secretary of Labor.

The effectiveness of political executives depends also on their length of service, because reorienting an agency that has developed its own momentum over a number of years is no task for the bird of passage. The reshaping of agency policy is an incremental process, a slow and cumulative chipping away and adding on in small pieces, and this requires persistence, ingenuity, and the building of political and administrative support. High turnover among political executives has been a serious problem.

The political executives, particularly the department heads, have important representational roles. Their selection is scrutinized carefully by the general public as well as by the members of Congress, by the members of the President's party, and by interest groups in an effort to perceive some signal indicating the direction in which the administration or the specific department will go. The political executives must work with these elements in the political process and their viewpoints, their records, and their reputations create expectations, either of confidence or distrust. President Kennedy's selection of Stewart Udall as Secretary of the Interior, while giving confidence to the West in general, created considerable anxiety among Californians, who were concerned for the fate of their dispute over the waters of the Colorado River with the Secretary's home state of Arizona. This anxiety was symbolically reduced by the appointment of an Under Secretary from California.

⚘ THE CIVIL SERVICE

Recruitment and Selection

As was noted earlier, the distinctive feature of the civil service is its recruitment and selection on the basis of merit. The concept of merit suggests that the choice of candidates for office depends on demonstrated competence measured by objective examination techniques. Ties of family, party affiliation, education at the "right" schools—all of which may be considered relevant in nonmerit systems—are disregarded in favor of measured capacity for administrative tasks.

A fundamental issue, however, is the kind of device used in measuring competence. Should one measure basic intelligence, which presumably indicates the general capacity to deal with complex problems, or specific skills and knowledge, which equip a person to perform the tasks of the immediate position for which one is recruiting? In general, the American answer to this question has been the latter. Recruitment and selection have been directed toward the choice of the best person for the position to be filled, with relatively less concern for general ability to assume the duties of that office and perhaps higher positions in the administrative hierarchy. In large part, this preference is an expression of the American egalitarian spirit, which emphasizes equal opportunity for all people for public employment. Quite the contrary practice is found in the British civil service, especially for the higher administrative positions, where the examinations are clearly geared to the classical and humanistic traditions of the major British universities. Our foreign service examinations come closest to the British type of examination—which partly explains the strong "Ivy League" representation in the Foreign Service.

In order to recruit and examine candidates for positions it is necessary to describe the duties of these positions and to classify them according to their placement in hierarchy, the difficulty of their performance, and the breadth of responsibility. Thus all the positions in the federal public service have been so classified, permitting standardization of job descriptions and facilitating a wide range of other important personnel actions. The doctrine of equal pay for equal work, for example, requires an analysis of duties in order to establish a basis of comparability. Promotions and transfers are facilitated by these job descriptions, making it possible to discover and utilize talent where needed. And training programs can be related to the duties attached to each level of position. The result in the federal government has been the classification of its employees into approximately 10,000 different classes.

A contrasting system of classification of positions follows the "rank" concept, in which individuals are selected for a given rank, with related pay and other perquisites, but their duties depend on whatever specific task they are called upon to perform. This is essentially the practice in the military services, and is found in many foreign bureaucracies. Recruitment for these services is often very restricted, even directly related to the class structure of the society. Partly for this reason the idea has been resisted in the United States. Suggestions in the late 1950s that a Senior Civil Service be created on this basis met with determined resistance, in spite of the fact that this Service would be "open," rather than reserved to a relatively restricted number who had entered at an early age. There are, however, several "closed" career systems in the federal civil service, notably the Public Health Service and the Foreign Service, wherein entrance into the service usually takes place at an early age and at the bottom of the career ladder, leading to higher positions in the service upon the completion of satisfactory service at lower levels. Even in the Foreign Service, however, there has been some effort to promote "lateral entry," that is, entrance for qualified people at higher levels as a means of "democratizing" that career service.

The federal government attempts to recruit qualified personnel in a highly competitive labor market, one in which the more immediately attractive incentives are normally found in private enterprise. Pay scales for administrative and technical personnel are generally higher in private industry, and personnel policies of corporations may be less hemmed in by rules and regulations that are imposed by Congress on public employees. The "image" of the public service often is a negative rather than a positive one. Among the better educated and higher occupational classes, there is a tendency to stereotype government service as excessive paper work and clerical duties. They do not perceive the possibility of realizing the goals of self-development and achievement that motivate the better educated population. The perceived values of public service tend to emphasize security rather than opportunities for service or exciting careers.

To meet this competition Congress has attempted to improve the conditions of public service. Facing a severe shortage of trained scientists and technical personnel, Congress established in 1958 several "super-grades," the appointment to which required approval by the Civil Service Comission, and for the highest grade, the approval of the President. The pay for the entire civil service was increased that year, but significantly so for the higher administrative levels. In 1962 Congress for the first time adopted the principle of comparability of federal pay scales with the pay given individuals performing similar duties in private enterprise. For many years this principle had been followed with regard to blue-collar employees and the lower clerical grades, but was not followed at the higher levels. Finally, in 1964 Congress passed a federal pay act which boosted federal salaries for administrative personnel to upper limits of $24,500. While not achieving "comparability," this pay raise at least made a significant move toward that standard.

In addition to improved pay, recent years have witnessed other forms of incentives for public service employment. Career development programs have been inaugurated, providing for in-service training as well as for more extensive educational programs at the university level. Special examinations have been devised to select especially qualified college graduates for intensive career development programs that will lead to accelerated movement into the higher echelons of the federal service.

In spite of the public's tendency to depict the bureaucracy as an undifferentiated mass of paper shufflers, studies of the occupational values of federal civil servants do not reveal that their daily lives are filled with unremitting boredom. In fact, the higher level administrators have found considerable challenge and excitement, quite comparable to that achieved by executives in the business world. Moreover the breadth of the concerns of the federal government, ranging from vital issues of national security to conservation of national resources, necessarily involve these officials in crucial decisions for the country's future.

The Problems of Neutrality and Loyalty

The fact that the administrator performs his duties in a political environment and that he is deeply involved in the policy-making process has been amply demonstrated. It is neither desirable nor possible that he remove himself from this highly charged political atmosphere because the bureaucrat brings to bear a wealth of experience and technical and administrative know-how without which the quality of decisions would be decidedly poorer.

But the bureaucrat faces unusually severe problems because he is not a politician in the usual sense of the word. He is a public employee and therefore must perform his duties in a nondiscriminatory way for all citizens, regardless of party or interest or other more personal considerations. Moreover, he must be protected against undue partisan influence in pursuing his duties, lest he be tempted to make decisions on the basis of partisan considerations rather than on the basis of criteria that promote the goals of the agency he serves. The history of the spoils system in the United States has led to legislative efforts to guarantee the position of the employee against the most severe forms of partisan intrusions in the administrative process.

Perhaps the most stringent limitation is found in the restriction on political activities by civil servants. Although civil servants may vote and discuss politics privately, they may not actively promote the interests of a political party, participate in campaigns, run for office, serve on party committees, or solicit funds. They are protected against unwarranted partisan pressures by prohibitions against party campaign solicitations, which traditionally constituted assessments on politically appointed officeholders.

In general terms, such restrictions may be necessary to ensure public confidence in the impartiality of federal civil servants. Yet the fact that they are civil servants does not necessarily diminish their interest in politics. There has been sentiment for revising these restrictions on political participation, particularly in granting to the public servant greater freedom in running for local office. At the present time, virtually the only elective office that a public official may hold is membership on a nonpartisan school board.

World War II intensified the government's concern for the loyalty and the security of its employees. Tight security regulations were imposed on vital defense activities during the war, and the highly publicized accusations of ex-Communists about infiltrations in the public service after the war made the Congress and the Executive extremely security conscious. After extensive investigation of the problem, President Truman inaugurated a loyalty program in 1947[4] which involved searching inquiries into the background of all civil servants; loyalty boards in each agency were empowered to consider evidence of disloyalty, with appeals available to a special board in the Civil Service Commission. Subsequently, during the Eisenhower administration, there was developed a combined interest in loyalty and security, the latter referring to questions of character—reliability, honesty, and morality. The heads of agencies were made responsible for the regulations, with no appeals beyond the agency itself. And all employees were again "cleared." In 1956, the Supreme Court ruled, however, that the security program for federal employees applied only to "sensitive jobs," such as in national defense, secret scientific research, or intelligence. In Britain the loyalty program had applied only to sensitive positions from its establishment in 1947.

Necessary as these actions were, and continue to be, they raise important questions of citizen rights as well as of desirable policy. The very definition

---

[4] The British security program was also set up in 1947. The fact that loyalty-security programs were set up in both countries by "liberal" administrations helped to remove the charge of partisan conservatism that might have been attached to such programs if set up by more conservative governments.

of loyalty is subject to varied interpretations, because opinions and general attitudes rather than specific overt acts are often questioned. Although there is no right to a job in the public service, a fair-minded government must give to an individual whose loyalty has been questioned every opportunity to demonstrate his loyalty.

⚬ THE FORMULATION OF THE BUDGET

The crucial decisions regarding the direction of public policy and the speed with which policy goals will be achieved are made in the formulation of the national budget. The bureaucracy plays a vital role in the process of making these decisions owing to its intimate acquaintance with existing programs, its capacity to estimate costs for new projects, and its vital stake in ensuring funding of its own programs.

The process of formulating the budget is a long and arduous one, encompassing a period of 18 months from the time the first estimates are asked for by the Bureau of the Budget until the budget is submitted to Congress. During this period, the bureaucracy, the political leadership of the department and agencies, the Bureau of the Budget, and the White House are engaged in a process of estimating costs, evaluating existing programs, projecting future needs, and guessing about what others are likely to accept or defend. There is nothing in government that so partakes of the nature of bargaining as does this struggle for a "fair" share of the public revenue.

This bargaining takes place because there are always more projects to be undertaken and more people to be served than there is money to accomplish these goals in the federal treasury. The budget is pre-eminently a means of establishing priorities among programs, all of which have value, but some of which may take precedence. This precedence may be determined in cost terms, in terms of human needs, or even esthetic values.

The national budget in the late 1960s now totals well over 100 billion dollars, a staggering figure which many people would like to see reduced. But it must be recognized that there are certain amounts built into the budget that cannot be tampered with. At least 40 percent of the budget is fixed by statute for which money must be appropriated. Moreover, the exigencies of crises, such as the Vietnam War, build constraints into the budget process that severely reduce the discretion of the budget planners. The size and character of the budget also reflect government fiscal policy in general. Will a larger budget increase inflationary pressures? Is it necessary to increase spending in order to counteract a recession or maximize employment? The budget presented to Congress is the President's budget and represents his estimate of the spending necessary or desirable in the ensuing fiscal year.

Control over budget formulation is centered in the Bureau of the Budget, which acts as the President's chief defender in his effort to protect his estimate of the amounts of money that should be spent. Budget examiners hold hearings and examine agency estimates, thus providing the Budget Director the information necessary to make final allocations in the budget recommended to Congress.

Criticisms of the budgetary process—that it has emphasized detail rather than purpose, that it has been too little concerned with long-range goals and alternatives—have resulted in important improvements in budget formulation. One of these is the development of advance planning, especially in the Department of Defense. The idea is that budget commitments should not be made without recognizing the implications of those commitments over a longer period of time. For the Department of Defense, this has meant the development of five-year program plans. Performance budgets have emphasized quantity and quality of program per unit of costs, thus helping to evaluate alternative levels and methods in achieving goals.

❧ A RESPONSIBLE BUREAUCRACY IN THE DEMOCRATIC SYSTEM

Large-scale enterprise, whether private or public, has resulted in the creation of bureaucratic structures of immense size and of immense power. In the public sector, these structures are capable of administering gigantic undertakings such as the worldwide security programs of the Department of Defense. Millions of citizens depend on the administration of programs that are vital to their health, education, mobility, employment, and general welfare.

The question of the responsibility of the bureaucracy immediately raises a second question: responsibility to whom or what? Clearly, the bureaucracy is not autonomous and self-directing, notwithstanding the degree of discretion granted to it. In the first place, the bureaucracy is responsible to the law. What Congress states to be its purpose and the methods to achieve it must necessarily be those subscribed to by administrators. Often what citizens complain of is not bureaucratic irresponsibility but bureaucratic fidelity to the wishes of the legislative branch. Secondly, the bureaucrat is responsible to the President or to subordinates to whom he has delegated his authority. The President is chief administrator of the United States government, backed by a national electoral majority. He may seldom actively intervene in the work of the bureaucrat, but his general philosophy and occasionally his specific decision must guide the bureaucrat's work. Thirdly, the bureaucrat has professional responsibility in the sense that there are imperatives of his own profession or discipline, be it engineering, accounting, or the law, which must guide his behavior. Fourthly, he has responsibility to the clients of his organization, who depend on its services and have developed expectations about the integrity and character of its actions. Finally, he has responsibility to the traditions and goals of his own organization, to defend them and to place them at the service of what he defines to be the public interest.

Because of the multiple foci of responsibility—and sometimes conflicting demands that are placed on him—the responsibility of the bureaucrat must be expressed largely in terms of his own integrity, his own sense of fairness, his own interpretation of what constitutes the public interest. The external controls that exist—the Congress and the courts—are effective in reinforcing this personal sense of responsibility and in establishing limits of irresponsible behavior. The bureaucrat has great power that is tempered by an awareness of conflicting values and the necessity of achieving a reconciliation of these values through patient encouragement of consensus rather than authoritative fiat. Most of all, he must ensure equitable treatment for all who depend on him. Calculated in these terms, the American bureaucracy has achieved a relatively high level of responsibility.

CHAPTER 21

THE AMERICAN
POLITICAL ECONOMY

⚓ THE AMERICAN ECONOMIC EXPERIENCE

The First New Nation

The economic experience of the United States cannot be described by any ism, slogan, or simple theory. Yet the basic fact of that experience is clear and disputed by no one: never have so many had it so good. Even Communist regimes define their future economic goal as reaching and overtaking the United States. This is a telling compliment.

The population of the United States increased 8 times between 1850 and 1960, yet its national income increased 40 times (in constant dollars). Work hours have been constantly shortened, and there is more leisure available than man has ever known before. At the same time, more Americans receive more education than ever before, mostly in public institutions maintained at public expense.

Though professional economists and social historians have been, and still are, in disagreement as to the whys and whens of the unparalleled American economic record, there seems to have been less disagreement among ordinary men who have to make a living rather than theorize about it. In the years 1820–1966, over 43 million persons from all over the world immigrated into the United States, far more than into any other country. These

542

millions were in search of the good life, of which the economic aspect was only a part. But it was an important part.

Not unexpectedly, the success of the American economic experience has been studied and analyzed throughout the world. Advanced and developing nations, Communist and non-Communist states see in the American level of living a goal to be attained. Goethe's famous phrase over a century ago—"Amerika, du hast es besser" ("America, you have it better")—succinctly expressed the then universal feeling that in America man could build a new life, both materially and spiritually. Above all, observers in older Western societies were impressed by the fact that in the United States the burden of the dead past was absent or relatively light, and that American society was concerned more with the future than with the past, just as young individuals tend to be more interested in their future than in their past.

More recently, and particularly since the end of World War II, the American economic experience has been of particular relevance to the newly developing nations. This interest stems not only from the deep concern of developing nations with rapid economic growth, of which the United States is a prime historical example, but also from the fact that, not so long ago, the United States itself was a new nation, politically trying to set up a workable system of constitutional government; and economically attempting to transform a relatively simple agrarian economy into an advanced mercantile and industrial economy. In fact, the United States may be called the "first new nation" in modern history because it was the first large colony to acquire freedom and independence from its imperial ruler through revolutionary means.

The elements that went into the making of the American economy from independence onward are therefore of enduring interest, particularly to the newly emerging nations that find themselves at the beginning of the road both politically and economically. Moreover, the study of the basic ingredients that went into the making and growth of the American economy is of more than purely historical value, for fundamentally they impinge upon issues that any new nation has to face today. While the intimate understanding of the evolution of the American economy and of its character today will not necessarily recommend its slavish imitation elsewhere, it may, at least, contribute to a better insight into what a new nation is up against economically, and what is the most successful approach to such problems. Also, a systematic analysis of the key elements in the evolution and character of the American economic system will show that, as any other economic system, it cannot be understood in purely economic or technological terms: the political context within which an economy operates, the moral commitments of the people, the social goals of society—all these are part of the economic system, just as much related to the final measurable economic output as are measurable elements like capital investment, manpower, or paved highways.

Attitudes Toward Life and Work as Economic Factors

In the contemporary world, too, it becomes increasingly clear that rapid economic growth through industrialization requires more than an official commitment to a particular economic system. Much of the difficulty in attaining rapid economic growth in the underdeveloped countries lies in the fact that it assumes the existence of basic drives and attitudes that cannot be as easily exported or taught as can technological skills. For example, a society whose spiritual outlook is dominated by a religion that denigrates this world and focuses on the world beyond will encounter a serious handicap in adopting economic values with an emphasis on this life and this world. Similarly, a society in which men, from time immemorial, have been accustomed to live and care only for today, will find it hard to get adjusted to the basic concept of saving (for the future) that is implied in a modern economic system that accumulates capital by withholding resources from immediate consumption. Fortunately for the United States, its dominant Protestant ethic of hard work in its early phase of economic development strongly discouraged consumption and encouraged frugality and saving, while at the same time stressing the notion that man's proper conduct in this world was a religious duty.

Another important point is the attitude toward work. Rapid economic growth assumes, and demands, a positive—and preferably an enthusiastic—interest in work, and does not look upon it as a curse to which mankind is condemned. In such a society, even wealthy individuals work, and often work harder than the less well-to-do. Work is almost a religion. In fact, in a highly productive economy like that of the United States, leisure decreases and work generally increases with higher social and economic status, whereas in a static, preindustrial society, work decreases and leisure increases the wealthier a person is. In the United States, for example, most physicians work more hours than do nurses or attendants, and most lawyers work a great deal more than do office secretaries. Whereas workers consider the 40-hour week as the upper limit, many top executives take a 60- or 70-hour week for granted.

By contrast, in preindustrial civilizations, work is still often considered a curse. Only those who have to work, do so. Work is merely a means to an end, to avoid hunger and suffering. He who has amassed enough wealth to live comfortably stops working, and spends his time on the pleasures of life. Even ordinary workers, in fields and factories, often follow this logic.

"... And, while each subsidiary company will have a certain amount of fiscal autonomy, all major policy decisions will rest with the parent corporation and its board of directors, however...." Ruge; in *Saturday Review*, 1966.

The porter in India who stops working in the middle of the day because he has earned enough for the day, the rubber tapper in Liberia who works for a week or two and then takes off until he needs money again—these are not isolated examples. Many an American or European entrepreneur who sets up shop in underdeveloped countries knows that regularity of work and the willingness to work when one can afford not to do so are not traits inborn in man, but have to be learned the hard way.

An explicit commitment to either capitalism or communism does not resolve all difficulties of a static, traditional society that rapid economic development seeks to overcome. Some of the problems that capitalist economies have had to face also appear under communism. After thinking that rapid economic progress through communism merely means the adoption of new methods of technology or administrative organization, some underdeveloped countries are discovering that communism, like capitalism, is more than a form of economic organization, and that it, too, rests on a set of values and attitudes that go with the specific processes of Communist economic change. An important difference lies, of course, between the Communist and the capitalist response to these difficulties of adaptation. Capitalism seeks to bring about new attitudes and values without coercion, by creating new psychological wants and expectations that cannot be fulfilled in the framework of old attitudes. This method succeeds in some cases, but not in others, as history has shown. Communism seeks to modify basic attitudes by force. But it, too, has had failures, because force also has its limitations, just as freedom does.

For example, Soviet and East European economic advisers in Castro's Cuba have been often reported as being sharply critical of what seems to them the "lackadaisical" and "happy-go-lucky" attitude of Cubans, even of dedicated Communist Cubans. In Russia, Eastern Europe, and China the Communist version of Puritanical devotion to toil and frugality, necessitating sharp cuts in consumption of the good things here and now, has worked to a varying degree, but it has worked. What worries Soviet advisers in Cuba is whether "communism can work in the tropics," which implies the recognition that economic development under communism requires more than government ownership of all productive property, politically supported by the single totalitarian party. The United States, too, has often experienced the difficulties of "capitalist democracy in the tropics" in Asia, Africa, and Latin America.

⚹ FROM RUGGED INDIVIDUALISM TO GOVERNMENT RESPONSIBILITY IN ECONOMIC AFFAIRS

In its early phases, capitalism was highly individualistic in outlook, although the emergent mercantile and capitalist classes did not hesitate to demand all sorts of government protection and subvention. The dominant view was that the individual must be free to pursue his own interest, free from government interference. It was this emphasis on "rugged individualism" that later subjected the capitalist system to many criticisms and reforms. Yet it should not be forgotten that the highly individualistic streak in early capitalism was not the result of a deficient, heartless ethics, but the product of circumstances. First, it must be recalled that capitalism developed as a reaction against the economic system that preceded it— mercantilism, under which the purpose of economic activity was the enhancement of the power of the state rather than individual welfare. Also, under mercantilism economic activity was minutely regulated by either governmental authorities or by private guilds and trade associations. As a result, individual economic initiative was often stifled.

It is not unnatural that in its early phase capitalism overreacted to both the purposes and procedures of mercantilism. If mercantilism stressed public purpose and public policy at the expense of individual choice and discretion, early capitalism overreacted by emphasizing individual freedom of action as against public responsibility. If mercantilism prescribed detailed regulation of economic activity through governmental and quasi-public bodies, early capitalism overreacted to what it considered a lot of unnecessary "red tape" by allowing the individual maximum discretion and choice in his economic operations. Economically, the American Revolution was part of the general protest of early capitalist entrepreneurs against the mercantilist policies of the British empire.

Moreover, early capitalism could emphasize extreme individualism because of the nature of the economy which then prevailed. In its early stage of development, the technologically most efficient unit of production was relatively small, whether in manufacturing, merchandising, servicing, or farming. Typically, the family unit supplied management, capital, and most or all of the required labor. The strong belief in unfettered individualism, therefore, was not only the expression of economic ideologies, but also of objective technological and economic facts.

Yet even in its early formative phase, capitalism did not propose, nor did it realize, the extreme version of the laissez-faire "night-watchman state." In his *Wealth of Nations* (1776), Adam Smith clearly stated that government had not only the duty to defend its citizens against foreign aggression and domestic oppression and injustice, but also to erect and maintain public works and institutions "which it can never be for the interest of any individual, or small number of individuals, to erect and maintain," but which would be of great benefit and profit to society as a whole. Such public works and institutions included, according to Adam Smith, not only physical assets like roads, canals, and harbors, but also intangible assets like popular education and public health measures, such as the prevention of the spread of dangerous communicable diseases. What Smith had in mind as the proper sphere of government activity is what is called in current economic terminology the "infra-structure" of society, or the framework of a modern economy, which is the responsibility of government, because private individuals or corporations will not find it possible or profitable to provide such an "infra-structure" with their own resources. With respect to economic policy, Adam Smith favored high wages for the workers as being advantageous to society as a whole; he also felt the government had the right and duty to intervene in the case of trade monopolies, particularly where vital commodities, such as bread or other basic foods, were involved.

Although it is true that the scope of governmental intervention was narrowly conceived by the early capitalist state and its ideological defenders, there was generally no commitment to an abstract or philosophical dogma of laissez-faire for its own sake. After Jeremy Bentham, for example, returned from a prolonged visit to Russia, he was convinced that the

economic *"agenda"* in Russia made substantially more governmental action necessary than would be the case in his native England in the late
eighteenth or early nineteenth centuries. As he grew older and saw the
effects of the growing industrialization of Britain, Bentham became eager
to use political means—universal suffrage, for example—to alleviate the
results of industrial capitalism. John Stuart Mill is another famous figure of
the nineteenth century who started out as an out-and-out laissez-faire
individualist in economic policy, but gradually shifted his position toward
the acceptance of public responsibility in an industrial society. As a libertarian, he was convinced that a modern economy wholly managed and
owned by a centralized government would be incompatible with individual
liberty. Yet as a utilitarian he kept an open mind, and was willing to
embrace broad social and economic policies within the capitalist system
aiming at the correction of its abuses.

✕ AMERICAN ATTITUDES TOWARD GOVERNMENT INTERVENTION IN THE ECONOMY

The Dominance of Empiricism

The dominant empirical and pragmatic outlook of Americans is not the
result of philosophical ideas as formulated by great thinkers from John
Locke to William James and John Dewey, but reflects the experience of
the frontier. Survival and prosperity depended on the ability to adapt to
new and rapidly changing conditions rather than on the capacity to spin
out intellectual arguments to their logical conclusion. In politics and economics, too, this pragmatism became manifest at an early stage. The
framers of the Constitution, for example, did not aim at a logically consistent and "pure" political system, but at one that would work. Generally
believing in the principle of liberty, they nevertheless recognized the
existence and continuance of slavery. Generally believing in the sovereignty
of the people, they nevertheless introduced a quasi-monarchical institution—the Presidency—and a quasi-aristocratic one—the Senate—side by
side with the popularly elected Congress. The framers wanted neither pure
monarchy, nor pure aristocracy, nor pure democracy—and to this day the
American political system has elements of all three.

In economics, too, this pragmatism has prevailed from the very beginnings of the American experience. While the ideas of Adam Smith and
laissez-faire were considerably in vogue in the late colonial and early

independence periods, they did not have the dominance they enjoyed in England. As the leaders in the Industrial Revolution, the British entrepreneurs found laissez-faire not only intellectually convincing but also economically profitable, for under laissez-faire, particularly as applied on an international scale, the British economy stood to benefit greatly in competition with the less-developed nations.

The proper perspective for an understanding of the early American economic principles and policies cannot be fruitfully gained by relating them to Adam Smith or any doctrine of laissez-faire, but by looking at the problems facing "new nations" today. On gaining independence, the political framework of the economy under the Articles of Confederation inevitably led to the fragmentation and "Balkanization" of the economy, which was one of the main reasons for creating a federal union, economically based on one free market, with one uniform currency, one national policy in foreign trade, one system of postal communication and highways, and one national policy of taxing and spending for the common defense and the "common welfare." The framers clearly realized that there could be no powerful and prosperous nation without national economic policies, and therefore, in the listing of the powers of Congress in Article I, for example, economic powers are more specifically spelled out than any other category. Although these powers do not add up to any complete and clear-cut system or "ism," they at least reflect the view of the Founding Fathers that government is not an inactive bystander in the economic process.

Hamiltonianism Versus Jeffersonianism

From the early days of the Republic, therefore, all levels of government—federal, state, and local—were involved in direct governmental action in the field of economic development. As early as 1791, Alexander Hamilton in his *Report on Manufactures* asked Congress for governmental support of American manufacturing, regardless of whether such a policy harmonized with the then prevailing laissez-faire doctrines of Adam Smith. This policy of protective tariffs for "infant industries" in newly developing nations has, since then, been imitated in many places—Europe, Australia, Asia, and South America.

Another important measure of early direct intervention took the form of federal investment in the Bank of the United States (set up in 1791), a practice widely followed today under similar circumstances in developing nations. States and local governments went even further than did the federal government. Many state and local governments invested directly in the building of canals, turnpikes, mills, and railroads—the framework of the economy. Government on all levels felt it had to act because private capital—domestic or foreign—was not sufficiently available, and also because in some cases the profitability of "infra-structure" enterprises might be visible in relation to the whole economy, but not to an individual investor. Seymour Martin Lipset, in his *First New Nation: The United States in Historical and Comparative Perspective*, aptly summarizes the early American period in the following words: "The story of state and local investment in early economic development in the United States clearly justifies the conclusion that government in this period played a role corresponding to that envisaged in most new nations today."[1] What is called Hamiltonianism in the American political and economic tradition, is no more than the first instance of a newly developing nation using its governmental resources—administrative, legal, and financial—in behalf of deliberately planned rapid economic growth.

Where there is change, there is opposition to change. Jefferson and Jeffersonianism, reflecting the more static elements of the small farmer and the small man in his workshop and trade, opposed the expansion of industry, because the small man in town and country might be reduced to insignificance as the result of big business power. Yet economic Jeffersonianism was bound to lose to Hamiltonianism in the early days of the American Republic, just as a century and a half later the simple agrarianism of Gandhi lost to Nehru, the Hamilton of the Republic of India. Like Hamilton, Nehru firmly believed that India's future as a progressive and prosperous nation could be achieved only through rapid economic development, and that government had to play a substantial, and often leading, role in achieving that goal. In India, Hamiltonianism is called "state socialism," seeking to combine strong government in the economy with the goals of greater equality and social responsibility for the welfare of the individual.

The Rise of Laissez-Faire

The doctrine of laissez-faire, with its insistence on governmental noninterference in the economy, gained in the United States in the middle of the nineteenth century—only after private skills, capital, and managerial ability had accumulated. Again, this rise of laissez-faire ideas reflected facts, not theories. The most important fact was that industrial production gradually increased its share of national output, until by the end of the Civil War it passed agriculture in the production of wealth. Supported by vast natural resources, by a free market of continental dimensions, and by a ceaseless stream of energetic immigrants, industry became the dominant element in

[1] (New York: Basic Books, 1963), p. 54.

American society. As a result, the "image" of industry and industrialists also changed in the eyes of the public. Whereas "American industrialists in the half century after 1812 were hated by southern planters, vilified by New England radicals, despised by landed gentry and Quaker merchants,"[2] the following half century witnessed the dominance of business in most phases of American life. Calvin Coolidge's famous dictum: "The business of America is business" was not an epigrammatic summary of all American history, but merely reflected the dominant outlook of two generations of American life, stretching roughly from the 1870s to the end of the 1920s.

The ideological rationalization of laissez-faire was provided by Herbert Spencer, particularly his *Social Statics* (1850). Relatively unsuccessful in his native England, Spencer became the idolized fountain of wisdom in the American business community, providing "scientific proof" that monopoly and the amassing of wealth through paying low wages merely confirmed the general law of nature of the "survival of the fittest." While England turned to Bentham and John Stuart Mill toward the end of the nineteenth century, and neglected Spencer (his *Social Statics*, for example, took ten years to sell out in its first English edition), American businessmen barely knew that Bentham and Mill existed, and worshipped Spencer. This disparity largely reflected the fact that British business had passed the zenith of its power and influence at the very time when American business and industry approached dominance.

The Decline of Laissez-Faire

Yet even at the peak of business power, there were dissenting elements. The Granger and Populist movements, mostly active in the agrarian Midwest and West, were audible protests against the ruthless practices of industrial and financial monopolies as well as against their excessive influence in Washington and the state capitals. Toward the end of the nineteenth century, as the growth of big corporations, trusts, and monopolies showed that economic power in a democracy might become too independent and oppressive, the countermovement of "trust-busting" developed. The small farmer, artisan, and worker realized that if Jeffersonianism—or the protection of the little man against the big fellow—was to be realized, big government had to be used against big business, thus in effect becoming Hamiltonians of a sort. By contrast, the erstwhile Hamiltonians—businessmen, industrialists, financiers—became Jeffersonians (or so they claimed), for they invoked the Jeffersonian principles of states' rights

[2] Thomas C. Cochran and William Miller, *The Age of Enterprise: A Social History of Industrial America* (New York: Harper & Row, 1961), p. 119.

and individual liberty against centralized power in Washington. In that transfiguration of Jeffersonianism, a billion-dollar corporate giant asking for freedom from government intervention pretended to be no different in principle from the small grocery-owner fighting for his economic and political freedom.

From the beginning of this century, the dogmas of laissez-faire came under increasing attack from all sides. Intellectually, the works of Thorstein Veblen—perhaps the most original American social scientist of the last hundred years—popularized the notion of business as a system of power and its paradoxical position in a democratic society. Politically, an important segment of the Republicans under Theodore Roosevelt's leadership began to challenge the uncontrolled powers of big business. From Theodore Roosevelt's "Square Deal" a straight line led to Woodrow Wilson's "New Freedom" and to Franklin D. Roosevelt's "New Deal." All these new freedoms and deals reaffirmed the original principle of American public policy that government must intervene in social and economic affairs if private enterprise is either so powerful as to challenge popular government or so inefficient as to produce economic crises and depressions.

Laissez-faire did not die a sudden death in American thought and public policy. Despite the popularity of Franklin Roosevelt's New Deal policies during his first term, the Republicans put up a laissez-faire candidate, Governor Landon of Kansas, in 1936, but he lost 46 states out of 48 in a landslide victory for Roosevelt. The Republican candidates from 1940 to 1960 were committed to varying degrees of governmental action in the economy; perhaps because they lost, with the exception of General Eisenhower in 1952 and 1956, the Republican party made one more try in 1964 to present a candidate who was not "an echo" of Democratic governmental activism in the economy. Senator Goldwater's crushing defeat in 1964 showed that the American people, when presented with a clear choice between economic laissez-faire and governmental activism in economic affairs, prefer activism to laissez-faire.

Yet there was one remarkable difference between the elections of 1936 and 1964. In 1936, Governor Landon enjoyed the almost unanimous support of the business community, particularly of big business, which had organized the Liberty League as a high-powered and highly financed pressure group against the New Deal. By contrast, in the three decades between 1936 and 1964, the American business community had become deeply divided: "The newly rich and the shopkeepers, auto dealers, realty men and other small businessmen still tended for Barry, but a large number of the top brass of older and larger firms took the lead in the 'Business for Lyndon' movement."[3] In this new "mainstream" of American eco-

[3] *Wall Street Journal*, February 2, 1965.

nomic attitudes—inconceivable in the 1930s—Henry Ford II and Walter Reuther jointly rejected Senator Goldwater and amicably worked for the re-election of the "Great Society" candidate, Lyndon Johnson. While such consensus may not always go on in this breadth, it is unlikely to split into two opposing camps fighting for or against laissez-faire.

In sum, to the present generation of Americans the New Deal of the 1930s may appear as the great watershed of American economic policy, ending the "traditional" American attitude of laissez-faire by establishing government policies and leadership in economic matters. Looked at from the broader perspective of American history as a whole, the picture is exactly the reverse: the five decades from the late 1870s to the late 1920s were the exception rather than the rule. During that period, and during that period only, can the philosophy of laissez-faire and the power of the business community be said to have been predominant. Since the 1930s more than a shift of power from business to government and labor has occurred. The businessman has ceased to be the lawgiving and ideal-setting center of American life. Other heroes are now rivaling the businessman in popular esteem: politicians, medical researchers, astronauts, nuclear physicists, and space scientists.

⅍ THE CONSTITUTION AND ECONOMIC POLICIES

Flexibility of Constitutional Language

The Constitution has been invoked to justify low and high taxes, laissez-faire and government intervention in economic affairs, and the priority of economic rights over human rights and vice versa. As has been true so often, in the long run the Supreme Court also followed election results in this area. In the era of laissez-faire, or from about 1880 to the 1930s, the Supreme Court struck down many economic reforms, particularly of the states, such as minimum wages for women, limitations on hours of employment, and price controls. Since the middle 1930s, the Court has recognized the fact that the majority of the people need, and desire, government action in economic matters, and has consistently refused to interfere with such policies, state or federal, on constitutional grounds.

The language of the Constitution is flexible enough to allow both a narrower—laissez-faire—interpretation and a broader interpretation, such as was used, for example in an earlier period by the Supreme Court under Chief Justice Marshall and, more recently, under Chief Justice Warren. The powers of Congress to "lay and collect taxes" (Article I, Section 8), to "provide for the common defense and general welfare of the United States," and to regulate interstate commerce, can be used for governmental economic policies that go beyond anything that has been done so far.

Under its war and commerce powers, the federal government has not only built arsenals, atomic installations, and missile bases, but it is also generating and supplying electricity, through the Tennessee Valley Authority (TVA), for 5 million people in seven states, combined with many other activities aiming at a general economic development of the region. As to the constitutional purpose of "general welfare," it is difficult to say dogmatically what type of general welfare would be unconstitutional. If the federal government can lay and collect taxes for the general welfare, it can also spend such revenue on broad social objectives, such as a redistribution of wealth—the progressive income tax, sanctioned by the Sixteenth Amendment, is specifically designed to do just that, in addition to its purpose of raising revenue.

Private Property and Eminent Domain

Under the Fifth and Fourteenth Amendments, private property may be taken by the federal or state governments, provided due process is observed, the property so taken is for public use, and just compensation is paid. The key phrase is "public use." The Courts at one time interpreted public use in a very narrow sense—that is, the private property taken had to be used by a governmental authority or by the general public. More recently, courts have taken a much broader approach. A city may, for example, condemn slum dwellings, and build public housing projects on that land for "persons of low income." In the first test case on this issue, decided by the New York Court of Appeals, the state's highest court, in 1936 (*New York City Housing Authority* v. *Muller*), the main issue was the meaning of "public use." The property owners argued that public housing projects for "persons of low income" was "class legislation" not meeting the constitutional standard of public use, because only low-income persons were eligible for the public housing project and they alone would use it. By contrast, the court took a broader view and interpreted "public use" to mean "benefit to the public": "But the essential purpose of the legislation is not to benefit that class or any class; it is to protect and safeguard the entire public from the menace of the slums."[4]

Moreover, in later cases the courts have decided that condemned property of private owners need not be turned over to public ownership for purposes of redevelopment. In fact, most of the large-scale redevelopment

[4] For a fuller discussion, see William Ebenstein, *The Law of Public Housing* (Madison, Wis.: University of Wisconsin Press, 1940).

programs for big cities involve billions of investment. State and city governments therefore gladly turn over such projects of urban renewal to
private groups of investors, if such can be found. In 1954, the Supreme
Court held, in a case dealing with a redevelopment program in Washington, D.C. (*Berman* v. *Parker*), that, after private property is condemned
for a public purpose, it may be redeveloped by private enterprise. Also,
broadening the concept of "public use," the Court held that the removal
of physical blight need not be the sole purpose of redeveloping an entire
city area: "If those who govern the District of Columbia decide that the
Nation's capitol should be beautiful as well as sanitary, there is nothing in
the Fifth Amendment that stands in the way." We thus see that massive
urban renewal on a hitherto unprecedented scale—one of the foremost
needs of this and the next generation—will not in any way be limited by
constitutional restraints. Rather, the obstacles to overcome are the apathy
of the affluent who have fled to the suburbs, the timidity of government
agencies, and the reluctance of taxpayers to pay the bill for the inevitably
high cost of urban renewal.

Eminent domain, or the right of the state to take private property for
public use, goes back to the Middle Ages. In the medieval concept of
feudalism, the king was considered as the ultimate owner of all property,
and he could assert that right whenever a public need required him to do
so. Thus, before the coming of the capitalist era, private property was not
considered an absolute or a "sacred" right but a "bundle" of specific rights
and duties that fitted into a larger whole. The rise of economic individualism, of capitalism, weakened this concept, but did not completely destroy
it. As unbridled economic individualism has given way to a reawakening of
a sense of communal responsibility, the concept of eminent domain is
likely to be broadened to include an increasing array of purposes in which
the community claims precedence over individual property rights.

This does not signify a necessary drift toward socialism and public
ownership, for as we saw in the previous illustration of urban redevelopment, private property condemned for a public use may then be turned
over by the public authority to private enterprise for uses determined by
the public authority. In effect, ownership of the property remains in
private hands, but the purposes of such property, its uses, are determined
and planned by public authorities.

This shows again the basically undogmatic and pragmatic approach in
the United States. Some may argue that in this approach capitalism is still
preserved because private enterprise is used for redevelopment; others, in
turn, may view this method as coming close to socialism, for the use of
property is no longer solely determined by private individuals but by a
governmental body.

"Business Affected with a Public Interest"

The undogmatic nature of American governmental economic policies in relation to the Constitution, as interpreted by the courts, can perhaps best be seen in the characteristically American concept of "business affected with a public interest." In 1877, the Supreme Court had to decide whether an Illinois statute fixing maximum rates charged by grain elevators was constitutional. In upholding the statute (*Munn* v. *Illinois*, 1877), the Court laid down the principle that government regulation, including price control, is constitutional in the case of businesses "affected with a public interest." Looking back to the (precapitalist) Common Law, the Court found that when private property is "affected with a public interest, it ceases to be *juris privati* only." The Court then went on to deduce governmental regulation from public interest: "When, therefore, one devotes his property to a use in which the public has an interest, he, in effect, grants to the public an interest in that use, and must submit to be controlled by the public for the common good, to the extent of the interest he has thus created."

The courts have never drawn up a list of businesses affected with a public interest and therefore subject to governmental regulation. Insurance companies, tobacco warehouses, milk producers and marketers, coal producers, and many other types of businesses have been held to be subject to regulation with prices—in some cases, minimum prices and in other cases, maximum prices. The Supreme Court has pointed out that "public interest" is not a mystical quality that inheres in some types of business but not in others. Public interest means no more, the Court held in *Nebbia* v. *New York* (1934), "than that an industry, for adequate reason, is subject to control for the public good." Regulation for the sake of regulation is thus unconstitutional; but regulation that is not arbitrary or unreasonable is constitutional.

No Specific Theory Enshrined in the Constitution

The absence of a clearly defined economic theory about the nature and limits of governmental policies in economic affairs has been most clearly stated by Justice Holmes. In 1905, the Supreme Court (in *Lochner* v. *New York*) struck down a New York statute limiting the hours of work in bakeries to 10 hours per day and to 60 hours per week, such limitation being held by the Court's majority to be a deprivation of liberty without due process. This majority decision—a high point of dogmatic laissez-faire argumentation in the Court's history—was sharply attacked by Justice

Holmes in one of his most famous dissenting opinions: "The Fourteenth Amendment does not enact Mr. Herbert Spencer's *Social Statics*." Holmes went on to say that *"a constitution is not intended to embody a particular economic theory, whether of paternalism and the organic relation of the citizen to the state or of laissez-faire"* (italics ours).

One of the most frequently used arguments in favor of laissez-faire and against any government action in economic matters is that "one thing leads to another," and that once government intervenes in economic life, the "road to serfdom" (the title of F. A. Hayek's famous book) is inevitable.[5] In less analytical terms, this logic is often expressed in the American phrase "creeping socialism." In 1911, the Supreme Court upheld the constitutionality of an Oklahoma statute that subjected state banks to assessments for a Depositors' Guaranty Fund (*Noble State Bank* v. *Haskell*). In challenging the constitutionality of the statute, the appealing bank argued along the customary lines of "one thing leading to another." Speaking this time for the majority of the Court, Justice Holmes rebutted such argumentation as follows: "It is asked whether the State could require all corporations or all grocers to help to guarantee each other's solvency, and where we are going to draw the line? But the last is a futile question, and

[5] F. A. Hayek, *The Road to Serfdom* (Chicago: University of Chicago Press, 1944).

"And when they get their Great Society, you can be damned certain they'll want a *Greater* Society." Drawing by D. Fradon;
© 1965 The New Yorker Magazine, Inc.

we will answer the others when they arise." Holmes's view has been confirmed by the passage of time: to this day, the Supreme Court has not had to deal with the issue whether Oklahoma (or any other state) could constitutionally subject all corporations or all grocers to guarantee each other's solvency, although state banks were required to do so in Oklahoma by a state statute of 1907. In this case, as in so many others, one thing did not lead to another.

⅍ THE CORPORATION IN THE AMERICAN ECONOMY

The Corporate Share of Business

Of the 5 million business firms (excluding farming and the professions), about 1.3 million are corporations. In trade, services, and construction, the unincorporated form of business (individual ownership or partnership) predominates. By contrast, the corporation is very strong in manufacturing, mining, transportation, finance, and utilities. In these sectors, corporations account for over 90 percent of activity.

Corporations account for about 55 percent of gross national product and for 65 percent of all business activity, whereas in 1870 the corporate share in business activity was only 21 percent. Whereas most corporations are small, nearly all large businesses are corporations.

The five sectors of the economy that are predominantly corporate have two important characteristics. First, these five sectors hold the "commanding heights" of the economy, for they include the basic industries (steel, chemicals, petroleum), banking, and transportation. Second, within these five sectors, the large corporation has a decisive position in assets, sales, and profits.

Concentration of Economic Power

According to the 1966 *Report* of the Joint Economic Committee of Congress, the 200 largest manufacturing corporations held 55 percent of all manufacturing assets (corporate as well as noncorporate) in 1962 as compared with 47 percent in 1947. If this rate of increasing concentration should continue, the 200 largest manufacturing corporations may control two thirds of all manufacturing assets by 1975.

The automotive industry is a good illustration of concentration in manufacturing. In 1921, there were 87 manufacturers of cars; now, there are only 4. Of these, General Motors produces over one half of all automobiles; in addition, it is the largest producer of locomotives and of intercity and transit buses, and a major producer of trucks, diesel engines, earth-moving equipment, and home appliances. Through its foreign subsidiaries, General Motors is also the leading car manufacturer in Canada and Australia, holds second place in West Germany, and third place in Britain. In 1965, it employed 3 percent of all employees in manufacturing in the United States; its profits, after taxes, were $2.1 billion, or 5 percent of all corporate after-tax profits; its sales in the United States alone amounted to about $19 billion, or nearly 3 percent of gross national product; its worldwide sales of $21 billion were larger than the gross national product of all but a dozen countries in the world; its tax bill (federal, state, local, and foreign) was $2.6 billion, and it paid about 5 percent of all corporate income taxes in the United States; it paid to its 1.25 million shareholders $1.5 billion in dividends, or nearly 9 percent of all corporate dividends, or more than two and a half times as much as the dividends paid by the entire steel industry.

Industries in which the four leading companies produce more than half of the entire output include primary aluminum, locomotives, tin cans, cigarettes, computers, typewriters, tires, tractors, steel, organic chemicals, and synthetic fibers. This is not a complete listing, and the share of the largest four companies ranges from 51 to 95 percent in their respective industries. Below the 50 percent mark, the number of goods in which the four largest companies account for 25 to 49 percent of total output comes to about 500, ranging all the way from pianos (49 percent) to pharmaceuticals (25 percent).

Concentration in Banking, Insurance, and Utilities

In some major nonindustrial sectors, concentration is even larger than in industrial ones. In banking, the 50 largest banks account for over one third of the assets and deposits of all banks (14,000 in number). The largest bank, the Bank of America, has about 10 percent of the deposits and assets of the largest fifty banks, or about 4 percent of the assets and deposits of all American banks. The top five banks account for about 12 percent of assets and deposits of the nation's 14,000 banks.

In life insurance, concentration is also heavier than in industrial corporations. The combined assets of the largest 50 companies (out of 1,600 in all) are about 80 percent of the total; among the top 50, the top 5 alone account for nearly one half of the assets of all 1,600 companies. The largest single life insurance company, the Metropolitan, has 13 percent of the assets of all insurance companies. As to life insurance in force: the ratio of concentration with respect to the top 50, the top 5, and the top 1 is about the same as in the case of assets.

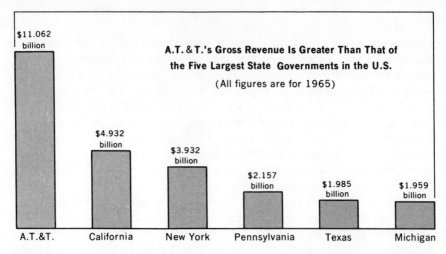

FIGURE 21-1. A.T.&T.'s Gross Revenue in 1965 Compared with That of the Five Largest State Governments in the United States. (Adapted from *The New York Times.* © 1964, 65, 66 by The New York Times Company. Reprinted by permission.)

In public utilities (communications, gas, electric energy), concentration is probably more extreme than in any other segment of the economy. This sector contains the corporation with the largest assets in the world, American Telephone and Telegraph, whose assets are over $35 billion. A.T.&T. accounts for over one third of the assets of the largest 50 utilities and for 40 percent of the revenues of the largest 50 utilities. (See Figure 21-1.) In its own field, the A.T.&T. operates 85 percent of the national total, the remaining 15 percent of telephones being operated by about 2,600 smaller independent companies. A.T.&T. is a leader, not only in the telephone business, but also in many phases of electronics and space communications.

The Advantage of the Large Corporation in Research

The importance of the giant corporations can be seen in *research*. There are over 15,000 firms doing research in their own laboratories. The largest 44 companies in this group employ 45 percent of all technicians and scientists, and spend 50 percent of all the money devoted to research and development in the entire country. There is also much concentration in research and development in terms of geography. According to a study of *Fortune* (March 1966), California received, in 1961–1965, 38.5 percent of all federal research and development funds. The National Aeronautics and Space Administration (NASA), with an annual research and development budget of over $5 billion, spends about 45 percent of its commitments in

California. This percentage accurately reflects the number of California scientists and engineers in NASA's thirty-five major contractors—44 percent of the whole nation's. Also, about half of all American Nobel Prize winners are in California. The top five metropolitan areas that are richest in scientific and technical personnel (New York City, Washington, D.C., Los Angeles, San Francisco, Boston) account for over one third of the national total.

Size is an important factor in obtaining government contracts; annual federal expenditure on goods and services runs to about $50–$60 billion, or about 8 percent of the gross national product. The bulk of government procurement is military: 25 large corporations typically receive about one half of all military contracts. Through subcontracting, some of the work is spread among smaller companies, but about 60 percent of contract dollars still remain with the few giant companies. In the field of military research, the share of large corporations is even more impressive. Small business typically receives only about 2–3 percent of such work.

Rates of Profit

Rates of profit also increase with corporate size of assets. In manufacturing corporations (accounting for over one half of all corporate profits), the average rate of after-tax profit on sales in 1964 was 5.2 percent. However, this rate of profit was only 2.3 percent for corporations with assets under $1 million, but was 6.4 percent for corporations with assets of $100 million and over. Between these two extremes, the same pattern prevails: as the assets of the corporation go up, its rate of profit goes up, too, although not always in a completely proportionate manner. The role of giant corporations is particularly impressive: in the first quarter of 1964, according to an analysis of *U.S. News & World Report* (June 1, 1964), the top 8 corporations earned 25 percent of all corporate profits; the top 72 corporations earned 43 percent of all corporate profits. The 57 percent went to the remaining 1.3 million corporations.

Concentration in Labor Unions

Before we leave the subject of concentration in business, it may be noted briefly that organized labor shows a very similar trend. Of 180 national labor unions with a total membership of 18 million, the 5 largest unions have a combined membership of about 5 million, or over one fourth of the total. More than half of all union members are in the largest 15 unions. Contrary to the popular belief that big unions are no more than a reflection of big business, three of the biggest half dozen unions (teamsters, machinists, and carpenters) are concentrated in small and medium-sized businesses; only 2 of the 5 largest unions (auto and steelworkers) are in industries dominated by large corporations.

ﾞ CURBING CONCENTRATION OF ECONOMIC POWER

The Rise of Trusts

The era after the Civil War was characterized not only by rapid industrialization and the appearance of big business organizations, but also by various monopolistic devices which enabled a single corporation to control an entire industry. The most effective of these devices was the *trust*. Through a trust agreement, stock of competing corporations was handed over to a board of trustees in return for "trust certificates." The trustees were then in a position to fix prices and exclude competition in an entire industry. Later, the term "trust" came to mean any big corporation that had large power in its industry. Particularly in political parlance, "trust-busting" and "anti-big business" became virtually identical. This terminological ambiguity of the word "trust" reflected from the beginning the suspicion that mere bigness is, or may be, a threat to the free market, although no specific acts of restraint of trade are committed by the big corporation.

The first major trust was formed in 1882 by John D. Rockefeller out of about 40 oil companies, and his Standard Oil Company controlled 90 to 95 percent of the petroleum industry in the United States. Trust agreements in other industries followed swiftly; around the turn of this century 26 corporations controlled 80 percent or more of the output in their fields, and 8 corporations controlled 90 percent or more. This degree of monopolistic concentration was unique in two respects: it has never happened at any time in any other modern economy, and in the United States, too, it had never happened before, and is very unlikely ever to happen again.

The Sherman Anti-Trust Act

Since the states were powerless to curb these monopolistic giants (and in many states there was not even the desire to do any curbing), pressure for federal action against monopolies became more and more intensive because they were national in scope and impact. Bipartisan support for the defense of the free market against restraint of trade through monopolies resulted in the Sherman Act of 1890, the first major piece of antitrust legislation in the United States (and in any Western country).

The Sherman Act has two important provisions. First, it declares illegal "every contract, combination in the form of trust or otherwise, or conspiracy, in restraint of trade or commerce among the several states or with foreign nations." The second main provision declares any person guilty of a misdemeanor who "shall monopolize, or attempt to monopolize, or combine or conspire with any other person or persons, to monopolize any part of the trade or commerce among the several states, or with foreign nations." In the first section of the Sherman Act, "contract," "combination," or "conspiracy" are involved, applying to collusive activities of two or more persons. The most typical violations of restraint of trade outlawed by this provision are conspiratorial price-fixing, agreements to eliminate competition, or the dividing up of markets. In the second main provision of the Sherman Act, illegal action of one person or corporation is sufficient, if it aims at monopoly.

The restriction on interstate and foreign trade has been interpreted broadly by the courts. Thus restraints of trade within a single city or state are held illegal if they significantly impinge on interstate commerce. As to foreign trade, agreements between American corporations and foreign corporations reducing competition in the United States exports or imports are illegal. Even agreements among foreign corporations are held illegal if they aim at price-fixing or other anticompetitive or monopolistic practices in the United States.

Breakup of Monopolies

In the first phase of its operation, the most notable successes in breaking up monopolies were scored against Standard Oil of New Jersey and the American Tobacco Company, both cases decided by the Supreme Court in 1911. Like Standard Oil of New Jersey, American Tobacco had bought up its competitors, and finally controlled 95 percent of the cigarette industry. In both cases, practices used by either or both monopolies included cutthroat competition; compelling competitors to join the monopoly or get out of business; discriminatory freight-charge arrangements with the railroads; industrial bribery and espionage; dividing up the market through exclusive agreements among subsidiaries to eliminate competition; and controlling the sources of raw materials in a monopolistic manner. There was hardly an offense against competition not committed by either or both companies.

Both monopolies were ordered to dissolve. In the case of Standard Oil of New Jersey (*Standard Oil Company of New Jersey* v. *U.S.*, 1911), several new Standard Oil companies of a regional nature (such as of California, Indiana, or Ohio) emerged as independent companies, and although Standard Oil of New Jersey is still the largest oil company in the world, it is no longer a monopolist. As an international company it is closely followed in size by the Royal Dutch Petroleum Company, and as an American company it has to face the competition of such giants as Texaco, Gulf Oil, and many others. Although the Sherman Act did not transform Standard Oil of New Jersey into a small, independent wildcat drilling operation, it did break up a monopoly. The periodic "price-wars" in the retail price of gasoline indicate that there is some real competition in this area.

The American Tobacco Company was dissolved, as a result of the Supreme Court decision in 1911 (*U.S.* v. *American Tobacco Co.*), into three major and eleven small companies. For a long time, American Tobacco still remained the largest single corporation in the cigarette industry, but for a number of years now it has dropped to second place.

The third major antimonopoly case involved the steel industry, and was directed against the United States Steel Corporation (*U.S.* v. *U.S. Steel Corp.*, 1920). U.S. Steel was formed in 1901 out of nine large previous corporations, and by 1908 accounted for slightly over one half of steel production. Suit against it was brought in 1912, and finally decided by the Supreme Court in 1920. The Court did not order its dissolution, because it found that competition still existed, and that U.S. Steel had discontinued its famous "price-fixing dinners" and other "predatory" and anticompetitive practices. Judge Gary, U.S. Steel's head in its early days, had followed the policy of not allowing it to grow beyond one half of the entire industry, and his policy paid off.

Interestingly enough, in the case of U.S. Steel the facts of economic life accomplished what the Supreme Court refused to do: whereas in 1908 U.S. Steel's share in steel production was 50.9 percent of the industry, it gradually declined, and in the 1960s has hovered around 25 percent of steel production. It is still the largest single steel corporation, and is still on many an occasion the "price leader" in its industry. But it is unlikely ever to regain the borderline monopoly position it occupied early in this century.

Criminal Prosecutions Under the Sherman Act

Under the Sherman Act, the Department of Justice can bring both civil and criminal suits against persons or corporations charged with violations under its provisions. In criminal actions, the penalty for each violation may be a fine not exceeding $50,000 (originally only $5,000) or imprisonment not to exceed one year, or both. Criminal proceedings are instituted only in flagrant cases of deliberate violation of the law, and within that category, jail sentences are given in particularly extreme cases. Prison sentences have ranged from four hours to three years (for three violations), but terms generally tend to be short. For example, in 1961, 29 leading manufacturers of heavy electrical equipment and 45 of their top officials were sentenced by a federal court for price-fixing. These companies controlled 95 percent of the business, amounting to about $2 billion in annual sales. Fines of $1.9 million were imposed, 7 executives were sent to prison for 30 days each, and 21 executives were given suspended short prison sentences and put on probation.

However, the Sherman Act also provides that persons who have suffered injury as a result of anticompetitive practices may bring "treble damage" lawsuits against the perpetrators of such practices. As a result of the criminal conspiracy trial against the electrical equipment manufacturers in 1961, about 1,100 treble damage suits were brought against the 29 manufacturers by states, cities, public utilities, and other customers. These lawsuits cost the companies about $400 million in damages, most cases never going to court but being settled by negotiation. Over three quarters of this huge sum were paid out by General Electric and Westinghouse, the remaining damage awards being paid by the other 27 companies.

In addition to trusts and monopolies in tobacco and petroleum, monopolistic conditions in meat-packing, railroading, powder, and other industries were terminated or substantially reduced in the first two decades after the Sherman Act. The coming of World War I marked a halt, because in wartime many industrial practices are tolerated or even encouraged for the sake of winning the war. The 1920s saw a strong return of economic conservatism; this laissez-faire policy was rejected by the people in the election of 1932, but it took the Supreme Court several more years to catch up with the election results. From the late 1930s, a new era of judicial interpretation began, which went beyond some of the basic concepts of even vigorous Court action before World War I.

A New Approach in the Fight Against Monopoly: The Factor of Size

The breakthrough occurred in the aluminum industry (*U.S.* v. *Aluminum Company of America*), decided by the federal Court of Appeals as the court of last resort in 1945. At the time of bringing the lawsuit against Alcoa, the company controlled over 90 percent of primary aluminum production in the United States. Until the Alcoa case, the government always felt it had to prove "predatory practices" and "unworthy motives" of a company before it could be held an illegal monopoly: "The law does not make mere size an offense" (*U.S.* v. *U.S. Steel Corporation*, 1920). In the Alcoa case, the Court of Appeals expressed the new doctrine that mere monopolistic size was enough to constitute a monopoly, even if no specific "predatory practices" could be charged, because the very possession of monopolistic power meant that Alcoa would sell at a price fixed by itself, with no interference from nonexisting competitors. Alcoa was ordered to dispose of its Canadian interests, but was otherwise left intact. Instead of breaking it up, the government turned over wartime production facilities to Alcoa's two emerging rival companies, Reynolds Metals and Kaiser Aluminum, to create more balanced competition. Alcoa is still the largest aluminum producer, but its share has dropped from 90 percent to around 33 percent of the aluminum industry, and its two nearest rivals mentioned above now account together for slightly over one half of total aluminum output.

Expanding Governmental Protection of the Free Market: The Clayton Act

Although the Sherman Act was a big step forward in the protection of the free market, it suffered from two basic defects. First, it was couched in such general language that the courts had almost complete discretion to determine what such general terms as "restraint of trade" or "monopolize" meant. As the Supreme Court itself recognized (*Apex Hosiery Co.* v. *Leader* [1940]), "the courts have been left to give content to the statute," because the "prohibitions of the Sherman Act were not stated in terms of precision or of crystal clarity." The second main defect was, at least until the Alcoa case in 1945, that the Sherman Act dealt with accomplished facts: it was punitive rather than preventive.

The desire for specific anticompetitive prohibitions and for preventive action found its legislative expression in the Clayton Act and the Federal Trade Commission Act of 1914. The Clayton Act outlawed price discrimination, such as selling below cost to drive competitors in specific areas out of business, or granting large buyers price concessions that go beyond the cost-saving resulting from large sales to one buyer; exclusive dealing, or the sale of goods to a dealer on condition that he refrain from buying such goods (or related goods) from another company; tie-in sales, compelling the buyer to buy articles B and C if he wants to obtain article A; interlocking directorships, or serving on the board of directors of two or more competing companies; and acquisitions of share capital of competing corporations.

All these practices are illegal when the "effect may be to substantially lessen competition or tend to create a monopoly." Here lies perhaps the biggest difference between the Clayton Act and the Sherman Act. Whereas the Sherman Act seeks to remedy past offenses, the Clayton Act looks to the probable future: all the government has to prove is that anticompetitive acts *may* result in less competition, or that they *tend* to create a monopoly.

The Federal Trade Commission was entrusted with the administration and enforcement of the provisions of the Clayton Act, sharing these activities with the Department of Justice. In setting up the FTC, the Act of 1914 also provided that "unfair methods of competition in commerce and unfair or deceptive acts or practices in commerce" are illegal. The outlawry of unfair and deceptive methods goes even beyond the prohibited practices of the Sherman and Clayton Acts, for the FTC goes after unfair and deceptive methods regardless of whether they are used in competition or not. The aim here is to protect the buyer and consumer against unfair and deceptive practices rather than to prevent monopolies. Misrepresentation in advertising and, more lately, packaging are the most frequent abuses handled by the FTC. Unfair practices include false or misleading advertisements, claiming false endorsements, commercial bribery or spying, deceptive pricing, and "payola." In advertising, for example, calling one's product perfect, marvelous, wonderful, stunning, the best, or by any other superlatives, is allowed. But suggesting that "calories don't count" in a dietary regime is deceptive.

Curbing the Urge to Merge

Section 7 of the Clayton Act forbade acquisition of share capital of one company by another, if both were in a competitive position. If one company buys up another competing company, such mergers are called *horizontal*. But under the Clayton Act, two other types were permissible until 1950: *vertical* mergers (or "integration") between a supplier and a customer, as for example, between a manufacturer of steel ingots and an iron ore mining company or between a shoe manufacturer and a retail chain outlet; and *conglomerate* mergers, or the merging of two corporations in different lines of business. This loophole was closed by Congress in 1950, when it forbade such acquisitions and mergers if substantial reduction of competition would be the probable effect "in any line of commerce in any section of the country."

In 1957, for example, the Supreme Court decided that DuPont had to dispose of its ownership of 23 percent of General Motors stock, acquired by it in 1917. DuPont became the main supplier to General Motors of fabrics and paints used in the manufacture of cars. Because General Motors typically produces half or more of all American cars, DuPont thus acquired a vast assured market. The Supreme Court (in *United States* v.

DuPont, 1957) held that "the inference is overwhelming that DuPont's commanding position was promoted by its stock interest and was not gained solely on competitive merit."

However, even relatively small companies have been held to violate the prohibition of vertical mergers. In *Brown Shoe Co.* v. *United States* (1962), the Supreme Court held the merger between Brown Shoe Company, a shoe manufacturer, and the R. G. Kinney Company, a shoe retail chain, illegal, although Brown Shoe Company produced only 4 percent of the nation's footwear, and the Kinney Co. had only 1.2 percent of total national retail shoe sales.

Particularly attacked by the federal government are conglomerate mergers, where the acquiring company has such vast financial resources that future competition in the acquired company's business might thereby be weakened. For example, a federal court in 1966 held the proposed acquisition of the Potash Company of America by Standard Oil of New Jersey illegal.

The danger of conglomerate mergers was vividly described by a leading student of monopoly, Walter Adams:

> I venture to say that if General Motors suddenly decided to enter the ice cream industry and to capture 20, or 40, or 100 per cent of the sales, it could easily do so and be assured of success. It would matter little whether General Motors is an efficient ice cream manufacturer, or whether its ice cream is indeed tastier than more established brands. By discrete price concessions, by saturation advertising, by attractive promotional deals, it could commit its gargantuan financial power to the battle until only so much competition as General Motors is prepared to tolerate would be left in the industry.[6]

The Primacy of Political over Economic Values

Is competition between many small businesses economically more efficient than "price leadership" and other practices in industries with few large companies? Economists have argued over this issue for a long time, but so far no consensus of scholarly analysis or opinion has emerged. However, public policy in curbing monopoly and bigness and in encouraging small business is not based only on economic, but also on political considerations.

In the *Brown Shoe Co.* case, the Supreme Court conceded that some of the results of the merger between a shoe manufacturer and a shoe store chain "are beneficial to the customer." But the Court went on to say, that

---

[6] Testimony given, on January 24, 1959, before the Subcommittee of the Senate Committee on the Judiciary.

"we cannot fail to recognize Congress' desire to promote competition through the protection of viable, small, locally owned business. Congress appreciated that occasional higher costs and prices might result from the maintenance of fragmented industries and markets. It resolved these competing considerations in favor of decentralization. We must give effect to that decision."

The Overall Trend

How serious the merger problem is can be seen from the 1966 *Report* of the Joint Economic Committee. Mergers in manufacturing alone rose from an annual average of 200 to 300 in the early 1950s to over 1,000 in the mid-1960s. In the years 1961–1965, the number of acquisitions of large companies averaged about 75 per year, and their total assets, averaging $2.7 billion annually, have thus been transferred to still larger companies. Two-thirds of all large acquisitions in the years 1948–1965 were made by the 200 largest corporations.

The greatest effect of American public policies aimed at excessive concentration of economic power has been twofold. First, the phenomenon of an entire industry being dominated by one company, as happened in numerous industries early in this century, has disappeared. Second, the very existence of anticoncentration policies produces effects that cannot be statistically measured. In every area of policing, one can only measure the number of violations of the law, but there is no way of knowing to what extent crimes are not being committed because of the presence of a police force. Much of the effectiveness of policing depends on the will of the community to supply the police with enough resources. In 1966, the Antitrust Division of the Department of Justice had about 275 on its professional staff, of whom only 25 were economists. The Division brings annually only about 40 to 90 cases to court, and its relatively small professional legal and economic staff has to face some of the highest-priced lawyers and economists working for large corporations.

Above all, enforcement of antimonopolistic practices and the defense of the free market depend on a political factor: how much interest can be aroused among the people, in Congress, and in the White House to watch over trends toward bigness in the economic field. Until World War I, the issue seemed clear: bigness itself seemed suspect. Since that time, the attitude of many Americans toward big business and concentrated economic power has become more ambiguous. On the one hand, there is a tendency to approve of large corporations as having mightily contributed to the highest living standard of any society in history, and as typically paying higher wages than industries with small-scale competitive units, such as retail trade, services, or farming. On the other hand, Americans have a deep suspicion of concentrated power, whether political or economic, and are therefore willing to curb concentrated economic power.

Whereas to many liberals, antimonopolistic policies in the United States are not vigorous enough, most foreign observers are impressed by the "aggressive interventionist spirit in this instance and the readiness with which private enterprise is guided by official directives, based on a good deal of discretion."[7] The developing economic union of the Common Market countries is increasingly strengthening antimonopoly policies, consciously seeking to learn from the successes and failures of the American experience. The Common Market, with a population almost as large as that of the United States, offers dangerous possibilities for monopolistic practices, and the size of the market alone has suddenly made the American experience more relevant. In Britain, too, both under Conservative and Labour governments, there has been a recent surge of awareness of the dangers of uninhibited corporate growth, and the American experience serves in many respects as a guide for public policy. Just as American federalism may still contribute a great deal to evolving large-scale political unions in the future, American antitrust and antimonopolistic policies may serve a similar function in the economic field, as large-scale economic communities on the model of the Common Market evolve in various parts of the world.

[7] Andrew Shonfield, *Modern Capitalism: The Changing Balance of Public and Private Power* (New York: Oxford University Press, 1965), p. 329.

CHAPTER 22

ECONOMIC POLICIES:
ENDS AND MEANS

⚜ GOVERNMENT AND LABOR

Under the common law, combinations of any sort—in any field of economic activity, by employers or workers—were illegal conspiracies. This approach of the common law rested on the facts of the economy: essentially agrarian, the economy did not possess any sharp disparities. Artisans and merchants were small, and workers did not have to face giant enterprises, but could bargain with a small artisan or merchant on a nearly equal basis.

These conditions, however, have radically changed with the rise of modern industrial economy. There is no longer the sameness or similarity of size throughout the economy. Combination may be a threat in one branch of the economy, but a necessity in another. For this reason, the policies against monopoly and other forms of combinations are not applied in some areas.

Areas Exempt from Antimonopoly Policies

Public utilities such as gas and electric companies, communications such as telephone and radio and television broadcasting, transportation companies such as railroads, are exempt from the provisions of antimonopoly laws

571

to the extent that their activities are regulated by state and federal regulatory commissions—the Interstate Commerce Commission, the Federal Power Commission, the Federal Communications Commission.

Agriculture is another area in which combination is not only tolerated, but often governmentally encouraged and sponsored in various allocation and marketing programs, through which farmers are to be assured minimum prices for some of their products. The Clayton Act itself specifically exempted farmers' mutual help organizations from its antimonopoly provisions.

The Rationale Behind the Encouragement of Combination of Labor

The most important exemption, however, from the general principle against combination is with respect to labor. Here, the purpose of public policy is to make possible the democratic method of bargaining between employers and workers. However, in a corporate economy the individual worker does not possess bargaining power in dealing with his employer. His employer (or prospective employer) is not as eager a buyer of his individual labor power as he is an eager seller of his services. An employer of

"Do you think I *want* to let you go, Haley? We're both victims of the system."
Drawing by Lorenz; © 1962 The New Yorker Magazine, Inc.

10,000 workers who lets one man go, loses $\frac{1}{100}$ of 1 percent of his work force, and at worst, if he cannot find immediate replacement, has to get along without this small fraction of his labor force. A worker who loses his job, or does not get it, has to forgo 100 percent of his wage. Only if workers combine in a union, can they match the bargaining power of the employer. This is particularly true when the employer himself does not act alone, but acts with other employers in a particular line of business or locality in determining wage rates or other working conditions.

The Norris–La Guardia Act

The Clayton Act specifically exempted labor unions from its provisions against illegal conspiracies in restraint of trade, as long as unions were carrying out their "legitimate objects." However, the interpretation by the courts of the "legitimate objects" of unions did not bring about the results labor had hoped for. Another two decades had to pass before organized labor was afforded genuine relief. In 1932, the Norris–La Guardia Act limited the use of the injunction against labor unions. Until that time, the injunction was probably the most important method of employers to break strikes, for disobedience to a court order is contempt of court punishable by immediate imprisonment. The Act also forbade the "yellow-dog contract," under which workers had to pledge themselves not to join a union as a condition of employment.

The National Labor Relations Act: The Magna Carta of Labor

The National Labor Relations Act of 1935 (often referred to as the Wagner Act, named after its chief author, Senator Robert Wagner of New York) finally brought organized labor what it wanted. The two most important provisions of the Act were (1) employees were given the right to organize unions and take part in their activities, without restraint or coercion by employers in the excercise of their rights; (2) employees were given the right to bargain collectively with the employers through their elected representatives, and the employer could not refuse to bargain. Employers were also forbidden to set up "company unions" (that is, unions controlled by the employers), to discriminate against union members, or to dismiss or otherwise penalize a worker for having exercised his rights under the Act.

The philosophy of the National Labor Relations Act was based on the democratic principle that social conflicts should be settled through peaceful negotiation rather than through violence. The Fascist state denies that social conflicts are real, because members of the same "race" or folk must all have the same interest; Communists argue that in a classless society there can be no social conflicts, and therefore strikes, for example, are outlawed under both totalitarian systems. If disagreements among different social groups do occur in a Fascist or Communist state, the government claims to be the sole judge of what is the general interest of the community.

By contrast, in the democratic philosophy as it underlies the National Labor Relations Act, all that government seeks to do is to provide the "rules of game" under which peaceful settlements of social conflicts can be arrived at. Unions and managements are not compelled, under the Act, to agree; they are merely compelled to bargain their disputes collectively. If they do not agree, strikes (by employees) and lockouts (by employers) are still legal, but the hope of democratic government—borne out on the whole, by the experience of collective bargaining—is that people who talk to each other across a bargaining table will more likely agree than if they do not do so.

The Act also set up, for its enforcement, the National Labor Relations Board (NLRB), an independent regulatory body made up of five members, appointed by the President, with the consent of the Senate, for five years. One of its main functions is to determine, in case of disagreement, who the legitimate representative union of workers is, and to hold supervised elections to make that determination, in instances where several unions claim to represent the majority of the employees. In addition, the NLRB has the authority to investigate charges of unfair labor practices, and to issue "cease and desist orders" in the light of its findings.

The Taft-Hartley Act

As a result of the National Labor Relations Act and the prolabor attitude of the New Deal Administration under Franklin D. Roosevelt, union membership jumped from 3.6 million in 1935 to over 10 million in 1941. Yet, as time went on, the feeling grew that the pendulum had swung too far in the direction of labor, and that a new balance between labor and management had to be sought. This led to the Labor-Management Relations Act of 1947, commonly referred to as the Taft-Hartley Act. The two basic principles of the Wagner Act—the right of labor to organize unions and to bargain collectively—were preserved, but important restrictions on labor were added. Some of the most important innovations of the Taft-Hartley Act are:

1. A cooling-off period of 80 days, initiated by the President in cases of threatening or actual strike situations, if he finds that stoppage of work would imperil national health or safety. Since 1948, such cooling-off

periods have been invoked about 1.5 times per year on the average, in industries such as maritime transportation, atomic energy, aircraft production, and steel. In a number of instances, this method has worked.

2. Prohibition of the *closed shop*, under which an employer can hire only persons who are union members. The *union shop* was allowed to continue: under the union shop arrangement, new employees must join the union, provided a majority of the workers has voted in favor of a union shop, and provided union shops are not forbidden by state "right to work" laws.

3. Unfair labor practices by unions. Whereas the Wagner Act focused on unfair labor practices by employers, the Taft-Hartley Act made numerous labor practices by unions illegal. Such prohibitions include the following: the refusal to bargain collectively; coercion of, or discrimination against, employees for exercising their rights; sympathy strikes, or strikes by a union aimed at forcing an employer other than one's own to recognize a union not recognized by the National Labor Relations Board; secondary boycotts, or the refusal by a union to deal in any way with companies that deal with the employer with whom the union is in dispute; and jurisdictional strikes, in which the dispute between unions is about which union is to represent a particular category of workers. Under this ban, a union cannot strike to force the employer to recognize one union rather than another; it cannot practice featherbedding—that is, forcing employers to pay for work not done or not intended to be done; and it cannot make contributions of union funds in federal elections.

The Landrum-Griffin Act

A decade after Taft-Hartley, Congress passed another major reform as the result of congressional investigations of abuses in labor-management relations. The chief objective of the Labor-Management Reporting and Disclosure Act of 1959, commonly referred to as the Landrum-Griffin Act after its House sponsors, was to protect union members against improper union practices.

First, the reform gave union members a "bill of rights," guaranteeing them the secret vote in union elections, "reasonable rules and regulations" for participation in union meetings, full and fair hearings in disciplinary proceedings of unions, the right to appear before a governmental body without union coercion or interference, and the right to sue unions in a federal court for infringing any of the "bill of rights." The threat or use of force by unions in interfering with these rights became a federal crime, subject to a fine up to $1,000 and imprisonment up to one year.

The second main objective of the Landrum-Griffin Act was to strengthen the character of leadership positions in unions as positions of trust and responsibility. The misappropriation or embezzlement of union funds became a federal crime, and union officials handling union money have to be bonded. Unions may lend to their officers a maximum of $2,000, to avoid the previous practice of some union leaders of borrowing hundreds of thousands of dollars for private business ventures—and worse. Unions have to submit annual financial reports to the Secretary of Labor; as the financial assets of American unions now exceed $5 billion, this is one of the most important provisions of the Act—protecting the financial integrity of union management.

Finally, the Act had three provisions aimed directly at a hoodlum element that had penetrated a few unions: first, there is the prohibition of picketing for the purpose of extortion; second, there is the prohibition for management to pay, or for union officers to receive, bribes for "sweetheart contracts," that is, labor contracts between union leaders and management that are favorable to management and that corrupt union leaders arrange against payment of cold cash. Lastly persons convicted of serious felonies are barred from holding union offices for at least five years.

The Question of Compulsory Arbitration

On the whole, government intervention in labor-management relations has attained its objective of industrial peace. Because strikes receive newspaper attention, it is often forgotten that the average annual loss of working time through strikes is only slightly more than $\frac{1}{10}$ of 1 percent. In isolated cases, there may be a move toward compulsory arbitration, as happened in 1963, when Congress imposed compulsory arbitration in railroad disputes over work rules, particularly over the problem of featherbedding. But on the whole, the United States is unlikely to imitate other democratic nations in which compulsory arbitration has been more widely used. Australia and New Zealand, both frequently under Labour governments, have most vigorously practiced compulsory arbitration in serious labor disputes; Norway, Denmark, and Sweden, largely governed by Labor governments in the last three decades, have also used it on many occasions. France has repeatedly seized plants and drafted workers into the armed forces in serious strike situations. Britain had compulsory arbitration in World Wars I and II, and operates an industrial disputes' tribunal for the settlement of major labor conflicts.

In the United States, there was no compulsory arbitration in World Wars I and II, although there was strong government intervention through the War Labor Board. Yet industrial peace was no less effectively maintained than in Britain, which had compulsory arbitration in wartime. Yet, as the congressional requirement of compulsory arbitration in 1963 in the railroad dispute has shown, there is a growing inclination not to allow strikes in vital industries upon which the very existence of the nation's economy depends, such as in transportation, steel, or defense industries. But even without such legislative action, the federal government under Presidents Eisenhower, Kennedy, and Johnson has directly intervened in the settlement of strikes or in preventing threatening work stoppages. In several instances, the President himself (or the Vice-President acting for him) has thrown his influence into such disputes. Such *ad hoc* presidential intervention may suffice for an experimental period. But in the long run, it is possible that the traditional American distaste for compulsory arbitration and direct governmental settlement of labor disputes will be overcome, and that the United States will move in the direction of other Western democracies that have accepted the necessity of compulsory arbitration in major labor disputes imperiling the safety and health of the nation.

The Growth of the Welfare State and Industrial Peace

The expansion of the welfare state in the United States may also gradually lessen disputes between labor and management. One of the main reasons, for example, that there are so few strikes in Sweden, despite the long rule of a pro-union Labor government, is that there is relatively little left to strike about: working hours, vacations, sick leave, unemployment relief, and pensions are regulated by law, and are not left to labor-management bargaining. To some extent, the expanding welfare in the United States will accomplish the same results, but at a slower rate and in more limited areas, for neither labor nor management is willing to hand over to government the settlement of as many social and economic issues as is done in Sweden or Britain. For this reason, it is more likely that either informal governmental intervention in labor disputes through "guidelines" or presidential action, or possibly the more drastic method of congressional legislation requiring compulsory arbitration in specific industries will gain ground in the United States. The power of both organized labor and the corporations is tremendous: if either is abused, the even greater power of the United States government will have to be used.

ʚ PUBLIC POLICIES FOR ECONOMIC GROWTH AND STABILITY

The Employment Act of 1946

The principal legal commitment of national policy to maintain economic stability and encourage economic growth is expressed in the Employment Act of 1946. Little known to the general public, it is one of the most important Acts of Congress in this century. At the end of World War II, there was widespread apprehension that the rapid demobilization of over 10 million men in the armed forces combined with the ending of war production would—almost inevitably, some thought—bring about a severe economic depression, possibly worse than the Great Depression of the early 1930s. To forestall such developments, Congress passed the Employment Act in 1946.

The Act declared that it is the "continuing policy and responsibility of the Federal Government" to create and maintain "conditions under which there will be afforded useful employment opportunities, including self-employment, for those able, willing, and seeking work, and to promote maximum employment, production, and purchasing power." The Act, further, provided that the President transmit annually to Congress by January 20 an "Economic Report," presenting an analysis of the state of the economy during the preceding year, the prospects and needs for the coming year, and programs and legislative proposals for the maximum utilization of manpower and resources.

The Joint Economic Committee and the Council of Economic Advisers. The Act also set up two Committees: first, the Joint Economic Committee, composed of eight members of the Senate and eight members of the House of Representatives. Its main function is to serve "as a guide" to congressional committees dealing with legislation relating to the *Economic Report*, and to submit to Congress annually by March 1 its own findings and recommendations with respect to presidential proposals in the Economic Report. The second Committee set up by the Employment Act of 1946 is the Council of Economic Advisers in the Executive Office of the President. The Council consists of three members, appointed by the President with the consent of the Senate; he also designates one of the three members as chairman. The main function of the Council is to assist the President in the preparation of the annual Economic Report, and to "develop and recommend to the President national economic policies" aiming at full employment of manpower and resources. As do the President and the Joint Economic Committee, the Council publishes an annual Report.

The influence of the Joint Economic Committee and the Council of Economic Advisers has gradually grown beyond original expectations. The Joint Economic Committee was fortunate enough to have among its members men such as Senators Paul Douglas (a leading economist before his election to the Senate), Jacob Javits, John F. Kennedy, Robert Taft, and Representatives Richard Bolling, Christian Herter, and Wright Patman. The Council of Economic Advisers, both under Democratic and Republican administrations, has had among its members some of the nation's outstanding economists, and expertise always commands respect in the United States.

The main burden of formulating economic policies falls on the Council of Economic Advisers. It has no authority to compel any government agency or any private individual to do anything or to abstain from doing anything. Its sole influence derives from its ability to correctly analyze conditions and trends in the economy, and to propose policies and plans which convince the President and Congress.

Under the Kennedy and Johnson administrations in particular, the Council has grown in stature, mainly because the "new economics" (first propounded by John Maynard Keynes in the 1930s) promoted by the Council was adopted by Congress and the executive branch—and it worked. In the 1950s, the average annual rate of growth of the American economy was 2.3 percent. In 1961–1965, the average annual growth rate (in constant dollars) approached 5 percent. Whereas in the 1950s, the American economic rate of growth was only about one half of the Soviet rate, in the first half decade of the 1960s it matched the Soviet growth rate. To give an idea of what rapid growth means in the United States: in 1965, for example, the gross national product increased by 47 billion dollars. In only seven countries in the world did the *total output* of goods and services in 1965 match or exceed this *increase*.

The "New Economics": The Use of Fiscal and Monetary Policies

The basic concept of the "new economics" is twofold: to use fiscal and monetary policies as instruments of economic stability and growth. The purpose of both "tools" of economic policy is *to match* at all times, as much as is feasible, *total spending* ("aggregate demand") *with productive capacity* in the economy.

The Use of Fiscal Policies. If total spending is below productive capacity, or threatens to fall below it, the government can do one of two things (or both) in fiscal policy: it can either increase government spending, thus driving up demand, or it can cut taxes so that private individuals and businesses have more money to spend on consumer goods and to invest in productive facilities. This dual policy of both cutting taxes and increasing government expenditures was followed from 1961 on.

President Kennedy favored a sizable cut in taxes, although the budget was in a state of deficit. After his assassination, President Johnson persuaded Congress to enact the Revenue Act of 1964 and the Excise Tax Reduction Act of 1965. Although both tax-cut Acts reduced taxes by $16 billion, federal revenue did not decline, but increased by $9 billion in 1964–1965, because the increased spending by private individuals and corporations increased business activity and reduced unemployment to such an extent that more tax revenue was generated than would have been under the previous higher tax and excise rates.

The drop in unemployment was one of the most dramatic developments. The rate of unemployment dropped from 5.7 percent in 1963 to below 4 percent in 1966, the lowest rate in 13 years. This figure was still higher than in most Western European countries, some of which (like Germany, France, Sweden, and Switzerland) have for years suffered from a labor shortage, met only by recruiting large numbers of foreign workers from all over Europe—from Portugal to Greece.

The "new economics" as practised since the early 1960s has had to face the threat of inflation since 1966. Inflation means that, if all productive capacity is fully employed, excessive demand cannot stimulate more production, but merely drives prices upward. Fiscal policy can, then, be effectively used by increasing taxes, though the budget may have a surplus, or by cutting down government expenditures. In the first method, the spending of private individuals is reduced, and in the second method that of government. The federal annual expenditures alone amount to about 20 percent of the gross national product; if the expenses of state and local governments are added, government expenditures in the United States amount to about 30 percent of the gross national product. This provides government with a powerful leverage in influencing the total spending in the economy. In addition to fiscal measures, behind which there is the force of law, the government may also resort to admonition and guidelines. Thus President Johnson asked business in 1966 to cut down on new investments in plant expansion, and a number of top executives immediately responded that they would make such cuts wherever feasible. Similarly, the government has, in recent years, asked banks and corporations with foreign interests to reduce investments and loans abroad to lessen the drain on American resources.

The Use of Monetary Policies. The second main instrument of government policy in promoting economic stability and growth is monetary. Unlike fiscal policy, which is handled by the federal government, monetary policy is handled by the Federal Reserve System, a semi-independent body set up in 1913. The system is made up of twelve regional Federal Reserve Banks, owned by the private member banks that are members of the system. Nearly one half of the 14,000 banks in the United States are members of the Federal Reserve System, but this half controls over 80 percent of bank assets and deposits. The system is directed by a Board of

Governors in Washington, made up of seven men, appointed by the President with the consent of the Senate. To make the Board politically independent, its members are appointed for staggered 14-year terms, and members may not be reappointed for a second term. One of the main powers of the Board of Governors is to set the interest rate at which it lends money to private banks, which in turn make loans to businesses or individuals. A raise of the interest rate is applied in inflationary or near-inflationary periods; its purpose is to decrease the demand for credit. Thus less money enters the spending stream in the economy, and there is therefore less pressure on existing resources. By contrast, when there is a slack in the economy—manpower and resources being underemployed—a decrease in the interest rate, or "easy money," stimulates the demand for credit, and these additional funds enter the spending stream by increasing expansion of plants, inventories, and the production of consumer goods.

The federal government itself is the largest borrower of money in the entire economy. Like all debtors, it therefore has a vested interest in "easy money," whereas as the representative of the national interest it should welcome high interest rates when inflationary pressures show up. Not infrequently, the federal government resists increases of the interest rate, either because such raises are never politically popular or because the federal government is too concerned with its own problems as a debtor. For example, in December, 1965, the Federal Reserve Board increased the interest rate that private banks have to pay on loans from the Federal Reserve Banks ("rediscount rate") from 4 to 4½ percent, the highest since 1931. Because private banks must make some profit, the lowest rate of interest that they charge preferred (large) borrowers ("prime rate") is at least ½ percent higher than what they have to pay themselves. President Johnson attacked the Board's action, but it stuck to its decision. Such presidential opposition is often just "for the record." In actuality, the Board's unpopular decisions—invariably when it raises the interest rate— may be a boon to the President because he may realize that they may be necessary, although he naturally prefers popular displeasure to be diverted from the White House to the "Fed."

Limits of Monetary Policies

The great—and as yet not completely resolved—dilemma in using monetary tools in economic policy has both an economic and a political aspect. Economically, the manipulation of credit volume and interest rates does not seem to have the same predictable results that are inherent in fiscal policies. When the government increases expenditures or cuts taxes in time of underemployed manpower or resources, money immediately enters the spending stream and stimulates production and investment. By contrast, even the policy of very low interest rates during the Great Depression in the 1930s did not have the desired effect in any decisive manner. If credit is easily available at low interest rates, potential borrowers may still abstain from borrowing if they feel very pessimistic about the future of the economy.

Similarly, in a period of inflation or near-inflation, fiscal policies have also proved more predictable than monetary policies. If the government spends less and increases taxes, such actions have an almost immediate effect in lowering demand for goods and services by cutting down the spending power of both private individuals and governmental bodies. By contrast, if credit is made tight and interest rates are raised, overly optimistic individuals or corporations may still borrow money to increase plant facilities, to buy consumer goods on credit, or to purchase stocks in a rising stock market. Conversely, there have been times when "tight money" has been more than effective, that is, where it has curbed inflation too drastically by creating unemployment.

In most Western nations, the bias in recent years has been in favor of full employment at the price of "a little inflation" (say, an annual increase of prices by about 2–3 percent). In the United States, there has been more reluctance to accept this politically important choice in putting full employment ahead of the stability of the currency, perhaps because the influence of financial orthodoxy is still stronger than in most other Western nations, and possibly also because the United States as the financial center of the non-Communist world—the dollar serving as a kind of international currency—feels a special responsibility to keep the value of its currency as stable as possible.

Federal Insurance of Deposits and Credits

Because the safety of credit affects both the stability and growth of the economy, the federal government is involved in various programs. The Federal Deposit Insurance Corporation (FDIC) insures deposits in banks up to $10,000 for each account. Nearly all of the country's 14,000 banks participate in this program. Set up in 1933, at the depth of the Great Depression, the purpose of federally insured bank deposits is to remove the fear of "runs" on individual banks or the entire bank system, which had previously occurred from time to time, resulting in economic and financial chaos. The Federal Savings and Loan Insurance Corporation insures savings deposits up to $10,000 per account that are held in savings and loan associations that participate in the program. To get an idea of the dimensions of these two federally sponsored insurance programs: in 1966, the

total amount of individual savings accounts in banks was above $150 bil-
lion, and over $100 billion in savings and loan associations. The over-
whelming majority of American families have a direct stake in these
insurance programs that protect their hard-earned savings.

In the field of foreign trade, the federal government established in 1934
the Export-Import Bank of Washington to facilitate foreign trade through
credit, particularly where private banks are unwilling or unable to assume
the risks. Such risks may be political, as in trade credits granted to Communist governments or to politically unstable non-Communist countries,
or where the credits are for projects with uncertain financial returns. In the
years 1945–1964, the Export-Import Bank granted over $9 billion in foreign
trade credits, and in most recent years, the annual amount of credit has
frequently exceeded $½ billion.

☙ BUILT-IN STABILIZERS OF THE ECONOMY

In addition to *ad hoc* public policies aiming at economic stability, governmental intervention and long-range policies have developed "built-in stabi-
lizers" that tend to lessen the impact of sharp upswings or declines in
economic activity.

Government Spending

First, there is the size of government itself, employing (on the federal,
state, and local levels) *one seventh* of the civilian labor force. In 1929,
government expenditures (federal, state, and local) were well below 10
percent of gross national product. In the 1960s, this percentage had risen
to about 30 percent of gross national product. This percentage of government expenditures is still considerably lower than in Britain, France,
Canada, and West Germany, to mention but a few major Western countries.

Unlike families and business enterprises, which in the long run must
spend less when they take in less, government (particularly on the federal
level) can keep on spending more than it receives through the process of
borrowing. In fact, since Keynes, government *should* increase its expenditures in times of shrinking economic activity to make up for the loss of
demand on the part of family households and private businesses. Moreover, about half of federal expenditures go into goods and services which
the federal government buys from private sources. This item alone
amounts to 10 percent of the gross national product. Since some government contracts extend over several years—particularly in the electronic,

aircraft, and space industries—such purchases of goods and services provide a cushion against sudden declines of at least some branches of the economy.

Furthermore, when business declines, tax collections also decline, and thus take away less purchasing power from private families and businesses, particularly corporations, which pay about half of their profits as taxes. High corporate taxes still enable corporations to maintain dividend payments, for with declining earning there is also a corresponding drop in tax payments. Assuming a corporation earns $1 million a year after paying state and local taxes, its federal tax bill is $480,000. Its net profit would be $520,000. Of this amount, about half, or $¼ million, would typically be paid out as dividends to stockholders, the remaining $270,000 being retained for improvement of productive facilities. If, after state and local taxes, the earnings should go down by 10 percent, from $1 million to $900,000, the federal tax liability would drop from $480,000 to $432,000, but the corporation could still well afford to maintain its payment of dividends of $¼ million out of "after-tax" profits of $468,000, while reinvesting only $218,000 (instead of $270,000 of the preceding year) in its own business. As a result of such decline in earnings, the government "absorbs" half of the lost earnings, whereas the stockholders keep on getting their dividends.

The Importance of "Transfer Payments"

An even more important "built-in" stabilizer in the economy derives from the phenomenal growth of "transfer payments" (payments not resulting from current production, such as public and private pensions, social security benefits, unemployment insurance, veterans' benefits, and the like). In 1929, transfer payments amounted to only 1.6 percent of total personal income. In 1965, the share of transfer payments in personal income had risen to 7.5 percent. Most of these payments, such as pensions or social security benefits, remain stable in recessions. Some types of transfer payments even rise in recessions; for example, as unemployment increases, unemployment assistance payments increase. In some recent (and relatively brief) recessionary periods, as in 1960–1961, personal income increased more than national income declined. The decline of national income showed up in lower corporate profits rather than in lower personal income. At times this phenomenon of rising personal income during a decline of national income has produced the hitherto new phenomenon of rising prices of consumer goods and services during a recession, as happened during the brief recessions of 1957–1958 and 1960–1961.

ℳ GOVERNMENT BY GUIDELINES

Until recently, the concept of "business affected with a public interest" was applied to specific businesses or industries; only in wartime the whole economy acquired public interest, and wage and price controls were applied throughout the economy. In normal times, it was thought that government had to make a reasonable case for interfering with the movement of prices and wages.

President Kennedy and the Steel Industry (1962)

This traditional pattern of governmental economic policy has changed since 1962. In that year, the major steel companies announced a substantial increase in steel prices; President Kennedy reacted swiftly, attacked the announced price rises as inflationary and detrimental to the public interest, and insisted, by various veiled and not-so-veiled threats, that the steel companies rescind the increases. Within a few days, the disagreement became more than a struggle between two principles—free price determination by business versus government control—or even between two impersonal forces—government versus the steel industry—but it appeared to the public as a struggle between the President of the United States and the chairman of the board of the U.S. Steel Corporation, who took the lead in defending the price increases. The steel industry backed down, particularly after it became clear that the preponderance of public opinion was on the side of the President.

Guidelines on Wages and Prices

Since that struggle in 1962, various federal agencies, led by the Council of Economic Advisers, have issued *guidelines,* or *guideposts,* with respect to wage and price policies to be followed by business and labor. The overall purpose of these guidelines is to avoid inflation through rising wages or prices. At first, the Council of Economic Advisers laid down the general principle, for example, that wages not be raised above the rise in productivity. In 1964, the Council more specifically recommended the figure of 3.2 percent as the guideline for wage increases because that figure was considered the recent average annual rise of labor productivity. With respect to prices, the Council of Economic Advisers recommended stable levels in industries enjoying average productivity increases. Both in the area of wages and prices, exceptions were admitted where productivity or other factors (such as capital availability or rate of unemployment or existing wage levels) were above or below the national average.

Controlling prices is not a novelty in the American economy. The independent regulatory commissions (such as the Interstate Commerce Commission, established in 1887, the Federal Communications Commission, in 1934, the Civil Aeronautics Board, in 1938), all are empowered to regulate the rates that may be charged by railroads, telephone and telegraph companies, or airlines. But this type of regulation differs from regulation by "guidelines" in several important respects. First, the traditional regulatory agencies apply only to industries and services that are monopolies or quasi-monopolies and are franchised by a public authority. By contrast, guideline regulation applies—in intent at least—to the whole economy. Second, the independent regulatory commissions were set up by acts of Congress, after the issues and merits were debated in the customary manner. The guidelines are not issued by Congress but by federal officials such as the Council of Economic Advisers or the Treasury or the Department of Commerce. Then, in the case of the regulatory agencies there is judicial review of their decisions because they have legal, binding force. In regulations by guideline, there is no judicial review because they are merely "recommendations" that should be "voluntarily" complied with by management and labor; as a result, no specific penalties can be attached to the guidelines if violated.

Some Major Guideline Tests

Major tests for economic regulation by guidelines occurred on several occasions. In 1965, price increases of aluminum and copper were rescinded after vigorous protests by leading administration spokesmen. In addition to the usual weapons the President possesses, the federal government also threatened to unload aluminum and copper from its own stockpile of both materials and thus drive the prices back to what it considered noninflationary.

In 1966, Bethlehem Steel Corporation, the second largest in the industry, announced a price increase of $5 a ton of structural steel. High federal officials immediately attacked this price increase as inflationary and unjustified; a few days later, U.S. Steel announced a price increase of $2.75 per ton. This was accepted by the federal government, and the whole industry shortly fell in line. Between the price increase announced by Bethlehem, which the federal government rejected, and the more moderate increases by U.S. Steel, which the government accepted, there was a good deal of activity in Washington. Government officials urged the other steel companies not to follow Bethlehem's lead, and asked U.S. Steel top officials to come to Washington to hear the administration's side. Government officials also asked high executives in other industries to persuade the steel industry not to go along with a $5 a ton increase. Out of all this activity came the decision of U.S. Steel to increase the price of structural steel by only $2.75 a ton. Later in 1966, the steel companies increased the price of sheet steel by $3 a ton—without any interference by the government. Guidelines were not invoked, perhaps because the increase was moderate and also because it was shrewdly announced by the steel companies during the airline strike, when it was clear that the striking airline machinists paid no attention to guidelines on wage increases.

"A New Breed of Corporate Cat"?

Compliance of the steel industry early in 1966 with the demands of the federal government and regulation by guidelines was motivated by several factors. First, there was, and still is, the fear that if guidelines are not followed, direct controls of prices and wages will replace the less definite method of guidelines. Second, in many industries, particularly in defense-related ones, the government wields much power as a buyer and customer. Third, the most powerful weapon of the President is his ability to mobilize public opinion, particularly in a period of cold war (or localized hot war as in Korea in the 1950s and in Vietnam in the 1960s), in the name of patriotism versus "profiteering." Finally, the present generation of management leaders are different from the executives in the 1920s or 1930s. The *Wall Street Journal* describes the change as follows: "Increasing numbers of today's top corporate officials believe in a sizable Government role as a philosophic matter.... They grew up with the John Maynard Keynes economic philosophy, not with Adam Smith's. 'There's a new breed of corporate cat,' is the way one top Treasury Department official puts it."[1]

So far, the federal government has generally not lost in cases of major defiance of guideline regulation, whenever it chose to resist such defiance. This latter qualification is of the greatest importance. The United Auto Workers won a 3-year contract in 1964 which, according to many, represented an annual increase of 5 percent in wages and fringe benefits, considerably more than the 3.2 percent permissible upper limit fixed by guidelines on wage increases. Aluminum and construction workers obtained, in 1965, wage increases considerably above the guidelines ceiling, as did airline machinists after a long strike in 1966. The argument has been proposed, probably with some degree of validity, that a Democratic administration is more likely to enforce guidelines on prices rather than on wages,

[1] *Wall Street Journal*, January 13, 1966.

"I'm afraid this is going to play hell with the Presidential guidelines."
Drawing by Ed Fisher; © 1966 The New Yorker Magazine, Inc.

just as a Republican administration—if it were to follow such a policy—
might be more adamant on guidelines on wages than on prices.

Areas in Which Guidelines Are Less Effective

However, there are factors at work here that transcend narrow political
partisanship. Guidelines on prices have been most effective in industries
that produce a basic product, such as steel, copper, or aluminum, and that
are dominated by a relatively small group of companies. Price increases
therefore have occurred in food, clothing, lumber, furniture, appliances, and
many other products, in which there is substantial competition on the
supply side of the market. In the area of services, guidelines are most
ineffective: medical services, for example, have been one of the elements of
living costs that has risen very fast in recent years. The same is true of
other services.

With respect to wages, it must be remembered that only about one
quarter of American wage and salary earners are unionized. Whereas it is
true that the high-wage element of the labor force is best organized (as in
steel, automobiles, coal, trucking), and often sets wage levels that influence
the wages of the entire labor force, the fact remains that in specific cases,
guidelines can operate only where organized labor meets organized business. Where there is little unionization, as in white-collar and service

employment, wages and salaries can rise substantially without such rises being exposed to the limelight of publicity.

The Issue of Responsible Economic Power Under the Rule of Law

Government by economic guidelines as developed under the Kennedy and Johnson administrations does not solve the problem of responsible economic power, but it is at least a recognition that it exists, that it is here to stay, and that some public policies must be devised to cope with it. Until a generation ago, the American public barely recognized that a big corporation or labor union was more than a magnified corner grocery store or grocery clerk, that it was a vast aggregate of quasi-governmental power. Today, it is increasingly recognized that corporations and unions are among the crucial centers of power, and that, like all power, their power, too, must be subjected to constitutional limits if it is to be legitimate power. Guidelines are the first step in this direction—improvised, informal, proceeding from case to case.

Before too long, some more formal and institutionalized methods will have to be found if the public interest in vital economic areas is to be protected by established procedures based on the rule of law. In the meantime, experience will teach how the hitherto experimental and informal approach that bypasses Congress and the courts can be brought into more orderly procedures. Government by guidelines possesses an inherent element of veiled threat of penalty, and the rule of law requires that punishment be clearly defined in advance by a legislative body, and that courts have the power to review their legality and constitutionality.

❦ FEDERAL SUBSIDIES

The federal subsidy program is another direct federal economic policy aiming at stability in selected sectors, although it may also pursue other objectives, such as raising income (as in farming) or output (as in air or sea transportation). In a study of the Joint Economic Committee of Congress in 1965, *Subsidy and Subsidy-Effect Programs of the U.S. Government*, the mere listing of the programs filled over eight pages. Between 1950 and 1965, the total amount spent on federal subsidy programs came to $88 billion, and the long-term trend per average year has been upward. In the 1960s, federal subsidy programs have often exceeded $8 billion per year, of which about 60 to 65 percent go to agriculture.

Subsidies to Business: Transportation

Business gets about 20 percent of the total subsidy amount. Historically, the federal government has always been concerned with encouraging all forms of transportation. In the nineteenth century, for example, land grants to railroads created fabulously wealthy railroad magnates, but railroads spanning the continent were built at great speed. Land grants to railroads in the years 1850–1871 amounted to 183 million acres, valued at over $400 million. In addition to land grants, federal and state contributions to the construction of railroads came close to $1 billion. The Urban Mass Transportation Act of 1964 authorized the expenditure of $375 million by state and local agencies for the improvement of mass transportation services in large metropolitan areas. Because there is a strong feeling against public ownership of railroad commuter services in metropolitan areas, public funds will increasingly be spent on this segment of the railroad industry.

Air carriers have been another main recipient of federal subsidies. Annual subsidies to air carriers have amounted to about $85 million in recent years, most of which sum goes to small local service carriers. With expanding business in air transportation the need for up-to-date airports has constantly grown. Under federal-aid airport programs, nearly $1 billion was spent in the years 1947–1966. More recently, the federal government has committed itself to about $2 billion in helping private aircraft manufacturers to develop supersonic aircraft. Although this revolutionary type of aircraft will obviously have great implications for defense, private air carriers will substantially benefit from this development. Not included in the above subsidy figures are various government expenditures that directly benefit private air carriers, such as airport facilities, navigation aids, aeronautical research conducted by government agencies, and the sale of surplus planes.

Direct aid to shipping goes back to 1789, when the First Congress passed legislation in favor of American vessels. Mail subsidies have been granted to maritime carriers since 1845. Under the Merchant Marine Act of 1936, the federal government has two major subsidy programs for American shipbuilding and shipping. First, there is the *construction-differential* subsidy. Under this program, the federal government pays an American citizen the cost differential between constructing a vessel in the United States (to be used in its foreign commerce) and the estimated lower cost of constructing it in a foreign shipyard. The subsidy can go up to one half of the cost of building the vessel in the United States. In the years 1950–1964, construction-differential subsidies came to $600 million. The second maritime aid program is the *operating-differential* subsidy. It covers—out of federal funds—the cost differential between operating expenses of an American vessel used in foreign commerce and estimated operating costs of a vessel of a foreign country that is in substantial competition with the subsidized American vessel. During the period 1947–1964, $1.7 billion was paid out in operating-differential subsidies.

Subsidies Through Postal Services

The reported postal budgetary deficit for the eight years 1955–1963 was $5.6 billion. First class mail and airmail are the only two services in which the United States Post Office consistently makes a profit. Second class mail, which carries mainly newspapers and magazines, is the biggest single money-losing service, accounting in an average year for about 40 to 50 percent of the total Post Office deficit. The main justification for this subsidy to publishers of newspapers and periodicals—running annually to about $300 million in the 1960s—is that it is in the public interest to stimulate the widest distribution of such reading materials through below-cost postal rates. Advertisers in newspapers and magazines also benefit from this subsidy because they can increase sales through advertising at the expense of the taxpayer. Because the reading public is unorganized, whereas the publishers of newspapers and periodicals are both well organized and very powerful, Congress has so far not been eager to tackle the problem of second class mail deficits.

Subsidies in Research and Development

The officially labeled "subsidy programs" of the federal government of about $8 billion per year do not give the complete picture. If one adds subsidy programs not so labeled, one arrives at federal subsidy expenditures for the benefit of private business that are more than double the cost of officially labeled "subsidy programs." For example, research and development expenditures amounted to about $24 billion in 1966, or over 3 percent of the gross national product. Of this vast sum, the federal government contributes two thirds, or $16 billion, whereas industry contributes the remaining one third. Yet although private industry pays only for one third of the cost, it performs about three fourths of all research and development. Thus, industry received about half of its research and development costs from the federal government in 1966.

It is hardly surprising that the emphasis in industrial research and development is on development rather than on basic research, because development is the area that produces profits. In basic research, which costs about $2 billion annually, industry carries on only one fourth of the total effort, of which nearly half is paid by the government. The main work in basic research, nearly half of the total, is done by universities and colleges, most of which is paid for by the federal government. Private business benefits immensely from these federal subsidies particularly in the electronics, aircraft, and computer industries. These are highly profitable industries in the United States, and their products lead the world in technological advances. There are, for example, more American-made planes and computers in use in the world today than aircraft and computers of all other nations put together, and American electronics and office machine manufacturers maintain worldwide production and sales facilities.

The officially labeled "subsidy programs" of the federal government also do not include veterans' benefits, federal grants-in-aid to the states, the latter item alone amounting to nearly $14 billion in 1966. Of these $14 billion, about $4 billion alone went for subsidies to highway construction, directly benefiting business in general and the automotive and trucking industries in particular.

❦ GOVERNMENT AND AGRICULTURE

Agriculture is the sector of the American economy in which the intervention of government is more clearly, and more strongly, visible than in any other branch of the economy. Public policies in agriculture are not marginal as in some other areas, but provide the setting within which the American farmer can function and maintain his economic identity and existence. In no other Western nation is there the strong commitment of government to the maintenance of a healthy farm economy that has evolved in the United States. Yet this deepening involvement of government in American farming is not the result of a preconceived theory that has been methodically put into practice, but rather the cumulative response to practical needs and problems as they have arisen.

The Main Problem of Farming: Overproduction

The main problem of American farming is its tremendous capacity to produce an ever-increasing amount of food and fibers with less and less land and manpower. In popular thinking, the technological revolution of the last century is identified with increased industrial productivity. In the United States, however, agricultural productivity in recent decades has grown at a faster rate than that of the whole economy. Between 1950 and 1965, for example, productivity in farming (or output per man-hour) increased by about 110 percent, whereas in the nonfarm sector of the economy the increase was only about 40 percent. This means, productivity in farming in these fifteen years increased at a rate that was almost three times as fast as in the nonfarm economy.

The demand for farm products is relatively "inelastic," which means that, as incomes of consumers go up, only a small fraction goes into more and better foods, because there is a natural limit to what a person can eat or drink. The extra income goes into other goods and services. Thus fewer and fewer farm workers and less and less farm land are needed to meet the requirements of food production for domestic consumption and foreign exports. Between 1950 and 1965, for example, farm production rose by 35 percent, but with 45 percent fewer man-hours and 11 percent less cropland. About one sixth of cropland has been withdrawn from production through various government subsidy programs, and more and more people have left the land, about 1 million annually, or almost 3,000 daily. This has resulted in a sharp decrease of the farm population: whereas in 1920, the farm population was still over 30 percent of the total population, in 1965 the figure had dropped to 6.4 percent of the population. The number of farms in 1940–1965 declined from about 6.4 million to about 3.2 million, or by one half.

Most of the farms that have disappeared were small and submarginal, unable to make a decent living. The farms that have remained have increased in size and income, and about one third of current farm families gross over $10,000 in sales. They are still mostly family farms, but they are much more efficient than the older, small farms, and they produce for the market rather than for their own subsistence. These farmers possess great technological skill, are highly trained, and have large capital investments. The enormous productive capacity of these affluent farmers, about one third of the total, is in sharp contrast with the poor third of farm families, whose annual sales gross well below $5,000 per annum.

Disadvantages of Unregulated Competition in Farming

Industry is able to adjust production to demand, because relatively few enterprises are in charge of the industrial process. This is not a "natural process," but the result of government and law that permit a structure of industrial enterprise in which such "private planning" is possible. By contrast, farm production is determined by several millions of production units. Ignorance of market conditions, anticipation of bad weather conditions which may, or may not, materialize, and excessive optimism of the individual farmer that he can beat the next fellow—all may combine in producing unbridled competition with a disastrous imbalance between production and demand for farm products. Such an imbalance is quickly reflected in falling prices at times when demand for farm products declines or merely fails to increase as rapidly as productivity. For example, between 1929 and 1933, farm output dropped by only 6 percent, but farm products dropped by 63 percent in price, or over ten times as much. By contrast, during those four years of the Great Depression production of farm implements dropped by 80 percent, but prices declined by only 6 percent, because an industry dominated by a few large corporations could regulate production more effectively by cutting output to a level at which it was still profitable, particularly since prices in such "oligopolistic" industries do not necessarily reflect supply and demand but are "administered prices," or prices set by either tacit agreement among a few firms or by the exercise of "price leadership" on the part of the largest single firm.

Reasons Behind Government Aid to Farming

The rationale behind government aid to farming is based on several factors. First, there is the factor of social justice, according to which the farm sector of the economy should be entitled to share fairly in the general prosperity of the nation. Second, there is the economic consideration, according to which an ailing agriculture cannot but have harmful effects on the rest of the economy. A prosperous agriculture is an important market for many products and services that come from the nonfarm branches of the economy. In some Midwest and Mountain states, farming is the principal economic activity on which the other sectors of the economy depend for their prosperity and stability.

Finally, and in the eyes of some perhaps the most important factor, there are the intangible values of the individualism and independence of the farm community: farming is the only major industry left in which the traditional American values seem to survive. Many people—including urban dwellers—feel that a prosperous farm economy is indispensable for the moral, spiritual, and political "health" of the nation. From Jefferson on, there has always been a streak of romantic idolization of farming in the American tradition, perhaps because it was the farmer who opened the frontier and who was the dominant figure in the early phase of American history.

"Parity" Prices

Although aid to farming goes back to the earliest days of the Republic, the current massive and detailed aid and regulation of agriculture started under

President Franklin D. Roosevelt in the early 1930s. Often set up as emergency measures, the basic policies and institutions of the farm program in the 1930s have continued to the present, and there has been no partisan disagreement about the overall objective of federal responsibility for a healthy farm economy. The key economic concept in aid to farming is "parity" between prices of farm products and nonfarm products. (See Figures 22–1 to 22–4.) The period of 1909–1914 was chosen as the base period because the purchasing power of farm products during those five years was considered a fair and reasonable one by Congress in the 1930s. Whenever the farmer receives less for what he sells relative to what he has to pay for what he buys than in the "base period," parity declines in proportion. If, for example, the farmer had to sell 100 bushels of wheat in 1909–1914 in order to buy 100 articles X, but could purchase only 80 articles X through the sale of 100 bushels of wheat in 1965, the parity ratio went down from 100 to 80. The purpose of "price support" policies of the federal government since the 1930s has been to make sure that the parity ratio does not drop below a certain level in predetermined "basic" commodities. In general, price support policies have ranged from 60 to 90 percent of parity.

Contrary to a widely held belief that the prices of all, or nearly all, farm products are supported by government aid and regulation, this is not true. In a typical year, about 55 to 60 percent of all market sales are outside of price support programs. The main commodities that benefit from price support programs are the "basic" commodities such as cotton, wheat, corn, tobacco, rice, and peanuts, and some "nonbasic" commodities such as dairy products, soybeans, cottonseed, sorghum grain, oats, and barley. More than 80 percent of all government support aid goes into five highly competitive commodities—cotton, wheat, corn, sorghum grain, and dairy products—although these five categories represent only 40 percent of the value of all farm sales. Yet these are the products in which competition is the stiffest, in which the dangers of overproduction are the largest, and in which whole geographical areas are affected.

The Commodity Credit Corporation

The main instrumentality of supporting prices is the Commodity Credit Corporation (CCC). Set up by executive order in 1933, the CCC was chartered as an agency of the United States in 1948. It is governed by a board of directors of seven, made up of the Secretary of Agriculture who is

Percent of 1910–1914

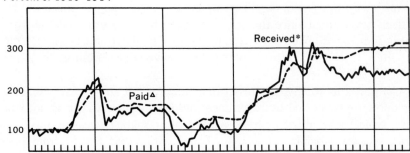

Percent of Parity

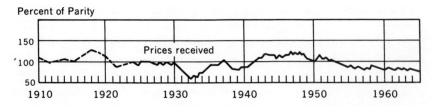

* Monthly data.
△ Includes interest, taxes, and wage rates. Annual average data, 1910 to 1923; by
  quarters, 1924 to 1936; by months, 1937 to date.

FIGURE 22–1. Indexes of Prices Received and Paid by Farmers, 1910–1964.
During this period, the prices of things which farmers buy have generally gone
up more than the prices of things farmers sell. Farmers' prices went above parity
in three periods marked by war: World War I, World War II, and the Korean
war. (SOURCE: *Statistical Abstract of the United States 1965*. Based on data
from Department of Agriculture, Economic Research Service.)

Farm Population Has Sharply Declined. . .

Millions of Persons

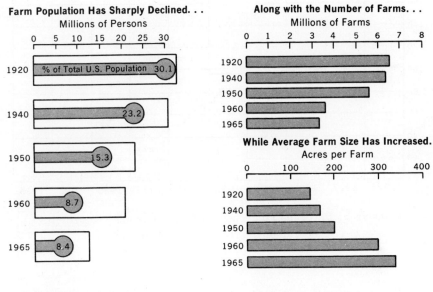

Along with the Number of Farms. . .

Millions of Farms

While Average Farm Size Has Increased.

Acres per Farm

**Although Farm Share of Gross
National Product Has Declined. . .**

Net Income per Farm Has Increased.

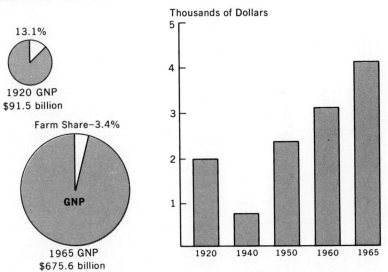

FIGURE 22–2. Changes in Agricultural Production and Farm Population.
(Adapted from U.S. Department of Agriculture and
U.S. Department of Commerce.)

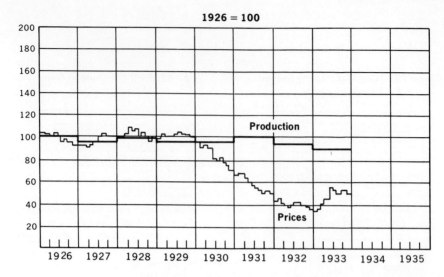

FIGURE 22–3. Prices and Production for Farm Commodities, 1926–1933.
(Adapted from U.S. Department of Agriculture,
Bureau of Agricultural Economics.)

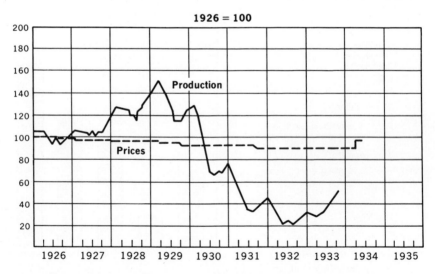

FIGURE 22–4. Prices and Production for the Farm Implements Industry, 1926–
1933. (Adapted from U.S. Department of Agriculture,
Bureau of Agricultural Economics.)

chairman, and six members appointed by the President with the consent of the Senate. The main activity of the CCC is to support prices of commodities specified by law and listed above. The CCC buys some farm products in the open market. The more common procedure is for the individual farmer to obtain a loan from the CCC when his crop is ready for marketing. The loan is equivalent to the support price of the commodity. If the market price of the commodity goes above the support price, the farmer sells his crop in the open market, repays the loan, and keeps the difference between the support price and the higher market price. If at the time the loan becomes due the market price has not risen to the level of the support price, he forfeits his crop by not repaying the loan, and the CCC keeps the crop. In effect, therefore, the loan constitutes a guaranteed price for the farmer's crop, the government bearing all the risks if prices drop.

This price support policy has been an expensive business for the federal government over the years. In the years 1933–1964, the CCC loaned—under the price support program alone—over $42 billion, and its loss on these loans amounted to $13 billion. In addition, the CCC lost, in the period 1933–1964, $11 billion on related programs (wartime consumer subsidy programs, acreage diversion payments in feed grains and wheat, commodity export programs). Total losses of the CCC on price support and related programs thus came to over $24 billion in 1933–1964.

A New Approach to Farm Price Supports

Until 1962, the price support programs kept prices so high, and generally well above world market levels, that the American consumer had to pay artificially high prices, and that, in addition, the exporter found it difficult to sell abroad. Since agricultural exports amount to about one quarter of all American exports, the price support program aiming at high prices had particularly harmful effects on exports; the CCC found itself burdened with vast stocks of farm commodities, the value of which might be as high as $10 billion, and the storage costs alone came close to $1 billion annually in some years.

Beginning in 1962, the federal government embarked on a new approach, first suggested by Secretary of Agriculture Brannan in 1949. Under this plan, market prices are supported by the government at a much lower level than previously. The farmer receives a cash subsidy making up the difference between the low market price supported by the government and the "fair price" the government judges the farmer ought to receive. As a result, the farmer gets a satisfactory price, the consumer enjoys a relatively low market price, the processor of foods and fibers can buy commodities at low prices, and the exporter can compete again in world markets. In 1962, this system was introduced with respect to corn; wheat came into the program in 1963, and cotton in 1965. As a result of the program, the storage of corn by the government was cut in half in 1962–1965, and exports rose sharply. For the first time in three decades, there seems to be reasonable hope that this approach will work more efficiently than the old system of supports at high price levels, although the taxpayer will continue to pay about $4 billion to $5 billion annually in keeping the new program going.

Another aspect of price supports for farm programs—the reduction of crop acreage—has been continued and strengthened under the new program. Various programs of acreage allotments, land diversion, and soil conservation have been applied since the 1930s. Removing land from cultivation not only contributes to less production and therefore to greater price stability, but also expands available resources for recreation and conservation. Acreage allotted to wheat was cut, for example, from 73 million acres in 1950 to 50 million acres in 1964. Corn acreage was reduced from 82 million acres in 1960 to 67 million acres in 1961. However, limiting acreage is not the final answer to excessive farm production. Farmers can circumvent controlled acreage programs by more intensive cultivation on the allotted acreage. Capital thus used in more intensive cultivation, some economists argue, might be put to better use in other sectors of the economy that do not have to depend on government support.

Disposal of Surplus Food

Accumulating vast stocks of farm products, the federal government was—and still is—faced with the problem of what to do with them. In 1954, Congress passed the Agricultural Trade Development and Assistance Act, commonly referred to as Public Law 480. The main purpose of PL 480 was to dispose of the government-stored stocks in an orderly fashion. Most of the surplus food has been given away or sold to foreign countries (such as India, for example). But even when such surplus food is sold, payment is made, not in dollars, but in local "soft" currencies, which the United States then lends to the foreign country for development purposes. In effect, therefore, PL 480 has become one of the most important instruments of foreign aid and foreign policy. In this "Food for Peace" program, the United States often even pays the shipping costs for the transportation of the food to the receiving countries. A smaller portion of the surplus food is used for subsidized welfare programs at home, such as school lunches and food stamp plans. In the first ten years of PL 480, the foreign food disposal came to over $18 billion, of which over $1 billion went into transportation costs, and the domestic disposal amounted to a little under $2 billion. The combined cost of price support programs in 1933–1964— $24 billion—and of disposal programs in 1954–1964—$20 billion—thus reached the staggering figure of $44 billion.

Costs and Benefits

A study on the relation of farm program benefits and costs, made for the Senate Committee on Agriculture and Forestry, showed that in the years 1961–1963 net farm income averaged about $12.6 billion per year. Had there been no price support and acreage diversion programs, net farm income would have averaged only $6 billion, or less than half of actual income. The cost of the price support and acreage diversion programs to the CCC came to about $2.8 billion annually. Thus, each $100 of CCC expenditures on price support and acreage diversion programs increased farm incomes by $236.[2]

Other Farm-Aid Programs

Price support and acreage diversion programs are the two most important methods of government aid to farming, but in addition there are numerous other ways, not always statistically measurable in terms of cost, through which government helps the farmer.

Under the agricultural Conservation Program, the government shares with farmers the cost of soil-building and water-conserving improvements. The Farmers Home Administration makes loans to farmers to operate or buy family farms, to build homes or essential farm buildings, and it enables laborers and sharecroppers to become independent farmers. The Federal Crop Insurance Corporation insures farmers against loss of crops through bad weather, insects, or disease. The Rural Electrification Administration makes loans, generally to public bodies and cooperatives, to bring electric services to rural areas that are not adequately supplied. Such loans are made at the exceedingly low rate of 2 percent per annum, and may be repaid up to 35 years. In marketing, there are numerous programs—some

[2] *Farm Program Benefits and Costs in Recent Years: A Comparison of Costs and Programs* (Washington, D.C.: Library of Congress, Legislative Reference Service, 1964), pp. 2–3.

informational, others regulatory—that help the farmer to market his products to his best advantage.

Finally, there is the general activity of the Department of Agriculture providing constant information, services, and guidance to farmers. In agricultural research, the Department of Agriculture is generally recognized to be one of the world's leading research centers in both the natural and social science aspects of farming. Historically, the Department of Agriculture has always employed much more personnel than either the Department of Commerce or the Department of Labor. In 1965, for example, the Department of Agriculture employed 96,000 persons, as compared with 38,000 employed by the Department of Commerce, and 9,000 employed by the Department of Labor. While these comparative figures do not tell the whole story, they show that farming is not a neglected area in economic policies.

The Outlook for Governmental Farm Policies

It is one of the ironies of American society that the one segment of the economy which in the popular image symbolizes the time-honored American virtues of sturdy individualism and independence is more minutely regulated by, and dependent on, government than any other branch of economic activity. Although the United States is the most advanced industrial nation in the world, it supports its shrinking farm community more generously and more effectively than any other country, even where agriculture is the mainstay of the entire economy.

Government aid to farming in the United States in the years to come may gradually decline, probably not as a result of opposition by urban taxpayers who have to foot the bill, but as a result of growing population at home and greater use of farm products in helping underdeveloped countries. India alone has been receiving about one fourth to one fifth of the American wheat crop in recent years, and if the United States should be willing to assume greater commitments in foreign aid than in the past, the demand for American food may greatly increase. Also, as living standards rise in Europe, Japan, and other parts of the world, there may be more demand for American products, such as feed grains for livestock. Finally, there is the possibility that, in the event that relations with Russia and China greatly improve, more food will be sold to Communist countries, either in cash or on more lenient credit terms, such as Canada has been doing.

Until these possibilities materialize, the basic pattern of government aid for farming will remain in the form of price support and acreage diversion programs.

CHAPTER 23

THE WELFARE STATE

The growth of the welfare state is the result of long-term structural changes in American society and of specific political demands made by the people of government. In the United States, welfare state policies have not been the product of a master plan or ideology, but of the slow and cumulative responses to practical situations. The Constitution states in the Preamble that one of the main purposes of forming this nation is to "promote the general welfare."

⚘ REASONS FOR THE GROWTH OF THE WELFARE STATE

Changing Structure of the Population

The first structural change is the rapid urbanization of American society. Whereas in 1910 less than half of the American people lived in urban areas, in 1960 70 percent were urban residents. By the year 2000, four out of five Americans will live in urban areas. Within urban areas, there is growing concentration of population in metropolitan areas. Currently, over one third of the American people live in metropolitan areas of over 1 million; that proportion is growing, too, as more people move into suburbs that cluster around large metropolitan centers.

The anonymity of urban life makes the needy person dependent on public assistance, because the community ties of small-town or rural life are gone. Moreover, the number of those needing public welfare in cities is growing faster than is the population of the cities. As the middle- and high-income groups have left the "central cities" for the suburbs, their place has been taken by low-income groups, inevitably creating problems of govern-mental aid. In New York City, for example, about 800,000 middle- and upper-income people moved to the suburbs in the two decades after World War II, and their place has been taken by lower-income groups, mostly Negroes and Puerto Ricans.

The second structural change is in the age composition of the popula-tion. The old and the young grow at a faster rate than the population as a whole. In 1930, the age group over 65 was 6.6 million, or 5.4 percent of the population. In 1964, the absolute number had risen to nearly 18 million, or 9.4 percent of the population—almost twice the proportion as compared with 1930. The age group under 14 was 36 million in 1930, or 29 percent of the population. In 1964, the absolute number had risen to 56 million, or 31 percent of the population. If one considers the fact that more than half of the high school graduates go on to college, one gets the following figures for 1964: out of a population of 191 million, 78 million were 21 or under, and 18 million were 65 and over. If we look upon the age group of 21–65 as the productive group, we find that its 95 million had to support the 96 million of those under 21 and over 65. The year 1964 was the first year in American history when the productive element was less than half of the population. This does not take into account the fact that not all in the productive age group of 21–65 actually work.

This structural change in the age composition of the population is ag-gravated by growing urbanizaton. For in a farm economy, the very young and the very old can do all kinds of chores and part-time work, for which no provision has as yet been made in the urban economy. Thus, govern-ment must step in and fill the growing gap between the productive minority and the unproductive majority of the population.

The Political Factor: The Welfare State as a Response to Popular Demands

The third major reason for the growth of the welfare state is political. Where constitutional government has been firmly established, as in North America, Northwestern Europe, Australia, New Zealand, and Uruguay, the use of the vote, of free labor unions, and of a free press proved powerful weapons in the arsenal of social reform. Democracy in a capitalist society can work only—at least with respect to social and economic issues—if the propertied classes are willing to share their good fortune with the less fortunate ones. If the well-to-do cannot stand the thought of parting with some of their property through progressive income taxes, relief for the needy, and similar policies, democracy may become the victim of Rightist, Fascist, or other antidemocratic movements, as has happened in more than one country in this century.

The democratic process itself inevitably leads to social change and reform, because for many it is the main instrument through which they can hope to improve their lot. Free labor unions, for example, are not a new principle subverting democracy, but are simply the application of the established democratic principle of freedom of association to the realm of social relations. The demand for educational opportunity is not the product of "statist" thinking, but the logical consequence of an advanced economy that demands constantly rising educational standards from its work force. Similarly, economic performance in an advanced industrial society also requires high standards of health.

If private industry itself were able and willing to provide such educational and health needs, there would be no reason for government to take over these responsibilities. In the pre-industrial society, the landlord assumed such responsibilities as a matter of course. But in the modern industrial society, as Tocqueville clearly saw in his *Democracy in America*, the employer no longer feels the same sense of responsibility—and the vacuum is inevitably filled by government.

The Welfare State and the Voter

Because the number of voters who need *some* form of public aid is vastly greater than that of the well-off who can go it alone, it comes as no surprise that welfare expansion is "good politics." Particularly in a two-party system, this fact is evident: both parties show a natural tendency to promising more and more social welfare. No party has a monopoly in promoting welfare policies. In Britain, the Conservative party has ruled most of the time in the last four decades, because it has avoided the impression that it is the party of the rich and opposed to welfare state measures. And it has been able to avoid such an impression, not by any clever publicity or gimmickry, but by the simple device of actually promoting social change and welfare. By contrast, the Republican party in the United States has shown deep cleavages within its ranks on the issue of the welfare state. Candidate Goldwater's statement early in the presidential campaign in 1964 that he would prefer private, voluntary social insurance to the compulsory public system that has been law since 1935 probably did not add to his chances of being elected President. By contrast, following the Goldwater disaster in 1964, Republican John Lindsay—a "me-too"

Republican of the most advanced tendency—managed to get elected mayor of New York City in 1965, the first Republican in a generation.

This is not to suggest that politicians view welfare politics solely from the vote-getting angle. Many political leaders—in both parties—favor such policies because they sincerely believe in human welfare, but they are not displeased that what seems the right thing to do also pays off politically. As in so many other instances, actions need not fail in order to establish their virtuous character.

Welfare Policies as Insurance Premiums

Welfare state policies can also be viewed as insurance premiums which the better-off pay in the interests of social and political stability. This applies to both welfare policies inside a country and to assistance to other countries. It is perhaps no coincidence that states with the most advanced welfare state policies also enjoy the highest degree of political stability—the Scandinavian countries, Britain, Holland, Switzerland, Australia, New Zealand, Israel, Canada, and Uruguay—to mention but a few. Political stability cannot be ensured solely by political instruments—constitutions, free elections, a free press, and the right to vote—but must have a solid foundation of social and economic equity and justice. If people are to feel that they have a stake in their community, the best way of ensuring that feeling is to give them the stake rather than the substitutes of exhortation and indoctrination. To the extent that this sense of identification is absent in substantial segments of the population, crime and violence—political and nonpolitical, if a clear boundary between the two can always be drawn—are very likely consequences.

❧ SOCIAL SECURITY

Social security is the provision to a working person and his family of a guaranteed income in the case of retirement, unemployment, disability, or death. In other advanced industrial societies, social security also protects the population against the economic hazards of illness—but not yet in the United States, or only to a limited extent since 1965. Until the Great Depression of the 1930s, the generally accepted attitude in the United States was that each individual was responsible for planning ahead for emergencies resulting from loss of income. If he was unable to do so, his family or friends were expected to help. From the turn of the century, state and local authorities gave some assistance in extreme cases, but each state felt that, in order to attract business, it had to provide a favorable "business climate," which means low taxes—and therefore few welfare services.

It took the shattering experience of the Great Depression to break down the dogmas of traditional individualistic ideology and to realize that the facts of the 1930s were not the facts of a century earlier. Hard as it may seem for the present generation—reared in comparative prosperity and well-being—to visualize, for several years during the Depression about 1 out of 4 in the labor force was out of work, and about 1 family out of 3 received relief in some form or another.

Because state and local governments had shown themselves unable to make an effective response to the critical situation, it became finally clear to most people, in and out of Congress, that the American economy had become a *national economy*, and that only the national government could provide the resources and administrative machinery of a system of economic security. This was accomplished in the Social Security Act of 1935, the most important in this area until that time, and still the greatest single Act of Congress relating to social security. Before it was passed by Congress, dire predictions were made by some that the nation could not afford to provide protection against the economic hazards of retirement, disability, or death, and that social security, federally set up and administered, would be the first step at least toward socialism, if not communism or fascism. Yet in the end, the Social Security Act was passed by a vote of 372 to 33 in the House and 77 to 6 in the Senate.

The Act was hardly a new policy in Western societies, whether in Europe or in other continents. Germany was the first nation to set up an old-age pension and disability system in 1889, followed by Britain in 1908, France in 1910, and Sweden in 1913. By the time the Social Security Act was passed in 1935, over fifty nations had adopted systems which generally were far more comprehensive in scope than that of the American social security system. Rather than being an innovating revolution, the Social Security Act of 1935 might more appropriately be called a delayed reaction to modern economic life—long overdue.

Old-Age, Survivors, and Disability Insurance

Although, as we shall soon see, social security provides for several other contingencies, to most people it is almost synonymous with old-age, survivors, and disability insurance (OASDI). The popular identification of social security with these three types of protection rests on the fact that they are its most important part, affecting more people than any other form of social security. In 1965, 64 million people were insured under OASDI, and 20 million people received benefits totaling over $17 billion.

OASDI covers nearly all forms of employment and self-employment, citizens as well as noncitizens. Federal and railroad employees are covered by separate retirement systems. As to state and local government employees: coverage cannot be compulsory, because under our federal system the national government cannot tax state governments and their subdivisions. However, the states may voluntarily join the social security system, and more than three fifths have done so. Similarly, there is no compulsory OASDI for nonprofit organizations of an educational, religious, charitable, or scientific character, because such entities are tax-exempt. However, such organizations may join the social security system by waiving their tax exemption for this specific purpose. In fact, nearly all nonprofit organizations of this type have joined—teachers and administrative employees in private schools and colleges are probably the largest single group benefiting from social security in this category. Well over 90 percent of all gainfully employed (including self-employed) persons are now covered by social security.

A few marginal groups are not included: for example, self-employed persons who earn under $400 a year; domestic workers who earn less than $50 from one employer in one quarter; and farm workers who earn less than $150 from one employer in one year. Since the OASDI portion of the social security system is based on the insurance principle, persons of such low earnings cannot build up enough assets to warrant OASDI benefits on a strictly actuarial basis. Yet students of OASDI have often pointed to the oddity that those who earn the least and therefore need protection the most are excluded from OASDI because of the dogma that benefits must be financed on an insurance basis, the costs being borne by employees, employers, and self-employed persons—but not out of general federal revenues.

However, it seems likely that the day may come before very long when the lowest income receivers will be included in OASDI. The first important break with the strict insurance concept of OASDI came in 1966, when Congress passed a law granting old-age pensions to persons over 72 regardless of any previous work experience or not. The pension is fixed at the extremely moderate level of $35 per month for a single person or $52.50 for a couple if both are over 72. Even these low benefits are reduced by the amount such persons receive from welfare or public pension systems. But it is the first recognition that the insurance principle is not an idol to be worshipped without any compromise, and that general government revenue may be used to remedy hardship situations that cannot be alleviated through the application of "sound" actuarial insurance principles.

OASDI is financed by social security taxes paid by employees, employers, and self-employed persons. The maximum annual earning on which social security taxes are paid is $6,600. In 1966, the rate of contribution under

OASDI was 3.85 percent each for the employee and his employer, and this rate was scheduled to rise to 4.85 percent each by 1973. In the case of self-employed persons, the contribution rate in 1966 was 5.80 percent, and scheduled to reach 7 percent by 1973. Payments made under OASDI are deposited in a special trust fund, administered by the Secretary of the Treasury, the Secretary of Labor, and the Secretary of Health, Education and Welfare. Annual intake of the trust fund has been around $20 billion in the last several years, but is scheduled to go up sharply, as the contribution rates are scheduled to go up considerably until 1973. Also, average earnings are constantly rising, as does the covered labor force in line with the growth of the population. Full benefits are paid on retirement at 65, or in case of death or disability before that age, provided the insured person is "fully insured." Full insurance is the amount of time prescribed by law as the minimum period of coverage. Thus a person who retired at 65 (or became disabled or died before that age) in 1966 needed 3¾ years of "credit" in the insurance system. This minimum time needed for full insurance is steadily going up, and is scheduled to reach 10 years by 1991.

Monthly individual retirement benefits ranged from a minimum of $44 to a maximum of $136 in 1966, the latter to go up to $168 within the next several years. Monthly payments to family members of a retired, disabled, or deceased person are made in the following categories:

Children under 18 (under 22, if full-time students);
Disabled children regardless of age, if they became disabled before they were 18;
A wife or widow, regardless of her age, if she cares for a disabled child or one that is under 18;
A wife aged 62 or older or a widow 60 or older, regardless of whether there are children entitled to monthly benefits;
A dependent husband or widower aged 62 or older.

Maximum family benefits per month were $309 in 1966, and were scheduled to go up to $368 during the following several years. Average monthly payments to a retired worker in 1966 were about $90, and if he had a wife over 62, average combined payments came to about $140. Unless a retired person has some savings or benefits from a private pension plan, the old-age pension alone is, for the average person, distinctly on the low side. However, since the number of persons who have high annual earnings that are covered by insurance—up to $6,600—is constantly going up, the average monthly benefits for insured persons and their families in the 1970s and 1980s will be considerably higher. The present relatively low average benefits reflect the fact that average earnings were considerably lower in the past than they are now and are likely to be in the future.

Private Pensions

Both public and private pension funds have played an increasingly important role. As public pension funds have gone up in size, private pension funds have not declined, but, instead, have been going up at an even faster rate than public funds. In 1940, public pension funds (social security trust fund, federal civil service retirement system, state and local government retirement systems) amounted to $4.5 billion, whereas private pension funds were only $2.4 billion. In 1964, public pension funds had assets of $69.9 billion, whereas private pension fund assets had jumped to $77.2 billion. Combined public and private pension fund assets thus increased *twenty times* in the years 1940 to 1964. Over 25 million workers are now covered by private pension funds (who are generally also covered by OASDI), and over 3 million currently receive private pensions (in addition to their social security benefits). It is estimated that by 1980, 42 million workers (or 60–65 percent of the nonfarm labor force) will be covered by private pension funds, that 6.6 million will then receive private pensions, and that the assets of private pension funds will amount to about $225 billion.

A big snag in private pension schemes is that they are generally set up for the benefit of workers in major industries (automobiles, steel) in which wages are highest. Low-paid workers in small businesses generally cannot look forward to a company pension, for only larger corporations can afford such schemes. The advantageous position of the better-paid worker in private pension schemes is underscored by the fact that the employer contributions to pension funds run to over 85 percent, whereas in OASDI, employers and employees each pay the same amount. The main defect in private pension schemes is that, in most cases, the insured employee loses his pension rights when he changes jobs, whereas under the social security system pension, rights are not affected by changing the place of employment. In 1965, the President's Committee on Corporate Pension Funds and Other Private Retirement and Welfare Programs recommended that pension rights in private pension schemes also be "portable," if a worker changes jobs. Such a reform would greatly stimulate the mobility of the labor force, thus benefiting employees, employers, and the economy as a whole.

Much of the phenomenal growth of private pension funds is the result of the fact that they do not pay taxes on employer contributions or on income from investments. The employer who contributes to the pension fund for the benefit of his employees may deduct such payments from his taxable income. Such contributions are also not taxed as current compensation of employees. Taxation is deferred until the employee receives his pension benefits—generally his tax rate is then much lower than during his employment period, and several times lower than if the employer had to pay taxes on his contributions at the time of depositing them in the pension fund. Nor do private pension funds pay taxes when earning income on their investments. Here again, the tax is paid—at a very low rate—by the employee at the time of receiving such income as a portion of his pension benefits. The federal government loses several billions annually through this favorable tax treatment of private pension funds, and Congress could therefore—if it wanted to do so—grant such tax privileges only to private pension funds that carry "portable" pension rights. The trend is in this direction, but full portability—as under OASDI—is still a long way off.

Unemployment Insurance

Unlike OASDI, which is directly administered by the federal government, unemployment insurance is a joint federal-state effort. The Social Security Act of 1935 set up this joint scheme to make it more adaptable to varying levels of wages and living costs in different parts of the country. The federal-state scheme did not replace inadequate state programs, but set up something new in the field of unemployment insurance. Wisconsin passed an unemployment insurance law in 1932, but benefit payments started only in 1936. Here again, the United States was hardly a pioneer, for most other Western societies had had various types of unemployment insurance long before 1935.

In this federal-state program, state participation was virtually compelled—or, at least, so strongly encouraged that no alternative of nonparticipation was left open. The law required that employers pay a federal unemployment insurance tax of 3 percent on the first $3,000 dollars of an employee's annual wages, but that 90 percent of this payroll tax would not be collected, if the employer's state had a federally approved state unemployment insurance program. If a state were not to take part in this joint unemployment insurance plan, the employers would still have to pay the payroll tax, but the state unemployed would receive no benefits from those taxes that went directly to the federal government. By 1937, all states in the Union had passed unemployment insurance laws.

The federal government sets minimum standards of law and administration, but the states determine who is to be covered, how large contributions are to be, how large benefits are to be, and for how long. The federal government collects from employers a tax of 0.4 percent on the first $3,000 of wages of covered employees, and the funds thus received are used for employment security programs. The federal government not only pays part of the administrative costs of state unemployment insurance, but also makes loans and grants subsidies to the states from time to time.

As to coverage: in 1966, about 80 percent of the civilian labor force was covered by unemployment insurance programs. Federal law excludes from coverage farm workers, domestic workers, state and local government employees, and employees of nonprofit organizations. The most general exclusion is of workers in a firm employing fewer than four persons. Here again, individual states have been more lenient than the federal law. Thus, 20 states cover employers of one or more employees, and several more cover employers with fewer than four employees. Some of the categories not covered under federal law are covered by state programs: 25 states cover state and local government employees, a few states cover employees of nonprofit organizations, and a handful of states have special provisions for farm and domestic workers.

The financing methods also show a good deal of variation. By federal law, the unemployment tax needs to be paid, by the employer only, on the first $3,000 of a worker's pay. Yet over a dozen states push the taxable base higher up—from $3,300 in Tennessee to $7,200 in Alaska. Although 47 states follow the federal law and require only the employer to pay the unemployment insurance tax, 3 states also levy a very small tax on employees. As to the rate of the employer's tax: the national average in 1964 was 2.20, but in some states it was only slightly above 1 percent on the taxable portion of the wage, whereas in others the rate exceeded 3 percent. In general, wealthier industrial states levy a higher tax so that they can pay higher benefits. Average weekly payments to unemployed workers also vary widely. The average weekly payment in 1964 was $36, or 36 percent of the average weekly pay of covered workers. Minimum payments per week are under $10 in several states, about $10 to $15 in most states, but go up as high as $25 in California. Maximum weekly payments range from $30 to $55, plus allowances for dependents in about a dozen states. The maximum period during which payments are made to insured workers is generally 26 weeks, but in some states it goes as high as 39 weeks. The actual average period during which unemployed persons received benefits in 1964 was, however, only 13 weeks.

Manpower Training

Unemployment insurance is the answer for workers who are temporarily out of work, but are able to find new employment within a reasonably short period. But there are those who find it difficult to obtain employment because they do not have the basic skills required, either because their training has been deficient or because their acquired skills have become obsolete. Such persons tend to become unemployable, and after they have exhausted unemployment aid, they depend on long-term relief for the most meager subsistence.

To remedy this situation, Congress passed in 1962 the Manpower Development and Training Act (MDTA). Under MDTA, vocational education programs are carried on by state agencies, whereas on-the-job training can be given by employers themselves. Ninety percent of the cost is borne by the federal government; allowances to workers being trained may be granted for a whole year, and there are also family allowances. If the worker being trained or retrained has to leave his regular place of residence, he also receives the costs of transportation to and from the training facility as well as a separate maintenance allowance. The annual number of workers in the MDTA program was over 100,000 in 1963, and climbed to over 200,000 in 1965. The average cost per trainee in vocational education programs came to about $1,900, and the average cost per trainee in on-the-job programs was only about $500—in both cases the costs were considerably less than protracted unemployment and relief payments over many years, not to mention the unproductive nature of the latter. The self-respect a person gains through being able to earn his own living can, of course, not be expressed in dollars.

Encouraging Labor Mobility

Unemployment tends to be a long-drawn-out condition for workers who either possess few marketable skills or whose skills become obsolete because of a general decline of the industry in which they work, or who live in a depressed, labor-surplus, area. Helping workers in labor-surplus areas to move to labor-shortage areas has therefore become an increasing concern of industrial societies. In 1963, Congress authorized "labor mobility demonstration projects" on a small scale, and authorized up to $5 million a year for such pilot programs. Relocation assistance included travel allowances for the worker and his family from his home to his new work place; removal allowances for the shipping of household goods; and settling-down allowances, paying for living expenses while traveling to the new location and for living expenses until receipt of the first paycheck in the new job. All in all, 1,200 persons in 14 states were relocated in this manner in 1963–1965—hardly a monumental effort in view of the fact that in some counties (in West Virginia, for example) the unemployment rate in 1965, an exceptional boom year, was still between 10 to 20 percent, or 3 to 5 times as high as in the rest of the country.

Comparing the few small-scale relocation pilot projects in the United States with relocation policies in nine other countries (in Western Europe,

Scandinavia, and Canada), a study of the Joint Economic Committee in 1966 found that the United States is way behind these other Western nations. All have long abandoned small pilot projects, and have settled policies in this field that encompass more phases of assistance, and help more workers.

Sweden has probably developed the most impressive relocation program. Although the Swedish unemployment rate since the end of World War II has averaged well below 2 percent (or about one half to one third of the U.S. rate), Sweden has made a systematic effort to encourage workers to move from labor-surplus to labor-shortage areas. In addition to a wide variety of assistance to the relocating worker and his family, the Swedish government has made a special effort in behalf of workers in chronically depressed areas. One factor that often deters persons in such areas from leaving is the necessity to take a loss in selling their homes, because their value declines in depressed areas. The government therefore passed legislation in 1964 compensating homeowners for any losses in the market values of their homes.

In the opinion of Swedish economists, employers, and workers, their extensive and advanced relocation system is not only more humane than the system encouraging workers to vegetate inertly on permanent relief in depressed areas, but is also less costly than the protracted unproductive relief expenses for unemployed workers who do not move on to new job opportunities. The Swedish government's expenditure on relocation assistance in fiscal 1964–1965 (July 1, 1964–June 30, 1965) was proportionately 24 times higher than the similar pilot effort in the United States. Considering that the unemployment rate in 1964–1965 was about 2½ times higher in the United States than in Sweden, the Swedish relocation effort was proportionately about 60 times larger than that of the United States.[1]

Public Assistance

In addition to setting up insurance programs against the economic hazards of old age, death, disability, and unemployment, the Social Security Act of 1935 established public assistance programs for those who were not covered by insurance programs. Whereas insurance programs derive their income from contributions of employers and employees, assistance programs are financed out of general tax revenues. The Social Security Act of 1935 established three assistance programs: Old-Age Assistance (OAA), Aid to

[1] Fuller comparative data on relocation programs in the United States, Canada, Britain, France, Norway, Denmark, Holland, Belgium, West Germany, and Sweden will be found in *Programs for Relocating Workers Used By Governments in Selected Countries*, Economic Policies and Practices, Paper No. 8, Washington, D.C., Joint Economic Committee of Congress, 1966.

Family Income in Constant (1964) Dollars: 1947 to 1964

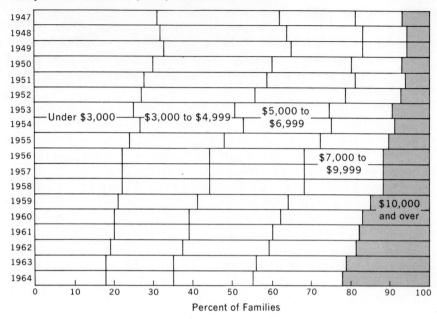

FIGURE 23–1. Adapted from *Current Population Reports,*
Series P–60, No. 47, Bureau of the Census.

Dependent Children (ADC), and Aid to the Blind (AB). In 1950, a fourth program was added: Aid to the Permanently and Totally Disabled (APTD).

All four programs are administered by the states, but the federal government contributes heavily (60 percent in 1964) through grants-in-aid to the states. However, the federal government requires minimum standards of financial soundness and administration (for example, administrative personnel in these assistance programs must be recruited on the merit principle). Otherwise, states have wide discretion to decide the criteria of need and the level of benefits. Thus average monthly benefits in old-age assistance in 1964 were $80, but there were wide discrepancies between Mississippi ($39 per month) on the low end and California and Wisconsin ($110 per month) on the high end of the scale.

Several hundred thousand persons receive both old-age pensions under OASDI and old-age assistance, if their old-age pensions are too low. However, as the benefits under OASDI have increased, there has been a decline of old-age assistance recipients from 2.8 million in 1950 to 2.2 million in 1964, although the number of persons aged 65 and over went up by about 50 percent during that period. The greatest increase in the number of assistance recipients has been in the aid to dependent children program:

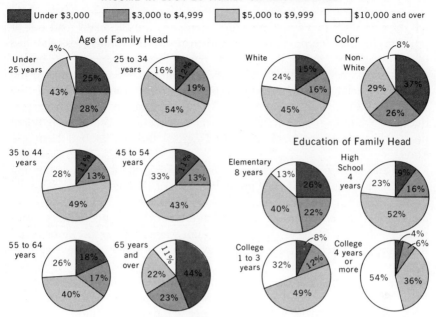

INCOME IN 1964 BY FAMILY CHARACTERISTICS

■ Under $3,000   ▨ $3,000 to $4,999   ▨ $5,000 to $9,999   □ $10,000 and over

FIGURE 23–2. Adapted from *Current Population Reports,*
Series P–60, No. 47, Bureau of the Census.

their number jumped from 2.2 million in 1950 to 4.3 million in 1964. The
total number of persons receiving public assistance under the four major
programs was in excess of 7 million in 1964, and the number has been
increasing at a much faster rate than the U.S. population. Total assistance
benefits for 7 million recipients in 1964 were $5.1 billion, or slightly over
$60 per month for the average recipient.

Impact of Social Security and Assistance Programs on Poverty

Poverty has consistently declined in the United States since the end of
World War II. In 1947, the rate of poverty was 32 percent of the population; in 1964, the rate had dropped to 18 percent. But 18 percent still
meant that 34 million out of 190 million Americans were poor, poverty
being defined generally as incomes under $1,500 for single persons, with
$500 added for each dependent (the poverty line for a family of four
would thus be $3,000). (See Figures 23–1 and 23–2.) In 1964, 43 per-
cent of the poor were children under 18, and 16 percent were 65 years or
older. For them, improved social security and public assistance benefits are
the main hope of rising above the poverty line. The remaining 41 percent
of the poor were between 18 and 65, in the productive age, and for them

job opportunities in a full-employment economy are the main road out of poverty. In the decade from the mid-1950s to the mid-1960s, the loss of output due to unemployment was about $260 million, or $26 billion per year (in constant dollars). There is also a loss of production due to the effects of racial discrimination: according to the 1966 *Report* of the Council of Economic Advisers, the American economy would have produced $22 billion more in 1965—or over 3 percent of the gross national product—if the educational levels of Negroes and whites had been the same.

Full employment is, as we saw in the preceding chapter, not something that just happens, or that the "invisible hand" of the market providentially brings forth, but the result of cooperative efforts of government, business, and labor. Even employment does not automatically remove poverty, for a worker who in 1966 received the minimum wage of $1.25 per hour could not support himself and a wife and two children above the poverty line. Moreover, only 36 million out of 60 million were covered by minimum wage laws; paradoxically, most of those who were covered needed coverage least, because they generally earned considerably above the minimum level, whereas those low-paid workers who needed protection most were not covered.

However, there is no doubt that the core of poverty is in the 59 percent of the poor who are either under 18 or over 65—the group that must largely depend on higher insurance or assistance benefits for a substantial improvement of its condition. In fiscal 1965, about $40 billion of personal income derived from public "transfer payments" (that is, payments not derived from current production), such as social security benefits, public pensions, public assistance, and the like. Of this sum, about one half, or $20 billion, went to persons who were below the poverty line, or were raised above it by such payments. One half of the poor received no public transfer payments. According to the 1966 *Annual Report* of the Council of Economic Advisers, $12 billion was needed in fiscal 1965 to wipe out completely the poverty-income gap of the remaining poor. Twelve billion dollars is a great deal of money—but the increase of gross national product in 1964 was $38 billion, and $47 billion in 1965. Thus, by devoting less than one third of either year's *increase* in gross national product, poverty (at least as statistically defined) could have been eliminated altogether. The question for the American people, therefore, is not one of being able to wipe out poverty, but of political decision.

Comparing the portion of the national income devoted to social insurance and major types of social welfare in various Western countries, the Joint Economic Committee found in 1965 that in the United States the share was 4.8 percent, whereas it was 9.2 percent in Sweden, 10.6 percent

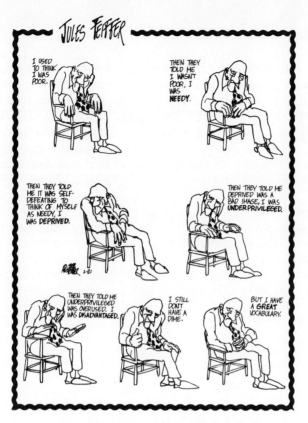

Jules Feiffer; in *New Republic*, 1965.

in Britain, and between 12 and 14.4 percent in the six Common Market Countries.

Table 23–1 has two interesting features. First, the scope of American social welfare is much more limited than in the other countries. There are no family allowances in the United States, under which every family receives a monthly allowance per child, the cost generally borne by the employer or the government, or both. In the field of health expenditures, the establishment of medical care for the aged in 1966 will somewhat increase the proportion of American national income spent on health, but since only persons over 65 are covered by medicare, the overall picture will not greatly change. Moreover, even in the most developed American program—OASDI—the ratio of expenditures to national income is considerably lower in the United States than in other countries.

The second feature that emerges from the table is even more impressive. Contrary to the common notion that social welfare is the first step to socialism, Sweden and Britain—the two countries in the table with the strongest Socialist labor movements—spend proportionately less of their

TABLE 23–1. *Social Security Expenditures of Common Market Countries— Sweden, the United Kingdom, and the United States—as Percent of National Income, by Major Types of Coverage, 1962*

Country	Total	OASDI	Sickness and Maternity Insurance	Unem- ployment Insurance	Work Accident Insurance	Family Allow- ances
Belgium	13.4	4.7	3.6	1.1	1.0	3.0
France	13.4	3.9	4.1	0.0	1.1	4.3
Germany (Fed- eral Republic)	14.4	8.1	4.5	0.4	0.8	0.6
Italy	12.0	4.7	2.9	0.6	0.6	2.9
Luxembourg	13.7	6.3	3.1	0.0	1.8	2.5
Netherlands	12.0	5.7	3.6	0.6	0.4	1.7
Sweden	09.2	5.1	2.2	0.2	0.2	1.6
United Kingdom	10.6	4.2	5.1	0.3	0.3	0.6
United States	04.8	3.6	0.1	0.7	0.3	—

SOURCE: Adapted from *European Social Security Systems: A Comparative Analysis of Programs in England, Sweden, and the Common Market Countries, Together with a Description of the U.S. System*, Washington, D.C., Joint Economic Committee of Congress, 1965.

national income on social welfare than do countries in which capitalist ideologies and governments are more strongly entrenched, such as France, West Germany, Belgium, and Italy. In line with this phenomenon, the United States could treble its social welfare expenditures and still be merely in step with Germany, France, or Belgium. Finally, it should be borne in mind, when one is examining the above comparative table, that per capita income in the United States is double that in the other Western countries, so that spending the same ratio of national income on social welfare would be much less of a burden on the American economy.

❧ HEALTH AND MEDICARE

Government Involvement in Health Services

Public responsibility for minimum health standards affecting the safety of the community is one of the oldest functions of government, going back to colonial times, and beyond that to Elizabethan England. The Public Health Service of the United States was founded in 1789, and originally provided for all medical and hospital needs of merchant seamen in federal hospitals. Today, the Public Health Service provides such services not only for about 120,000 merchant seamen, but also for 340,000 Indians, and several other groups, totaling about 800,000. In addition, the federal government provides, in federally operated hospitals, for the health needs of 22 million war veterans, and for 3 million members of the armed forces (active and retired), plus 4 million of their dependents. Thus, over 30 million persons out of about 200 million receive health and hospital services directly from the federal government, in federal hospitals, staffed by federally appointed physicians. This figure does not include the health and hospital services provided for several millions by state, county, and local authorities.

The Public Health Service, through the National Institutes of Health (NIH), has increasingly also supported medical research, both in its own facilities and by giving grants to other research agencies. In 1957, all medical research in the United States—private and public—amounted to under $500 million, of which NIH contributed about one half. In 1967, total allocations exceeded $2 billion, of which about 60 percent came out of NIH grants.

In 1965, Congress passed a three-year, $340 million program, to set up regional medical centers throughout the United States, in order to extend the benefits of latest medical advances from a few major medical centers to thousands of hospitals and millions of patients throughout the nation. Initially, these regional centers—tying together medical schools, teaching hospitals, and research centers—will concentrate on three principal killers: heart diseases, cancer, and stroke. But there is little doubt that this federal involvement in financing regional centers will before long include other major diseases.

Critical Shortages of Health Personnel

In the area of physical and professional medical resources, the federal government has also been very active in recent years. Under the 1946 Hill-Burton Act for hospital grants, the federal government has granted $2.4 billion during 1947–1965 toward a total investment of $7.7 billion in hospital construction.

In the area of professional health personnel, the shortage in the United States has been critical for many years. The ratio of doctors per 10,000 population has been about 14—lower than in Western countries such as Austria, Argentina, West Germany, Italy, and Israel, and much lower than in Communist states such as Hungary, Czechoslovakia, and the Soviet Union. In the Soviet Union the ratio of doctors to 10,000 population is 22, or about half as much more than in the United States, and the Soviets annually graduate about 28,000 doctors, or almost 4 times as many as the United States. The shortage has been so severe in the United States that thousands of foreign doctors have had to be imported from abroad, including doctors from underdeveloped countries in Asia and Latin America, where standards of medical training are not always up to accepted American standards.

In 1963, Congress passed the Health Professions Educational Assistance Act authorizing grants for the building of medical and dental schools as well as loans for medical and dental students. In 1964, Congress passed the Nurse Training Act, under which the federal government makes grants for the construction of nursing schools, the expansion of training programs, and for loans to nursing students. In 1965, Congress went a step further, and established for the first time scholarships for needy students in all health fields. Medical training is so expensive that 40 percent of medical students are drawn from families with incomes in the top 8 percent. The average cost of four years in medical school is over $12,000, after which there is a loss of earnings during one year of internship or of three years of residency for the specialist. Putting all costs together (including four years of college prior to medical school), one of the nation's leading medical experts, Dr. Howard A. Rusk, estimated that the total cost of training a general practitioner in 1959 was $47,000, and $67,000 for a specialist.[2]

Medicare: Toward a National Health Insurance Program?

Although health has been traditionally considered, like education, the area of state rather than federal activity, the federal involvement in health programs dramatically increased after World War II. The year 1964 was a landmark, because for the first time in American history federal health expenditures ($4.6 billion) surpassed state expenditures ($4.4 billion). Yet despite these considerable expenditures, one element was still missing: the direct protection of individuals against the hazards of illness, both medically and financially.

In 1949, President Truman proposed a national health insurance program to be financed—as are other aspects of social security—through a payroll tax. But the country was not ready for it. The fight against a national health insurance program was led by the American Medical Association under the banner of fighting "socialized medicine." Health insurance was first introduced in 1883 in Germany, and the man who was responsible for it, Prince Otto von Bismarck, was hardly a "premature" Socialist Similarly, the many countries which set up broad health insurance schemes in the late nineteenth or early twentieth centuries, did so under non-Socialist governments, but the AMA propaganda campaign, run at great expense by a leading public relations firm, accomplished its purpose.

After another decade, Congress passed, in 1960, the Kerr-Mills Act,

[2] *New York Times*, November 15, 1959.

which increased federal grants to the states for medical assistance to the needy aged who were on relief. This was only "more of the same," but in addition the Act introduced a new form of medical state aid that would go to the "medically indigent." This new feature meant that the federal government would offer matching grants to the states to help those over 65 who were not poor enough to receive public assistance, yet were not financially able to pay their own medical bills. The states were left free to join or not to join the program, to determine who was eligible, and how much the benefits would be. By 1965, ten states still had not joined.

One of the main arguments against a general health insurance program, even if limited to those over 65, was the tremendous growth of private health insurance—hailed as the American answer to the "menace" of the "un-American" scheme of "socialized medicine." True, the proportion of Americans who took out some form of private health insurance rose from 9 percent in 1940 to 80 percent in 1965. Yet benefits under such insurance covered only 25 percent of the cost of illness in 1965. More serious still is the fact that the old and the poor often could not afford to buy private health insurance, or if they were over 65, found it difficult to obtain insurance because of the higher risk involved. Yet persons over 65 need health

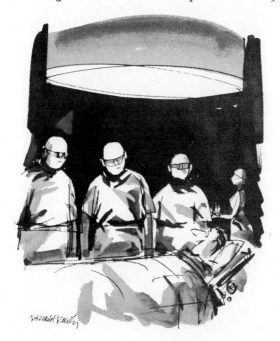

"I'd just like to mention, Doctor, that I was against Medicare." Drawing by Donald Reilly; © 1965 The New Yorker Magazine, Inc.

protection more than younger age groups. In 1965, for example, persons over 65 were 9 percent of the population, but occupied 27 percent of the nation's hospital beds.

In 1965, Congress finally made the historic decision of providing health insurance for all persons over 65 by passing the Health Insurance for the Aged Act, popularly known as "medicare." Under this program, 17 million persons covered by social security automatically received medicare benefits, starting July 1, 1966. An additional 2 million persons over 65, who were not covered by social security, were also declared eligible for medicare by merely registering with the local Social Security office. Those who reach the age of 65 in 1968 or thereafter, will be eligible for medicare only if they will have paid the medicare payroll tax for a specified period.

There are two plans under medicare. The basic plan covers hospital insurance, and provides for the following benefits:

1. *Up to ninety days of hospitalization for each spell of illness. For the first sixty days of the hospital stay, the patient pays only $40. During the next thirty days, he pays $10 per day. Medicare pays the rest.*
2. *Up to one hundred days of convalescence in a hospital or nursing home, but only if this care starts within fourteen days after leaving the hospital. The patient pays nothing for the first twenty days of such "extended care," and $5 per day for the following eighty days.*
3. *Up to one hundred home visits by nurses or other health personnel (but not doctors), within a period of 365 days following release from a hospital or nursing home. Medicare pays the entire bill.*
4. *Out-patient diagnostic tests in a hospital for a 20-day period. The patient pays the first $20 plus 20 percent of the rest of the bill. Medicare pays the remaining cost.*

This hospital insurance of the basic medicare program is financed by a new payroll tax. In 1966, employer and employee each had to pay 0.35 percent on the first $6,600 of the wage or salary, and this tax was scheduled to go up to 0.80 percent by 1987. The same rates apply to self-employed persons over 65. A separate Federal Hospital Insurance Trust Fund administers the contributions of employers, employees, and self-employed persons.

The second major insurance under medicare covers doctors' bills. This supplementary plan requires voluntary enrollment by persons over 65, and costs $3 per month. In the first period of enrollment in 1966, more than 90 percent of persons over 65 enrolled. The patient receives the following benefits in each calendar year, for which he pays $50 plus 20 percent of the rest. Medicare pays the difference.

1. *All doctors' bills, whether at home, in the doctor's office, or in a clinic or hospital.*

2. Up to 100 home visits by nurses and health personnel, even if the patient has not been hospitalized. This is in addition to the 100 home visits included in the basic plan of hospital insurance.
3. Diagnostic tests, X rays, lab tests, and similar services in or out of hospital, and rental of medical equipment, such as iron lungs, wheelchairs, if ordered by a doctor for use in the patient's home.

The following health services are not covered either by the basic hospital plan or by the supplementary medical insurance: drugs used outside a hospital or nursing home, routine physical examinations, dental care, eyeglasses, or hearing aids.

All the benefits under the hospitalization and supplementary insurance for doctors' bills are thus available to persons over 65 for $36 per year, as compared with the cost of $240 per year charged by private insurance companies for such coverage.[3]

State Medicare Programs

Unlike nearly all other national health insurance programs in Western countries, medicare in the United States is limited to persons over 65. Yet the medicare law of 1965 contains a provision which indirectly breaks through the age limit of 65. Under that provision, the federal government contributes varying grants to state medicare programs for families with dependent children "whose income and resources are insufficient to meet the costs of necessary medical services." There is no age limit in this provision, and it is up to the states to decide at what income level medical need begins.

A number of states made use of this provision even before the federal medicare program went into effect on July 1, 1966. On April 30, 1966, for example, Governor Rockefeller of New York signed the New York State medicare program, calling it "the most significant social legislation in three decades." Under the New York State medicare plan, medicare services are available to families with an annual net (or after tax) income of $6,000 for a family of four or $7,700 for a family of six, that is, to about 20 to 30 percent of the state's population. Eligible families earning more than $4,500 a year must pay 1 percent of their income toward medical bills. The New York State program offers not only the hospital and medical services provided by federal medicare for persons over 65, but also provides for eyeglasses, dentures, and a few other services not provided by federal medicare.

The combination of federal medicare for persons over 65 with the New York State medicare program "has made it logical for Congress," the *New*

[3] *Consumer Reports,* 31 (June, 1966), p. 290.

York Times commented editorially, "to begin thinking seriously about the desirability of providing comprehensive health insurance for all Americans" (May 1, 1966). There is little doubt that federal medicare is not the end, but the beginning of a prepaid national health insurance program for Americans of all ages. As in other countries, such a program will not come in one sweep, but by stages.

✻ THE EXPANDING FEDERAL EFFORT IN EDUCATION

The Role of Education in the American Development

Among the elements that contributed to rapid economic growth in the United States from its very inception, education deserves an important place. This does not mean that the purpose of education is economic growth, but that there can be no rapid economic growth without education. No ill-educated nation has ever attained significant economic progress, and no highly educated nation has ever been extremely poor. The United States was the first modern nation to make education—from kindergarten to college and university—available to all through public, tax-supported schools.

The first state university was established in 1785 by the State of Georgia, followed by North Carolina in 1789. Jefferson founded the University of Virginia in 1816, and from then on public colleges and state universities proliferated throughout the land. Before the Civil War, 182 colleges and universities existed in the United States—more than in any other country in the world. In 1862, the Morrill, or Land Grant, Act provided federal public lands to the states and territories for the purpose of creating and maintaining colleges and universities.

Although private colleges and universities continue to play a vital part in American higher education, increasingly the center of gravity in American education—both in quantity and quality—is moving into the area of publicly supported institutions. In 1950, about half of the American college students were in public colleges; in 1965, the number rose to two thirds, and was expected to reach four fifths by 1975. In his message to Congress, January 12, 1965, President Johnson, asking for vast new federal funds for education, pointed out that the college enrollment in the United States had risen by 80 times since 1900, as contrasted with an increase of population that was less than threefold. Although the population of the United States is only 6 percent of the world's, it has one third of the world's college professors and students and one quarter of the world's institutions of higher learning.

Socialism Discovers the American High School

Yet the American high school is as unique as the American college and university. Whereas in other countries, the secondary school is set up in two types—an academic type for a small minority that leads to college, and a vocational type that ends at ages 14 or 15 for the mass of the people—the American high school is unique in being generally set up in one type that ends at age 18, or the entrance age to college. The main advantage of the American system is that the decision about going on to college or not is made at age 18, whereas in other countries it must be made at the ages of 10 or 11.

What is in the United States an accepted principle of the American idea of equality, is in many other countries an issue of socialism versus conservatism. Thus, the British Labour Government moved in 1965 to adapt the British system to the American concept. Of British secondary schools in 1965, 180 "comprehensive schools" combined academic and vocational preparation, akin to the American pattern. But side by side with this small number, there were 1,300 "grammar schools" (academically oriented) and 3,900 "modern schools" (vocationally oriented). It is interesting that in recent years Sweden, governed by a Socialist party for three decades, has come closest to the American pattern of high school education, as a result of which more young people receive a secondary education best suited to their needs, combined with a constant increase of high school graduates who go on to college. Again, what has been done in Sweden—not nearly on the relative scale of the United States—in the name of the Socialist ideal of equality has been done in the United States on a proportionately much larger scale in the name of the American ideal of equality of opportunity.

The Magnitude of the Educational Effort

Over one quarter of the entire American population is involved in education. In the fall of 1965, out of a population of 192 million, 54 million were enrolled in schools (from grade school to college), 2.3 million were teaching, and 200,000 served as administrators in the nation's schools. The educational effort thus included nearly 30 percent of the population—by far the largest single "industry" in the United States, and one that grows much faster than the economy as a whole. This growth of education is reflected in the financial effort. In 1929, private and public expenditures on education were 3.1 percent of gross national product; in 1965, the percentage was 6.2, or exactly double, and it is constantly rising. As a result, average levels of education have risen enormously. In 1900, 6 out of 100 17-year-olds graduated from high school. In 1965, the figure rose to over 75. In the ten years of 1955–1965, college enrollments alone doubled from 2.7 to 5.4 million. In 1965, 54 percent of high school graduates went on to college, as compared with only 34 percent in 1940, and the ratio will before too long be 75 out of 100 high school graduates.

Federal Aid to Education

Until 1965, federal involvement in education was generally specific or on an *ad hoc* basis. Traditionally, education has been thought of as the domain of state and local authorities, and federal involvement on a large, and general, scale was fought off on two grounds: First, the states' righters claimed that federal aid would mean federal control and uniformity. Second, there was the religious issue; if federal money were to benefit parochial (mostly Roman Catholic) schools, the objection was raised that the separation of state and church would thereby be violated. If federal aid would be withheld from Roman Catholic schools, members of that faith in Congress opposed federal aid to schools on the grounds of anti-Catholic discrimination. The combination of (generally) southern states' righters and northern Roman Catholic leaders thus seemed to create an insurmountable obstacle.

Federal involvement in education was therefore confined to specific areas, in which there was either an identifiable federal interest or an element of pork-barrel politics. Educational grants to veterans after World War II clearly involved a federal responsibility to members of the United States armed forces. Federal aid to "federally impacted areas" (that is, areas suffering from additional educational burdens because of sizable defense installations or similar activities) was a mixture of both federal interest and local politics. The school lunch program was a device to raise the performance level of school children through better nutrition, but it also helped to dispose of surplus farm products.

The National Defense Education Act of 1958

The successful launching of the first satellite (*sputnik*) by the Soviets in 1957 shocked the nation into the realization that, after the battle for quantity in education was almost won, the battle for quality had conspicuously lagged. Congress therefore enacted in 1958 the National Defense Education Act (NDEA), the first federal general education act, though still largely confined to one level, colleges and universities. It was a billion dollar program, designed to aid the nation's defense capacity through the strengthening of science, mathematics, and foreign languages in colleges and universities. In addition to generous graduate fellowships, the Act (and its subsequent amendments) provided for student loans to needy students. The loan is interest-free while the student attends college, and the interest is only 3 percent during the 10-year repayment period after graduation. During the 1965–1966 school year, 400,000 students, or about 1 out of 15, had NDEA loans. However, half the loan is forgiven if the student goes into teaching after graduation. If, after graduation the student teaches in "poverty-area schools" for seven years, the loan is entirely forgiven.

As time went on, several of the social sciences and English were added to the physical sciences, mathematics, and foreign languages. The Act also extended matching grants to the states for the purchase of equipment in public schools and for loans to private schools in the "defense" fields of instruction.

In 1963, Congress passed legislation authorizing $1.2 billion for grants and loans to public and private colleges for the construction of classroom buildings. The importance of this legislation lay in the fact that education rather than defense was the target, whereas under NDEA the pretense was kept up that the purpose of aid was national defense, although—as in the case of supporting the improved teaching of English—the link to defense might not always be clearly visible to the naked eye.

The Elementary and Secondary Education Act of 1965

Direct federal aid to elementary and secondary schools was legislated by Congress in 1965 in the Elementary and Secondary Education Act. Like the establishment of social security in 1935 and medicare in 1965, this is one of the great legislative breakthroughs in the history of social welfare in the United States. Federal aid to elementary and secondary schools was made possible in 1965 because of three factors: first, the realization that, owing to the growing interdependence of states and communities, quality differentials were a national concern. During the 1964–1965 school year, expenditures per pupil in public elementary and secondary schools ranged from $273 in Mississippi to $790 in New York. (See Figure 23-3.) Because of the great mobility of the population, poor levels of education in one state affect all other states. Second, aid to education was justified as a main line of attack on poverty, which President Johnson had stressed in his 1964 campaign and in his subsequent legislative proposals to Congress. Third, the Congress elected in 1964 was the most liberal Congress in over a

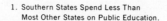

1. Southern States Spend Less Than
Most Other States on Public Education.

(Total per Pupil Public Education 1965-66)

| | Under $500 | | $500 to $700 | | Over $700 |

(U.S. Average, $630)

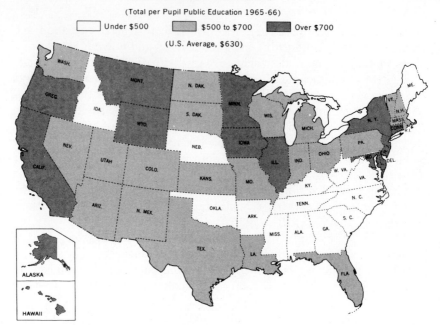

2. This has Resulted in a High
Rate of Illiteracy in the Region.

(Percent of Population 14 Years Old and Over Unable to Read or Write)

| | Under 1% | | 1% to 3% | | Over 3% |

(U.S. Average, 2.4%)

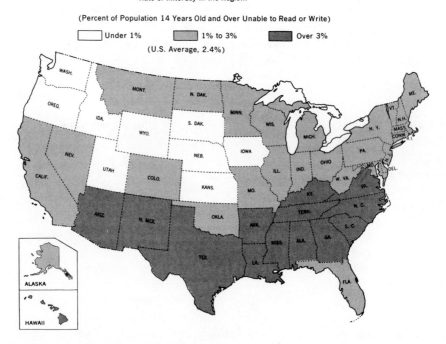

FIGURE 23-3. Regional Imbalance in Public Education, and U.S. Government
Efforts to Correct It. (Adapted from *The New York Times.* © 1964, 65, 66 by
The New York Times Company. Reprinted by permission.)

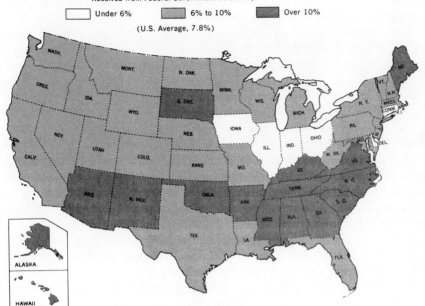

3. The Government's Aid Program, Therefore,
   Has Concentrated on the South.

   (Percent of Public Education Expenditure
   Received from Federal Government 1965-66)

   Under 6%   6% to 10%   Over 10%

   (U.S. Average, 7.8%)

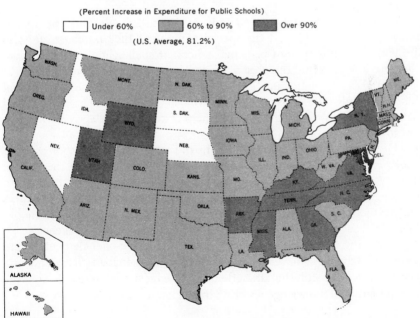

4. Because of Federal Aid and Increased
   Spending by Most States, Total Expenditures
   for Public Education Have Increased Sharply
   in the Last Ten Years, Notably in the South.

   (Percent Increase in Expenditure for Public Schools)

   Under 60%   60% to 90%   Over 90%

   (U.S. Average, 81.2%)

FIGURE 23-3. (*Continued*)

generation. Many of the "freshmen" in Congress strongly favored President Johnson's aid to education programs.

The Elementary and Secondary Education Act of 1965 aims, in principle, at aiding school districts with specified numbers or percentages of pupils from low-income families. However, funds under the Act are, in fact, available to 95 percent of all school districts, for all a school district needs to be eligible for federal aid is to show that 3 percent of its pupils, or 100 pupils (whichever is less), are from poor families. Areas with a higher percentage of low-income families receive proportionately more. Thus, under the Act, Mississippi was scheduled to receive 15 percent of its school budgets from federal funds, whereas in California and New York the percentages would only be 2.3 and 3.6 respectively. In effect, therefore, the Act shares with other social welfare policies the feature of redistribution of resources through the transfer of wealth from more affluent to less affluent groups and geographical areas.

Of the $1.3 billion earmarked for the first year (fiscal 1966) under the Act, over $1 billion was assigned to the general purpose of strengthening education in aid-receiving school districts, including the building of school facilities and the hiring of teachers for new programs. The emphasis of the Act is on services that improve education rather than on routine services. Typical services financed under the Act include preschool or after-school programs, guidance counseling, educational radio and television, speech therapy, remedial education, mobile services, and equipment and facilities.

Funds under the Act can go only to public schools, but the special programs they set up, and the special equipment they purchase, are also available to children from parochial schools if such schools qualify under the criterion of having the prescribed number of children from low-income families. Because parochial schools cannot directly receive any federal funds, the state-church issue was thus avoided, at least to the satisfaction of Congress. The intent of the law is to help educationally deprived children, not to aid religion.

The second major target of aid is in the area of library resources, textbooks, and other instructional materials. In 1965, at the time of the passage of the Act, more than two thirds of public elementary schools, with over 10 million children, had no school libraries at all! Again, such library resources and textbooks are also available for use by children in parochial schools, but title in such materials remains vested in public educational agencies.

Finally, the Act also provides for the setting up of model elementary and secondary schools to develop and test new educational methods and programs, as well as for the strengthening of educational research and the dissemination of knowledge resulting from such research.

With respect to the issue of potential federal control over elementary and secondary education, the Act specifically prohibits any federal officer "to exercise any direction, supervision, or control over the curriculum, program of instruction, administration, or personnel of any educational institution or school system, or over the selection of library resources, textbooks, or other printed or published instructional material by any educational institution or school system."

The Higher Education Act of 1965

The single most important provision of the Higher Education Act of 1965 is the allocation of substantial funds for direct federal undergraduate scholarships for needy students. They range from $200 to $800 per year, with a bonus of $200 added if the student is in the top half of his class. Funds for 1965–1966 were assigned for well over 100,000 students or nearly one out of ten entering freshmen students. In addition, the government also insures loans for undergraduate and graduate students, up to $1,000 and $1,500 per year, respectively. If the loan recipient is from a family whose annual earnings are under $15,000, the government pays all the interest while the student is in college, and half the interest after he leaves college. Needy students may benefit from a "work-study" program in colleges, toward the cost of which the federal government contributes 90 percent. More than 700,000 are aided by the loan and work-study programs.

The Act also authorizes federal funds for "developing institutions," mostly Negro colleges in the South, and for equipment and library resources for institutions that especially need them. In line with the growing urbanization of society, the Act provides funds for "community services" and adult education to be offered by urban colleges and universities; such community services by colleges in urban areas are designed to do for the cities what the county agent has done so successfully for the farmer for many decades. One of the most interesting provisions of the Act is the creation of a National Teacher Corps, made up of experienced teachers and teacher-interns. Such teams receive up to two-year teaching assignments in schools attended mainly by pupils from low-income families, and are sent only by local request.

The Attack on Poverty Through Training and Education

As average living standards of the American people have gone up to unprecedented levels, the public awareness of the still remaining poverty has proportionately increased. This is not as paradoxical as it seems. For as the vast majority of the people live in greater and greater comfort, as poverty therefore becomes rarer, it becomes more news. In a poor nation like India, poverty is hardly news, for over 90 percent of the people live in abject poverty. Even in the United States, as recently as 1947, 32 percent of the people were poor, at least by American standards. Yet there was less talk of poverty in 1947 than in 1964, when the percentage had been cut to 18. As poverty becomes less common, the realization grows that it is not inevitable or necessary at all, and that it can be almost entirely eliminated if the nation makes the political decision to do so. This explains why the richest nation in the world has, in recent years, been more concerned about poverty than any other country, rich or poor.

The Economic Opportunity Act of 1964 (EOA), commonly called the "Anti-Poverty Act," is the first congressional commitment to attack the roots of poverty, rather than—as has been traditionally the case—to alleviate its symptoms. (See Figure 23–4.) Sample studies of recipients of aid to dependent children have shown, for example, that 40 percent of the parents of such children were themselves raised by families which were on public relief. As to education, two thirds of families classified as poor were revealed to be headed by persons with less than an eighth-grade education. Of these undereducated heads of poor families, two thirds in turn came from families whose heads also had not gone beyond the eighth grade.

The main target of EOA is therefore youth, and the main instrument is training and education. Many culturally and socially deprived children start elementary school without being ready for it. They often come from homes in which there is little or no communication on a literate level, in which a book is unheard of, in which the vocabulary is primitive, and in which the child has not learned simple abstractions, such as long and short. The mental and physical health of many of these underprivileged children may have been so neglected that they are not fit to attain even moderate levels of training and education. As time goes on, their insufficiencies become cumulative, and they fall behind more and more. Traditional education then seems to have the effect of progressively lowering their intelligence and scholastic performance.

Figures 23–5 and 23–6 show two interesting facts. First, IQ scores of New York City pupils rise from third grade (98.6) to eighth grade (100), in terms of the national score (100), whereas during that same period the IQ of Central Harlem (Negro) children declines from 90.6 to 87.7. Second, in reading comprehension, New York City children are roughly in line with national averages. But Central Harlem children, who, at the end of the third grade, have a reading comprehension level of 2.5 grades, drop to sixth-grade comprehension levels (6.0) at the end of the eighth grade. Disadvantaged children thus decline in intelligence and reading comprehension the more traditional education they get in elementary schools.

Negroes Have Less Chance Than White Students To Get a High School Education

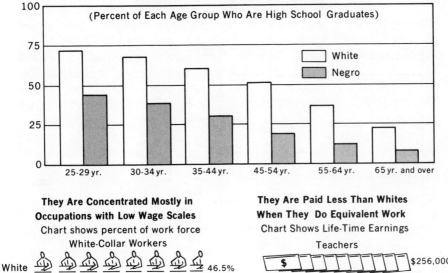

(Percent of Each Age Group Who Are High School Graduates)

White
Negro

25-29 yr.   30-34 yr.   35-44 yr.   45-54 yr.   55-64 yr.   65 yr. and over

They Are Concentrated Mostly in Occupations with Low Wage Scales

Chart shows percent of work force

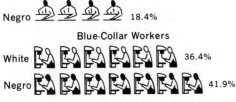

White-Collar Workers

White 46.5%

Negro 18.4%

Blue-Collar Workers

White 36.4%

Negro 41.9%

Service Workers

White 10.8%

Negro 31.4%

Farm Workers

White 6.3%

Negro 8.3%

They Are Paid Less Than Whites When They Do Equivalent Work

Chart Shows Life-Time Earnings

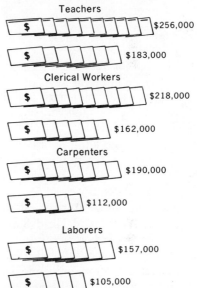

Teachers

$ $256,000

$ $183,000

Clerical Workers

$ $218,000

$ $162,000

Carpenters

$ $190,000

$ $112,000

Laborers

$ $157,000

$ $105,000

Their Current Rate of Unemployment Is More Than Twice as Great

White 4.3%   (Percent of each Work Force Unemployed)

Negro 9%

FIGURE 23–4. Disparities in Negro and White Education and Employment. (Adapted from *The New York Times.* © 1964, 65, 66 by The New York Times Company. Reprinted by permission.)

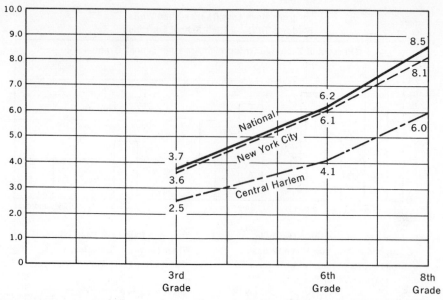

FIGURE 23–5. Median Equivalent Grades in Reading Comprehension for Central Harlem and New York City Pupils Compared to National Norms. (SOURCE: Prepared for *Youth in the Ghetto: A Study of the Consequences of Powerlessness and a Blueprint for Change*, Harlem Youth Opportunities Unlimited, Inc., p. 190. From Francis Keppel, *The Necessary Revolution in American Education*, New York, Harper & Row, 1966, p. 40.)

One of the most ambitious programs, *Project Head Start*, was therefore instituted in the summer of 1965 under the antipoverty Act. Over half a million children of *preschool age*—about half of the children from poor families entering school for the first time each fall—took part in the program, operated in 2,500 urban and rural communities throughout the nation. Year-round Head Start programs for over 100,000 children were also set up. In both summer and year-round programs, the children receive, in addition to educational stimulation and broadening, a balanced diet and medical attention, often provided by volunteer doctors. One such medical group in Boston discovered that 71 percent of the participating children had physical or emotional problems that required further professional diagnosis and treatment. The aim of Head Start is to help the whole child, and above all to help him get ready for the public school for which he would otherwise be unprepared.

Another major target group are boys and girls in the 16–21 age bracket, particularly those that are neither in school nor on a job. The antipoverty Act has two programs for them. First, the *Neighborhood Youth Corps* aims at providing for persons between 16 and 21 years the opportunity of receiving more formal education by staying in, or returning to, school, or of receiving vocational training through full-time or part-time work, par-

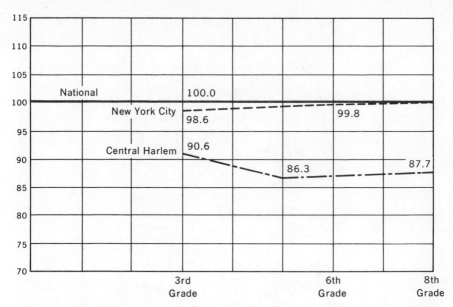

FIGURE 23–6. Median IQ Scores for Central Harlem and New York City Pupils Compared to National Norms. "IQ tests, originally believed to assess innate intellectual capacity, are now understood to be influenced by cultural and educational opportunities. Whatever the weaknesses of these scores as a test of intelligence, the above chart does show that the 'capacity' of children in Central Harlem declines between the third and sixth grades, rising slightly between the sixth and eighth grades, while the scores of children in New York City as a whole rise slightly from grades three to eight." (SOURCE: Prepared for *Youth in the Ghetto: A Study of the Consequences of Powerlessness and a Blueprint for Change*, 1964, Harlem Youth Opportunities Unlimited, Inc., p. 193. From Francis Keppel, *The Necessary Revolution in American Education*, New York, Harper & Row, 1966, p. 42.)

ticularly in schools, libraries, hospitals, and similar nonprofit institutions. About 350,000 young people were thus employed in 1966. The second method of helping the 16–21 age group is the *Job Corps*. It provides education and training in rural conservation and urban training centers, where the enrollees (about 30,000 in 1966) live, learn, and receive work-training.

One of the most important activities of the antipoverty Act is the *Community Action Program* (CAP), which receives about one half of antipoverty funds. The philosophy behind CAP is that the poor will most quickly improve their condition if they can learn to help themselves. Typical activities include day care for children, literacy courses for adults, legal aid, consumer education, neighborhood organizations and services. In some areas, CAP also operates birth control centers—the first federally supported birth control effort in the United States. Of all CAP activities, the Head

December 20, 1964
Heritage. Drawing by Bill Mauldin. From *I've Decided I Want My Seat Back*
by Bill Mauldin. Copyright 1962, 1963, 1964 by Bill Mauldin. Reprinted
by permission of the author and Harper & Row, Publishers.

Start Projects have been the most successful, and the ones that have caught the public imagination the most. Finally, under the antipoverty program a domestic Peace Corps, called *VISTA* (Volunteers in Service to America), has been set up, for which men and women 18 to 80 may volunteer for service in depressed areas or among disadvantaged groups.

The importance of education in antipoverty programs has been dramatically shown by the experience of two cities, Chicago and New York. In Chicago, the number of relief recipients dropped by 9 percent in the years 1962–1965, mostly because they are assigned to literacy courses and vocational training operated directly by the Chicago Board of Education. By contrast, during the same four years, the number of relief recipients in New York increased by 48 percent, and this increase is at least in part due to the fact that New York does not require such educational endeavor on the part of welfare receivers.[4]

The lessening or elimination of poverty is not the only beneficial result of providing education for the disadvantaged. Numerous studies of political attitudes have shown that the more a person is educated, the more he is open to considering new ideas and willing to tolerate the expression of even the most unorthodox ideas by others. Interest in public affairs also

4 *New York Times*, January 12, 1966.

goes up as one's education rises. An increase in the general level of education, then, improves not only the economic health of society but the quality of democracy in the body politic as well.

The war on poverty includes not only new and expanded programs in health, education, manpower training, and urban development, but also in area and regional development. In the last category, the best-known program of regional renewal is that of the Appalachian 11-state region in the Southeast, the largest impoverished region in the whole country. Emphasis is on road construction and other "infra-structure" elements of potential development, such as vocational schools, land improvement, health facilities, and better utilization of timber and water resources.

⚘ HOUSING AND URBAN RENEWAL

Just as the creation of a Cabinet-level Department of Health, Education and Welfare in 1953 was a belated recognition of social welfare as a national responsibility, the creation of the Cabinet-rank Department of Housing and Urban Development (HUD) in 1965 finally took official cognizance of the fact that the urbanization of American society had created problems that were beyond the capacity of state and local governments.

Federal activities in housing and urban renewal are centered in four major areas. Insurance is the oldest. During the Great Depression, the federal government entered the home-financing business on a small scale in 1932. In 1934, the Federal Housing Administration (FHA) was set up to encourage the flow of private mortgage funds through federal insurance. During the years 1934–1964, the FHA insured $96 billion of mortgage money, of which about half was still to be repaid at the end of 1964. The Veterans Administration insures loans to World War II and Korea veterans. Between 1945 and 1964, 6.3 million veterans received such VA insured loans totaling $60 billion. In addition, the VA has also, since 1950, made direct loans to veterans, amounting to $2.3 billion. Direct loans have also been made to farmers by the Farmers Home Administration, for college housing, and for urban renewal planning.

In addition to insuring and making home loans, the federal government has made direct grants to cities, mostly for urban renewal. Direct federal capital grants may pay for two thirds to three fourths of urban renewal projects. What dent even such sizable grants will make on urban renewal is open to speculation, because estimated costs for the renewal of American cities run into the hundreds of billions.

Finally, federal activity in housing is effected through subsidies. The

Public Housing Administration (PHA) was created in 1937 to help local housing authorities clear slums and build public housing for low-income families. The local housing authorities own and manage these housing projects, but the federal government grants or insures loans to public housing authorities, and also makes annual subsidies to cover the difference between operating costs and rents received. Such direct subsidies to local housing authorities amounted to $1.4 billion during the years 1937 to 1964, and 2.1 million persons lived in almost 600,000 units thus subsidized. Considering that since 1950 the annual number of housing units started has averaged around 1.5 million, the total number of public housing units in three decades has been only less than one half of all housing built in one year.

More recently, the federal government has embarked on a new method of housing subsidies. In 1966, Congress authorized an initial $12 million for a "rent-subsidy" demonstration program. Under this program, the federal government pays directly to the landlord the difference between the fair market rents and one fourth of the tenant's income. The argument put forth by the supporters of this program is that it is cheaper than traditional slum-clearance projects, and that it takes such subsidized tenants out of the hard-core slums and distributes them among middle-income families. The main argument of the opponents of rent subsidies, apart from the financial cost, is the reverse: that it is a form of "forced socioeconomic integration."

A leading student of American urban problems reported in 1964 an estimate, according to which it would take, at the current rate, about 400 years to eliminate existing slums in the United States; but in the meantime "eight times as many new slums will have come into existence."[5] This is a sober reminder that the "Great Society" (at least in housing and urban renewal) is not about to be realized, despite the increasing effort on the part of the federal government. The American people have the resources and know-how to restore to the urban and metropolitan centers the architectural dignity and cultural leadership they once possessed. Whether this restoration will occur, or whether decay—architectural, social, economic, and cultural—will transform big cities into tax-supported reservations for the disadvantaged and the poor, this may well be the dominant domestic issue in the next thirty years of American politics. The basic decision about the shape of American urban life still has to be made. Government cannot play the role of a *deus ex machina*. In a democracy, it will only do what the people want it to do.

[5] Edward C. Banfield, "The Key Problem of the City," *The Harvard Review*, 2 (Fall, 1964), 21.

CHAPTER 24

AMERICAN
FOREIGN POLICY

❧ FROM COLONY TO WORLD POWER

Never before in history has a nation been catapulted as rapidly as the
United States from the colonial status of insignificance to world leadership.
Starting with a population of about 3 million at the time of attaining
independence, the United States now numbers about 200 million, the
fourth most populous nation in the world, exceeded only by China, India,
and the Soviet Union. Beginning its economic career as a simple farm
community, having little impact on the international economy, it is now
the most advanced industrial society, producing over one third of the
world's goods and services, although possessing only 6 percent of the
world's population. Militarily weak at the outset, the United States has
become, since World War II, the strongest military force on earth. Long a
disciple of Europe in science and education, the United States now leads
the world as the most important center of learning and scientific advance.

Inward-looking in its early years, seeking to go it alone by opening up the
vast stretches of an empty continent, deliberately shunning entangling
commitments to traditional rivalries and alliances, the United States now
finds itself in a position where the whole world is of concern to its present
and future.

641

The Cost of Keeping America's Place in the World

In Washington's days, the Department of State had about a half dozen officials, including the Secretary of State, and its budget was $6,600. The entire diplomatic service spent about $40,000 annually, a paltry sum even in those days, when the dollar was worth much more than now. Today, government activity in the international field dominates everything else. Since the 1950s, annual government expenses on national defense has regularly exceeded one half of the federal budget. If one adds space research and technology (much of which is related to defense), the foreign service, foreign aid, veterans' benefits, and the interest on the national debt (mostly the result of past wars), one finds that about two thirds of the federal budget is devoted to maintaining America's place in the world. (See Figures 24–1 and 24–2.) The same holds true of federal employment. Of the nearly 3 million civilian employees of the federal government, well

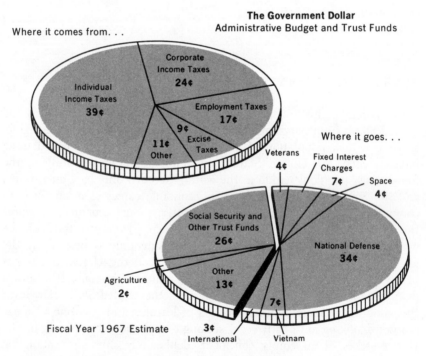

FIGURE 24–1. The Sources and Distribution of the Government Dollar.
(SOURCE: *The Budget in Brief: Fiscal Year 1967*,
Bureau of the Budget, 1966.)

Billions of Dollars

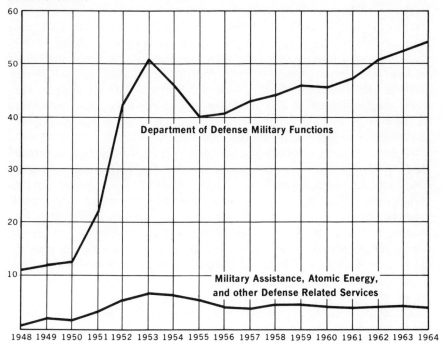

FIGURE 24–2. Expenditures for National Defense, 1948–1964.
(Adapted from *Congress and the Nation*, Washington, D.C.,
Congressional Quarterly Service, 1965, p. 239.)

over one half work for the Department of Defense, the Department of
State, and the various agencies related to defense or international affairs.

Domestic and Foreign Affairs

The paramount importance of foreign relations goes beyond statistically
provable facts and figures. It has become increasingly difficult to keep
"domestic" issues neatly separate and distinguishable from "foreign" policy
issues. Tariff and immigration laws obviously concern other nations very
closely. From the American viewpoint, an increase in tariffs on coffee or
bananas may affect only a fraction of 1 percent of the whole American
economy, but the nations affected by such tariff changes may depend for
60 to 70 percent of their foreign currency earnings on exports to the
United States.

Even without initiating any specific policy, the United States—solely
because it is what it is—profoundly affects the rest of the world. The whole
non-Communist world, for example, keenly watches the performance of
the American economy at all times. If the American economy is buoyant

and expanding, the outlook for shared prosperity in many other nations looks bright. If American economic activity is sluggish, if Wall Street sneezes, tremors immediately seize many another nation. The same holds true of noneconomic issues. To most Americans, equal rights for Negroes are a strictly domestic affair. To hundreds of millions throughout the world—among whites as well as among non-whites—racial equality is the crucial test of judging American fitness for international leadership, because the vast majority of the human race is not white.

That the American people have not fully adjusted to the prime importance of foreign affairs can be seen in the selection of presidential candidates without much experience in world affairs in this century. In the earlier days of the Republic, six Secretaries of State became President: Jefferson, Madison, Monroe, John Quincy Adams, Van Buren, and Buchanan. Paradoxically, although experience in foreign affairs for the presidential office has become infinitely more important in this century than in the last, no Secretary of State in this century has become President. Perhaps as the nation has become more democratic in the sense of being more responsive to demands by specific major groups, it puts a special premium on the ability to recognize and meet such demands rather than on experience in foreign policy, in which domestic pressure groups play a much less important role.

❧ DEMOCRACY AND FOREIGN POLICY

Inherent Tensions Between Democracy and Foreign Policy

Is there, then, an inherent tension between democracy and the successful conduct of foreign relations? Alexis de Tocqueville, although viewing the American experiment in democracy with friendly sympathy, had grave doubts whether democracy and foreign affairs were compatible:

> Foreign politics demand scarcely any of those qualities which a democracy possesses; and they require, on the contrary, the perfect use of almost all those faculties in which it is deficient. Democracy is favorable to the increase of the internal resources of the State; it tends to diffuse a moderate independence, it promotes the growth of public spirit, and fortifies the respect for law in all classes of society; and these are advantages which only exercise an indirect influence over the relations which one people bears to another. But a democracy is unable to regulate the details of an important undertaking, to persevere in design, and to work out its execution in the presence of serious obstacles. It cannot combine its measures with secrecy, and will not await their consequence with patience.[1]

[1] Alexis de Tocqueville, *Democracy in America* (London: Longmans, 1835), vol. 1, pp. 236–237.

There is little doubt that, whether Tocqueville is basically right or not, some of his criticisms are amply borne out by historical experience. Many a democracy has dearly paid for preferring butter to guns too long, pursuing the good life in the wishful hope that critical situations will fade out of existence by not paying attention to them.

In World War I, the United States entered the conflict in 1917 and then proceeded to build up its military strength. When World War II broke out in 1939, the United States was virtually disarmed, and was shaken out of its lethargy only after the fall of France in 1940, when the invasion and conquest of Britain by Nazi Germany looked imminent. Immediately after World War II was over, the nation disarmed at the fastest possible rate, throwing away the fruits of military victory in a fitful attempt to return to normalcy, just as it had done after World War I. The Communist take-over of Czechoslovakia in 1948 and the attempted Communist conquest of Korea in 1950 rudely awakened the American people from its desire to meet its international responsibilities with as little military preparedness as possible. Yet even the lesson of Korea was quickly unlearned: the major American strategy in the 1950s centered on nuclear weapons, because it was argued that nuclear weapons yield "more bang for a buck" than conventional instruments of warfare. The military involvement in Vietnam under the Johnson administration showed that nuclear weapons are of little use in fighting guerrillas in the jungles of Southeast Asia.

Weakness of the Rule of Law and of a Sense of Community

Another inherent tension—or even incompatibility, some would argue—between democracy and foreign affairs lies, as Tocqueville clearly saw, in the different qualities required for their successful operation. The two fundamental features of democracy—the rule of law and the consciousness of community—exist but in a rudimentary form among independent nations. In a democracy, the rule of law means not only that there is a legal answer to every problem and conflict, but also that the rule of law is mindful of legitimate interests, and that it is enforced by an impartial authority. If the law is unjust, the pressure of the community will eventually bring about its substitution by a just rule. By contrast, in the society of nations, binding international law is still in its infancy, struggling for recognition and respect, and lacking an essential feature of national law—a machinery of impartial adjudication and enforcement. Thus every nation—particularly if it happens to be a Great Power—is judge and policeman in its own cases.

Paradoxically, therefore, the more civilized and nonviolent a democratic nation becomes in its internal institutions and behavior, the more peaceful and frank the outlook and conduct of its people, the more it may find it difficult, as a nation, to survive and prosper in the semianarchy of international affairs, in which secrecy, suspicion, and violence always lurk in the background. This paradox is rooted in the very origins of democracy. Both in antiquity and in modern times, democracy developed in response to urgent domestic problems, such as the relations between different social classes, between religion and government, and between government and the governed. Specific democratic solutions to such domestic issues have been found and tested by experience, but the same cannot be said of the conduct of foreign relations. If democratic states dealt only with other democratic states, a common pattern of institutions and behavior might develop, because there would be a "common agreement on fundamentals" in interstate relations.

However, in the society of nations, democratic states have to conduct foreign relations not only with other democracies but also with authoritarian and totalitarian regimes. In such encounters, the democratic nation is only too easily inclined to project its own peaceful intentions on undemocratic nations and to disbelieve their aggressive intentions until it is too late. Before 1914, many persons in the Western democracies thought that the Kaiser was just blustering, and that German ambitions for imperial expansion by force should not be taken too seriously. Before World War II, the democracies again refused to believe—until it was almost too late—that Hitler, Mussolini, and Tojo meant exactly what they said, that is, to impose fascism on the whole world. In the case of communism, too, the world might have been spared a great deal of grief if Lenin's concept of spreading communism by revolution and armed force had been taken at its face value.

Even though democracy and foreign policy show inherent contradictions, which to some observers appear incompatible, in fact such contradictions are not as serious as they might seem in theory. For as democracy is practiced by human beings, it ceases to be a perfect abstraction or ideal, and inevitably partakes of the frailties and ambivalences of man. Democracy is not a method of eliminating aggressive and domineering impulses in man, but of channeling them into acceptable activities.

In its conduct of foreign relations, too, a working democracy tries to steer a middle course between the two extremes of absolute morality and absolute ethical cynicism. What the philosophy of anarchism is in domestic politics, pacifism—or the refusal to use force under any circumstances—is in the conduct of foreign relations. Although democracies recognize the right of individuals to be pacifists (and, as in the United States and Britain, exempt them from military service), no democracy has adopted pacifism as a national policy in its relations with other nations.

From the viewpoint of most democrats, the policy of not resisting aggression—whether in domestic or foreign affairs—is not evidence of a higher morality, but is a violation of the duty to resist evil, and is bound to produce more violence, not less.

Collective Defense Agreements as a Substitute for the Rule of Law

Thus it is argued by some historians that Germany and Austria-Hungary might not have unleashed World War I in 1914 had they known in advance that Britain (and, later, the United States) would fight on the side of France and Russia. Similarly, in the 1930s, the Fascist aggressor states assumed (or at least hoped) that the United States would not enter the conflict, and this uncertainty was, again, a contributing factor in shaping Fascist aggressive plans leading to war. The Communist take-over of Eastern Europe by Soviet armed force after World War II showed that Soviet imperialism followed the pattern of Fascist expansion. Yet the United States still did not react with a basically new foreign policy. Only after Czechoslovakia was communized in 1948 did the conviction grow in the United States that American policies of waiting and seeing would lead to eventual major conflict, as they had done in 1914 and 1939. Seeking to learn a lesson from the errors of the past, the United States therefore joined with other like-minded nations in setting up the North Atlantic Treaty Organization (NATO) in 1949. Its most important provision is in Article 5, in which members of NATO "agree that an armed attack against one or more of them in Europe or North America shall be considered an attack against them all." Similar collective defense agreements were made with the Latin American nations in 1947 and Southeast Asia nations in 1954 (SEATO). Such defense pacts, in which the United States is a member, are no absolute protection against aggression, but they tend to lessen that danger.

Korea is a case in point. The invasion of South Korea by North Korea in 1950 occurred after the United States had failed to specifically include South Korea in the American "defense perimeter," where aggression would be resisted by American armed force. Counting on this ambiguity, the Communists in North Korea, backed by Russia and Red China, felt encouraged to attack South Korea. Yet, their calculation proved wrong, since President Truman immediately dispatched air and naval forces to Korea. After three years of heavy fighting, the invasion was stopped, and the Republic of Korea was saved from Communist subjugation. In 1953, the United States and the Republic of Korea signed a mutual defense pact. Since then, Korea has been left alone, and one reason for this may be the knowledge of would-be aggressors that this is no longer 1950, and that an attack against Korea would result in an immediate military response by the United States. The United States has also similar bilateral defense pacts with Taiwan (Republic of China) and Japan.

❦ THE EMPHASIS ON POWER AND NATIONAL INTEREST

In the 1920s and 1930s, the Western democracies—both students and practitioners of foreign policy—disregarded power as a key element in world politics, and hoped that peace could be maintained solely through international treaties outlawing war and through appeals to morality. This neglect of the role of power by the democracies encouraged the Fascist states to prepare for aggressive war, and led the Soviet Union to believe that the Western democracies were decadent and on the way out as major forces in world affairs.

After World War II, the pendulum of opinion and criticism often swung to the other extreme, and power, or national interest, became the sole yardstick by which some students and diplomats judged foreign policy. According to this view, foreign policy should pursue only the national interest, and must avoid the tempting chimeras of "legalistic" and "moralistic" ideas. In analyzing American diplomacy between 1900 and 1950, George F. Kennan, the most distinguished American representative of the "national interest" school of thought, comes to the following conclusion: "I see the most serious fault of our past policy formulation to lie in something that I might call the legalistic-moralistic approach to international problems."[2]

The "national interest" school deserves credit for reminding the United States that there can be no realistic foreign policy without the recognition of the factors of power and national interest. The danger in powerful democracies has, on the whole, been the underuse rather than the overuse of power, and a healthy reminder that American foreign policy must never forget power and national interest can be of very great value. Also, the emphasis on national interest as a key element in the making of foreign policy is a useful antidote against unctuous hypocrisy that often hides the pursuit of very material interests.

Difficulty of Defining the National Interest

Foreign policy, however, is not only the pursuit of national interest. In the first place, there is the difficulty of defining what the national interest is.

[2] George F. Kennan, *American Diplomacy: 1900–1950* (Chicago: University of Chicago Press, 1951), p. 95.

Disagreements over issues of American foreign policy are not only between "idealists" seeking to uphold moral standards in international life and "realists" coldly pursuing the national interest, but also among those who agree that the national interest should guide American foreign policy but who differ over what the national interest is in a particular case.

After the United States defeated Mexico in 1846 and took over half of its territory, some Americans urged that all of Mexico plus a few Central American republics ought to be taken over. Those who opposed such a policy did so, among other reasons, on the ground that such excessive imperialist aggrandizement of the United States would not be in the American interest, because it might permanently poison U.S.–Latin American relations. A century later, when Mexico nationalized the oil industry and expropriated several American oil companies in 1938, some Americans urged tough action against Mexico in order to protect the national interest. President Roosevelt, in resisting such a policy, also thought of the national interest: he was sure that war would soon descend upon the world, and that a friendly Mexico (which in World War I almost sided with America's enemies) and a friendly Latin America would be vital in the coming world conflict. His policy was confirmed by subsequent events. When the United States was drawn into World War II, all Latin American republics (with the exception of Fascist-dominated Argentina) quickly declared war on the Rome-Berlin-Tokyo Axis, and Mexico, in particular, made an important contribution to the American war effort.

No Sharp Distinction Between Morality and National Interest

Secondly, the sharp differentiation between morality and interest in the conduct of foreign relations becomes blurred on closer inspection. Moral action would be meaningless if it always demanded a sacrificial or suicidal posture, for then only angels or saints could act morally. Moral action on the part of an individual or a nation does not require self-restraint to the point of self-destruction, but allows the pursuit of one's interests, provided such interests are subjected to rational examination, and provided they are related to the interests of others over a long period of time.

In its domestic policy, too, the democratic state recognizes that men naturally wish to pursue their interests, and does not consider such a natural desire as immoral. All that the democratic philosophy requires is that the pursuit of one's interests—whether in the case of an individual or a nation—take into account the long-term interests of all, including one's own interest. Those statesmen who have despised the critical, rational examination of the national interest and have shown no consideration for other nations, have not fared better than those who have pursued their nations' interests in a spirit of moderate self-restraint and consideration for others.

If democratic nations like the United States insist on civilian supremacy over the military, they do so primarily not out of some ideological or idealistic love of peace and rejection of militarism as a way of life, but because democratic nations have the sincere conviction that "war is too important to be left to the generals," as the French statesman Georges Clemenceau put it. In the view of democrats, the civilian mind is more likely to pursue national objectives in the light of long-term considerations and overall political factors, whereas the military mentality may be more inclined to concentrate on immediate and tangible results that can be obtained by the use of armed force. The temptation for "final" military solutions is by no means without appeal in democracies too.

In the Korean War, for example, General MacArthur publicly criticized the American policy of confining the war to Korea, and was eager to carry the war to the Chinese "sanctuary," thus ending the Chinese threat "once and for all." President Truman asserted the constitutional tradition of civilian supremacy by firing the general for his impetuous criticisms, and stuck to his concept of confining the war to the Korean theater of operations because of the larger political issues involved. At the time, a substantial segment of American public opinion sided with General MacArthur, but in the end President Truman's judgment was accepted as having served the American national interest more effectively, particularly by avoiding a possible world war.

In another famous conflict situation, the Cuban missile crisis of 1962, President Kennedy was urged by many to follow up the removal of Soviet missiles from Cuba by an invasion aiming at the forcible overthrow of Fidel Castro by American armed force. Yet President Kennedy refused to invade Cuba, partly at least because he felt that such an action might do irreparable damage to long-range United States–Latin American relations.

✻ DEMOCRATIC CONTROL OF FOREIGN POLICY

From Jefferson on, democratic leaders and thinkers have known that democracy requires not only an interested public, a people that cares about public affairs, but also an informed and educated public. In domestic affairs, information is backed up by personal experience. The average voter thus feels he can judge public issues on the basis of interest, personal involvement, and information. Also, special interest groups perform an important function in this process, for in trying to promote a cause, they disseminate information, slanted and one-sided as it may be.

Low Level of Interest and Information in Foreign Affairs

By contrast, in foreign affairs the citizen of a democratic country has neither the intensity of interest nor the level of information that he brings to bear on domestic issues. The more important an issue of foreign policy is, the more it affects the nation as a whole, but by the same token it seems to affect the citizen less as an individual. Where any foreign policy issue directly affects a particular group—as when workers get thrown out of jobs because of tariff cuts on a specific article—those affected take an intense interest and express it as loudly as they can. But where an issue of foreign policy goes beyond the interests of a special group, the effect is often that no one in particular—at least among the mass of the voters—seems to get aroused.

Part of the lack of interest in foreign affairs is due to lack of knowledge and information. The majority of Americans have never lived in foreign countries, and the millions of tourists who do visit other countries hardly acquire knowledge that can be a solid basis for informed judgment. Moreover, even those who stay abroad for extended periods of time—as in the case of armed forces personnel and their families—often live in American enclaves, shut off from the native people by barriers of language and the PX (Post Exchange) system, which supplies most foods and other necessary goods to the Americans stationed abroad. These little Americas—nearly fully self-sufficient—exist all over the world, wherever sizable numbers of Americans are stationed, and by living in such an enclave one can easily get along without any contacts with local people. From the supermarket to the baseball field and American school—everything is most efficiently organized and provided, but the "inmates" of these enclaves might just as well have never left their hometowns.

The Growing Role of Science and Technology

Another source of ignorance lies in the changing nature of foreign policy. As science and technology have increasingly come to determine the complicated weapons on which the United States must rely in the last resort, the layman—and even most congressmen, high executive officials, and newspaper commentators are in this category—feels more bewildered than ever. As foreign policy has become more and more determined by scientific and technological developments, strategy, too, has become increasingly removed from the range of interest or understanding of the average citizen. When he therefore encounters terms such as megatons, fissionable material, clean and dirty bombs, spasm warfare, controlled reprisals, flexible responses, escalation, and de-escalation, he may easily throw up his hands in despair and feel that all this is beyond his grasp, and ought to be decided by experts.

Foreign affairs have thus become the domain of "small" publics, made up largely of scientists, professional strategists, government policy-makers, and of highly influential small private groups such as the Council on Foreign Relations. Although hard thinking in these small groups goes on all the time, few pronouncements on foreign policy by these experts ever reach the daily paper or television screen. It could perhaps be argued that the very smallness and *expertise* of such "small publics" in the field of foreign policy may help to eliminate demagoguery and keep thought on a high level. But even if such were the case, the problem of democratic control of foreign policy—as of any policy—would thereby not be solved, for under democratic control the people control the experts, high-minded as they may be, and not vice versa.

The Changing Role of Congress

In its power to appropriate money, Congress still tries to maintain some substance of control over foreign policy. This is particularly noticeable in areas that do not require highly specialized information and in which the issues involved can be easily grasped. This happens annually, for example, in discussions, by Congress, of foreign aid. All the traditional formal and informal practices of Congress come into play: those who oppose aid to Yugoslavia finally give in if Spain gets its cut, and partisans of massive aid to India must make concessions on aid to Pakistan—all this is in the classical pattern of congressional treatment of foreign affairs.

But in the crucial decisions affecting the expenditure of billions of dollars on new weapons systems, not to mention their effect on national security and survival, Congress, too, must ultimately rely on the testimony of the experts as filtered through by the responsible executive officials in the Defense and State Departments. Finally, when a critical situation develops, as under Eisenhower in the Middle East, under Kennedy in Cuba, and under Johnson in Southeast Asia, Congress feels it has no alternative but to give the President virtual carte blanche because he, and he alone, is in possession of the relevant data, some of them secret, assembled by thousands of persons throughout the world.

Veto-Limits of Public Opinion

This does not mean that democratic control of foreign policy is totally gone. Public opinion and Congress still serve an important function in setting some veto-limit to foreign policy proposals. President Truman found that public opinion would not stand for his proposal of sending a regular and permanent ambassador to the Vatican. In 1937, President Roosevelt made his famous "quarantine speech," in which he urged the American people to join with the other Western democracies in quarantining the Fascist aggressor powers, Germany, Italy, and Japan. But the public was not ready for this policy, and the President became so discouraged that for over half a year he stayed away from major public discussions of foreign policy. However, it may be that even these traditional veto-limits of public opinion are now receding more and more from the center of decision-making, for in the nuclear age decisions have often to be made more speedily than in the past.

Bipartisanship in Foreign Policy

The inherent tension between democracy and foreign policy can also be seen in the concept and practice of bipartisanship. After President Woodrow Wilson's debacle in the Senate over the issue of American membership in the League of Nations, later Presidents have made it a point to consult in advance with congressional leaders of both parties on important foreign policy matters. The aim has been to build a foreign policy that could be accepted by both parties. In 1940, immediately after the fall of France, President Roosevelt appointed Republican Henry L. Stimson (who had served as Secretary of State under Hoover) as Secretary of War, and Republican Frank Knox, a newspaper publisher, as Secretary of the Navy. After World War II, bipartisanship received its strongest support from Republican Senator Arthur Vandenberg. Before World War II a confirmed isolationist, he changed his mind during the war, and became convinced that the United States could not evade the responsibilities of leadership. As the most influential Republican in the Senate Committee on Foreign Relations, Vandenberg more than any other public figure helped to hammer out a bipartisan foreign policy on the American role in the United Nations, aid to Greece and Turkey, the Marshall Plan, and the setting up of the North Atlantic Treaty Organization.

President Eisenhower, a strong believer in bipartisan foreign policy, experienced his main difficulties in his own party rather than with the Democrats. Both he and Secretary of State Dulles continued the internationalist policies of Presidents Roosevelt and Truman, and the main core of isolationist opposition was in the Republican rather than in the Democratic party. Eisenhower did not appoint high-ranking Democrats to important foreign policy positions, perhaps because he felt he could in any case count on congressional Democratic support, and also because after twenty years of Democratic administrations in Washington the Republicans had a natural tendency to "make a clean sweep" in the capital, and bring new faces into top positions.

President Kennedy continued the practice adopted by President Franklin Roosevelt, and appointed three high Eisenhower officials to important positions. Former Secretary of State Christian Herter was appointed Special Representative for Trade Negotiations; Under Secretary of State Douglas Dillon was appointed Secretary of the Treasury; and Henry Cabot Lodge, the United States Ambassador to the United Nations under Eisenhower, and Nixon's running mate in 1960, became Ambassador to South Vietnam. In addition, Kennedy appointed Robert S. McNamara, a Republican top executive of the Ford Motor Company, as Secretary of Defense. President Johnson retained McNamara, Dillon, and Lodge in their positions but did not appoint other Republicans to major assignments. As in the case of Eisenhower, Johnson encountered his major foreign policy troubles—as over the intervention in the Dominican Republic in 1965 and the conduct of the war in South Vietnam—among elements in his own party.

If bipartisanship in foreign policy merely means that vital issues of American security be considered by everybody, regardless of party, in a rational and objective manner, and that foreign policy issues not be exploited for partisan purposes, there is no special problem of democratic government here, for the same attitude should ideally prevail in domestic politics too. However, the problem arises when bipartisanship in foreign policy leads to an excessive emphasis on "closing the ranks," "standing shoulder to shoulder," and unity for the sake of unity. Bipartisanship may then become a threat to the functioning of traditional democratic processes.

When Adlai Stevenson, in his race for the Presidency in 1956, proposed an international ban on H-bomb tests, he was bitterly attacked for having dared to deviate from what was then considered a principle of bipartisan policy, and his proposal did him politically no good, although it was hardly discussed on its merits. Yet in 1963, Stevenson's proposal was vindicated by the treaty between the United States, the Soviet Union, and Great Britain to ban above-ground nuclear tests.

Another illustration of the dangers of bipartisanship foreclosing calm reflection and critical discussion on a vital issue is provided by the American attitude toward diplomatic recognition of Red China. After the decision was taken not to recognize Red China when it won the civil war in 1949, nonrecognition became a bipartisan dogma. For years, persons who questioned the wisdom of nonrecognition did not dare to raise the issue in public, lest they be painted with the brush of "Communist fellow traveler" or be charged with the political crime of being "soft on communism." Regardless of the merits of the issue, bipartisanship in this vital area of American foreign policy removed an important issue from the normal processes of unhindered debate.

Fundamentally, democracy recognizes that opponents of the government are just as loyal to the nation as is the government, because democratic theory draws a sharp distinction between government and nation. By contrast, totalitarian regimes know of no "loyal opposition," and because they identify government with nation, opponents of the government are branded as traitors to the nation. To the extent that bipartisanship in foreign policy fosters the illusion that because a specific policy has been adopted by the majorities of both parties, government and nation have become identical, the real danger arises that people in a democracy forget that under the democratic concept, loyalty to the nation is independent of agreement with government policies. In a democracy, no issue is ever beyond, or above, critical appraisal, and no policy is so sacred that it may not be attacked without fear of political penalty or ostracism.

The Problem of Foreign Relations of Private Corporations

Finally, democratic control of foreign relations encounters a difficult problem in an area which the general public is hardly aware of: the conduct of foreign relations by large private corporations with important interests in other nations. Generally, American corporations prefer to deal directly with foreign governments rather than through American diplomatic officials, and the latter may themselves not always be too eager to be drawn into such deals. At times, agreements between American corporations and foreign governments acquire a momentum of their own, which is not always in harmony with aims and purposes of national policy. Before World War II, for example, American companies supplied Japan with vital raw materials (scrap iron, petroleum) at a time when conflict between Japan and the United States seemed highly likely. While official American policy aimed at weakening Japan's war-making potential, some American companies kept on strengthening it, as long as no direct violation of the law was involved.

After World War II, American policy in the Near East has looked upon Israel as an element of stability and as an important counterweight to Communist influence in some Arab states. Israel has therefore received substantial American diplomatic, economic, and military aid. By contrast, big American oil companies with immense financial interests in the Near and Middle East have favored the Arab states whose goodwill means millions of profits to the oil companies. Whereas treaties and agreements of the United States are subject to congressional debate and approval, agreements of private companies with foreign governments are subject to no such checks, and even shareholders, the owners of corporations, have very little to say in this as in other corporate policies.

Dealing with foreign governments is for many American companies a part of regular business rather than an occasional occurrence. Large corporations with extensive international interests have therefore developed foreign policies of their own, carried out by their own foreign service. A leading American political economist, with considerable private and governmental experience in the international field, describes this development as follows: "Some companies with large and widespread overseas interests frequently maintain their own edition of a tiny State Department. Their overseas subsidiaries, branches, and representatives report more or less regularly. Their economic departments keep them informed on business and financial conditions. They have their own resident or traveling diplomats." However, in some cases these corporations diplomats report not only on foreign governments, but also on American diplomatic officials abroad, "rating them according to their probable usefulness in advancing or protecting the company's interests."[3]

✄ IDEOLOGICAL BURDENS OF AMERICAN FOREIGN POLICY

There is no major country in the world in which there is as much general popular agreement as in the United States on the existing social, economic, and political order. Socially, there is no hereditary aristocracy—or even the memory of one—and, on the other hand, there is no landless peasantry historically descending from a class of serfs, as in so many other countries in Europe, Asia, and Latin America. Economically, the system of private enterprise has been so successful that—with necessary modifications and adaptations—it is accepted by nearly all Americans as the only conceivable form of economic organization. Politically, there is no sharp ideological or class gap between the two major parties, and their similarities have driven many foreigners to despair when trying to figure out the differences between Republicans and Democrats. There have been no powerful Fascist, Communist, or other extremist political movements in American history, and representative government based on the rule of law seems the only desirable form of government to nearly all Americans.

[3] A. A. Berle, *The 20th Century Capitalist Revolution* (New York: Harcourt, Brace & World, 1954), pp. 132, 135.

Rigid Commitment to Private Enterprise in Foreign Aid

In dealing with foreign nations, the United States therefore not infrequently tends to project its own experience of liberal capitalism as not only the best for itself, but as the only one suitable for other nations, particularly for the newly emerging societies that are still searching for appropriate economic and political institutions. India is a case in point. With a population of about 500 million, India is the most populous democracy in the world. India's ability to maintain constitutional government since gaining independence in 1947, despite abject poverty and Red China's military pressure, has been one of the most miraculous achievements in the history of any nation. Many students of the underdeveloped countries feel that, as India goes, so will the majority of the "Third World" go. If India fails by comparison with Red China, many of the underdeveloped countries may well follow the Chinese model of intransigent totalitarian communism rather than the Indian model of combining moderate Socialist planning with constitutional government.

Yet, American aid to India has not measured up, in the eyes of many qualified students and of some high American policy-makers, to the needs of India and the national interest of the United States, because India's leadership and some of its policies have expressed a commitment to some Socialist ideas. In practice, this commitment has meant two things. First, a desire to raise the cultural and economic level of the Indian masses above the present level of backwardness and poverty. Secondly, the commitment to socialism has meant, not a commitment to total public ownership of the means of production, but a larger role of government in the economy than is customary in more advanced Western countries.

For example, in the early 1960s India negotiated with the United States for several years in order to build a huge state-owned steel mill that would increase her annual steel production from about 6 million tons to about 10 million tons for a population of nearly 500 million (the United States, with a population of about 200 million, produces over 130 million tons of steel annually). India was finally turned down because Congress did not wish to promote socialism in India, although President Kennedy supported the Indian project. American dogmatism gave the Soviet Union the opportunity to immediately offer to build the steel mill for India, which greatly increased Soviet prestige and influence in India as well as in other underdeveloped countries.

What was overlooked in this case, as in other similar cases, by American policy-makers is that rapid development of a steel industry in India is basically no different from the development of new "frontier" industries in advanced countries. In the United States, for example, atomic energy, supersonic aircraft, and communication by satellites have been, and are being, developed very largely by government financing and regulation, for only the government has the resources to finance such basic developments that are bound to be profitless for some time. Yet in India (as in other underdeveloped countries) the rapid development of steel production or the manufacture of conventional aircraft may be just as basic to its economy, at its stage of development, as the rapid development of a sophisticated and expensive space technology or of supersonic aircraft is for the United States.

The Role of Government in Underdeveloped Countries

Moreover, the American prejudice against a larger government role in underdeveloped countries overlooks the fact that these countries are in a hurry, and are eager to advance toward a productive industrial economy as rapidly as possible. Because skilled technical manpower, capital, and managerial ability are extremely scarce in underdeveloped countries, there has to be some rationing of these scarce human and material resources; only the government can be in charge of that rationing process, and in many cases it alone is qualified to do the job.

Yet despite all the talk of socialism in India, for example, its government takes a much lesser share of the gross national product than does government in the "capitalist" United States. In India, government spends about 15 percent of the gross national product, whereas in the United States, government (on all levels) spends about 30 percent of the gross national product. In agriculture, American policy has for long been far more regulatory than in India, and although in industry and transportation there is proportionately more government ownership and regulation in India than in the United States, India follows a pragmatic course of experimentation and is by no means addicted to any dogma of public ownership, which instils such fears in some American policy-makers. As an American economist has put it:

> We commonly allege that the Indian policy is doctrinaire—specifically, socialistically doctrinaire. But on the relative merits of private versus public ownership of industry, Indian policy, though strikingly different from ours, is exploratory, self-corrective to a degree and capable, as the record shows, of moving either toward or away from private ownership. The most conspicuous difference between domestic policy in the United States and in India is that U.S. policy is rigid in restricting public owner-

ship to few fields, is less open, less exploratory, more governed by doctrine than is the Indian.[4]

Economic Planning and Democratic Socialism in the "Third World"

The choice in most underdeveloped countries is not between liberal capitalism and democratic socialism, but between totalitarian communism and economic planning based on the rule of law. To the extent that some underdeveloped countries manage to combine democratic government with planning and some public ownership, such combination is the most effective antidote to communism, and therefore in the interest of international stability and American foreign policy.

Whereas socialism is a "minus-word" in the American political vocabulary, it is a "plus-word" throughout the rest of the world. By extending American rejection of domestic socialism to foreign nations, the United States creates substantial barriers of communication and influence between itself and other countries, particularly in the "Third World," where socialism has the same positive appeal today that democracy had in the nineteenth century in Western nations.

From the viewpoint of American national interest, support of democratic socialism and state planning in other countries, particularly in the "Third World," would probably be a more effective policy than the insistence on "free enterprise" in a dogmatic manner. In 1963, for example, the State Department released a Presidential Committee's Report on foreign aid, in which the following recommendation was made: "We believe the U.S. should not aid a foreign government in projects establishing government-owned industries and commercial enterprises which compete with existing private endeavors."[5] The United States itself could not pass such a rigid test too well. The federal government owns about one third of all the land in the United States, and is engaged in hundreds and hundreds of businesses and services that run into billions every year, raising complaints from electrical contractors, telephone companies, travel bureaus, power companies, and health insurance companies, to mention but a few. In the United States, such government activities are not attributed to socialism, but to national security, internal government "housekeeping," or to the "Great Society"—any label will do as long as it is not called socialism.

[4] Charles E. Lindblom, "Has India an Economic Future?" *Foreign Affairs*, 44 (January, 1966), 251.
[5] *The Scope and Distribution of United States Military and Economic Assistance Programs*, Report to the President of the United States from the Committee to Strengthen the Security of the Free World (Washington, D.C.: Department of State, 1963), p. 5.

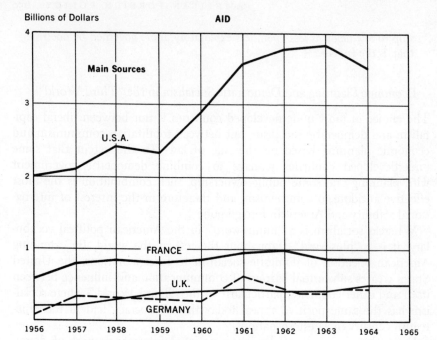

Billions of Dollars   **AID**

Main Sources

U.S.A.

FRANCE

U.K.

GERMANY

1956   1957   1958   1959   1960   1961   1962   1963   1964   1965

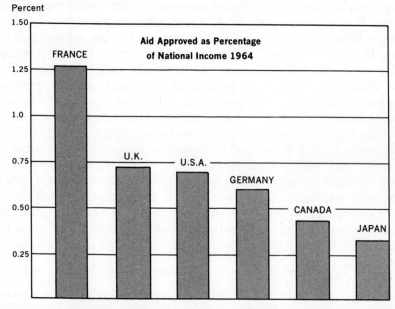

Percent

Aid Approved as Percentage
of National Income 1964

FRANCE

U.K.

U.S.A.

GERMANY

CANADA

JAPAN

FIGURE 24–3. Comparative Expenditures for Foreign Aid, by the United States,
France, Germany, and the United Kingdom. (Adapted from
Lloyd's Bank Review, No. 80, April 1966.)

The Alliance for Progress

In the Alliance for Progress, the ambitious aid program for Latin America set up by President Kennedy in 1961, there is the first indication that foreign economic aid need not be tied to any rigid dogma of free enterprise. The establishment of communism in Cuba brought the realization that Latin America had to undergo radical changes, and that the choice lay between peaceful methods and Communist methods. Whereas in other foreign aid programs the emphasis has generally been on staying out of the domestic affairs of the aid-recipient, in the Alliance for Progress the United States seeks to induce Latin American governments to bring about drastic social changes, such as redistribution of wealth through tax reform, and basic economic changes, such as land reform, previously considered by many Americans as socialistic. Should the Alliance for Progress succeed to a considerable extent, American policy toward other underdeveloped areas might then move away more markedly from its current fixation on spreading capitalism abroad.

Rigid ideological commitment to private enterprise has also blocked the formulation of economic aid to developing nations on a long-term basis and on a much larger scale than has been the case so far. Whereas the United States still provides more aid than does any other single nation, it is remarkable that aid as a percentage of the national income has dropped from about 2.7 percent in 1946 to about 0.5 percent in 1966. Moreover, other nations, such as France and Britain, spend a higher share of their national incomes on aid to developing nations than does the United States, although the per capita income of the United States is more than double that of France or Britain. (See Figures 24-3 and 24-4.) Finally, the mix in aid has substantially changed in the direction of loans rather than outright grants. This, too, partly flows from the fear that grants have a "socialistic" flavor of giving something for nothing, whereas loans can be justified as being "sound business deals."

Ideological Blocks in American Relations with
Advanced Countries: The Case of Britain

The ideological fixation on the dogma of liberal capitalism has also not been very helpful in American foreign relations with advanced nations, both democratic and Communist. Thus during the first Labour government in Britain after World War II (1945–1951), Britain was criticized by

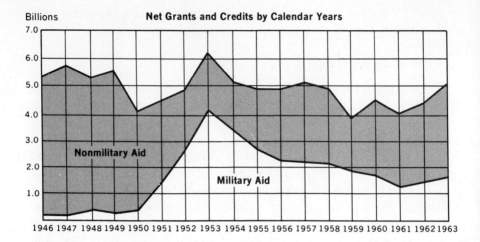

Billions   **Net Grants and Credits by Calendar Years**

Nonmilitary Aid

Military Aid

1946 1947 1948 1949 1950 1951 1952 1953 1954 1955 1956 1957 1958 1959 1960 1961 1962 1963

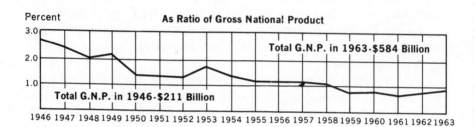

Percent   **As Ratio of Gross National Product**

Total G.N.P. in 1963-$584 Billion

Total G.N.P. in 1946-$211 Billion

1946 1947 1948 1949 1950 1951 1952 1953 1954 1955 1956 1957 1958 1959 1960 1961 1962 1963

FIGURE 24–4. Ratio of Foreign Aid Expenditures to G.N.P. (Adapted
from *Congress and the Nation,* Washington, D.C.,
Congressional Quarterly Service, 1965, p. 162.)

some American public figures for committing itself too deeply to socialism;
the fear was expressed that the alliance value of Britain was doubtful
because Britain engaged in "socialized medicine," nationalized a few
industries and services, all of which, so it was argued by some, might in the
end lead to some form of communism. During the later Labour government
under Harold Wilson, these fears greatly subsided, partly because the
Labour government supported the United States on most issues, even on
Vietnam, and partly because the independent (or anti-American, as some
phrased it) policies of General de Gaulle proportionately increased the
value of British friendship and goodwill. Also, British Labour largely
abandoned public ownership as a basic policy—for reasons of its own, to be
sure, and not in order to please American public opinion—but to many
Americans this change of internal policy revived the image of the British
people as being basically sound and sober.

❧ THE PROBLEM OF COMMUNISM

Failure to Distinguish Between Different Kinds of Communism

In dealing with Communist nations, also, our foreign policy has often been hampered by ideological stumbling blocks. Since all Communist regimes reject both liberal democracy and the capitalist economy, many persons have drawn the conclusion that all Communist systems and nations are alike and ought to be treated in the same way. The Soviet Union, Red China, Yugoslavia, Poland, Hungary, Rumania, Cuba—all too many Americans, in and out of Congress, consider them so much alike that one overall policy with one final objective—"total victory"—seems to be indicated. The policies of aiding Yugoslavia militarily and economically and of giving economic assistance to Poland have therefore often been attacked as aid to communism rather than as instruments of strengthening the desire for national independence in both countries. This failure to distinguish between different brands of communism overlooks a general problem that is relevant to specific policies toward particular Communist states: what matters to the United States most in the behavior of any other country is, not whether it practices economic individualism or collectivism, or whether it is politically democratic or authoritarian or totalitarian, but whether its conduct as a member of the society of nations is peaceful or aggressive.

The Issue of Communism

President Kennedy, in an interview with the editor of *Izvestia* on November 28, 1961, defined the issue of communism more clearly than had any other President:

> Where we feel the difficulty comes is the effort by the Soviet Union to communize, in a sense, the entire world. If the Soviet Union were merely seeking to protect its own national interests, to protect its own nation security, and would permit other countries to live as they wish—to live peace—then I believe that the problems which now cause so m' sion would fade away.
>
> We want the people of the Soviet Union to live in peace same for our own people. It is this effort to push outward system, on to country after country, that represents threat to peace. If the Soviet Union looked only and to providing a better life for its people u'

*I think there would be nothing that would disturb the relations between
the Soviet Union and the United States.*

The President then stated that, contrary to the wartime agreements at
Yalta and Potsdam in 1945, the Soviet Union did not permit free elections
in Eastern Europe and, instead, had imposed communism by armed force.
The President then added his view on the American attitude of communism coming into power through a free election:

*If the people of any country choose to follow a Communist system in a
free election, after a fair opportunity for a number of views to be presented, the United States would accept that. What we find to be objectionable, and a threat to the peace, is when a system is imposed by a
small militant group by subversion, infiltration, and all the rest.*

So far, no Communist regime has ever been set up after a free election,
and thus President Kennedy's commitment to accept such an election
result has never been tested in practice. Fidel Castro announced shortly
after his victory in the civil war in 1958 that free elections would be held
within a short time, but he has failed to live up to his promise.

Communism and Free Elections

In the Vietnam conflict, this issue became an important policy matter.
Until the end of 1965, the prevailing attitude in Washington was to
prevent South Vietnam's communization under all circumstances. From
the end of 1965 on, Secretary of State Dean Rusk and other high government spokesmen expressed the view, paralleling that of President Kennedy
cited previously, that the United States would recognize a Communist
government in South Vietnam, provided it came into existence as a result
of free elections rather than of internal revolution aided by aggression from
the outside. North Vietnam and the Viet Cong, however, rejected the
American proposal, because their view of the preconditions of free elections radically differed from that of the United States.

Military Intervention in the Dominican Republic

Ane of communism and free elections had prime importance in the
inter intervention in the Dominican Republic in April, 1965. The
milita followed a revolution against the existing unconstitutional
force in which had ousted the legally elected president by armed
proportio fore the democratic uprising in 1965 could take on the
tarily, wit ll-fledged civil war, the United States intervened mili-
 objective of protecting the security of American

citizens and, more importantly, of preventing a Communist take-over, because Castro-type elements were alleged to have infiltrated the democratic movement of rebellion. The United States managed to set up an inter-American force in the Dominican Republic, headed by a Brazilian officer. One of the main criticisms of American intervention, in the United States as well as abroad, was that its purpose was to crush democracy in the Dominican Republic out of fear of communism, and that the antidemocratic military junta could count on indefinite American support.

Yet, efforts of the United States and a number of Latin American republics to stabilize the political situation finally succeeded. On June 1, 1966, a free election—watched by observers of the Organization of American States (OAS)—was held, in which a moderately conservative democrat, Joaquin Balaguer, was elected President, and Communist numerical strength was shown up to be very small. The free election in the Dominican Republic confirmed that the purpose of American intervention was not to aid reactionary, militaristic regimes, but to make constitutional government on the basis of free elections a reality, and that communism can more decisively be defeated at the polls rather than at the barricades. Although the outcome of the American intervention in the Dominican Republic was viewed less critically after its purpose was achieved, the troublesome question of American intervention in the internal affairs of other states—without the request by a legitimate government—in order to save democratic processes or, at least, to stave off the danger of a Communist take-over still remained unanswered.

Three Types of Military Intervention

The three major military interventions of the United States since the end of World War II presented three types of problems. American intervention in Korea in 1950 was hardly open to any serious challenge. It was caused by the invasion of South Korea by regular armies of Communist North Korea; the government of South Korea asked for aid, to which the United States quickly responded, and the United Nations authorized and recommended military aid to embattled South Korea.

In South Vietnam, the situation was more complex. There, the Communist attempt to take over the government by civil war also caused the United States to intervene militarily, but the judgment of the American intervention depended on the evaluation of the role of North Vietnam and Communist China in the conflict. Although North Vietnam sent war matériel and regular troops to South Vietnam, and Red China sent war matériel, there was much debate over the question of whether the conflict was primarily an internal civil war, or whether the conflict was largely due to the aid given to the Viet Cong by Communist North Vietnam and Red China. On the first supposition, it was argued by some, the United States had no right to intervene by armed force in an internal conflict of another nation, and could not play the role of "policing the world," even if it were asked by one of the parties in the civil war to intervene militarily. On the second supposition, American intervention could be more properly justified, since its purpose would then be to aid an independent state against armed aggression from the outside.

In the Dominican intervention, an entirely different type of situation developed: there, the United States intervened without being asked by either of the two civil war factions to do so, and the clearly stated objective was to prevent a Communist take-over, even if no intervention from an outside Communist state had to be resisted. Does the American policy of allowing no Communist take-over from within, without any outside aggression or direct aid, apply only to the Caribbean area with its sensitive role in defending American security? Does it apply to all of the Western Hemisphere under a new version of the Monroe Doctrine? Or does it apply to the whole world? These are questions which may come up again in the next decade or two, but so far no firm American doctrine has been developed on these issues.

✻ THE ELEMENT OF UNCERTAINTY IN MAJOR POLICY AREAS

The uncertainty over these crucial policy issues keeps not only other nations—including the Communist states—guessing, but also produces a sense of anxiety in the United States. This came out clearly during the South Vietnam intervention, when more Americans opposed military action than in any previous armed conflict involving the United States. Although such dissenters were in a minority, they were a sizable minority, about one third of those interviewed in public opinion polls.

Effects of Sudden American Leadership

This uncertainty over crucial policy issues stems in part from the fact that the United States has been catapulted into a position of world leadership before going through any lengthy period of apprenticeship, such as was experienced by all other major world powers in past history. The common law method of building up principles by proceeding from case to case over many centuries might have been adequate for domestic disputes between individuals in a simple agrarian society. In American foreign relations today, the absence of clear-cut principles in some major policy areas is a source of weakness, because decisions have often to be made very quickly.

Moreover, American history—until the burdens of leadership fell upon the United States—has been an almost uninterrupted success story, not only in the eyes of Americans, but also of other people. The idea that all problems are soluble, and are quickly soluble, is deeply ingrained in American thought and experience. The motto of the Seabees in World War II: "If it's difficult, we'll do it right away; if it's impossible, it may take us a little time," succinctly reflects the American temper for which nothing is impossible.

Learning to Live with Frustration

This attitude has worked miracles in internal American development, but may be a liability in foreign relations. In foreign affairs, the path of necessity and wisdom may often be to wait patiently, to live with frustration, and not to pursue a course of action based on the slogan of "Let's get it over with." Apart from the Civil War, the American experience has known relatively little of the tragic element of life that older nations take for granted both in their domestic and foreign affairs.

"It's ironical. Our Peace Corps built their brickyard." Drawing by W. Miller; © 1963 The New Yorker Magazine, Inc.

Throughout the whole nineteenth century, for example, Britain and Russia had conflicting interests in Asia, and continuous Russian territorial expansion, bringing Russian power close to the Indian borders, led many to foresee and apprehend a major Russian-British collision as inevitable. Yet Britain adjusted itself to the persistent pressure, and apart from the relatively minor Crimean War of 1854–1856, in which Russia was arrayed against Turkey, France, and Britain, the nineteenth century came to an end without a major Russian-British war. Long schooled in world affairs, the British had learned that some deep-seated international tensions cannot be removed by a single dramatic action, but must be lived with for a long time, until a major turn of events creates a new international environment. At the beginning of the twentieth century, Russia and Britain gradually drew closer as a result of German ambitions to become the dominant land power on the Eurasian continent and to gain naval supremacy on the high seas.

When the cold war started in 1947, all too many Americans were eager to get it over with as soon as possible. One of the causes behind the temporary hysteria of the McCarthy period in the early 1950s was the inability of some Americans to understand and admit that the problem of communism throughout the world was not decided solely in the Department of State, and that China was not lost by President Truman or Secretary of State Dean Acheson, but was won by the Chinese Communists in a long and bloody civil war. The illusion of unlimited American power led many to believe that if things went wrong anywhere in the world as viewed from the vantage-point of American national interests, only treason in high places in Washington could be responsible for such "un-American" behavior of foreign nations.

Similarly, after the foreign aid program had been in operation for a few years, many Americans, including members of Congress, expressed disappointment that progress in underdeveloped countries seemed so slow, and that aid funds were no better than "water down the drain." Since annual per capita income in many underdeveloped countries is between $100–$200 (in India, it is only about $75), it will take a long time at best before their economies approach present Western levels, which are 20 to 30 times higher.

The cold war may go on for generations (still a better prospect than an early decisive hot nuclear war), although the Soviet Union may some day be replaced by Red China as the major protagonist. Or new issues, such as the population explosion, may take the place of the issues of both Russia and China. In 1960, the world's population was 3 billion; by the year 2000, it is expected to double to 6 billion. And most of the increase will occur in the hungry nations of the world.

❧ THE LONG-RANGE CHALLENGES TO AMERICAN FOREIGN POLICY

Gradually, the realization begins to dawn on American policy-makers that the hard and long challenge to American foreign policy is more than this or that country, or this or that ideology. The protracted cold war with hunger and poverty throughout the world is likely to last even longer than the conflict with communism, because communism is only the froth on the surface of much bigger problems. If communism cannot be tackled with some single dramatic action or policy that will assure "total victory" and the "final solution" of the problem, the larger issues on which communism feeds are even less likely of such quick and dramatic resolution.

The Widening Gap Between Rich and Poor Countries

In the world today, there are 27 nations classified as rich, in which the per capita annual income is $750 or over (in the United States it is about $3,000). These 27 nations have 25 percent of the world's population, but 75 percent of its wealth. On the other extreme, there are 38 very poor nations (including India), where annual per capita income is under $100. What is most alarming is that the gap between the rich and the poor countries is persistently widening, not narrowing, because in the poor countries population is increasing at a faster rate than national income, whereas in the rich countries the reverse is true. Thus, in half of the 80 underdeveloped countries of the world, annual per capita incomes are rising by only 1 percent, and by the end of the century, they will amount to about $170, as compared with a projected annual per capita income of $4,500 in the United States.

The Rise of Violence Throughout the World

The widening gap between the wealthy and the poor nations is reflected in the growing incidence of violence throughout the world. In a major address on May 18, 1966, Secretary of Defense Robert S. McNamara cited the following facts and figures on internationally significant outbreaks of violence in the years 1958–1966: the number of such instances of violence was 164, involving 82 different governments. In 15 cases, such violence occurred in military conflicts between two states, yet in no case was there a formal declaration of war. During the period of 1958–1966, internationally significant violence occurred in 87 percent of the very poor nations, in 69

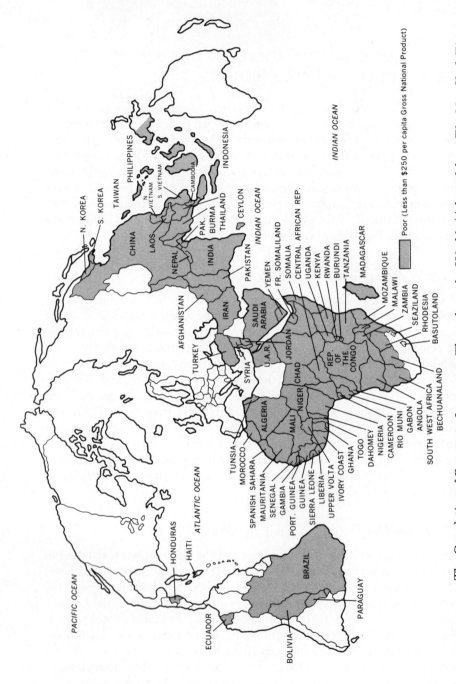

FIGURE 24–5. The Correlation of Poverty to Insurgency Throughout the World. (Adapted from *The New York Times*. © 1964, 65, 66 by The New York Times Company. Reprinted by permission.)

Poor (Less than $250 per capita Gross National Product)

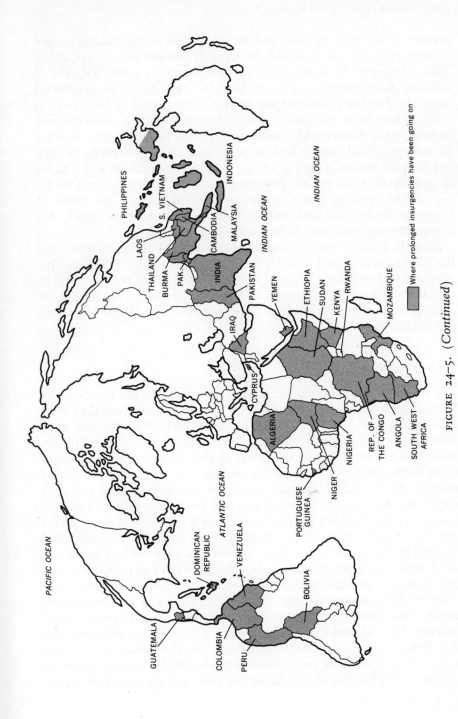

FIGURE 24-5. (Continued)

PACIFIC OCEAN

GUATEMALA
DOMINICAN REPUBLIC
COLOMBIA
VENEZUELA
PERU
BOLIVIA

ATLANTIC OCEAN

PORTUGUESE GUINEA
NIGER
NIGERIA
REP. OF THE CONGO
ANGOLA
SOUTH WEST AFRICA
MOZAMBIQUE
RWANDA
KENYA
SUDAN
ETHIOPIA
YEMEN
IRAQ
CYPRUS
ALGERIA

INDIAN OCEAN

PHILIPPINES
S. VIETNAM
INDONESIA
LAOS
THAILAND
BURMA
CAMBODIA
MALAYSIA
PAK.
INDIA
PAKISTAN

INDIAN OCEAN

Where prolonged insurgencies have been going on

percent of the poor nations, and in 48 percent of the middle-income nations. Throughout that period, the trend of violence was up, not down. Thus, whereas at the beginning of 1958 there were 23 protracted cases of violence, their number rose to 40 by 1966. Also, the total number of outbreaks of violence increased year by year, from 34 cases in 1958 to 58 in 1965. "There is an irrefutable relation between violence and economic backwardness," Secretary McNamara said, and he predicted more violence for the years ahead, mainly because of the widening gap between the rich and the poor nations. (See Figure 24–5.) While communism was a factor in some cases, it was not the dominant factor: in only 38 percent of the 149 internal uprisings were Communists involved. Even if the threat of Communist subversion and revolutionary activities were to vanish, the deeper structural imbalance in the world would still exist.

Since the forces of violence and disorder have been on the increase since the conclusion of World War II, American foreign policy cannot be classified as a striking success, if one of its main objectives has been, and still is, the building of a stable world order, in which each nation can develop its political and economic institutions without the constant threats of internal and external violence.

The Task Ahead

The task confronting the American people is staggering, but the challenge to its understanding and imagination is even more revolutionary than to its material resources. The Marshall Plan after World War II—"the most unsordid act of any nation in history," as Winston Churchill called it— saved Western Europe from the threat of violence and upheaval brought about by the ravages of a devastating conflict. The complexity of a similar program for the underdeveloped nations is infinitely greater, and of a magnitude that has not permeated as yet the minds of the American people and therefore has not produced as yet a new turn in our relations with the world. Whereas the Marshall Plan could be organized and financed by the United States alone, imposing only a temporary burden on the American taxpayer, the task confronting the well-off nations now is one that no nation can singlehandedly meet with any prospect of success.

United States association with the emerging European Economic Community (the Common Market nations of France, West Germany, Italy, Belgium, Holland, and Luxembourg) is the first condition, assuming also that Britain and Canada will before long join this community of free nations. Such a new policy will require a fundamental change of American attitudes, for while the United States has aided and applauded the evolution of the European Economic Community, it has stood aside insofar as a more intimate and formal association is concerned.

Will the United States repeat the errors of Britain on the issue of the Atlantic Community and the Common Market? If Britain had joined the Common Market in its first phase in the early 1950s as a "charter member," it would undoubtedly have been its natural leader from the very outset. By waiting over a decade, and finally applying in 1963, Britain had to experience the humiliation of being turned down because of French opposition.

If the United States associates itself with Western Europe (and Canada) while its strength and vitality are still at their peak, it will be the natural leader of the Atlantic Community, the largest area of freedom in the world, and one that would dynamically expand by the sheer force of its example and accomplishments. If the United States should repeat the error of Britain in the 1950s, and wait too long before it seeks a more permanent association with Western Europe, perhaps when its strength and influence are on the decline, it might experience the same humiliation that was inflicted on Britain in 1963.

However, American leadership in a closer association of the free nations of the Atlantic Community is only the first step. The purpose of close association between the free nations of the Atlantic Community—initially Western Europe, Britain, Canada, and the United States—cannot be to form a "rich men's club" for mutual protection and convenience, but to strengthen the peace and stability of the whole world by helping the poorer nations to develop at the fastest possible rate. In such an association, the United States will have a better chance of inducing other wealthy nations to contribute their share to the common betterment of mankind. There is no reason why the American citizen should have to carry a greater military and financial burden than the citizen of other wealthy nations, whose stake in the maintenance of international peace and stability is just as great as that of the American people.

It is in this long-range area of creative political planning and innovation that United States foreign policy can make its greatest contribution—and perhaps will have to make it—if the nation is to survive in an environment of freedom rather than turn into a garrison state heading toward inevitable conflict and disaster.

Advantages of Totalitarian Foreign Policy

In short-term policy, aggressive totalitarian states—fascism yesterday, communism today—have an advantage that cannot easily be met. In this short-term range, it is true that the United States is often put into a position of reacting to what the Soviet Union or Red China are doing, starting a civil war here, subverting a government there, and always keeping the United States and its allies guessing where the next strike will occur. Democratic nations cannot imitate aggressive totalitarian states in this short-term policy range; democracies are slow enough in resisting aggression, and cannot—if they are to remain true to their character and goals—act aggressively in order to keep the tactical advantage of keeping the other side guessing.

Democratic Opportunities in Long-term Innovation

But in the area of long-range political planning, the democracies have the advantage if they are willing to use it. Here, the democracies need not react, but can initiate and innovate. The creation of the Common Market was the greatest single blow at world communism, although not a shot was fired, for it was inspired by a great idea quite independently of the existence of communism.

The founders of this nation created a single political community out of 13 sovereign states, not in order to spite King George, but because it seemed to them a great idea to expand opportunity on this Continent and to attract people from all over the world to share in the opportunities of a free society. Even if communism were to disappear from the face of the earth tomorrow, the free nations of Western Europe and North America will some day—perhaps in the not too distant future—associate themselves in a new community of freedom, in which the United States can make a contribution worthy of its ideals and its experience.

Before his death in 1959, Secretary of State John Foster Dulles proposed that NATO be transformed from a purely military organization into a broader political, economic, and cultural community of nations, since the military link alone could not outlast the military threat causing the creation of the alliance in the first place. Secretary Dulles' thinking has been confirmed by events. As the threat of Soviet military aggression against Western Europe receded in recent years, NATO military headquarters were ordered to leave France and had to be moved to Belgium in 1966. Not having progressed beyond the purely military concept toward a more closely knit community in political and economic affairs, NATO has in the end even lost much of its military usefulness, because long-term military commitments cannot be separated from nonmilitary ties.

In our age of over-kill, the struggle between the Communist and non-Communist states, particularly in influencing the direction of events in the "Third World," will not be determined by the side that has more thermo-

November 23, 1964
"Why do you Americans stay where you're not wanted?" Drawing by Bill
Mauldin. From *I've Decided I Want My Seat Back* by Bill Mauldin.
Copyright 1962, 1963, 1964 by Bill Mauldin. Reprinted by
permission of the author and Harper & Row, Publishers.

nuclear weapons, because both sides already have hundreds of times more
than they need to destroy the whole world. In the current "balance of
terror," that idea will prevail which shows itself more creative of life,
human dignity, and freedom. No single nation is strong enough to impose
its will on the rest of the world. Nations gain in strength and in friends
and allies in proportion to their ability to pursue foreign policies that are
also in the interest of other nations.

The Paradox of Power and Influence

Before the United States attained the status of a superpower after World
War II, its influence in the world was much greater than its "raw power."
During the nineteenth century, for example, the United States got along
without Information Agencies in foreign countries, explaining and justifying American policies. The tens of millions of immigrants who came here
from all over the world did not need any official American propaganda to
explain the United States to them. During the eighteenth and nineteenth

centuries, liberals everywhere looked upon the United States as the "conscience of democracy," the haven of the lowly and oppressed from all four corners of the globe.

Paradoxically, as American power reached its zenith after World War II, as it became the shield that protects the non-Communist nations from Communist aggression, it lost much of its previous influence, for it ceased to be regarded as the conscience of democracy. For the first time in American history the necessity arose to explain the United States and its foreign policies to other nations. If the contemporary struggle in the world will be decided in the minds of men rather than on the battlefields, the performance of American ideas and institutions at home will be closely watched by the rest of the world.

In 1776, the worldwide impact of the American call for freedom, of defiance of privilege and authority, was enhanced by America's economic and political weakness. Having attained vast material power, unprecedented in history, can the United States survive in a dangerous world, live up to its original ideals, and strengthen and expand freedom and welfare throughout the world? Or will it travel the road of other great powers in history that went down, failing to see that power can endure only if it is justified, not by those who possess it, but by those who do not?

THE DECLARATION OF INDEPENDENCE, 1776

WHEN IN THE COURSE of human events, it becomes necessary for one people to dissolve the political bands which have connected them with another, and to assume among the Powers of the earth, the separate and equal station to which the Laws of Nature and of Nature's God entitle them, a decent respect to the opinions of mankind requires that they should declare the causes which impel them to the separation.

We hold these truths to be self-evident, that all men are created equal, that they are endowed by their Creator with certain unalienable Rights, that among these are Life, Liberty and the pursuit of Happiness. That to secure these rights, Governments are instituted among Men, deriving their just powers from the consent of the governed, That whenever any Form of Government becomes destructive of these ends, it is the Right of the People to alter or to abolish it, and to institute new Government, laying its foundation on such principles and organizing its powers in such form, as to them shall seem most likely to effect their Safety and Happiness. Prudence, indeed, will dictate that Governments long established should not be changed for light and transient causes; and accordingly all experience hath shown, that mankind are more disposed to suffer, while evils are sufferable, than to right themselves by abolishing the forms to which they are accustomed. But when a long train of abuses and usurpations, pursuing invariably the same Object evinces a design to reduce them under absolute Despotism, it is their right, it is their duty, to throw off such Government, and to provide new Guards for their future security.—Such has been the patient sufferance of these Colonies; and such is now the necessity which constrains them to alter their former Systems of Government. The history of the present King of Great Britain is a history of repeated injuries and usurpations, all having in direct object the establishment of an absolute Tyranny over these States. To prove this, let Facts be submitted to a candid world.

He has refused his Assent to Laws, the most wholesome and necessary for the public good.

He has forbidden his Governors to pass Laws of immediate and pressing importance, unless suspended in their operation till his Assent should be obtained; and when so suspended, he has utterly neglected to attend to them.

He has refused to pass other Laws for the accommodation of large districts of people, unless those people would relinquish the right of Representation in the Legislature, a right inestimable to them and formidable to tyrants only.

He has called together legislative bodies at places unusual, uncomfortable, and distant from the depository of their Public Records, for the sole purpose of fatiguing them into compliance with his measures.

He has dissolved Representative Houses repeatedly, for opposing with manly firmness his invasions on the rights of the people.

He has refused for a long time, after such dissolutions, to cause others to be elected; whereby the Legislative Powers, incapable of Annihilation, have returned to the People at large for their exercise; the State remaining in the mean time exposed to all the dangers of invasion from without, and convulsions within.

He has endeavoured to prevent the population of these States; for that purpose obstructing the Laws of Naturalization of Foreigners; refusing to pass others to encourage their migration hither, and raising the conditions of new Appropriations of Lands.

He has obstructed the Administration of Justice, by refusing his Assent to Laws for establishing Judiciary Powers.

He has made Judges dependent on his Will alone, for the tenure of their offices, and the amount and payment of their salaries.

He has erected a multitude of New Offices, and sent hither swarms of Officers to harass our People, and eat out their substance.

He has kept among us, in times of peace, Standing Armies without the Consent of our legislature.

He has affected to render the Military independent of and superior to the Civil Power.

He has combined with others to subject us to a jurisdiction foreign to our constitution, and unacknowledged by our laws giving his Assent to their acts of pretended legislation:

For quartering large bodies of armed troops among us:

For protecting them, by a mock Trial, from Punishment for any Murders which they should commit on the Inhabitants of these States:

For cutting off our Trade with all parts of the world:

For imposing taxes on us without our Consent:

For depriving us in many cases, of the benefits of Trial by Jury:

For transporting us beyond Seas to be tried for pretended offences:

For abolishing the free System of English Laws in a neighboring Province, establishing therein an Arbitrary government, and enlarging its Boundaries so as to render it at once an example and fit instrument for introducing the same absolute rule into these Colonies:

For taking away our Charters, abolishing our most valuable Laws, and altering fundamentally the Forms of our Governments:

For suspending our own Legislature, and declaring themselves invested with Power to legislate for us in all cases whatsoever.

He has abdicated Government here, by declaring us out of his Protection and waging War against us.

He has plundered our seas, ravaged our Coasts, burnt our towns, and destroyed the lives of our people.

He is at this time transporting large armies of foreign mercenaries to compleat the works of death, desolation and tyranny, already begun with circumstances of Cruelty & perfidy scarcely paralleled in the most barbarous ages, and totally unworthy the Head of a civilized nation.

He has constrained our fellow Citizens taken Captive on the high Seas to bear Arms against their Country, to become the executioners of their friends and Brethren, or to fall themselves by their Hands.

He has excited domestic insurrections amongst us, and has endeavoured to bring on the inhabitants of our frontiers, the merciless Indian Savages, whose known rule of warfare, is an undistinguished destruction of all ages, sexes and conditions.

In every stage of these Oppressions We have Petitioned for Redress in the most humble terms: Our repeated Petitions have been answered only by repeated injury. A Prince, whose character is thus marked by every act which may define a Tyrant, is unfit to be the ruler of a free People.

Nor have We been wanting in attention to our British brethren. We have warned them from time to time of attempts by their legislature to extend an unwarrantable jurisdiction over us. We have reminded them of the circumstances of our emigration and settlement here. We have appealed to their native justice and magnanimity, and we have conjured them by the ties of our common kindred to disavow these usurpations, which, would inevitably interrupt our connections and correspondence. They too have been deaf to the voice of justice and of consanguinity. We must, therefore, acquiesce in the necessity, which denounces our Separation, and hold them, as we hold the rest of mankind, Enemies in War, in Peace, Friends.

We, therefore, the Representatives of the united States of America, in General Congress, Assembled, appealing to the Supreme Judge of the world for the rectitude of our intentions, do, in the Name, and by Authority of the good People of these Colonies, solemnly publish and declare, That these United Colonies are, and of Right ought to be Free and Independent States; that they are Absolved from all allegiance to the British Crown, and that all political connection between them and the State of Great Britain, is and ought to be totally dissolved; and that as Free and Independent States, they have full Power to levy War, conclude Peace, contract Alliances, establish Commerce, and to do all other Acts and Things which Independent States may of right do. And for the support of this Declaration, with a firm reliance on the Protection of Divine Providence, we mutually pledge to each other our Lives, our Fortunes and our sacred Honor.

※※

THE CONSTITUTION OF THE UNITED STATES

[*Preamble*]

WE THE PEOPLE of the United States, in Order to form a more perfect Union, establish Justice, insure domestic Tranquility, provide for the common defence, promote the general Welfare, and secure the Blessings of Liberty to ourselves and our Posterity, do ordain and establish this Constitution for the United States of America.

ARTICLE 1

Section 1

[*Legislative Powers*]

All legislative Powers herein granted shall be vested in a Congress of the United States, which shall consist of a Senate and a House of Representatives.

Section 2

[*House of Representatives, How Constituted, Power of Impeachment*]

The House of Representatives shall be composed of Members chosen every second Year by the People of the several States, and the Electors in each State shall have [the] Qualifications requisite for Electors of the most numerous Branch of the State Legislature.

No Person shall be a Representative who shall not have attained to the Age of twenty five Years, and been seven Years a Citizen of the United

States, and who shall not when elected, be an Inhabitant of that State in which he shall be chosen.

Representatives and direct Taxes shall be apportioned among the several States which may be included within this Union, according to their respective Numbers, which shall be determined by adding to the whole Number of free Persons, including those bound to Service for a Term of Years, and excluding Indians not taxed, three fifths of all other Persons. The actual Enumeration shall be made within three Years after the first Meeting of the Congress of the United States, and within every subsequent Term of ten Years, in such Manner as they shall by Law direct. The Number of Representatives shall not exceed one for every thirty Thousand, but each State shall have at Least one Representative; and until such enumeration shall be made, the State of New Hampshire shall be entitled to chuse three, Massachusetts eight, Rhode-Island and Providence Plantations one, Connecticut five, New York six, New Jersey four, Pennsylvania eight, Delaware one, Maryland six, Virginia ten, North Carolina five, South Carolina five, and Georgia three.

When vacancies happen in the Representation from any State, the Executive Authority thereof shall issue Writs of Election to fill such Vacancies.

The House of Representatives shall chuse their Speaker and other Officers; and shall have the sole Power of Impeachment.

Section 3

[The Senate, How Constituted, Impeachment Trials]

The Senate of the United States shall be composed of Two Senators from each State, chosen by the Legislature thereof, for six Years; and each Senator shall have one Vote.

Immediately after they shall be assembled in Consequence of the first Election, they shall be divided as equally as may be into three Classes. The Seats of the Senators of the first Class shall be vacated at the Expiration of the second Year, of the second Class at the Expiration of the fourth Year, and of the third Class at the Expiration of the sixth Year, so that one third may be chosen every second Year; and if Vacancies happen by Resignation, or otherwise, during the Recess of the Legislature of any State, the Executive thereof may make temporary Appointments until the next Meeting of the Legislature, which shall then fill such Vacancies.

No Person shall be a Senator who shall not have attained to the Age of thirty Years, and been nine Years a Citizen of the United States, and who shall not, when elected, be an Inhabitant of that State for which he shall be chosen.

The Vice President of the United States shall be President of the Senate, but shall have no Vote, unless they be equally divided.

The Senate shall chuse their other Officers, and also a President pro tempore, in the Absence of the Vice President, or when he shall exercise the Office of President of the United States.

The Senate shall have the sole power to try all Impeachments. When sitting for that Purpose, they shall be on Oath or Affirmation. When the President of the United States [is tried] the Chief Justice shall preside: And no Person shall be convicted without the Concurrence of two thirds of the Members present.

Judgment in Cases of Impeachment shall not extend further than to removal from Office, and disqualification to hold and enjoy any Office of honor, Trust or Profit under the United States: but the Party convicted shall nevertheless be liable and subject to Indictment, Trial, Judgment and Punishment, according to Law.

Section 4

[Election of Senators and Representatives]

The Times, Places and Manner of holding Elections for Senators and Representatives, shall be prescribed in each State by the Legislature thereof; but the Congress may at any time by Law make or alter such Regulations, except as to the Places of chusing Senators.

The Congress shall assemble at least once in every Year, and such Meeting shall be on the first Monday in December, unless they shall by Law appoint a different Day.

Section 5

[Quorum, Journals, Meetings, Adjournments]

Each House shall be the Judge of the Elections, Returns and Qualifications of its own Members, and a Majority of each shall constitute a Quorum to do Business; but a smaller Number may adjourn from day to day, and may be authorized to compel the Attendance of absent Members, in such Manner, and under such Penalties as each House may provide.

Each House may determine the Rules of its Proceedings, punish its Members for disorderly Behaviour, and, with the Concurrence of two thirds, expel a Member.

Each House shall keep a Journal of its Proceedings, and from time to time publish the same, excepting such Parts as may in their Judgment require Secrecy; and the Yeas and Nays of the Members of either House on any question shall, at the Desire of one fifth of those Present, be entered on the Journal.

Neither House, during the Session of Congress, shall, without the Consent of the other, adjourn for more than three days, nor to any other Place than that in which the two Houses shall be sitting.

Section 6

[Compensation, Privileges, Disabilities]

The Senators and Representatives shall receive a Compensation for their Services, to be ascertained by Law, and paid out of the Treasury of the United States. They shall in all Cases, except Treason, Felony and Breach of the Peace, be privileged from Arrest during their Attendance at the Session of their respective Houses, and in going to and returning from the same; and for any Speech or Debate in either House, they shall not be questioned in any other Place.

No Senator or Representative shall, during the Time for which he was elected, be appointed to any civil Office under the Authority of the United States, which shall have been created, or the Emoluments whereof shall have been encreased during such time; and no Person holding any Office under the United States, shall be a Member of either House during his Continuance in Office.

Section 7

[Procedure in Passing Bills and Resolutions]

All Bills for raising Revenue shall originate in the House of Representatives; but the Senate may propose or concur with Amendments as on other Bills.

Every Bill which shall have passed the House of Representatives and the Senate, shall, before it becomes a Law, be presented to the President of the United States; if he approve he shall sign it, but if not he shall return it, with his Objections to that House in which it shall have originated, who shall enter the Objections at large on their Journal, and proceed to reconsider it. If after such Reconsideration two thirds of that House shall agree to pass the Bill, it shall be sent, together with the Objections, to the other House, by which it shall likewise be reconsidered, and if approved by two thirds of that House, it shall become a Law. But in all such Cases the Votes of both Houses shall be determined by yeas and Nays, and the Names of the Persons voting for and against the Bill shall be entered on the Journal of each House respectively. If any Bill shall not be returned by the President within ten Days (Sundays excepted) after it shall have been presented to him, the Same shall be a Law, in like Manner as if he had signed it, unless the Congress by their Adjournment prevent its Return, in which Case it shall not be a Law.

Every Order, Resolution, or Vote to which the Concurrence of the Senate and House of Representatives may be necessary (except on a question of Adjournment) shall be presented to the President of the United States; and before the Same shall take Effect, shall be approved by him, or being disapproved by him, shall be repassed by two thirds of the Senate and House of Representatives, according to the Rules and Limitations prescribed in the Case of a Bill.

Section 8

[Powers of Congress]

The Congress shall have the Power To lay and collect Taxes, Duties, Imposts and Excises, to pay the Debts and provide for the common Defence and general Welfare of the United States; but all Duties, Imposts and Excises shall be uniform throughout the United States.

To borrow Money on the credit of the United States;

To regulate Commerce with foreign Nations and among the several States, and with the Indian Tribes;

To establish an uniform Rule of Naturalization, and uniform Laws on the subject of Bankruptcies throughout the United States;

To Coin Money, regulate the Value thereof, and of foreign Coin, and fix the Standard of Weights and Measures;

To provide for the Punishment of counterfeiting the Securities and current Coin of the United States;

To establish Post Offices and post Roads;

To promote the Progress of Science and useful Arts, by securing for limited Times to Authors and Inventors the exclusive Right to their respective Writings and Discoveries;

To constitute Tribunals inferior to the supreme Court;

To define and punish Piracies and Felonies committed on the high Seas, and Offences against the Law of Nations;

To declare War, grant Letters of Marque and Reprisal, and make Rules concerning Captures on Land and Water;

To raise and support Armies, but no Appropriation of Money to that Use shall be for a longer Term than two Years;

To provide and maintain a Navy;

To make Rules for Government and Regulation of the land and naval Forces;

To provide for calling forth the Militia to execute the Laws of the Union, suppress Insurrections and repel Invasions;

To provide for organizing, arming, and disciplining, the Militia, and for governing such Part of them as may be employed in the Service of the

United States, reserving to the States respectively, the Appointment of the Officers, and the Authority of training the Militia according to the discipline prescribed by Congress;

To exercise exclusive Legislation in all Cases whatsoever, over such District (not exceeding ten Miles square) as may, by Cession of particular States, and the Acceptance of Congress, become the Seat of the Government of the United States, and to exercise like Authority over all Places purchased by the Consent of the Legislature of the State in which the Same shall be, for the Erection of Forts, Magazines, Arsenals, dockYards, and other needful Buildings;—And

To make all Laws which shall be necessary and proper for carrying into Execution the foregoing Powers, and all other Powers vested by this Constitution in the Government of the United States, or in any Department or Officer thereof.

Section 9

[Limitation upon Powers of Congress]

The Migration or Importation of such Persons as any of the States now existing shall think proper to admit, shall not be prohibited by the Congress prior to the Year one thousand eight hundred and eight, but a Tax or duty may be imposed on such Importation, not exceeding ten dollars for each Person.

The Privilege of the Writ of Habeas Corpus shall not be suspended, unless when in Cases of Rebellion or Invasion the public Safety may require it.

No Bill of Attainder or ex post facto Law shall be passed.

No Capitation, or other direct, Tax shall be laid, unless in Proportion to the Census or Enumeration herein before directed to be taken.

No Tax or Duty shall be laid on Articles, exported from any State.

No Preference shall be given by any Regulation of Commerce or Revenue to the Ports of State over those of another; nor shall Vessels bound to, or from, one State, be obliged to enter, clear, or pay Duties in another.

No Money shall be drawn from the Treasury, but in Consequence of Appropriations made by Law; and a regular Statement and Account of the Receipts and Expenditures of all public Money shall be published from time to time.

No title of Nobility shall be granted by the United States: And no Person holding any Office of Profit or Trust under them, shall, without the Consent of the Congress, accept of any present, Emolument, Office, or Title, of any kind whatever, from any King, Prince, or foreign State.

Section 10

[Restrictions upon Powers of States]

No State shall enter into any Treaty, Alliance, or Confederation; grant Letters of Marque and Reprisal; coin Money; emit Bills of Credit; make any Thing but gold and silver Coin a Tender in Payment of Debts; pass any Bill of Attainder, ex post facto Law, or Law impairing the Obligation of Contracts, or grant any Title of Nobility.

No State shall, without the Consent of [the] Congress, lay any Imposts or Duties on Imports or Exports, except what may be absolutely necessary for executing its inspection Laws: and the net Produce of all Duties and Imposts, laid by any State on Imports or Exports, shall be for the Use of the Treasury of the United States; and all such Laws shall be subject to the Revision and Controul of [the] Congress.

No State shall, without the Consent of Congress, lay any Duty of Tonnage, keep Troops, or Ships of War in time of Peace, enter into any Agreement or Compact with another State, or with a foreign Power, or engage in War, unless actually invaded, or in such imminent Danger as will not admit of delay.

ARTICLE 2

Section 1

[Executive Power, Election, Qualifications of the President]

The executive Power shall be vested in a President of the United States of America. He shall hold his Office during the Term of four Years, and, together with the Vice President, chosen for the same Term, be elected as follows.

Each State shall appoint, in such Manner as the Legislature thereof may direct, a Number of Electors, equal to the whole Number of Senators and Representatives to which the State may be entitled in the Congress: but no Senator or Representative, or Person holding an Office of Trust or Profit under the United States, shall be appointed an Elector.

The Electors shall meet in their respective States, and vote by Ballot for two Persons, of whom one at least shall not be an Inhabitant of the same State with themselves. And they shall make a List of all the Persons voted for, and of the Number of Votes for each; which List they shall sign and certify, and transmit sealed to the Seat of the Government of the United States, directed to the President of the Senate. The President of the Senate shall, in the Presence of the Senate and House of Representatives, open all the Certificates, and the Votes shall then be counted. The Person having the greatest Number of Votes shall be the President, if such Number be a Majority of the whole Number of Electors appointed; and if there be more than one who have such Majority, and have an equal Number of Votes, then the House of Representatives shall immediately chuse by Ballot one of them for President; and if no Person have a Majority, then from the five highest in the List the said House shall in like Manner chuse the President. But in chusing the President, the Votes shall be taken by States, the Representation from each State having one Vote; A quorum for this purpose shall consist of a Member or Members from two thirds of the States, and a Majority of all the States shall be necessary to a Choice. In every Case, after the Choice of the President, the Person having the greatest Number of Votes of the Electors shall be the Vice President. But if there should remain two or more who have equal Votes, the Senate shall chuse from them by Ballot the Vice President.

The Congress may determine the Time of chusing the Electors, and the Day on which they shall give their Votes; which Day shall be the same throughout the United States.

No person except a natural born Citizen, or a Citizen of the United States, at the time of the Adoption of this Constitution, shall be eligible to the Office of President; neither shall any Person be eligible to that Office who shall not have attained to the Age of thirty five Years, and been fourteen Years a Resident within the United States.

In Case of the Removal of the President from Office, or of his Death, Resignation, or Inability to discharge the Powers and Duties of the said Office, the Same shall devolve on the Vice President, and the Congress may by Law provide for the Case of Removal, Death, Resignation or Inability, both of the President and Vice President, declaring what Officer shall then act as President, and such Officer shall act accordingly, until the Disability be removed, or a President shall be elected.

The President shall, at stated Times, receive for his Services, a Compensation, which shall neither be encreased nor diminished during the Period for which he shall have been elected, and he shall not receive within that Period any other Emolument from the United States, or any of them.

Before he entered on the Execution of his Office, he shall take the following Oath or Affirmation:—"I do solemnly swear (or affirm) that I will faithfully execute the Office of the President of the United States, and will to the best of my Ability, preserve, protect and defend the Constitution of the United States."

Section 2

[Powers of the President]

The President shall be Commander in Chief of the Army and Navy of the United States, and the Militia of the several States, when called into the actual Service of the United States; he may require the Opinion, in writing, of the principal Officer in each of the executive Departments, upon any subject relating to the Duties of their respective Offices, and he shall have Power to grant Reprieves and Pardons for Offences against the United States, except in Cases of Impeachment.

He shall have Power, by and with the Advice and Consent of the Senate, to make Treaties, provided two thirds of the Senators present concur; and he shall nominate, and by and with the Advice and Consent of the Senate, shall appoint Ambassadors, other public Ministers and Consuls, Judges of the supreme Court, and all other Officers of the United States, whose Appointments are not herein otherwise provided for, and which shall be established by Law: but the Congress may by Law vest the Appointment of such inferior Officers, as they think proper in the President alone, in the Courts of Law, or in the Heads of Departments.

The President shall have Power to fill up all Vacancies that may happen during the Recess of the Senate, by granting Commissions which shall expire at the End of their next Session.

Section 3

[Powers and Duties of the President]

He shall from time to time give to the Congress Information of the State of the Union, and recommend to their Consideration such Measures as he shall judge necessary and expedient; he may, on extraordinary Occasions, convene both Houses, or either of them, and in Case of Disagreement between them, with Respect to the Time of Adjournment, he may adjourn them to such Time as he shall think proper; he shall receive Ambassadors and other public Ministers; he shall take Care that the Laws be faithfully executed, and shall commission all the Officers of the United States.

Section 4

[Impeachment]

The President, Vice President and all civil Officers of the United States, shall be removed from Office on Impeachment for, and Conviction of, Treason, Bribery, or other high Crimes and Misdemeanors.

ARTICLE 3

Section 1

[*Judicial Power, Tenure of Office*]

The judicial Power of the United States, shall be vested in one supreme Court, and in such inferior Courts as the Congress may from time to time ordain and establish. The judges, both of the supreme and inferior Courts, shall hold their Offices during good Behavior, and shall, at stated Times, receive for their Services, a Compensation, which shall not be diminished during their Continuance in Office.

Section 2

[*Jurisdiction*]

The judicial Power shall extend to all Cases, in Law and Equity, arising under this Constitution, the Laws of the United States, and Treaties made, or which shall be made, under their Authority;—to all Cases affecting Ambassadors, other public Ministers and Consuls;—to all Cases of admiralty and maritime Jurisdiction;—to Controversies to which the United States shall be a Party;—to Controversies between two or more States;—between a State and Citizens of another State;—between Citizens of different States;—between Citizens of the same State claiming Lands under Grants of different States, and between a State, or the Citizens thereof, and foreign States, Citizens or Subjects.

In all Cases affecting Ambassadors, other public Ministers and Consuls, and those in which a State shall be Party, the supreme Court shall have original Jurisdiction. In all the other Cases before mentioned, the supreme Court shall have appellate Jurisdiction, both as to Law and Fact, with such Exceptions, and under such Regulations as the Congress shall make.

The Trial of all Crimes, except in Cases of Impeachment, shall be by Jury; and such Trial shall be held in the State where the said Crimes shall have been committed; but when not committed within any State, the Trial shall be at such Place or Places as the Congress may by Law have directed.

Section 3

[*Treason, Proof and Punishment*]

Treason against the United States, shall consist only in levying War against them, or in adhering to their Enemies; giving them Aid and Comfort. No Person shall be convicted of Treason unless on the Testimony of two Witnesses to the same overt Act, or on Confession in open Court.

The Congress shall have Power to declare the Punishment of Treason, but no Attainder of Treason shall work Corruption of Blood, or Forfeiture except during the Life of the Person attainted.

ARTICLE 4

Section 1

[Faith and Credit Among States]

Full Faith and Credit shall be given in each State to the public Acts, Records, and judicial Proceedings of every other State. And the Congress may by general Laws prescribe the Manner in which such Acts, Records and Proceedings shall be proved, and the Effect thereof.

Section 2

[Privileges and Immunities, Fugitives]

The citizens of each State shall be entitled to all Privileges and Immunities of Citizens in the several States.

A Person charged in any State with Treason, Felony, or other Crime, who shall flee from Justice, and be found in another State, shall on Demand of the executive Authority of the State from which he fled, be delivered up, to be removed to the State having Jurisidiction of the Crime.

No person held to Service or Labour in one State, under the Laws thereof, escaping into another, shall, in Consequence of any Law or Regulation therein, be discharged from such Service or Labour, but shall be delivered up on Claim of the Party to whom such Service or Labour may be due.

Section 3

[Admission of New States]

New States may be admitted by the Congress into this Union; but no new State shall be formed or erected within the Jurisdiction of any other State; nor any State be formed by the Junction of two or more States, or Parts of States, without the Consent of the Legislatures of the States concerned as well as of the Congress.

The Congress shall have Power to dispose of and make all needful Rules and Regulations respecting the Territory or other Property belonging to the United States; and nothing in this Constitution shall be so construed as to Prejudice any Claims of the United States, or of any particular State.

Section 4

[Guarantee of Republican Government]

The United States shall guarantee to every State in this Union a Republican Form of Government, and shall protect each of them against Invasion; and on Application of the Legislature, or of the Executive (when the Legislature cannot be convened) against domestic Violence.

ARTICLE 5

[Amendment of the Constitution]

The Congress, whenever two thirds of both Houses shall deem it necessary, shall propose Amendments to this Constitution, or, on the Application of the Legislatures of two thirds of the several States, shall call a Convention for proposing Amendments, which, in either Case, shall be valid to all Intents and Purposes, as Part of this Constitution, when ratified by the Legislatures of three fourths of the several States, or by Conventions in three fourths thereof, as the one or the other Mode of Ratification may be proposed by the Congress; Provided that no Amendment which may be made prior to the Year One thousand eight hundred and eight shall in any Manner affect the first and fourth Clauses in the Ninth Section of the first Article, and that no State, without its Consent, shall be deprived of its equal Suffrage in the Senate.

ARTICLE 6

[Debts, Supremacy, Oath]

All Debts contracted and Engagement entered into, before the Adoption of this Constitution, shall be as valid against the United States under this Constitution, as under the Confederation.

This Constitution, and the Laws of the United States which shall be made in Pursuance thereof; and all Treaties made, or which shall be made, under the Authority of the United States, shall be the supreme Law of the Land; and the Judges in every State be bound thereby, any Thing in the Constitution or Laws of any State to the Contrary notwithstanding.

The Senators and Representatives before mentioned, and the Members of the several State Legislatures, and all executive and judicial Officers, both of the United States and of the several States, shall be bound by Oath or Affirmation, to support this Constitution; but no religious Test shall ever be required as a Qualification to any Office or public Trust under the United States.

ARTICLE 7

[Ratification and Establishment]

The Ratification of the Conventions of nine States, shall be sufficient for the Establishment of this Constitution between the States so ratifying the Same.

done in Convention by the Unanimous Consent of the States present the Seventeenth Day of September in the Year of our Lord one thousand seven hundred and Eighty seven and of the Independence of the United States of America the Twelfth In witness whereof We have hereunto subscribed our Names.

New Hampshire	JOHN LANGDON NICHOLAS GILMAN
Massachusetts	NATHANIEL GORHAM RUFUS KING
Connecticut	WM SAML JOHNSON ROGER SHERMAN
New York	ALEXANDER HAMILTON
New Jersey	WIL: LIVINGSTON DAVID BREARLY WM PATERSON JONA: DAYTON
Pennsylvania	B. FRANKLIN THOMAS MIFFLIN ROBT MORRIS GEO. CLYMER THOS. FITZSIMONS JARED INGERSOLL JAMES WILSON GOUV MORRIS
Delaware	GEO. READ GUNNING BEDFORD jun JOHN DICKINSON RICHARD BASSETT JACO: BROOM

Maryland	{ JAMES McHENRY DAN OF ST THOS. JENIFER DANL CARROLL
Virginia	{ JOHN BLAIR— JAMES MADISON JR.
North Carolina	{ WM BLOUNT RICHD DOBBS SPAIGHT. HU WILLIAMSON
South Carolina	{ J. RUTLEDGE CHARLES COTESWORTH PINCKNEY CHARLES PINCKNEY PIERCE BUTLER
Georgia	{ WILLIAM FEW ABR BALDWIN

AMENDMENTS TO THE CONSTITUTION

[The first ten amendments were proposed by Congress on September 25, 1789; ratified and adoption certified on December 15, 1791.]

AMENDMENT I

[Freedom of Religion, of Speech, and of the Press]
Congress shall make no law respecting an establishment of religion, or prohibiting the free exercise thereof; or abridging the freedom of speech, or of the press; or the right of the people peaceably to assemble, and to petition the Government for a redress of grievances.

AMENDMENT II

[Right to Keep and Bear Arms]
A well regulated Militia being necessary to the security of a free State, the right of the people to keep and bear Arms, shall not be infringed.

AMENDMENT III

[Quartering of Soldiers]
No Soldier shall, in time of peace be quartered in any house, without the consent of the Owner, nor in time of war, but in a manner to be prescribed by law.

AMENDMENT IV

[Security from Unwarrantable Search and Seizure]
The right of the people to be secure in their persons, houses, papers, and effects, against unreasonable searches and seizures, shall not be violated, and no Warrants shall issue, but upon probable cause, supported by Oath or affirmation, and particularly describing the place to be searched, and the persons or things to be seized.

AMENDMENT V

[Rights of Accused in Criminal Proceedings]
No person shall be held to answer for a capital, or otherwise infamous crime, unless on a presentment or indictment of a Grand Jury, except in cases arising in the land or naval forces, or in the Militia, when in actual service in time of War or public danger; nor shall any person be subjected for the same offense to be twice put in jeopardy of life or limb; nor shall be compelled in any criminal case to be a witness against himself, nor be deprived of life, liberty, or property, without due process of law; nor shall private property be taken for public use, without just compensation.

AMENDMENT VI

[Right to Speedy Trial, Witnesses, etc.]
In all criminal prosecutions, the accused shall enjoy the right to a speedy and public trial, by an impartial jury of the State and district wherein the crime shall have been committed, which district shall have been previously ascertained by law, and to be informed of the nature and cause of the accusation; to be confronted with the witnesses against him; to have compulsory process for obtaining witnesses in his favor, and to have the Assistance of Counsel for his defence.

AMENDMENT VII

[Trial by Jury in Civil Cases]
In Suits at common law, where the value in controversy shall exceed twenty dollars, the right of trial by jury shall be preserved, and no fact tried by a jury, shall be otherwise reexamined in any Court of the United States, then according to the rules of the common law.

AMENDMENT VIII

[Bails, Fines, Punishments]
Excessive bail shall not be required, nor excessive fines imposed, nor cruel and unusual punishments inflicted.

AMENDMENT IX

[Reservation of Rights of the People]
The enumeration in the Constitution, of certain rights, shall not be construed to deny or disparage others retained by the people.

AMENDMENT X

[Powers Reserved to States or People]
The powers not delegated to the United States by the Constitution, nor prohibited by it to the States, are reserved to the States respectively, or to the people.

AMENDMENT XI

[Proposed by Congress on March 4, 1794; declared ratified on January 8, 1798.]

[Restriction of Judicial Power]
The Judicial power of the United States shall not be construed to extend to any suit in law or equity, commenced or prosecuted against one of the United States by Citizens of another State, or by Citizens or Subjects of any Foreign State.

AMENDMENT XII

[Proposed by Congress on December 9, 1803; declared ratified on September 25, 1804.]

[Election of President and Vice-President]
The Electors shall meet in their respective states, and vote by ballot for President and Vice-President, one of whom, at least, shall not be an inhabitant of the same state with themselves; they shall name in their ballots the person voted for as President, and in distinct ballots the person voted for as Vice-President and they shall make distinct lists of all persons voted for as President, and of all persons voted for as Vice-President, and of the number of votes for each, which lists they shall sign and certify, and transmit sealed to the seat of the government of the United States,

directed to the President of the Senate;—The President of the Senate shall, in the presence of the Senate and House of Representatives, open all the certificates and the votes shall then be counted;—The person having the greatest number of votes for President, shall be the President, if such number be a majority of the whole number of Electors appointed; and if no person have such majority, then from the persons having the highest numbers not exceeding three on the list of those voted for as President, the House of Representatives shall choose immediately, by ballot, the President. But in choosing the President, the votes shall be taken by states, the representation from each state having one vote; a quorum for this purpose shall consist of a member or members from two-thirds of the states, and a majority of all the states shall be necessary to a choice. And if the House of Representatives shall not choose a President whenever the right of choice shall devolve upon them, before the fourth day of March next following, then the Vice-President shall act as President, as in the case of the death or other constitutional disability of the President.—The person having the greatest number of votes as Vice-President, shall be the Vice-President, if such number be a majority of the whole number of Electors appointed, and if no person have a majority, then from the two highest numbers on the list, the Senate shall choose the Vice-President; a quorum for the purpose shall consist of two-thirds of the whole number of Senators, and a majority of the whole number shall be necessary to a choice. But no person constitutionally ineligible to the office of President shall be eligible to that of Vice-President of the United States.

AMENDMENT XIII

[Proposed by Congress on January 31, 1865; declared ratified on December 18, 1865.]

Section 1

[Abolition of Slavery]
Neither slavery nor involuntary servitude, except as a punishment for a crime whereof the party shall have been duly convicted, shall exist within the United States, or any place subject to their jurisdiction.

Section 2

[Power to Enforce This Article]
Congress shall have power to enforce this article by appropriate legislation.

AMENDMENT XIV

[Proposed by Congress on February 20, 1933; declared ratified on 1868.]

Section 1

[Citizenship Rights Not to Be Abridged by States]

All persons born or naturalized in the United States, and subject to the jurisdiction thereof, are citizens of the United States and of the State wherein they reside. No State shall make or enforce any law which shall abridge the privileges or immunities of citizens of the United States; nor shall any State deprive any person of life, liberty, or property, without due process of law; nor deny to any person within its jurisdiction the equal protection of the laws.

Section 2

[Apportionment of Representatives in Congress]

Representatives shall be apportioned among the several States according to their respective numbers, counting the whole number of persons in each State, excluding Indians not taxed. But when the right to vote at any election for the choice of electors for President and Vice-President of the United States, Representatives in Congress, the Executive and Judicial officers of a State, or the members of the Legislature thereof, is denied to any of the male inhabitants of such State, being twenty-one years of age, and citizens of the United States, or in any way abridged, except for participation in rebellion, or other crime, the basis of representation therein shall be reduced in the proportion which the number of such male citizens shall bear to the whole number of male citizens twenty-one years of age in such State.

Section 3

[Persons Disqualified from Holding Office]

No person shall be a Senator or Representative in Congress, or elector of President and Vice-President, or hold any office, civil or military, under the United States, or under any State, who, having previously taken an oath, as a member of Congress, or as an officer of the United States, or as a member of any State legislature, or as an executive or judicial officer of any State, to support the Constitution of the United States, shall have engaged in insurrection or rebellion against the same, or given aid or comfort to the enemies thereof. But Congress may by a vote of two-thirds of each House, remove such disability.

Section 4

[What Public Debts Are Valid]

The validity of the public debt of the United States, authorized by law, including debts incurred for payment of pensions and bounties for services in suppressing insurrection or rebellion, shall not be questioned. But neither the United States nor any State shall assume or pay any debt or obligation incurred in aid of insurrection or rebellion against the United States, or any claim for the loss or emancipation of any slave; but all such debts, obligations and claims shall be held illegal and void.

Section 5

[Power to Enforce This Article]

The Congress shall have power to enforce, by appropriate legislation, the provisions of this article.

AMENDMENT XV

[Proposed by Congress on February 26, 1869; declared ratified on March 30, 1870.]

Section 1

[Negro Suffrage]

The right of citizens of the United States to vote shall not be denied or abridged by the United States or by any State on account of race, color, or previous condition of servitude.

Section 2

[Power to Enforce This Article]

The Congress shall have power to enforce this article by appropriate legislation.

AMENDMENT XVI

[Proposed by Congress on July 12, 1909; declared ratified on February 25, 1913.]

[Authorizing Income Taxes]

The Congress shall have power to lay and collect taxes on incomes, from whatever source derived, without apportionment among the several States, and without regard to any census or enumeration.

AMENDMENT XVII

[Proposed by Congress on May 13, 1912; declared ratified on May 31, 1913.]

[Popular Election of Senators]

The Senate of the United States shall be composed of two Senators from each State, elected by the people thereof, for six years; and each Senator shall have one vote. The electors in each State shall have the qualifications requisite for electors of the most numerous branch of the State legislatures.

When vacancies happen in the representation of any State in the Senate, the executive authority of such State shall issue writs of election to fill such vacancies: *Provided,* That the legislature of any State may empower the executive thereof to make temporary appointments until the people fill the vacancies by election as the legislature may direct.

This amendment shall not be so construed as to affect the election or term of any Senator chosen before it becomes valid as part of the Constitution.

AMENDMENT XVIII

[Proposed by Congress on December 18, 1917; declared ratified on January 29, 1919.]

Section 1

[National Liquor Prohibition]

After one year from the ratification of this article the manufacture, sale, or transportation of intoxicating liquors within, the importation thereof into, or the exportation thereof from the United States and all territory subject to the jurisdiction thereof for beverage purposes is hereby prohibited.

Section 2

[Power to Enforce This Article]

The Congress and the several States shall have concurrent power to enforce this article by appropriate legislation.

Section 3

[Ratification Within Seven Years]

This article shall be inoperative unless it shall have been ratified as an amendment to the Constitution by the legislatures of the several States, as provided in the Constitution, within seven years from the date of the submission hereof to the States by the Congress.

AMENDMENT XIX

[Proposed by Congress on June 4, 1919; declared ratified on August 26, 1920.]

[Woman Suffrage]

The right of citizens of the United States to vote shall not be denied or abridged by the United States or by any State on account of sex.

Congress shall have power to enforce this article by appropriate legislation.

AMENDMENT XX

[Proposed by Congress on March 2, 1932; declared ratified on February 6, 1933.]

Section 1

[Terms of Office]

The terms of the President and Vice President shall end at noon on the 20th day of January, and the terms of Senators and Representatives at noon on the 3rd day of January, of the years in which such terms would have ended if this article had not been ratified; and the terms of their successors shall then begin.

Section 2

[Time of Convening Congress]

The Congress shall assemble at least once in every year, and such meeting shall begin at noon on the 3rd day of January, unless they shall by law appoint a different day.

Section 3

[Death of President Elect]

If, at the time fixed for the beginning of the term of the President, the President elect shall have died, the Vice President elect shall become President. If a President shall not have been chosen before the time fixed for the beginning of his term, or if the President elect shall have failed to qualify, then the Vice President elect shall act as President until a President shall have qualified; and the Congress may by law provide for the case wherein neither a President elect nor a Vice President elect shall have qualified, declaring who shall then act as President, or the manner in which one who is to act shall be selected, and such person shall act accordingly until a President or Vice President shall have qualified.

Section 4

[Election of the President]

The Congress may by law provide for the case of the death of any of the persons from whom the House of Representatives may choose a President whenever the right of choice shall have devolved upon them, and for the case of the death of any of the persons from whom the Senate may choose a Vice President whenever the right of choice shall have devolved upon them.

Section 5

Sections 1 and 2 shall take effect on the 15th day of October following the ratification of this article.

Section 6

This article shall be inoperative unless it shall have been ratified as an amendment to the Constitution by the legislatures of three-fourths of the several States within seven years from the date of its submission.

AMENDMENT XXI

[Proposed by Congress on February 20, 1933; declared ratified on December 5, 1933.]

Section 1

[National Liquor Prohibition Repealed]

The eighteenth article of amendment to the Constitution of the United States is hereby repealed.

Section 2

[Transportation of Liquor into "Dry" States]

The transportation or importation into any States, Territory, or possession of the United States for delivery or use therein of intoxicating liquors, in violation of the laws thereof, is hereby prohibited.

Section 3

This article shall be inoperative unless it shall have been ratified as an amendment to the Constitution by conventions in the several States, as provided in the Constitution, within seven years from the date of the submission hereof to the States by the Congress.

AMENDMENT XXII

[Proposed by Congress on March 21, 1947; declared ratified on February 26, 1951.]

Section 1

[Tenure of President Limited]
No person shall be elected to the office of the President more than twice, and no person who has held the office of President, or acted as President for more than two years of a term to which some other person was elected President shall be elected to the office of the President more than once. But this Article shall not apply to any person holding the office of President when this Article was proposed by the Congress, and shall not prevent any person who may be holding the office of President, or acting as President, during the term within which this Article becomes operative from holding the office of President, for acting as President during the remainder of such term.

Section 2

This Article shall be inoperative unless it shall have been ratified as an amendment to the Constitution by the legislatures of three-fourths of the several States within seven years from the date of its submission to the States by the Congress.

AMENDMENT XXIII

[Proposed by Congress on June 17, 1960; declared ratified on March 29, 1961.]

Section 1

[District of Columbia Suffrage in Presidential Elections]
The District constituting the seat of Government of the United States shall appoint in such manner as the Congress may direct:

A number of electors of President and Vice President equal to the whole number of Senators and Representatives in Congress to which the District would be entitled if it were a State, but in no event more than the least populous State; they shall be in addition to those appointed by the States, but they shall be considered, for the purposes of the election of President and Vice President, to be electors appointed by a State; and they shall meet in the District and perform such duties as provided by the twelfth article of amendment.

Section 2

The Congress shall have power to enforce this article by appropriate legislation.

AMENDMENT XXIV

[Proposed by Congress on August 27, 1962; declared ratified on January 23, 1964.]

Section 1

[Bars Poll Tax in Federal Elections]
The right of citizens of the United States to vote in any primary or other election for President or Vice President, for electors for President or Vice President, or for Senator or Representative in Congress, shall not be denied or abridged by the United States or any State by reason of failure to pay any poll tax or other tax.

Section 2

The Congress shall have power to enforce this article by appropriate legislation.

AMENDMENT XXV

[Submitted for ratification on August 20, 1965.]

Section 1

In case of the removal of the President from office or of his death or resignation, the Vice President shall become President.

Section 2

Whenever there is a vacancy in the office of the Vice President, the President shall nominate a Vice President who shall take office upon confirmation by a majority vote of both Houses of Congress.

Section 3

Whenever the President transmits to the President pro tempore of the Senate and the Speaker of the House of Representatives his written declaration that he is unable to discharge the powers and duties of his office, and until he transmits to them a written declaration to the contrary, such powers and duties shall be discharged by the Vice President as Acting President.

Section 4

Whenever the Vice President and a majority of either the principal officers of the executive departments or of such other body as Congress may by law provide, transmit to the President pro tempore of the Senate and the Speaker of the House of Representatives their written declaration that the President is unable to discharge the powers and duties of his office, the Vice President shall immediately assume the powers and duties of the office as Acting President.

Thereafter, when the President transmits to the President pro tempore of the Senate and the Speaker of the House of Representatives his written declaration that no inability exists, he shall resume the powers and duties of his office unless the Vice President and a majority of either the principal officers of the executive department or of such other body as Congress may by law provide, transmit within four days to the President pro tempore of the Senate and the Speaker of the House of Representatives their written declaration that the President is unable to discharge the powers and duties of his office. Thereupon Congress shall decide the issue, assembling within forty-eight hours for that purpose if not in session. If the Congress, within twenty-one days after receipt of the latter written declaration, or, if Congress is not in session, within twenty-one days after Congress is required to assemble, determines by two-thirds vote of both Houses that the President is unable to discharge the powers and duties of his office, the Vice President shall continue to discharge the same as Acting President; otherwise, the President shall resume the powers and duties of his office.

BIBLIOGRAPHY

CHAPTER 1 ❧ DEMOCRACY AS A SYSTEM OF VALUES

BECKER, CARL L. *Freedom and Responsibility in the American Way of Life.* New York: Knopf, 1945.

BERLIN, ISAIAH. *Two Concepts of Liberty.* New York: Oxford University Press, 1959.

BROGAN, D. W. *America in the Modern World.* New Brunswick, N.J.: Rutgers University Press, 1960.

EBENSTEIN, WILLIAM. *Modern Political Thought: The Great Issues,* 2d ed. New York: Holt, Rinehart and Winston, 1960.

HARTZ, LOUIS. *The Liberal Tradition in America.* New York: Harcourt, Brace & World, 1955.

LERNER, MAX. *America as a Civilization.* New York: Simon and Schuster, 1957.

LIPSET, SEYMOUR MARTIN. *Political Man.* Garden City, N.Y.: Doubleday, 1960.

MYERS, HENRY ALONZO. *Are Men Equal? An Inquiry into the Meaning of American Democracy.* Ithaca, N.Y.: Cornell University Press, Great Seal Books, 1955.

PADOVER, SAUL K. *The Meaning of Democracy: An Appraisal of the American Experience.* New York: Praeger, 1963.

PENNOCK, J. ROLAND. *Liberal Democracy: Its Merits and Prospects.* New York: Holt, Rinehart and Winston, 1950.

PERKINS, DEXTER. *The American Way.* Ithaca, N.Y.: Cornell University Press, 1957.

707

CHAPTER 2 ⚘ DEMOCRACY, AUTHORITARIANISM,
TOTALITARIANISM

ARENDT, HANNAH. *The Origins of Totalitarianism*, 2d ed. New York: World Publishing, Meridian Books, 1958.
BARBU, ZEVEDEI. *Democracy and Dictatorship*. New York: Grove Press, 1956.
BURCH, BETTY B. *Dictatorship and Totalitarianism*. Princeton, N.J.: Van Nostrand, 1964.
CANTRIL, HADLEY. *The Politics of Despair*. New York: Collier, 1961.
EBENSTEIN, WILLIAM. *Fascist Italy*. New York: American Book, 1939.
EBENSTEIN, WILLIAM. *The Nazi State*. New York: Holt, Rinehart and Winston, 1943.
EBENSTEIN, WILLIAM. *Today's Isms: Communism, Fascism, Capitalism, Socialism*, 5th ed. Englewood Cliffs, N.J.: Prentice-Hall, 1967.
FISCHER, LOUIS. *The Life of Lenin*. New York: Harper & Row, 1964.
FRIEDRICH, CARL J. (ed.). *Totalitarianism*. Cambridge, Mass.: Harvard University Press, 1954.
KOESTLER, ARTHUR. *Darkness at Noon*. New York: New American Library, Mentor Books, 1948.
METZ, HAROLD, and C. A. H. THOMSON. *Authoritarianism and the Individual*. Washington, D.C.: The Brookings Institution, 1950.
ORWELL, GEORGE. *1984*. New York: New American Library, Signet Books, 1950.
SHIRER, WILLIAM L. *The Rise and Fall of the Third Reich*. New York: Simon and Schuster, 1960.
WETTER, GUSTAV A. *Soviet Ideology Today*. New York: Praeger, 1965.
WHITAKER, ARTHUR P. *Spain and the Defense of the West*. New York: Praeger, 1962.
YANG, C. F. *Chinese Communist Society*. Cambridge, Mass.: Massachusetts Institute of Technology Press, 1965.
ZAWODNY, J. K. *Death in the Forest: The Story of the Katyn Forest Massacre*. Notre Dame, Ind.: Notre Dame University Press, 1962.

CHAPTER 3 ⚘ DEMOCRACY: ITS PSYCHOLOGICAL
FOUNDATIONS

ADORNO, T. W., and others. *The Authoritarian Personality*. New York: Harper & Row, 1950.
ALEXANDER, FRANZ. *Our Age of Unreason*. Philadelphia: Lippincott, 1942.
CANTRIL, HADLEY. *Human Nature and Political Systems*. New Brunswick, N.J.: Rutgers University Press, 1961.
DAVIES, JAMES C. *Human Nature in Politics*. New York: Wiley, 1963.
DOLLARD, JOHN, and others. *Frustration and Aggression*. New Haven: Yale University Press, 1939.

FROMM, ERICH. *Escape from Freedom*. New York: Holt, Rinehart and Winston, 1941.
HOFFER, ERIC. *The True Believer*. New York: Harper & Row, 1951.
LASSWELL, HAROLD D. *Power and Personality*. New York: Norton, 1948.
LINDNER, ROBERT. *Must You Conform?* New York: Holt, Rinehart and Winston, 1956.
STANTON, ALFRED H., and STEWART E. PERRY (eds.). *Personality and Political Crisis*. New York: Free Press, 1951.
WALLAS, GRAHAM. *Human Nature in Politics*. London: Constable, 1908.

CHAPTER 4 ❧ THE ECONOMIC ENVIRONMENT
OF DEMOCRACY

ARNOLD, THURMAN W. *The Folklore of Capitalism*. New Haven: Yale University Press, 1937.
BAZELON, DAVID T. *The Paper Economy*. New York: Random House, 1963.
BEARD, CHARLES A. *The Economic Basis of Politics*. New York: Knopf, 1922.
FRIED, ALBERT, and RONALD SANDERS (eds.). *Socialist Thought: A Documentary History*. Garden City, N.Y.: Doubleday, Anchor Books, 1964.
FRIEDMAN, MILTON. *Capitalism and Freedom*. Chicago: University of Chicago Press, 1962.
HACKER, LOUIS M. *American Capitalism*. Princeton, N.J.: Van Nostrand, 1957.
LIPSET, SEYMOUR MARTIN. *The First New Nation: The United States in Historical and Comparative Perspective*. New York: Basic Books, 1963.
MORGAN, H. WAYNE (ed.). *American Socialism: 1900–1960*. Englewood Cliffs, N.J.: Prentice-Hall, 1964.
POLANYI, KARL. *The Great Transformation*. New York: Holt, Rinehart and Winston, 1944.
POTTER, DAVID M. *People of Plenty: Economic Abundance and the American Character*. Chicago: University of Chicago Press, 1954.
SCHUMPETER, JOSEPH A. *Capitalism, Socialism, and Democracy*. New York: Harper & Row, 1942.
SHONFIELD, ANDREW. *Modern Capitalism: The Changing Balance of Public and Private Power*. New York: Oxford University Press, 1965.
THOMAS, NORMAN. *Socialism Re-examined*. New York: Norton, 1963.
WILSON, HAROLD. *The Relevance of British Socialism*. London: Weidenfeld & Nicolson, 1964.

CHAPTER 5 ❧ CONSTITUTIONAL GOVERNMENT

BEARD, CHARLES A. *An Economic Interpretation of the Constitution of the United States*. New York: Macmillan, 1913.
BROWN, ROBERT E. *Charles Beard and the Constitution: A Critical Analysis of "An Economic Interpretation of the Constitution."* Princeton, N.J.: Princeton University Press, 1956.

FARRAND, MAX (ed.). *The Records of the Federal Convention of 1787*, 4 vols. New Haven: Yale University Press, 1911, 1937.

HOLCOMBE, ARTHUR N. *The Constitutional System*. Chicago: Scott, Foresman, 1964.

KELLY, ALFRED H., and WINFRED A. HARBISON. *The American Constitution: Its Origins and Development*, 3d ed. New York: Norton, 1963.

MCILWAIN, CHARLES H. *Constitutionalism Ancient and Modern*. Ithaca, N.Y.: Cornell University Press, 1940.

MCLAUGHLIN, ANDREW C. *The Confederation and the Constitution, 1783–1789*. New York: Collier, 1962.

MITCHELL, BROADUS, and LOUISE MITCHELL. *A Biography of the Constitution of the United States*. New York: Oxford University Press, 1964.

SMITH, DAVID G. *The Convention and the Constitution: The Political Ideas of the Founding Fathers*. New York: St. Martin's, 1965.

VAN DOREN, CARL. *The Great Rehearsal: The Story of the Making and Ratifying of the Constitution of the United States*. New York: Viking, 1948.

WARREN, CHARLES. *The Making of the Constitution*. Boston: Little, Brown, 1928.

CHAPTER 6 ❦ THE VITALITY AND ADAPTABILITY OF THE CONSTITUTION

CROSSKEY, WILLIAM W. *Politics and the Constitution in the History of the United States*, 2 vols. Chicago: University of Chicago Press, 1953.

HOLCOMBE, ARTHUR N. *The Constitutional System*. Chicago: Scott, Foresman, 1964.

MCLAUGHLIN, ANDREW C. *A Constitutional History of the United States*. New York: Appleton-Century-Crofts, 1935.

MCWHINNEY, EDWARD. *Comparative Federalism*. Toronto: University of Toronto Press, 1962.

ORFIELD, LESTER B. *The Amending of the Federal Constitution*. Ann Arbor, Mich.: University of Michigan Press, 1942.

PRITCHETT, C. HERMAN. *The American Constitution*, chs. 3, 4. New York: McGraw-Hill, 1959.

READ, CONYERS (ed.). *The Constitution Reconsidered*, part 3. New York: Columbia University Press, 1938.

SWISHER, CARL B. *American Constitutional Development*, 2d ed. Boston: Houghton Mifflin, 1954.

CHAPTER 7 ❦ FEDERALISM

ANDERSON, WILLIAM A. *The Nation and the States, Rivals or Partners?* Minneapolis: University of Minnesota Press, 1955.

COMMISSION ON INTERGOVERNMENTAL RELATIONS. *Report to the President*. Washington, D.C.: U.S. Government Printing Office, 1955.

GOLDWIN, ROBERT A. (ed.). *A Nation of States: Essays on the American Federal System*. Chicago: Rand McNally, 1963.

LEACH, RICHARD H., and REDDING S. SUGG, JR. *The Administration of Interstate Compacts*. Baton Rouge, La.: Louisiana State University Press, 1959.
LILIENTHAL, DAVID E. *TVA: Democracy on the March*. New York: Harper & Row, 1953.
MACMAHON, ARTHUR W. (ed.). *Federalism: Mature and Emergent*. Garden City, N.Y.: Doubleday, 1955.
PRITCHETT, C. HERMAN. *The American Constitution*, part 2. New York: McGraw-Hill, 1959.
RIKER, WILLIAM H. *Federalism: Origin, Operation, Significance*. Boston: Little, Brown, 1964.
WHEARE, KENNETH C. *Federal Government*, 4th ed. New York: Oxford University Press, 1964.
WHITE, LEONARD D. *The States and the Nation*. Baton Rouge, La.: Louisiana State University Press, 1953.

CHAPTER 8 ⚹ LAW AND THE COURTS

DOUGLAS, WILLIAM O. *We the Judges*. Garden City, N.Y.: Doubleday, 1956.
FRANKFURTER, FELIX, and JAMES M. LANDIS. *The Business of the Supreme Court: A Study in the Federal Judicial System*. New York: Macmillan, 1928.
GROSSMAN, JOEL B. *Lawyers and Judges: The ABA and the Politics of Judicial Selection*. New York: Wiley, 1965.
HART, HENRY M., JR., and HERBERT WECHSLER. *The Federal Courts and the Federal System*. Brooklyn, N.Y.: Foundation, 1953.
JACOB, HERBERT. *Justice in America*. Boston: Little, Brown, 1965.
MAYERS, LEWIS. *The American Legal System*. New York: Harper & Row, 1955.
MURPHY, WALTER F., and C. HERMAN PRITCHETT. *Courts, Judges, and Politics: An Introduction to the Judicial Process*. New York: Random House, 1961.
PRITCHETT, C. HERMAN. *The American Constitution*, chs. 7, 8. New York: McGraw-Hill, 1959.
SMALL, NORMAN J. (ed.). *The Constitution of the United States of America: Analysis and Interpretation*. Washington, D.C.: U.S. Government Printing Office, 1964.

CHAPTER 9 ⚹ THE SUPREME COURT AND JUDICIAL REVIEW

BEARD, CHARLES A. *The Supreme Court and the Constitution*. Englewood Cliffs, N.J.: Prentice-Hall, 1962.
BICKEL, ALEXANDER M. *The Least Dangerous Branch*. Indianapolis, Ind.: Bobbs-Merrill, 1962.
BLACK, CHARLES L., JR. *The People and the Court: Judicial Review in a Democracy*. New York: Macmillan, 1960.
CARR, ROBERT K. *The Supreme Court and Judicial Review*. New York: Holt, Rinehart and Winston, 1942.
CORWIN, EDWARD S. *The "Higher Law" Background of American Constitutional Law*. Ithaca, N.Y.: Cornell University Press, 1955.

DEAN, HOWARD E. *Judicial Review and Democracy.* New York: Random House, 1966.

JACKSON, ROBERT H. *The Supreme Court in the American System of Government.* Cambridge, Mass.: Harvard University Press, 1955.

MURPHY, WALTER F. *Congress and the Court.* Chicago: University of Chicago Press, 1962.

PRITCHETT, C. HERMAN. *Congress Versus the Supreme Court, 1957–1960.* Minneapolis: University of Minnesota Press, 1961.

PRITCHETT, C. HERMAN. *The Roosevelt Court: A Study in Judicial Politics and Values, 1937–1947.* New York: Macmillan, 1948; Octagon, 1963.

ROCHE, JOHN P. *Courts and Rights: The American Judiciary in Action.* New York: Random House, 1961.

SHAPIRO, MARTIN. *Law and Politics in the Supreme Court.* New York: Free Press, 1964.

SWISHER, CARL B. *The Supreme Court in Modern Role.* New York: New York University Press, 1958.

CHAPTER 10 ❧ LIBERTY

BERNS, WALTER. *Freedom, Virtue and the First Amendment.* Baton Rouge, La.: Louisiana State University Press, 1957.

BROWN, RALPH S., JR. *Loyalty and Security.* New Haven: Yale University Press, 1958.

CHAFEE, ZECHARIAH, JR. *Free Speech in the United States.* Cambridge, Mass.: Harvard University Press, 1941.

CHASE, HAROLD W. *Security and Liberty: The Problem of Native Communists, 1947–1955.* New York: Doubleday, 1955.

FELLMAN, DAVID. *The Constitutional Right of Association.* Chicago: University of Chicago Press, 1963.

FELLMAN, DAVID. *Religion in American Public Law.* Boston: Boston University Press, 1965.

FREUND, PAUL A., and ROBERT ULICH. *Religion and the Public Schools.* Cambridge, Mass.: Harvard University Press, 1965.

FRIEDMAN, MILTON. *Capitalism and Freedom.* Chicago: University of Chicago Press, 1962.

HORN, ROBERT A. *Groups and the Constitution.* Stanford, Calif.: Stanford University Press, 1956.

KALVEN, HARRY, JR. *The Negro and the First Amendment.* Columbus, Ohio: Ohio State University Press, 1965.

KONVITZ, MILTON R. *Fundamental Liberties of a Free People: Religion, Speech, Press, Assembly.* Ithaca, N.Y.: Cornell University Press, 1957.

KURLAND, PHILIP B. (ed.). *The Supreme Court and the Constitution.* Chicago: University of Chicago Press, 1965.

MANWARING, DAVID R. *Render unto Caesar: The Flag-Salute Controversy.* Chicago: University of Chicago Press, 1962.

MEIKLEJOHN, ALEXANDER. *Political Freedom.* New York: Harper & Row, 1960.

OAKS, DALLIN (ed.). *The Wall Between Church and State*. Chicago: University of Chicago Press, 1963.
PRITCHETT, C. HERMAN. *The American Constitution*, part 6. New York: McGraw-Hill, 1959.
ROCHE, JOHN P. *The Quest for the Dream*. New York: Macmillan, 1963.
SHAPIRO, MARTIN. *Freedom of Speech: The Supreme Court and Judicial Review*. Englewood Cliffs, N.J.: Prentice-Hall, 1966.

CHAPTER 11 ❧ EQUALITY AND CIVIL RIGHTS

BERMAN, DANIEL M. A *Bill Becomes a Law: The Civil Rights Act of 1960*. New York: Macmillan, 1962.
BICKEL, ALEXANDER M. *Politics and the Warren Court*. New York: Harper & Row, 1965.
BLAUSTEIN, ALBERT P., and CLARENCE C. FERGUSON, JR. *Desegregation and the Law*. New York: Vintage Books, 1962.
CARR, ROBERT K. *Federal Protection of Civil Rights*. Ithaca, N.Y.: Cornell University Press, 1947.
CONGRESSIONAL QUARTERLY. *Revolution in Civil Rights*. Washington, D.C.: Congressional Quarterly Service, 1965.
FELLMAN, DAVID. *The Defendant's Rights*. New York: Holt, Rinehart and Winston, 1958.
GOLDWIN, ROBERT A. (ed.). *One Hundred Years of Emancipation*. Chicago: Rand McNally, 1964.
GRIMES, ALAN P. *Equality in America*. New York: Oxford University Press, 1964.
HARRIS, ROBERT J. *The Quest for Equality*. Baton Rouge, La.: Louisiana State University Press, 1960.
LEWIS, ANTHONY. *Gideon's Trumpet*. New York: Random House, 1964.
LEWIS, ANTHONY. *Portrait of a Decade*. New York: Random House, 1964.
PELTASON, J. W. *Fifty-Eight Lonely Men: Southern Federal Judges and School Desegregation*. New York: Harcourt, Brace & World, 1961.
PRITCHETT, C. HERMAN. *The American Constitution*, part 7. New York: McGraw-Hill, 1959.
U.S. COMMISSION ON CIVIL RIGHTS. *Report, Book 1, Voting; Book 2, Education*. Washington, D.C.: U.S. Government Printing Office, 1961.
VOSE, CLEMENT E. *Caucasians Only*. Berkeley, Calif.: University of California Press, 1959.

CHAPTER 12 ❧ PUBLIC OPINION AND ELECTORAL BEHAVIOR

ALMOND, GABRIEL A. *The American People and Foreign Policy*. New York: Harcourt, Brace & World, 1950.
BERELSON, BERNARD, and MORRIS JANOWITZ. *Reader in Public Opinion and Communication*, 2d ed. New York: Free Press, 1966.

BERELSON, BERNARD, and others. *Voting: A Study of Opinion Formation in a Presidential Campaign*. Chicago: University of Chicago Press, 1954.

BURDICK, EUGENE, and ARTHUR J. BRODBECK (eds.). *American Voting Behavior*. New York: Free Press, 1958.

CAMPBELL, ANGUS, and others. *The American Voter*. New York: Wiley, 1960.

CATER, DOUGLASS. *The Fourth Branch of Government*. Boston: Houghton Mifflin, 1959.

DAVIES, JAMES C. *Human Nature in Politics*. New York: Wiley, 1963.

KEY, V. O., JR. *Public Opinion and American Democracy*. New York: Knopf, 1961.

KEY, V. O., JR. *The Responsible Electorate*. Cambridge, Mass.: Harvard University Press, 1966.

LANE, ROBERT E. *Political Life*. New York: Free Press, 1959.

LANE, ROBERT E., and DAVID O. SEARS. *Public Opinion*. Englewood Cliffs, N.J.: Prentice-Hall, 1964.

LAZARSFELD, PAUL F., and others. *The People's Choice: How the Voter Makes Up His Mind*, 2d ed. New York: Columbia University Press, 1948.

MILBRATH, LESTER W. *Political Participation*. Chicago: Rand McNally, 1965.

RIVERS, WILLIAM L. *The Mass Media*. New York: Harper & Row, 1964.

SCHRAMM, WILBUR. *Process and Effects of Mass Communications*. Urbana, Ill.: University of Illinois Press, 1965.

CHAPTER 13 ✻ THE AMERICAN PARTY SYSTEM

AND

CHAPTER 14 ✻ POLITICAL PARTIES IN ACTION

ALEXANDER, HERBERT E. *Financing the 1964 Election*. Princeton, N.J.: Citizens' Research Foundation, 1966.

BINCKLEY, W. E. *American Political Parties: Their Natural History*, 3d ed. New York: Knopf, 1958.

BONE, HUGH A. *American Politics and the Party System*, 3d ed. New York: McGraw-Hill, 1965.

CHAMBERS, WILLIAM N. *Political Parties in a New Nation: The American Experience, 1776–1809*. New York: Oxford University Press, 1963.

DAVID, PAUL T., and others. *The Politics of the National Party Conventions*. Washington, D.C.: The Brookings Institution, 1960.

DUVERGER, MAURICE. *Political Parties: Their Organization and Activity in the Modern State*. New York: Wiley, 1956.

ELDERSVELD, SAMUEL J. *Political Parties: A Behavioral Analysis*. Chicago: Rand McNally, 1964.

GOLDMAN, RALPH M. *The Democratic Party in American Politics*. New York: Macmillan, 1966.

HEARD, ALEXANDER. *The Costs of Democracy*. Chapel Hill, N.C.: University of North Carolina Press, 1960.

KEY, V. O., JR. *Politics, Parties and Pressure Groups*, 5th ed. New York: Crowell, 1964.

LEISERSON, AVERY. *Parties and Politics.* New York: Knopf, 1958.

Moos, MALCOLM. *The Republicans.* New York: Random House, 1956.

OGDEN, DANIEL, JR., and ARTHUR L. PETERSON. *Electing the President: 1964.* San Francisco: Chandler, 1964.

POLSBY, NELSON W., and AARON B. WILDAVSKY. *Presidential Elections: Strategies of American Electoral Politics.* New York: Scribner, 1964.

SORAUF, FRANK J. *Political Parties in the American System.* Boston: Little, Brown, 1964.

CHAPTER 15 ❧ POLITICAL INTEREST GROUPS

BELL, DANIEL (ed.). *The Radical Right.* Garden City, N.Y.: Doubleday, 1963.

BLAISDELL, DONALD C. *American Democracy Under Pressure.* New York: Ronald, 1957.

BLAISDELL, DONALD C. "Unofficial Government: Pressure Groups and Lobbies." *The Annals of the American Academy of Political and Social Science,* Vol. 319, September, 1958.

ENGLER, ROBERT. *The Politics of Oil.* New York: Macmillan, 1961.

GROSS, BERTRAM. *The Legislative Struggle.* New York: McGraw-Hill, 1953.

HOLTZMAN, ABRAHAM. *Interest Groups and Lobbying.* New York: Macmillan, 1966.

JACOBS, PAUL J., and SAUL LANDAU. *The New Radicals.* New York: Random House, 1966.

LANE, EDGAR. *Lobbying and the Law.* Berkeley, Calif.: University of California Press, 1964.

LUCE, PHILLIP ABBOTT. *The New Left.* New York: McKay, 1966.

McCONNELL, GRANT. *Private Power and American Democracy.* New York: Knopf, 1966.

MILBRATH, LESTER W. *The Washington Lobbyists.* Chicago: Rand McNally, 1963.

MONSEN, R. JOSEPH, JR., and MARK W. CANNON. *The Makers of Public Policy.* New York: McGraw-Hill, 1965.

TRUMAN, DAVID. *The Governmental Process.* New York: Knopf, 1951.

ZEIGLER, HARMON. *Interest Groups in American Society.* Englewood Cliffs, N.J.: Prentice-Hall, 1964.

CHAPTER 16 ❧ CONGRESS: MIRROR OF THE NATION

AND

CHAPTER 17 ❧ CONGRESS: SOURCE OF PUBLIC POLICY

BERMAN, DANIEL. *In Congress Assembled: The Legislative Process in the National Government.* New York: Macmillan, 1964.

BOLLING, RICHARD. *House Out of Order.* New York: Dutton, 1965.

CARROLL, HOLBERT N. *The House of Representatives and Foreign Affairs,* rev. ed. Boston: Little, Brown, 1966.

CLAPP, CHARLES L. *The Congressman: His Work as He Sees It.* Washington, D.C.: The Brookings Institution, 1963.

CLARK, SENATOR JOSEPH S. *Congress, the Sapless Branch.* New York: Harper & Row, 1964.

FREEMAN, J. LEIPER. *The Political Process: Executive Bureau-Legislative Committee Relations.* New York: Random House, 1955.

FROMAN, L. A., JR. *Congressmen and Their Constituencies.* Chicago: Rand McNally, 1963.

GALLOWAY, GEORGE B. *History of the House of Representatives.* New York: Crowell, 1961.

GRIFFITH, ERNEST. *Congress, Its Contemporary Role,* rev. ed. New York: New York University Press, 1961.

HACKER, ANDREW. *Congressional Districting: The Issue of Equal Representation.* Washington, D.C.: The Brookings Institution, 1963.

HARRIS, JOSEPH P. *The Advice and Consent of the Senate.* Berkeley, Calif.: University of California Press, 1953.

HARRIS, JOSEPH P. *Congressional Control of Administration.* Washington, D.C.: The Brookings Institution, 1964.

MATTHEWS, DONALD R. *U.S. Senators and Their World.* Chapel Hill, N.C.: University of North Carolina Press, 1960.

PEABODY, ROBERT L., and NELSON W. POLSBY (eds.). *New Perspectives on the House of Representatives.* Chicago: Rand McNally, 1963.

ROBINSON, JAMES A. *Congress and Foreign Policy-Making,* Dorsey, 1962.

ROBINSON, JAMES A. *The House Rules Committee.* Indianapolis: Bobbs-Merrill, 1963.

TAYLOR, TELFORD. *Grand Inquest.* New York: Simon and Schuster, 1955.

TRUMAN, DAVID B. *The Congress and America's Future.* Englewood Cliffs, N.J.: Prentice-Hall, 1965.

TRUMAN, DAVID B. *The Congressional Party.* New York: Wiley, 1959.

CHAPTER 18 ❦ THE PRESIDENCY

AND

CHAPTER 19 ❦ PRESIDENTIAL LEADERSHIP

BINCKLEY, WILFRED E. *President and Congress,* 3d ed. New York: Random House, 1962.

BURNS, JAMES MACGREGOR. *Presidential Government.* Boston: Houghton Mifflin, 1966.

CORNWELL, ELMER E., JR. *Presidential Leadership of Public Opinion.* Bloomington, Ind.: Indiana University Press, 1965.

CORWIN, EDWARD S. *The President: Office and Powers, 1787–1957,* 4th ed. New York: New York University Press, 1957.

FENNO, RICHARD F. *The President's Cabinet.* Cambridge, Mass.: Harvard University Press, 1959.

FINER, HERMAN. *The Presidency: Crisis and Regeneration.* Chicago: University of Chicago Press, 1960.

HORN, STEPHEN. *The Cabinet and Congress*. New York: Columbia University Press, 1960.

HYMAN, SIDNEY. *The American President*. New York: Harper & Row, 1954.

KALLENBACH, JOSEPH E. *The American Chief Executive*. New York: Harper & Row, 1966.

KOENIG, LOUIS W. *The Chief Executive*. New York: Harcourt, Brace & World, 1964.

KOENIG, LOUIS W. *The Invisible Presidency*. New York: Holt, Rinehart and Winston, 1960.

LASKI, HAROLD J. *The American Presidency*. New York: Grosset & Dunlap, 1960.

LONGAKER, RICHARD P. *The Presidency and Individual Liberties*. Ithaca, N.Y.: Cornell University Press, 1961.

NEUSTADT, RICHARD E. *Presidential Power*. New York: Wiley, 1960.

ROSSITER, CLINTON. *The American Presidency*. New York: Harcourt, Brace & World, 1960.

SORENSEN, THEODORE C. *Decision Making in the White House: The Olive Branch or the Arrows*. New York: Columbia University Press, 1963.

WHITE, WILLIAM S. *The Professional: Lyndon B. Johnson*. Boston: Houghton Mifflin, 1964.

WILLIAMS, IRVING G. *The American Vice Presidency: A New Look*. New York: Random House, 1954.

CHAPTER 20 ❧ RUNNING THE NATIONAL GOVERNMENT

APPLEBY, PAUL. *Policy and Administration*. University, Alabama: University of Alabama Press, 1949.

BERNSTEIN, MARVER H. *The Job of the Federal Executive*. Washington, D.C.: The Brookings Institution, 1958.

BLAU, PETER. *The Dynamics of Bureaucracy*. Chicago: University of Chicago Press, 1955.

HEADY, FERREL. *Public Administration: A Comparative Perspective*. Englewood Cliffs, N.J.: Prentice-Hall, 1966.

HYNEMAN, C. S. *Bureaucracy in a Democracy*. New York: Harper & Row, 1950.

KILPATRICK, FRANKLIN P., MILTON C. CUMMINGS, JR., and M. KENT JENNINGS. *The Image of the Federal Service*. Washington, D.C.: The Brookings Institution, 1964.

MANN, DEAN E. with JAMESON W. DOIG. *The Assistant Secretaries*. Washington, D.C.: The Brookings Institution, 1965.

SAYRE, WALLACE. *The Federal Government Service: Its Character, Prestige, and Problems*, 2d ed. Englewood Cliffs, N.J.: Prentice-Hall, 1965.

SIMON, HERBERT A. *Administrative Behavior*, 2d ed. New York: Macmillan, 1957.

STEIN, HAROLD (ed.). *Public Administration and Policy Development*. New York: Harcourt, Brace & World, 1952.

Van Riper, Paul P. *History of the United States Civil Service.* New York: Harper & Row, 1958.

Warner, W. L., and others. *The American Federal Executive.* New Haven: Yale University Press, 1963.

White, Leonard D. *The Federalists* (1948); *The Jeffersonians* (1951); *The Jacksonians* (1954); *The Republican Era* (1957). New York: Macmillan.

Wildavsky, Aaron. *The Politics of the Budgetary Process.* Boston: Little, Brown, 1954.

CHAPTER 21 ❦ THE AMERICAN POLITICAL ECONOMY

Berle, Adolf A. *The American Economic Republic.* New York: Harcourt, Brace & World, 1963.

Cochran, Thomas C. *The American Business System: A Historical Perspective, 1900–1955.* New York: Harper & Row, Harper Torchbooks, 1962.

Fuller, John G. *The Gentlemen Conspirators: The Story of the Price-Fixers in the Electrical Industry.* New York: Grove, 1962.

Ginzberg, Eli, and others. *The Pluralistic Economy.* New York: McGraw-Hill, 1965.

Kaplan, A. D. H. *Big Enterprise in a Competitive System,* rev. ed. Washington, D.C.: The Brookings Institution, 1964.

Lilienthal, David E. *Big Business: A New Era.* New York: Harper & Row, 1953.

Mansfield, Edwin (ed.). *Monopoly Power and Economic Performance.* New York: Norton, 1964.

Mason, Edward S. (ed.). *The Corporation in Modern Society.* Cambridge, Mass.: Harvard University Press, 1959.

Maurer, Herrymen. *Great Enterprise: Growth and Behavior of the Big Corporation.* New York: Macmillan, 1955.

Means, Gardiner C. *The Corporate Revolution in America: Economic Reality vs. Economic Theory.* New York: Crowell-Collier, 1962.

Mendelson, Wallace. *Capitalism, Democracy, and the Supreme Court.* New York: Appleton-Century-Crofts, 1960.

Sutton, Francis X., and others. *The American Business Creed.* Cambridge, Mass.: Harvard University Press, 1956.

Warner, W. Lloyd. *The Corporation in the Emergent American Society.* New York: Harper & Row, 1962.

CHAPTER 22 ❦ ECONOMIC POLICIES: ENDS AND MEANS

Anderson, James E. *Politics and the Economy.* Boston: Little, Brown, 1966.

Beard, Charles A. *Public Policy and the General Welfare.* New York: Holt, Rinehart and Winston, 1941.

Bernstein, Peter L. *The Price of Prosperity.* Garden City, N.Y.: Doubleday, 1962.

BUNZEL, JOHN H. *The American Small Businessman*. New York: Knopf, 1962.

GALBRAITH, JOHN K. *American Capitalism: The Concept of Countervailing Power*. Boston: Houghton Mifflin, 1952.

GUTMANN, PETER M. (ed.). *Economic Growth: An American Problem*. Englewood Cliffs, N.J.: Prentice-Hall, 1964.

HIGBEE, EDWARD. *Farms and Farmers in an Urban Age*. New York: Twentieth Century Fund, 1963.

MUND, VERNON A. *Government and Business*, 4th ed. New York: Harper & Row, 1965.

MUSOLF, LLOYD D. *Government and the Economy*. Chicago: Scott, Foresman, 1965.

REAGAN, MICHAEL D. *The Managed Economy*. New York: Oxford University Press, 1963.

ROSTOW, EUGENE V. *Planning for Freedom: The Public Law of American Capitalism*. New Haven: Yale University Press, 1959.

SAULNIER, RAYMOND J. *The Strategy of Economic Policy*. New York: Fordham University Press, 1963.

SHISTER, JOSEPH, and others (eds.). *Public Policy and Collective Bargaining*. New York: Harper & Row, 1962.

WERNETTE, JOHN PHILIP. *Government and Business*. New York: Macmillan, 1964.

CHAPTER 23 ❧ THE WELFARE STATE

BATOR, FRANCIS M. *The Question of Government Spending: Public Needs and Private Wants*. New York: Harper & Row, 1960.

CLARK, KENNETH. *Dark Ghetto*. New York: Harper & Row, 1965.

CORNUELLE, RICHARD C. *Reclaiming the American Dream*. New York: Random House, 1965.

DE GRAZIA, ALFRED (ed.). *Grass Roots Private Welfare*. New York: New York University Press, 1957.

GALBRAITH, JOHN K. *The Affluent Society*. Boston: Houghton Mifflin, 1958.

HARRINGTON, MICHAEL. *The Other America*. New York: Macmillan, 1962.

HEILBRONER, ROBERT L. *The Limits of American Capitalism*. New York: Harper & Row, 1966.

KEPPEL, FRANCIS. *The Necessary Revolution in American Education*. New York: Harper & Row, 1966.

MILLER, HERMAN P. *Rich Man, Poor Man*. New York: Crowell, 1964.

MOYNIHAN, DANIEL P. *The Negro Family: The Case For National Action*. Washington, D.C.: U.S. Department of Labor, 1965.

PHELPS, EDMUND S. (ed.). *Private Wants and Public Needs*. New York: Norton, 1962.

SELIGMAN, BEN B. (ed.). *Poverty as a Public Issue*. New York: Free Press, 1965.

THEOBALD, ROBERT. *Free Men and Free Markets*. Garden City, N.Y.: Double-day, Anchor Books, 1965.
TUNLEY, ROUL. *The American Health Scandal*. New York: Harper & Row, 1966.

CHAPTER 24 ☙ AMERICAN FOREIGN POLICY

BAILEY, THOMAS A. *The Man in the Street: The Impact of American Public Opinion on Foreign Policy*. New York: Macmillan, 1948.
BALDWIN, DAVID A. *Foreign Aid and American Foreign Policy*. New York: Praeger, 1966.
BELOFF, MAX. *Foreign Policy and the Democratic Process*. Baltimore: Johns Hopkins, 1955.
CARLETON, WILLIAM G. *The Revolution in American Foreign Policy: Its Global Range*. New York: Random House, 1964.
COHEN, BERNARD C. *Foreign Policy in American Government*. Boston: Little, Brown, 1965.
GERBERDING, WILLIAM P. *United States Foreign Policy: Perspectives and Analysis*. New York: McGraw-Hill, 1966.
GOLDWIN, ROBERT A. (ed.). *America Armed: Essays on United States Military Policy*. Chicago: Rand McNally, 1963.
GORDON, MORTON, and KENNETH N. VINES. *Theory and Practice of American Foreign Policy*. New York: Crowell, 1955.
HEILBRONER, ROBERT L. *The Great Ascent: The Struggle for Economic Development in Our Time*. New York: Harper & Row, Harper Torchbooks, 1963.
HORELICK, ARNOLD L., and MYRON RUSH. *Strategic Power and Soviet Foreign Policy*. Chicago: University of Chicago Press, 1966.
KENNAN, GEORGE F. *American Diplomacy: 1900–1950*. Chicago: University of Chicago Press, 1951.
LERCHE, CHARLES O. *America in World Affairs*. New York: McGraw-Hill, 1963.
McCORD, WILLIAM. *The Springtime of Freedom: Evolution of Developing Societies*. New York: Oxford University Press, 1965.
McLELLAN, DAVID S. *The Cold War in Transition*. New York: Macmillan, 1966.
PALMER, NORMAN D. *South Asia and United States Policy*. Boston: Houghton Mifflin, 1966.
RUBIN, SEYMOUR J. *The Conscience of Rich Nations: The Development Assistance Committee and the Common Aid Effort*. New York: Harper & Row, 1966.
STRAUSZ-HUPÉ, ROBERT, and others. *Protracted Conflict*. New York: Harper & Row, 1963.
TARR, DAVID W. *American Strategy in the Nuclear Age*. New York: Macmillan, 1966.

INDEX

Abbate v. *United States* (1959), 273
Abolitionist party, 340
A Book v. *Attorney General of Massa-
  chusetts* (1966), 230–231
Abrams v. *United States* (1919), 244–245
Accommodations, public, 256–257
Acheson, Dean, 410–411, 668
Acreage, reduction of crop, 600
Adams, John, 207, 319
  as Federalist, 141, 506
Adams, John Quincy, 320, 644
Adams, Sherman, 487
Adams, Walter, 568
Adamson v. *California* (1947), 268
Adkins v. *Children's Hospital* (1923), 214
Administration, tone of, 485–486
Administrative Procedure Act and public
  hearings, 382
Administrators, and Congress, 418–419
  recruiting able, 470
  and technical specialists, 528
Admission of new states, 166–168
Advertising, institutional, 379
Age composition of population, 605
Aged, medicare for, 623–625
Agencies, administrative, appeals from
  orders, 191
  executive directives, 467–468
  and guidelines, 418
  justification for, 523–524
  and pressure groups, 382

procedures, 528–531
Aggression, and democracy, 646–648
  and frustration, 77–78
Agricultural committees, congressional,
  429–430
Agricultural Conservation Committee,
  529–530
Agricultural Trade Development and Assistance Act, 600
Agriculture, exempt from Clayton Act,
  572
  and federal subsidy, 589, 594–602
Aid, foreign, and Congress, 652–653,
  657–658
  as percentage of national income,
  661–662
Aid to the Blind (AB), 616
Aid to Dependent Children (ADC), 610,
  616
Aid to the Permanently and Totally Disabled (APTD), 616
Air carriers, subsidies to, 590
Alabama, 227, 235, 236, 237, 259, 271–
  272
  Birmingham demonstrators, 260
  and NAACP, 237
  Negro candidates, 255
Alaska, 403, 613
  statehood, 167, 170
  voting age, 308
Alexander of Russia, Tsar, 156

Mississippi, 254, 616
 and schools, 259, 260, 629, 630
 violence in, 268, 309–310
 voting requirements, 254, 308, 309–310
Missouri, 200, 257
Missouri ex rel. Gaines v. *Canada* (1938), 257
Missouri Plan, 200
Mobility, social, and government-run economy, 89–90
 in United States, 31, 113
Monarchy and democracy, 32
Money and economics, 93
Monopolies, breakup of, 563–564
 fight against, 565–570
 and news coverage, 293–294
 and states' rights, 551–552
Monroe, James, 320
Montana, 111
Morality and national interest, 649–650
Morgan v. *Virginia* (1946), 256
Mormons, 239
Morrill Act of 1862, 177, 626
Morris, Gouverneur, 125, 127
Morse, Wayne, 428
Motion pictures, censorship, 222
 obscenity, 230–231
Moyers, Bill D., 487
Multiparty system, 341–343
Munn v. *Illinois* (1877), 556
Murdock v. *Pennsylvania* (1943), 239
Mussolini, Benito, 36, 40, 69, 81–82

National Aeronautics and Space Administration (NASA), 491, 494, 495, 523
National Association for the Advancement of Colored People (NAACP),
 and courts, 258–259, 383
 mass demonstrations, 379–380
 right to join, 237
NAACP v. *Alabama* (1958), 237
NAACP v. *Button* (1963), 237
National Association of Manufacturers, 379, 384–385
National Defense Education Act of 1958, 628–629
National Farmers' Union, 386, 387
National Institutes of Health, 621
National interest, foreign policy and, 648–650
National Labor Relations Act of 1935 (Wagner Act), 222, 573–574
National Labor Relations Board (NLRB), 574, 575
 interpreting laws, 176, 212, 530
National Recovery Act, 222

National Security Act of 1947, 490
National Security Council (NSC), 477, 490
 and foreign policy, 495
National States' Rights Party, 340, 393
National Teacher Corps, 633
National Urban League, 379
Nationalism and Communists, 60–61
Nationalization and Socialists, 108–110
Nations, underdeveloped, attitude toward work, 544–545
 and authoritarianism, 45
 and civil service, 515
 and communism, 48–51, 56–61, 661, 674
 investing in, 96–97
 nationalism and racism, 60–61
 and public ownership, 109–110
 and socialism, 103–104, 109–110, 657–659
 and U.S. experience, 543
 violence in, 669, 672
Natural Gas Act, 212
Nazi Germany, 13–14, 23, 24
 anti-Hitler plot, 81
 appeal of fascism, 53, 55–56
 lesson of, 35–36
 and race, 37, 53
 and religion, 26
 role of military, 54
 trials under, 47
 turncoats of, 83
 wartime travel documents, 82–83
 See also Hitler, Adolf
Near v. *Minnesota* (1931), 227
Nebbia v. *New York* (1934), 249
Nebraska, 300, 353
Negroes, 114, 253, 407
 and constitutional amendments, 143
 and demonstrations, 236
 disadvantaged children, 633
 and foreign affairs, 644
 as freedmen, 222
 and free speech, 234
 and housing, 262–263
 on juries, 271
 and libel, 229
 mass demonstrations, 279–380
 and public accommodations, 256–257
 Ralph Bunche, 13
 and Republican party, 322
 and SNCC, 48, 380
 suffrage, 253–256, 307–310
 and urbanization, 605
 voting habits, 302
Nehru, Jawaharlal, 103, 109

Tennessee Valley Authority
(Continued)
as government corporation, 182, 525, 554
Terminiello v. *Chicago* (1949), 234
Territories, federal, 170, 171
incorporated, 170
Texas, 166, 167–168, 259
tidelands oil, 168
white primary, 254
Texas v. *White* (1869), 166
"Third World," 657, 659, 673–674
Thomas, Norman, 110, 111
Thornhill v. *Alabama* (1940), 235
Thurmond, Strom, 454
Tidelands oil controversies, 168, 383
Tocqueville, Alexis de, democracy and foreign affairs, 644–645
equality in America, 30, 76, 113–114
and industrial capitalism, 86–87, 606
and power of the people, 99
Totalitarianism, in Asia, 33
and authoritarianism, 46–47
Communist, 35–42
control of mass media, 291
and degradation, 47–48
and democratic language, 42
and economic development, 48–51
Fascist, 35–42
goals and means, 34–35
ideology, 36–39
and individuality, 16, 65
interest groups in, 375–376
lesson of, 36
nihilism of, 47–48
one-party states, 343
prospects of, 61–62
and public opinion, 280
and racism, 48
and reality-principle, 66–67
and rule of law, 19–20
and schools, 75
and science, 5–9
and subversion, 672–673
and trials, 15, 47
and women, 72–73
Trade agreements program, 491
Trade associations, as lobbyists, 384–386
Trade credits, 583
Training, manpower, 613–614
Transfer payments, 584, 618
Transportation, Department of, 492
Treaties, 420–422, 478–479
Trials, purge, 47, 81
and double jeopardy, 273
Trop v. *Dulles* (1958), 274

Trotsky, Leon, 58–59
Truman, Harry S, 89, 485–486, 503
and atomic bomb, 152, 475
election of, 289, 323
Fair Deal, 110, 466
and foreign affairs, 479, 668
and Korea, 647, 650
as leader, 70, 506
loyalty program, 538
and MacArthur, 650
national health insurance, 446, 622–626
on Presidency, 471, 488, 508
and Sherman Act, 562–567
and steel mills, 209
Supreme Court appointment, 196
and Vatican, 653
and veto, 502
as Vice-President, 152, 475, 496
Twentieth Amendment, 461
Twining v. *New Jersey* (1908), 268
Tyler, John, 463

Udall, Stewart, 534
Ullmann v. *United States* (1956), 151, 268
Unemployment, and fascism, 55
fiscal and monetary policies, 579–582
insurance, 584, 612–613
relocation assistance, 614–615
and vocational education, 613–614
Unions, and Landrum-Griffin Act, 575–576
and Taft-Hartley Act, 575
Unitary system, 159, 161
in Great Britain, 336, 337
United Auto Workers, 587
United Mine Workers, 388
United Nations, 493, 494
and Senate, 420, 421
United States, communism in, 41, 227, 244–245, 245–246, 392–393; and Congress, 419–420, 424–425 and Smith Act, 212, 216
fascism in, 41
and future, 672–676
and Great Depression, *see* Depression
influence today, 641, 643–644, 675–676
leftists, new, 392–393
Radical Right in, 52–53, 393–396
social reform in, 103
socialism in, 110–115
as world power, 641–643, 666–668, 675–676
U.S. v. *Aluminum Co. of America* (1945), 565